THE HOME FRONT ENCYCLOPEDIA

THE HOME FRONT ENCYCLOPEDIA

◆

United States, Britain, and Canada in World Wars I and II

VOLUME ONE: WORLD WAR I

James Ciment

EDITOR

Thaddeus Russell

CONTRIBUTING EDITOR

A B C ◆ C L I O

Santa Barbara, California • Denver, Colorado • Oxford, England

Cataloging-in-Publication Data is available through the Library of Congress
ISBN: 1-57607-849-3   ISBN-13: 978-1-57607-849-5
E-ISBN: 1-57607-875-2   ebook ISBN-13: 978-1-57607-875-4

This book is also available on the World Wide Web as an eBook.
Visit abc-clio.com for details.

Acquisitions Editor: Simon Mason
Production Editor: Christine Marra
Editorial Assistant: Gayle Woidneck
Media Editor: Jason Kniser
Production Manager: Don Schmidt
Manufacturing Coordinator: Paula Gerard

ABC-CLIO, Inc.
130 Cremona Drive, P.O. Box 1911
Santa Barbara, California 93116-1911

This book is printed on acid-free paper. ∞
Manufactured in the United States of America

CONTENTS

—————◆—————

LIST OF ENTRIES

◆

VOLUME ONE: WORLD WAR I

World War I: Topics

VOLUME TWO: WORLD WAR II

World War II: Biographies

World War II: Topics

VOLUME THREE: DOCUMENTS

THE HOME FRONT
ENCYCLOPEDIA

WORLD WAR I

INTRODUCTION

———————— ◆ ————————

Few nations go to war expecting a long, bloody, and futile struggle. Certainly, Britain and the British people did not when they marched off to fight—flags waving, bands playing—in the summer of 1914. But they were wrong, and that wrongness became apparent in very short time. The mass British and French offensives of 1915 produced more casualties than the decade of warfare following the French Revolution.

During the relatively long peace since the end of the Napoleonic wars a century earlier, Europe had changed. New and lethal weaponry—notably, the machine gun and long range artillery—had been invented and deployed. More significantly, society itself had been transformed. The democratic and industrial revolutions of the nineteenth century had forged the modern nation, capable of turning out masses of machines and vast armies of patriotic young men. The result was unprecedented slaughter on the battlefield.

World War I—or the Great War, as contemporaries soon came to call it—changed the world, destroying one set of empires (German, Russian, Austro-Hungarian, Ottoman) while weakening others (French and British). It also unleashed new political forces, most notably bolshevism in Russia and nationalism in the colonial world beyond European shores.

But those are subjects for books about the political and diplomatic dimensions of the Great War. This is a volume dedicated to the home front, specifically that of the three major English-speaking allies—Britain, Canada, and the United States. Here, too, the change wrought by the conflict was profound and far-reaching.

For Britain in particular, the war represented an unprecedented challenge to its very being. Dependent upon foreign trade—both with Europe and its colonial possessions overseas—the country found itself increasingly isolated as German submarines, or U-boats, patrolled the shipping lanes and sent hundreds of vessels and millions of tons to the bottom of the sea. The country was forced to restructure its economy and its government to meet the twin goals of keeping a massive military machine in the field and, more to the point of this book, feed, clothe, and sustain the morale of a home front that had been turned into an armory.

Old shibboleths of free-market capitalism were tossed aside—in Britain and, to a lesser extent, Canada, and the United States, too—as governments took heretofore unimagined direction of their national economies "for the duration." Goods were rationed, prices and wages frozen, and travel restricted. The first great planned economies of modern times were not in the communist countries that arose after 1917 but in the belligerent powers of World War I. The regimentation that soldiers had known since the first days of organized conflict at the dawn of civilization had now come—albeit in modified form—to the civilian populations they were defending, and for similar reasons. In an age of total warfare, all of society—military and civilian, men and women—had to be regimented before it could be mobilized for the all-encompassing goal of defeating the enemy, who was doing much the same thing. Even thought itself—as the propaganda efforts of the great powers made clear—was manipulated, regimented, and controlled. In the United States, especially, civil liberties—including such constitutionally protected rights as free speech and free assembly—came under an assault never before seen in the nation's history, even during the arguably greater threat of the Civil War.

The war also upended social relations, especially as they pertained to women. Never before, in so short a time, did the women of the United States, Britain, and Canada leave their homes for gainful employment. With the economy fully mobilized and millions of men in uniform on faraway battlefields, women went to work in manufacturing jobs previously considered inappropriate for the "weaker sex." But more than in just defense plants, women became much more visible throughout society, particularly in labor-strapped Britain where women carried the mail, handled the cash, and even wielded the police officer's baton. While the armistice would lead to a general retreat for women—both voluntary and forced—back into the domestic sphere, not all returned. Moreover, the war years heralded changes that would become irreversible later in the century.

The war also had an impact on class and race relations. In Britain and, to a lesser extent, Canada, labor unions and the workers they represented enjoyed an unusual degree of influence over politics and the economy, a result of cooperation with government agencies and industrial leaders over wages, prices, and work conditions. African Americans in the United States did not wield such influence, but the war accelerated the move from Southern farm to Northern factory, establishing the foundation of urban African American communities, more self-assured and more politically influential, than anything seen since the days of Reconstruction a half-century earlier.

The war also led to domestic political change. With the significant exception of the socialist left in the United States, virtually all persons of all political stripes in the three countries considered in this volume enthusiastically embraced the war when it began. But as the war dragged on and the casualties mounted, people began to question the wisdom of their leaders—"stupid . . . and without imagination or heart," as British philosopher Bertrand Russell described them—and even the political system that gave rise to them. While none of the three English-speaking countries went through the kinds of political convulsions that pulsed through Russia, Germany, and even France, all experienced a turn to a harsher, more divided politics. In Britain, Conservative gains in the 1918 elections forced the government to take a tougher role with Germany at the Versailles Peace Conference. The prowar results of the 1917 Canadian elections further exacerbated relations between the English-speaking majority—always more committed to the war effort—and the French-speaking minority. But it was in the United States—ironically, having suffered the least number of casualties relative to its population than the other two—where the war had the greatest political effect. Isolationists voted down U.S. participation in the postwar League of Nations and then captured the White House and Congress, spelling an end to two decades of government activism.

Perhaps the greatest tragedy of World War I—aside from the legions of dead, orphaned, and widowed citizens—was the fact that it did not change things enough, for, within a generation, Europe and the world would once again be plunged into a conflict of even greater global proportions.

James Ciment

WORLD WAR I: BIOGRAPHIES

A

Addams, Jane

Social reformer, pacifist, and suffragist, Jane Addams (1860–1935) was born in Cedarville, Illinois, the eighth child of a successful miller, banker, landowner, and longtime state senator of Illinois. Her mother died when she was only three. After graduating from Rockford Female Seminary in 1881, she traveled in Europe for several years, returning to Chicago to found Hull House in 1889 with Ellen Gates Starr. The settlement house, based on London's Toynbee Hall, was intended to assimilate immigrants into the dominant culture, but it also became a center for the arts, education, civic reform, and multiethnic social life.

As Europe moved toward war, Addams became deeply involved in the peace movement. In 1915 she presided over the International Congress of Women at The Hague, from which came the Women's International League for Peace and Freedom and the Women's Peace Party, pacifist organizations of mostly middle- and upper-class women. The party's twenty-five thousand adherents called for arbitration of the European conflict by a conference of neutral parties. Economist Emily Balch, Dr. Alice Hamilton, and Addams presented their proposal to every member of the U.S. Senate and House and were largely ridiculed for their efforts. Addams in particular was attacked in the press for being unpatriotic and was expelled from the Daughters of the American Revolution.

In February 1917, Addams was one of a committee of five urging President Woodrow Wilson to find a way to avert U.S. entry into the war. But by then, Wilson had become committed to intervention, and Addams left the meeting in "deep dejection." In 1918, Herbert Hoover recruited Addams to his Department of Food Administration. She toured the country making speeches encouraging the conservation and increased production of food. She was criticized by some pacifists who felt that any support of the war effort was morally wrong.

After the war, Addams traveled to Europe with the Friends Service Committee and the Hoover Commission, distributing food, making note of the effects of deprivation, and arguing that peace would be impossible until hunger was eradicated. She strongly supported formation of the League of Nations.

Jane Addams was awarded the Nobel Prize for Peace in 1931, an honor she shared with Nicolas Murray Butler. She died in 1935 after surgery for cancer.

Among her extensive writings on her philosophy of peace are *Democracy and Social Ethics*

Jane Addams, founder of Chicago's Hull House, actively fought U.S. entry into World War I. (Library of Congress)

(1902), *Newer Ideals of Peace* (1906), *The Long Road of Woman's Memory* (1916), and *Peace and Bread in Time of War* (1922), as well as her classic *Twenty Years at Hull-House* (1910), and *The Second Twenty Years at Hull-House* (1930).

Betty Burnett

See also: Pacifists (WWI); Women's International League for Peace and Freedom (WWI); Biographies: Hoover, Herbert Clark (WWI); Documents: *Bread and Peace in Time of War,* 1922

REFERENCES

Elshtain, Jean Bethke. *Jane Addams and the Dream of American Democracy.* New York: Basic Books, 2001.

Elshtain, Jean Bethke, ed. *The Jane Addams Reader.* New York: Basic Books, 2001.

Anderson, Sherwood

Sherwood Anderson (1876–1941) was a prolific but, according to most literary scholars, a minor American literary figure of the twentieth century, but his experimental short stories were influential and he encouraged such younger authors as Ernest Hemingway, William Faulkner, and Thomas Wolfe. Anderson's most famous work, *Winesburg, Ohio,* was a series of short stories about a Midwestern town. The work displays Anderson's common themes of small-town life, the search for individual truth, and the perils of materialism.

Anderson was born on September 13, 1876, in Camden, Ohio, and spent most of his youth in the small town of Clyde, Ohio, the prototype for the fictional Winesburg. He did not begin writing in earnest until he was nearly forty years old, following a legendary midlife crisis. Up to that time, Anderson had worked as an advertising salesman and copywriter in Chicago and founded a mail-order business in Elyria, Ohio.

Married to Cornelia Lane since 1904, he had three children and lived the life of a typical Midwestern businessman and family man—that is, until November 1913, when Anderson abruptly walked out of his office and disappeared for four days. He turned up in a Cleveland hospital and rededicated his life to the artistic side he had long buried. Anderson left his wife and family, returned to his advertising job in Chicago, and began publishing short stories. His first novel, *Windy McPherson's Son,* appeared in 1916 and was embraced by critics and young writers. The story, largely autobiographical, was about a young man who turns his back on business and materialism to become a truth-seeker. Anderson's second novel, *Marching Men* (1917), did little to advance his reputation.

Anderson began writing the stories of Winesburg, Ohio, in 1915 and worked on them for several years. They appeared in book form in 1919. Critics hailed the work for its unique use of interrelated individual stories and Anderson's evocative, but not explicit, prose. *Winesburg, Ohio* made Anderson a leader in the literary revolution that occurred after World War I. It was his most significant work and also the end of his most successful writing stage. Anderson's next novels—*Poor White* (1920), *Many Marriages* (1923), and *Dark Laughter* (1925)—were uneven and showed his inability to completely inhabit the genre. His short story collections such as *The Triumph of the Egg* (1921), *Horses and Men* (1923), and *Death in the Woods and Other Stories* (1933), however, contained outstanding and inventive stories. He published the autobiography *A Story Teller's Story* in 1924.

Anderson was generous with his encouragement of other writers, most younger and more educated than himself. He convinced Hemingway to visit Paris rather than Italy, helped Faulkner publish his first novel, and his influence is evident in the works of Wolfe. Although he was always midwestern in sentiment, Anderson moved to the South in 1927, a change reflected in later works such as *Perhaps Women* (1931) and *Beyond Desire* (1932), both about the effects of industrialization. He bought two newspapers near his country home in Marion, Virginia in 1927 and thoroughly enjoyed his work as a country editor, reporter, and columnist. His work in nonfiction continued with *No Swank* (1934) and *Puzzled America* (1935), which profiled common Americans living during the Great Depression and the New Deal.

Anderson was married four times, the last to Eleanor Copenhaver. She turned his attention to social causes, which were evident in his last novel, *Kit Brandon: A Portrait* (1935), and his

last published work, *Home Town* (1940), a long essay illustrated with photos from the Farm Service Administration. In 1941, he was on his way to South America with Eleanor to observe the lives of common men there when he swallowed a toothpick at a cocktail party and died. Several works appeared after his death, including *Sherwood Anderson's Memoirs* (1942), a collection of his newspaper writings, and several collections of letters.

Melissa Stallings

See also: Literature (U.S., WWI); Biographies: Hemingway, Ernest (WWI)

REFERENCES

Rideout, Walter. *Sherwood Anderson: A Collection of Critical Essays.* Englewood Cliffs, NJ: Prentice Hall, 1974.

Taylor, Welford. *Sherwood Anderson.* New York: F. Ungar Publishing Co., 1977.

Townsend, Kim. *Sherwood Anderson.* Boston: Houghton Mifflin, 1987.

White, Ray. *Winesburg, Ohio: An Exploration.* Boston: Twayne Publishers, 1990.

Arbuckle, Roscoe "Fatty"

Known for his baby face and a rotund shape that contributed to his almost acrobatic physical humor, early comic movie star Roscoe "Fatty" Arbuckle began on the vaudevillian stage as a singer but soon found that his talent for controlling his large frame played well on film. Starting as a nameless Keystone Kop for Mack Sennett in 1905 (for a mere $5 a day), Arbuckle's career took off during World War I.

During the first years of the war, Arbuckle continued to work for Sennett at Keystone Stu-

Like many stars of the new movie industry, comic actor Roscoe "Fatty" Arbuckle used his fame to sell Liberty Loans during World War I. Here he puts up posters in New York's Times Square. (National Archives.)

dios but had advanced to directing and starring in his own shorter one- and two-reel films and working occasionally with up-and-comer Charlie Chaplin. Although a prolific period for Arbuckle, producing seventy-nine films between 1914 and 1916, he sought to have greater control over his pictures and developed a personality for his lovable Fatty character. While Sennett encouraged disorganized improvisation in his own films to achieve laughs, Arbuckle, trained on the stage, had more of an appreciation for careful timing.

Lou Anger, an executive at Paramount, approached Arbuckle in 1916 with an irresistible deal: He would be paid $1,000 a day, receive partial profits from his films amounting to $1 million after three years, and most importantly, have full creative control.

Shortly after finalizing his deal with Paramount, on Labor Day 1916, Arbuckle developed an excruciatingly painful boil above his knee. His wife, Minta Durfee, finally found a physician to look after Arbuckle on the holiday. Arbuckle was prescribed heroin for the pain, and he soon became dependent on the drug. Lou Anger had told Minta that a publicity tour was scheduled for February 1917, and so Fatty was checked into a hospital for drug treatment, losing almost one hundred pounds of his signature weight. Arbuckle, true to his word, finished the publicity tour, though to complete it he was again receiving daily injections of heroin. When Arbuckle could not obtain heroin, he would self-medicate with alcohol, an addiction he would also struggle with throughout his career.

Despite his personal troubles, Arbuckle still made a success of himself at Paramount, finally giving his Fatty character depth and producing twenty-three films between 1917 and the end of World War I in 1919. His first film with Paramount, *The Butcher Boy* (1917), introduced him to the young actor Buster Keaton. The two became good friends and often collaborated on projects. During the war, Keaton was drafted for entertainment purposes, but Arbuckle could not enlist because he was officially one hundred pounds over the army's limit. However, Arbuckle contributed to wartime efforts by raising money through his performance in a Liberty Bond short film, performing vaudeville and acrobatics for soldiers, and visiting orphanages. He also anonymously donated a trainload of tobacco to American troops.

Although Arbuckle's lucrative period at Paramount was cut short by scandal—specifically, the death of a young starlet in his hotel room in 1921—he flourished under his own creative control during World War I, and his name remains synonymous with the well-timed physical comedy of the silent film period, placing him in the ranks of legends such as Chaplin and Keaton.

Kathryn Bergeron

See also: Film (U.S., WWI); Biographies: Chaplin, Charlie (WWI); Keaton, Buster (WWI)

REFERENCES

Oderman, Stuart. *Roscoe "Fatty" Arbuckle: A Biography of the Silent Film Comedian, 1887–1933*. Jefferson, NC: McFarland and Company, Inc., 1994.

David Yallop. *The Day the Laughter Stopped: The True Story of Fatty Arbuckle*. New York: St. Martin's Press, 1976.

Armstrong, Louis

The founder of modern jazz and one of the most influential musical artists in American history, Louis Armstrong (1901–1971) excelled as a singer, trumpet player, bandleader, and motion-picture star for more than fifty years. He single-handedly defined the primary role of the

Louis Armstrong, whose career was just taking off during World War I, had become a national icon by World War II. (Library of Congress)

creative soloist in any jazz ensemble, recorded dozens of legendary record albums, radio performances, and television broadcasts, and became the most emulated jazz musician in history.

A native of New Orleans, Armstrong (better known later in life as "Satchmo") grew up poor and was forced to work as a child to help his family survive. In 1912 he was arrested for allegedly firing a pistol into the air on New Year's Eve and placed by police into the Colored Waif's Home for Boys as punishment. It was there that he learned to play the coronet under the instruction of Peter Davis, who directed the Waif's Home Band. He rose quickly through the ranks to become the band leader by 1913. His astounding musical skill and virtually limitless potential quickly brought him to the attention of the famous New Orleans trumpet player Joe "King" Oliver, who tutored him between 1914 and 1917 while Armstrong played in local clubs and sold newspapers or delivered coal on the side to feed himself, his mother, and his sister.

In 1918, Armstrong turned seventeen and married a New Orleans prostitute named Daisy Parker. He also devoted himself full time to a career as a trumpeter and singer, and played with the Kid Ory band before Fate Marable hired him in 1919 to perform on steamboats that cruised the Mississippi River. He held that position until he moved to Chicago to join King Oliver's band in 1922, at which time his success as a musician was assured.

Lance Janda

See also: Jazz (WWI); Music (U.S., WWI); Biographies: Armstrong, Louis (WWII)

REFERENCES

Bergreen, Laurence. *Louis Armstrong: An Extravagant Life.* New York: Broadway Books, 1997.

Giddins, Gary. *Satchmo: The Genius of Louis Armstrong.* New York: Da Capo Press, 2001.

Asquith, Herbert Henry

British Prime Minister and leader of the Liberal Party from 1908 to 1916, Herbert H. Asquith (1852–1928) had attempted to deal with extraordinary domestic political and social issues facing Great Britain when he suddenly became a wartime prime minister in 1914. His personal style, however, was not suited to the task of full-scale, modern, industrialized war. After a short period of unanimous political support, Asquith was attacked by members of the opposition and his own Liberal Party for failures on the military fronts and unpopular decisions on the home front, such as conscription. However, it was the failure of industry to supply sufficient munitions and the unending carnage of the Somme offensives that proved Asquith's undoing, and he was ousted from his position in December 1916.

Herbert H. Asquith was born into a middle-class family in Yorkshire on September 12, 1852. He attended Balliol College, Oxford, in 1870 and became a lawyer in 1876. Asquith was elected to the House of Commons as a Liberal member from East Fife in 1886, a position he held for thirty-two years. He served as home secretary under William Gladstone from 1892 to 1894, until the Liberals were defeated. During the Boer War, Asquith objected to British tactics to suppress the South Africans, especially the use of concentration camps. When the Liberals regained the government in 1906, he became Chancellor of the Exchequer. During this period, Asquith espoused views supporting Britain's imperial policies abroad but opposed women's suffrage at home.

In April 1908, Asquith became prime minis-

Herbert Henry Asquith led the Liberal Party and served as British Prime Minister during the first two years of World War I. But criticism about his war leadership led to his downfall at the end of 1916. (Library of Congress)

ter of a new Liberal government and was immediately faced with domestic issues such as Parliamentary reform and Irish home rule. Asquith also promoted social welfare efforts, such as old-age pensions and unemployment insurance. During the diplomatic crisis of July–August 1914 that led to the outbreak of war, Asquith and his foreign secretary, Sir Edward Grey, attempted to maintain British neutrality, but the German invasion of Belgium in early August propelled British intervention. When he ordered the British Expeditionary Force (BEF) to France, Asquith, like most leaders at the time, believed the war would be over in a few months.

Asquith quickly found the support in war

that he had sought during peacetime. He organized a War Council that included men of dominating personalities, such as David Lloyd George, Winston Churchill, and Lord Kitchener. Uncertain of his personal capabilities, Asquith relied perhaps too heavily on the advice of his council, in particular Secretary of War Kitchener. When stalemate on the Western Front prompted seeking other, more creative, options, Asquith was approached by Lloyd George and Churchill to support the Dardinelles expedition in 1915. When that option ended in a bloodbath on the Gallipoli Peninsula, the Conservative and Labor parties seized upon Asquith's growing list of failures and disappointments.

The final straw was the "shell scandal," in which Asquith was indicted for failing to mobilize Great Britain's resources for total war, resulting in inadequate ammunition for the army in France. When Sir John French told a war correspondent about the lack of sufficient or adequate artillery shells, the *London Times* published a series of articles critical of the governments' war-making abilities. This challenge to the Liberal Party grew when the Conservative leader, Andrew Bonar Law, and Asquith's Liberal challenger, Lloyd George, brought pressure to abandon the all-Liberal administration. As a result, Asquith was forced into a coalition government in May 1915, and he appointed Lloyd George to lead the new Ministry of Munitions.

Forced into the unenviable role as a compromiser, Asquith reluctantly assented to conscription on January 5, 1916, when he introduced a bill to add more than two million men to sustain British Army strength. Asquith's choice of Douglas Haig as field commander brought new concerns because the general insisted on an all-out effort to break the German line on the Western Front. In July 1916, Haig undertook the Somme offensive, which resulted in more than five hundred thousand British casualties and lasted until November with little appreciable gains for the sacrifice endured. Asquith was held accountable for these casualties, which included his eldest son, Raymond.

By 1916 a culmination of misfortunes permanently affected Asquith's position, including opposition to conscription, the Easter rebellion in Ireland, and increased shipping losses from U-boats. Variously accused of indifference, drunkenness, and adultery, Asquith was judged an out of touch war leader. In December he found was outmaneuvered in a scheme by Lloyd George in which he would be excluded from a War Committee that would exercise draconian powers to lead Britain to victory. Asquith at first agreed, but then declined to accept the arrangement, forcing Lloyd George to resign. Asquith further misjudged his position when he offered his own resignation, expecting it to be rejected by a majority in Parliament. Instead, it was accepted and Asquith was forced to resign as Prime Minister on December 5, 1916.

Asquith found himself as the leader of the opposition, where he vainly denied that he had mismanaged the war. The extent of his failure would be manifested during the election of December 1918, when he was defeated for the seat from East Fife, which he had held for thirty-two years. However, he returned to the House of Commons in 1920 and accepted honors making him a Knight of the Garter and chancellor of Oxford University. He was appointed to the House of Lords as First Earl of Oxford and Asquith in 1925.

Steven J. Rausch

See also: Armaments Industry (WWI); Conscription (UK, WWI); Conservative Party (UK, WWI); Easter Rising (WWI); Labour Party (UK, WWI, WWII); Liberal Party (UK, WWI); Biographies: Kitchener, Horatio Herbert (WWI); Law, Andrew Bonar (WWI); Lloyd George, David (WWI)

REFERENCES

Cassar, George H. *Asquith as War Leader.* London and Rio Grande: The Hambledon Press, 1994.

Jenkins, Roy. *Asquith.* New York: Chilmark Press, 1964.

Spender, John A., and Cyril Asquith. *Life of Herbert Henry Asquith.* 2 vols. London: Hutchinson, 1932.

B

Baker, Newton Diehl

Newton Diehl Baker (1871–1937), secretary of war during World War I, was born in Martinsburg, West Virginia. He graduated from Johns Hopkins University, where he studied under Woodrow Wilson, in 1892. After graduating with a law degree from Washington and Lee University in 1894, he practiced law for a time in his hometown. Moving to Cleveland in 1899, Baker quickly became part of the large, reform-minded network of young professionals in the city. He was involved in the settlement house movement, the local Council of Sociology, the Municipal Association, and the YMCA, and he played a significant role in establishing the city's juvenile court.

In 1902 Mayor Tom Johnson appointed him assistant law director. He became city solicitor in 1903. Baker accepted the leadership of the city's Democratic Party after Johnson's death, running successfully for mayor himself in 1912. That same year, Baker supported Woodrow Wilson's bid for the presidency. Declining Wilson's offer to become secretary of the interior in 1913, Baker accepted the position of secretary of war in 1916, after the resignation of his predecessor, Lindley M. Garrison. Before the war's outbreak, Baker had to steer a careful course between those opposed to entering the war and those who argued for preparedness, and he began by supporting a bill giving the federal government more control over the National Guard.

Newton Baker, U.S. Secretary of War from 1916 to 1921 was critical to the Woodrow Wilson Administration's efforts to mobilize the nation's resources and manpower during World War I. (Library of Congress)

Although the bill passed, it immediately sparked controversy in the War Department. It was the first of many difficulties Baker would have to moderate. Baker's early tenure was also complicated by the Pancho Villa affair in Mexico, in which the military sought to take steps against the Mexican revolutionary whose forces attacked the American town of Columbus, New Mexico, in 1915, by sending forces into Mexico in retaliation. Both Baker and Wilson had not desired such a punitive response. During the Great War, Baker was responsible for drafting, training, supplying, and mobilizing the country's two million troops as swiftly and efficiently as possible. By early 1918, when businesses came under the direct supervision of the War Industries Board, Baker focused his attention on the coordination of American troop and supply movements in the field. When the war was over, he oversaw the decommissioning of troops and the cancellation of war contracts and helped Wilson promote the League of Nations.

In 1921, Baker returned to Cleveland and the law firm he had established in 1916. In his remaining years he also served on the committees of numerous community agencies.

Paul Hillmer

See also: Demobilization (WWI); League of Nations (WWI); War Industries Board (WWI)

REFERENCES

Beaver, Daniel R. *Newton D. Baker and the American War Effort.* Lincoln: University of Nebraska Press, 1966.

Bara, Theda

A top film star and sex symbol in the World War I era, Theda Bara was born Theodosia Goodman in Cincinnati, Ohio, in 1890. As a child, she had a natural talent for song and dance, and worked in the local theater. Her future in the entertainment business was sealed when, in the early part of the twentieth century, her family moved to New York City. There she performed at a Yiddish theater and worked with a touring company. With the advent of motion pictures, she began to work in bit parts, eventually making her debut in the 1915 film, *The Stain.*

Bara's penchant for scanty clothes, exotic makeup, and dark dyed hair made her a natural for femme fatale roles, and she was cast as a seductive vampire in the 1915 classic, *A Fool There Was.* The movie was a success and launched Bara into instant stardom. Her famous line in the film, "kiss me, my fool," became a well-used phrase in the American lexicon of the time, and her dark, mysterious, exotic image generated an obsessive interest in her by the public.

The popularity of the film soon found Bara in a rapid succession of movies in which she played a seductress and murderess. She tried to break out of the mold and play other types of roles, but audiences preferred that she play a vamp.

An active supporter of the American war effort in World War I, Bara participated in Liberty Bond drives. In 1918 she took part in a drive in which movie stars sold the bonds. Bara's take was $56,950 worth of bonds, well past the expected $50,000 quota. She also enjoyed a certain popularity with the troops, who adopted her and showered her with gifts.

Following World War I, the interests of movie audiences changed. Soldiers came back from the war with more sophisticated tastes than the simple vamp roles played by Bara. Her roles in movies became infrequent and she went back to the stage. She eventually married and acted in the occasional movie and stage production. She died in 1954.

Kelly M. Jordan

See also: Film (U.S., WWI); War Bonds (WWI)

REFERENCES

Genini, Ronald. *Theda Bara: A Biography of the Silent Screen Vamp, with a Filmography.* Jefferson, NC: McFarland and Co., 1996.

Golden, Eve. *Vamp: The Rise and Fall of Theda Bara.* Vestal, NY: Emprise Publishers, 1996.

Keesey, Pam. *Vamps: An Illustrated History of the Femme Fatale.* San Francisco: Cleis Press, 1997.

Barrymore, John

A member of the great Barrymore acting family and a film star of the silent era, John Barrymore was born in 1882 in Philadelphia, Pennsylvania. Born into a family of acting legends, his parents were often on tour, leaving Barrymore at boarding schools. This contributed to a wild, troublesome youth, which extended into his adult years.

At the turn of the century, Barrymore studied art in England, and then worked as a cartoonist for the *New York Evening Journal.* His initial foray into acting was as a way to supplement his income, but soon acting overtook his art career.

Barrymore's first acting job came in 1903 in Chicago, with McKee Rankin and Nance O'Neill's Touring Company. By the end of the year, he was in New York for a role in the comedy, *Glad of It.* Barrymore's gift for comedic performance was a hit with audiences and soon led to a part in the comedy, *The Dictator.* Playing a drunken telegraph operator with great success, Barrymore toured with the production for a year. His first starring performance was in *The Boys of Company "B"* and was followed by other popular performances in *The Stubborn Cinderella* (1908–1909) and *The Fortune Hunter* (1909–1910).

The advent of film saw Barrymore's career shift from the stage to movies. Riding on his stage success, the actor easily landed a contract with the Famous Players Film Company. By 1913 he appeared in his first motion picture, *An American Citizen.*

During World War I, Barrymore's popularity with audiences continued to climb. Interested in joining the war effort, the actor applied for officer's training but failed the physical exam. His focus thus remained in his craft; his handsome looks and athleticism made him both a film and stage idol. His comedic performances brought relief to wartime audiences. While he pursued his comedic film career, Barrymore also began to explore dramatic roles on the stage. His 1917–1918 performance in *Peter Ibbetson* was a hit, as was *Redemption* (1918) and *The Jest* (1919).

In the 1920s Barrymore achieved one the greatest feats for a dramatic actor: the opportunity to play the lead in Shakespeare's *Richard III* and *Hamlet.* Barrymore's passionate performances moved audiences in both America and England. Following this achievement, the actor continued to appear in many films from the mid-1920s to the 1930s. Among some of his most popular were *State's Attorney* (1932), *A Bill of Divorcement* (1932), and *Topaz* (1933).

In later years, acute memory loss attributed to alcoholism and hard living plagued Barrymore's career. Movie studios became reluctant to work with him; by 1941 he had appeared in his final film, *Playmates.* Radio shows were kinder to the actor, who was allowed to read from scripts. From the mid-1930s on, he worked in radio, and appeared regularly on Rudy Vallee's *Sealtest Show* until his death in 1942.

Kelly M. Jordan

See also: Film (U.S., WWI)

REFERENCES

Fowler, Gene. *Goodnight Sweet Prince.* New York: Viking Press, 1943.

Kobler, John. *Damned in Paradise: The Life of John Barrymore.* New York: Atheneum, 1977.

Norden, Martin F. *John Barrymore: A Bio-Bibliography.* Westport, CT: Greenwood Press, 1995.

Baruch, Bernard

Bernard Mannes Baruch (1870–1965) made millions as a speculator and investor on Wall Street and attributed his wealth to decisions made by the U.S. government. In 1912, he entered politics as a major financial supporter of Democratic presidential candidate Woodrow Wilson.

When World War I began, Baruch gave his money to the war effort. He believed that the stability of the American financial markets and the American economy depended upon preparedness. He owned no munitions stocks because he feared that a financial interest in any product connected to war would risk compromising his position as a spokesman for preparedness. Although Baruch purchased Anglo-French war loans in the fall of 1915, he focused on American military and industrial preparedness for war. He gave $10,000 to Major General Leonard Wood to help finish building roads at the reserve officer's camp that Wood founded at Plattsburgh, New York. After the United States entered the war, Baruch bought $5 million of the first issue of Liberty Loans.

Baruch sought a Businessman's Commission that would synchronize plans for industrial mobilization, and in October 1916, a weaker version of what he had suggested came into being. The Wilson Administration established a Council of National Defense—consisting of the secretaries of War, Navy, Interior, Commerce, Labor, and Agriculture—to direct the home front in time of war. An Advisory Commission was established to help out the Council. Baruch was named as an advisor, much to his surprise.

Baruch never ran for public office. He was of German Jewish stock and believed that as a Jew, although not a devout one, he would never have a chance to be elected. As anti-German hysteria gripped the United States during the war, Baruch managed to avoid doubts about his patriotism. His father, a well-known physician, was asked to pledge allegiance to the United States by a magazine that promised to forward his response to the Justice Department for appropriate action. When the senior Baruch swore loyalty to the United States, the issue died quickly.

Baruch, a tall cheerful man with boundless energy and an ego to match the size of his fortune, served as chairman of the raw materials and minerals section of the Advisory Commission. He lined up supplies to meet the government's vast emergency demands. It was Baruch's idea that prices should be controlled to reduce civilian hardship and to deprive businessmen of an undeserved profit.

In July 1917, the Wilson Administration created the War Industries Board (WIB) to succeed the Advisory Commission. Baruch continued to head the raw materials and minerals section of the new body. He moved up to serve as chairman of the board for the last eight months of the war. The WIB disbanded with the signing of the Armistice. Baruch served as an economic advisor to Wilson at the Paris Peace Conference. In subsequent years, Baruch continued as a contributor to the Democratic Party and as an advisor to presidents.

Caryn E. Neumann

See also: Council of National Defense (WWI); War Industries Board (WWI); Biographies: Wood, Leonard (WWI)

REFERENCES

Baruch, Bernard M. *Baruch*. New York: Holt, 1960.
Grant, James. *Bernard M. Baruch: The Adventures of a Wall Street Legend*. New York: Simon and Schuster, 1983.

Beard, Charles A.

One of the greatest American intellectuals of the twentieth century, Charles Austin Beard (1874–1948) published landmark works in both political science and history and served as a staunch defender of academic freedom during World War I.

Born in Knightstown, Indiana, in 1874, Beard completed a doctorate at Columbia in 1904 and returned to accept a teaching position there in 1907. He produced his first textbook (*American Government and Politics*) in 1910, and demonstrated a remarkable gift for teaching and a progressive approach to education. His 1913 masterpiece was *An Economic Interpretation of the Constitution*. Critics raged against his contention that greed strongly influenced the authors of the American Constitution, but the book became an international bestseller and catapulted Beard into a leading role as a critic of traditional views of American life.

When World War I began the following year, Beard supported U.S. neutrality and subsequently endorsed the American declaration of war on Germany in 1917 (a position he later recanted). He was enraged, however, by the firing of three Columbia faculty members by university president Nicholas Murray Butler for their criticism of U.S. entry into the conflict. Beard saw their dismissal as part of a larger pattern of social and governmental suppression of dissent unleashed by the war and as an assault on academic freedom. He responded by resigning

The preeminent American historian of the early twentieth century, Charles Beard of Columbia University supported President Woodrow Wilson's decision to bring the United States into World War I, but he vigorously protested university president Nicholas Murray Butler's decision to dismiss anti-war professors. (Library of Congress)

from Columbia, castigating Butler in his letter of resignation, and never returning to academia.

For the rest of his days, Beard pursued an extraordinarily productive and lucrative career as a revisionist historian and social critic whose books sold an estimated twelve million copies during his life. He died in New Haven, Connecticut on September 1, 1948.

Lance Janda

See also: Intellectuals (WWI); Biographies: Butler, Nicholas Murray (WWI)

REFERENCES

Barrow, Clyde W. *More Than a Historian: The Political and Economic Thought of Charles A. Beard.* Somerset, New Jersey: Transaction Publishing, 2000.

Beale, Howard K., ed. *Charles A. Beard: An Appraisal.* Lexington, KY: University of Kentucky Press, 1951.

Benson, A. L.

Allan Louis Benson (1871–1940) was a journalist and member of the Socialist Party during World War I. Benson was born in Plainfield, Michigan and attended public schools. He became a journalist, working for papers in Chicago, Salt Lake City, and San Francisco. Between 1897 and 1906, he was managing editor for two Detroit newspapers. He then spent a year as managing editor for the *Washington Times.* His travels across the United States and experiences as a newspaperman made him sympathetic to the Socialist point of view, and he began writing pamphlets with a Socialist slant; these included *Socialism Made Plain: Why the Few Are Rich and the Many Poor* and *Confessions of Capitalism,* both published in 1904. During the 1908 presidential campaign, Benson published *What Help Can Any Workingman Expect from Taft or Bryan?,* encouraging workers to vote for Socialist Party candidates.

As Benson's political convictions became stronger, he retired from the newspaper profession in 1907 and supported himself by the sales of his pamphlets and by writing for left-wing and Socialist journals. In 1911, his pamphlet *The Usurped Power of the Courts* sold more than one million copies. He followed with *The Truth About Socialism* (1913), which went through nine editions, and *The Growing Grocery Bill* (1912), which sold one million seven hundred thousand copies. Benson was an active campaigner for the presidential campaign of Eugene V. Debs in 1912. That election marked the high point of the Socialist Party's electoral success. Although defeated, Debs received one million votes for president, the highest amount a third-party candidate had received in a generation. Hundreds of Socialists were elected to local offices, from which they hoped to begin changing society.

In 1914, World War I broke out in Europe. Like many other groups, the Socialist Party blamed it on imperialism and bourgeois capitalism. The party adopted an antiwar stand. Benson wrote *A Way to Prevent War* (1915) and *Inviting America to War* (1916) to set out the Socialist Party's position. When the 1916 presidential campaign came around, the Socialists hoped to capitalize on the general American opposition to involvement in the war and increase their share of the votes. Because Debs was ill, he declined to be the party's candidate for president. Instead, Benson was nominated by a direct mail vote by the membership. At the national convention, Benson asked for Kate Richards O'Hare—a well-known socialist orator, writer, and spokesman for sexual emancipation—to be his running mate. A woman was too controversial for the party, however, and they nominated Socialist writer George Kirkpatrick instead.

Benson and the Socialists continued their antiwar platform. Benson vowed that a declaration of offensive war would be made by him only after a referendum by the voters of the entire country. He also criticized Woodrow Wilson for his support for preparedness, believing it was a way of drawing the United States into war. Finally, Benson criticized American industrialists for producing war goods for the Allies and for promoting American entry into war as a means of increasing their profits. Benson proved to be a disappointing candidate after the dynamic

Debs, however. Wilson's claim that he had kept the country out of war attracted many antiwar voters. Workers, the Socialists natural supporters, were also drawn to Wilson because of his record of pro-labor actions. In the election, Benson received a disappointing 3.2% of the votes, down from the 6% Debs received in 1912.

Within six month after the election, the United States declared war on Germany. The Socialist Party issued a paper blaming both Germany and the Allies equally for the outbreak of war. The party also opposed conscription and continued their antiwar stand. Benson felt he could no longer support those positions and resigned from the Socialist Party in 1918. He continued to write on various topics, including a biography of Daniel Webster in 1929. He died in Yonkers, New York, in 1940.

Tim J. Watts

See also: Socialist Party (WWI); Biographies: Debs, Eugene V. (WWI)

REFERENCES

Esposito, Anthony V. *The Ideology of the Socialist Party of America, 1901–1917.* New York: Garland, 1997.
Trachtenberg, Alexander, ed. *The American Socialists and the War.* New York: Garland, 1973.
Weinstein, James. *The Decline of Socialism in America, 1912–1925.* New Brunswick, NJ: Rutgers University Press, 1984.

Berger, Victor

An Austrian immigrant, U.S. congressman, and cofounder of the Socialist Party of America, as well as a teacher and newspaper publisher, Victor Berger (1860–1929) was the first Socialist to be elected to Congress. During World War I, he was an ardent opponent of U.S. involvement in the conflict. Berger was charged with violating the Espionage Act, found guilty, and sentenced to twenty years in prison. While appealing his conviction, Berger was reelected to Congress. A year later, the Supreme Court reversed his sentence and Berger was allowed to take his seat in the House. Berger remained an outspoken advocate of freedom of speech and left a legacy as to the rights of citizens during wartime.

Born on February 28, 1860, in the Nieder-Rehbach region of Austria-Hungary, Victor Louis Berger was the son of innkeepers Ignatz and Julia Berger. After attending the Universities of Vienna and Budapest, Berger emigrated with his family to the United States in 1878 at the age of eighteen. The Berger's settled in Bridgeport, Connecticut. Three years later, in 1881, Berger moved to the German-speaking enclave of Milwaukee, Wisconsin and was employed in a series of odd jobs before becoming a teacher. He quickly became a leader in the city and developed an interest in the radical politics that permeated such immigrant epicenters. He embraced socialism, and lost his job because of his radical beliefs. Initially a member of the Socialist Labor Party, Berger, along with the Socialist Party presidential candidate Eugene V. Debs and others, left the Socialist Labor Party three years later and began the Socialist Party of America. This new creation of Berger and Debs had the greatest power of all Marxist associations in U. S. history.

Meanwhile, Berger embarked on a newspaper publishing career. He served as both editor and publisher of the *Wisconsin Vorwaerts* from 1892 to 1898, the *Social Democratic Herald* from 1901 to 1913, and the *Milwaukee Leader* from 1911 to 1929. All were German-language newspapers that catered to the strong German American population in Wisconsin. In his position as editor, Berger was able to shape the socialist minds in his area. In 1910, Berger was elected to the city council and then, later that same year, was elected to the U. S. House of Representatives. He was the first Socialist to be elected to Congress.

Initially a supporter of violence as a way to promulgate socialist values, Berger soon changed his thinking on the subject. In his first term, Berger introduced bills to provide pensions for the elderly, improve workers' conditions in the District of Columbia, dismantle the Senate and the presidential veto, and put the ownership of several corporations in the hands of the public. When the United States entered into World War I, Berger opposed it, and his newspaper, the *Leader,* had its second-class mailing permit taken away. The *Leader* was said to have violated the Espionage Act and Berger was brought to trial for conspiracy to violate said act. In 1918, he was reelected to his seat in the House and in 1919 he was convicted of the charges against him. In 1921, the Supreme Court reversed his conviction and Berger did not have to serve his twenty-year sentence. While awaiting his appeal, the House refused to allow Berger to take his seat in the sixty-sixth Congress. He was reelected again in 1922, 1924, and 1926. By the end of the 1920s, socialism had lost its savor and was replaced by other left-wing groups, as was Berger in the House. Berger retired to Wisconsin to work on local politics and was killed in a traffic accident on July 16, 1929.

Philine Georgette Vega

See also: Espionage Act (WWI); Socialist Party (WWI); Biographies: Debs, Eugene V. (WWI); Documents: Espionage Act, June 15, 1917

REFERENCES

Miller, Sally M. *Victor Berger and the Promise of Constructive Socialism, 1910–1920.* Westport, CT: Greenwood Press, 1973.

Berlin, Irving

Irving Berlin (1888–1989), born Isidore Baline, was more successful at articulating American values and attitudes than any other composer of the twentieth century. Every major period of cultural development in America between 1910 and 1970 had a hit song by Irving Berlin that summed up how Americans were feeling at the time. *Alexander's Ragtime Band,* (1911), *Blue Skies* (1927), and *Let's Have Another Cup of Coffee* (1932) helped promote a mainstream attitude that was not only politically correct but socially affirmative.

Berlin's wartime songs are perhaps the most frankly propagandistic because of the urgent need for morale-boosting material; his large group of WWI songs helped bolster American courage at home and at the front. A sampling of patriotic songs from this period includes *Let's All Be Americans Now* (1917), *For Your Country and My Country* (1917), *Oh, How I Hate to Get Up in the Morning* (from the musical, *Yip! Yip! Yaphank*) (1918), *The Blue Devils of France* (1918), *Dream on Little Soldier Boy* (1918), *Over the Sea Boys* (1918), *We're on Our Way to France* (1918), *Good-bye France* (1918), and *I've Got My Captain Working for Me Now* (1919). All these songs were broadcast over the airwaves in the tense, expectant nights at home, and played upon the lips of many fighting men as they descended to the trenches of doom.

Irving Berlin could always come up with easily memorable slogans capable of expressing the essence of popular attitudes. His masterful ability to write lyrics with transparent propagandistic content, combined with a talent for tuneful, catchy melodies, raise him from the status of a mere composer to a cultural icon, a permanent fixture in the history of World War I.

Richard Freeman-Toole

See also: Music (WWI); Songs (U.S., WWI); Biographies: Berlin, Irving (WWII)

REFERENCES

Jablonski, Edward. *Irving Berlin: American Troubadour.* New York: Henry Holt, 1999.

Borden, Robert Laird

If World War I was the most significant event in modern history, its effect was no less profound on Robert Laird Borden. Born in the village of Grand Pré, Nova Scotia, in 1854, more than a decade before the British North American provinces united to form the Dominion of Canada, he entered politics largely because of his strong belief in the moral obligation of those who are able to serve their community. Thus, when Sir Charles Tupper, a family friend and then prime minister, asked him in 1896 to seek election to the House of Commons, he left his lucrative law practice in Halifax, by then the largest in the Maritime provinces, recognizing that Tupper's government was in danger of being defeated by the Liberal Party led by Wilfrid Laurier.

The Tupper government was defeated but Borden was elected and four years later he succeeded Tupper as leader of the Conservative Party. He led the party unsuccessfully through the 1904 and 1908 elections and almost certainly would have returned to Halifax had fate not intervened. When the Laurier government announced first that it would build a Canadian navy rather than contribute directly to the Royal Navy's struggle to maintain supremacy over the German high seas fleet, and then that it had negotiated a reciprocity (free trade) agreement with the United States, Borden's patriotic feelings and sense of duty to the preser-

vation of the British empire and Canada's proud place in it were aroused. He rallied the Conservative Party, which had hitherto been sharply divided over his progressive inclinations and unsteady leadership, and succeeded in forcing an election in 1911, which the Conservatives won.

Thus, Borden found himself in office when World War I broke out in August 1914. Although the Canadian people generally supported Canada's participation in the war because of the historic British connection and strong emotional and kinship ties to the old country, it was not long before disagreement over the extent of Canadian participation emerged. Borden quickly became convinced that the war was not merely a conflict between rival European empires but a moral struggle between civilization, represented by Britain, and barbarism, represented by Germany. The possibility that barbarism might triumph over civilization was unthinkable, so it logically followed, in Borden's mind, that there could be no limit to the extent of the Canadian contribution.

Accordingly, when voluntary enlistments failed to keep pace with the demands of the Flanders slaughterhouse, Borden's original commitment of twenty-five thousand troops rose steadily to five hundred thousand, an unsustainable number. He responded by introducing conscription, along with an increasingly elaborate regulatory system designed to control production, distribution, wages, and prices. In the end, he even rewrote the electoral laws to ensure his government's reelection in 1917.

A curiously unpartisan man for a politician, he began life as a Liberal—his cousin was Laurier's minister of militia (defense) for fifteen years—and won the 1911 election because of significant support from Liberals in Ontario and Nationalists in Quebec. In 1917 he formed a coalition with proconscription Liberals and sincerely offered to resign in favor of Laurier if he would support conscription. This did not happen, and Borden ended up leading an overwhelmingly English-speaking Protestant prowar coalition against a predominantly French-speaking Catholic opposition.

Borden was roundly denounced at the time and later for aspiring to dictatorship, for attempting to destroy democracy, for being anti-French (because it was believed that conscription would recruit more French Canadians than English Canadians, who had volunteered in greater numbers), and even for being a Communist when he nationalized the privately owned railways, which were facing bankruptcy. He was none of these and indeed found most of his actions in 1917–1918 as distasteful as did his critics. He was a man of deep convictions whose greatest compliment was to describe a man as earnest, and he believed that it was his profound responsibility to do what was required to achieve the necessary goals.

In the end, Canada's contribution to the war was significant—more than six hundred thousand men, as well as a large financial and economic contribution—and at the cost of bringing Canada to the verge of civil war. A side effect was the destruction of the Conservative Party in both Quebec and the Prairie provinces, a political reality that has deeply affected the Canadian political process to the present.

Borden retired in 1920, exhausted from the physical and mental strain, and enjoyed the last seventeen years of his life more than the previous twenty. He emerged as a respected elder statesman with a deserved international reputation, lectured at universities and received honorary degrees, and spent a lot of time with his books. A scholarly, erudite, passionate man, he had hoped to contribute to the progressive reform movement in his political career but ended up appearing to be a callous, bigoted imperialist who sacrificed Canadian interests to the demands of British imperialism. He could,

however, take satisfaction in the knowledge that he had advanced Canada's constitutional status significantly from the level of a semicolonial dominion to that of an autonomous nation. Borden died in 1937.

Brian Tennyson

See also: Conscription (Canada, WWI); Conservative Party (Canada, WWI); Mobilization (Canada, WWI); Biographies: Hughes, Sir Sam (WWI); Laurier, Sir Wilfrid (WWI); Documents: Speech to the Canadian Club, December 29, 1914; Appeal for National Service, October 23, 1916

REFERENCES

Borden, Robert Laird. *Robert Laird Borden: His Memoirs.* Edited by Henry Borden. 2 vols. Toronto: Macmillan, 1938.

Borden, Robert Laird. *Letters to Limbo.* Edited by Henry Borden. Toronto: University of Toronto Press, 1971.

Brown, Robert Craig. *Robert Laird Borden.* 2 vols. Toronto: Macmillan, 1975–1980.

Brown, Robert Craig, and Ramsay Cook. *Canada 1896–1921: A Nation Transformed.* Toronto: McClelland and Stewart, 1974.

English, John. *The Decline of Politics: The Conservatives and the Decline of the Party System, 1901–1920.* Toronto: University of Toronto Press, 1977.

Morton, Desmond, and J. L. Granatstein. *Marching to Armageddon: Canada and the Great War, 1914–1919.* Toronto: Lester and Orpen Dennys, 1989.

Bourassa, Henri

Grandson of the legendary Louis-Joseph Papineau, who led the campaign for responsible government in Lower Canada (Quebec) that culminated in the Patriote uprising of 1837, and son of Napoleon Bourassa, an artist, architect, and novelist, Henri Bourassa (1868–1952) carried on the family tradition of independent thinking and powerful advocacy and made a profound contribution to the political crisis that brought Canada to the verge of civil disruption during World War I.

Elected at the age of twenty-eight to the House of Commons in the great Liberal victory of 1896, Bourassa was widely regarded as a young man with a brilliant future. Ethnic nationalism was a growing force in Canada, and national leaders such as Wilfrid Laurier sought acceptable compromises, but Bourassa sought to protect French language rights and Roman Catholicism, not merely in his own province but throughout Canada. He dreamed of an autonomous Canada within the empire that recognized equal rights for both cultures throughout the country. These were radical ideas at the time.

He broke with Laurier in 1899 over the government's decision to send troops to support Britain in the South African War and became hostile a decade later when Laurier agreed to create a Canadian navy. Bourassa saw these decisions as unnecessary responses to imperialist pressure that would inevitably drag Canada into foreign wars. Not surprisingly, he was one of the founders of the Nationalist League in 1903, and in 1910 he established the nationalist newspaper, *Le Devoir.*

In a catastrophic political miscalculation, he collaborated with the Conservative Party in the 1911 election, forming what Laurier called an "unholy alliance," which succeeded in destroying the Liberal government. The new Borden government had won enough seats in Canada outside Quebec that it did not need Nationalist support, however, so that when Canada entered World War I, it was ruled by a party whose support was almost entirely English-speaking and Protestant, while the official opposition in the House of Commons was made up largely of French-speaking Catholics, mostly from Quebec.

Bourassa reluctantly supported Canadian participation in the war, recognizing Canada's moral obligations to Britain, but insisted that participation should be voluntary. Thus, when Borden introduced conscription, Bourassa led a powerful opposition campaign in Quebec that contributed to the polarization of the country between English-speaking Protestants, who supported conscription (assuming that it was largely French Canadians who would be conscripted), and French-speaking Catholics, who largely opposed it. Bourassa's outrage over conscription was fuelled in part by the Ontario government's determination to virtually eliminate French language instruction in schools located in francophone communities in that province. Borden won the 1917 election, in which conscription was the major issue, but Laurier and Bourassa carried all but three of Quebec's seats. The country was on the verge of civil war when, mercifully, World War I came to an end.

In the post-war years, Bourassa continued to be a vigorous spokesman for the nationalist cause. But he was increasingly regarded as too moderate and was supplanted by the more radical Abbé Lionel Groulx, a priest and popular historian who believed that Quebec's cultural and religious survival could be assured only through political independence.

Henri Bourassa is a tragic figure whose dream of an autonomous bicultural and bilingual Canadian nation that recognized Quebec's distinctiveness was sidelined by the conflicting ethnic nationalist antipathies to which he made a significant contribution during World War I. Nevertheless, when he died in 1952, following a similar though lesser political crisis over conscription during World War II, B. K. Sandwell correctly observed in *Saturday Night* that "all the constitutional issues which he espoused during the first fifty years of his life and for which he was repaid by being denounced as a traitor by a fair share of the English-speaking public have become established constitutional practices."

Brian Tennyson

See also: Conscription (Canada, WWI); Liberal Party (Canada, WWI); Biographies: Borden, Robert Laird (WWI); Laurier, Sir Wilfrid (WWI)

REFERENCES

Armstrong, Elizabeth. *The Crisis of Quebec, 1914–1918.* New York: Columbia University Press, 1937.

Laurendeau, André. "Henri Bourassa." R. L. Mac-Dougall, ed. *Our Living Tradition,* 4th Series. Toronto: University of Toronto Press, 1962.

Levitt, Joseph, ed. *Henri Bourassa on Imperialism and Bi-Culturalism, 1900–1918.* Toronto: Copp Clark, 1970.

Murrow, Casey. *Henri Bourassa and French-Canadian Nationalism.* Montreal: Harvest House, 1968.

O'Connell, M. P. "The Ideas of Henri Bourassa." *Canadian Journal of Economics and Political Sciences* 19, no. 3 (August 1953): 361–376.

Wade, Mason. *The French Canadians 1760–1945.* Toronto: Macmillan, 1955.

Bourne, Randolph

Writer, cultural critic, and pacifist during World War I, Randolph Bourne (1886–1918) was born in Bloomfield, New Jersey, to Charles Bourne, a ne'er-do-well businessman, and Sara Barrett. Physically deformed from the misuse of forceps at birth and several childhood illnesses, Bourne's odd appearance often isolated him from his peers even though he was affable and gregarious by nature.

When he was a child, his parents separated due to his father's alcoholism, and he grew up in the home of his mother's uncle. When he

was ready to attend Princeton, his uncle had a sudden reversal of fortunes and Bourne was forced to take a number of odd jobs, including work in a factory that permanently instilled in him a deep sympathy for the working class. By 1909 he had saved enough money to enter Columbia University. He received his bachelor's degree in 1913.

While a student, Bourne was exposed to the ideas of Friedrich Nietzsche, George Santayana, William James, and John Dewey. Politically he became a devoted Socialist. Unlike other reformers of the period who focused their energy on social and political institutions, Bourne focused his on culture. He was critical not only of outmoded genteel Victorian values but also of the emerging mass consumer market and its materialistic mores. To reform American culture, Bourne believed more emphasis had to be placed on youth. Bourne considered youth not just a transient stage in life but also a regenerative attitude of questioning and challenging established authority and maintaining an open mind. Bourne was also critical of the "melting pot," which he considered coercive. America would be stronger if its culture was an amalgamation of various ethnic composites instead of strictly Anglo American.

During World War I, Bourne broke with other intellectuals and remained a steadfast and vocal opponent of American involvement. He feared the war would kill the youth of America both literally and figuratively. Moreover, he feared that the coercion of wartime unity would crush his dreams of a pluralistic, multiethnic culture.

Bourne died in New York City, a victim of the influenza epidemic of 1918. In addition to writing hundreds of articles for such magazines as *Seven Arts, Dial, New Republic,* and *The Masses,* he wrote *Youth and Life* (1913), *Gary Schools* (1916), and *Education and Living* (1917). Two more books *Untimely Papers* (1919) and *The His-*

tory of a Literary Radical (1920) were published posthumously.

Gregory Dehler

See also: Censorship (WWI); Influenza Epidemic of 1918 (WWI); Pacifists (WWI); Red Scare (WWI); Socialist Party (WWI)

REFERENCES

Clayton, Bruce. *Forgotten Prophet: The Life of Randolph Bourne.* Baton Rouge: Louisiana State University Press, 1984.

Vaughan, Leslie. *Randolph Bourne and the Politics of Cultural Radicalism.* Lawrence: University of Kansas Press, 1997.

Bryan, William Jennings

William Jennings Bryan (1860–1925) was a captivating orator who espoused populist social reform and pacifism and lost three presidential elections (1896, 1900, 1908) as the Democratic Party candidate. He served as secretary of state in Woodrow Wilson's cabinet.

When World War I erupted in 1914, the American public vociferously rejected involvement in European affairs and the Wilson administration urged that Americans adopt a stance of "absolute neutrality" and "impartiality and restraint." Bryan was the country's most powerful and eloquent voice of pacifism. A high moral purpose guided Bryan's advocacy on the issues that defined his legacy: a national income tax, a bimetal monetary policy (unlimited silver and gold reserves versus a single, limited gold standard), and tariffs to protect small farmers. Bryan saw himself upholding the "everlasting" ideals of American democracy promulgated by Thomas Jefferson and Andrew Jackson.

In 1894, Bryan became editor-in-chief of the Omaha *World Herald.* In 1901 in Lincoln, Nebraska, he founded his own weekly newspaper, the *Commoner,* which became an influential voice against the war. Woodrow Wilson appointed Bryan his secretary of state in 1912. Unlike Wilson, however, Bryan never wavered on the principle of neutrality. In 1915, prompted by the sinking of the *Lusitania,* Bryan resigned as secretary of state to protest what he saw as the Wilson administration's deviation from neutrality.

Born in Salem, Illinois, Bryan grew up in a devoutly religious home. His father, Silas, was a state senator and a state judge. Bryan graduated valedictorian from Illinois College in 1881, spent two years at Union College of Law in Chicago, and then married Mary Baird. He practiced law in a small Illinois town, Jacksonville, for five years. He did not distinguish himself until he moved to Lincoln, Nebraska and formed a law partnership with an old friend. Plunging into local politics, Bryan excelled as a populist orator, arguing for tariffs and bimetallism to protect farmers against speculators and big business interests.

Bryan's rise was swift. From 1891 to 1895, he served as one of Nebraska's Democratic representatives to the U.S. Congress. As a delegate at the 1896 Democratic National Convention in Chicago, Bryan delivered his most famous oration, the "Cross of Gold" speech: "You shall not press down upon the brow of labor this crown of thorns. You shall not crucify mankind upon a cross of gold," he intoned in conclusion. He was just thirty-six and had not sought office. However, his speech so moved the delegates that Bryan was swept up in a tide of popular support and won the party's nomination to face the Republican candidate, William McKinley, governor of Ohio.

Believing Woodrow Wilson to be a man who "listens to his conscience," Bryan worked hard to help Wilson, the governor of New Jersey, win the Democratic presidential nomination in 1912. In a risky move, Wilson asked Bryan to be his secretary of state. Perhaps Wilson thought that bringing Bryan into the fold would hold back Bryan's inevitable criticism of his administration. Bryan agreed on condition that Wilson allow him to negotiate a series of international peace treaties. Bryan managed to negotiate pacts with thirty nations, including France, Britain, and Italy. On May 7, 1915, a German submarine torpedoed the British liner *Lusitania,* killing some twelve hundred passengers, including one hundred twenty-eight Americans. Hardliners in the Cabinet wanted—at the very least—that Germany be made to apologize. Bryan argued that the *Lusitania* was carrying munitions; he wanted Wilson to issue a warning to Americans not to sail on the ships of belligerent nations in the war. The Cabinet argued for a month about what to write Germany about sinking the *Lusitania.* Bryan pointed to his thirty peace pacts and said the arbitration rules they contained should be used to handle the *Lusitania* incident. And if Germany was going to be reprimanded, said Bryan, so too should Britain, for interfering with American trade. Bryan's proposals were rejected and he was sharply rebuked by Wilson, for "unjustly" labeling "good Americans" pro-British or pro-German. Bryan told Wilson that he would not sign the official communiqué to Germany and was resigning his post. At his last Cabinet meeting, on June 8, Bryan said, "I must act according to my conscience."

After the war, Bryan devoted himself to the fundamentalist religious movement. He defended its creationist tenets in the 1925 Scopes "Monkey" trial in Dayton, Tennessee. Bryan served as a prosecutor in the trial of a high-school biology teacher, John Scopes, who had violated a newly enacted state law banning the teaching of evolution. Bryan argued that par-

ents had the right to decide what their children should be taught. Said Bryan: "Shall we be detached from the throne of God and be compelled to link our ancestors with the jungle—tell that to these children?" In defending Darwin's theory of evolution, Scope's lawyer, Clarence Darrow, tarnished Bryan's reputation by maneuvering him into defending absurd positions. But Scopes lost his case and was ordered to pay a $100 fine. Although Bryan won the grueling, two-week trial, he died exhausted five days after the verdict was announced.

Tony Osborne

See also: Isolationism (WWI); *Lusitania,* Sinking of (WWI); Pacifists (WWI); Biographies: Wilson, Woodrow (WWI)

REFERENCES

Glad, Paul W. *McKinley, Bryan, and the People.* Philadelphia and New York: J. B. Lippincott, 1964.

Koenig, Louis W. *Bryan.* New York: G. P. Putnam's Sons, 1971.

Burleson, Albert Sidney

Albert Sidney Burleson (1863–1937) served as postmaster general during World War I. After Burleson received his law degree from the University of Texas at Austin in 1884, he developed an interest in Texas politics. Burleson became an active member of the Democrat Party, and developed a close friendship with Edward M. House. By 1899, Burleson was elected to Congress. During his tenure in Congress, he supported legislation designed to improve agricultural conditions in the South. In 1913, Edward House recommended Burleson for a cabinet position in the administration of President

Woodrow Wilson, and the president appointed Burleson as postmaster general.

Following the U.S. entrance into World War I, Congress established the Espionage Act, which enabled the postmaster general to ban from the mail any publications that promoted treason and insurrection among the American public. Burleson used the powers under the act to deny mailing privileges to any organization or group that expressed opposition to U. S. involvement in the war, such as *American Socialist, New York Call,* and *Milwaukee Leader.* Burleson justified his actions by asserting that these publications encouraged socialist ideas. The postmaster general also refused to deliver *The Masses* in the mail. The editor of *The Masses* maintained that the magazine was a pacifist publication, but Burleson remarked that the magazine had Socialist writers who promoted their ideologies in the periodical. Some individuals believed that the postmaster general's actions infringed on Americans' rights, but President Wilson expressed only limited opposition toward Burleson's policies.

In October 1917, Congress enacted the Trading with the Enemy Act, which required editors of all foreign-language newspapers to submit their work to the postmaster general before publication. The act also stipulated that foreign-language newspapers had to translate in English any editorials relating to the war. The translation of these newspapers represented an expense, so many foreign-language periodicals went bankrupt during the war.

By 1918, Burleson continued to deny mailing privileges to publications that he regarded as undermining U.S. war efforts. For example, he banned the *Nation* from the mail because it criticized union leaders. While the postmaster general stated that he was serving American interests, this incident caused Wilson to finally intervene and reprimand Burleson for his actions.

Burleson's censorship of foreign-language periodicals and socialist publications caused anarchists to target him following the war. In May 1919, postal authorities found thirty-four bombs addressed to Burleson and other prominent government officials.

Following Burleson's retirement as postmaster general in 1921, he returned to Austin, Texas. In 1930, Baylor University awarded him an honorary law degree. Although Burleson distanced himself from politics during his retirement, he campaigned in favor of Franklin D. Roosevelt during the presidential election of 1932. On November 24, 1937, Burleson died at his home in Austin.

Kevin M. Brady

See also: Espionage Act (WWI); Socialist Party (WWI); Biographies: Wilson, Woodrow (WWI)

REFERENCES

Murphy, Paul L. *World War I and the Origins of Civil Liberties in the United States.* New York: Norton, 1979.
Scheiber, Harry N. *The Wilson Administration and Civil Liberties, 1917–1921.* Ithaca: Cornell University Press, 1960.

Burns, William John

William John Burns (1861–1932) was one of the leading American detectives of the early twentieth century. Besides hunting down counterfeiters, he exposed corruption by public office holders. During World War I, Burns and his operatives provided security against sabotage by German agents and assisted the U.S. government's counterespionage efforts. His tenure as director of the Federal Bureau of Investigation (FBI) was marked by investigations of radicals, the Ku Klux Klan, and political favoritism.

Burns was born in Baltimore in 1861, but he moved with his family to Columbus, Ohio, when he was a boy. When his father was elected police commissioner, the teenage Burns honed his detective skills as an amateur sleuth and soon established a regional reputation. In 1885, he determined that a number of voter tally sheets for a recent election were frauds and helped to convict a ring of arsonists. In 1889, Burns joined the U.S. Secret Service. He helped break up several notorious counterfeiting rings and solved the theft of $30,000 in double-eagle gold pieces from the San Francisco Mint. Burns's success as a detective was aided by his recognition that publicity was as important as skill.

In 1903, the Department of the Interior asked Burns to investigate land frauds in Oregon, Washington, and California. He turned up evidence that resulted in more than one hundred indictments and thirty-three convictions, including that of U.S. Senator John H. Mitchell. In 1905, San Francisco civic leaders asked Burns to head an investigation of that city's government, resulting in a fourteen-year prison term for Abraham Ruef, the city's political boss. Burns left the Secret Service in 1909 to establish the William J. Burns National Detective Agency in New York. His clients included the American Banker's Association, with more than twelve thousand members. Hotel chains and other trade associations were also customers. In 1910, Burns solved his most sensational case to date. That year, a bomb destroyed the building of the *Los Angeles Times,* an antiunion newspaper, and killed twenty people. Burns believed it was the work of the International Association of Bridge and Structural Ironworkers. After he and his agents rounded up enough evidence, they spirited two union leaders out of Indiana and back to California to stand trial. After protesting their innocence, the two confessed to the bombing, helping to fuel antilabor and antiradical sentiment in the country. Burns wrote

about his detective experiences in catching the bombers in *The Masked War* (1913).

When World War I broke out in 1914, many American manufacturers began supplying the Allies with munitions and military equipment. Evidence quickly surfaced that the Germans were planning acts of sabotage. J. P. Morgan, acting as the purchasing agent for the British and French governments, hired Burns's detective agency to provide security for manufacturers doing business with those governments. Burns's agents supervised the loading of supplies and rode the trains that carried munitions to the ships carrying equipment overseas. Burns also provided men for security in factories making munitions.

On July 30, 1916, the Black Tom terminal in New York harbor, an important staging point for munitions ships headed for Europe, exploded. Although the explosion was assumed to be an accident, the Lehigh Valley Railroad hired Burns to investigate. Burns's agents provided evidence that indicated German saboteurs had caused the explosion.

Burns and his agents could be ruthless in their investigations, often overstepping the law. In 1917, his agents were caught wiretapping telephones and breaking into offices to copy papers. They investigated radical groups as well as Germans and were accused of urging suspects into illegal acts. When a bomb rocked Wall Street in 1920, Burns blamed it on communists and offered a $50,000 reward for the perpetrators. Later, one of his operatives claimed to have sent bomb threats before the explosion. Critics suspected Burns had arranged the bombing to implicate radicals and to promote his own image.

In 1921, Attorney General Harry M. Daugherty appointed Burns to head the FBI. He became the first man to use the title of director. Because Burns remained in New York much of the time, his assistant director, J. Edgar Hoover, performed most of the daily work. As director,

Burns continued his war on radicals, but he also investigated the Ku Klux Klan. Burns's term as director was controversial. He authorized the same sort of illegal methods his detectives had used previously, and he investigated political opponents to obtain discrediting information. On May 10, 1924, Attorney General Harlan Fiske Stone fired Burns. He was later indicted for having agents spy on jurors in the corruption trials of the Teapot Dome conspirators. Burns died in 1932 in his retirement home in Sarasota, Florida.

Tim J. Watts

See also: Federal Bureau of Investigation (WWI, WWII); Sabotage and Spies (WWI)

REFERENCES

Adams, Samuel Hopkins. *Incredible Era: The Life and Times of Warren Gamaliel Harding.* Boston: Houghton Mifflin, 1939.

Caesar, Gene. *Incredible Detective: The Biography of William J. Burns.* Englewood Cliffs, NJ: Prentice-Hall, 1968.

Butler, Nicholas Murray

Nicholas Murray Butler (1862–1947) was a peace activist and president of Columbia University who supported American actions during the war and worked afterward to strengthen international institutions that promoted world order.

Butler became interested in peace issues in 1898, when Czar Nicholas of Russia called for an international peace conference to be held at The Hague. In the years that followed, he participated in several peace conferences and played a significant role in convincing Andrew Carnegie to provide $10 million to found the Carnegie Endowment for International Peace.

When World War I broke out in Europe, Butler supported President Wilson's call for strict neutrality and halted the Carnegie Endowment's publication of works deemed too supportive of any of the belligerent nations. Convinced that the United States had no interest in the conflict, Butler opposed increased military expenditures, cofounded with Lillian Wald and Oswald Garrison Villard the American League to Limit Armaments, and initially supported the Columbia University faculty's academic freedom to speak out against the war. As U.S. intervention in Europe became more likely, however, Butler's stance on the war changed. For example, during the presidential election of 1916, he joined Republican candidate Charles Evans Hughes in attacking Wilson for not increasing America's defenses. After the United States entered the war, he denounced war dissenters and formally withdrew the Columbia faculty's freedom to publicly oppose the conflict.

When the war ended, Butler expressed ambivalence about the League of Nations covenant. Although he supported the League's determination to address the economic and social conditions in underdeveloped nations, he disliked the influence that the covenant would give European powers over the United States.

Christy Jo Snider

See also: Pacifists (WWI); Biographies: Hughes, Charles Evans (WWI); Villard, Oswald Garrison (WWI); Wald, Lillian (WWI)

REFERENCES

Marrin, Albert. *Nicholas Murray Butler.* Boston: Twayne Publishers, 1976.

Herman, Sondra R. *Eleven Against War: Studies in American Internationalist Thought, 1898–1921.* Stanford, CA: Hoover Institution Press, 1969.

C

Castle, Vernon and Irene

Irene and Vernon Castle were one of the great dancing teams of the early twentieth century. Born Vernon Blythe in Norwich, England, Vernon Castle (1887–1918) immigrated with his family to America in 1906, changing his last name the following year. Although trained as an engineer at the University of Birmingham, Castle pursued roles in musical theater, becoming known for his comical drunk performances. In 1910, he met dancer Irene Foote (1893–1969), the daughter of a doctor, when she was cast in *Summer Widowers*. The two married in May 1911 and were touring Europe when the play closed abruptly, stranding them in Paris.

To support themselves, the Castles became nightclub performers, specializing in a dancing act that blurred the line between audience and entertainer—they would emerge from the seated patrons to lead social dancing. This popular act brought them to New York cabarets and the Keith Vaudeville theaters, although the Castles were, with the guidance of agent Elizabeth Marbury, becoming known as high-class promoters of elegant ballroom dancing, paid by the social elite to attend their parties and give instruction. Almost single-handedly, the Castles redefined social dance from a rowdy, déclassé activity dominated by polkas to a graceful, upper-middle-class hobby suitable for mass consumption. By 1914, the year in which their textbook *Modern Dancing* appeared, the Castles had introduced the Castle Walk and the Castle House Rag and were franchised in a range of consumer products from clothing to records. They also merchandized dancing instruction, opening the Castle House Studio in New York. Irene Castle's sophisticated chic was widely copied, including her bobbed hair and stylish evening gowns. The Castles also appeared in short films, and a biographical movie, *The Whirl of Life* (1915), reached a large international audience.

At the outbreak of World War I, Vernon Castle enlisted in the Royal Flying Corps in Great Britain, while Irene appeared in a patriotic serial, *Patria* (1917–1918) in which she heroically foiled spies and promoted the American war effort. Vernon returned to America as a flying instructor for U.S. pilots; on February 15, 1918, he died in a training accident at Fort Worth, Texas.

Irene married three more times and continued dancing, but she never found a partner as successful as Vernon. In the 1930s, she choreographed routines for Hollywood studios and became a passionate advocate for animal rights. She died in Eureka Springs, Arkansas, on January 25, 1969.

Margaret Sankey

See also: Film (U.S., WWI); Music (U.S., WWI)

REFERENCES

Castle, Irene. *My Husband.* New York: Scribner, 1919.
———. *Castles in the Air.* Garden City, NY: Doubleday, 1958.
Cooks, Susan, "Passionless Dancing and Passionate Reform: Respectability, Modernism, and the Social Dancing of Irene and Vernon Castle." In *The Passion of Music and Dance,* ed. William Washabaugh. New York: Oxford University Press, 1998.

Cather, Willa

Often considered among the best American novelists, Willa Cather (1873–1947) published twelve novels as well as short fiction and poetry from 1903 to 1940. Through most of her career, Cather's novels won both popular and critical acclaim. Much of her work is set in Nebraska, where she spent her adolescence and young adulthood before moving to New York; her vision of the American Southwest also plays an important part in her work. Her writing has been labeled an examination of regional American cultures and landscapes, nostalgic, religious, modernist, feminist, and lesbian. However, although each of these interpretations has been forwarded, each has also been shown to inadequately encompass her multifaceted work. Perhaps her most frequently read book is *My Ántonia* (1918), a portrait of an immigrant woman's endurance on the Nebraskan prairie.

Cather's Pulitzer Prize–winning "war book," *One of Ours* (1922), was a popular success but drew criticism from reviewers, who found it sentimental and naïve following e.e. cummings's and John Dos Passos's post-war novels of disillusionment. *One of Ours* follows a frustrated and emasculated Nebraskan who briefly finds fulfillment fighting and dying in World War I. Cather was motivated to write the novel after her cousin died in combat; she felt a close kinship with him and was inspired by his letters to his mother. Whereas earlier critics saw simply a demonstration of war's redemptive power, recent readers have identified a more conflicted depiction of the war's effect.

Believing that "the world broke in two in 1922 or thereabouts," Cather felt uneasy with the modern sense of isolation and materialism, and much of her writing addresses the struggle to find meaning in the face of loss and restrictive conditions.

Lisa Schreibersdorf

See also: Literature (U.S., WWI)

REFERENCES

Lee, Hermione. *Willa Cather: A Life Saved Up.* London: Virago, 1989.

Catt, Carrie Chapman

A leading figure in the women's suffrage movement and a peace advocate during World War I, Carrie Chapman Catt (1859–1947) was born Carrie Clinton Lane in Ripon, Wisconsin. Her family moved to Charles City, Iowa, during her youth. After graduating from Iowa State College in 1880 and working as a reporter in California, she returned to Iowa to organize the Iowa Woman Suffrage Association. Later, she was chairperson of the National American Woman Suffrage Association (NAWSA) and president of the International Woman Suffrage Alliance.

In 1915, Miram Leslie gave the NAWSA almost $1 million, which allowed Catt to initiate her "winning plan." Instead of holding Democrats in state and local offices responsible for the failure of suffrage laws, she began a massive drive on the federal level to ensure a constitutional amendment. Because Catt and most of the other NAWSA leaders were publicly opposed to America's entry into World War I, those with hawkish outlooks declared their opposition to suffrage. Jane Addams and Catt were so committed to their views that they formed the Woman's Peace Party at the onset of the war. The party marched on Capital Hill with the slogan that "Real Patriots Keep Cool." Individuals such as Theodore Roosevelt and organizations such as the National Security League saw their lobbying, speeches, and protests as mutinous and unpatriotic. Through magazines, newspapers, and radio, prowar opponents attacked suffrage leaders, coining the slogan, "Real Patriots Fight Hard."

However, Catt's efforts and tireless lobbying were rewarded on January 10, 1918, when the Congress passed the Nineteenth Amendment to the Constitution, which granted "The Right of Women Citizens to Vote." By August 1920, the amendment was ratified. She then became the first president of the League of Women Voters, which sought to educate women on the intelligent use of their new right to vote.

After the war ended, Catt supported the League of Nations and in 1925 formed the Committee on the Cause and Cure of War. She remained opposed to most military conflicts until her death in New Rochelle, New York in 1947.

T. Jason Soderstrum

See also: National Security League (WWI); Pacifists (WWI); Women (U.S., WWI); Documents: Women's Suffrage Speech to Congress, 1917

REFERENCES

Fowler, R. B. *Carrie Catt: Feminist Politician.* Boston: Northeastern University Press, 1986.

Peck, Mary Gray. *Carrie Chapman Catt: A Biography.* New York: H. W. Wilson Company, 1944.

Van Voris, Jacqueline. *Carrie Chapman Catt: A Public Life.* New York: Feminist Press at City University of New York, 1987.

Chaplin, Charlie

Sir Charles Spencer Chaplin (1889–1977) was born on April 16, 1889, in Walworth, London, to vaudevillians Charles Sr., an alcoholic, and Hannah Hill, a schizophrenic. They soon separated. Charles Sr. died of alcoholism in 1901. Charlie and his elder half brother, Sydney, endured the Lambeth Workhouse in East London and the Hanwell School for Orphans and Destitute Children.

Chaplin entered show business at age five. A job with the Karno Fun Factory brought him to the United States in 1912. Mack Sennett of the Keystone Film Company noticed Chaplin's masterful slapstick comedy in 1913 and signed him to a contract. Chaplin created the Little Tramp persona and soon became world famous.

By 1917 Chaplin, a perfectionist, obtained creative control over his films and earned $1 million per picture. After working for various film companies, Chaplin joined with Mary Pickford, Douglas Fairbanks, and D. W. Griffith to establish United Artists in 1919.

Chaplin used movies to promulgate his left-

America's leading comic film star during World War I, Charlie Chaplin is seen here in his signature role as the "tramp." (Library of Congress)

ist political sympathies. In 1936, Chaplin's film *Modern Times* depicts the bleak circumstances of the working class and the poor. "Talkie" films emerged in 1927, but he did not appear in one until 1940, with *The Great Dictator*, a comedy that ridiculed Adolf Hitler. He received several Oscar nominations.

Chaplin's unconventional lifestyle, typical for Hollywood, irritated the establishment and resulted in great press copy. In 1918, he married Mildred Harris; the marriage did not survive the death of their baby, Norman Spencer. He married Lita Grey (Lillita McMurray) in 1924; they had two sons, Charles III and Sydney, but divorced two years later. The exhilarating divorce testimony led to a public campaign against him. In 1936, he married Paulette Goddard, but they divorced in 1942. Chaplin finally

found happiness at age fifty-four with eighteen-year-old Oona O'Neill, daughter of playwright Eugene O' Neill and Agnes Boulton O'Neill. The well-suited couple had eight children. Oona became his emotional anchor. Chaplin brought his mother Hannah to Hollywood in 1921, where she died in 1928.

Chaplin's refusal to become an American citizen, claiming he was an internationalist citizen of the world, angered the American establishment and resulted in a vindictive campaign against him. Chaplin was charged with the Mann Act but was acquitted. The volatile actress Joan Barry accused Chaplin of fathering an out-of-wedlock child with her. Blood tests disproved his paternity but that evidence was not allowed into California court records. Despite his innocence, Chaplin paid out $75 a week for twenty-one years.

He was suspected of being a Communist and accused of committing un-American activities. The FBI's J. Edgar Hoover was assigned to find cause to terminate his U.S. residency. Hoover could never determine that Chaplin was a Communist. Chaplin left a $2 million surety bond with the IRS before he made a 1952 visit to England. Hoover then had the INS revoke his reentry. Chaplain never received an apology for these blatant miscarriages of justice.

Chaplin moved to Vevey, Switzerland, in 1952. His genius was eventually recognized by his peers, and he received numerous awards for his contribution to cinema. He had made seventy-one short films and seventeen feature films. Chaplin died at Vevey on December 25, 1977, and was buried in Corsier-Sur-Vevey Cemetery.

Annette Richardson

See also: Film (U.S., WWI); Biographies: Fairbanks Sr., Douglas (WWI); Griffith, D. W. (WWI); Hoover, J. Edgar (WWI); Pickford, Mary (WWI)

REFERENCES

Chaplin, Charlie. *My Autobiography*. Harmondsworth: Penguin, 1964.

———. *My Life in Pictures*. Secaucus, NJ: Castle, 1982.

Robinson, David. *Chaplin: His Life and Art*. London: Collins, 1985.

Scheide, Frank, and Hooman Mehran. *Chaplin: The Dictator and the Tramp*. London: British Film Institute, 2004.

Vance, Jeffrey. *Chaplin: Genius of the Cinema*. New York: Harry N. Abrams, 2003.

Churchill, Winston

A major figure in the British government during World War I—he held a multiple portfolio as minister of munitions, secretary of state for war, and secretary of state for air—Sir Winston Leonard Spencer Churchill was born at his family's ancestral home Blenheim Palace, Oxfordshire, England, on November 30, 1874. His father was Lord Randolph Churchill, a descendant of John Churchill, first duke of Marlborough, and his mother, Jeannette (Jenny) Jerome, was an American socialite. Lonely, neglected, and unwanted, he became rebellious, ruinously impulsive, and fiercely independent. Churchill was educated at Harrow, where he failed most of his subjects but excelled in English.

After graduating eighth in his class from Sandhurst, the nation's premier military academy, Churchill served as a professional cavalry officer in India with the 4th Hussars from 1895 to 1899, when he resigned his commission to enter politics. He wrote dispatches from areas of conflict, beginning his lifelong literary career. In South Africa, he helped rescue an armored train ambushed by Boers. He was taken prisoner but escaped; his story, when publicized, mesmerized the British public. Returning as a military hero, he ran as a Tory for Oldham in 1900 and won. He joined the Liberals in 1904, became president of the Board of Trade, and was home secretary from 1910 to 1911.

Churchill married Clementine Hozier on September 12, 1908, at St. Margarets in Westminster. They had five children, one of whom died in infancy. They purchased Chartwell in 1922, and it remained their home throughout their marriage.

Churchill was first lord of the admiralty from 1911 to 1915. His important reforms created the Admiralty War Staff, a Home Fleet, and Royal Navy Staff College. He significantly increased Britain's naval strength. Churchill would often disagree with his professional advisers and override their decisions. Consequently, he was responsible for the failure of Gallipoli, the fiasco that showed appalling judgment and caused needless loss of lives. The government fell over this disaster.

Churchill served as lieutenant colonel of the Sixth Royal Fusiliers, serving in France for six months into early 1916. As minister of munitions as of July 1917, he endorsed the Zeebrugge raid of April 1918. He was simultaneously secretary of state for war and secretary of state for air from 1918 to 1922 as well as secretary of state for the colonies in 1921.

In 1924, Churchill was chancellor of the exchequer under the Baldwin government and responsible for the disastrous return of the gold standard, which caused deflation, massive unemployment, and eventually, the miners' general strike of 1926. To earn additional income, he wrote *World Crisis and Marlborough: His Life and Times, History of the English Speaking Peoples*.

Churchill was strongly disliked for his support of King Edward VIII, who abdicated in December 1927 over his constitutional and religious inability to marry twice-divorced American Mrs. Wallis Warfield Simpson. The Church of England forbade divorce and both of her husbands were still alive. Moreover, Churchill was a critic of Chamberlain's appeasement policy toward Hitler and he seemed a lone voice against the German dictator's territorial ambitions. But with Hitler's victories in Europe, Churchill's position became more tenable. In 1940 he again became first lord of the admiralty, and in May he became prime minister of an all-party government. He was also minister of defense. King George VI relied heavily on Churchill, and they eventually reached a mutually respectful working relationship.

Churchill galvanized the British people with his inspirational speeches. In one speech he said, "We shall defend ourselves, whatever the cost may be, we shall fight on the beaches, we shall fight on the landing grounds, we shall fight in the fields, and in the streets, we shall fight in the hills; we shall never surrender." He elicited unprecedented patriotism.

Churchill made strong alliances with U.S. President Franklin Delano Roosevelt. Their collaboration secured fundamental supplies and kept the North Atlantic shipping route open. The Lend Lease Program—offering U.S. warships on loan in exchange for Britain leasing some of its bases to the United States—was initiated. Churchill established the Special Operations Executive, which cultivated espionage, counterespionage, covert operations, and partisan operations in most of the occupied territories. Churchill was involved in redrawing the post World War II boundaries at the Yalta and Potsdam Conferences. At the end of the war, Churchill was accorded the singular honor of appearing with the Royal Family on the balcony of Buckingham Palace on VE Day.

Churchill lost the 1945 election. He wrote *The Second World War,* for which he won a Noble Prize for Literature. He was reelected prime minister in 1951 and served until 1955, when he permanently retired.

Churchill experienced poor health the last few years of his life. On January 24, 1965, he suffered a severe cerebral hemorrhage and died. He was accorded a magnificent state funeral, with more than one hundred representatives from around the world bidding him farewell. Churchill is buried at St. Martin's Churchyard at Bladon near his ancestral home.

Annette Richardson

See also: Biographies: Churchill, Winston (WWII)

REFERENCES

Blake, Robert, and William Roger Louis, eds. *Churchill: A Major New Assessment of His Life in Peace and War.* Oxford: Oxford University Press, 1993.

Gilbert, Martin. *Finest Hour: Winston S. Churchill, 1939–1941.* London: Heinemann, 1983.

Hough, Richard. *Winston and Clementine: The Triumphs and Tragedies of the Churchills.* New York: Bantam Books, 1991.

Jenkins, Roy. *Churchill: A Biography.* New York: Farar, Straus and Giroux, 2001.

Manchester, William. *Visions of Glory, 1874–1932.* Boston: Little, Brown and Company, 1983.

———. *The Last Lion: Winston Spencer Churchill, Alone 1932–1940.* London: Little Brown and Company, 1988.

Clark, James "Champ"

James Beauchamp Clark (1850–1921), a prominent Democratic leader from Missouri, was the Speaker of the House of Representatives at the time of the First World War. He was born March 7, 1850, near Lawrenceburg, Kentucky, to John Hampton Clark and Aletha Beau-

A strong critic of America's entry in World War I, House Speaker Champ Clark tried futiley to block the Woodrow Wilson Administration's measures to impose a military draft. (Library of Congress)

champ. Clark began his career as an attorney and then became an editor. He was a member of the House since 1893. With an interregnum in the year 1896, Clark remained as a member in the succeeding Congresses through his death in 1921.

He unsuccessfully ran for the position of house minority leader in 1903 against John Sharp Williams. The Speaker of the House, Joseph Cannon, had used arbitrary methods in legislative procedures and Clark organized a strong opposition to this. Clark became the Speaker in 1911, replacing Cannon. The political skill of Clark was evident in checking William Howard Taft's legislation between 1910 and 1914. At the Baltimore Democratic convention in 1912, Clark lost the presidential

nomination on the eighty-fourth ballot to Woodrow Wilson, the governor of New Jersey. The Eastern banks of New York City had a lot of financial clout due to the Federal Reserve Act of 1913. Clark had opposed the act and two federal reserve banks in St. Louis and Kansas.

Advocating a policy of isolationism, Clark was prominent in opposing the U.S. entry into the First World War and almost created a schism in the party. Genevieve Bennett, his wife, pursued an active role in politics, supporting her husband and criticizing the president on various issues. Wilson had proposed the idea of expanding the regular army and stressed the need for a national draft policy. Clark vehemently criticized the Compulsory Military Service Bill and tried to initiate an investigation into the conditions of imprisoned conscientious objectors of the war. He was also not in favor of the creation of a volunteer army. However, the president succeeded in the passage of the Selective Services Act in May 1917, bringing three million people into the army. Another two million joined voluntarily. By the end of the year, the American Expeditionary Force had arrived in Europe.

Clark was the minority leader in the sixty-sixth Congress. He also wanted withdrawal of American troops from Communist Russia; U.S. forces, along with other Western allies, had entered that country shortly after World War I in support of anti-communist forces. After the end of WWI, the treaty of Versailles and the League of Nations attracted considerable opposition in the United States. The Republicans captured both houses of Congress, and Clark lost to Theodore Hukriede in the elections. He died shortly afterward in his home in Washington, D.C., on March 2, 1921. Although Clark lost the presidential nomination before the war as well as his congressional seat after the war, he left his mark in American politics. His son, Joel Bennett Clark, was the senator from Missouri from 1932 to 1945.

Patit P. Mishra

See also: Conscientious Objectors (WWI); Conscription (U.S., WWI); Democratic Party (WWI); Elections of 1920 (WWI); Isolationism (WWI); Biographies: Wilson, Woodrow (WWI)

REFERENCES

Clark, Champ. *My Quarter Century of American Politics.* 2 vols. New York: Harper, 1969 (reprint from 1920).

Garraty, John A., and Mark C. Carnes. *American National Biography,* vol. 4; *Clark, Champ.* New York: Oxford University Press, 1999.

Morrison, Geoffrey F. "A Political Biography of Champ Clark." Ph.D. dissertation, St. Louis University, 1972.

Clarkson, Grosvenor

Grosvenor Clarkson (1882–1937) was a publicist who was active in the preparedness movement before the United States entered World War I. He then played an important role in the volunteer committees formed to mobilize opinion and resources after the American declaration of war. Clarkson left one of the most detailed descriptions of the War Industries Board under Barnard Baruch, considered a starting point for those doing research on that agency.

Clarkson was born in 1882 in Des Moines, Iowa. His father was a lifetime member of the Republican party and had once served as chair of the National Committee. Theodore Roosevelt appointed the elder Clarkson surveyor of the port of New York.

Clarkson attended private schools before becoming a reporter in 1900 on the *New York Mail and Express.* He later served as special agent for the U.S. General Land Office in New Mexico. By 1909, Clarkson had returned to New York City to take up a career in advertising. He did some publicity work for the automobile industry, where he came to the attention of Howard Coffin, vice president of the Hudson Motor Company. Coffin was convinced that the United States would eventually enter World War I, and he urged the creation of a board that could help plan for the industrial mobilization that would be necessary. When the Naval Consulting Board was established in early 1916, Coffin was appointed to head it. Recognizing the need for someone to handle publicity, he nominated Clarkson. Clarkson saw the potential in the position and quickly accepted.

Clarkson's first job was to assist with a nationwide survey of industrial plants that could help supply necessary products to the navy. Because the survey was voluntary, Clarkson's most important task was to convince industrialists and engineers to complete the forms. He also prepared an educational program to show businesses why preparedness was important to the country.

On August 29, 1916, Congress established the Council of National Defense and an advisory board. The Council was comprised of six members of the Cabinet, and the advisory board consisted of seven leaders of industry. The advisory board was intended to help prepare for a national industrial mobilization. Coffin became chair of the board and requested Clarkson as secretary. Clarkson's job was to act as chief administrative assistant to the director, keeping all the records and issuing all public statements for the group. He assisted with policy decisions as well.

Public education in preparedness was an important part of Clarkson's job. After the United States declared war on Germany on April 6, 1917, his duties included encouraging support for the war effort, including support for the draft and industrial mobilization. In May 1918, Clarkson began organizing economic reconstruction and readjustment work by the council, with an emphasis on the effects of demobilization on the cost of living.

The Council of National Defense organized state and local committees to continue its work at lower levels. Eventually, 48 state committees, 4,000 county committees, 162,000 city and town committees, and 18,000 committees for women were organized. As secretary, Clarkson maintained direct contact with each of the 184,000 committees. On August 29, 1918, the Council authorized the Field Division, which combined all the committees into one unit, and Clarkson served as a member of the governing board and director. The Field Division played an important role in communicating the national security needs of the federal government to local bodies.

Clarkson became acting director of the Council of National Defense in July 1918. He was appointed permanent director in November 1918. The end of the war did not end the Council's work. Clarkson believed the Council could play an important role during peacetime. He organized an employment committee to help demobilized veterans find jobs and tried to set up a coordinating committee to maintain an inventory of American industry.

In 1920, Clarkson retired from the Council of National Defense. He was determined to write the history of the wartime work of the committees that supervised American industrial mobilization. With financial support from Bernard Baruch, he published *Industrial America in the World War: The Strategy Behind the Line 1917–1918* in 1923. Although it has biases, the book remains the standard introduction to American industrial mobilization in World War I.

Clarkson later became a senior fellow and councilor of the Engineering Economic Foundation. He spent his remaining years writing about economics and national defense. He died in New York City on January 23, 1937.

Tim J. Watts

See also: Advertising (WWI); Council of National Defense (WWI); Mobilization (U.S., WWI); War Industries Board (WWI); Biographies: Coffin, Howard E. (WWI)

REFERENCES

Breen, William J. *Uncle Sam at Home: Civilian Mobilization, Wartime Federalism, and the Council of National Defense, 1917–1919.* Westport, CT: Greenwood Press, 1984.

Clarkson, Grosvenor. *Industrial America in the World War: The Strategy Behind the Line, 1917–1918.* Boston: Houghton Mifflin, 1923.

Cobb, Ty

Arguably the greatest baseball player of all time, Tyrus Raymond Cobb (1886–1961), "The Georgia Peach," dominated the game during the early twentieth century. He retired in 1928 with 4,191 hits, a lifetime .367 batting average (still a record), 892 stolen bases, and 2,245 runs. During a twenty-four year career, he batted over .400 three times and under .320 only once.

Born in Narrows, Georgia, Cobb combined strong physical skills with a fierce determination to win and an intellectual approach to baseball that included studying opposing pitchers and the science of hitting, throwing, fielding, and running the bases. He strongly believed in playing as hard as possible to intimidate opponents both physically and psychologically and prided himself in outsmarting other teams.

After joining the Detroit Tigers as a rookie in 1905, Cobb quickly established himself as one of the most consistent and exciting players in baseball. He won twelve league batting titles (including nine in a row from 1907 through 1915), hit .420 in 1911, and performed well even as a player-manager in Detroit and

Arguably the greatest baseball player of the early twentieth century, slugger Ty Cobb had some of his best seasons during World War I. (Library of Congress)

Philadelphia in the mid-1920s. During World War I, he batted between .368 and .383 from 1914 through 1917, stole ninety-six bases in 1915, and provided fans with a welcome distraction from the horrors of war while helping to reinforce baseball's prominence as the national game.

Although he never won a World Series championship and was often criticized for his rough style of play, his racism, and his difficult personality, Cobb probably had the last laugh on his critics. He became the first inductee into the National Baseball Hall of Fame in 1936, and made millions investing in the stock market before his death in 1961.

Lance Janda

See also: Baseball (WWI)

REFERENCES

Cobb, Ty, Al Stump, and Charles C. Alexander. *My Life in Baseball: The True Record.* Lincoln: University of Nebraska Press, 1993.

Stump, Al. *Cobb: A Biography.* Chapel Hill, NC: Algonquin Books, 1994.

Coffin, Howard E.

Howard E. Coffin (1873–1937) was an engineer and industrialist who worked for American industrial mobilization during World War I. He was especially interested in aircraft production and technology.

Coffin was born near Milton, Ohio, and studied at the University of Michigan. He left school in 1896, before completing his degree, and worked at the post office. However, the university allowed him to continue his experiments in its engineering workshops, where he built a one-cylinder gas engine and a steam-powered car that he used on his mail route. Coffin returned to the university in 1900 but left again in 1902 to head Oldsmobile Company's Motor Works' experimental engineering department. He continued to advance in rank with other manufacturers, until he helped found the Hudson Motor Car Company in 1910.

Coffin was active in industrywide concerns, including engineering societies, and was a charter member of the Society of Automotive Engineers. He recognized that the automotive industry was hampered by costly patent lawsuits and the lack of standards. Coffin was one of the men credited with pushing the Patent Cross-License Agreement through in 1915. This agreement allowed all automobile manufacturers to use innovations patented by others by paying a fee. He also helped establish agreements to standardize basic automobile parts and materials. By doing so, production increased and costs were held down, making automobiles more affordable.

When World War I broke out in Europe, it quickly became apparent that it would be an industrial war. Interested Americans watched as European countries mobilized their economies and industries to an unprecedented degree. Coffin and like-minded men began to consider how to apply lessons learned in Europe to the United States. In mid-1915, Secretary of the Navy Josephus Daniels formed a Naval Consulting Board to advise him on technology and science related to naval mobilization. Coffin was among the industrialists asked to join. The most active subdivision of the Board was the Industrial Preparedness Committee, under Coffin. Finding that the navy and army had no idea of America's potential to produce arms, he supervised a nationwide survey of factories to assess what military-related products they could produce. The work was performed voluntarily and without public financing. The survey laid the groundwork for an efficient industrial mobilization.

Coffin took his efforts to a higher level in 1916. The National Defense Act of that year authorized formal planning for mobilization. The army appropriations that followed on August 29, 1916, included a rider that formed the Council of National Defense and an advisory commission. The commission was composed of seven leaders in their fields who could plan and coordinate industrial mobilization. President Woodrow Wilson appointed Coffin to the commission in October 1916, along with prominent men such as Holliss Godfrey of Drexel, Samuel Gompers of the American Federation of Labor, and Franklin H. Martin, director general of the American College of Surgeons. At their first meeting in December 1916, the commission agreed to undertake a complete survey of American industry and how it could be used to produce military supplies. They expected their work to take up to three years. They also agreed to form subcommittees on particular industries, with each headed by a member of the commission.

Coffin headed up the Aircraft Board. He recognized that American aircraft lagged far behind European developments and recommended a large increase in the manufacturing capacity for aircraft. He also suggested that standardization of parts and production of a few types of machines would be most efficient. Coffin also oversaw the beginning of a powerful aircraft engine that could be used in all types of aircraft. This project became the Liberty engine, one of the most significant American contributions to aircraft development.

The commission's work was hampered, however, because it could only make suggestions; it had no power to make things happen. Soon after the United States entered the war, public unhappiness with the confusion of American industrial mobilization reached a high level.

Criticism fell especially on Coffin, who had become chair of the Aircraft Production Board. He had spoken publicly of thousands of American aircraft leading the way to victory in Europe, but Americans learned that no American-designed aircraft was comparable to those of the Europeans. Under fire, Coffin resigned from the Board in March 1918.

Coffin returned to his business but remained a supporter of the air industry. In 1925, he was a founder of National Air Transport, which became United Air Lines. During the Depression, Coffin advised his friend Herbert Hoover to use his powers as commander in chief to improve conditions. Coffin opposed the New Deal and Franklin Roosevelt. He died in 1937 of an apparently accidental gunshot wound at his nephew's house at Sea Island, Georgia.

Tim J. Watts

See also: Mobilization (U.S., WWI); National Defense Act (U.S., WWI)

REFERENCES

Courson, Maxwell Taylor. *Howard Earle Coffin: A Prince of Detroit and King of the Georgia Coast.* Lanham, MD: University Press of America, 1998.

Kennedy, David M. *Over Here: The First World War and American Society.* New York: Oxford University Press, 1980.

Cohan, George M.

George M. Cohan (1878–1942) was one of the most popular songwriters and performers of the first two decades of the twentieth century. He dominated Broadway and popular music like few performers before him. Cohan came to his success honestly, with natural talent. He was born into a family of vaudeville performers and was on stage with his father, mother, and younger sister at an early age. He began to write skits and songs for the family when he was a teenager, even though he had almost no formal education. Cohan's first musical opened on Broadway in 1901, but it was not a success. The early works that followed were criticized for their weak plots, but Cohan's scores were highly regarded. His first real success was *Little Johnny Jones,* opening in 1904, which included favorites such as "The Yankee Doodle Boy" and "Give My Regards to Broadway." Two years later, Cohan introduced "You're a Grand Old Flag" in another musical. Cohan's music, with its naïve and patriotic sentimentality, captured the imagination of many, especially recent immigrants.

Cohan continued his success on Broadway with both musicals and nonmusicals. He also worked with his partner, Sam H. Harris, to produce several minstrel shows that toured the country. He divorced his first wife in 1907, but remarried later that year. In 1916, Cohan's sister died of heart disease, leaving a husband and son. A year later, Cohan's father died. The elder Cohan had been both mentor and best friend, and his death dealt Cohan a serious personal blow.

When the United States entered World War I on April 6, 1917, Cohan was determined to do what he could for the war effort. Intensely patriotic, he had always claimed that he was born on the fourth of July, sharing his birthday with the United States. Cohan spent much of his time at benefits, raising money for soldiers and their families. He also appeared at many war bond rallies, to encourage civilians to support the war effort, and always drew a big crowd. To raise money for the Red Cross, Cohan made his first appearance in a play by another writer. Beginning in May 1918, he took a role in J. Hart-ley Manner's *Out There* for eight benefit performances. Cohan appeared with an all-star cast, and the play made a three-week tour of major American cities after its New York run. It ended up grossing $600,000.

Cohan's most memorable contribution to World War I was his composition of "Over There" in 1917. It became the "theme song" of the American Expeditionary Force and was performed constantly. Cohan later related that he composed the song during a forty-five-minute commuter train ride from his home in New Rochelle to his office in New York City. The song had a simple melody and simple patriotic verses that promised that the Yanks were coming and that they would end the war. The confident message resonated with the American public and the soldiers. The song became Cohan's most frequently published and played composition. More than 1.5 million copies of the sheet music for "Over There" were sold. For the mechanical instrument rights alone, Cohan received $25,000, which he donated to soldiers' funds and other patriotic charities. The following year, Cohan wrote a follow-up song, "When You Come Back, and You Will Come Back." Although its popularity did not approach that of "Over There," the later song was also popular throughout the war, with its message of hope for the future and comfort for homesick boys.

Cohan continued to write and produce after the war. His dominance of Broadway declined, but he remained an entertainment giant. When the next world war broke out, his patriotic songs gained a new popularity. In 1942, President Franklin Roosevelt presented Cohan with the Congressional Medal of Honor in recognition of his contributions to the war efforts. Cohan died on November 5, 1942, the same year that the story of his life came out in the movie *Yankee Doodle Dandy.*

Tim J. Watts

See also: Music (U.S., WWI); Songs (U.S., WWI); Theater (WWI); Documents: Over There, 1917

REFERENCES

Cohan, George M. *Twenty Years on Broadway and the Years It Took Me to Get There.* New York: Harper and Bros., 1925.
McCabe, John. *George M. Cohan, the Man Who Owned Broadway.* Garden City, NY: Doubleday, 1973.
Morehouse, Ward. *George M. Cohan, Prince of the American Theatre.* Philadelphia: J. B. Lippincott, 1943.

Coolidge, Calvin

Known for his efforts to break a key post–World War I strike in Boston while governor of Massachusetts and later as the president of the United States from 1923 to 1929, Calvin Coolidge (1872–1933) was born in Plymouth Notch, Vermont, the son of John Calvin Coolidge, a farmer and storekeeper, and Victoria Moor.

After graduating from Amherst College in 1895, Coolidge read law in Northampton, Massachusetts, and entered local politics as a Republican. From 1898 to 1918 he served as city councilman, city solicitor, state legislator, state senator, president of the state senate (the highest ranking Republican in Massachusetts at the time), and lieutenant governor. In 1918 he was elected governor and followed a policy of frugal government and law and order. During the Boston Police Strike of September 1919, Coolidge gained national fame by supporting the firing of the striking policemen and publicly declaring the supremacy of the public good over the right to strike.

In 1920 Coolidge was nominated and elected vice president of the United States on

President Calvin Coolidge permitted U.S. loans to Germany to help that country pay off its World War I reparations debts to France, Britain, and other allies. (Library of Congress)

the Republican ticket. After the death of Warren G. Harding in 1923, Coolidge was sworn in as the thirtieth president of the United States by his father, a notary public. Amid the unraveling scandals of his predecessor, Coolidge exerted calm and honesty. In 1924 he was elected handsomely in his own right. As president, Coolidge followed a policy of tax reduction, government reform, privatization, frugality, international arms control, federal debt reduction, and the enforcement of prohibition. Coolidge was adamant that the Allies repay their debts from World War I, and sanctioned the Dawes Plan (1924) and the Young Plan (1929), which stabilized the European economy. Coolidge was hampered by the division of the Republicans in Congress into warring Eastern conservative and Midwestern progressive wings.

After the presidency, Coolidge wrote his *Autobiography*, several magazine articles, and a nationally syndicated newspaper column. He died of a heart attack while shaving at his home in Northampton.

Gregory Dehler

See also: Boston Police Strike (WWI); Elections of 1920 (WWI); Republican Party (WWI); Biographies: Harding, Warren Gamaliel (WWI)

REFERENCES

Coolidge, Calvin. *The Autobiography of Calvin Coolidge.* New York: Cosmopolitan Book Corporation, 1929.

Ferrell, Robert H. *The Presidency of Calvin Coolidge.* Lawrence: University of Kansas Press, 1998.

Sobel, Robert. *Coolidge: An American Enigma.* Washington, DC: Regnery, 1998.

White, William Allen. *Calvin Coolidge, the Man Who Is President.* New York: Macmillan, 1925.

Cowley, Malcolm

An independent and critical literary voice, Malcolm Cowley (1898–1989) had a firsthand acquaintance with many of the most notable literary voices of his generation and an intimate knowledge of many of the milieus in which they worked. He became a chronicler of the literary movements and personalities of the interwar years, providing subsequent generations of readers with a sense of that period that remains engagingly immediate and consistently perceptive.

Born in Belsano, Pennsylvania, Cowley graduated from Harvard University in 1920 and received a *diplôme* from the Université de Montpelier in 1922. In between, he served with the American Ambulance Service and then the American Army in France. Although he subsequently held a number of editorial positions with leading periodicals and visiting professorships at prestigious universities, his period of greatest influence on American letters may have coincided roughly with his term as literary editor of the *New Republic* from 1929 to 1944.

Cowley's most well-known work is *Exile's Return: A Narrative of Ideas* (1934). Although some commentators on Cowley's work have argued that *A Second Flowering: Works and Days of the Lost Generation* (1973) is a more thoroughly considered and more elegant book, all of Cowley's subsequent work, including *A Second Flowering*, has been measured against *Exile's Return*.

The thesis of *Exile's Return* is that the so-called "lost generation" actually found itself and its sense of literary purpose through its self-imposed exile in Europe in the 1920s. Having passed from upbringings in small-town America through the almost inconceivable horrors of the Great War, these writers relocated themselves in their work, recovering literarily, if not literally, an American geographical and cultural landscape that they could comprehend and measure themselves against more clearly from a distance. Furthermore, Cowley argues that it was the economic and political crises of the 1930s that actually undermined the sense of purpose that had so animated the work of many of these writers, forcing them finally to confront the Great War in its impending and still more terrible reincarnation. Most of Cowley's generation did return to the United States in the 1930s but, ironically, experienced a sense of disconnection rather than of reconnection.

If Cowley's stature has diminished with each decade, it can be attributed to the contrast between his personal interest in the works that he felt compelled to write about and the increasing emphasis in the academy on critical theory.

Indeed, because he is so identified with the writers of his period, his insights on those who have remained prominent have become so widely disseminated that they now seem readily apparent, and much of the criticism he produced on those writers who are no longer widely known has come to seem a historical curiosity.

Martin Kich

See also: Literature (U.S., WWII)

REFERENCES

Eisenberg, Diane U. *Malcolm Cowley: A Checklist of His Writings.* Carbondale: Southern Illinois University Press, 1975.

Faulkner, D. W. "Malcolm Cowley and American Writing." *Sewanee Review* 98 (Spring 1990): 222–235.

Shi, David E. "Malcolm Cowley and Literary New York." *Virginia Quarterly Review* 58 (Autumn 1982): 575–593.

Simpson, Lewis P. "Cowley's Odyssey: Literature and Faith in the Thirties." *Sewanee Review* 89 (Fall 1981): 520–539.

Travis, Trysh. "The Man of Letters and the Literary Business: Re-Viewing Malcolm Cowley." *Journal of Modern Literature* 25 (Winter 2001–2002): 1–18.

Young, Philip. "For Malcolm Cowley: Critic, Poet, 1898–." *Southern Review* 9 (1973): 778–795.

Croly, Herbert

New York journalist and editor of the *New Republic,* a widely read journal during World War I, Herbert Croly (1869–1930) was born into a family of journalists. Croly entered the business at an early age, after the death of his father. At the time of the outbreak of World War I, Croly was asked to become the first editor of the *New Republic,* and he cemented his position in wartime political philosophy with his editorials and "who's who" list of journal contributors.

Herbert David Croly was born on January 23, 1869, to David Goodman and Jane Cunningham Croly, both famous journalists and intellectuals in their own right. This environment fostered Croly's mental development. He was educated at private schools in New York City before beginning Harvard University in 1886. In 1888, Croly returned to New York to care for his ill father, who died in 1889. Croly then took over two of his father's publications, the *Real Estate Record and Builders' Guide* and the *Architectural Record.* Within a few years, Croly returned to Harvard to complete his education, but he continued to encounter difficulties and finally, after two more attempts, left Harvard in 1899 without a degree.

After serving as the editor of the *Architectural Record* for some time, Croly began work on a monograph, *The Promise of American Life,* which was published in 1909. Essentially, this book was a commentary on various American problems, including the destruction of trusts. Former president Theodore Roosevelt was marveled by the book and began a friendship with Croly. Roosevelt believed that much of what Croly wrote in his book was akin to his own beliefs. Soon thereafter, Croly assisted Roosevelt in his Progressive campaign in 1912 but refused to join the party. After that brief venture into politics, Croly was asked to write biographies and even guest lecture at Harvard.

Croly's biggest opportunity came when Willard and Dorothy Straight, wealthy reformists, offered him the editorship of a new journal, which they would fund. This journal entitled the *New Republic,* was to bring political commentary, which Croly was now known for, to a national audience. The first issue hit the newsstands in November 1914. It was well received by the critics and the public alike. It sold

875 copies, but by 1915 the circulation reached 15,000.

During the first years of publication, the journal was engrossed in World War I and its political, economic, and social ramifications. Originally, the *New Republic* supported neutrality for the United States, but Croly changed his mind after the sinking of the *Lusitania*. While strongly advocating Woodrow Wilson's declaration of war on Germany, Croly vehemently opposed Wilson's Versailles Treaty. For Croly, the Versailles Treaty and the League of Nations were a violation of Wilson's idealism and both would only further international tensions. The circulation of the *New Republic* reached as high as 43,000 during the war but waned in the 1920s. Through the 1920s, the journal took a stand on the rebirth of conservatism. Croly continued to serve as editor of the *New Republic* until his death on May 17, 1930.

Philine Georgette Vega

See also: Journalism (U.S., WWI); League of Nations (WWI)

REFERENCES

Levy, David W. *Herbert Croly of the New Republic: The Life and Thought of an American Progressive.* Princeton, NJ: Princeton University Press, 1985.

cummings, e.e.

Like many of his literary contemporaries, poet e.e. cummings (1894–1962) participated in the First World War by joining the ambulance corps. However, because of his interest in seeing the world, he signed up for the Norton-Harjes Ambulance Service, a branch of the Red Cross that served the French army. Already a pacifist, cummings (he preferred to spell his name with

A poet of idiosyncratic verse, e.e. cummings joined a number of other American writers and artists serving in the Ambulance Corps during World War I. (Library of Congress)

all lower case letters) had experiences in the ambulance corps and, later, in a detainment camp that solidified his suspicions of anything institutionalized and reinforced his emphasis on nonconformity—views he would maintain throughout his writing career. *The Enormous Room* (1922) is cummings's semiautobiographical account of his experience during the war.

When cummings arrived in Paris to report for duty, he and William Slater Brown, whom he had met on the passage over, were separated from their unit. The two were somehow forgotten, and the young Americans spent the next five weeks enjoying the culture and attractions of the city before they were eventually tracked down and sent to join their unit, Section Sanitaire XXI, in Germaine, France.

Cummings did not adjust well after he

joined his unit, particularly because his superior attempted to run the ambulance corps in military fashion. Besides, he found here the same prejudices and patriotic rhetoric he was hoping to escape. He and Brown created further resentment by fraternizing with the French soldiers. From these soldiers, they learned about the unrest and mutinies among the French ranks, knowledge that Brown argues was the cause of their eventual arrest. Other accounts suggest that the two were arrested due to comments censors found in Brown's letters—and that cummings was considered guilty by association (an association some claim was emphasized by their superior).

After their arrest, cummings and Brown were both sent to Dépôt de Triage, La Ferté-Macé, the focal point of *The Enormous Room.* The large room in which they and the other inmates lived gives the novel its title, for it is in this context that cummings demonstrates most clearly his ideology of the dominion of the human spirit over the body; he is less concerned with the poor living conditions than the ability of humanity—at the level of the individual—to demonstrate goodwill toward one another, even in the midst of squalor. This is in contrast to the dehumanizing institutions (that is, governments) that initiate and engage in war and more specifically oppress persons who fail to conform to the standards of society.

Cummings remained at the detainment camp for about three months until he was finally released and returned to the United States, thanks mainly to letters and inquiries made by his father. Brown, however, was sent to Précigne, a full-fledged concentration camp, and released several months later. Upon his return, cummings was urged by his father to file an international lawsuit. Unwilling to do this, he compromised by writing the story of his experience, the text that would become *The Enormous Room.*

Cummings eventually returned to New York, where he had been residing, and tried to pick up his life as an artist. However, his encounter with the war was not over. Still eligible for the conscription but feeling the war was soon to end, he felt he could wait out General Crowder's "work or fight" edict, so he did not make any attempt to find more "essential" work than his art—despite his father's encouragement. He was drafted in July 1918. Cummings's unit never left Camp Devon, where he was stationed, and he was finally discharged six months later, still only a private.

Although cummings was not cut out for military duty, his experience during the First World War was a defining moment for his ideology; the antiestablishment and nonconformist themes dominate his poetry. Many critics claim that cummings's continued emphasis on the individual demonstrates a weakness, becoming repetitious; others claim he refined his themes as he matured as an artist. Regardless, he focused his efforts on raising humanity up above the status quo.

W. Todd Martin

See also: Censorship (WWI); Literature (U.S., WWI); Pacifists (WWI)

REFERENCES

cummings, e.e. *The Enormous Room.* Foreword by Richard S. Kennedy. New York: Liveright, 1978 (reprint from 1922).

Forrest, David. "William Slater Brown and *The Enormous Room.*" *Spring: The Journal of the E. E. Cummings Society* 1 (October 1992): 87–91.

Kennedy, Richard S. *Dreams in the Mirror: A Biography of E. E. Cummings.* New York: Liveright Publishing Corporation, 1980.

Vernier, J. P. "E. E. Cummings at La Ferté-Macé." *Journal of Modern Literature* 7 (1979): 345–349.

Wickes, George. "e. e. cummings at War." *Columbia Forum* 12.3 (Fall 1969): 31–33.

Curtis, Edwin Upton

Edwin Upton Curtis (1861–1922) was the Boston police commissioner in 1919, when nearly the entire police department went out on strike. Curtis was a Republican politician who had served in several city offices, including that of mayor. During his time in office, Curtis earned a reputation as a reformer. In December 1918, Governor Samuel McCall appointed him Boston police commissioner, an appointment that reflected the deep political divisions in Massachusetts at the time. Boston was heavily Democratic, but the remainder of the state was dominated by the Republicans. In 1885, the legislature passed a law requiring that Boston's police commissioner be appointed by the governor. Boston's mayor had no police powers.

During 1919, the United States was swept by a wave of strikes and terrorism, generally blamed on the Communists. The disorders in the wake of World War I gave rise to the red scare, and many Americans feared anything that raised the specter of worker revolution. In Boston, the most important labor issue involved the police department. Three grievances were raised by the police. The first was the failure of wages to keep pace with wartime inflation. Although they received a raise in May 1919, Boston's policemen still had difficulty making ends meet. They were also upset about the hours they had to work and the poor living conditions in their station houses. Police leaders found Curtis unsympathetic.

The Boston Social Club functioned as a de facto union for the police. Curtis refused to deal with its leaders and appointed his own grievance committee. On August 9, 1919, the Social Club applied for a charter as a local of the American Federation of Labor (AFL), and on August 15, the Club became Local 16,807. Curtis had already warned the police against forming a union. On August 11, he amended the police department's rules to bar members from joining any organization with outside ties and threatened to dismiss any policeman who became a member of the AFL.

On August 26 and 29, Curtis suspended nineteen policemen for union activities. Mayor Andrew Peters tried to mediate a settlement by appointing a panel of Boston citizens to review the situation. The panel recommended that the police form an independent union, but Curtis refused to accept it. He considered the mayor's actions to be unlawful interference. When Curtis fired the suspended policemen on September 8, three-quarters of the police force went out on strike the following afternoon.

Within hours, unruly mobs began to riot, and the few policemen and volunteers were unable to control the situation. Although Curtis claimed to have the situation in hand, looting and arson broke out. After three days, Governor Calvin Coolidge called out the National Guard, who restored order. At least eight people died and more were wounded. With order restored, Curtis fired all 1,147 policemen who had gone out on strike. He hired replacements from World War I veterans. By December 13, 1919, the new police force was in place and the National Guard was withdrawn.

Curtis remained in office until his death in 1922. His actions and those of Coolidge against the union were widely approved. In the context of the red scare, union actions that seemed to threaten the public order were viewed as a step to "sovietization." Coolidge's actions in particular were highly regarded, and propelled him to the vice presidency in 1920.

Tim J. Watts

See also: American Federation of Labor (WWI, WWII); Boston Police Strike (WWI); Red Scare (WWI); Biographies: Coolidge, Calvin (WWI)

REFERENCES

Russell, Francis. *A City in Terror: The 1919 Boston Police Strike.* New York: Viking Press, 1975.

Sobel, Robert. *Coolidge: An American Enigma.* Washington, DC: Regnery Publications, 1998.

White, John Randall. *A Triumph of Bureaucracy: The Boston Police Strike and the Ideological Origins of the American Police Structure.* Ann Arbor, MI: University Microfilms International, 1982.

D

Daniels, Josephus

Josephus Daniels, secretary of the navy during World War I, newspaper editor, progressive, and ambassador to Mexico, was born in Washington, North Carolina, in 1862. He was educated in Wilson, North Carolina, but left before graduating to become editor and eventual owner of a local newspaper. He attended law school at the University of North Carolina at Chapel Hill (UNC) and then acquired a weekly paper in Raleigh, North Carolina. He also served as state printer for several terms, beginning in the late 1880s.

Later, as editor and owner of the *Raleigh North Carolinian,* Daniels made his mark as a Southern Progressive. He promoted federal aid for education and supported the creation of North Carolina State College in 1887, now North Carolina State University. Daniels distrusted big business, especially the tobacco trust. In many respects, he followed the traditional Populist platform of the late nineteenth century in his support of antitrust legislation, a state railroad commission, free silver, direct elections of senators, and a graduated income tax. He also favored women's suffrage, workmen's compensation, and the regulation of child labor. However, his progressivism did not extend to race relations.

A close friend of Woodrow Wilson, he was appointed secretary of the navy when the former assumed the presidency in 1913. He served for both of Wilson's terms. Daniels became known to the sailors as "Uncle Josephus" because he devoted much of his energies to improving their station in life, especially their educational opportunities, often over objections from senior officers. He also banned the use of alcohol in areas frequented by sailors and cleaned up red light districts near navy bases. By doing so, he improved the civilian view of sailors.

As with his interest in sailors, Daniels's Progressive views influenced his response to corporate power during his tenure. He protected the naval oil reserves from big business and, in keeping with his hatred of trusts, worked to break up collusion in the steel industry. He even went so far as to build the navy's own armor plate and projectile plant in Charleston, West Virginia. Daniels also served on the Council of National Defense, which oversaw the American war effort, and as a member of the Committee on Public Information, the group most responsible for propaganda and censorship.

After the war, he returned to North Carolina and assumed the editorship of the *Raleigh News and Observer*. In 1932, he supported his former assistant secretary at the Navy Department, Franklin Delano Roosevelt (FDR), for the presidency. Although the two men had their differences, and Roosevelt had not always proven to be a loyal assistant secretary, they came to admire one another. In 1933, FDR appointed Daniels to serve as ambassador to Mexico.

After serving abroad for eight years, Daniels returned to the United States in 1941 due to his wife's illness. Once again, he resumed his role as editor of the *News and Observer*. In this role, he opposed compulsory military service after World War II. In later years, he came to regret his earlier views concerning race relations. He remained active, both politically and professionally, until his death from pneumonia in January 1948.

Jonathan F. Phillips

See also: Committee on Public Information (WWI); Council of National Defense (WWI); Journalism (U.S., WWI)

REFERENCES

Cooling, Benjamin Franklin. *Gray Steel and Blue Water Navy: The Formative Years of America's Military-Industrial Complex, 1881–1917*. Hamden, CT: Archon Books, 1979.

Cronon, David, ed. *The Cabinet Diaries of Josephus Daniels, 1913–1921*. Lincoln: University of Nebraska Press, 1963.

Daniels, Jonathan. *The End of Innocence*. Philadelphia: J. B. Lippincott Company, 1954.

McKenna, Richard. "The Wreck of Uncle Josephus," in Robert Shenk, ed. *The Left-Handed Monkey Wrench: Stories and Essays by Richard McKenna*. Annapolis: Naval Institute Press, 1986.

Morrison, Joseph L. *Josephus Daniels: The Small-d Democrat*. Chapel Hill: University of North Carolina Press, 1966.

Urofsky, Melvin I. "Josephus Daniels and the Armor Trust." *North Carolina Historical Review* 45, no. 3 (July 1968).

Darrow, Clarence

Clarence Seward Darrow (1857–1938) was one of the most storied figures in American legal history. Born near Kinsman, Ohio, Darrow was raised by parents regarded as heretics in their community. They encouraged him to question everything. Spending a brief stint as a school teacher, where he passed on his parents' philosophy to his students, Darrow turned to law school in 1877, attending only one year before his admission to the Ohio bar. Moving to Chicago in 1887, he quickly became involved in efforts to free anarchists charged with murder during the infamous Haymarket Riot in 1886. Darrow spent several years defending the cause of labor until 1912, when he was charged with bribing two jurors in the McNamara case. He was acquitted, but many have suggested he was guilty.

Although an ardent pacifist, Darrow came to believe the Great War was necessary. Nonetheless, he made the unpopular decision to defend the rights of conscientious objectors in 1917. "If a man's religion tells him he must not kill," Darrow asserted, "then he cannot kill even to defend himself and his home . . . This may seem like suicidal nonsense to . . . 99 per cent of us but . . . we have to grant them the right to follow the will of their God. That is what democracy means."

In 1918, Great Britain's government chose

Darrow to help them gain the sympathy and support of Americans. He spent four months in London, and then returned to Chicago and gave only one speech, in which he offered $1,000 to anyone who could prove a German had cut off the hand of a French or Belgian child.

Darrow defended eleven Italian anarchists in Wisconsin, winning acquittal for nine on appeal and convincing the governor to pardon the other two. In Chicago he fought against the government's attempts to use the Overthrow Act to hastily and unjustly imprison anyone suspected of advocating the overthrow of the government. He successfully defended Arthur Person, a Swedish immigrant from Rockford, Illinois, who was persecuted for his affiliation with the Communist Labor Party.

Darrow's fame spread further in the postwar era. His most notable cases include the Loeb-Leopold, Ossian Sweet, and notorious Scopes "Monkey" trials.

Paul Hillmer

See also: Anarchists (WWI); Communist Party (U.S., WWI); Pacifists (WWI)

REFERENCES

Darrow, Clarence. *The Story of My Life.* New York: Charles Scribner's Sons, 1932.

Stone, Irving. *Clarence Darrow for the Defense.* Garden City, NY: Doubleday, 1941.

Debs, Eugene V.

Eugene Debs (1855–1926) was a labor organizer who founded the American Socialist Party. Debs ran for the U.S. presidency five times

Socialist Party leader Eugene Debs was arrested and imprisoned for opposing America's participation in World War I. He was pardoned by President Warren Harding in 1921. (Library of Congress)

(1900, 1904, 1908, 1912, 1920), and he was imprisoned in 1918 under the Espionage and Sedition Acts for criticizing America's entry into World War I.

Eugene Debs, a deeply committed pacifist and spellbinding orator, was a major voice of opposition throughout America's involvement in World War I. As leader of the Socialist Party, Debs renounced violent revolution in favor of peaceful, democratic social reform. As a third-party candidate in the 1912 presidential elections, Debs garnered nearly one million votes, while more than one thousand of his party's members filled public office.

The Espionage Act of 1917 made it a crime to criticize the war effort, and the Sedition Act of 1918 criminalized the criticism of government. In June 1918 Debs spoke at a Socialist rally in Canton, Ohio. He denounced World War I as a manifestation of capitalist exploitation of the labor class. Debs was immediately arrested. At his trial several weeks later, he argued his own case. In his speech to the jury, Debs quoted passages from the U.S. Constitution to challenge the legitimacy of the Espionage and Sedition Acts. Despite his reasoned eloquence, Debs was sentenced to ten years in prison but served just two-and-a-half before being pardoned by President Warren G. Harding on Christmas Day, 1921. After the war, his old nemesis, President Woodrow Wilson, refused to commute the sentence. However, President Warren Harding pardoned Debs in 1921.

Debs was born in Terre Haute, Indiana. At the age of fourteen he became a locomotive fireman; in 1879 he became city clerk of Terre Haute; and from 1885 to 1887 he was a member of the Indiana legislature. In 1894 Debs led the most famous nineteenth century railroad strike, the Pullman Strike in Chicago. President Grover Cleveland used army troops to break the strike, and in 1895 Debs was sentenced to six months in jail, where he read Karl Marx and became a socialist.

Tony Osborne

See also: Censorship (WWI); Espionage Act (WWI); Pacifists (WWI); Sedition Act (WWI); Socialist Party (WWI); Documents: Anti-War Speech, June 16, 1918

REFERENCES

Salvatore, Nick. *Eugene V. Debs: Citizen and Socialist.* Urbana: University of Illinois, 1982.

Young, Marguerite. *Harp Song for a Radical.* New York: Alfred A. Knopf, 1999.

DeMille, Cecil B.

Cecil Blount DeMille (1881–1959) was an actor, screenwriter, motion picture and radio director and producer, and corporate executive whose award-winning productions ranged from silent films to Hollywood extravaganzas based on biblical stories. In 1913, Samuel Goldwyn, Jesse L. Lasky, and DeMille founded the Jesse L. Lasky Feature Play Company, for which he served as the director-general. In 1916, this company and Adolph Zukor's Famous Players Film Company purchased 50 percent of the stock in Paramount Pictures Corporation and merged. DeMille spent most of his career at Paramount. Along with Oscar Apfel, he directed the first noteworthy feature-length movie to be filmed in Hollywood, *The Squaw Man* (1914). For his 1915 film, *The Warrens of Virginia,* DeMille and the cameraman Alvin Wyckoff introduced an innovative lighting technique referred to as "Rembrandt Lighting" that used spotlights to create more natural looking light and shade.

DeMille's earliest films helped shape a market for mass entertainment and featured western American or melodramatic romance themes. Other 1915 titles include *The Girl of the Golden West, The Wild Goose Chase,* and *The Cheat.* As the Great War intensified, he directed patriotic war films that supported Great Britain and France and denounced Germany. *Joan the Woman* (1917) retells the story of Joan of Arc but is set in the European trenches. DeMille, a frequent speaker at war bond rallies, successfully boosted popular sentiment in favor of U.S. participation in the war through his films of war intrigue and romance, such as *The Little American* (1917) and *Till I Come Back To You* (1918).

After the United States joined the conflict, DeMille organized the 51st Southern California Home Guard and equipped seventy-five men with a machine gun, rifles, and ammunition. He reportedly paid full salary to the dependents of those family men in his employ who entered the service. In the spring of 1918, DeMille schemed to assume control of the national film industry under the guise of helping the government eliminate pro-German propaganda and activity. He planned to personally finance, appoint, and manage government-approved overseers who would investigate movie houses, exhibitors, and employees. But while a special agent for the Justice Department in Los Angeles approved the idea, the quasigovernmental spy organization, the American Protective League (APL), disliked the competition and offered to take charge. DeMille's idea was never implemented.

Diane M. T. North

See also: American Protective League (WWI); Film (U.S., WWI)

REFERENCES

Birchard, Robert S. *Cecil B. DeMille's Hollywood.* Lexington: University Press of Kentucky, 2004.

DeMille, Cecil B. *The Autobiography of Cecil B. DeMille.* Edited by Donald Hayne. Englewood Cliffs, NJ: Prentice-Hall, 1959.

Dempsey, Jack

One of the dominant figures in American sports during his reign as heavyweight champion of the world from 1919–1926, Jack Dempsey (1895–1983) pioneered modern boxing with a mix of speed, grace, and power that propelled him to a 64-6-9 record and 49 knockouts before his retirement in 1940. He rose to prominence steadily throughout World War I and today ranks among the greatest heavyweight boxers in history.

Born William Harrison Dempsey in Manassa, Colorado, Jack worked in copper mines as the young son of a poor timber and mining family, and from 1911 to 1916 fought in dozens of small mining towns under the name "Kid Blackie." During this era, Dempsey fought as many as one hundred unrecorded fights, in addition to sixty-seven officially sanctioned bouts between 1914 and 1918. After going professional in 1914, he became one of the most recognizable and admired sports heroes in the country, a man almost universally admired for

Heavyweight champion of the world from 1919 to 1926, American boxer Jack Dempsey rose to fame shortly before and during World War I. (Library of Congress)

his legendary toughness and respected for his devastating left hook and overall skill. His talents and what critics saw as a streak of brutality reached their apex in 1919, when Dempsey defeated Jess Willard for the world heavyweight title and left Willard with two broken ribs, a closed eye, a broken jaw, and a partial loss of hearing after only three rounds.

The Willard fight earned Dempsey the nickname "The Manassa Mauler," and he defended his title six times over the next seven years while dominating the sports scene of the 1920s. He was finally defeated by Gene Tunney in two remarkable bouts in 1926 and 1927, after which he boxed in exhibition matches until his retirement. He then became a successful and famous restaurant owner in New York City and died in 1983.

Lance Janda

See also: Biographies: Willard, Jess (WWI)

REFERENCES

Kahn, Roger. *A Flame of Pure Fire: Jack Dempsey and the Roaring '20s*. Orlando, FL: Harcourt Trade Publishers, 1999.
Roberts, Randy. *Jack Dempsey: The Manassa Mauler*. Urbana: University of Illinois Press, 2003.

Dewey, John

An early twentieth-century American philosopher, John Dewey (1859–1952) was born in Burlington, Vermont, to store owner Archibald Sprague Dewey and philanthropist Lucina Artemesia Rich. An unexceptional student at the lower levels, he completed high school in three years and entered the University of Vermont at age sixteen, where he thrived, graduating second in his class in 1878.

After teaching in Pennsylvania and Vermont, Dewey earned a Ph.D. in philosophy at Johns Hopkins University in 1884. He obtained a position at the University of Chicago, to head its new department of philosophy, psychology, and pedagogy. Dewey acquired a strong interest in contemporary social problems through contacts with social activists and was strongly influenced by Henry George, a radical writer, and the pragmatism philosophy of William James.

Consequently, he focused his energies on the philosophy of education. Using his own progressive approach to education, his experimental Laboratory School at the University of Chicago closed after three years because results were found to be inconclusive. Dewey then obtained a position at Columbia University in New York, where he stayed until his formal retirement in 1932. In 1899 Dewey published *School and Society* to wide acclaim. In search of finding a suitable education system for the United States, Dewey traveled to China, Japan, Turkey, and Mexico to determine their failures and successes. His trip to the Soviet Union, where he was pleased to find an education system shaped to fit its society, resulted in extreme criticism in the United States.

Dewey disliked linear models of thinking and critiqued the traditional rote learning of dead facts without an accompanying explanation. He railed against dogmatic instruction. Dewey realized that the United States was modernizing. He felt that pedagogy should accompany that growth and fully develop each student's potential, which in turn, would contribute to a thriving democratic society. The intellect of students could be broadened through active learning, that is, by way of conducting projects that would result in reflective and critical thinking skills. He postulated that this experience would in turn provide useful habits and skills allowing larger problems to be solved. This theory set pedagogy on its head. Unfortunately, extreme perversions of Dewey's progressive education were practiced by some educators and in later years led him to denounce their methods.

Dewey was a prolific writer, writing more than forty books. He published *My Pedagogic Creed* in 1897, *Democracy and Education* in 1916, and numerous other books, all pertaining to his interest in using education to improve individualism that would ultimately perfect democracy. He also wrote more than seven hundred articles and innumerable lectures and speeches throughout his career.

Dewey's political activism reflected his pedagogical theories, which infuriated those holding a right-wing mentality. He became a member of the National Association for the Advancement of Colored People, the American Civil Liberties Union, the Socialist Party, the Progressive Party, and the League for Independent Political Action. Believing that students should be active participants in their education, he funded various student organizations that would provide early initiation into the machinations of society.

After Dewey's retirement from teaching in 1929 and a subsequent ten-year emeritus stint, he devoted himself to writing. He died on June 1, 1952, in New York. His idea of providing society's members with maximum experimentation and personal growth was unique. He called for a liberalism of thought that brought the United States into the modern era.

Annette Richardson

See also: Civil Liberties (WWI); Intellectuals (WWI); National Association for the Advancement of Colored People (NAACP) (WWI); Progressivism (WWI); Socialist Party (WWI)

REFERENCES

Boydston, Jo Ann. *The Collected Works of John Dewey.* 37 vols. Carbondale: Southern Illinois University Press, 1967–1991.

Bullert, Gary. *The Politics of John Dewey.* Buffalo, NY: Prometheus Books, 1983.

Dewey, John. *How We Think: A Restatement of the Relation of Reflective Thinking to the Educative Process.* Boston: D. C. Heath, 1933.

Ryan, A. *John Dewey and the High Tide of American Liberalism.* New York: W. W. Norton, 1995.

Dos Passos, John

The life of author John Dos Passos (1896–1970) spanned two world wars. His World War I experiences informed his early novels. His radical ideas inspired his greatest literary achievements.

John Dos Passos was named Jack Madison at his birth in 1896. Lucy Addison Sprigg Madison, his socially prominent mother, told her family the child was born in Chicago, Illinois, on January 14. Jack's father, John Dos Passos Sr., a corporate lawyer, was married to Mary Hays. Jack Madison spent much of a lonely childhood in Europe with his mother. He attended Peterborough Lodge, a boarding school in Hampstead near London, and Sidwell Friends School in Washington, D.C., and graduated from Choate in Wallingford, Connecticut. Although not immediately made public, on June 21, 1910, three months after the death of his wife, Dos Passos Sr. married Lucy Madison—seven years after the death of her husband. On July 13, 1912, Jack Madison signed the register at Young's Hotel in Boston as John Rodirigo Dos Passos Jr. In 1916, he graduated cum laude from Harvard, where his many friends included e.e. cummings and Robert Nathan.

A few days after the United States entered World War I (April 1917), Dos Passos, a pacifist, joined the Norton-Harjes Ambulance Service, an organization similar to the American Field Service. He had just arrived in New York from Spain because of his father's death. On June 20, he sailed to France aboard the *SS Chicago.* The ship, filled with Ivy League men as well as some nurses, debutantes, and other volunteers, was just two days behind the first convoy of American soldiers. When Norton-Harjes, along with other volunteer American ambulance services, became part of the U.S. Army, Dos Passos enrolled in the American Red Cross and headed for the Italian front. While there, a Red Cross censor recommended his discharge because of leftist ideas Dos Passos expressed in his letters. On June 20, Dos Passos went to Paris to address these accusations and discovered that the U.S. government had brought charges against him for draft evasion. Dos Passos had been ordered to report to his draft board for a physical soon after he sailed with his Norton-Harjes unit. Although his friend Wright McCormick had notified the draft board accordingly, it was never recorded. While awaiting a hearing in Paris, Dos Passos volunteered for the grisly job of carting gigantic loads of amputated limbs from the hospital to the dump.

Dos Passos returned to the United States to resolve the charges he faced. At the request of his mother's sister, Mary Lamar Gordon, James Brown Scott, president of the Carnegie Peace Foundation and a major in the Red Cross Judge Advocates Corp, wrote a letter that helped exonerate him. Scott also enabled Dos Passos, despite eyesight poor enough for rejection, to enlist in the U.S. Army Medical Corps. Dos Passos reported to Camp Crane, Allentown, Pennsylvania, on September 26, 1918,

was appointed acting quartermaster sergeant, and was quarantined because of the flu epidemic. Sent next to Camp Merritt, on November 11, 1918, he sailed for France amidst rumors of the Armistice. By November 28, when he crossed the channel, the war was over. After he marched his men into a wall during a demonstration for a visiting colonel, Dos Passos was stripped of his rank and remained a private throughout the rest of his service. Stationed in Paris, he continued to write, took sketching classes, suffered a bout of the rheumatic fever that afflicted him throughout his life, and attended the Sorbonne under the auspices of the U.S. Army Overseas Educational Commission. He was then posted to Gièvres, to be mustered out of the army. After weeks of hard labor, he went AWOL for twenty-two hours to Tours, tracked down the file, the misplacement of which prevented his discharge from the army, obtained the necessary papers, and upon return to Gièvres, was discharged on July 11, 1919. He went to England and Spain.

After World War I, Dos Passos traveled and wrote novels based on his war experiences, including *One Man's Initiation, 1917* (1920) and *Three Soldiers* (1921). Many critics praised his honesty about the horrors of war; others attacked him bitterly for killing the glory-of-war mystique that sends men to their death with a sense of accomplishment. *Manhattan Transfer* appeared in 1925. His best-known work, the trilogy *U.S.A,* was published in 1938. It consisted of *42nd Parallel* (1930), *1919* (1932), and *The Big Money* (1936). Despite a sometimes negative press about their experimental style and radical content, these novels established John Dos Passos as a major American literary figure and led Jean-Paul Sartre to proclaim him "the greatest writer of our time."

Dos Passos gradually became disenchanted with leftist causes because of Soviet leader

Joseph Stalin's tyranny, the realization that communism demanded total allegiance to the party line and permitted no intellectual independence, and the murder, allegedly by communist assassins, of close friend José Robles, a professor at Johns Hopkins.

By the time the United States entered World War II, Dos Passos's literary reputation was sinking, but his writing was still in demand. In 1944, he published *State of the Nation,* a nonfiction account of workers in war industries—their reaction to rationing, higher taxes, morale, racial tensions, and rumors about workers loafing in shipyards and steel mills. It originated with articles he wrote for *Liberty* magazine. In December 1944, Dos Passos left for the Pacific Theater of War on assignment as a war correspondent for *Life* magazine. On October 10, 1945, Dos Passos left for Europe to report for *Life* on the Nuremberg trials. In 1945, he completed *Tour of Duty,* a book of essays about what soldiers thought about the war. *District of Columbia* (1952), a trilogy consisting of *Adventures of a Young Man* (1939), *Number One* (1943), and *Grand Design* (1949), never attained the popularity or critical acclaim of *U.S.A.,* which appeared in a new edition with illustrations by Reginald Marsh in 1946.

In 1957, Dos Passos was elected to the American Academy of Arts and Letters, and was awarded the National Institute's Gold Medal for fiction. He completed four more novels, *Chosen Country* (1951), *Most Likely to Succeed* (1954), *The Great Days* (1958), *and Midcentury* (1961). *The Head and the Heart of Thomas Jefferson* (1954) and *The Shackles of Power, Three Jeffersonian Decades* (1966), reflect his abiding interest in American history. His literary reputation revived during the 1960s, but despite his prolific output, he was beleaguered by money problems throughout his life. Most of his small inheritance was dissipated by poor oversight or was tied up in litigation, and publishers devoured his book advances by billing him for the cost of advertising. He died September 27, 1970, in Baltimore, Maryland.

Miriam Steinhardt Soffer

See also: Ambulance Drivers (WWI); Censorship (WWI); Civil Liberties (WWI); Communist Party (U.S., WWI); Conscientious Objectors (WWI); Journalism (U.S., WWI); Literature (U.S., WWI); Pacifists(WWI); Biographies: Dos Passos, John (WWII)

REFERENCES

Carr, Virginia Spencer. *John Dos Passos: A Life.* Garden City, NY: Doubleday, 1984.

Ludington, Townsend. *The Fourteenth Chronicle, Letters and Diaries of John Dos Passos.* Boston: Gambit, 1973.

Rohrkemper, John. *John Dos Passos: A Reference Guide.* Boston: G. K. Hall, 1980.

DuBois, W. E. B.

William Edward Burghardt (W. E. B.) DuBois (1868–1963) was an African American intellectual, early sociologist, writer, editor, critic, and activist born in Great Barrington, Massachusetts. The first African American to earn a Ph.D. from Harvard University, DuBois dedicated more than ten years to the sociological study of black America. Increasingly alarmed by the virulent racism found particularly in the South, he became critical of Booker T. Washington, who encouraged African Americans to accept their lot—at least in the short term—and gain acceptance through hard work, thrift, and patience. DuBois's *The Souls of Black Folk*

(1903) included a chapter attacking Washington's tactics, which he believed merely entrenched racism.

As a participant in the Niagara Movement, which focused primarily on attacking Washington, DuBois figured prominently in the establishment of the National Association for the Advancement of Colored People (NAACP). As longtime editor of its magazine, *The Crisis,* DuBois sparked controversy during the First World War. Germany, DuBois claimed, was attempting to seize France's and Britain's interests in Africa. Although these other countries were far from guiltless in their dealings with Africans, Germany, with its own Prussian version of a white supremacy doctrine, was far worse. A German victory, he predicted, would unleash "a world war of races." His July 1918 editorial, suggesting that blacks suppress their "special grievances" until the war was over, alarmed many African Americans.

However, by May 1919, Dubois expressed frustration and disillusionment: "We return. We return *from fighting.* We *return fighting.*" He later confessed in 1938's *Dusk of Dawn,* "I doubt if the triumph of Germany could have had worse results than the triumph of the Allies."

Growing increasingly radical by the mid-1940s, DuBois feuded with the NAACP and the U.S. government. In 1961 he joined the Communist Party, moved to Ghana, and later renounced his American citizenship.

Paul Hillmer

See also: African Americans (WWI); National Association for the Advancement of Colored People (NAACP) (WWI); Documents: Return Soldiers, May 1919

REFERENCES

Moon, Henry Lee, ed. *The Emerging Thought of W. E. B. DuBois.* New York: Simon and Schuster, 1972.

Lewis, David Levering, ed. *W. E. B. DuBois.* 2 vols. New York: H. Holt, 1993–2000.

E

Eastman, Crystal

Crystal Eastman (1881–1928) was an activist, a lawyer, a pacifist, a journalist, and a feminist who shaped civil liberties beliefs and legislation during the World War I period. Eastman engaged in the fight for labor rights, woman's suffrage, and the campaign against entry into World War I. Later, Eastman was responsible for the birth of the American Civil Liberties Union (ACLU) and the formulation of the Equal Rights Amendment (ERA).

Crystal Eastman was born in Glenora, New York, to Congregational Church ministers Samuel and Bertha Eastman. Educated at Vassar College and Columbia University, and second in her class at New York University School of Law, Eastman was active in the Greenwich Village community. While working at the Greenwich House, a settlement house, she met Paul U. Kellogg, a social activist who hired her to work on the Russell Sage Foundation's Pittsburgh Survey, which probed labor conditions. Her final product, *Work Accidents and the Law,* published in 1910, was considered groundbreaking and led New York Governor Charles Evans Hughes to name her to the New York State Commission on Employers' Liability and Causes of Industrial Accidents, Unemployment and Lack of Farm Labor. The first woman to serve on this board (from 1909–1911), she was involved in writing the first workers' compensation statute. From 1913 to 1914, she was an investigating attorney on the U. S. Commission on Industrial Relations.

In Milwaukee, while married to her first husband, Wallace Benedict, Eastman became a radical feminist and was partly responsible for the establishment of the Congressional Union. As World War I became a reality, she included the antiwar movement in her activism and organized the U. S. Woman's Peace Party with Jane Addams. She served as the head of the New York branch and was also the executive director of the American Union Against Militarism.

After her divorce and remarriage in 1916 to Walter Fuller, a British poet, Eastman continued to advocate against the war, the draft, and other such issues. Eastman also held civil liberties during wartime of the utmost importance and founded the National Civil Liberties Bureau, a forerunner of the ACLU. Eastman was blacklisted during the Red Scare of 1919 to 1921. When the war was over, she turned her energies to the women's rights movement and authored the ERA in 1923. Eastman continued to write for *Equal Rights,* a journal, and *Time and Tide,* a weekly feminist newspaper. On July

The daughter of Congregational Church ministers, Crystal Eastman was an activist, lawyer, pacifist, journalist, and feminist who shaped civil liberties beliefs and legislation during the World War I period. (Library of Congress)

8, 1928, at the age of forty-eight, Eastman died from nephritis.

Philine Georgette Vega

See also: American Union Against Militarism (WWI); Journalism (U.S., WWI); Pacifists (WWI); Red Scare (WWI); Women (U.S., WWI); Biographies: Eastman, Max Forester (WWI)

REFERENCE

Law, Sylvia A. "Crystal Eastman: NYU Law Graduate," *New York University Law Review* 66 (1991): 1963–1994.

Eastman, Max Forester

Max Eastman (1883–1969) was a well-known Socialist and radical who opposed American entry into World War I. During the war, his first journal was silenced by the U.S. government, and he was put on trial twice for violating the Espionage Act. Eastman spent time in the Soviet Union after the war and became a supporter of Leon Trotsky. Disillusioned by Joseph Stalin's excesses, he moved to the extreme right by the 1950s.

Eastman was the son of two Congregationalist ministers, born in Canandaigua, New York. Well educated, he studied philosophy under John Dewey at Columbia University from 1907 to 1910. Eastman finished all requirements for his Ph.D., but refused to submit his dissertation, although Dewey had already approved it. He was determined to avoid academics and become a poet. In 1911, he moved with his older sister Crystal to Greenwich Village. Eastman soon became a socialist and feminist.

Eastman's growing fame as a writer and radical soon won him an invitation to edit a Socialist monthly journal entitled *The Masses*. It was on the verge of bankruptcy when he took over, but he quickly transformed it into one of the most important left-wing periodicals in American history. Eastman ran it as a cooperative, with anyone who contributed having a say in how the journal operated. His charm and winning personality attracted contributions from leading writers and artists who were Socialists, including John Reed, Sherwood Anderson, Carl Sandburg, and Stuart Davis. *The Masses* was soon thriving, with its attacks on the established order. Eastman and his magazine were once sued by the Associated Press for criminal libel but won.

When World War I broke out, Eastman adopted an antiwar stand. He countered the

Editor of the left-wing journal The Masses, *Max Eastman opposed U.S. entry in World War I. The U.S. Post Office refused to deliver the magazine during the war, but was overruled by a federal court. (Library of Congress)*

preparedness movement with cartoons and editorials condemning militarism. Some issues of *The Masses*, such as that for July 1916, were completely devoted to antiwar materials. When the United States entered the war in April 1917, Eastman continued to oppose the war. He also attacked efforts to mobilize American society and to restrict individual rights such as freedom of speech. Eastman traveled across the country in August 1917 to call for peace.

As a result of Eastman's political stand, federal authorities sought to shut down *The Masses*. Under the terms of the Espionage Act, the Post Office declared the August 1917 issue unmailable for its cartoons and editorials. Al-

though a U.S. District Court judge ordered the issue to be mailed on July 26, the Circuit Court immediately overturned his ruling. The September issue was published as scheduled, but the Post Office rescinded *The Masses'* second-class postage permit, citing its failure to mail the August issue as grounds. Unable to mail to subscribers, Eastman was further hampered because many newsstands refused to sell *The Masses* due to its radical viewpoint. A combined November-December issue was the last issue. Undeterred, Eastman and his sister founded another journal in 1918. That journal, entitled *The Liberator*, was owned by the Eastmans and had many of the same contributors. Eastman had encouraged John Reed to go to Russia in 1917 to report on the revolution there, and *The Liberator* published many of Reed's reports.

Meanwhile, Eastman and six of his associates from *The Masses* were indicted for conspiracy to obstruct military recruitment and opposition to the draft, activities outlawed by the Espionage Act. Many others who spoke out against American involvement in World War I were sent to prison on similar charges. When brought to trial in April 1918, however, Eastman soon won over members of the jury. His eloquence and good looks while testifying won praise even from hostile observers. The trial ended in a hung jury. A second trial was held in September 1918. Again, Eastman was the star of the proceedings. He gave a three-hour summation to the jury that won over several members. Once again, the trial ended in a hung jury. The federal government declined to prosecute him again, since the war ended in November.

After the war, Eastman continued to praise the Bolshevik Revolution in *The Liberator*. In 1922, he moved to the Soviet Union to witness the Revolution firsthand. He became friends with Trotsky and began translating his works. Eastman left the Soviet Union in 1924 and published Lenin's warning against Stalin. His attack on Stalin isolated Eastman from most other American leftists during the 1920s and 1930s. He later broke with Trotsky and moved radically to the right. He published several works critical of Stalin and Marxism in 1940 that are still regarded as among the best of their kind. In the 1950s, Eastman—who by the post-war period had come to believe that communism was the greatest danger facing the world—praised Joseph McCarthy's witch hunt for Communists. By the time Eastman died in 1969, he had become a political moderate.

Tim J. Watts

See also: Espionage Act (WWI); Journalism (U.S., WWI); Socialist Party (WWI); Biographies: Anderson, Sherwood (WWI); Eastman, Crystal (WWI); Reed, John (WWI)

REFERENCES

Cantor, Milton. *Max Eastman.* New York: Twayne, 1970.

Giffen, Frederick C. *Six Who Protested: Radical Opposition to the First World War.* Port Washington, NY: Kennikat, 1977.

O'Neill, William L. *The Last Romantic: A Life of Max Eastman.* New York: Oxford University Press, 1978.

Ellington, Duke

Prolific composer, bandleader, and recording artist Edward Kennedy "Duke" Ellington (1899–1974) was born in Washington, D.C. He began his piano career at the age of seven. By the time he reached his teens, Ellington had dropped out of school and was writing his own music. He performed with bands in the D.C. area, eventually joining a group called the Washingtonians.

In 1923, the band relocated to New York City and played at the Hollywood Club. The following year, the group did its first recording; by 1927 they scored their first hit, "East St. Louis Toodle-oo." Ellington became the leader of the band (the Duke Ellington Band) when they moved to the Cotton Club, a job they held for more than three years. Their recordings soon grew, as did the number of their hits.

By 1929, Ellington's band appeared in the Broadway musical *Show Girl* and were soon featured in their first film, *Check and Double Check.* In 1931 the band left the Cotton Club to tour and establish themselves as the leaders of the swing era, with hits such as "Sophisticated Lady" (1933) and "Stormy Weather" (1933). The band continued their prosperity throughout the 1930s, in film, on stage, and on the road.

During World War II, the Duke Ellington Band was one of the most popular groups in the country. During the 1940s, the addition of artist and composer Billy Strayhorn marked a change in their sound. This was evident in their hit, "Take the A Train," a song many considered to be the defining tune of the swing era. A ban on recording brought by the American Federation of Musicians during the war shifted Ellington's focus to recitals at Carnegie Hall and working on his compositions. More movies followed, including *Cabin in the Sky* and *Reveille with Beverly,* two films popular in wartime America.

Following World War II, Ellington continued to compose and record albums. His musical dominance ended, but it did not affect his recordings or tours. He continued to generate new material and work on other projects. In 1946 he worked on the Broadway musical *Beggar's Holiday,* and in 1950 he wrote the score for the film *Asphalt Jungle.* In the late fifties and into the sixties, Ellington continued to record, tour, and write music for films. His work on the movie *Paris Blues* was nominated for an Academy Award in 1961. Ellington continued his career until his death in 1974.

Kelly M. Jordan

See also: Jazz (WWI); Music (U.S., WWI); Biographies: Ellington, Duke (WWII)

REFERENCES

Hasse, John Edward. *Beyond Category: The Life and Genius of Duke Ellington.* New York: De Capo Press, 1995.

Lawrence, A. H. *Duke Ellington and His World: A Biography.* New York: Routledge, 2001.

Nicholson, Stuart. *Reminiscing in Tempo: A Portrait of Duke Ellington.* Boston: Northern University Press, 1999.

Europe, James Reese

A noted composer and orchestra conductor, James Reese Europe (1880–1919) popularized ragtime dances and did much to promote jazz during World War I. After playing the jazz circuit, he enlisted with the New York National Guard and provided both entertainment and battlefield support for the troops before he met his tragic death at the hand of one of his band members.

James Reese Europe was born on February 22, 1880, in Mobile, Alabama. He was the son of IRS employee Henry J. Europe and his wife, Lorraine. After Reconstruction, the family had to move to Washington, D.C., because Henry lost his job and had to take a new position with the United States Postal Service. By most accounts, the entire Europe family was musical; James was able to attend the M Street High School for blacks, where he studied violin, piano, and composition.

In 1900, Europe moved to New York City and became part of the emerging black musical theater culture. He worked steadily as a composer and musical director over the next six years. Europe worked on "Memphis Students," *A Trip to Africa, Shoo-Fly Regiment,* and *Reel Mom.* In 1910, he established the Clef Club of New York, a musicians union for African Americans. The Clef Club under Europe did much to promote and protect the talent of black musicians and was a powerful force in the city. That same year, Europe conducted a one-hundred-member orchestra at the Manhattan Casino in Harlem, and on May 2, 1912, he directed one hundred twenty-five people at Carnegie Hall for the *Symphony of Negro Music.* Along with other notable black conductors, Europe was able to shatter the once-Anglo hold over Carnegie Hall and was asked back in both 1913 and 1914.

Vernon and Irene Castle asked Europe to codirect their dance team, which he did. They then toured the country and opened a dance studio and supper club in New York City. During this period, Europe collaborated with the Castles on popularizing ragtime dances, including their famous fox-trot. Because of his success with the Castle duo, Europe and his orchestra, the Society Orchestra, were offered a record contract with Victor Records. This was the first such deal for a black orchestra.

When World War I broke out, Europe joined the Fifteenth Infantry Regiment of the New York National Guard, the first black regiment to be organized, and also joined a French combat group and became the 369th Infantry Regiment. After boot camp in South Carolina, the infantry was sent to France, where Europe served as bandmaster and commander of a machine gun company. Europe was the first black officer to command troops into battle during

World War I. The "Hellfighters," as the Fifteenth Regiment was called, became highly decorated, and his band became famous in Europe for introducing non-American audiences to jazz.

Upon his return, Europe's band was paraded on Fifth Avenue. He signed a second record contract and set out on a nationwide tour. On May 9, 1919, Europe was stabbed by a bandmate during a concert in Boston and died. Europe was given a public funeral in New York City—the first for an African American. He was buried in Arlington National Cemetery with military honors.

Philine Georgette Vega

See also: African Americans (WWI); Jazz (WWI); Music (U.S., WWI); Biographies: Castle, Vernon and Irene (WWI)

REFERENCES

Badger, Reid. *A Life in Ragtime: A Biography of James Reese Europe.* New York: Oxford University Press, 1995.

F

Fairbanks Sr., Douglas

Born in Denver, Colorado, Douglas Fairbanks (1883–1939) was one of the leading movie actors of the silent era of American cinema. He was the fourth son of Charles and Ella Ullman. When Charles Ullman abandoned the family in 1888, Ella returned to the name of her first husband, John Fairbanks, and all the children adopted it. Beginning in local theater, Fairbanks soon joined regional traveling companies and discovered a knack for physical comedy that suited his athletic and energetic style. He half-heartedly held several traditional jobs in sales and brokerage before committing himself to acting. In 1907, Fairbanks married Anna Elizabeth Sully, the daughter of a wealthy cotton broker who attempted to sway him from the theater, but a 1908 economic downturn destroyed the Sully family fortune and Fairbanks ended up supporting his in-laws as an increasingly popular juvenile comedy lead.

In 1915, Fairbanks signed a contract with the Triangle Fine Arts Company and appeared in silent films, the first of which was *The Lamb*. His success as a film actor came in 1916 with *His Picture in the Paper*, which capitalized on his ability to do stunts. Secure in his popularity as a leading man, Fairbanks acted as a spokesman for the Boy Scouts, promoting exercise, positive thinking, and sexual self-control, including marital fidelity. This was ironic, because beginning in 1917, Fairbanks had begun a secret affair with Mary Pickford, "America's Sweetheart," who was both married and a devout Roman Catholic.

During World War I, Fairbanks, who was too old to enlist, organized fundraisers for the Red Cross, including a spectacular rodeo in Hollywood. He appeared in short propaganda films, including *Swat the Kaiser!*, and traveled the country with Pickford selling Liberty Bonds. At several stops, he increased sales by taking outlandish physical challenges from local businessmen who promised to buy bonds.

Unhappy with Triangle, Fairbanks, Pickford, Charlie Chaplin, and Cecil B. DeMille founded United Artists in January 1919. This was the first studio owned and controlled by actors, giving the quartet extraordinary power to choose material and negotiate with theater chains. Secure in their popularity, Fairbanks and Pickford divorced their respective spouses, rode out the scandal, and married on March 28, 1920, before embarking on a popular tour of Europe. In the postwar film industry, Fairbanks found his niche as an action hero and made the transition to sound through roles in *The Mark of*

Although too old to enlist, early Hollywood icon and action hero Douglas Fairbanks appeared in propaganda films during World War I, as well as touring the country to pitch Liberty Bonds. (Library of Congress)

Zorro, Three Musketeers, Robin Hood, and *The Thief of Baghdad,* although age began to make swashbuckling more difficult. Pickford and Fairbanks traveled to both Fascist Italy and Soviet Russia in 1926 and were photographed giving the Fascist salute as well as meeting Sergei Eisenstein to view *Battleship Potemkin.*

Increasingly separated by work and interests, Fairbanks and Pickford separated in 1932 and divorced in January 1935, prompting calls of immorality and the unseemliness of America's first film couple making divorce acceptable. Fairbanks married Lady Sylvia Ashley on

March 7, 1936, and lived in England, returning in September 1939 when WWII broke out. He died in Los Angeles of a massive heart attack on December 10, 1939.

Margaret Sankey

See also: Film (U.S., WWI); Biographies: Chaplin, Charlie (WWI); Griffith, D. W. (WWI); Pickford, Mary (WWI)

REFERENCES

Carey, Gary. *Doug and Mary.* New York: E. P. Dutton, 1977.
Hancock, Ralph. *Douglas Fairbanks, the Fourth Musketeer.* New York: Holt, 1953.
Herndon, Booten. *Mary Pickford and Douglas Fairbanks.* New York: Norton, 1977.

Filene, Edward

Businessman and American government consultant on logistics and manpower, Edward Filene (1860–1937) was the second son of Clara Ballin and Wilhelm Katz, a German Jew from Posen who changed his name to Filene upon immigrating to New York. Edward and his brother Lincoln helped build a family mercantile store into a large Boston department store before inheriting control of the business at their father's retirement in 1890. Although Edward was disappointed that family demands kept him from a university education, he and Lincoln were innovators in their field, developing procedures to track fads, cultivate manufacturers, and train clerks in customer service that was so helpful they referred people to other stores if Filene's could not satisfy. Filene's Bargain Basement, begun in 1909, was a new con-

Boston department store magnate Edward Filene used his stores to sell war bonds in World War I. The military also consulted him on logistical and supply questions. (Library of Congress)

cept in retailing and offered other businesses a chance to liquidate inventory, while shoppers learned to grab deals. The store also offered extensive insurance benefits, profit sharing, a medical clinic, and an employee-run restaurant, and the Filene Cooperate Association board with employee representatives to arbitrate disputes. Filene's was one of the first to promote women as executives.

Edward was an active Democrat and a longtime supporter of Franklin Roosevelt. He lobbied for social reforms, including workers' compensation and protections for working women, and supported Lincoln Steffen's journalistic exposé of the corruption in Boston politics. The store attorney was Louis Brandeis, who was encouraged to take on cases of social justice. Support for Brandeis's Supreme Court appointment opened the Filenes to attacks by anti-Semites. A 1907 trip to India inspired Edward to promote the legalization of credit unions, succeeding in 1909 in Massachusetts and then nationally. Edward was active in the U.S. Chamber of Commerce, and helped found the Boston City Club to bring together Jewish, Catholic, and old New England leaders in the interest of good city government.

Edward, an intrepid traveler, was in Paris at the beginning of World War I and organized Americans in France to aid refugees and remain out of harm's way. As a member of the Chamber of Commerce, he was consulted by the government as an expert on logistics and financing. The store helped to promote and sell war bonds, and they paid employees in military service the difference between their military pay and their civilian salary.

Edward remained active in Europe, touting the League of Nations. In 1924 he attended the negotiations on the Dawes plan on reparations, and he sponsored an international essay contest on achieving world peace.

In 1928, Edward's younger brother Lincoln and executives forced Edward out of real power at Filene's (which shortly thereafter became Federated Department Stores) but allowed him to remain president. Now free to travel, Edward visited Soviet Russia, protested against Japanese aggression in Asia, and became more involved in Jewish refugee work and opposition to Hitler's German regime. With Captain George Finlay and IBM, Edward invented the simultaneous translation devices used at the Nuremburg trials and the United Nations. In 1936, he endowed Clyde Miller's Institute for Propaganda Research. Edward Filene died in Paris on September 26, 1937.

Margaret Sankey

See also: Business (U.S., WWI); League of Nations (WWI)

REFERENCES

Berkley, George E. *The Filenes*. Boston: International Pocket Library, 1998.

Johnson, Gerald. *Liberal's Progress*. New York: Coward McCann, 1948.

La Dame, Mary. *The Filene Store: A Study of Employees' Relation to Management in a Retail Store*. New York: Russell Sage Foundation, 1930.

Martin, Christopher. "Edward A. Filene and the Promise of Industrial Democracy." Ph.D. dissertation, University of Rochester, 2002.

Flynn, Elizabeth Gurley

A lifelong radical and acclaimed public speaker, Elizabeth Gurley Flynn (1890–1964) was a dedicated advocate for men and women imprisoned or facing deportation for violating antisubversive laws during World War I and the postwar Red Scare.

Elizabeth Gurley Flynn joined the Industrial Workers of the World (IWW) in 1906, when she was just sixteen. She was indicted in 1917 for antiwar propaganda, which was actually a pamphlet she had written for a 1913 IWW strike, and charged with violating the Espionage Act. The charges were eventually dropped. In 1918, with help from the Civil Liberties Bureau, she founded the New York–based Workers' Defense Union (WDU). A coalition of labor unions and other working-class groups, the WDU assisted individuals arrested under the Espionage Act, the Sedition Act, and the Alien Act. Flynn worked to publicize these cases and to raise money for the prisoners and their families.

After the war, Flynn continued to work for labor defense. She actively protested the Palmer Raids, and raised money to assist men and women arrested during the raids and awaiting possible deportation. For seven years, Flynn and the WDU worked diligently, if unsuccessfully, to save Sacco and Vanzetti from the electric chair. When the WDU merged with another defense organization in 1925, Flynn left to become secretary of the American Fund for Public Service (the Garland Fund), which financed various left-wing causes, including the Sacco-Vanzetti campaign. For the rest of her life, Flynn remained an active radical. She joined the American Communist Party in 1926, an affiliation for which she was ousted from the American Civil Liberties Union in 1940. In 1951, Flynn was arrested as a Communist under the Smith Act and sentenced to three years in prison. She remained a Communist until her death in Moscow in 1964.

Mary Ann Trasciatti

See also: Alien Act (WWI); Civil Liberties Bureau (WWI); Communist Party (WWI); Espionage Act (WWI); Industrial Workers of the World (WWI); Palmer Raids (WWI); Red Scare (WWI); Sacco and Vanzetti Case (WWI); Sedition Act (WWI); Biographies: Palmer, Alexander Mitchell (WWI)

REFERENCES

Camp, Helen C. *Iron in Her Soul: Elizabeth Gurley Flynn and the American Left*. Pullman: Washington State University Press, 1995.

Flynn, Elizabeth Gurley. *The Rebel Girl: An Autobiography, My First Life (1906–1926)*. New York: International Publishers, 1973.

Ford, Henry

Pioneer automobile manufacturer and pacifist, Henry Ford (1863–1947) was born on a farm in Springwells (now Greenfield) Township, located in Wayne County in Michigan. As a schoolboy, Ford was not good at reading or writing, but he was proficient in arithmetic and fascinated by machinery. He left the farm for Detroit in 1879, and worked as an apprentice in several companies. He returned home in 1882, and six years he later married Clara Bryant. Ford's father gave him forty acres of land as a wedding gift, but Henry refused to farm. He and his wife moved to Detroit in 1891,

Automobile pioneer and industrialist Henry Ford was a determined pacifist. But his privately organized diplomatic mission to Europe in 1915 failed to bring an end to fighting in World War I. (Ford Motor Company)

where he found employment as a night engineer for the Edison Illuminating Company.

In 1896, Ford built his first experimental car, which he called a quadricycle. It had four bicycle tires and weighed only five hundred pounds. Ford made a second car in 1899 that he drove between Detroit and Pontiac. This successful motoring demonstration convinced William H. Murphy, a wealthy Detroit lumber merchant, to assist Ford in establishing the Detroit Automobile Company. Ford left the Edison Illuminating Company to serve as superintendent in charge of production at Detroit Automobile. This company failed in November 1900 but was briefly reconstituted in November 1901 as the Henry Ford Company. Ford was fired from this company in March 1902 for indulging in car racing.

In 1903, Ford established the Ford Motor Company in partnership with James Couzens, the Dodge brothers, and others. The Ford family took control of the company after Henry acquired a majority interest in 1907. In October 1908, Ford Motor unveiled the Model T, the world's first mass-produced automobile; fifteen million units were sold before Model T production ended in 1927. Ford Motor became the world's largest automobile company by wedding a cost-efficient mass-production system with an automated assembly line to rapidly manufacture standardized automobiles. Ford took a paternalistic interest in his employees, and his company became famous for paying high wages. In January 1914, Ford introduced the $5 an hour and eight-hour-day labor system at his company. Ford Motor workers were therefore paid roughly double the ordinary wage for industrial workers and labored fewer hours. In return, Ford expected his workers to staunchly oppose unionism.

Ford declared himself a pacifist and opposed American involvement in World War I. In an attempt to end the war, Ford commanded a privately organized peace ship, the *Oskar II,* that sailed Europe in December 1915, but the result was a dismal failure. After the United States entered the war, he reversed his pacifist position, helping the country by producing ambulances, airplanes, munitions, tanks, and submarine chasers. In 1918, Ford ran for the U.S. Senate, but was narrowly defeated.

Yoneyuki Sugita

See also: Business (U.S., WWI); Pacifists (WWI)

REFERENCES

Batchelor, Ray. *Henry Ford, Mass Production, Modernism and Design.* Manchester: Manchester University Press, 1994.
Wood, John C., and Michael C. Wood, eds. *Henry Ford: Critical Evaluations in Business and Management.* New York: Routledge, 2003.

Fosdick, Raymond

Raymond Fosdick (1883–1972), social worker, writer, lawyer, and chairman of the Commission on Training Camp Activities (CTCA) during World War I, was born to a family of educators in Buffalo, New York. He attended Colgate for two years before transferring to Princeton, where he completed his undergraduate studies, earned a master's degree, and came under the tutelage of Princeton's president, Woodrow Wilson. Inspired by Jacob Riis's *How the Other Half Lives* and the settlement house movement, he later worked for social activist Lillian Wald in New York while attending New York Law School and clerking in a law office. He then entered public service in the City Commissioner of Accounts office, where he investigated political corruption.

In his remarkably varied career, Fosdick studied police administration in Europe, served on various boards of education, represented the United States as Under Secretary General of the League of Nations, and examined liquor control policy. He was elected president of the Rockefeller Foundation in 1936 and worked there until his retirement in 1948. Although he was a partner of the Curtis, Fosdick, and Belknap law firm from 1920 until 1936, he devoted the great majority of his efforts to public service.

During World War I, Fosdick served as chairman of the CTCA for the War and Navy Departments. He ran the two organizations as one. Inspired in part by the deplorable conditions and prurient activities surrounding army camps on the Mexican border in 1916, the CTCA had three primary goals: improve the morale of soldiers and sailors, provide socially acceptable outlets for servicemen including athletics, and educate the troops on various public health issues. The CTCA oversaw the war camp activities of the YMCA, the American Library Association, and the Playground and Recreation Association. The YWCA, the Knights of Columbus, and the Jewish Welfare League also participated.

During the war, the commission embarked upon an aggressive public education campaign against venereal disease. The CTCA was created before the Selective Service Act of 1917, but it was this legislation that gave Fosdick's commission the enforcement power it needed. The act enabled President Woodrow Wilson to create "around all military camps, broad zones in which prostitution was outlawed." In addition, the legislation also proscribed the sale of alcohol to uniformed personnel. Although organizations such as the American Social Hygiene Association had pushed for greater awareness of venereal disease for years, the army had a more utilitarian purpose: maximizing the number of "effectives" from the vast sea of recruits and draftees. For many men, the commission's "fit to fight" program was the first and only sex education they received in their lives. The army and the CTCA were surprisingly open and frank about a subject that many considered taboo. As historian David Kennedy noted, "the army contributed to the demythologizing of erotic life by bringing sexual matters into the arena of public discourse." In addition to his leadership of the commission, Fosdick participated in other wartime duties, both as an advisor to the War Department in France and later as an aide to General John J. Pershing. Fosdick traveled throughout France and reported on troop conditions during demobilization in 1919. He later assisted Pershing at the Paris Peace Conference.

In 1958, Raymond Fosdick published the well-respected *Chronicle of a Generation: An Autobiography.* The work provides an insider's view of progressivism and is essential reading for anyone interested in the progressive underpinnings of the war effort. He died in Newtown, Connecticut, in 1972.

Jonathan F. Phillips

See also: Conscription (U.S., WWI); YMCA and YWCA (WWI)

REFERENCES

Dawley, Alan. *Changing the World: American Progressives in War and Revolution.* Princeton, NJ: Princeton University Press, 2003.

Fosdick, Raymond. *Chronicle of a Generation: An Autobiography.* New York: Harper and Brothers, Publishers, 1958.

Kennedy, David M. *Over Here: The First World War and American Society.* New York: Oxford University Press, 1980.

Frankfurter, Felix

Felix Frankfurter (1882–1965), a prominent American judge and law professor, was known for his liberal views. Son of Leopold Frankfurter, a Jewish merchant, and Emma Winter, he was born in Vienna, Austria, on November 15, 1882. He emigrated to the United States in 1894 along with his family and graduated from Harvard Law School. Frankfurter was assistant attorney in the State of New York (1906–1908) and a legal officer in the Bureau of Insular Affairs, War Department (1919–1914) before becoming a professor at Harvard Law School.

He belonged to the group of jurists who gave a human touch to legal affairs and stressed social interests and needs, and the collective good of society. When the United States entered the First World War, Frankfurter became secretary and counsel of the president's Mediation Commission in 1917 and assistant to secretary of labor from 1917 to 1918.

A man of progressive outlook who moved beyond the confines of academic affairs, he came into the limelight from 1916 onward. The nomination of the first Jewish person, Louis D. Brandeis, to the Supreme Court by Democratic President Woodrow Wilson was attacked by anti-Semites, business groups, and Boston Brahmins. Frankfurter supported Brandeis by writing articles in the *New Republic,* founded by like-minded liberals. In Washington, he was becoming influential appointing law clerks at the behest of Brandeis and the legendary Justice Oliver Wendell Holmes. In addition, a bill introduced in 1914 to give self-independence to the Philippines was drafted mainly by Frankfurter.

The War and Navy Departments were setting up agencies for fixing wage and labor policies. The president appointed Frankfurter director of the War Labor Policies Board, which standardized wages and hours. A National Labor policy was also enunciated. About four million workers were put in jobs related to the war by the newly constituted United States Employment Service. Frankfurter had also investigated a number of cases concerning labor disputes and controversies.

He held the position of U.S. Army Major, JAG Corps between 1917 and 1920. In January 1918, Frankfurter was asked to suggest a panel of experts to advise the president on the terms of peace with the Germans. He also participated in the Paris Peace Conference as a member of the Zionist delegation. Frankfurter also directed his attention toward the erosion of civil rights over the Red Scare from communist Russia. He was one of the founding members of the American Civil Liberties Union (ACLU), which was set up in 1920. The career of Frankfurter reached its apogee when he became the third Jewish judge of the Supreme Court in 1939 amidst much opposition. He was also a prolific writer. He died in Washington on February 22, 1965. An ardent advocate of constitutional rights and democratic norms, Frankfurter influenced America judicial process for a long time.

Patit P. Mishra

See also: American Federation of Labor (WWI, WWII); Civil Liberties (WWI); Espionage Act (WWI); Paris Peace Conference (WWI); Sacco and Vanzetti Case (WWI); Supreme Court (WWI); War Labor Board (WWI); Biographies: Wilson, Woodrow (WWI)

REFERENCES

Frankfurter, Felix. *Felix Frankfurter Reminisces: Recorded in Talks with Harlan B. Phillips.* New York: Reynal, 1960.

———. *Law and Politics: Occasional Papers of Felix Frankfurter, 1913–1938.* New York: Capricorn Books, 1962.

Hirsch, H. N. *The Enigma of Felix Frankfurter.* New York: Basic Books, 1981.

G

Garfield, Harry

Son of President James A. Garfield, Harry Garfield (1863–1942) did not follow his father into the political realm, opting instead to become an ardent Wilsonian. He was influential in shaping World War I economic ideology on the home front. Garfield witnessed his father's assassination in 1881 and had to deal with that memory for the rest of his life. He graduated from Williams College, and taught before entering the law school at Columbia University. He also studied at Oxford University and the Inns of Court.

With his brother, James Rudolph Garfield, he opened an Ohio law firm in 1888. While practicing law, Garfield formed the Cleveland Trust Company and actively acquired interests in southeastern Ohio railroads and coal operations. In addition, Garfield organized the Cleveland Chamber of Commerce in 1893 and the Cleveland Municipal Association in 1896. A career in politics seemed next in line for Garfield, but he did not follow his family tradition. He opted for a career studying public affairs when Woodrow Wilson asked him to join the faculty at Princeton University as a professor of government. Years later, Garfield became president of Williams College.

Garfield believed in the power of education in society. While initially undecided about the U.S. declaration of war, Garfield trusted Wilson's decision. Garfield also joined Herbert Hoover's Food Administration, which regulated wheat prices. Within months, Wilson named Garfield head of the Fuel Administration. Garfield served in this capacity for two years, seeking cooperation between industry and government; a stand that brought resentment in Washington. He also faced serious criticism for the administration's 1918 decision to shut down factory production for a week east of the Mississippi in order to save much needed fuel for the war effort in Europe. Despite public concerns, Garfield was able to bring control to the fuel industry in the United States.

When the armistice was declared on November 11, 1918, Garfield tried unsuccessfully to have the Fuel Administration operate until June 1919. He also lobbied Wilson unsuccessfully to create organizations like the Fuel Administration for regulating other valuable commodities. In the wake of growing labor tensions, Garfield quit the Wilson administration in December 1919.

Garfield maintained his belief in international relations and advocated the ratification of the Versailles Treaty. In 1921, he founded the Institute of Politics at Williams College, a think tank funded by Wilsonians and the Carnegie Corporation. In 1923 Garfield was appointed president of the American Society of International Law. Later, in 1930 he joined the board of trustees of the World Peace Federation and also oversaw the organization's committee that was studying and making recommendations on the Kellogg-Briand Pact.

Philine Georgette Vega

See also: Food Administration (WWI); Fuel Administration (WWI); Biographies: Hoover, Herbert Clark (WWI); Wilson, Woodrow (WWI)

REFERENCES

Cuff, Robert. "Harry Garfield, The Fuel Administration, and the Search for Cooperative Order during World War I," *American Quarterly* 30 (1978): 39–53.

Jamaican-American Marcus Garvey organized the black nationalist movement around his Universal Negro Improvement Association before, during, and after World War I. (Library of Congress)

Garvey, Marcus

Black leader, ideologue, and entrepreneur, Marcus Moziah Garvey (1887–1940) was born in St. Ann's Bay, Jamaica. Friendly with white students throughout his childhood, white parents began to separate their children from him in his early teens. Disillusioned and frustrated, he left school at fourteen, moving to Kingston around 1906. Influenced by the anticolonialist movement, he joined the National Club, which espoused "self-government within empire." He traveled through Central America and lived in London from 1912–1914. There he met another important influence, Egyptian journalist Duse Mohammed. Returning to Jamaica in mid-1914, he cofounded the Universal Negro Improvement Association (UNIA), which sought economic empowerment and political self-determination for dark-skinned peoples. First visiting the United States in 1916, Garvey traveled to thirty-eight states and established UNIA headquarters in large Northern ghettos, including Harlem. His call for the recovery of a proud African past and power through economic independence found some sympathy upon his arrival, but African American frustration during and immediately after the Great War led thousands more to view Garvey as a kind of prophet.

His "theology" of race pride was widely disseminated in *The Negro World* newspaper.

By 1919, the UNIA claimed a membership of about two million, though exact numbers were never clear. Members who wed often sought Garvey's blessing. "Garvey children" were taught about heroic black men and women and the tenets of the UNIA. In New York, they were even issued their own birth certificates. Garvey and the UNIA launched a number of black-owned businesses, including the ill-fated Black Star Line Steamship Company. The grandest scheme was the "Back to Africa Movement," which encouraged a group of blacks to establish an independent settlement in Liberia.

Garvey's emphasis on racial separation even led him to endorse the Ku Klux Klan because they sought the same end. He became a target of attacks by leaders such as W. E. B. DuBois and A. Philip Randolph.

Garvey presided in military regalia over a 1920 UNIA convention that boasted delegates from twenty-five countries and a parade of fifty thousand through the streets of Harlem, but the UNIA's business methods led to his arrest for mail fraud in 1922. He was imprisoned in 1925, pardoned by Calvin Coolidge, deported as an undesirable alien in 1927, and died in relative obscurity.

Paul Hillmer

See also: African Americans (WWI); Biographies: DuBois, W. E. B. (WWI); Randolph, Asa Philip (WWI); Documents: Speech on East St. Louis Riot, July 8, 1917

REFERENCES

Cronon, David. *Black Moses: The Story of Marcus Garvey and the Universal Negro Improvement Association.* Madison: University of Wisconsin Press, 1955.

Lewis, Rupert. *Marcus Garvey: Anti-Colonial Champion.* Trenton, NJ: Africa World Press, 1988.

George V, King

George Frederick Ernest Albert (1865–1936; reigned 1910–1936) was born at Marlborough House in London on June 3, 1865, the second son of Edward and Alexandra, Prince and Princess of Wales. Despite the efforts of his tutor, the Reverend J. N. Dalton, George was a less than average student and a troublesome child.

At age twelve, George became a naval cadet and thrived in the military routine, finding his forte as commander of a torpedo boat in 1889. George's naval career ended upon the death of his brother, Albert Victor, Duke of Clarence, who died of pneumonia on January 14, 1892. Second in line to the throne, George took crash courses on the British Constitution, became Duke of York, and gained entry to the House of Lords. His self-declared motto in life became "duty, dignity, and diligence," but he became known as a stickler for detail and order.

On July 6, 1893, George married his deceased brother's fiancée, Mary of Teck, daughter of Prince Francis, Duke of Teck and his wife Mary Adelaide, Duchess of Teck. The couple lived at the York Cottage, on the royal estate at Sandringham, and had six children. George was devoted to his wife and she, in turn, remained loyal and obedient to him. Both were reserved and raised their children in strict fashion, which some say led to emotional problems for the children later in life.

On May 6, 1910, King Edward VII died and King George V and Queen Mary were crowned on June 22, 1911, at Westminster Abbey. More than six hundred royal family members witnessed the impressive ceremony. Upon his ascension, George faced a brewing constitutional

Descended from German royalty, King George V changed the name of England's royal family from the Teutonic Saxe-Coburg Gotha to the British-sounding Windsor during World War I. (Reynolds and Taylor, Collier's Photographic History of the European War, *1916*)

crisis over the House of Lords' rejection of the 1910 budget; they wanted to retain absolute veto over financial matters. It was resolved when George threatened to create two hundred fifty new Liberal Party peers. The Lords acquiesced and the Parliament Bill of 1911 was passed.

George and Mary were the first British monarchs to visit India. They were crowned with the magnificent Imperial Crown at the Delhi Durbar on December 11, 1911, and were granted the titles of Emperor and Empress of India.

World War I caused many problems for George, from both a family and monarchical perspective. George, separately and sometimes with Mary, made hundreds of visits to the Western front. On August 14, 1916, he visited the troops at the site of the Battle of the Somme

and gave a rousing speech. Over the course of the war, George made nearly five hundred trips and visited more than three hundred hospitals to cheer the troops.

In 1917, public anti-German agitation led George to take the prudent step of changing the royal family name from Saxe-Coburg Gotha to Windsor, after the ancient castle. All British-born family members lost any titles or connections to Germany. Bowing to rising republican fervor, George also denied asylum to his Russian cousin Tsar Nicholas II and his family; the decision cost the lives of the Russian leader and his family, as they were murdered by Bolshevik revolutionaries in 1918.

George appointed Britain's first Labour prime minister, Ramsay MacDonald, in 1924. George also played a role in the General Strike in 1931. George persuaded MacDonald to form a coalition government consisting of Conservatives, Liberals, and Labour to fight the Depression, which had led to the strike. Passage of the Statute of Westminster in 1931 provided greater autonomy for the former settler colonies of Britain—Australia, Canada, New Zealand, and South Africa—and made George the titular head of each country, as their own "king."

George had always been a heavy smoker. He suffered from repeated bronchial infections and died of influenza on January 20, 1936. He was succeeded by his eldest son, Edward Prince of Wales.

Annette Richardson

See also: Biographies: Lloyd George, David (WWI)

REFERENCES

Arthur, Sir George. *King George V.* London: Jonathan Cape, 1939.

Edwards, Anne. *Matriarch: Queen Mary and the House of Windsor.* New York: William Morrow, 1984.

Gore, John. *King George V: A Personal Memoir*. London: Murray, 1941.

Judd, Denis. *The Life and Times of George V*. London: Weidenfeld and Nicolson, 1973.

Rose, Kenneth. *King George V*. London: Weidenfeld and Nicolson, 1984.

Gifford, Walter

Walter Sherman Gifford (1885–1966) played an important role in helping the U.S. government establish the industrial potential of the country before and during World War I. His command of statistics and how they could be interpreted to determine the condition of American industry helped leaders make informed decisions about production.

Gifford was born in 1885 at Salem, Massachusetts. A scholarly child, he entered Harvard at the age of sixteen and finished in three years (but took his degree a year later, with the class of 1905). Although he had hoped to go into engineering, he took a job in 1904 as an accounting clerk at Western Electric. Gifford was imbued with the idea that talent and determination would lead him to success with a large corporation. A year after being hired, he transferred to Western Electric's New York office as assistant treasurer. Gifford became fascinated with the different ways statistics and numbers could be used to express information. The graphic charts he prepared caught the eye of Theodore N. Vail, president of AT&T, parent company of Western Electric. After a short stint managing a copper mine in Arizona, Gifford was promoted by Vail to become chief statistician for AT&T in 1911. For the next five years, he gathered information for the executives at AT&T so they could make policy.

When World War I broke out in Europe in 1914, Gifford became convinced that America needed to prepare for war. In August and September 1915, he enrolled in the military training school at Plattsburgh, New York. He made important connections with others in business and industry who felt as he did. In 1916, Howard Coffin recommended that Gifford be appointed by President Woodrow Wilson as supervising director of the Committee on Industrial Preparedness of the Naval Consulting Board. Like other businessmen at the time, Gifford kept his job in private industry and donated his time and work to the country for $1 a year. This advisory group of volunteers was charged with preparing a statistical analysis of more than twenty-seven thousand factories and other manufacturing concerns that could be used for national defense. The work was paid for by private funds and industry management provided the information voluntarily. With the statistics that Gifford collected, a tentative plan was drawn up for how American industry could support naval mobilization.

Gifford was able to continue his work at a higher level later in 1916, when Congress passed the Army Appropriation Act on August 29. A rider to the bill authorized a Council of National Defense comprised of six members of the Cabinet. An advisory board of not more than seven men was also authorized. The Naval Consulting Board was used as the model for the advisory board. Some of the members were the same, and Gifford was invited to participate as the director of the board. He cut short his honeymoon to come to Washington in October 1916 and begin organizing the board's administration.

The advisory board first met in December 1916 in a Washington hotel room. The seven members assumed the chairs of committees on different parts of the U.S. economy. As director, Gifford coordinated their work and maintained a central repository of their suggestions. One of the first steps taken by the board was a national survey of all industries, to provide information for a plan for general mobilization. Once again, Gifford collected the statistics and molded them into formats that helped decision making. The advisory board had no power to compel industries to follow their suggestions, but their recommendations formed the basis of America's mobilization for war in 1917.

Throughout the war, Gifford continued his government work. He became especially knowledgeable about munitions. In July 1918, he was sent to Paris to represent the American government as secretary of the U.S. section of the Inter-Allied Munitions Council. He remained there until September. In October 1918, Vail requested that the secretary of war release Gifford from his government positions, so he could resume vital work with AT&T. Because AT&T held a virtual monopoly over the vital telephone communication system, the secretary was happy to comply. By the end of the war, Gifford had taken a new position as vice president at AT&T.

Gifford became president of AT&T in January 1925, before he was forty years old. Under his leadership, the company expanded enormously. By the time he left the presidency in 1948, most American homes had a telephone. Cutting-edge research had been performed by AT&T's Bell Labs in all forms of communication technology as well. After serving as ambassador to Great Britain from 1950 to 1953, Gifford retired. He died on May 7, 1966, in New York City.

Tim J. Watts

See also: Council of National Defense (WWI)

REFERENCES

Brooks, John. *Telephone: The First One Hundred Years.* New York: Harper and Row, 1976.

Page, Arthur W. *The Bell Telephone System.* New York: Harper and Bros., 1941.

Gilman, Charlotte Perkins

Born in Hartford, Connecticut, Charlotte Perkins Gilman (1860–1935), author, pacifist, and women's rights activist, was the third child (but second surviving child) of Frederick Beecher Perkins, a writer and librarian, and Mary Ann Fitch Wescott. After her father abandoned the family in 1861, Gilman lived on the fringes of the Beecher family, attending formal schooling sporadically and occupying a tenuous position in both the intellectual family and the respectable middle class. She taught art

Feminist intellectual Charlotte Perkins Gilman helped co-found the American wing of the Women's Peace Party, an anti-war political movement that also fought for women's right to vote during World War I. (Library of Congress)

and painted greeting cards for several years before marrying Charles Walter Stetson, a painter from Rhode Island, on May 2, 1884. After giving birth to her only child, Katherine, in 1885, Gilman increasingly felt trapped by the rigid expectations of women and tormented by depression. This only increased after a "rest cure" under the care of Dr. Weir Mitchell, a misogynistic and patronizing experience that inspired Gilman's most famous short story, "The Yellow Wall Paper" (1892).

Gilman left Stetson and moved to California, where she lived with the family of her childhood friend Grace Channing and pursued writing and lecturing to support herself and to protest against the status of women and the necessity for social reform. She became the center of scandal when Stetson met, courted, and married Channing, and Gilman sent Katherine to live with them, remaining friendly to her ex-spouse the rest of her life. Through Bellamy Nationalism and contacts with the British Fabian Society, Gilman met prominent reformers such as Jane Addams and Florence Kelly, and increasingly advocated that women become society's reformers. On June 12, 1900, Gilman married her first cousin, George Houghton Gilman, a lawyer.

Her first book, *Women and Economics* (1898), criticized female dependence on men, particularly wives on husbands, and used the social sciences to illustrate the ways in which women's limited roles retarded both their own development and human society. She followed this with *Concerning Children* (1900), *The Home* (1903) and *Human Work* (1904), in which she suggested that communal cooking, day care, and professional women would aid natural selection and economic development and improve the world. As the sole writer for the journal *Forerunner* (1909–1916), she suggested a world in which limiting sex roles could be replaced by gender equality, peace, and opportunity. An outsider because she rejected feminism (preferring to be a humanist) and Marxism, her ideas and fiction nonetheless sparked interest in women's place in society.

Before and during WWI, Gilman used her lectures and publishing to advocate for pacifism and a peace settlement, as well as to draw attention to the plight of the Armenians in the Ottoman Empire. In 1915, she co-founded the American wing of the Women's Peace Party with Florence Kelley and Jane Addams, although the 1917 Espionage Act crippled the group's activities. Gilman's novel *Herland* (1915) and her study *Man Made World* (1911) placed the blame for international tensions and war on "masculinized" society and offered a utopian alternative. Her last work, *His Religion and Hers* (1923), critiqued women's place in Western religious thought.

Gilman retired to California and committed suicide while suffering the final stages of breast cancer on August 17, 1935, two months before the release of her autobiography, *The Living of Charlotte Perkins Gilman*.

Margaret Sankey

See also: Espionage Act (WWI); Journalism (U.S., WWI); Pacifists (WWI); Biographies: Addams, Jane (WWI); Kelley, Florence (WWI)

REFERENCES

Gilman, Charlotte Perkins. *The Living of Charlotte Perkins Gilman: An Autobiography*. Madison: University of Wisconsin Press, 1991.

Hill, Mary. *Charlotte Perkins Gilman: The Making of a Radical Feminist: 1860–1896*. Philadelphia: Temple University Press, 1980.

Lane, Ann. *To Herland and Beyond: The Life and Work of Charlotte Perkins Gilman*. New York: Pantheon, 1990.

Gish, Lillian

The leading actress of the silent film era, Lillian Gish (1896–1993) was born Lillian Diana de Guiche in Springfield, Ohio, to James Leigh de Guiche and Mary Robinson McConnell de Guiche, both of whom descended from pioneer stock. She had a sister, Dorothy, who also became an actress. James de Guiche left his wife and daughters.

Lillian was not formally educated but grew to appreciate literature, history, religion, and drama. Her childhood was spent alternatively as a trouper working on the stage and at the homes of relatives when her mother was temporarily impoverished.

Lillian first acted on stage in 1902, to support the family income, by performing at The Little Red School House in Rising Sun, Ohio. She toured with her mother and sister from 1903 to 1904. In 1905, Gish danced in a Sarah Bernhardt production in New York City.

Gish made her film debut in 1912, starring with her sister in *An Unseen Enemy,* directed by the influential D. W. Griffith. In 1913, she played in *A Good Little Devil.* In *The Mothering Heart,* Gish played the suffering heroine role to its fullest extent by taking advantage of her fragile stature that masked an innate emotional strength. She used these characteristics in *Broken Blossoms,* a role where she underplayed the terror her character was experiencing and let the audience empathize with her feelings. Her unique acting ability was also evident in *Way Down East,* as she baptized a baby near death. Another example is *The Wind,* in which she wanders near death through the streets of Montmartre. This style soon made her an American icon and the First Lady of Silent Pictures.

In 1915, Gish rose to stardom as Elsie Stoneman in *The Birth of a Nation,* the controversial film directed by Griffith. She embodied the

Arguably the most popular Hollywood actress during World War I, Lillian Gish starred in numerous films in the first half of the twentieth century. (Library of Congress)

American heroine, and during World War I her popularity knew no bounds.

The Gish/Griffith collaboration ended in 1922. She initially joined the Tiffany Company and then joined MGM in 1925, where she starred in *La Bohème* and *The Scarlet Letter* (both in 1926). She was released from her contract in 1928. She made her first "talking" film, *One Romantic Night,* in 1930, and then returned to the stage. Thereafter she worked in radio. Gish appeared on television for the first time in 1948 in *The Late Christopher Bean.* She presented lectures on "Lillian Gish and the Movies: The Art of Film, 1900–1928" through a Philco Playhouse production.

Gish acted in more than one hundred films in her seventy-five-year career (from 1912 to 1987), including the 1946 *Duel in the Sun,* for which she was nominated for her only regular Academy Award (Best Supporting Actress). Gish's popularity was maintained throughout her career. In 1971, Gish received an honorary Academy Award, The American Film Institute Life Achievement Award, as well as the D. W. Griffith Award for lifetime achievement. She wrote several books and starred in *The Whales of August* in 1987. Gish died on February 27, 1993.

Annette Richardson

See also: Film (U.S., WWI); Biographies: Griffith, D. W. (WWI)

REFERENCES

Affron, Charles. *Lillian Gish: Her Legend, Her Life.* New York: Scribner, 2001.

Barry, Iris, and Eileen Bowser. *D. W. Griffith: American Film Master.* Garden City, NY: Doubleday, 1965.

Everson, William K. *American Silent Film.* New York: Oxford University Press, 1978.

Frasher, James E., ed. *Dorothy and Lillian Gish.* New York: Scribner, 1973.

Gish, Lillian, with Ann Pichot. *Lillian Gish: The Movies, Mr. Griffith and Me.* Englewood Cliff, NJ: Prentice Hall, Inc., 1969.

Glass, Carter

As a U.S. Representative, Secretary of the Treasury, and Senator, Carter Glass (1858–1946) promoted sound money policies and internationalism during the World War I era, and was instrumental in the creation of the Federal Reserve System and the Federal Deposit Insurance Corporation (FDIC). Glass became an expert in finance in the House of Representative's Banking and Currency Committee. Chairing the committee from 1913 to 1919, he headed efforts to reform the nation's financial policies. In 1913, he authored the Federal Reserve Act, which established the central banking system that supports and regulates lending institutions. At the close of World War I, President Woodrow Wilson appointed Glass secretary of the Treasury. Secretary Glass consolidated the government's war debt into the Victory Loan, enabling the United States to settle its wartime expenses. As a U.S. senator, he coauthored major banking legislation and encouraged intervention in World War II before the 1941 attack on Pearl Harbor.

Before entering the U.S. Congress in 1903, Glass rose to prominence in Virginia politics. He edited and owned the *Lynchburg News,* a forum he used to promote educational and labor reforms. In 1899, he won election to the state senate, where he advocated states' rights and measures meant to restrict the African American vote. As a Democratic delegate to the 1901–1902 Virginia constitutional convention, he lobbied for literary tests and poll taxes, which would prevent several thousand formerly eligible poor and largely African American voters from participating in the 1904 presidential election.

In 1907, an economic downturn prompted a run on the nation's banks. Scores of financial institutions collapsed after panicked depositors withdrew their savings. Glass, as chairman of the House Banking and Currency Committee in 1913, investigated proposals to ensure the availability of money and credit. Like other conservative Democrats, he favored installing a system of privately owned and controlled regional banks, while progressive politicians favored a publicly owned and controlled system.

In a compromise with the new president, Woodrow Wilson, Glass determined that the Federal Reserve Banks would be owned by private bankers but overseen by a central governing board appointed by the president. Glass's 1913 Federal Reserve Act established the Federal Reserve System, the Federal Reserve Note, and the Federal Reserve Board.

In 1916, Glass assisted the passage of the Federal Farm Loan Act to provide low-interest loans to farmers and ranchers. Two years later, he left the House to replace William McAdoo as Wilson's secretary of the Treasury. Serving in the year following the World War I armistice, he floated the $5 billion Victory Loan to pay off the nation's war debt.

Glass returned to Congress as a senator in 1920. His senate career peaked during the Great Depression when he coauthored the Banking Act of 1933 with Representative Henry Steagall. The Glass-Steagall Act separated commercial and investment banking and established FDIC insurance for bank deposits. He defended the gold standard throughout the 1930s and sought early intervention in World War II. Declining health, however, prevented him from taking an active role in the war effort.

Jane Armstrong Hudiburg

See also: Agriculture (WWI); Banking and Finance (WWI); Democratic Party (WWI); Federal Reserve (WWI); War Bonds (WWI); Biographies: Wilson, Woodrow (WWI)

REFERENCES

Bright, Christopher John. "'Proud to Lend My Name and Whatever Strength I May Have': U.S. Senator Carter Glass and World War II Interventionism." *Southern Historian* 22 (2001): 66–80.

Glass, Carter. "The Opposition to the Federal Reserve Bank Bill." *Proceedings of the Academy of Political Science* 30 (1971): 37–43 (reprint of 1913 article).

Wilson, Harold. "The Role of Carter Glass in the Disfranchisement of the Virginia Negro." *The Historian* 32 (November 1969): 69–82.

Godfrey, Hollis

Hollis Godfrey (1874–1936) was a noted engineer, scientist, and educator of the early twentieth century. He was among those Americans who believed that scientific management could alleviate the country's problems. He also believed that war with Germany was inevitable and therefore the United States needed to prepare for an industrial mobilization. Godfrey later took credit for suggesting the idea of a Council of National Defense to plan American mobilization before the war broke out.

Godfrey was born in Lynn, Massachusetts. He was a good student and soon discovered a talent for solving engineering problems. Godfrey was a graduate of Tufts, Harvard, and MIT. Godfrey observed some of the problems the United States was experiencing in mobilizing for the Spanish-American War. He realized that modern warfare was industrialized warfare, and military success depended on industrial and economic mobilization. Successful mobilization, in turn, depended on planning.

Godfrey became an advocate of scientific management and efficiency studies. He spent the first part of his career teaching at MIT and working as a consulting engineer. He also wrote a number of short stories that indicated his faith in science as a means of insuring peace. The most notable was *The Man Who Ended War* (1907), about an inventor of a ray that dissolved warships without harming individuals. In 1913, Godfrey was hired by the trustees of the Drexel Institute to study the school and suggest changes. His recommendations were adopted, and he was hired as president. During his eight-year administration, Godfrey transformed Drexel into an accepted university. He consolidated the different departments into four schools, with the emphasis on technology and practical arts. In 1919, Godfrey instituted a cooperative education program, in which seniors spent most of their final year working in business and industry in their field. They were then able to use these connections to obtain positions.

Godfrey's enduring passion, however, was to apply his ideas of scientific management to national policy. On a trip abroad in 1906, he met Sir Henry Campbell-Bannerman and Winston Churchill. The two were developing the idea of a council for imperial defense that would study the threats to the empire and how the empire's resources could be used in its defense. Godfrey was inspired to seek the same for the United States. He watched as proposals for such a U.S. council in 1910 and 1912 were rejected by Congress. With the outbreak of World War I, Godfrey became convinced that the United States would eventually enter the war and that it was vital for the country to be prepared. In the spring of 1916, he decided to do more than just write articles. He approached the leading advocate of preparedness, General Leonard Wood, with his plan for a committee to survey industry and plan for mobilization. Wood approved Godfrey's plan and facilitated his meeting with Secretary of War Lindley Garrison and Secretary of Commerce William Redfield. Godfrey also met with members of Congress, who introduced bills to authorize a Council of National Defense. The bill was attached as a rider to the Army Appropriations Bill and passed on August 29, 1916.

Godfrey's plan called for a Council of National Defense, comprised of six members of the Cabinet. They were to be advised by a council of no more than seven leading men from business and industry. President Woodrow Wilson appointed the advisory board in October, and Godfrey was one of those selected. The advisory board first met on December 6, 1916, in Washington. They planned a national survey of industries and organized themselves into seven committees, each headed by one member. Godfrey took charge of the committee on science and research, which included education. He gathered information on resources, individuals, and industries in areas considered vital to national security. Godfrey continued to serve on the advisory board after the United States entered World War I.

Godfrey returned to his position at Drexel University at the end of the war. He resigned in 1921 and took a position as president of the Engineering Economic Foundation. Godfrey died on January 17, 1936, at Duxbury, Massachusetts.

Tim J. Watts

See also: Council of National Defense (WWI); Biographies: Wood, Leonard (WWI)

REFERENCES

Clarkson, Grosvenor B. *Industrial America in the World War: The Strategy Behind the Line 1917–1918.* Boston: Houghton Mifflin, 1923.

Cuff, Robert D. *The War Industries Board: Business-Government Relations During World War I.* Baltimore, MD: Johns Hopkins University Press, 1973.

Goldman, Emma

Emma Goldman (1869–1940) was a political activist, an anarchist, a lecturer, and a writer. She

Anarchist writer and agigator, Emma Goldman vociferously opposed World War I, one of the political stances that got her imprisoned in 1917 and deported to communist Russia in 1919. (Library of Congress)

campaigned for various causes, including birth control, women's rights, and factory reform. She was born in Russia in 1869 and emigrated to the United States in 1885, where she lived with her sister's family in Rochester, New York. She married at the age of nineteen, but the marriage collapsed just ten months later. Yearning for more opportunities, she moved to New York City in 1889. Influenced by her adventurous spirit and memories of the radical culture of St. Petersburg in her youth, she joined the burgeoning anarchist movement of Alexander Berkman.

In her first major undertaking in the movement, she and Berkman planned the assassination of Henry Clay Frick, a prominent industri-

alist, in an attempt to spark worker unrest. When the plot failed, Berkman was interred for his participation. Although Goldman was never tried, her continued activism on behalf of workers, namely her attempts to incite labor riots, as well as her involvement in the women's rights movement through the illegal distribution of birth control literature, prompted her imprisonment by the early 1890s. Undeterred, Goldman continued such crusades for workers and women over the next few years (although she never actively promoted the suffrage campaign).

The promotion of these ideals was largely accomplished through the publication of her anarchist monthly, *Mother Earth*, founded in 1906. The journal allowed Goldman and her colleagues to comment on the current state of politics, discuss labor concerns and problems, and offer essays and poems on various topics with the expressed purpose of spreading anarchist ideas to a wider audience. Financial problems eventually doomed the journal's future, but by the 1910s Goldman's priorities had shifted as well.

As World War I began across Europe, she became an outspoken advocate for peace. Goldman was imprisoned again in 1917 for her anti-war demonstrations, particularly her protests against conscription. She repeatedly affirmed the absurdity of military buildup to secure national defense, stating that "the contention that a standing army and navy is the best security of peace is about as logical as the claim that the most peaceful citizen is he who goes about heavily armed." These perceived subversive activities eventually pushed the American government to revoke her citizenship and deport her, along with other "Reds," to Russia in 1919.

Life under communist rule shocked and horrified Goldman, and she immediately mounted campaigns to overturn the new oppressive regime. When such efforts failed to facilitate change, Goldman, frustrated at her lack of progress, left Russia for Western Europe in 1921. She spent the last two decades of her life traveling between Canada and Europe (largely Great Britain and France), still actively advancing the cause of anarchism. She even went to Spain in the late 1930s to contribute to the anarchist cause during its civil war. She died in Toronto in 1940.

Rachel Finley-Bowman

See also: Anarchists (WWI); Communist Party (U.S., WWI)

REFERENCES

Drinnon, Richard. *Rebel in Paradise: A Biography of Emma Goldman.* Chicago: University of Chicago Press, 1982.

Goldman, Emma. *Living My Life.* Volumes 1 and 2. New York: Alfred A. Knopf, 1931.

Gompers, Samuel

Labor activist and founder of the American Federation of Labor (AFL), Samuel Gompers (1850–1924) served as president from the organization's inception in 1886 until his death in 1924. Appointed to the War Committee on Labor during World War I, Samuel Gompers helped mobilize domestic labor and helped found the International Labor Organization (ILO) during the Versailles Treaty negotiations in 1919.

Born in London, England, on January 26, 1850, Gompers immigrated to America in 1863. He initially apprenticed as a shoemaker but switched to cigar making in early adolescence. Gompers's trade brought him to New

Founder and president of the American Federation of Labor, Samuel Gompers worked with management and government to assure labor peace during World War I. (National Archives)

York in 1863, where he spent hours toiling in large sweatshops for low wages.

In 1885, he was promoted to head the Cigar Makers Union Local 144. Gompers's experience as a specialized labor representative prompted him to question the political and social goals of contemporary labor unions. Gompers felt that labor organizations should focus more on immediate tangible improvements in the lives of workers rather than on lofty political goals. As such, Gompers left the Cigar Makers Union a year later to found the AFL, a close cooperation of various labor organizations focused more on economic issues rather than long-term social reform.

Gompers helped revolutionize labor relations in the early twentieth century through the use of collective bargaining and legislative action. Operating under the principle that labor interests were neither inferior nor superior to corporate interests, Gompers and the AFL sought to gain higher wages and shorter workdays through the use of strikes and boycotts.

The organization was most successful under President Woodrow Wilson, whose administration focused on progressive reform in all areas of life between 1913 and 1921. Wilson and Gompers worked together on the subject of labor reform to ensure that issues dealing directly with workplace safety and worker compensation were brought to the forefront of American politics. During World War I, Wilson appointed Gompers to the Council of National Defense, where he helped create the War Committee on Labor. Gompers, in turn, used his political role to persuade Wilson to devise a wartime labor policy that explicitly articulated government support for independent trade unions and collective bargaining. This policy was the first of its kind in American history, and as such its effect on the labor populace was deeply felt. Labor union membership skyrocketed by the end of the war.

In addition to his interest in domestic labor, Gompers expressed concern over international labor conditions. Although he lived most of his life in America, Gompers was familiar with the European model of labor unions. In acknowledgment of his personal interest and past experiences, President Wilson sent Gompers to the Paris Peace Conference as a labor advisor in 1919. Gompers not only lent his particular brand of politics to the discussion but was also instrumental in the establishment of the ILO under the authority of the League of Nations.

Gompers died in 1924 while attending a Congress of the Pan-American Federation of Labor in Mexico City. His innovations and advancements in labor relations would later establish the foundations for Franklin Roosevelt's New Deal.

Catherine Griffis

See also: American Federation of Labor (WWI, WWII); Paris Peace Conference (WWI); Trade Unions (U.S., WWI); Documents: On U.S. Conscription Policy, 1917

REFERENCES

Gompers, Samuel. *Seventy Years of Life and Labor: An Autobiography.* Ithaca: ILR Press, 1984.

Livesay, Harold C. *Samuel Gompers and Organized Labor in America.* Boston: Little, Brown Press, 1978.

Gregory, Thomas W.

U.S. attorney general during World War I, Thomas Gregory (1861–1933) was born to Francis and Mary Gregory in Crawfordsville, Mississippi. His father was a Confederate physician who was killed in the service of the Confederate army. After a childhood on a plantation, Gregory attended Southwestern Presbyterian University, graduating in 1883. He then studied law at the University of Virginia for a year before transferring to the University of Texas. He graduated in 1885 and married Julia Nalle in 1893. They had four children.

A practicing attorney in Austin from 1885 to 1913, Gregory established a partnership in 1900 with Robert L. Batts and a third partnership with Victor Lee Brooks in 1908. The firm represented Texas in an antitrust case against

Waters-Pierce Oil Company, a branch of Standard Oil. They won the case and soon Gregory was elevated to the status of a prominent Democrat in the state. From 1891 to 1894, he served as Austin's assistant city attorney. Ideologically, Gregory was a moderate. He supported the limitation of corporate dominance, supported prohibition, was almost mute on women's suffrage, and took a stand against the Ku Klux Klan and anti-Semitism. Counter to the majority of Southerners, Gregory advocated African American education and did not support lynching.

After supporting Woodrow Wilson's run for the presidency in 1912, Gregory was rewarded with a position as special assistant to the attorney general of the United States. In that capacity, he tried a case that broke the New York, New Haven, and Hartford railroad monopoly. In 1914 Gregory become attorney general.

During World War I, Gregory did much to broaden the power of the Justice Department. He repealed the Alien and Sedition Acts of 1798 and replaced them with the Espionage Act (1917) and the Sedition Act (1918). The latter set parameters for punishment of those who spoke out against the war and government. Gregory was adamant about the enforcement of these laws as well as selective service and the Alien Anarchist Act (1918).

Gregory realized the atmosphere of fear in the United States during the war. He sought German spies and enabled the Justice Department's Bureau of Investigation to cooperate with several other government agencies and two hundred fifty thousand volunteers to form the American Protective League (APL). The APL detained two thousand three hundred aliens and sent two hundred twenty thousand people to trial for violation of the draft and other offenses. His office and the APL dismantled the Industrial Workers of the World, a radical dissident group, and imprisoned more than one hundred of its leaders. Because of his vehement prosecution of antigovernment and antiwar suspects, Gregory was not without his critics.

He resigned his post as attorney general in May 1919 and served as Wilson's advisor at the Paris Peace Conference. Later that year, he served on Wilson's Second Industrial Conference and tried to ameliorate relations between labor and management. His semiretirement was spent practicing law in both D.C. and Houston, Texas. Gregory maintained a devotion to Wilson and adamantly supported him. Later, Gregory supported Franklin Roosevelt; he died after meeting FDR at a New York hotel in 1932.

Philine Georgette Vega

See also: Alien Act (WWI); American Protective League (WWI); Espionage Act (WWI); Sedition Act (WWI)

REFERENCE

Anders, Evan. "Thomas Watt Gregory and the Survival of His Progressive Faith," *Southwestern Historical Quarterly* 93 (July 1989): 1–24.

Grey, Zane

One of the best-selling American novelists of all time, Zane Grey (1872–1939) saw his work on the annual top ten lists nine times between 1915 and 1924. His books have been integral in defining the western genre as we know it. Born Pearl Zane Grey in Zanesville, Ohio, Grey published more than sixty books in his lifetime (other manuscripts were published posthumously); more than one hundred feature films have been based on his books. Grey's novels are characterized by vivid descriptions of western landscapes. His plots follow hardy heroes, at home or learning to feel at home on the land, who fall in love with capable heroines and overcome adversities, usually in lawless environments. His best-known books include *Riders of the Purple Sage* (1912), *The U.P. Trail* (1918), and *The Vanishing American* (1925). Grey's writing reflects his social Darwinist philosophy and manifests contemporary ideas about the vanishing American frontier, the manly virtues of restraint and ruggedness, and the restorative power of adventure and wilderness.

Although often described as purely escapist and nostalgic, Grey researched locations, industries, and events as he wrote about them, and many of his novels deal with current political circumstances. Several of Grey's novels are set during or in the wake of World War I and concern the effect of war and the government's treatment of veterans. The home front and battlefield get the most extensive treatment in *Desert of Wheat* (1919), which tells the story of a German American wheat farmer struggling to define his patriotic duty and finally fulfilling that duty by enlisting in the U.S. army and fighting in Europe. During World War I, Grey's books were among the soldiers' favorites.

Lisa Schreibersdorf

See also: Literature (U.S., WWI)

REFERENCE

Kimball, Arthur. *Ace of Hearts: The Westerns of Zane Grey.* Fort Worth: Texas Christian University Press, 1993.

Griffith, D. W.

Born David Llewelyn Wark Griffith Griffith (1875–1948) was a pioneering movie director of the silent era in American film history. He grew up in Kansas and worked as a journalist after leaving school. In 1897, he became an actor and joined the Mefferty Stock Company in Louisville, Kentucky. For the next ten years, Griffith toured America with different theater companies while writing his own plays. Failing to gain work as a playwright, Griffith landed a position with a movie studio, Biograph Company, as a writer, an actor, and eventually a director. From 1909–1913, he directed more than four hundred fifty short films, most of them lasting less than fifteen minutes.

During these years, Griffith introduced many innovations in film, including crosscutting, tracking shots, close-ups, and flashbacks, and fought for the opportunity to make longer films. Leaving Biograph in 1913, Griffith embarked on his most ambitious film to date. Based on the novel *The Clansmen* by Thomas Dixon, *The Birth of a Nation* was instantly hailed as a work of genius. An intense, emotionally charged film about the Civil War and Reconstruction, it featured sweeping battle scenes and moments of tender human drama. The film's success established movies as a popular and persuasive form of entertainment and was a major step forward in the establishment of film as a legitimate work of art. When critics attacked the film's controversial and heroic depiction of the Ku Klux Klan, Griffith argued that films shared the same protection of free speech as literature and other forms of art.

Griffith poured his energy and profits into his next work, *Intolerance.* Two years in the making, the film featured three parallel stories of injustice set in ancient Babylon, renaissance France, and modern slums. Ambitious in both set construction and storytelling, critics applauded *Intolerance* for its further innovations in filmmaking, but audiences stayed away and Griffith barely recouped the film's costs. In 1917, Griffith accepted an invitation from the British government to make a film. After touring European battlefields for research, Griffith made *Hearts of the World,* which depicted the suffering of women and children in a French village behind German lines in World War I.

Returning to the United States in 1919, Griffith, along with Mary Pickford, Douglas Fairbanks, and Charles Chaplin, founded United Artists. After directing a few box office failures, Griffith adapted a play, *Way Down East,* and achieved the largest box office success of his entire career. Hampered by alcoholism, Griffith continued to make films throughout the 1920s, but none achieved the success of *Way Down East* or *The Birth of a Nation.* His last completed film, *The Struggle,* was pulled from theaters after only a week. Although financially comfortable, he was forgotten by the film industry. He died on July 22, 1948.

Jason Dikes

See also: Film (U.S., WWI); Propaganda (U.S., WWI); Biographies: Chaplin, Charlie (WWI); Fairbanks Sr., Douglas (WWI); Pickford, Mary (WWI)

REFERENCES

Barry, Iris. *D. W. Griffith: American Film Master.* New York: Doubleday, 1965.

Simmon, Scott. *The Films of D. W. Griffith.* Cambridge: Cambridge University Press, 1993.

Although his film Birth of a Nation *was protested by African Americans as a racist view of history, direct D.W. Griffith was hired by the British government to make a propaganda film. (Library of Congress)*

H

Haig, Douglas

A career soldier whose name is synonymous with the carnage on the Western Front, Douglas Haig (1861–1928) led the British Expeditionary Force (BEF) to victory at great cost during World War I. He is both infamous for ordering offensives at the Somme River and the third battle of Ypres that cost almost a million British casualties, and celebrated for finally defeating the German army in 1918.

Born in Edinburgh, Scotland, and educated at Oxford and Sandhurst, Haig was commissioned into the 7th Hussars and served in Egypt, South Africa, and India. He fought against the Mahdi in 1898 and in the Second Boer War from 1901 to 1902, and rose steadily through the ranks to command the I Corps of the BEF during the German invasion of France in 1914. Haig distinguished himself during the first battle of Ypres and was rewarded with command of the First Army in February 1915, then elevated to lead the BEF in December after engineering the dismissal of his predecessor, Sir John French.

Haig desperately tried to restore mobility to the Western Front, launching massive offensives with unprecedented artillery bombardments in the hope of smashing the barbed wire, trenches, and machine gun emplacements that made large-scale movement virtually impossible. He launched his first great offensive near the Somme River on June 1, 1916, losing 60,000 casualties the first day. Undaunted, Haig continued the assault until November, when 420,000 British and 200,000 French soldiers lay dead or wounded. German casualties were also heavy, but Haig had little to show for the bloodletting. He duplicated that experience in 1917, launching an ill-fated offensive near the village of Passchendaele known as the third battle of Ypres. Between July and November, he lost two hundred seventy-five thousand men in an agonizing campaign plagued by torrential rains and great seas of mud, and again he achieved nothing to compensate for the loss of life. Haig rebounded to fight a solid defensive battle in Flanders during the great German offensive of 1918, subordinated himself to overall French command under Ferdinand Foch, and in August launched a successful attack near Amiens. His armies advanced steadily until November, when Germany called for an armistice and World War I mercifully came to a close.

Critics have argued furiously over Haig's legacy ever since. Detractors vilify him as a dimwitted, cold-hearted, and unimaginative com-

Commander of the British Expeditionary Force on the Western Front in World War I, Douglas Haig was criticized for launching offensives at the Sommes and Ypres rivers that cost nearly a million casualties. Here Haig, in dark uniform, reviews troops with French Marshal Ferdinand Foch days after the Armistice ending the war in November 1918. (National Archives)

mander who, surrounded by sycophants, lived in an elegant chateau fifty miles behind the front, dined on French cuisine, took daily horseback rides, and slept peacefully in a warm bed while thousands of his men died in the mud. They argue that he was a romantic fool who used nineteenth century tactics during a twentieth century war, and point to his lifelong faith in the cavalry (Haig helped reintroduce the lance to cavalry units) as proof that he was a stubborn traditionalist who never adapted to the obvious need for new ideas in light of the destructive power of artillery, machine guns, and poison gas. Finally, they suggest his zealous religious beliefs and unshakable confidence in

his own divine mission made him a difficult subordinate for British Prime Minister David Lloyd George, that his incompetence led to the deaths of an entire generation of British men, and that he achieved victories only under French command and after the slaughter of thousands had finally worn down the German army.

His defenders argue that Haig was a humane leader whose meticulous plans attempted to minimize casualties. They credit him with choosing a strategy of attrition that ultimately defeated the German army, and point out that between August and November 1918 his armies won the greatest succession of victories in the history of the British Army. More importantly, they suggest Haig was limited in his options by the demands of coalition warfare, and that he and all other World War I generals were trapped between the destructive power of artillery and machine guns and the lack of radios, modern tanks, and effective aircraft that could have broken the power of the trenches. No one, they argue, found a way to win without great loss of life during the war, and though Haig endured much criticism in Britain for his enormous casualty lists, David Lloyd George never replaced him with anyone better.

Haig was made First Earl of Bemersyde in 1919 to honor his wartime service, and organized the Royal British Legion to care for wounded veterans. He remained a controversial figure in Britain until his death in 1928.

Lance Janda

See also: Mobilization (UK, WWI); Biographies: Lloyd George, David (WWI); Kitchener, Horatio Herbert (WWI)

REFERENCES

DeGroot, Gerard J. *Douglas Haig, 1861–1928.* London: Unwin Hyman, 1989.

Johnson, J. H. *Stalemate! The Great Trench Warfare Battles of 1915–1917.* London: Weidenfeld and Nicholson, 1995.

Prior, R., and T. Wilson. *Passchendaele: The Untold Story.* New Haven, Connecticut: Yale University Press, 1976.

Terraine, John. *Douglas Haig: The Educated Soldier.* London: Orion Publishing Group, 1963.

Winter, Denis. *Haig's Command: A Reassessment.* New York: Viking Press, 1991.

Hall, G. Stanley

A trained theologian, G. Stanley Hall (1844–1924) earned the first Ph.D. in psychology awarded in the United States and went on to build the foundations for the study of the discipline in the United States. Although his life was riddled with tragedy, Hall made a successful career validating psychoanalysis, educational psychology, and gender differences.

Born on February 1, 1844, in Ashfield, Massachusetts, Hall was the son of Granville Hall, a farmer, and Abigail Hall, a local leader. In 1867, he graduated from Williams College and went on to attend Union Theological Seminary. While studying there, Hall had the opportunity to study in Berlin for fifteen months, where he embraced the philosophical works of Hegel. He obtained a degree in divinity from Union in 1870 but did not enter into a career in that field, Instead, he taught philosophy and literature at Antioch College from 1872 to 1876. Hall furthered his own education at Harvard University under the tutelage of William James. In 1878, Hall earned the first Ph.D. in psychology awarded in the United States.

He authored the now standard work *Philosophy in the United States,* and returned to Germany, which had become a hotbed of psychological study in the late 1800s. After two years, a marriage, and two children, Hall returned to the United States. He continued to seek a professorship while lecturing and writing. Soon Hall turned his research interests to pedagogy and was finally offered a position as a lecturer at Johns Hopkins University in 1882. Two years later, he was appointed a full professor of psychology, the first of its kind in the United States. After only meager success with his psychological laboratory, Hall organized the American Journal of Psychology in 1887. In 1892, he founded the American Psychological Association and sat as its first president.

After an 1888 move to Worcester, Massachusetts, Hall was appointed as the first president of Clark University. Given free reign to recruit professors, Hall hired some of the best scientific minds of the time, including Franz Boas, John Ulric Nef, C. O. Whitman, and Albert A. Michelson. After severe monetary problems and a disillusioned sponsor, local businessman Jonas Clark, the project to set up a psychology-oriented faculty soon fell apart in 1892 when the majority of the faculty was lured by the upstart University of Chicago. This only further compounded the pain of the 1890 deaths of his wife and daughter.

Despite these setbacks, Hall once again embraced the study of educational psychology and established the Pedagogical Seminary in 1891. Three years later Hall became the first president of the National Educational Association's child study department. He embraced a romantic notion of childhood, one that staved off all adult requirements until actual adulthood. He also purported the beliefs that gender played a role in a person's mental abilities. Hall invited Sigmund Freud and Carl Jung to Clark University in 1909 and further advocated psychoanalysis.

Hall retired in 1920. He died in 1924, willing his estate to the university for the development of further psychological research. While the Progressive Era of social reforms in the early twentieth century did much to stunt his popularity, Hall will be remembered as one of the founders of psychological studies in the United States.

Philine Georgette Vega

See also: Intellectuals (WWI)

REFERENCES

Ross, Dorothy. *G. Stanley Hall: The Psychologist as Prophet.* Chicago: University of Chicago Press, 1971.

Harding, Warren G.

The twenty-ninth president of the United States, Warren Gamaliel Harding (1865–1923) was born in the hamlet of Blooming Grove, Ohio, to George T. Harding, a farmer and doctor, and Phoebe Dickerson, a midwife. After attending Ohio Central College, Harding moved with his family to Marion, Ohio, at the age of seventeen. After several failed career attempts, Harding became a reporter, and in 1884 he and two partners purchased the failing Marion *Star.* As editor, he turned the newspaper into a financial success.

A Republican, he was elected in 1899 to the state senate. Seen as one who could bring harmony to discordant factions, Harding was rewarded in 1902 with the nomination to lieutenant-governor. In 1910 Harding lost the race for Ohio governor. Four years later, he was elected to the United States Senate, where he served on several committees but offered no significant legislation.

In 1920 Harding received the Republican nomination for president of the United States. Believing the American people wanted calm and confidence, Harding conducted a "front porch" campaign on a platform of normalcy that promised to restore America to the calm and prosperity of the McKinley years. He was elected in a landslide. As president, Harding advocated governmental efficiency; international cooperation and arms reduction but not membership in the League of Nations; high tariffs; privatization; tax cuts; and pro-business appointments and policies. His cabinet was a mixture of highly able men and incompetent cronies. The latter group created an atmosphere of scandal that plagued Harding. The breaking Teapot Dome Scandal and the need to escape the national capital led Harding to take a trip to Alaska in the summer of 1923. Never a well man, he had a heart attack, be-

The majority of Americans wanted a return to "normalcy" and isolationism from world affairs in the wake of World War I. Republican presidential candidate Warren G. Harding (right) won on both issues in the 1920 election campaign. (Corbis)

came ill, and died of thrombosis in a San Francisco hotel room. He was succeeded by Calvin Coolidge.

Gregory Dehler

See also: Elections of 1920 (WWI); Republican Party (WWI); Documents: On Normalcy, May 14, 1920

REFERENCES

Downes, Randolph, *The Rise of Warren Gamaliel Harding, 1865–1920.* Columbus: Ohio State University Press, 1970.

Sinclair, Andrew. *The Available Man: The Life behind the Masks of Warren Gamaliel Harding.* New York: Macmillan, 1965.

Hart, William S.

Silent-film star William S. Hart (1864–1946) built a career in westerns early in the twentieth century. Although he was in his fifties when World War I began, too old to enlist, Hart played an active role through fundraising and supporting the American war effort.

William Surrey Hart was born on December 6 in Newburgh, New York. The year of his birth is still in some dispute; most likely it was 1864. The Hart family later moved to Minnesota, and then to New York City. Hart took on a series of odd jobs and eventually began his acting career as a Shakespearean actor on Broadway. In 1914 he signed with Thomas Ince's New York Motion

Picture Company and moved west to Hollywood.

Following the smash success of 1903's *The Great Train Robbery,* Hollywood westerns had become increasingly formulaic. Hart saw an opportunity to revive the genre by focusing on realism. He hired real Sioux Indians, who pitched their teepees near his film sets. He began directing and acting in his own productions, churning out films including *The Bargain* (1914), *The Roughneck* (1915), and *The Taking of Luke McVane* (1915), the last of which introduced Hart's pinto horse, "Fritz," to movie audiences. In the spring of 1915, Hart moved with Ince to the newly formed Triangle Film Corporation. Hart made seventeen films for Triangle, among them *Hell's Hinges* (1916), *The Return of Draw Egan* (1916), and *The Gun Fighter* (1917). In 1917 he moved to a new motion picture company, Artcraft. As part of the deal, Hart was able to form his own production company, William S. Hart Productions.

When the United States entered World War I in 1917, Hart joined other silent-film stars in pitching himself wholeheartedly into the war effort. In the spring of 1917, Hart embarked on a five-week, coast-to-coast tour for the First Liberty Loan Drive, appearing in thirty-four cities in just thirty-one days. Later that year he again helped sell war bonds for the Second Liberty Loan Drive by participating in the Mickey Neilan-directed propaganda film *War Relief,* along with Mary Pickford, Douglas Fairbanks, and other stars of the day. As part of the Third Liberty Loan Drive in April 1918, Hart once again promoted the program. He traveled across the western United States while Pickford, Fairbanks, and Charlie Chaplin toured the east. He and his pony also raised money for the American Red Star Animal Relief, a charity that provided hospitals and veterinarians for the thousands of horses, mules, and dogs wounded during the war. The 159th California

Infantry choose Hart as their godfather, adopting the name of "Bill Hart Two-Gun Men."

Hart made his last film, *Tumbleweeds,* in 1925. The movie was a box office disappointment, and Hart retired to his ranch in Newhall, California, soon after. He died in Los Angeles in 1946. His home and ranch is now a public museum.

Eileen V. Wallis

See also: Film (U.S., WWI); War Bonds (WWI)

REFERENCES

Davis, Ronald L. *William S. Hart: Projecting the American West.* Norman: University of Oklahoma Press, 2003.

Hart, William S. *My Life East and West.* Boston: Houghton Mifflin, 1929.

Haynes, George Edmund

The son of economically disadvantaged and poorly educated parents, author and civil rights activist George Edmund Haynes (1880–1960) managed to obtain a high-quality education and a position of influence in the growing African American sociological movement. Committed to her children's education, Mattie Sloan moved from Pine Bluff, Arkansas, to Hot Springs so that Haynes and his sister could have better opportunities in life. Haynes attended Fisk University and then Yale University. He obtained an MA in sociology from Yale in 1904 and was then awarded a scholarship to Yale's Divinity School. However, Haynes was unable to pursue further education at that time because he had to assist with the financing of his sister's education.

Haynes took a job as secretary for the Colored Men's Department of the International

YMCA in 1905. He kept this job until 1908, taking coursework at the University of Chicago in the summer. When Haynes left the YMCA, he began advanced studies in sociology at Columbia University and in social work at the New York School of Philanthropy. Haynes became the first African American to graduate with a Ph.D. from Columbia. His research focused on the black population of New York City and brought attention to the growing urban group.

Much of Haynes's work in New York was directed toward advancing colored citizens. He became affiliated with the National League for the Protection of Colored Women (NLPCW) and the Committee for Improving the Industrial Conditions of Negroes in New York (CHCN). Through his work with both organizations, Haynes befriended Frances Kellor and Ruth Standish Baldwin, leaders in the black community. All three were concerned with the dearth of college-trained black social workers. In an effort to provide an adequate training ground for young social workers, Haynes and Baldwin founded the Committee on Urban Conditions among Negroes (CUCAN) in 1910, which eventually merged with the NLPCW and CHCN to form the National League on Urban Conditions among Negroes (National Urban League) in 1911. Haynes was not as radical as other black leaders of the time, such as Booker T. Washington and W. E. B. DuBois.

Around the time he founded CUCAN, Haynes returned to Fisk University, where he took a position as a professor of economics and was influential in establishing a sociology department. Haynes hired Eugene Kinckle Jones to oversee CUCAN in his absence, with Haynes traveling to New York City every six weeks and every summer. In 1916, Jones was able to convince the board of CUCAN to make him coexecutive with Haynes, and in 1917 Jones was made executive secretary outright. Haynes then took a position with the government in 1918 as the director of Negro Economics. This position was under the auspices of the Department of Labor. His three-year tenure in the position led to extensive research and a book titled *The Negro at Work during World War I*, published in 1921.

Haynes spent his retirement with the Federal Council of Churches working on race relations. He continued his research and published his findings on behalf of the black community. Haynes also lobbied for antilynching laws and for freedom for the Scottsboro boys. During the New Deal, he chaired the Joint Committee on National Recovery (1933–1935), which advocated a fair share for blacks during the Depression. In the latter years of his life, Haynes taught at the City College of New York.

Philine Georgette Vega

See also: African Americans (WWI); National Urban League (WWI); YMCA and YWCA (WWI); Biographies: DuBois, W. E. B. (WWI); Kellor, Frances (WWI)

REFERENCES

Perlman, Daniel. "Stirring the White Conscience: The Life of George Edmund Haynes." Ph.D. dissertation, New York University, 1972.

Hays, Will H.

A lawyer by profession, Will Hays (1879–1954) occupied a number of political offices in his native Indiana until June 1918, when he was selected to be the chairman of the Republican National Committee. He was chosen because of his successful leadership of the Indiana Republican Party and his ability to reconcile Republicans caught up in the Roosevelt-Taft split of

1912. As RNC chairman, Hays helped the Republican Party regain control of Congress in 1918 and later helped direct Warren Harding's election as president in 1920. In the Harding campaign, Hays used modern advertising techniques, such as film, sound recording, and electronic wire photo transmission to get Harding's message to voters across the country. He even hired an advertising expert, Albert Lasker, owner of Chicago's Lord and Thomas agency, to assist him.

After the election, Hays was tapped by Harding to become postmaster general. He established the Post Office Welfare Department, extended rural free delivery of mail, restored second-class mailing privileges for newspapers, and reduced post office expenses by $15 million.

In 1922, Hays became chairman of the Motion Picture Producers and Distributors of America. The film industry had been rocked by a number of scandals, and Hollywood hoped Hays could help them refurbish its image. The MPPDA soon became better known as the Hays Office, and came to reflect its namesake's rural small-town values.

The Motion Picture Production Code that Hays produced barred scenes depicting "excessive and lustful kissing, lustful embracing, suggestive postures and gestures." It also protected ministers from being used as "comic characters or as villains."

Hays presided over Hollywood until 1945, when he resigned in response to a growing chorus of dissent from filmmakers chafing under his code. He remained active in the film industry as an adviser to the Motion Picture Association of America, which later became involved with the House Un-American Activities Committee's search for communists in Hollywood. He died in 1954.

John Morello

See also: Film (U.S., WWI); Republican Party (WWI)

REFERENCES

Garraty, John. *American National Biography*. Vol. 10. New York: Oxford University Press, 1999.
Hays, Will H. *The Memoirs of Will H. Hays*. Garden City, New York: Doubleday Press, 1955.

Haywood, William "Big Bill"

Born in Salt Lake City, William Haywood's life as the son of a former Pony Express rider was poverty-stricken and difficult, a factor that led him to pursue a life of labor activism as a leader of the radical Industrial Workers of the World union. By age ten, Haywood (1869–1928) left formal schooling to work in the local mines, a task made more difficult by a childhood accident that left him blind in his right eye. As a silver miner in Idaho, Haywood became interested in the activities of the Western Federation of Miners. In 1896, he joined the union, quickly rising through its ranks to become secretary-treasurer. A charismatic and knowledgeable speaker, Haywood became a powerful force among the poor, embittered, and overworked miners, often moving secretly from camp to camp to avoid company harassment while he encouraged strikes and confrontation.

By 1902, Haywood was a coleader of the WFM, but his incendiary style clashed with that of his partner, Charles Moyer, who favored negotiation, not violence. Haywood, however, continued to incite bombings, intimidation, and showdowns with nonunion miners and company leaders, including the sabotage of a train in Independence, Colorado, in 1904. Haywood's biggest plot erupted in 1905, when

For his opposition to U.S. participation in World War I, Industrial Workers of the World union leader William "Big Bill" Haywood was sent to prison for seditious activities. (Library of Congress)

Idaho officials arrested Harry Orchard for the assassination of former Idaho governor Frank Steubenberg. Orchard confessed to being an agent of the WFM and named Haywood, Moyer, and George Pettibone as his superiors, all of whom were arrested in a raid by Pinkerton detectives and hustled to Boise for what became the "trial of the century."

Haywood, confined in the Idaho penitentiary awaiting trial, ran for governor of Colorado as a socialist, took a correspondence law course, and appealed his arrest to the U.S. Supreme Court, which condemned the methods of the arrest but let it stand.

Defended by Clarence Darrow and prosecuted by U.S. Senator William Borah, Haywood's trial began in 1907. Darrow insisted that Haywood had been framed by a vast conspiracy of antiunion government officials and mine owners, and placed the blame for Steubenberg's murder of Orchard, the bomber. Borah, instead, brought out a litany of Haywood's previous shady activities, so convincing the spectators of a conviction that the *Idaho Statesman* printed a headline announcing the verdict as guilty. The jury, however, found Haywood not guilty, raising cries of jury tampering and bribery. Although found not guilty, Haywood broke with Moyer and left the WFM to involve himself with the far more radical Industrial Workers of the World (IWW) in 1908.

The IWW, or "Wobblies," was a far more international body than the WMF, not only advocating direct and violent confrontation but tied to the Socialist and Marxist movements of Europe. In the years leading up to WWI, Haywood became notorious as an atheist, a strike agitator, and an advocate of the Socialist International. Haywood denounced WWI as a conspiracy of capitalists and called on young workers to refuse to enlist. These activities led to his arrest by the federal government on charges of espionage and sedition, but he fled the country on bail in 1918 and immigrated to Russia. Hoping to play a large role in the Bolshevik Revolution, Haywood was quickly disappointed in both his status as a spokesperson for Lenin's regime and the actual reality of the worker's paradise it promised. Disillusioned and chronically ill, Haywood faded from public Soviet life and died in 1928. His remains were cremated and divided between burial in the Kremlin Wall near journalist John Reed and a Chicago monument to American workers.

Margaret Sankey

See also: Espionage Act (WWI); Industrial Workers of the World (WWI); Sedition Act (WWI)

REFERENCES

Carlson, Peter. *Roughneck: The Life and Times of Big Bill Haywood.* New York: W. W. Norton, 1983.

Conlin, Joseph Robert. *Big Bill Haywood and the Radical Union Movement.* Syracuse, NY: Syracuse University Press, 1969.

Dubofsky, Melvyn. *'Big Bill' Haywood.* Manchester, UK: Manchester University Press, 1987.

Hemingway, Ernest

One of the most influential novelists of the twentieth century, Ernest Hemingway (1899–1961) created a style of writing that seemed inseparable from a style of living. He cultivated a reputation as a writer who measured his achievement against only his own exacting expectations and standards, and yet he became a celebrity as much for his adventurous travels and pastimes as for his books. Throughout his life, he sought primal kinds of experiences that would test his capacity for stoic endurance, though he may have actually been seeking diversions from an ongoing and largely private struggle with profound psychological demons. Likewise, his prose had a surface spareness and directness through which fundamental truths could ostensibly be expressed and within which the underlying complexity and ambiguity of much of human experience could be credibly suggested, instead of being distorted by statement. This prose style has been much imitated, and the adjective *Hemingwayesque* has been applied to the work of writers from Dashiell Hammett to Robert Stone.

Born in Oak Park, Illinois, Hemingway enjoyed outdoor activities, such as hunting, fishing, and hiking, which took him out of that genteel community and into the wilderness of remote places such as Upper Michigan. After a brief but formative stint as a reporter with the *Kansas City Star,* he volunteered to serve in the First World War with the Red Cross ambulance corps. Assigned to the Italian army, he was wounded severely in the legs by Austrian canister shot and was decorated for valor. In very different ways, this traumatic experience became the basis for his second and third novels, *The Sun Also Rises* (1926) and *A Farewell to Arms* (1929). In *The Sun Also Rises,* the central character, Jake Barnes, maintains a fairly level-headed attitude toward the social excesses of the postwar period even though he himself has been emasculated by a wound he suffered during the war. The novel follows a group of his self-indulgent acquaintances from Paris to Pamplona, Spain. In the more directly autobiographical *A Farewell to Arms,* the main character, an ambulance driver named Frederick Henry, finally becomes profoundly disillusioned by the horrors of the Italian defeat at Capporeto and flees to Switzerland with the nurse who is pregnant with their child. The denouement is far from idyllic, however, because both she and the child die in childbirth.

During the Spanish civil war of the 1930s, Hemingway was a prominent supporter of the Republican cause. His novel, *For Whom the Bell Tolls* (1940), his play, *The Fifth Column* (1940), and several memorable short stories came out of his experiences in Spain. During World War II, he armed his yacht and volunteered to conduct antisubmarine patrols in the waters around Cuba. Later, he served as a correspondent with the Allied forces in Western Europe, and he created some controversy when it appeared that he had compromised his status as a noncombatant. Little of his Second World War experiences worked their way into his fiction after the war. The central character of *Across the River and into the Trees* (1950) is an army colonel who has passed his prime, and the submarine hunting is an element of the posthumously published novel, *Islands in the Stream* (1970). But Hemingway seems to have been unable to translate his experiences in the war into novels with the focused power of *The Sun Also Rises* and *A Farewell to Arms*. After barely surviving several debilitating airplane crashes in Africa, Hemingway entered into a steep physical and psychological decline that ended with his suicide by gunshot at his home in Ketchum, Idaho.

Martin Kich

See also: Ambulance Drivers (WWI); Literature (U.S., WWI)

REFERENCES

Baker, Carlos, ed. *Hemingway and His Critics*. New York: Hill and Wang, 1961.

Baker, Carlos. *Ernest Hemingway: A Life Story*. New York: Scribner, 1969.

Benson, Jackson. *Hemingway: The Writer's Art of Self-Defense*. Minneapolis, MN: University of Minnesota Press, 1969.

Gurko, Leo. *Ernest Hemingway and the Pursuit of Heroism*. New York: Crowell, 1968.

Meyers, Jeffrey. *Hemingway: A Biography*. New York: Harper, 1985.

Reynolds, Michael. *Ernest Hemingway*. Detroit: Gale, 2000.

Young, Philip. *Ernest Hemingway*. New York: Rinehart, 1952.

Young, Philip. *Ernest Hemingway: A Reconsideration*. New York: Harcourt, 1966.

Hillquit, Morris

Morris Hillquit (1869–1933), a Latvian-born American lawyer, was a prominent figure in the left-wing politics of the United States. He was born on August 1, 1869, in Riga and emigrated to New York City at the age of seventeen. He was a founding member of United Hebrew Trades, a union of poor Jewish garment workers established in 1888. After graduating from New York University Law School in 1893, he was busy with his legal career for six years. He officially changed his name from Moses Hillkowitz to Morris Hillquit in 1897.

In the early part of the twentieth century, socialism was becoming a force in American politics. The Socialist Party of America (SPA) was formed in 1901 from the merger of the Social Democratic Party and the Socialist Labor Party. Hillquit emerged as a prominent Socialist leader and became an important functionary of the party. A theoretician and tactician, he wrote *History of Socialism in the United States* (1903) and *Socialism in Theory and Practice* (1909). He became the director of the Rand School of Social Science in 1905. His political orientation was somewhat centrist, opposing both mild reforms and extreme radicalism. Belonging to the right-wing faction of the SPA, Hillquit began to exert considerable influence and was its representative in the executive committee of the Socialist and Labor International, an organization of left-wing social democratic parties around the world.

He ran unsuccessfully for the Congress in 1906 and 1908. The SPA had Eugene V. Debs as presidential candidate in the election of 1912, with Hillquit managing the party organization. He was the lawyer for the International Ladies' Garment Workers' Union from 1914 onward.

Like most socialists, Hillquit was opposed to the United States entry into the First World War. Socialist journals such as *The Masses, The Call, International Socialist Review,* and *The Revolutionary Age* argued that the war had been started by imperialist forces and the United States should remain neutral. Under the Espionage Act, it was an offense to express views detrimental to the war effort. Many socialists, including Eugene Debs, were persecuted for antiwar activities and charged with sedition. Hillquit was their defense lawyer. Hillquit was also the attorney for many labor unions.

In 1918, he ran for mayor of New York City and lost the election. He became anti-Communist after a split in the SPA over the question of the Russian Revolution. In 1933, he ran again for New York City mayor, receiving a quarter of a million votes. He died on December 31 of tuberculosis in New York.

Patit P. Mishra

See also: American Federation of Labor (WWI, WWII); Espionage Act (WWI); Biographies: Debs, Eugene V. (WWI)

REFERENCES

Hillquit, Morris. *Loose Leaves from a Busy Life.* New York: Da Capo Press, 1971.
———. *The History of Socialism in the United States.* New York: Dover Publications, 1972.

Hoover, Herbert Clark

The thirty-first president of the United States, Herbert Clark Hoover (1874–1964) was born in West Branch, Iowa. Orphaned before the age of nine, Hoover was raised by his uncle, a country doctor in Oregon. Graduating as a mining engineer from Stanford University's first class (1895), Hoover traveled the world for eighteen years, overseeing mining projects on four continents. In China during the 1900 Boxer Rebellion, Hoover gained valuable experience providing relief to foreigners caught in the mayhem.

While visiting London on personal business in 1914, Hoover was recruited by the U.S. Embassy to aid American travelers stranded by the Great War. In six weeks his committee helped approximately 120,000 Americans reach home. Known for his competence and conservative fiscal administration, he was named chairman of the American Commission for Relief in Belgium. In four years, the Commission fed and assisted about ten million civilians in Belgium and northern France, spending nearly $1.5 billion.

President Wilson called Hoover home after America's entry into the war and later appointed him head of the country's Food Administration. Hoover managed to increase food production, reduce domestic consumption, raise efficiency, stabilize prices, and improve distribution to Allied soldiers abroad—without dependence on rationing. After the Armistice was signed, the Allies put him in charge of alleviating Europe's widespread food shortages. Agencies under his management fed and clothed more than two hundred million people in more than thirty countries by 1920. Hoover also created the American Relief Administration, which used $100 million appropriated by Congress to provide aid and comfort to millions of malnourished and diseased children. It also fed millions of starving Ukranians from 1921–1923. Criticized for supporting Bolshevism, Hoover replied, "Twenty million people are starving. Whatever their politics, they shall be fed!"

Serving as secretary of commerce under Presidents Harding and Coolidge, Hoover won the presidency himself in 1928. Although begun with great optimism, his tenure was marred by the Great Depression. He lost his bid for reelection to Franklin Roosevelt in 1932.

Paul Hillmer

See also: Food Administration (WWI)

REFERENCES

Burner, David. *Herbert Hoover: A Public Life.* New York: Alfred A. Knopf, 1979.

Hoover, Herbert. *Memoirs.* 3 vols. New York: Macmillan, 1951–1952.

Hoover, J. Edgar

Born in Washington, D.C., John Edgar Hoover (1895–1972) joined the Justice Department in 1917 and became director of the scandal-ridden Federal Bureau of Investigation in 1924. Brought in as a reformer, Hoover was to lead the agency until his death in 1972, making him the longest serving head of a national police agency in history. During his tenure as FBI director, Hoover ruled the bureau with an iron hand and helped to establish both it and himself in the American mind as the embodiment of masculine virtue and the guardian of law, order, and national security. Following Hoover's death in 1972, accounts of his crude violations of civil liberties and far-reaching personal corruption, which he had sought to suppress over decades, surfaced, made him an object of ridicule to large sections of the general public even as the FBI named their new national headquarters after him.

The red scare, which began during World War I and accelerated in the immediate postwar period, was to be the foundation for J.

Future FBI director J. Edgar Hoover headed the U.S. Justice Department's Enemy Alien Registration Section during World War I. (Yoichi R. Okamoto/Lyndon B. Johnson Library)

Edgar Hoover's long career. Graduating from George Washington Law School and passing the bar, Hoover, the son of a minor Interior Department official who had retired due to severe depression, got a position as clerk in the Justice Department, which kept him from being drafted. Family influence, many believe, was essential in his gaining the position and draft deferment, which enabled him to support his parents, particularly his mother, with whom he would live for the rest of her life.

Hoover rose rapidly in the Justice Department and was chosen in 1918 by his supervisor, John Lord O'Brien, to direct a new Enemy Alien Registration section. Hoover's conservative religious outlook and emphasis on efficiency made him a zealous prosecutor of aliens and an advocate of the position that aliens from hostile foreign powers were not entitled to the constitutional protections of U.S. citizens.

The end of the war saw the end of the Enemy Alien Registration section, but Hoover lobbied O'Brien, who had returned to private practice, to intercede on his behalf with the new attorney general, A. Mitchell Palmer, to keep his job in the department.

As strikes swept the country, the press generally denounced trade unionists and immigrants as agents of a Bolshevik inspired world revolution. In 1919, Attorney General Palmer's Washington home was bombed by an anarchist, who was killed in the attack. Palmer responded by promoting Hoover and directing him, given his background in the Enemy Alien Registration section, to organize an attack on radicals and aliens. Hoover devised a scheme to launch national raids against radical organizations and arrest and deport as many radicals as possible. Under Palmer's auspices, Hoover became director of a new section, the General Intelligence Division of the Justice Department, to carry forward this campaign.

Through the division, Hoover began to amass files on a huge number of people, many of them U.S. citizens. Hoover focused primarily on the Communist movement, then developing rapidly, and sought to portray himself as the Justice Department's leading expert on communism and ways to combat it, a role he cultivated for the rest of his life. Having acquired files on more than two hundred thousand people by the end of 1919, Hoover gained Palmer's approval to launch a series of raids against radical groups. The raids, which occurred in thirty-three cities on January 2, 1920, were carried forward without arrest warrants, which were issued after the arrests. More than ten thousand people were arrested, although nearly half were shortly released, primarily because they were not aliens.

Hoover sought to use the raids to mobilize public opinion for mass deportations and to associate socialist and communist ideas with Soviet directed conspiracies. Hoover also gathered information on anyone connected to radical movements, expanding the files he had opened in the General Intelligence Division. By the time Warren Harding took office in 1921, those files numbered 450,000.

Under Hoover's influence, more than 1,600 deportation warrants were issued for those arrested in the raids. When Assistant Secretary of Labor Louis Post, a Progressive, used his influence to veto more than 1,000 warrants, Hoover opened a file on him. Hoover also sought to use the press to expand the red scare, authoring and disseminating material that warned daily of armed Communist uprisings, with May 1, 1920 (May Day), being the day for apocalyptic revolution. When May 1 passed uneventfully, the red scare began to decline.

Attacks on the red scare from prominent figures, including the former Republican presidential candidate Charles Evans Hughes, and

Palmer's disastrous attempt to gain the Democratic presidential nomination, effectively ended Hoover's campaign for mass deportations, although Hoover himself was present in New York when more than five hundred Palmer Raid political prisoners, including the anarchists Emma Goldman and Alexander Berkman, were deported.

The new conservative Republican administration under Harding was a boon to J. Edgar Hoover. First the new attorney general, Harry Daugherty, found that Hoover's files contained material on Harding's enemies among the Democrats, which Hoover dutifully supplied. Daugherty rewarded Hoover by appointing him assistant director of the Bureau of Investigation, under the leadership of William Burns, a former Secret Service official and director of a private detective agency popular with businessmen because of its antilabor activities.

As the Harding administration was overwhelmed by scandals, some concerning the Bureau of Investigation, Calvin Coolidge, who became president with Harding's death in 1923, appointed a leading progressive Republican, Harlan Fiske Stone, as attorney general. Although Stone had been a fierce opponent of the Palmer Raids and would later distinguish himself as a Progressive Supreme Court Justice, he listened to friends in the administration who suggested that J. Edgar Hoover was a man of unimpeachable integrity. Meeting with Stone on May 10, 1924, Hoover accepted the position of acting director, appealing to Stone's Progressive views with promises to take the Bureau out of politics, to make all appointments dependant on merit, and to assure that the Bureau would be completely under the control of the attorney general. His role as acting director lasted forty-eight years, and none of his promises were ever fulfilled.

Norman Markowitz

See also: Federal Bureau of Investigation (WWI, WWII); Palmer Raids (WWI); Red Scare (WWI); Biographies: Hoover, J. Edgar (WWII)

REFERENCES

Gentry, Curt. *J. Edgar Hoover, the Man and the Secrets.* New York: Norton, 1991.

Powers, Richard Gid. *Secrecy and Power: The Life of J. Edgar Hoover.* New York: The Free Press, 1988.

Summers, Anthony. *Official and Confidential: The Secret Life of J. Edgar Hoover.* New York: G. P. Putnam and Sons, 1993.

Theoharis, Athan. *The Boss: J. Edgar Hoover and the American Inquisition.* Philadelphia: Temple University Press, 1988.

———. *J. Edgar Hoover, Sex, and Crime, an Historical Antidote.* Chicago: Ivan Dee, 1995.

Houston, David F.

David Franklin Houston (1866–1940) served as secretary of agriculture in the Woodrow Wilson administration from 1913–1920.

Born in North Carolina, Houston and his family scrimped so that he could attend South Carolina College. Upon graduation, Houston accepted a fellowship from Harvard, earning a master's degree in political science. Following teaching and administrative positions at the University of Texas, Texas Agricultural and Mechanical College, and Washington University, Houston accepted Woodrow Wilson's call to serve as secretary of agriculture.

More of a conservative, academic economist than an agriculturalist, Houston entered into office as one of Wilson's moderate, Progressive reformers rather than a specialist in farm issues. Indeed, his first term as secretary of agriculture saw him more interested in reorganizing the department's numerous bureaus into effective service agencies, streamlining its delivery of scientific information to farmers, and improving both farm marketing and distribution rather than agricultural production. Houston encouraged the creation of demonstration farms and bolstered the nascent extension agent program through the Smith-Lever Act of 1914.

World War I brought Houston into almost immediate, albeit subdued, conflict with food administrator Herbert Hoover. The Food Production and Food Control Acts of August 1917 served in part to delineate their duties, but the struggle never fell far below the surface as Houston and Hoover contested for authority on the transportation, marketing, and consumption of food and fiber.

Although Hoover's labors may have been more obvious to the public, Houston's efforts to enhance farmers' productivity provided the food administrator with the raw material of his success and forever changed the role of the Department of Agriculture. Aided by the Smith-Lever-enhanced Extension Service and multitudes of new county agents holding traditional as well as emergency appointments, production rose. Throughout the war years, acreage under cultivation expanded by 11 percent, while agricultural production increased by 5 percent.

Farm productivity also benefited from Houston's support of the Wilson initiative to provide seeds and fertilizer at cost, as well as the creation of a seed loan fund for western, drought-stricken farmers in 1918. Additional aid to farmers, and ultimately the war effort, came in the form of programs to license farm equipment manufacturers, stockyards, grain and cotton warehouses, and fertilizer producers. To ensure the purchase of wholesome foodstuffs and adequate fiber for America's armed forces, as well as fair grading standards for farmers, Houston encouraged the inspection of agricultural products at central marketing locations.

At the war's conclusion, the Department of Agriculture clearly stood as a changed institution; compared to its prewar form, it claimed new functions, expanding the role and visibility of the agency. Houston did not, however, remain with the department to build upon his wartime successes. Rather he accepted Wilson's offer of the treasury secretariat, resigning from that post in 1921.

Following his retirement from government, Houston served as president of the Mutual Life Insurance Company of New York, as well as a director of American Telephone and Telegraph, and a director of the United States Steel Corporation. He remained active in business until his September 2, 1940, death in New York.

Kimberly K. Porter

See also: Agriculture (WWI); Food Administration (WWI)

REFERENCES

Clements, Kendrick A. *The Presidency of Woodrow Wilson.* Lawrence: University Press of Kansas, 1992.

Houston, David F. *Eight Years with Wilson's Cabinet, 1913–1920.* Garden City, NY: Doubleday, 1926.

Hughes, Charles Evans

Secretary of State and U.S. Supreme Court Chief Justice Charles Evans Hughes (1862–1948) was born in Glens Falls, New York. In 1884, he received an LLB with honors from Columbia University Law School. After passing the New York County bar examination, Hughes joined Chamberlain, Carter and Hornblower, a prestigious law firm in New York City. Hughes entered public life, serving two terms as governor of New York from 1907 and 1910. In 1910, he was appointed an associate justice to the U.S. Supreme Court. In 1916, he resigned his Supreme Court seat to accept the Republican Party's presidential nomination but met defeat at the hands of Woodrow Wilson. After the election, Hughes returned to the private practice of law in New York.

From 1921 to 1925, he served as secretary of state in the Warren Harding and Calvin Coolidge administrations. In his attitudes toward Europe, Hughes was a supporter of the American tradition of isolationism, which had as one its principles no alliances with any European nations. Nevertheless, Hughes played an enlightened role in helping to stabilize the financial situation in Europe following the end of World War II. He helped to realize the Dawes Plan, which was designed to aid Germany in paying reparations to the Allied powers, who in turn were obligated to repay their war debts to the United States. As for his views toward the Soviet Union, Hughes sought to change its behavior by using a nonrecognition policy based on excluding it from the world scene.

Hughes was also responsible for major policy achievements aimed at Asia. He succeeded in establishing the Washington Treaty System, which consisted of three separate treaties for maintaining peace and stability in the western Pacific region and Asia. The Five-Power Naval Treaty imposed limits on the capital ship strength of the major naval powers by freezing the status quo ratio. The Four-Power Treaty dissolved the Anglo-Japanese Alliance concluded in 1902 and brought mutual recognition of claimed territorial rights in the Pacific region. In the Nine-Power Treaty, the signatories agreed to respect the principles of the Open Door, the territorial integrity of China, and the autonomy of Chinese customs. This treaty also precipitated the evacuation of the Japanese army from the Shandong peninsula. As for

Latin America, Hughes played a bridging role, helping to shift American policy gradually away from the kind of active interventionism promoted first by Theodore Roosevelt and then by Woodrow Wilson toward the Good Neighbor Policy implemented by Franklin D. Roosevelt in the 1930s. Although the U.S. government justified interventions in Latin America on the grounds of national security and moral responsibility, Hughes held out a principle of hemispheric unity in association with Pan-Americanism. To bring stability and social order to Latin America, Hughes actively offered his services to settle disputes between neighboring countries.

Hughes resigned as secretary of state in 1925 and returned to his Wall Street law practice. In 1930, President Herbert Hoover appointed him to the position of Supreme Court chief justice.

Yoneyuki Sugita

See also: Elections of 1916 (WWI); Republican Party (WWI); Supreme Court (WWI)

REFERENCES

Margot, Louria. *Triumph and Downfall: America's Pursuit of Peace and Prosperity, 1921–1933.* Westport, CT: Greenwood Press, 2001.

Parrish, Michael E. *The Hughes Court: Justices, Rulings, and Legacy.* Santa Barbara, CA: ABC-Clio, 2002.

Hughes, Sir Sam

As minister of militia and defense from 1911 to 1916, Sam Hughes (1853–1921) played an essential role in preparing Canada for the Great War and, from 1914 to 1916, was the most important and dynamic leader of the Canadian war effort. Hughes authorized and oversaw the raising of several hundred thousand men for overseas service and put the country on a war-footing. But by 1916, corruption, scandal, inefficiency, and increasingly unbalanced behavior drove Canadian Prime Minister Sir Robert Borden to fire him from the cabinet.

Robert Borden's Conservatives defeated Sir Wilfrid Laurier's Liberal government in 1911, and the new prime minister appointed Sam Hughes as minister of the Department of Militia and Defence. Hughes was a good choice because of his intimate knowledge of the militia and his political influence as a prominent leader among the Orange lodges of Ontario. The new minister immediately made an impact and was able to pressure the cabinet into raising the budget for the militia. This additional defence funding was significant for Canadian politicians, who, although forced into thinking about increased defence spending during the naval debates of 1909, were more inclined to support settlement of the west, railway expansion, and infrastructure for the nation's staple-goods economy. Hughes also found new resources for cadet corps and rifle clubs across the country. He even advocated universal military service for young women, although that was too radical to be accepted at the time. Responsible for raising the militia establishment from 43,000 to 77,000, and warning of the need to prepare for an upcoming war with Germany, Hughes was derided by the Liberal opposition as a "martial madman."

When war came in August 1914, Hughes was thrust into the spotlight, which he gladly accepted, revelling in the publicity engendered by headline-grabbing diatribes and hyperpatriotic speeches. At the age of sixty-one, Sam Hughes was the driving force behind the initial Canadian war effort, and the minister was cocksure in the righteousness of the cause and in his own abilities. A product of the patronage-infused federal politics of nineteenth-century Canada, Hughes believed it his right to interfere with senior commanders and, along with men like Sir Max Aitken (later Lord Beaverbrook), orchestrated the rise and fall of his favorites. His incessant meddling undermined the emerging professionalism in the overseas Canadian Expeditionary Force (CEF).

Dedicated to the cause, Hughes was the politician most closely identified with the Canadian war effort. Yet Hughes kept power to himself and was most comfortable appointing friends and loyal supporters to run major military programs. He thought little of and cared less for the small number of staff-trained officers who had the knowledge of how to organize, train, and equip an army. Despite striving to see his "boys" cared for, as he often referred to the men of the CEF, Hughes's truculent, impetuous, and bullying nature made him enemies at every turn.

In 1914, Hughes had thrown out the pre-arranged mobilization plans and sent a personal plea to more than two hundred militia colonels across the country to raise a force for overseas service. With Canadians anxious to participate in this perceived war of justness and defense of liberty, there was little trouble filling the ranks. However, Hughes's mobilization was chaotic, and when a second division was raised for service, the professional staff officers quietly took over and restored the mobilization plans. Because Hughes had allotted wartime contracts primarily on the basis of companies' political connections to the ruling Conservative Party, most of the equipment produced, from boots to wagons to the infamous and useless MacAdam shovel, a combination shovel and sniper shield, were useless and of poor quality. All were quickly replaced overseas with British equipment. Far more damaging was the minister's misplaced faith in the Canadian-built Ross rifle. Hughes had long been a champion of the

Ross; even though prewar trials revealed a faulty design, he ordered that Canadian soldiers carry it into battle. At the Second Battle of Ypres in April 1915, the Ross proved a disastrous weapon that jammed in combat. Even after mounting evidence revealed that the Ross was a poor battlefield rifle, Hughes clung to this national weapon until 1916. Before that, though, the Canadian soldier had lost faith in their weapon—and in their minister.

Hughes's fellow ministers in Borden's cabinet increasingly viewed him as a liability, and his many inopportune speeches provided easy fodder for the opposition. Nonetheless, Hughes continued to play an essential role in coordinating the war effort in Canada. His greatest accomplishment, along with his rapid raising of the First Contingent in 1914, was the establishment of a munitions industry in Canada where none had existed before the war. Unfortunately, the ineffective system of contract distribution and quality control that he presided over forced the British, by the end of 1915, to intercede with their own organization, the Imperial Munitions Board.

Scandals had clung to the Conservative government from almost the first weeks of the war, and many of them centred on Hughes and his appointed cronies. By early 1916, investigations hinted at problems; Hughes survived the attacks but his friends began to distance themselves. Hughes was performing even more erratically by the summer of 1916 and refused to heed Borden's demands that he reform the Byzantine-like administrative structure of the Canadian forces in England. Consequently, the prime minister was forced to remove more power from Hughes and establish an overseas ministry. This Hughes found unacceptable, as it would mark the end of much of his influence. Always intemperate and uncontrollable, Hughes wrote an indiscreet letter to Borden, which the prime minister could not avoid; he asked for Hughes's resignation in November 1916.

While most historians ignore Hughes in the last five years of his life, he remained a military authority in parliament. After a failed attempt to raise a new war party, Hughes continued to support the Canadian war effort, lending his name and support to numerous patriotic home front movements. However, he is best remembered for his high-profile attack against Sir Arthur Currie, the Canadian Corps commander from 1917 onward. In early 1919, Hughes publicly accused Currie of needlessly butchering Canadian soldiers in fruitless and costly attacks on the Western Front. Although Hughes was viewed as an unstable and discredited force in parliament, his verbal assaults were reported throughout the country. Even in the last years of his life, Hughes remained a person to be reckoned with. After more than thirty years as a member of parliament, Hughes died in 1921 and was buried with full military honors.

Timothy Cook

See also: Conservative Party (Canada, WWI); Mobilization (Canada, WWI); Biographies: Borden, Robert Laird (WWI)

REFERENCES

Capon, Alan R. *His Faults Lie Gently: The Incredible Sam Hughes.* Lindsay: Floyd Hall, 1969.

Harris, Stephen. *Canadian Brass: The Making of a Professional Army, 1860–1939.* Toronto: University of Toronto Press, 1988.

Haycock, Ronald. *Sam Hughes: The Public Career of a Controversial Canadian, 1885–1916.* Ottawa: Canadian War Museum, 1986.

Morton, Desmond. *A Peculiar Kind of Politics: Canada's Overseas Ministry in the First World War.* Toronto: University of Toronto Press, 1982.

Hurley, Edward Nash

Edward Nash Hurley (1864–1933), a close friend and political ally of President Woodrow Wilson, helped create and organize the merchant shipping necessary to transport American troops and supplies to Europe in 1917 and 1918. Hurley also supervised the creation of an infrastructure to make the American merchant fleet supreme in the postwar years.

Hurley was born in Illinois and worked for the railroads, like his father. He became active in Chicago Democratic politics and was rewarded with several patronage jobs. His main profession, however, was that of businessman. In 1896, while working as a salesman, Hurley staked his future on a piston air drill. He mortgaged his home and formed the Standard Pneumatic Tool Company. Within three years, the dynamic Hurley was marketing his pneumatic products throughout the United States and Europe. The naval armaments race between Great Britain and Germany spurred steel shipbuilding, so the demand for Hurley's pneumatic riveting hammers was especially great. He sold his company in 1902 for over $1.25 million. Several years later, Hurley came out of retirement to found the Hurley Machine Company, one of the most successful manufacturers of household electrical appliances of the era.

Hurley remained interested in Democratic politics. In 1910, he worked with Princeton alumni in the Chicago area for Wilson's election as governor of New Jersey. Two years later, he helped drum up midwestern support for Wilson's presidential bid. Wilson sent Hurley to Latin America to investigate markets for U.S. businesses in 1914. In 1915, the president appointed him to the newly created Federal Trade Commission (FTC). Hurley later served as vice-chair and chair of the FTC. During his time at the FTC, he developed a belief that co-operation between business and labor, as well as between businessmen, was the key to success.

Hurley resigned from the FTC in February 1917. He was working for the Exports Council when Wilson asked him to head the U.S. Shipping Board in July 1917. The Board was created by the Shipping Act of September 7, 1916, to regulate maritime commerce and to create a public corporation to purchase, construct, equip, and maintain U.S. merchant ships. This corporation became the Emergency Fleet Corporation, created on April 16, 1917, and funded by a combination of private and public funds.

Personality and philosophical differences prevented the Shipping Board from making much progress toward its goal. Knowing very little about ships, Hurley was hesitant to accept the appointment, but he acquiesced because the war with Germany required firm action. He focused on policy questions and public relations, while bringing in talented business leaders to handle details such as contract negotiations and production operations. Hurley soon brought order to the Shipping Board and the Emergency Fleet Corporation. In March 1918, Wilson asked him to join the War Council.

As a businessman, Hurley recognized the value of a large merchant fleet after the war was won. He used the $3.5 billion appropriated by Congress to expand U.S. shipbuilding capacity. Three new shipyards were constructed, and liberal contracts were given to private contractors. Production was quickly stepped up. At the end of fiscal year 1917, American shipyards had produced 664,000 tons of merchant shipping. By the end of fiscal year 1918, the annual total was 1.3 million tons. A year later, production soared to 3.3 million tons. American merchant shipping tripled under Hurley. Men and supplies were able to flow to Europe in unprecedented numbers.

At the end of the war, Hurley served on the Supreme Economic Council and supervised the confiscation of German merchant shipping. He resigned from the Shipping Board in July 1919 and returned to private business. He died in Chicago in 1933.

Tim J. Watts

See also: Mobilization (U.S., WWI); Shipping (WWI); Biographies: Wilson, Woodrow (WWI)

REFERENCES

Hurley, Edward N. *The Bridge to France.* Philadelphia: J. B. Lippincott, 1927.
Safford, Jeffrey J. *Wilsonian Maritime Diplomacy, 1913–1921.* New Brunswick, NJ: Rutgers University Press, 1978.

J

Jackson, Joseph "Shoeless Joe"

Famed Chicago White Sox star Joseph "Shoeless Joe" Jackson (1889–1951) was born in Pickens County, South Carolina, to George and Martha Jackson, who were tenant farmers. When he was six years old, the family moved to Brandon, South Carolina, where Joe worked long hours as a cleanup boy at a textile mill. As a teenager he earned extra money playing for the company baseball team. Jackson's amazing hitting and fielding abilities quickly attracted attention. In 1907 he was signed by a semiprofessional team in Greenville, South Carolina.

The following year Connie Mack of the Philadelphia Athletics professional team purchased Jackson's contract. Unfortunately, Jackson had difficulty adapting to the big city and was subjected to relentless teasing by his teammates. He played in only ten games over two seasons. In 1910 Mack reluctantly sold Jackson to the Cleveland team. He batted .408 in 1911, but lost the batting title to Ty Cobb of the Detroit Tigers. Throughout Jackson's career he was continuously compared to Cobb, who seemed to best him each season by only a hair.

In 1915, the failing Cleveland team sold Jackson to the Chicago White Sox. Jackson was part of the world championship team in 1917.

The following season, to avoid military service during World War I, Jackson worked in a shipyard, but he spent most of his time playing ball for the company team. Returning to professional baseball in 1919, he batted .351 and led the White Sox to a pennant, but the team lost the World Series. In 1920 it was discovered that the series had been fixed. To this day there is still uncertainty over Jackson's role in the famous "Black Sox" scandal. His detractors argue that he accepted $5,000 cash from gamblers and had knowledge of the fix from the beginning. His supporters counter that Jackson tried to tip off Charles Comiskey, the team's owner, played at his usual high level, and was fooled by fast talking lawyers. In 1921 he was banned from baseball with seven other players.

Jackson spent the next decade and a half playing for semiprofessional teams, sometimes under an alias. All the time he tried to clear his name. He also engaged in several modest but successful business ventures. Jackson died of a heart attack in his home in Greenville, South Carolina. He is ineligible for the Baseball Hall of Fame despite a .356 lifetime batting average, third best of all time.

Gregory Dehler

See also: Baseball (WWI); Biographies: Cobb, Ty (WWI)

REFERENCES

Frommer, Harvey. *Shoeless Joe and Ragtime Baseball.* Dallas: Taylor Publishing, 1992.

Gropman, Donald. *Say It Ain't So, Joe! The True Story of Shoeless Joe Jackson.* New York: Carol Publishing, 1992.

Johnson, Hiram

As a governor of California, vice-presidential candidate, and U.S. senator, Hiram Johnson (1866–1945) espoused domestic reform and isolationism before becoming one of the harshest critics of President Woodrow Wilson's foreign policy during and after World War I. An opponent of both conservative Republicans and internationalist Democrats, the Progressive senator helped block ratification of the 1919 Versailles Peace Treaty with its controversial League of Nations clause.

Johnson rose to prominence as a San Francisco assistant district attorney known for prosecuting bribery cases involving city officials. In 1910, California's Lincoln-Roosevelt League, a Progressive Republican organization, persuaded him to run for governor to fight corruption at the state level. As governor, he shaped the face of western Progressivism, leading his state to adopt direct election of senators, the recall of elected officials, and the popular referendum. He fought against big business, created a state commission to regulate railroad rates, and worked with unions to protect working women and children.

In 1912, Johnson helped create the Progres-

From left to right, California Senator Hiram Johnson, Idaho Senator William Borah, and Illinois Representative Medill McCormick, Republicans all, resisted U.S. entry into World War I. (Library of Congress)

sive Party after the Republicans renominated the conservative William Howard Taft for president. As Theodore Roosevelt's running mate, he rallied California behind the new party before its defeat to the Democrat, Woodrow Wilson. Four years later, Johnson won election to the U.S. Senate as a Progressive Republican. While he voted for the United States to enter World War I in 1917, he opposed the draft and grew concerned that wartime mobilization undercut domestic reform, destroyed free speech, and gave disproportionate power to the president. Johnson considered Wilson's Fourteen-Point address in January 1918, including its call for a League of Nations, an attempt by the administration to remake the map of Europe at the expense of peace and democracy. The following summer, he was outraged by Wilson's decision to send troops to Russia in response to the Bolshevik Revolution.

For Johnson, the Versailles Peace Treaty negotiations, which involved little congressional input, represented the height of presidential arrogance. During the summer of 1919, he launched an antitreaty speaking tour, arguing that the League of Nations provision in particular would divert the nation's financial and military resources to maintaining Europe's territorial boundaries. In the Senate, he teamed with William Borah, Robert La Follette, and other "irreconcilables," who opposed the treaty even after the Foreign Relations Committee adopted reservations meant to limit the nation's commitment to the League. Johnson's group of isola-

tionist Republicans voted against both the original and modified versions of the treaty in November 1919 and March 1920, preventing its ratification. As a result, the United States never entered the League of Nations and had to sign a separate peace agreement with Germany.

Johnson remained an isolationist throughout his Senate career. In the 1930s, he led successful campaigns to curtail international loans and block the United States' membership in the World Court. He opposed the draft in 1940 and the Lend-Lease program in 1941 but voted for war after the attack on Pearl Harbor. Poor health limited his political involvement during the World War II era.

Jane Armstrong Hudiburg

See also: Fourteen Points (WWI); Isolationism (WWI); Progressivism (WWI); Republican Party (WWI); Biographies: La Follette, Robert Marion (WWI)

REFERENCES

DeWitt, Howard A. "Hiram Johnson and World War I: A Progressive in Transition." *Southern California Quarterly* 56 (Fall 1974): 295–305.

Lower, Richard Coke. *A Block of One: Hiram W. Johnson and the American Liberal Tradition.* Stanford: Stanford University Press, 1993.

———. "Hiram Johnson: The Making of an Irreconcilable." *Pacific Historical Review* 41 (November 1972): 505–526.

K

Keaton, Buster

One of the great comedic actors of the silent-screen era, Buster Keaton (1895–1966) not only starred in a number of now-classic films but also produced, directed, wrote, and edited many of those films. On screen, he was the embodiment of the ordinary man beset by extraordinary calamities. Because these characters were typically unflappably stoic in the face of whatever befell them, Keaton became known as the "Great Stone Face." The stories frequently demanded extremely acrobatic stunts that Keaton insisted on performing himself.

Keaton was born Joseph Francis Keaton VI in Piqua, Kansas. His parents had a vaudeville act, and at a very young age, Keaton began to perform with them at venues throughout the country. Because of his obvious gift for physical comedy, the act gradually included more and more gags that involved Keaton's catapulting himself over furniture or other elements of the stage set. Eventually these seemingly reckless pratfalls became the signature feature of his performances, and he was tagged with the nickname "the human mop."

Keaton's film career began with *The Butcher Boy* (1917), but it was quickly interrupted by the entry of the United States into the First World War. Keaton served with the American Expeditionary Force in France. When he returned to Hollywood, he developed his reputation in a series of quickly made but carefully conceived short films. These early films are *Convict 13, Neighbors, One Week,* and *The Scarecrow,* all released in 1920; *The Boat, The Goat, Hard Luck, The Haunted House, The High Sign, The Paleface,* and *The Playhouse,* all released in 1921; and *The Blacksmith, Cops, Daydreams, The Electric House, The Frozen North,* and *My Wife's Relations,* all released in 1922.

Keaton's success was a mixed blessing. Although it permitted him to begin making full-length feature films, he also lost complete artistic control over his films because the studios financing the films began to demand a voice in everything from the writing of the screenplays to the editing of the films. After making *The Balloonatic* (1923), *The Love Nest* (1923), and the film that is often cited as his masterwork, *The General* (1927), Keaton increasingly starred in films written by others for him. Some, such as *Steamboat Bill* (1928), were creditable, but many of the others made marginal use of his talents. His professional dissatisfactions exacerbated his deepening dependence on alcohol, and that dependence further eroded his film career.

Between 1930 and 1950, Keaton appeared in almost five dozen films, but they were so mediocre or his parts were so small that when he resurfaced in a brief, eponymous television series in 1950, many reviewers as well as viewers expressed surprise that he was still alive. In the decade before his death, however, he reestablished himself in the public consciousness and rehabilitated his reputation by taking small roles in major productions with large casts, including *Around the World in 80 Days* (1956), *It's a Mad Mad Mad Mad World* (1963), and *A Funny Thing Happened on the Way to the Forum* (1966). He also wrote a well-received autobiography, *My Wonderful World of Slapstick* (1960). In 1960, he received an Honorary Academy Award recognizing his achievements in the medium of film.

Martin Kich

See also: Film (U.S., WWI)

REFERENCES

Bengston, John. *Silent Echoes: Discovering the Early Hollywood through the Films of Buster Keaton.* Santa Monica, CA: Santa Monica Press, 2000.

Blesh, Rudi. *Keaton.* New York: Macmillan, 1966.

Dardis, Tom. *Keaton: The Man Who Wouldn't Lie Down.* New York: Scribner, 1979.

Lebel, Jean Patrick. *Buster Keaton.* Translated from French by P. D. Stovin. New York: Barnes and Noble, 1967.

Meade, Marion. *Buster Keaton: Cut to the Chase.* New York: HarperCollins, 1995.

Moews, Daniel. *Keaton: The Silent Features Close Up.* Berkeley, CA: University of California Press, 1977.

Rapf, Joanna E., and Gary L. Green. *Buster Keaton: A Bio-Bibliography.* Westport, CT: Greenwood, 1995.

Robinson, David. *Buster Keaton.* Bloomington, IN: Indiana University Press, 1969.

Wead, George. *Buster Keaton and the Dynamics of Visual Wit.* New York: Arno, 1976.

Wead, George, and George Lellis. *The Film Career of Buster Keaton.* Boston: G. K. Hall, 1977.

Kelley, Florence

Florence Molthrop Kelley (1859–1932) was a staunch pacifist who opposed the U.S. entry into World War I and a social reformer instrumental in securing protective legislation and privileges for men, women, and children laboring on the home front in early twentieth-century America. Kelley was well educated, a socialist, and a member of Jane Addams's Hull House, the National American Woman Suffrage Association, and the National Association for the Advancement of Colored People. She is perhaps most noted for battling sweatshops in Chicago and for founding, with Addams and others, the Women's Peace Party (WPP), which was a forerunner to the Women's International League for Peace and Freedom (WILPF).

Kelley was born into a prominent Quaker family on September 12, 1859, in Philadelphia. She studied at Cornell University and the University of Zurich, where she encountered the works of Karl Marx and Friedrich Engels and became an avowed Socialist. In Europe in 1884, Kelley married Lazare Wischnewetzky (also spelled *Wishnieweski*), a Polish-Russian physician and fellow member of the Socialist Labor Party. The couple moved to New York City in 1886 but separated five years later, whereupon Kelley moved to Chicago.

In the 1890s, Chicago teemed with poverty, slums, and horrific working conditions for its one million inhabitants, many of whom were immigrants. Kelley settled at the remarkable Hull House, where she joined Jane Addams,

Ellen Gates Starr, Julia Lathrop, and others in championing social reform. Kelley crusaded chiefly against sweatshops and the exploitation of women and children in manufacturing and became Illinois's first Chief Factory Inspector in 1893.

In 1899, Kelley moved back to New York City, took up residence at Lillian Wald's Henry Street Settlement, and became active in such organizations as the National Consumers' League (which promoted industrial reform through consumer activity), the National American Woman Suffrage Association, and the National Association for the Advancement of Colored People. Kelley was also a staunch pacifist who opposed the involvement of the United States in World War I.

Kelley rejoined Jane Addams and other feminists in forming the Woman's Peace Party (WPP) in Washington, D.C., in January 1915 in response to the outbreak of World War I. The WPP united women from many local organizations behind a platform calling for mediation for peace, disarmament, and women's suffrage. Several women from the United States and more than a thousand from warring nations and neutral countries alike overcame political obstacles and traveled to The Hague in 1915 for an international women's peace conference. However, when America entered the war, the U.S. WPP fractured as some members focused on providing war relief while others continued to refuse to support the conflict. At war's end, Kelley's WPP met in Zurich to protest the Versailles Treaty as being unfair to Germany; delegates there formed the Women's International League for Peace and Freedom (WILPF), which still exists today.

A prolific writer, Kelley's books include *Some Ethical Gains Through Legislation* (1905), *Modern Industry in Relation to the Family* (1914), *The Supreme Court and Minimum Wage Legislation* (1925), and *Autobiography* (1927). Florence Kelley died in Germantown, Pennsylvania on February 17, 1932.

Charles H. Wilson, III

See also: National Association for the Advancement of Colored People (WWI); National Consumers' League (WWI); Pacifists (WWI); Women (U.S., WWI); Women's International League for Peace and Freedom (WWI); Biographies: Addams, Jane (WWI); Wald, Lillian (WWI)

REFERENCES

Blumberg, Dorothy Rose. *Florence Kelley: The Making of a Social Pioneer.* New York: A. M. Kelley, 1966.

Foster, Carrie A. *The Women and the Warriors: The US Section of the Women's International League for Peace and Freedom, 1915–1946.* Athens, GA: University of Georgia Press, 1989.

Sklar, Kathryn Kish. *Florence Kelley and the Nation's Work: The Rise of Women's Political Culture, 1830–1900.* New Haven, CT: Yale University Press, 1995.

Kellogg, Frank B.

Frank Billings Kellogg (1856–1937) served as U.S. secretary of state from 1925–1929, during which time he completed his most important achievements. Chief among these was the Kellogg-Briand Pact of 1928, which prohibited war as an instrument of national policy.

Kellogg was born on December 22, 1856, in Potsdam, New York. He studied law and was called to the bar in 1877. He became a U.S. senator in 1917 and remained in the Senate until 1923, at which time he became the ambassador to Great Britain. In 1925, he returned

Secretary of State Frank Kellogg is best known for the post-World War I Kellogg-Briand Pact, written with French foreign minister Aristide Briand, calling for the outlawing of war as a means of resolving disputes among nations. (Library of Congress)

from his ambassadorial position to serve as secretary of state under President Calvin Coolidge. Kellogg showed an interest in persuading the world's nations to adopt a universal policy of disarmament. In 1927, for example, he was instrumental in designing a Geneva-based conference for the purpose of reducing naval armaments. Although this conference was unsuccessful, Kellogg remained optimistic about future developments.

By 1928, Kellogg was in communication with the French foreign minister, Aristide Briand, who had expressed a desire to create a bilateral treaty that outlawed war as an instrument of national policy. The devastating results of the First World War and the subsequent anti-

war fervor of the 1920s had led Briand and many others to support the abolition of war as a political tool. Kellogg suggested that the proposal be extended to all the world's nations. The resulting proposal became a multinational treaty and was signed by fifteen nations in Paris on August 27, 1928. It was officially known as the Treaty for the Renunciation of War, but was popularly referred to as the Kellogg-Briand Pact. Later, the treaty was almost universally ratified.

Although Kellogg received the Nobel Peace Prize in 1929, the Kellogg-Briand Pact did little to prevent aggressive actions in the 1930s. The Japanese incursion into Manchuria and the Italian invasion of Ethiopia resulted in a loss of faith with regards to the potential of the pact to halt aggression. Despite its failures, the treaty remains an important contributor to international law, in which war is usually seen as an unacceptable and aggressive act. This is in stark contrast to the traditional perception of war, which was seen as a legitimate tool of national policy. This change in international attitude is in large measure a result of the efforts of individuals like Frank Kellogg.

Gordon Stienburg

See also: Biographies: Coolidge, Calvin (WWI)

REFERENCES

Ellis, Lewis. *Frank B. Kellogg and American Foreign Relations: 1925–1929.* New Brunswick, NJ: Rutgers University Press, 1961.

Louria, Margot. *Triumph and Downfall: America's Pursuit of Peace and Prosperity, 1921–1933.* Westport, CT: Greenwood Press, 2001.

Kellor, Frances

Social scientist and reformer Frances Kellor (1872–1952) devoted her early professional career to protecting the rights of immigrants living in the United States. Following America's entry into World War I in 1917, Kellor, along with many others, shifted her focus and support to programs designed to rapidly assimilate immigrants into American society. Her work exemplifies national concerns about the foreign born during the war years.

Frances Alice Kellor was born on October 20, 1873. Unable to afford to finish high school, she instead worked as a typesetter and later as an investigative reporter. She became the protégé of two wealthy sisters, Mary and Frances Eddy, who offered to finance her education. Kellor enrolled at Cornell Law School in 1895, earned her law degree in 1897, and then moved on to the University of Chicago, where she had earned a scholarship to study sociology. While studying at Chicago, Kellor lived and worked at Hull House, a settlement house devoted to providing social services to immigrants. Immigration soon became the focus of Kellor's personal and professional interest. In 1908 Kellor conducted field research on immigration in New York City. The resulting report called for the creation of a New York Bureau of Industries and Immigration. The Bureau was created in 1910, and Kellor became its chairperson. Under her leadership the Bureau arbitrated labor disputes, educated immigrant workers about their legal rights, and proposed additions to state labor laws.

In 1912, Kellor left the Bureau to work with the Progressive Party. In 1914, she helped found the Committee for Immigrants in America, an organization that coordinated local, state, and national programs of immigrant education and assimilation. The outbreak of war in Europe raised concerns about the loyalty of foreigners in the United States. Kellor became convinced that America needed better "Americanization" programs that would help immigrants assimilate into society. Although she continued to plead for tolerance of ethnic and cultural differences, Kellor also appealed to American xenophobia and fears of internal sabotage to gain public support for Americanization.

Her greatest success in wartime Americanization came in 1915, when she helped create National Americanization Day, an event held on the Fourth of July. Organized by the Committee for Immigrants in America, more than one hundred cities participated. Immigrants turned out by the thousands to demonstrate their loyalty to the United States and their commitment to the war effort. Following this success, the Committee for Immigrants in America was absorbed into a new National Americanization Committee that continued to develop and promote Americanization programs. In 1916, Kellor published *Straight America*, a book that advocated strict naturalization policies and the compulsory Americanization of immigrants.

Kellor eventually shifted back toward greater tolerance of immigrants in the United States. But as the red scare took hold in the 1920s, Americanization fell out of favor in the face of increasing demands for immigration restriction. Kellor then embarked on a career in conflict resolution. She became an authority on using these tactics to settle labor disputes. Kellor died in 1952.

Eileen V. Wallis

See also: Progressivism (WWI); Red Scare (WWI); Sabotage and Spies (WWI)

REFERENCES

Faderman, Lillian. *To Believe in Women: What Lesbians Have Done for America: A History.* New York: Houghton Mifflin, 1999.

Fitzpatrick, Ellen. *Endless Crusade: Women Social Scientists and Progressive Reform.* New York: Oxford University Press, 1990.

Higham, John. *Strangers in the Land: Patterns of American Nativism.* New Brunswick: Rutgers University Press, 1955.

Kellor, Frances A. *Straight America.* New York: Macmillan Co., 1916.

Keynes, John Maynard

With *The Economic Consequences of the Peace* (1919), John Maynard Keynes (1883–1946) first made a name for himself on the world scene. Keynes had acquired his special knowledge of the economic situation of the world in 1919 largely thanks to his close association with the British war effort in his daily duties at the Treasury, which he joined in January 1915, leaving his Cambridge teaching commitments for the duration of the war. His main wartime preoccupations bore on Allied finance, specifically, how to support Russia's war effort while sustaining the Anglo-French front with American loans. He was also concerned about Britain's postwar difficulties, especially the convertibility of sterling and the related problem of the rate of exchange with the dollar, and he advised against an early abandonment of the gold standard. Domestic and international economic issues were inextricably linked in what came to be known as a World War.

But Keynes was involved in the war on a more personal plane, too, through the vexed question of conscription. Most of his close friends from the Bloomsbury Group were Liberal or Labour intellectuals who did not share in the Hang the Kaiser hysteria that inspired most of the press and urged the government to introduce compulsory military service. Keynes was de facto exempt from military conscription

thanks to his post at the Treasury. However, his biographers do not agree on the episode of February 1916, when he applied for formal exemption on grounds of conscience, sending a written statement that contained the classic arguments of liberal (antistate regimentation), not pacifist (antiwar), conscientious objection. He failed to appear at the hearing and therefore continued to benefit from de facto exemption and never became a "proper" conscientious objector. The fact remains that he never hesitated to use his authority as a senior civil servant to support his friends before the tribunals in charge of granting conscientious objector status, at the risk of entering into conflict with his political masters. The link between his personal objection to conscription and his economic expertise was provided by his argument that the country could not financially afford to raise the number of fully equipped divisions above a certain level, with the consequent ceiling on the number of men needed in the armed forces.

Thus, by the end of the Great War, Keynes was a controversial figure. His reputation in conservative circles as a maverick was reinforced by his increasing attacks against the orthodox policies that dominated official thinking in the interwar years, while the rise of Nazism in Germany seemed to vindicate his unheeded warnings against a "Carthaginian Peace" in 1919, which paradoxically played against him. Unsurprisingly, when war broke out again in September 1939, he had no official government function. This left him free to express unconventional opinions, which he did in two articles in *The Times* (November 14 and 15, 1939) titled "Paying for the War," which was the embryo for *How to Pay for the War: A Radical Plan for the Chancellor of the Exchequer*, the famous booklet published in February 1940. His plan was so radical that it met the hostility of both the right and the left. The objections of the right are easy to understand: whereas the official policy of the

Chamberlain Government continued to rest on the old principle of business as usual, Keynes insisted that only a total mobilization of national resources in men and goods could hope to win the war. It had to be a total war not in the sense that all atrocities and war crimes would be tolerated, but in the sense that all peacetime considerations of the allocation of national production lost their relevance in wartime. The left was suspicious of deferred pay proposals, whereby stringent wage restraint and punitive income tax would be made good after the war in the form of savings certificates. The debate took a different turn with the threat of German invasion after June 1940, and Keynesian techniques leading to a manpower budget were fully applied in the following months, with Keynes gradually acquiring a senior position at the Treasury once again. The first ever Keynesian budget, in April 1941, was a great success in that it sustained the war effort while checking inflation. By 1944, Keynes's unparalleled command of financial techniques made him the obvious choice to lead the British delegation at the Bretton Woods talks, which led to the creation of the International Monetary Fund. Yet Keynes never allowed the "dismal science" to absorb him entirely, and he was probably the prime actor in the transformation of the wartime Council for the Encouragement of Music and the Arts (CEMA), which he chaired, into the postwar Arts Council of Great Britain, which received its charter in July 1946, three months after Keynes's death.

Antoine Capet

See also: Conscription (UK, WWI); Economy (UK, WWI); Intellectuals (WWI);Biographies: Keynes, John Maynard (WWII)

REFERENCES

Moggridge, Donald E. 1995. *Maynard Keynes: An Economist's Biography.* London: Routledge, 1995.

Skidelsky, Robert. *John Maynard Keynes.* Volume 1: *Hopes Betrayed, 1883–1920.* London: Macmillan, 1983–2000.

———. *John Maynard Keynes.* Volume 3: *Fighting for Britain, 1937–1946.* London: Macmillan, 1983–2000.

Kitchener, Horatio Herbert

One of the most famous and experienced British soldiers of his generation, Horatio Herbert Kitchener (1850–1916), as secretary of state for war from 1914 to 1916 was responsible for raising a mass volunteer force to support the allied effort on the Western Front. Greatly revered by the army, Kitchener enjoyed an irreproachable public image; his impressive patrician bearing rendered him the perfect patriotic symbol. Stern, inscrutable, autocratic, and uncomfortable in the presence of politicians, whom he generally detested, Kitchener refused to delegate responsibility to subordinates, preferring to bury himself in his work. This characteristic was perhaps more a virtue than a vice, for on his shoulders rested responsibility for war strategy and imperial defense, not to mention the mobilization of the Empire's human and material resources. He disliked political debate and resented criticism, which naturally grew as the stalemate persisted amidst appalling losses. Notwithstanding his defects, Kitchener was practically unique in military circles in predicting a protracted conflict of at least three years' length. His estimate that casualties would run into the millions proved tragically prophetic.

Kitchener's reputation had been established during long and distinguished service in numerous colonial campaigns, including an abortive expedition to relieve General Gordon at Khartoum in 1884–85. As commander of the Anglo-Egyptian Army, he won victories at

Celebrated military leader and secretary of state for war in the early years of World War I, Horatio Herbert Kitchener organized Britain's volunteer military force for the conflict in Europe. (The Illustrated London News Picture Library)

Atbara and Omdurman in the Sudan in 1898, before being appointed chief of staff to Lord Roberts during the Boer War. As commander in chief in South Africa from November 1900 to May 1902, he instituted harsh measures against the Boers. As commander in chief in India from 1902 to 1909, he was promoted to field marshal in September 1909, and from 1911 to 1914 he served as viceroy of Egypt and the Sudan.

When the First World War broke out, Kitchener was fortuitously on home leave in London where, on August 6, 1914, he reluctantly accepted the post of secretary of state for war. He immediately understood the necessity of rais-

ing an army of unprecedented proportions. His historic call for volunteers produced the world's most famous recruiting poster, bearing Kitchener's own grim-faced, finger-pointing, paternalistic image and the compelling words, *Your country needs you!* His many schemes for recruitment created a rapid flood of volunteers. Within a month, half a million men had answered the call to arms, and by the end of February 1915 that figure had doubled.

The massive public response to Kitchener's summons disrupted the distribution of labor, particularly in factories, and posed severe problems in the supply of military equipment, uniforms, and weapons. Many recruits were consequently not adequately prepared for action when they crossed the Channel, some having trained for a time with broomsticks and obsolete rifles. Nevertheless, by 1915 Kitchener's initiative had provided the badly needed reinforcements required to replace the catastrophic losses suffered the previous year.

The consummate field commander, Kitchener was never adept as a grand strategist. This fact was glaringly revealed when, in March 1915, he reluctantly committed troops to fight the Turks on the Gallipoli peninsula. He offered the commander of the expedition the scantiest of instructions, formulated no proper strategy for the campaign, and neglected to organize the forces properly or provide sufficient reinforcements. Utter failure in that theater was compounded by the shell scandal of the same year—for which Kitchener was partly to blame—in which the woefully short supply of artillery shells partly contributed to costly failures on the Western Front.

Although his reputation suffered seriously as a result of these disasters, Kitchener remained in office: The government did not dare remove a man whose prestige remained so high in the public mind. Indeed, he still retained enough influence over military matters to replace French with a new commander in chief of British forces in France, Sir Douglas Haig. Still, with his powers impaired, Kitchener tendered his resignation in early 1916. The government refused it, but Kitchener's absence on an official visit to Tsar Nicholas of Russia in June gave the cabinet time to review strategy without his direct intervention. On June 5, Kitchener was drowned when HMS *Hampshire*, while en route to Russia, struck a mine and sank off the Orkney Islands.

Gregory Fremont-Barnes

See also: Conscription (UK, WWI); Economy (UK, WWI); Mobilization (UK, WWI); Biographies: Asquith, Herbert (WWI); Haig, Douglas (WWI)

REFERENCES

Cassar, George. *Kitchener: Architect of Victory*. London: W. Kimber, 1977.
Pollock, John. *Kitchener*. London: Constable, 2001.
Royle, Trevor. *The Kitchener Enigma*. London: M. Joseph, 1985.
Warner, Philip. *Kitchener: The Man behind the Legend*. London: Hamish Hamilton, 1985.

Kitchin, Claude

Claude Kitchin (1869–1923), attorney, U.S. representative from North Carolina, and house majority leader during World War I, was best known as an antimilitarist and outspoken opponent of President Woodrow Wilson's preparedness plan. Born into an eastern North Carolina farming family, Claude Kitchin's early years were shaped by his family's Populist ideals. After election to Congress in 1898, Kitchin allied himself with the William Jennings Bryan wing of the Democratic Party. In 1909, he joined the House Ways and Means Committee. Kitchin supported fellow southerner Woodrow Wilson for president in 1912. Three years later, he rose to the chairmanship of the committee and, in doing so, ascended to the position of House majority leader.

With the advent of hostilities in Europe, Kitchin became increasingly alarmed at the possibility of U.S. intervention in the Great War. Kitchin favored rigid impartiality regarding belligerents. He opposed Wilson's 1915 preparedness campaign and generally voted against increased military expenditures. He also railed against Secretary of War Garrison's continental army plan. However, he supported the Defense Act of 1916 because it strengthened the army, the service he considered essential for defense of the homeland, while he rejected pleas for naval expansion, which he feared might make the United States more inclined to involve itself in foreign wars. Kitchin also hoped to control the excesses of the steel industry by creating a government-owned armor plate plant.

Kitchin was both praised and vilified for his vote against the April 5, 1917, declaration of war. In a stirring late night speech before Congress, he stated that he would not let his country "pull up the last anchor of peace in the world." Expecting little support, he proclaimed that he was willing to walk "barefoot and alone." Surprisingly, his plea was supported by fifty other members, including five fellow southerners who had the courage to oppose a popular southern president.

After American involvement was assured, he supported the war effort. Kitchin favored taxes over loans as the best way to pay for the war because he did not want to unduly saddle future generations with war debt. Along with Senator Furnifold Simmons of North Carolina, head of the Senate Finance Committee, Kitchin designed a number of funding plans.

In the election of 1918, the Republicans gained control of the House of Representatives and Kitchin became the ranking minority member of Ways and Means. In an April 1920 speech before Congress, he staunchly opposed a separate peace with Germany, believing that it would allow Germany too much power in setting the terms for peace. At the end of the speech, he suffered a stroke and collapsed. After recovery, he briefly returned to his duties. However, continuing dizzy spells forced him to undergo brain surgery. Although he had yet to return to his duties, fellow Democrats elected him to the position of House minority leader in 1921. Kitchin contracted pneumonia during the winter of 1922–1923 and, after a lengthy illness, died on May 31, 1923.

Jonathan F. Phillips

See also: Isolationism (WWI); Biographies: Bryan, William Jennings (WWI)

REFERENCES

Arnett, Alex Mathews. *Claude Kitchin and the Wilson War Policies.* New York: Russell and Russell, 1937.

Cooper, John Milton, Jr. *The Vanity of Power: American Isolationism and the First World War, 1914–1917.* Westport, CT: Greenwood Publishing Company, 1969.

Daniels, Jonathan. *The End of Innocence.* Philadelphia: J. B. Lippincott Company, 1954.

Link, Arthur. *Wilson: Confusions and Crises, 1915–1916.* Princeton: Princeton University Press, 1964.

L

La Follette, Robert Marion

A longtime Progressive reformer dedicated to the more equitable distribution of wealth and power in the United States, Senator Robert La Follette (1855–1925) proclaimed, "War is the money changer's opportunity, and the social reformer's doom," and was vilified for his leadership of the opposition to America's entry into World War I. Following the American declaration of war, even as efforts were made to remove him from the Senate, La Follette continued to promote corporate regulation, tax reform, and individual rights and freedoms. He lived to see his antiwar stance vindicated and remained in the Senate as a leader for reform until his death in 1924.

Beginning in the late nineteenth century, frustrated by the corporate, political, and social corruption and greed emerging from the rapid industrialization and urbanization of the Gilded Age, La Follette embraced reforms ranging from the conservation of natural resources to nominations by primary elections (rather than by appointment or legislative selection). He came to the Senate in 1906, determined to implement at the national level the same reforms he had brought to Wisconsin in his three terms as governor. Although originally ostracized for his self-righteous fervor, La Follette's dedication to more aggressive and interventionist reforms, including the direct election of United States senators, and accelerated attacks on trusts and monopolies, slowly gained him the support of a core of fellow Progressive senators.

La Follette was horrified as President Woodrow Wilson's policy of strict isolationism concerning the Great War raging in Europe gradually gave way. The Wisconsin senator viewed the calls for military preparedness as thinly veiled efforts by corporations to increase war profiteering and throw off new governmental regulations. He predicted that America's entry would mark the end of hard-fought political, economic, and social reforms. When Wilson asked Congress for the authority to arm merchant ships, La Follette, despite rumors of plans of violence to be carried out against him on the floor of the Senate, organized a twenty-six-hour filibuster that began on March 4, 1917, preventing the vote.

Wilson denounced La Follette and his fellow noninterventionists as "a little group of willful men" who "have rendered the great Government of the United States helpless and contemptible." Former president Theodore Roosevelt joined the chorus calling for La Follette's removal from the Senate, comparing him to

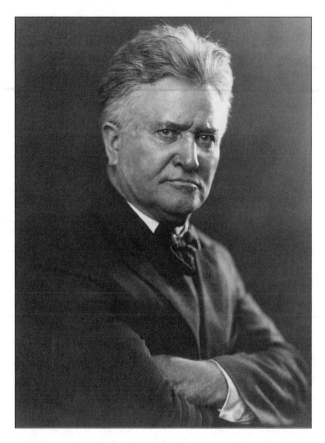

A Progressive Republican, Wisconsin Senator Robert La Follette organized a 26-hour filibuster against President Woodrow's Wilson's request to arm American merchant ships on the eve of U.S. entry into World War I. (Library of Congress)

Benedict Arnold and Judas Iscariat. Headlines proclaimed that the nation was united in its opposition to La Follette, and countless political cartoons presented him as in league with Germany's Kaiser. Opponents of the war, however, rejoiced in La Follette's actions. Labor leader and socialist Eugene Debs declared, "Let the Wall Street wolves and their prostitute press howl. The people will sustain you and history will vindicate you." At the subsequent emergency session of Congress the following month, La Follette was one of only six senators to vote against the declaration of war, generating renewed calls for his ouster from the Senate for disloyalty.

As La Follette anticipated, wartime concerns overshadowed efforts to further the domestic Progressive agenda. He continued to assert that America's entry was motivated more by corporate greed than by Wilson's stated goal of keeping the world safe for democracy, but he was not a pacifist. After his nation was committed to war, La Follette supported all but five of the sixty war measures proposed in Congress, but he also persisted in efforts to keep Progressive reform alive. His attempts to protect individual rights by ending the draft and overturning the Espionage Act failed, but he did enjoy some success in shifting the tax burden from customs and excise taxes to incomes, profits, and estates.

On September 17, 1917, La Follette gave a speech at the Nonpartisan League's convention in St. Paul, Minnesota that further crippled any attempts to promote his Progressive agenda during wartime. The audience was wildly receptive to his denunciation of American involvement in the war. However, in an Associated Press story that made headlines in more than a thousand papers across the country, La Follette was misquoted as saying, "We have no grievance against Germany." Former presidents Roosevelt and Taft as well as a number of senators, associations, newspapers, and organizations all called for La Follette's expulsion from the Senate. A formal investigation into La Follette's speeches and antiwar activities was launched by a senate committee.

Not all Americans joined in the vilification of La Follette. Citizens from across the country, especially the Midwest, supported his stance on the war, his right to free speech, and his willingness to stand up for his beliefs.

La Follette spent the bulk of 1918 immersed in the serious illness of his son and eventual successor, Robert M. La Follette Jr. As the interventionists became increasingly disenchanted with the war, especially its rising death toll as well as financial costs, La Follette's position was slowly vindicated. The Senate committee dropped its investigation into La Follette's loyalty, and the Associated Press issued a retraction and apology for its misreporting of the St. Paul speech.

As the war drew to a close, many who had originally denounced La Follette came to recognize that World War I was hardly the war to end all wars as promised by Woodrow Wilson, and congratulated La Follette for his courage, vision, integrity, and steadfast honesty. His efforts to implement meaningful reforms ceased only with his death in 1924.

Nancy C. Unger

See also: Espionage Act (WWI); Isolationism (WWI); Progressivism (WWI); Biographies: Berger, Victor (WWI); Debs, Eugene V. (WWI); Lane, Franklin (WWI); Roosevelt, Theodore (WWI); Wilson, Woodrow (WWI); Documents: Free Speech in Wartime, October 16, 1917

REFERENCES

Amchan, Arthur J. *The Kaiser's Senator: Robert M. La Follette's Alleged Disloyalty During World War I.* Alexandria: Amchan Publications, 1994.

Giffin, Frederick. *Six Who Protested: Radical Opposition to the First World War.* New York: Kennikat, 1977.

Ryley, Thomas. *A Little Group of Willful Men.* New York: National University Publications, 1975.

Unger, Nancy C. *Fighting Bob La Follette: The Righteous Reformer.* Chapel Hill: University of North Carolina Press, 2000.

Lane, Franklin

Franklin Lane (1864–1921) was a Canadian-born lawyer and journalist who served as inter-

state commerce commissioner and secretary of the Interior during the World War I period. After his parents moved to San Francisco, Lane was educated at the University of California, Berkeley and Hastings Law School. Lane decided not enter into a career in law, but rather took a position at the *San Francisco Chronicle* for three years. He then bought the *Tacoma Daily News* in 1891 and used his editorials to support Grover Cleveland and several Progressive reforms. When economic hard times hit the nation, the newspaper business began to fail and Lane was forced to join his brother's law firm.

While in San Francisco, Lane became involved in local politics and helped the effort to ratify a new city charter, which led to his being elected city attorney in three straight elections. Lane ran for governor of California in 1902. He lost even though Republicans had dominated state politics for some time. His failure to secure the position led to a meeting with Theodore Roosevelt. Roosevelt instantly liked Lane and later appointed him to the Interstate Commerce Commission (ICC). This was in 1906, when the Hepburn Act expanded the power of the ICC. Lane was so successful in his time as commissioner that President Taft kept him on the ICC throughout his presidency.

When Woodrow Wilson was inaugurated president, he appointed Lane as secretary of the Interior. The focus of Lane's early administration was the use of natural resources, especially on federal land. Congress assisted his call for action with the passage of the Reclamation Extension Act, the Alaskan Railroad Act, and the Alaskan Coal Leasing Act. All three were issued in 1914. Years later, in 1920, Congress further validated Lane's research findings with the Federal Water Power Act and the General Leasing Act. Lane was also influential in the passage of the National Park Serve Act of 1916 and in the solidification of the Indian Bureau under his command.

Lane supported his president with his World War I policies. He was on the Council of National Defense, which served a publicity function in the administration. Lane also advocated the Versailles Treaty in the Senate, but was never able to be a close advisor to Wilson because of his personality and relationships with opposing party members. Regardless of this, Lane was able to assert himself as a true leader in political movements of the time. In February 1920 he retired from politics to take a high ranking position in the private realm, as vice-president of Pan American Petroleum and Transport Company and Mexican Petroleum Company, which he held until he died in 1921.

Philine Georgette Vega

See also: Council of National Defense (WWI)

REFERENCE

Olson, Keith W. *Biography of a Progressive: Franklin K. Lane, 1864–1921.* Westport, CT: Greenwood Press, 1979.

Lansing, Robert

U.S. secretary of state during World War I, Robert Lansing (1864–1928) was born in Watertown, New York. After being admitted to the New York bar in 1889, he became a junior partner in the law firm of Lansing and Lansing. In 1890 Lansing married Eleanor Foster, whose father was a sophisticated international lawyer and diplomat who exerted considerable influence on Lansing's future career. Lansing served as U.S. counsel on many international arbitration cases. In 1906 he helped organize the American Society for International Law, and in 1907 he contributed to the establish-

ment of the American Journal of International Law. In March 1914, President Woodrow Wilson appointed him as counselor at the State Department. When William Jennings Bryan resigned as secretary of state in the spring of 1915, Wilson appointed Lansing in his place.

Because Lansing believed in a realist and pragmatist approach to international politics, he proposed that the United States should assume a dominant role in the politics in the Western Hemisphere but play a conciliatory role in relations with Japan in the East Asian and Pacific regions. Because Hughes was a hard-line realist, he believed that Germany could not be allowed to emerge as the dominant power in Europe. Consequently, he expected the United States to eventually intervene in World War I, even though Washington was officially declaring its neutrality. Although Wilson was the dominant figure making decisions about American foreign policy, Lansing was successful at persuading Wilson to adopt some of Lansing's views. Wilson accepted Lansing's advice that American citizens and bankers should be allowed to arrange loans for the Allied powers. Wilson also agreed to Lansing's strategy of arming U.S. merchant vessels in 1917.

When the United States entered World War I, Lansing paid much attention to containing Japanese expansionist sentiment toward China. His efforts here culminated in the Lansing-Ishii Agreement of November 1917, which recognized Japan's "special interest" in Manchuria and Inner Mongolia while embracing the American notion of open door principles for maintaining equal economic opportunity for all the nations and China's territorial integrity. The wording of this agreement, however, was so ambiguous that both Japan and the United States could interpret it as they liked. In the short run, the careful phrasing of the Lansing-Ishii Agreement apparently reduced tensions between Japan and the United States, but over the long run, the document's ambiguity served as one of the preconditions for the confrontation that eventually came in the Pacific War.

Lansing participated in the Paris Peace Conference after the end of World War I, but he objected to Wilson's strong commitment to establishing a League of Nations as well as to the Wilsonian notion of universal idealism. During U.S. Senate hearings on the Treaty of Versailles held in the summer of 1919, William C. Bullitt, another member of the U.S. delegation to the Paris Peace Conference, revealed Lansing's serious objections to Wilson's peace settlement terms. Partly because of this incident, Lansing resigned his office in February 1920 and returned to his law practice. After his retirement in 1925, he served as a trustee and later vice-president of the Carnegie Endowment for International Peace.

Yoneyuki Sugita

See also: League of Nations (WWI); Paris Peace Conference (WWI); Biographies: Bryan, William Jennings (WWI); Wilson, Woodrow (WWI)

REFERENCES

Hartig, Thomas H. *Robert Lansing: An Interpretive Biography.* New York: Arno Press, 1982.

Smith, Daniel M. *Robert Lansing and American Neutrality, 1914–1917.* New York: Da Capo Press, 1972.

LaRocca, Nick

A Louisiana-born cornetist and trumpeter who was one of the originators of Dixieland jazz, Nick LaRocca (1889–1961) was born to a New Orleans shoemaker and his wife and taught himself how to play the cornet and trumpet, and then began to play locally. After dropping out of high school, LaRocca joined the Papa Laine Reliance Band in 1912. In 1916, he moved to Chicago, which was becoming famous as a hotbed of jazz. That same year he formed the Original Dixieland Jazz Band, which quickly became successful. The band was asked to play Reisenweber's ballroom in 1917.

The successful performance at the famous musical venue led to record contracts with Columbia and Victor. From 1919 to 1920 the band toured and recorded more records in England. They returned to the United States in July 1920. They achieved more success over the next five years, until LaRocca had a nervous breakdown in 1925. He returned to New Orleans and gave up his music career.

While in his first retirement, LaRocca earned a living as a contractor. After establishing a business in New Orleans, he returned to the music world in July 1936. While his return was met with success, he retired a second and final time from the music industry in 1938. He finished working with his contracting business before he retired from that in 1958. LaRocca died in 1961, with little else known about his life.

Philine Georgette Vega

See also: Jazz (WWI); Music (WWI)

REFERENCE

Brun, H. O. *The Story of the Original Dixieland Jazz Band.* London: Sidgwick and Jackson, 1961.

Laurier, Sir Wilfrid

When war broke out in 1914, Wilfrid Laurier (1841–1919) had been an eloquent defender of liberal principles for the past twenty-seven years as leader of the Liberal party. As prime minister for fifteen of those years, he had emphasized the importance of compromise to maintain national unity between religious and linguistic groups. Although he strongly supported Canadian participation in the war, he inevitably became the leading spokesman against the imposition of conscription for service overseas.

He was first elected to the federal House of Commons in 1874 to represent the riding, or voting district, of Quebec East, and he entered Prime Minister Alexander Mackenzie's cabinet in 1877. He led the Liberal party while it was in the opposition from 1887 until he was elected prime minister in 1896. Some of the most important issues he dealt with as Canadian leader included educational rights for the Francophone and Catholic minorities in the Western provinces, changes to the increasingly important immigration policy, a balanced tariff policy, and the potentially explosive question of relations within the British Empire.

When Britain went to war in South Africa in 1899, Laurier adopted a conciliatory policy. Between Anglophone imperialists seeking a large Canadian contingent and Francophone nationalists seeking no Canadian involvement, he allowed some Canadian volunteers to join British forces. His defeat in 1911 was partly due to the issue of reciprocity with the United States and also due to another division between the two extremes on the imperial question. As Anglophone imperialists sought money for Britain's Royal Navy and Francophone nationalists preferred no navy, Laurier proposed a small Canadian navy, which satisfied neither side as they joined forces to defeat him and the Liberal party.

In August 1914 Conservative leader Robert Borden led a mostly united country to war. Because Canada automatically followed Britain into war, there was no separate Canadian declaration. Laurier supported the policy of participation and encouraged recruitment. He was insistent, however, that Ottawa should never force citizens to fight for Britain—a policy that French-speaking Canadians strongly opposed. Divisions between Francophones and Anglophones intensified in 1916 over Francophone rights in Ontario schools, but the question of conscription for service overseas became the dominant issue in 1917, with Laurier leading the opposition.

As casualties grew, Borden announced in May 1917 that the voluntary system was not yielding the numbers needed to maintain the Canadian army in the field, and he proposed that conscription be applied to ensure the necessary reinforcements. Borden had committed large numbers of Canadians to help Britain, but he was also aware that the more Canada contributed, the more its autonomy in the Empire was being advanced. He sought a coalition, but Laurier was unmoved by the arguments, and in June 1917 Laurier repeated his opposition to the principle of conscription. After Borden introduced his legislation, Laurier suggested an amendment that proposed a referendum on the question, but this was voted down. Reflecting the split throughout the country, many Francophone Conservatives sided with Laurier and many Anglophone Liberals sided with Borden.

The election of December 1917 confirmed the division in Canadian society. Many of the leading Anglophone Liberals joined the Conservatives in a Union government that won 153 seats across the country. The Liberals were limited to 82 seats, with 62 coming from Francophone Quebec, which remained united behind Laurier. Another issue that divided the two parties during the election was the right for women to vote: Borden's government had passed a law granting the vote to wives, widows, mothers, sisters, and daughters of persons serving (or having served) outside Canada in the war. Laurier complained that to limit the female vote this way was unjust discrimination, and he also criticized the removal of the vote for citizens of Canada from enemy countries naturalized after 1902.

Despite Laurier's continued appeals to the principles of liberty and the necessity for compromise to accommodate past promises made to French-speaking Canadians, Borden applied conscription to the end of the war in November 1918. Laurier also appealed to his Francophone followers to remain calm, particularly during riots in Quebec City in March and April 1918. He continued his attempts at rebuilding the Liberal party, calling for Unionist members to return, to his death in February 1919.

John MacFarlane

See also: Conscription (Canada, WWI); Liberal Party (Canada, WWI); Mobilization (Canada, WWI); Biographies: Borden, Robert Laird (WWI)

REFERENCES

Bélanger, Réal. "Wilfrid Laurier," in *Dictionary of Canadian Biography*. Toronto: University of Toronto Press, 2000.

Clippingdale, Richard. *Laurier: His Life and World*. Toronto: McGraw-Hill Ryerson, 1979.

Morton, Desmond. *A Peculiar Kind of Politics: Canada's Overseas Ministry in the First World War*. Toronto: University of Toronto Press, 1982.

Neatby, *H.B. Laurier and a Liberal Quebec: A Study in Political Management*. Toronto: University of Toronto Press, 1956.

Nicholson, G. W. L. *Canadian Expeditionary Force, 1914–19: The Official History of the Canadian Army in the First World War*. Ottawa: Queen's Printer, 1962.

Law, Andrew Bonar

Andrew Bonar Law (1858–1923) was one the shortest serving British prime ministers on record (209 days). His brief time in office (1922–1923) was followed by his death from cancer. Law's limited time in office, combined with his general melancholy and unobtrusive nature, gave him the epithet "the unknown Prime Minister." However, these generalities obscure his wartime partnership with the dynamic Liberal Prime Minister David Lloyd George.

Bonar Law's participation in the First World War is notable for several key achievements that deviated from his prewar political patterns. He became less partisan, and he relegated Ireland and tariff reform to the back burner for the duration of the war. After Britain's entry into the First World War in August 1914, Bonar Law offered a wartime political truce with Asquith's Liberal government. This gesture, while stemming from genuine patriotic impulses, would prove to be a political handicap for Conservatives, who had much to complain about, including the inefficient production of war material. A major crisis erupted in May 1915 when the *Times* published a sensational article by its military correspondent, Colonel Repington, who argued that the recent British failure at the Battle of Neuve Chapelle was due to inadequate production of shells. This Shells Scandal, combined with the resignation of Admiral Jackie Fisher over the Gallipoli expedition, led to the formation of a coalition government between Liberals and Conservatives. Conservatives expected to play a major part in the coalition, but Asquith's craftiness and Law's inability to push himself forward resulted in a Liberal dominated coalition.

Asquith's first coalition did not last, and in December 1916, Law was intimately involved in the formation of a new coalition government.

He supported a plan put forward by Edward Carson, Lloyd George, and others to set up a small war council responsible for controlling the course of the war while leaving Asquith as prime minister. Asquith refused to support this idea and resigned from office in December 1916. Law, as leader of the largest party in the House of Commons, would have been within his rights to form a government. Instead, he became a key partner in the coalition government formed by David Lloyd George.

Under the partnership of Bonar Law and David Lloyd George, Britain was given the political leadership it needed to triumph in the First World War. The general public at the time and historians ever since point to David Lloyd George's strengths as a wartime leader, with his soaring rhetoric, radical creation of a small war cabinet, and presidential style of leadership. What is often forgotten is how important Bonar Law was in making Lloyd George's unorthodox leadership style work.

Law made three principal wartime contributions. First, he served as the official political manager of the coalition: In his role as leader in the House of Commons, he kept a predominantly Conservative coalition firmly behind a formerly radical Liberal.

Second, Law was a foil to Lloyd George's more exuberant flights of fancy. The two men met daily to work out issues, and Lloyd George came to respect Law's cautious assessments of his wilder ideas. With Lloyd George's dynamism combined with Bonar Law's inherent conservatism, the two formed what Stanley Baldwin described as "the most perfect partnership in political history."

Third, Law ran a complex department as chancellor of the exchequer and brought forth two important wartime budgets, in which Britain raised a larger percentage of wartime expenses from revenue than any other combatant nation (although Law still kept income taxes for the highest incomes below 50%). He also supported the public subscription of long-term war loans. This move was opposed by the Treasury but turned out to be a stunning success.

The general election of December 1918 formed the last major wartime political contribution of Law. He fully accepted Lloyd George's analysis that the coalition should continue in the immediate aftermath of war and believed that Lloyd George played a key role in maintaining national unity and should have a fresh mandate in a postwar election. In the ensuing election, the Lloyd George coalition triumphed and was again dominated by Conservatives.

Bonar Law's wartime political contributions were crucial. He helped ensure that Lloyd George became prime minister. He prevented outright party strife from undermining the British war effort despite the acrimonious party relations that had existed before August 1914. Within the Lloyd George coalition, he acted as a force of stability and a political manager as well as running the Treasury. He also kept the Conservative Party together and would return in 1922 as its leader after it left the Lloyd George coalition. He suffered considerable personal tragedy; the First World War led to the death of two of his sons in military service. Despite these accomplishments and sacrifices, Bonar Law's refusal to put himself forward is most noticeable. Under both Asquith and Lloyd George, he was content to play the lesser role. Although this may have been understandable once the Lloyd George coalition was created, it was less understandable under Asquith. Bonar Law's personal reticence to put himself forward caused serious strains in the Conservative Party before December 1916 and may have not helped the overall British war effort.

Matthew Hendley

See also: Liberal Party (UK, WWI); Biographies: Asquith, Herbert (WWI); Lloyd George, David (WWI)

REFERENCES

Adams, R. J. Q. *Bonar Law.* Palo Alto, CA: Stanford University Press, 1999.
Blake, Robert. *The Unknown Prime Minister.* London: Eyre and Spottiswoode, 1955.

Lindsay, Vachel

It is easy for contemporary critics to minimize and even to dismiss the contributions of Vachel Lindsay (1879–1931) to American literature. His celebration of American rural life and traditional American values and his reliance on conventional poetic forms and techniques have made his poetry seem more dated than the works of his contemporaries with whom he has been most commonly grouped: Edgar Lee Masters, Edwin Arlington Robinson, and Carl Sandburg. Collectively, these poets became known as the "village school." The poems of Masters and Robinson, in particular, characteristically explore the debilitating effects of small-town life, providing a poetic corollary to the fictions of Sherwood Anderson and Sinclair Lewis. In contrast, Lindsay's work seems more sentimentally affirmative in the mode of the novels of Booth Tarkington and the paintings of Norman Rockwell.

Nonetheless, a case can be made that Lindsay did more than any poet of his generation to popularize a modern attitude toward poetry and that, like Sandburg, he demonstrated how folk materials could be effectively integrated into formal poetry. Furthermore, in his fascination with African American and Native American culture, Lindsay anticipated the emphasis on multiculturalism in American poetry of the last quarter century. In his attention to the oral qualities of poetry and his popularizing of public readings, he also is a notable forerunner of the current generation of performance poets.

Born in Springfield, Illinois, Lindsay grew up in an affluent but religiously strict household. His father was a physician and expected his son to follow him into the profession. Although Lindsay did study medicine for three years at Hiram College, he was simply not cut out to be a physician. He transferred to the Chicago Art Institute and then to the New York School of Art, but after half a decade of study, he was no closer to being a promising painter than he had been to being a physician. While working as a museum guide, he discovered that he had a gift for public speaking, and when he returned to Springfield, he began to lecture on American art and culture at the local Y.M.C.A.

Over the next decade, Lindsay also began to undertake long walking tours of one section after another of rural America. Although later admirers often characterized these walking tours as idyllic sojourns across bucolic landscapes, Lindsay himself described them as sometimes arduous tests of his ability to survive and of his commitment to his new vocation as a poet. In fact, he aimed on these walking tours to hone his own skills as a poet and to revitalize poetry as a broadly popular American genre. He gradually came to see himself as a distinctly American bard in the Whitmanesque tradition. What he experienced of America not only worked its way into his poems but also was chronicled in immensely popular prose accounts of his travels.

Sympathetic to Progressive causes, Lindsay nonetheless enlisted in the army when the United States entered World War I. His poems and prose of the period reflect his ambivalence toward America's and his own involvement in the war. Subsequently, his influence as a poet gradually leveled off and then declined.

Lindsay's most notable books of poetry are *Rhymes to Be Traded for Bread* (1912), *"General William Booth Enters into Heaven" and Other Poems* (1913), *"The Congo" and Other Poems* (1914), *"The Chinese Nightingale" and Other Poems* (1917), and *The Golden Whales of California and Other Rhymes in the American Language* (1920).

Martin Kich

See also: Literature (U.S., WWI)

REFERENCES

Bates, David W. "Lindsay's 'The Congo.'" *Explicator* 47 (Winter 1989): 44–45.

Engler, Balz. "Vachel Lindsay and the Town of American Visions." *Literature in Performance* 3 (November 1982): 27–34.

Gray, Paul H. "Performance and the Bardic Ambition of Vachel Lindsay." *Text and Performance Quarterly* 9 (July 1989): 216–223.

Guillory, Dan. "Tramping across America: The Travel Writings of Vachel Lindsay." *Midamerica: The Yearbook of the Society for the Study of Midwestern Literature* 27 (2000): 59–65.

Hallwas, John E., and Dennis J. Reader, eds. *The Vision of This Land: Studies of Vachel Lindsay, Edgar Lee Masters, and Carl Sandburg.* Macomb, IL: Western Illinois University Press, 1976.

Harris, Mark. *City of Discontent: An Interpretive Biography of Vachel Lindsay, Being Also the Story of Springfield, Illinois, USA, and of the Love of the Poet for That City, That State and That Nation.* Indianapolis, IN: Bobbs-Merrill, 1952.

Hummer, T. R. "Laughed Off: Canon, Kharakter, and the Dismissal of Vachel Lindsay." *Kenyon Review* 17 (Spring 1995): 56–96.

Massa, Ann. *Vachel Lindsay: Fieldworker for the American Dream.* Bloomington: Indiana University Press, 1970.

Masters, Edgar Lee. *Vachel Lindsay, a Poet in America.* New York: Scribner's, 1935.

Ruggles, Eleanor. *The West-Going Heart.* New York: Norton, 1959.

Taylor, Marjorie A. "Vachel Lindsay and the Ghost of Abraham Lincoln." *Centennial Review* 22 (1978): 110–117.

Wentworth, Michael. "'A Walk through the Paradise Garden': Vachel Lindsay's Idea of Kansas in Adventures while Preaching the Gospel of Beauty." *Midamerica: The Yearbook of the Society for the Study of Midwestern Literature* 20 (1993): 26–39.

Wesling, Donald. "What the Canon Excludes: Lindsay and American Bardic." *Michigan Quarterly Review* 21 (Summer 1982): 479–485.

Lippmann, Walter

A journalist, an author, and a political insider and advisor to Woodrow Wilson, Walter Lippmann (1889–1974) helped draft the Fourteen Points of Peace Program and the League of Nations covenant.

Lippmann was born in New York City. After graduating from Harvard University, where he became a Socialist, Lippmann worked for the muckraking journalist Lincoln Steffens. In the 1912 elections, Lippmann supported Theodore Roosevelt and the Progressive Party. In 1914 Lippmann helped found the *New Republic* magazine. In the 1916 elections, Lippmann campaigned for Woodrow Wilson, whose cabinet he joined as an assistant to the secretary of war. During World War I, Lippmann urged Wilson to create a government news agency that would advertise the war as making the world "safe for democracy." Lippmann designed the plans for an enormous clearinghouse to disseminate government information about the war effort: the Committee on Public Information (CPI), which mobilized communication specialists from all fields to shape public opin-

journalistic practices, and how the public uses stereotypes to understand the social world. In 1931 the New York *Herald Tribune* hired Lippmann to write a thrice-weekly column, "Today and Tomorrow," which was the nation's first analytical news column; hugely influential, it ran in syndication for more than thirty years.

Tony Osborne

See also: Censorship (WWI); Committee on Public Information (WWI); Intellectuals (WWI); Journalism (U.S., WWI); Propaganda (U.S., WWI); Biographies: Lippmann, Walter (WWII)

REFERENCES

Lippmann, Walter. *Public Opinion.* New York: Simon and Schuster, 1997.
Steel, Ronald. *Walter Lippmann and the American Century.* New York: Vintage Books, 1999.

Journalist and political advisor Walter Lippmann helped President Woodrow Wilson draft his Fourteen Points, a set of principles to establish peace and global order in the wake of World War I. (Library of Congress)

ion. Lippmann called this activity "manufacturing consent."

Lippmann drew upon his wartime experience to question the average citizen's role in democratic governance. He argued that public opinion is easily manipulated and thus contains no inherent wisdom, so an elite group of professionals should govern. Lippmann also criticized journalism for failing to fulfill its role in a democratic society: the public was ill served by newspapers simply offering facts devoid of any interpretive context. He called for a more scientific approach to journalism that aimed for the ideal of objectivity.

In 1922, Lippmann published his most influential book, *Public Opinion,* which examined

Lloyd, Harold

Along with Charlie Chaplin and Buster Keaton, Harold Lloyd (1893–1971) was one of the best-known comedic actors of the silent-film era. Extremely prolific (at one point he made a film every week), Lloyd was financially more successful than his fellow comedians, out grossing both Chaplin and Keaton. His most well-known character climbed the outside of a skyscraper and clung to a clock. This unprecedented stunt and Lloyd's plucky spirit made him a hit with audiences in the prosperous 1920s.

Lloyd was born in Burchard, Nebraska. His first performance was in theater, in a production of *Macbeth.* At the age of twelve, he appeared in *Tess of the D'Urbervilles* and thereafter was often employed as a child actor. In high school in San Diego, California, Lloyd played the lead in school plays and was employed in a variety of positions at local theaters. He had his first film role in 1912, working as an extra.

Lloyd moved to Los Angeles in 1913 and snuck onto the Universal Pictures lot. During 1913 and 1914, he hung around the lot looking for work, occasionally working as an extra. There, he met Hal Roach, who founded a production company in 1915 and hired Lloyd as his lead actor for $3 a day. They made a series of one-reel movies featuring Lloyd as "Willie Work" and "Lonesome Luke." Luke, a spin-off of Chaplin's "Little Tramp," was the focus of more than one hundred ten-minute silent pictures. The slapstick films were completely improvised and usually ended with Lloyd being chased by something silly and out-of-control.

In 1917, Lloyd developed what became his trademark character, a young man of average dress and build who could not be deterred from achieving success. Known as "Glasses" because of his distinctive horn-rims, the character was an instant hit with 1920's audiences. Lloyd's daredevil comedy style showcased the lengths the character would go to for success. One of the most indelible images of silent film is Lloyd hanging from the hands of a clock on a skyscraper in his attempt to "break in" to the business world in *Safety Last* (1923). Lloyd performed all his own stunts and lost a finger and thumb in a prop accident in 1919.

For five years Lloyd made a movie every week, writing the jokes and plots, directing, and starring. Films that came out of that era included *Doctor Jack* (1923), *Why Worry* (1923), *The Freshman* (1925), *For Heaven's Sake* (1926), *The Kid Brother* (1927), and *Speedy* (1928). Lloyd made his first "talking" picture, *Welcome Danger,* in 1929 and went on to appear in five others between 1930 and 1938. But the advent of sound in movies marked the end of Lloyd's career. He was also a victim of the Great Depression; the optimistic Glasses character was simply less popular with audiences. Lloyd retired from acting in 1947 and failed at an attempted comeback in 1950 with a sequel to *The Freshman, Mad Wednesday.*

Lloyd married Mildred Davis, his costar in *Why Worry,* in 1923, and they had three children. A 1927 *Variety* ranking of the twenty wealthiest members of the entertainment industry featured Lloyd as the only actor, due to shrewd investments and a tireless work ethic. Lloyd spent the 1950s and 1960s appearing at film festivals and was an active member of the Masons. He received an honorary Academy Award in 1952. Lloyd died in Los Angeles on March 8, 1971.

Melissa Stallings

See also: Film (UK, WWI)

REFERENCES

Dardis, Tom. *Harold Lloyd: The Man on the Clock.* New York: Viking Press, 1983.

Lloyd, Harold. *An American Comedy.* New York: Dover Publications, 1928, 1971.

Reilly, Adam. *Harold Lloyd: The King of Daredevil Comedy.* New York: Collier Books, 1977.

Schickel, Richard. *Harold Lloyd: The Shape of Laughter.* Boston: New York Graphic Society, 1974.

Lloyd George, David

No British politician in the First World War has been more controversial than David Lloyd George (1863–1945). Before 1914 he had built a strong reputation as a crusading radical Liberal opposition MP and minister. The First World War transformed Lloyd George's career. He would reorganize the munitions industry

Liberal Party leader David Lloyd George replaced Horatio Herbert Kitchener as British secretary of state for war upon the latter's death in 1916. In that position, George helped organize Britain's war effort. (Library of Congress)

have foreseen that David Lloyd George would be the man to help lead the country to victory. To the public, Lloyd George was a radical with an antiwar reputation and a passion for domestic reform. During the Boer War of 1899–1902, Lloyd George, then an opposition MP from rural Wales, won fame as pro-Boer. He was neither a pacifist nor an anti-imperialist but opposed the official rationale of the war. He felt the Boer War was not about defending the rights of English settlers in the Transvaal but was an attempt to bully a small nation. Before World War I, Lloyd George concentrated on domestic issues. His first ministerial position was as president of the Board of Trade from 1905–1908. Lloyd George's largest prewar achievements were as chancellor of the exchequer in the Liberal government of H. H. Asquith. He implemented noncontributory old-age pensions in 1908. His 1909 budget shifted the major source of government revenue from indirect to direct taxation and made income tax progressive based on income. In 1911, Lloyd George launched an ambitious scheme of insurance against illness and unemployment (the National Insurance Acts). In 1913, Lloyd George continued his radical initiatives with his Land Campaign, which attempted to limit the powers of rural landowners and create a better deal for agricultural workers and renters.

Lloyd George's greatest successes in the First World War before becoming prime minister came in providing financial stability, increasing production, and harnessing the industrial and financial might of Britain to the war effort. Lloyd George's initial wartime achievements, though substantial, pale in comparison to his year-long period as minister of munitions. In this post, his genius for innovation was triumphantly put on display. Lloyd George was given this position when Asquith was forced to form a wartime coalition in May 1915 with the

and eventually rise to become prime minister of a broad-based coalition. Lloyd George's government would undertake a number of vital innovations but was largely unable to alter the grand strategy of the war. Lloyd George's most important contributions to Britain's success in the First World War lay in his strong understanding of the need to sustain morale on the home front and his willingness to innovate whenever necessary. His failures during the war were most closely linked to his indirect methods.

When Britain began to consider entry into a continental war in late July 1914, few would

Conservatives. One of the issues leading to the formation of this coalition was a scandal that had arisen over inadequate shell production. Despite Lloyd George's efforts as chancellor, it was clear that the unprecedented scale of warfare on the Western Front was placing unbearable demands on existing British arms manufacturers. Lloyd George brought in large numbers of action-minded assistants to the new Ministry, including private businessmen such as Eric Geddes. Lloyd George divided the country into ten areas of production and gave each one a board of management. He held regular talks with private arms producers about increasing production and had more than sixty "national" shells and explosive factories built with state funding. By almost any measure of war efficiency, Lloyd George's tenure as minister of munitions was a triumph. Between May 1915 and July 1916, British production of shells had increased by 1,500 percent and machine gun production by 500 percent.

After successfully tackling the problem of munitions production, Lloyd George served as minister of war (July 1916 to December 1916), replacing Lord Kitchener. Kitchener had proved incompetent and many of his original duties as minister of war had been taken away from him. Such a reduced role did not suit the frenetic energies of Lloyd George. Although Lloyd George had definite strategic ideas of his own, he was unable to implement them. His only positive accomplishments while minister of war was to reorganize transport services for the British Army in France and Mesopotamia and to reinforce public commitment to the war effort.

Lloyd George's most important political position during the First World War was prime minister. He served as leader of a coalition government from December 1916 until October 1922. His postwar conduct, including his role in negotiating the Versailles Treaty, has not helped his historical reputation. However, during the First World War he was the man of the moment and his rise to the premiership was a vital ingredient in Britain's victory.

The maneuverings behind the emergence of Lloyd George as prime minister were complex. His first idea was to set up a small War Committee that would make the major decisions for the war. Lloyd George would be chairman but Asquith would remain as prime minister and could attend its meetings. Asquith was receptive to this idea at first but soon changed his mind. In a complicated series of events, Lloyd George resigned from office and was soon followed by Asquith. Lloyd George was able to create a new coalition government, which consisted mainly of Conservatives but also contained Labour Party figures and about half the Liberal Party. On December 7, 1916, David Lloyd George became prime minister and would remain so through the end of the First World War.

As Prime Minister, Lloyd George launched a series of major changes to Britain's wartime government. His regime was more efficient and businesslike in its conduct of war matters. His government also noted several major successes in keeping up public morale and launching wartime reforms. He was much less successful at challenging the entrenched position of the generals and making any notable changes to wartime grand strategy.

It is undeniable that Lloyd George made major alterations to the traditional form of British parliamentary government during the First World War. The most immediate change was his creation of a War Cabinet. Rather than a complementary decision-making structure to normal cabinet government, Lloyd George's War Cabinet replaced it. It had five permanent members (as opposed to Asquith's cabinet of twenty-three members) who met daily. Lloyd George set up new Ministries for Labour, Food, and Shipping and built up his own secretariat beyond the regular Civil Service. Ultimately, Parliament had the ability to make or unmake his administration. Lloyd George's reorganization of the wartime government gave a firmer lead to wartime decision making and gave the appearance of vigorous leadership at the highest levels.

Lloyd George's biggest wartime policy successes were on the home front. Due to his experience as chancellor of the exchequer and minister of munitions, he realized that Britain had to do more than send endless streams of soldiers to the Western Front. British industry and finance had an important role to play in any allied victory. Consequently, the British people had to be fully engaged in the war effort and resources had to be marshaled with maximum efficiency. To accomplish this, industrial production had to continue, food had to be allocated fairly, and manpower had to be used properly. For the most part Lloyd George succeeded in these areas. Lloyd George implemented a wide-scale system of food subsidies in 1917 and rationing by 1918, which ensured that the majority of the population was fed properly and fairly. He tried to keep the trade unions happy by avoiding industrial conscription and consulting widely with trade union leaders. As industrial unrest grew in 1917, Lloyd George appointed a number of commissions to inquire into the reasons for unrest, which mostly revolved around issues such as food, wages and exemptions from military service.

One of Lloyd George's most important realizations as prime minister was the need to offer reforms to the hard-pressed British people. The sacrifices of the First World War were total, and consequently the British people needed something to justify these sacrifices and give them hope for the future. Lloyd George fulfilled these hopes in the realms of education

and electoral reform with the Education Act of 1918 and the Representation of the People Act of 1918. The Education Act increased educational opportunities by making education compulsory up to age 14 and proposing a system of lifelong education from nursery school through adult education classes. The Representation of the People Act was an even greater success. It came about due to Britain's strict system of voter registration. If unchanged, this system would have disenfranchised all serving soldiers and most munitions workers. An interparty conference led by the Speaker of the House of Commons tackled this thorny issue in 1916 and began also to consider an extension of the franchise and other issues. The final act was extremely wide ranging. For the first time ever, some women were given the vote, conscientious objectors were disenfranchised, and all men over twenty-one were given the vote. This reform tripled the prewar franchise and ushered Britain into an age of mass democracy.

Lloyd George did make some positive military changes as prime minister, such as helping Britain implement a convoy system. In April 1917, Germany had declared unrestricted submarine warfare and was attempting to starve Britain into submission. Individual merchantmen sailing alone were being sunk with impunity by the Germans. The Admiralty was reluctant to embrace the solution of sailing multiple merchant ships in convoys with naval protection. Ultimately, Lloyd George helped force the issue and with the use of convoys, shipping losses fell considerably.

The German offensive of spring 1918, which is now understood to be the last gasp of the Kaiser's Army, was not Lloyd George's finest hour. After the massive British losses at Passchendaele, Lloyd George had resolved to reduce the number of soldiers available for the British generals to sacrifice. With America entering into the war, a defensive holding strategy was required. When the Austrians and Germans launched a successful attack on Italy in October 1917, Lloyd George sent four British divisions to assist the Italians. He also reduced the flow of British troops to Flanders while British troops took on more of the Allied line. Unfortunately for him, these indirect methods almost led to a German success. In May 1918, General Maurice wrote a letter to the British press challenging Lloyd George's claim that the Western Front had more British troops on January 1, 1918, than on January 1, 1917. Lloyd George transformed the matter into one of political confidence and with a deft speech in the House of Commons, deflected attention away from the main accusation. Although he won the debate and survived politically, he had distorted the truth considerably. For the election of December 1918, supporters of the coalition were deemed to be those who had voted for the government during the Maurice debate.

After the failure of the spring 1918 offensive and the arrival of American troops in large numbers, the tide of the war turned. By November 1918, the German Army had been forced out of large areas of Belgium and France. At this point, Germany had a revolution and its new government requested an armistice. When the armistice began on November 11, 1918, Lloyd George was acclaimed by all. In December 1918, he would lead his coalition government to a tremendous general election victory. In the afterglow of the armistice, Lloyd George was known as the "man who won the war." The postwar years would tarnish the luster of Lloyd George and he resigned as prime minister in October 1922, never to hold ministerial office again.

Lloyd George was crucial to the British war effort. He made major contributions in increasing munitions production, ensuring the full utilization of Britain's industrial and financial might, and keeping up public morale. As prime minister, his reorganization of British government was a major innovation and he did not neglect questions of social and electoral reform in wartime. However, to claim that Lloyd George "won the war" is misleading. He was unsuccessful in altering the basic grand strategy of the war and in some ways made things worse. Due to his uncertain political position he never launched a full-scale shake-up of British high command or a major redeployment of troops. His addiction to indirect methods helped make the German spring 1918 breakthrough possible and almost led to his political defeat in the Maurice Debate of 1918. Ultimately, Lloyd George helped Britain survive the war. Britain had never experienced a conflict of this severity before. Lloyd George's genius for innovation and ear for public morale helped Britain survive the onslaught without a major military breakdown (as in France and Russia) or political revolution (as in Russia, Germany, and Austria-Hungary). Lloyd George may not have single-handedly won the war, but his leadership ensured that Britain would emerge victorious without experiencing catastrophic upheaval.

Matthew Hendley

See also: Liberal Party (UK, WWI); Mobilization (UK, WWI); Biographies: Asquith, Herbert (WWI); Haig, Douglas (WWI); Kitchener, Horatio Herbert (WWI)

REFERENCES

Adams, R. J. Q. *Arms and the Wizard: Lloyd George and the Ministry of Munitions, 1915–1916.* College Station, TX: Texas A and M University Press, 1978.

Gilbert, Martin. *The First World War.* Toronto: Stoddart, 1994.

Grigg, John. *Lloyd George: From Peace to War, 1912–1916.* Berkeley: University of California Press, 1985.

Gullace, Nicoletta. *The Blood of Our Sons: Men,*

Women and the Renegotiation of British Citizenship during the Great War. New York: Palgrave Macmillan, 2002.

Keynes, John Maynard. "Mr. Lloyd George: A Fragment" in *Essays in Biography.* New York: Norton, 1951.

Pugh, Martin. *Lloyd George.* New York: Longman, 1988.

Lodge, Henry Cabot

Born into a prominent Boston family, Henry Cabot Lodge (1850–1924) led, as Senate majority leader, the forces in opposition to U.S. membership in the League of Nations. He attended Harvard University and Harvard Law School, eventually earning a doctorate and a law degree. During his youth in Boston, he became acquainted with Francis Parkman and Henry Adams, some of America's most prominent historians, and developed an affinity for the study of history. Early in his career he taught history at Harvard and edited *The North American Review* and the *International Review.* His twenty-six books included biographies of his ancestor George Cabot and luminaries of American history, such as Alexander Hamilton, George Washington, and Daniel Webster. With Theodore Roosevelt, he co-wrote *Hero Tales from American History.*

In 1880 he embarked on his public career by serving in the Massachusetts House of Representatives. Seven years later, he began the first of his three terms in the U. S. House of Representatives. Afterward, he was elected to the Senate and he served as a Republican senator from Massachusetts from 1893 until his death. In government, as in history, Lodge was a committed nationalist, who favored American expansion, a strong government, and a strong military, as had his heroes. Throughout his political career he remained close to Theodore Roosevelt, helping Roosevelt secure writing assignments, and later advancing Roosevelt's political career, particularly by helping to secure the position of assistant secretary of the navy for Roosevelt in President William McKinley's first administration. Only in 1912 would the two great friends part ways, when Roosevelt bolted the Republican Party to run for president on the Progressive ticket.

During his tenure in the Senate, Lodge distinguished himself as a staunch supporter of American overseas expansion and of the Spanish-American War and as an aggressive advocate of his concept of America's national interest. He later became the great opponent of Democratic President Woodrow Wilson. His battle with Woodrow Wilson came after the First World War, when Lodge, in his capacity as Senate majority leader, led the fight to keep the United States out of the League of Nations. Lodge's defeat of Wilson in the fight over the League humiliated the president and dealt a bitter blow to Wilson's pretensions as an international statesman. Late in his Senate career, he also restricted immigration by helping to pass the National Origins Act of 1924, and helped to keep the United States out of the World Court. Lodge died in 1924.

Mitchell McNaylor

See also: Isolationism (WWI); League of Nations (WWI); Republican Party (WWI); Biographies: Roosevelt, Theodore (WWI); Wilson, Woodrow (WWI); Documents: Against League of Nations, August 12, 1919

REFERENCES

Garraty, John Arthur. *Henry Cabot Lodge: A Biography.* New York: Alfred A. Knopf, 1953.

Lodge, Henry Cabot, ed. *Selections from the Correspon-*

dence of Theodore Roosevelt and Henry Cabot Lodge, 1884–1918. 2 vols. New York: Charles Scribner's Sons, 1925.

Lodge, Henry Cabot, ed. *The Senate and the League of Nations.* New York: Charles Scribner's Sons, 1925.

Widenor, William C. *Henry Cabot Lodge and the Search for an American Foreign Policy.* Berkeley: University of California Press, 1980.

Zimmermann, Warren. *First Great Triumph: How Five Americans Made Their Country a World Power.* New York: Farrar, Straus and Giroux, 2002.

Loew, Marcus

The founder of Metro-Goldwyn-Mayer (MGM), Marcus Loew (1870–1927) was born to Herman Loew and Ida Sichel, poor Jewish immigrants from Austria. He had to give up schooling at the age of six to support his family by becoming a newspaper hawker. He took up odd jobs such as working in a map-making plant, hand-printing sheets, and selling furs. He was highly ambitious and had a fascination for theaters. Carefully husbanding his savings, Loew was able to buy into penny arcades, or amusement halls that featured nickelodeons, or projectors which showed films to a single viewer, usually in league with partners. By the early 1900s, he was on his own, in sole possession of a number of penny arcades.

Exhibiting a marketing flavor in celebrating his thirty-fourth birthday, he gave free tickets to anyone having the same name as Marcus. Thus the foundation of the country's largest theater chain started. *The People's Vaudeville Company* became the world's fourth largest movie chain. The business spread rapidly to Boston, Philadelphia, and New York. He owned arcades in New York and the Penny Hippodrome, Cincinnati.

The motion picture industry was slowly picking up in the United States because of the entrepreneurial acumen of Marcus Loew and other Jewish immigrants, such as Adolph Zukor, Louis B. Mayer, and Samuel Goldwyn. *Loew's Theatrical Enterprises* was created in 1912. Loew became the owner of four hundred theaters spread across the country. With a capacity of 2,149, the *Loew's Yonge Street Theatre,* the largest theater in America up to that time, was opened to the public on December 15, 1913. After two months, an upper story was added, increasing seating by 1,410 people.

With an economic boom due to the outbreak of the First World War, important developments were taking place in the American movie industry. The European movie market was almost wiped out. Moviemakers were moving to the west coast, and by 1915, Los Angeles was producing about 60 percent of American films. With the increased profit, theaters became more luxurious. The development of the Hollywood star system created an aura of glamour. With singers, dancers, vaudeville performers, and newsreels, Loew's theaters were a source of mass entertainment. For production, a factory-like system became the norm for studios and mergers were occurring. By the end of the war, Loew's company was known as *Lowe's Incorporated.* He purchased the Metro Movie Studio in 1920. With assets of $25 million, he set up the premier studio, Metro-Goldwyn-Mayer (MGM) in 1924 out of business mergers with Metro Pictures (1915), Goldwyn Pictures Corporation (1917), and the Louis B. Mayer Pictures Company (1918).

He died on September 28, 1927, while constructing some new theaters. His sons, Arthur M. Loew and David L. Loew, followed in their father's business. *Loews Cineplex Entertainment,* set up in 1998, became one of the world's largest motion picture companies.

Patit P. Mishra

See also: Film (U.S., WWI); Theater (WWI); Biographies: Zukor, Adolph (WWI)

REFERENCES

Alleman, Richard. *The Movie Lover's Guide to Hollywood.* New York: Harper and Row, 1985.

Bowser, Eileen. *The Transformation of Cinema, 1907–1915.* New York: Scribner, 1990.

Everson, William K. *American Silent Film.* New York: Da Capo Press, 1998.

M

Man o' War

Bred by August Belmont from two famous racers, Fair Play and Muhubah, Man o' War—a leading race horse of the World War I era—was foaled on March 29, 1917. Concerned about the war and his coming participation in it, Belmont sold the colt at the 1918 Saratoga Yearling sale to Samuel Riddle for the bargain price of $5,000. Riddle, advised by his trainer Louis Festal, had high hopes for the product of two famous bloodlines, and debuted his find at Belmont in June 1919. Man o' War not only won at Belmont, but easily took the field at the Keene Memorial Stakes days later, then at Jamaica Park's Youthful Stakes eleven days after that. Despite being weighted with a record 130 pounds of jockey and gear, he continued to win, first the Hudson Stakes at the Aqueduct racetrack and then both the Tremont Stakes and the United States Hotel Stakes at Saratoga Springs, New York.

On August 13, 1919, however, Man o' War lost the Sanford Memorial Stakes at Belmont, suffering from a bad start (starting gates were not yet used, and Man o' War was facing backward when the race began), but performing with such power and effort that trainers and spectators knew the race had not really been won by Upset, first finisher, achieving the distinction of the only horse to beat Man o' War. This loss, however, was quickly redeemed by victories in a string of important races, including the Grand Union Hotel Stakes. In 1919, Man o' War experienced a growth spurt from 907 to 1,150 pounds, promising even more strength and endurance. Riddle and Feustal declined to enter their horse in the Kentucky Derby, preferring to train for the Preakness, which he won by a length and a half. Continuing to set American speed records in his next races (2:40: 4/5 for 1 5/8 miles), it became apparent that few owners wished to run their horses against Man o' War. However, his ferocious racing style had begun to exact a toll on his leg tendons.

The most worrisome argument for retirement came at the Kenilworth Park Gold Cup in 1920, where Festal learned that a saboteur had attempted to cut Man o' War's stirrups in an attempt to unseat his jockey. Anxious about other threats and possible damage from further racing, Riddle chose to retire his champion, declining match races for as much as $50,000. In an astonishing three-year racing career, Man o' War had been defeated only once, but had never raced in Kentucky, the heartland of American thoroughbred racing. Instead, Man o' War retired on January 7, 1921, and lived a quiet life as stud at Riddle's farm in Kentucky until his death at age thirty on November 1, 1947. His descendants, including War Admiral, Battleship, and Seabiscuit, form a dynasty of unrivaled speed and championship in American horse racing.

Margaret Sankey

REFERENCES

Anderson, C. W. *Horse of the Century: Man o' War.* New York: Macmillan, 1970.

Duke, Jacqueline, ed. *Thoroughbred Champions: Top 100 Racehorses of the 20th Century.* Lexington, KY: The Blood Horse, Inc., 1999.

Longrigg, Roger. *The History of Horse Racing.* New York: Stein and Day, 1972.

McAdoo, William

William McAdoo (1863–1941) served as Woodrow Wilson's secretary of the treasury before becoming a U.S. senator. Early in his treasury tenure, he set up a farm loan program and shaped the Federal Reserve Board's role in overseeing the nation's banking system. During World War I, McAdoo distributed loans to European powers, created the U.S. Shipping Board, administered the government's temporary takeover of the railroad industry, and promoted the Liberty Loan campaigns to pay for the war's expenses. In the Senate, he was a New Deal Democrat specializing in banking and financial issues.

McAdoo rose to prominence as an attorney and railroad executive in Tennessee. In 1889, he founded the Knoxville Street Railway Company, producing one of the first electrified street car lines. After moving to New York to sell railroad bonds, he started the Hudson and Manhattan Railway Company, which financed and constructed two underwater tunnels connecting New Jersey to the Manhattan subway system. Otherwise known as the Tubes, the McAdoo Tunnels opened to customers in 1909.

A well-known businessman, McAdoo supported Woodrow Wilson in his campaign for New Jersey governor in 1910. Two years later, as the vice-chairman of the Democratic National Committee, he helped direct Wilson's successful White House race. Once in office, the new president nominated McAdoo secretary of the Treasury, in part because McAdoo had no strong allegiance to Wall Street interests. The two men became father- and son-in-law in 1914 when McAdoo, then a widower, married Wilson's daughter, Eleanor.

In 1913, McAdoo worked with Senator Carter Glass to create the Federal Reserve System to support the nation's lending institutions. Glass wanted regional banks to be both owned and controlled by private bankers, but McAdoo favored a public organization. Wilson agreed to a compromise; the banks would be privately owned but supervised by a publicly appointed Federal Reserve Board.

After the onset of World War I in 1914, German submarine attacks made traveling through European waters hazardous and expensive. To preserve American trade, McAdoo proposed legislation allowing the U.S. government to regulate shipping rates, as well as construct and operate its own merchant vessels. The U.S. Shipping Board, created in 1916, maintained transatlantic trade throughout the war. McAdoo set up a similar program for railroads, placing the industry and its workers under federal control to ensure the transport of military equipment and personnel. The controversial measure, favored by government Progressives, was rescinded after the war ended. McAdoo paid for U.S. war expenses through higher taxes and the more popular Liberty Loan program. Inspired by patriotism and a major publicity campaign, American citizens eagerly bought the Treasury Department's gold savings bonds, contributing several billion dollars to the war effort.

At the close of the war, McAdoo resigned as secretary of the Treasury but remained active in Democratic politics. In 1924, he ran for president, but failed to win the nomination after a close primary race. From 1933–1939, he served in the U.S. Senate, where he worked closely with President Franklin Roosevelt to craft the New Deal's economic policies.

Jane Armstrong Hudiburg

See also: Banking and Finance (WWI), Federal Reserve (WWI); War Bonds (WWI); Biographies: Glass, Carter (WWI); Wilson, Woodrow (WWI)

REFERENCES

Broesamle, John J. *William Gibbs McAdoo: A Passion for Change, 1863–1917*. Port Washington, NY: Kennikat Press, 1973.

Kerr, K. Austin. "Decision for Federal Control: Wilson, McAdoo, and the Railroads, 1917." *Journal of American History* 54 (December 1967): 550–560.

Prude, James C. "Notes and Documents: William Gibbs McAdoo and the Democratic National Convention of 1924." *Journal of Southern History* 38 (November 1972): 621–628.

McClung, Nellie

Canadian women's activist Nellie Letitia Mooney (1873–1951) was born to Methodist John Mooney and Scottish Presbyterian Letitia McCurdy, near Chatsworth, Ontario. The family moved to their Millford, Manitoba, homestead on May 4, 1880. Since her prairie childhood, the feisty, explicitly forthright McClung never accepted the status quo. She would hate sexual inequality and the effects of alcohol on society her entire life. Formally schooled only from age ten to sixteen, her top entrance marks allowed attendance at the Normal School, from July 1889 to 1890. McClung began her teaching career in 1890 in a one-room schoolhouse and taught for five years.

McClung's teaching career ended when she married pharmacist Robert Wesley McClung on August 25, 1896. They had five children. Throughout their marriage, he firmly supported all her endeavors.

McClung wrote a best-seller, *Sowing Seeds in Danny* in 1908, based on her Western experiences and observations. She pursued writing short stories and numerous articles for various American and Canadian magazines. *The Second Chance* appeared in 1910. McClung had a strong involvement in the Woman's Christian Temperance Union.

In 1911, the McClungs moved to Winnipeg, Manitoba, where McClung commenced a heavy speaking schedule focused on women's rights. She joined The Canadian Women's Press Club and organized the Politic Equity League in 1913. McClung played the role of the Conservative Manitoba premier in the mock Parliament of Women in 1914. Her antics helped defeat the government. She evoked a strong surge of patriotism that facilitated Manitoba women receiving the vote on January 27, 1916.

McClung became an even stronger activist during World War I. In her 1915 book, *In Times Like These,* she advocated her ideology. She derided the degrading cruelty of the sweat shops and the need for higher education for women, an old-age pension, mother's allowances, women's property rights, medical care for school children, and public heath nursing care. She worked to reform all these social issues.

In 1915, the McClungs moved to Edmonton, Alberta, where she joined the Edmonton Equal Franchise League. On July 21, 1915, Alberta voted for Prohibition. Alberta women received the franchise on April 19, 1916. McClung toured the United States, where her witty, dynamic style was well received.

She attended the Women's War Conference at Ottawa in 1918 at Mackenzie King's invitation. Livid that the war cost sixty thousand Canadian casualties, McClung's fight for dower rights led to Alberta's Dower Act of 1917, granting women property rights. In 1918, the federal government passed the Women's Franchise Act, which meant that those over 21 could vote.

Her fame expanded when she addressed the Methodist Ecumenical Conference in Britain in 1921. McClung's book, *Purple Springs*, reflected her views of the suffrage movement. In 1921 she was elected as a Liberal member of the Legislature for Edmonton and served until 1926 but was not reelected. Her 1926 book, *The Stream Runs Fast*, depicts her political experience.

Although women had been legally recognized as persons in Alberta since 1917, this did not apply federally. McClung and her friends Henrietta Muir Edwards, Irene Parlby, Emily Murphy, and Louise McKinney were outraged that women were not considered persons under Section 24 of the British North American Act, preventing them from serving in the Senate. Their 1927 petition to correct this was rejected, but they boldly appealed the decision and won their appeal on October 18, 1929. This is also known as the Persons Case.

In 1933, the McClungs moved to their retirement home at Gordon Head, Vancouver Island, where Nellie wrote her two-part autobiography, *Clearing in the West*. She kept occupied with a syndicated column and short stories and remained active as a public lecturer. McClung was the only female Canadian delegate at the Geneva League of Nations meeting in 1938 but was profoundly disappointed with its ambiguous program.

McClung also was involved with the Canadian Authors Association. She was appointed as the first woman member of the CBC's first board of governors, serving from 1936 to 1942. During World War II she railed against the injustices accorded Japanese Canadians.

McClung's emotional health never completely recovered from the suicide of her eldest son, Jack, who had never been able to forget his war experiences. She had a heart attack in 1940. Nellie died on September 1, 1951, at Victoria, B.C., and is buried at Royal Oak Burial Park in Saanich.

Annette Richardson

See also: Journalism (Canada, WWI); Women (Canada, WWI)

REFERENCES

Benham, Mary Lile. *Nellie McClung* (revised edition). Markham, Ontario: Fitzhenry and Whiteside, 2000.

Hallett, Mary E., and Marilyn Davis. *Firing the Heather: The Life and Times of Nellie McClung*. Saskatoon: Fifth House, 1994.

Hancock, Carol L. *Nellie McClung: No Small Legacy*. Kelowna, British Columbia: Northstone, 1996.

MacPherson, Margaret A. *Nellie McClung: Voice for the Voiceless*. Montreal: XYZ, 2003.

McClung, Nellie L. *In Times Like These*. Toronto: University of Toronto Press, 1972.

———. *The Stream Runs Fast: My Own Story*. Toronto: Thomas Allen, 1945.

Savage, Candace. *Our Nell: A Scrapbook Biography of Nellie L. McClung*. Halifax, Nova Scotia: Goodread Biographies, 1985.

Warne, Randi R. *Literature as Pulpit: The Christian Social Activism of Nellie L. McClung*. Waterloo, Ontario: Wilfrid Laurier University Press, 1993.

McKenna, Reginald

Home secretary and chancellor of the Exchequer during the First World War, Reginald McKenna (1863–1943) occupied three ministerial posts in Britain's involvement in the war: First Lord of the Admiralty, 1908–1911, Home Office, 1911–1915, and the Treasury, 1915–1916. McKenna's role depended on two factors: very good relations with Prime Minister H. H. Asquith and very bad relations with the man who replaced him, David Lloyd George. McKenna's acceptance of conscription in December 1915 helped ensure the continuance of the government, and his steeling of Asquith's resolve in December 1916 helped ensure its fall. McKenna's importance, however, has not been reflected in his reputation or historical profile.

McKenna's expansion of the Royal Navy before the war was controversial, in a government elected to deal with social reform. He saw a supreme Royal Navy as a deterrent that, in the event of war, would ensure Britain's role as the arsenal of the allies and avoid conscription and other alien measures. This primarily defensive attitude to conflict typified McKenna's involvement on the home front, to where he was moved in 1911, after strategic disagreements over Britain's continental commitment, swapping places with Winston Churchill to become home secretary.

A home secretary's first priority is the maintenance of public order. The main risks—female suffragism and trade unionism—had been suspended for the duration of the war, but McKenna nevertheless countered threats to national security by overseeing the extension of the state into newspaper censorship and mail tampering and extending the use of compulsory powers. His approach toward conscientious objectors and enemy aliens proved very unpopular: too draconian for Liberals and too lax for Conservatives. Reacting to a spy fever stoked by the popular press and opposition politicians, McKenna's distaste at interning thousands without trial was matched only by his despair at continually being accused of being pro-German. McKenna's formal and unsympathetic public manner did not help, and the abuse from the press and the opposition that he received was unmatched by any other public figure during the war.

When Asquith reorganized the government in May 1915, he made a remarkable statement in not only retaining but also promoting his most unpopular minister. It was the right appointment but at the wrong time. Although the exchequer was McKenna's only real political ambition, he took over a disorganized and neglected department from Lloyd George, who believed that financial matters came a distant second to military success. Supported by John Maynard Keynes, McKenna's contention was that ultimate success could not be achieved with Britain bankrupted and world financial leadership having been passed across the Atlantic. In the face of popular and parliamentary pressure for escalation in the war effort, McKenna counseled caution. He raised taxes, introduced import duties, accepted conscription, and undertook other measures held to be illiberal, yet was still regarded by opponents as typical of Liberalism: ill-equipped to deal with the requirements of modern politics and of industrial warfare.

In December 1916, McKenna and others regarded as similarly old-fashioned were thrown out of office, never to return. He, with Keynes, spent the rest of the war promoting a negotiated settlement and generally sought to moderate the militant tone of the Lloyd George Coalition. His fate was to lose his seats in the election of 1918, and leave politics.

Martin Farr

See also: Conscription (UK, WWI); Economy (UK, WWI); Liberal Party (UK, WWI); Biographies: Asquith, Herbert (WWI); Lloyd George, David (WWI); Keynes, John Maynard (WWI, WWII)

REFERENCES

Brock, Michael, and Eleanor Brock, eds. *H. H. Asquith Letters to Venetia Stanley.* Oxford: Oxford University Press, 1982.

Clifford, Colin. *The Asquiths.* London: John Murray, 2003.

Farr, Martin. *Reginald McKenna 1863–1943, a Life.* London: Frank Cass, 2006.

McKenna, Stephen. *Reginald McKenna 1863–1943, a Memoir.* London: Eyre and Spottiswoode, 1948.

Skidelsky, Robert. *John Maynard Keynes, Volume One: Hopes Betrayed 1883–1920.* London: Macmillan, 1983.

Strachan, Hew. *Financing the First World War.* Oxford: Oxford University Press, 2004.

Mooney, Tom

Tom Mooney (1882–1942), a militant San Francisco labor leader, was born in Chicago. At the age of fourteen, he began work in the local factory. A precocious learner, at fifteen Mooney won an essay contest sponsored by a Socialist Magazine. The prize was a trip to an international socialist conference in Switzerland. There, and while traveling through Europe, Mooney learned more about socialism, and after his return, became a Socialist. He was a member of the Industrial Workers of the World (IWW) and the Socialist Party of America (SPA). The latter had been formed from a merger of the Social Democratic Party and the Socialist Labor Party in 1901.

Mooney attended the International Socialist Congress in Copenhagen and settled in San Francisco afterward. He published *The Revolt,* a Socialist newspaper. In 1911, he married Rena Hermann, who shared his ideology. Mooney actively campaigned for SPA President Eugene V. Debs in the presidential elections of 1908 and 1912. He gained prominence as an ardent socialist with a flair for writing and oratory. He campaigned for the release of jailed fellow workers of the IWW, and was himself framed on a charge of carrying explosives illegally and was behind bars for a year. Mooney opposed the entry of the United States in the First World War. From 1913 onward, Mooney was arrested frequently for organizing strikes. The Chamber of Commerce, Conservative city leaders, United Railroads, and the Pacific Gas & Electric Company considered him a dangerous enemy for his militant labor activities.

In July 1916, the atmosphere in the city of San Francisco was tense. The Chamber of Commerce had organized a Law and Order Committee to rid the city of militant elements, who opposed America's entry in the war and hampered business interests. On the Preparedness Day parade of July 22, 1916, a bomb exploded near the Ferry Building, killing ten and injuring forty. Mooney and his assistant, Warren K. Billings, were arrested. The trials, behind-the-scene machinations, trumped-up charges, and role of money and power made Mooney a martyr in labor circles. The office of the district attorney even arranged false witnesses. The jury consisted mostly of retired businessman and conservatives under the influence of the district attorney. After a hasty trial, Mooney was given capital punishment; Billings, life imprisonment, and Rena Mooney was acquitted.

Evidences began to accumulate pointing toward perjured evidence against Mooney. Public protests, international opinion, and the appeal of Liberals made the case a cause célèbre, similar to the Dreyfus case in France. President Woodrow Wilson directed the governor of California in 1918 to commute the death sentence of Mooney to life imprisonment just two weeks before the scheduled hanging. But the campaign to free Mooney went on, and he was given an unconditional pardon in January 1939 after spending twenty-two years in San Quentin for a crime he did not commit. He decided to give lectures on the New Deal and dangers of fascism. But the long stay in prison had made him weak. He died on March 6, 1942, after a protracted illness.

Patit P. Mishra

See also: Industrial Workers of the World (WWI); Socialist Party (WWI); Strikes, Labor (WWI); Trade Unions (U.S., WWI); Biographies: Debs, Eugene V. (WWI)

REFERENCES

Filippelli, Ronald L. *Labor in the USA: A History.* New York: Alfred A. Knopf, 1984.

Frost, Richard. H. *The Mooney Case.* California: Stanford University, 1968.

Gentry, Curt. *Frame-Up: The Incredible Case of Tom Mooney and Warren Billings.* New York: W. W. Norton and Company Inc, 1967.

Hale, Leslie. *Thirty Who Were Tried. Or Eternal Vigilance.* London: Victor Gollancz, 1955.

Hillquit, Morris. *The History of Socialism in the United States.* New York: Dover Publications, paperback, 1972.

Schlossberg, Joseph. *The Workers and Their World: Aspects of the Workers' Struggle at Home and Abroad.* New York: A.L.P. Committee, 1935.

Ward, Estolv Ethan. *The Gentle Dynamiter: A Biography of Tom Mooney.* Palo Alto, CA: Ramparts Press, 1983.

Morgan, J. P.

Influential American financier J. P. Morgan Jr. (1867–1943) was born in Irvington, New York, the son of John Pierpont Morgan, an investment banker. In 1889 he graduated from Harvard University. In 1890 he married Jane Norton Grew, daughter of Henry Sturgis Grew, a powerful merchant and manufacturer.

In 1890, Morgan briefly associated with Jacob C. Rogers, the Boston agent for his grandfather's merchant bank, Junius S. Morgan & Company. In 1891, he moved to New York to join his father's firm. In 1898, he was dispatched to Junius S. Morgan & Company in London to become a resident partner.

In January 1906, Morgan returned to New York. After his father's death in March 1913, J. P. Morgan Jr. assumed responsibility for J. P. Morgan & Company and inherited more than $50 million. In contrast to his father's authoritarian business style, Morgan held daily meetings and sought to reach decisions by consensus. Morgan lived in an age when New York was starting to replace London as the world's financial capital. Because the United States changed its financial status from a debtor to a creditor nation, J. P. Morgan & Company shifted its business emphasis from domestic to international loans.

When World War I broke out in Europe, J. P. Morgan Jr. actively supported Great Britain despite the official U.S. position of neutrality. In early 1915, Morgan became the purchasing agent for Great Britain and France. Between early 1915 and the U.S. entry into the war in April 1917, J. P. Morgan & Company purchased $3 billion in war supplies for Britain and France, receiving in return a commission of one percent. As President Wilson began removing government restriction on loans to belligerents in 1915, Morgan organized a syndicate of more than two thousand banks to underwrite a

A strong supporter of Britain in World War I, financier J. P. Morgan was London's main purchasing agent in the United States. (Library of Congress)

loan of $500 million in 5 percent bonds guaranteed by Great Britain and France. In the following two years, the total loan amount grew to reach $1.55 billion.

J. P. Morgan Jr. harbored an intense dislike for Jews and Roman Catholics, a fact that hurt his reputation when it became public. After World War I, he feared the emergence of a Communist influence in Central Europe and Russia, which led him to actively oppose Socialism in America. Morgan supported the kind of liberal world order advocated by President Woodrow Wilson and was especially supportive of Wilson's efforts to establish a League of Nations. In the 1920s, although he was a staunch supporter of the Republican Party, Morgan was uncomfortable with the Republican's isolationist policy. Because he believed in a liberal economic system, J. P. Morgan & Company floated a combined $1.7 billion worth of securities on behalf of major countries, including Great Britain, France, and Germany, between 1917 and 1926.

Alarmed by the conditions of economic chaos that had taken root in Germany in 1922, Morgan served on a committee of bankers in Paris to manage German war reparations. Morgan helped devise the Dawes Plan in 1924, which was intended to help Germany restructure its war reparations payment to the Allied powers. J. P. Morgan & Company underwrote a massive loan to Germany to accomplish the Dawes Plan. Taking matters a step further, in 1929 Morgan helped devise the Young Plan to reschedule German reparation debts. To promote the Young Plan, J. P. Morgan & Company implemented another loan to Germany that was worth nearly $100 million.

The New York stock market crashed on October 24, 1929. In response to this financial crisis, J. P. Morgan & Company took the initiative in organizing a bank consortium that included such leading banks as Bankers Trust, National City Bank, Chase National Bank, and Guarantee Trust. The consortium created a $240 million investment pool to help bring the panic in the stock market to an end, but the result was a dismal failure. Moreover, J. P. Morgan & Company lost more than half its capital. As part of New Deal reforms instituted in 1933 during the Franklin D. Roosevelt administration, the U.S. government separated commercial and investment banking services. As a result, in September 1935 J. P. Morgan & Company was divided into two firms: commercial banking operations were house under Morgan, while a new company, Morgan Stanley, assumed control of investment banking operations.

Yoneyuki Sugita

See also: Banking and Finance (WWI); War Bonds (WWI)

REFERENCES

Jackson, Stanley. *J. P. Morgan: The Rise and Fall of a Banker.* London: Heinemann, 1984.

Markham, Jerry W. *From J. P. Morgan to the Institutional Investor (1900–1970).* New York: M. E. Sharpe, 2002.

Morton, Jelly Roll

Born Ferdinand Joseph Lamothe in New Orleans, Louisiana, jazz pioneer "Jelly Roll" Morton (1890–1941) was abandoned by his father early in his life. His mother, Louise, married William Mouton, now Morton. After his mother passed away when he was fourteen, Morton and his sisters moved in with their grandmother. Shortly thereafter, his grandmother forced him to move out when she found out that he earned money as a pimp, among other disreputable occupations.

Little is known about Morton's formal musical training except that he was taught early on by Tony Jackson, a local pianist. The rest of his training is believed to have been acquired by simply absorbing what New Orleans had to offer musically. In the early part of the twentieth century, Morton published several pieces of piano music. From there, Morton toured the South extensively, which further added to the diverse musical exposure that influenced his craft. In 1907 Morton expanded his travels to include locations outside the Deep South, and in 1911 he came north to New York City, where famed jazz composer James P. Johnson heard him. Morton then went west to Los Angeles.

Los Angeles at the time was a growing center of music and culture transferred from New Orleans, and many famous musicians made the commute from New Orleans to Los Angeles. Morton did not spend a lot of time in Los Angeles, leaving for Chicago in 1922. Morton did not enjoy his time in Chicago. It was an epicenter for darker-skinned black musicians, a group that Morton had previously distanced himself from in New Orleans. He considered himself a Creole. As a result, Morton did not record with Louis Armstrong, among other musical legends of the time. Morton made his style of music unique from the norms of the day and maintained a popularity all his own.

After a period of great success in Chicago, Morton moved to New York in 1928. Once again Morton was dismayed at the uniformity in the music he found. By the 1930s, his style was no longer popular and his career began to decline, so he opened a club in Washington, D.C. Although his recordings and performances began to wane, Morton was able to gain notoriety for laying down interview tracks on the history of jazz for the Library of Congress. He died in 1940 in Los Angeles after suffering a heart attack.

Philine Georgette Vega

See also: Jazz (WWI); Music (U.S., WWI)

REFERENCE

Williams, Martin. *Jelly Roll Morton.* London: Cassell, 1962.

Muck, Karl

Karl Muck (1859–1940) was the long-time conductor of the Boston Symphony Orchestra, well respected for his mastery of Wagner. His career in the United States ended during World War I, when he was accused of being an enemy alien for refusing to play the *Star Spangled Banner* during a concert. Muck's undeniable German nationalism ran counter to the strong patriotism and anti-German bias during the war.

Muck was born in Darmstadt in Bavaria. His father was his first music teacher. Muck later studied classical music at the Universities of Heidelberg and Leipzig, receiving a Ph.D. from the latter in 1880. His talent was quickly noticed, and he was soon conducting with an opera company in Zurich. During this time, Muck obtained Swiss citizenship. By 1886 he was conducting a traveling Wagner company and had earned a reputation as a great interpreter of that composer. In 1892 he became first conductor at the Berlin Royal Opera. Over the next decade, he conducted at performances throughout Germany and the rest of Europe.

In 1906, Muck was lured to the United States to conduct the Boston Symphony Orchestra. Major Henry L. Higginson, founder and benefactor of the symphony, had heard Muck and hoped he could give the fledgling orchestra instant credibility. For the next two years, Muck remained with the symphony, and then returned to Germany. Higginson persuaded Muck to return in 1912 as permanent conductor. Under Muck, the Boston Symphony Orchestra traveled the United States and became one of the most respected symphonies in this country.

Muck never concealed his German heritage or nationalism. Many classical musicians in the United States at the time were German or of German descent. Muck hired many fellow German musicians and conducted rehearsals in German. After World War I broke out in 1914, tension developed between those who favored the Allies and those Americans whose ancestors came from the Central Powers. Commentators such as former president Theodore Roosevelt made matters worse by calling for citizens to be "one hundred percent American."

When the United States declared war on Germany on April 6, 1917, the anti-German sentiment became much greater. The Justice Department had already developed a list of Germans in the United States who might have violated neutrality laws. At least sixty-three individuals were arrested immediately after the war broke out. Muck's pro-German attitude attracted attention. Muck's personality made him many enemies; he held most Americans who attended his performances in contempt and considered that they had no taste. Appeals to Major Higginson to dismiss Muck had no effect.

In November 1917, the Boston Symphony Orchestra was performing for a group of nine ladies' organizations in Providence, Rhode Island. Although the organizers had requested the *Star Spangled Banner* be played, Muck refused. He considered the piece unsuitable for a symphony. He also opposed any mixing of art and politics. The episode caused a national uproar and was widely reported. Higginson made a number of excuses for Muck, and later performances included the *Star Spangled Banner.* However, the damage had been done. Government agents investigated Muck's personal life. They found he was having an affair with a woman in Boston who was half his age. Authorities let him know that he was facing prosecution under the Mann Act. Muck agreed to internment as an enemy alien instead on March 25, 1918. He was removed as conductor of the Boston Symphony Orchestra and placed in an internment camp at Fort Ogelthorpe, Georgia the next day. Muck remained in detention until June 1919, when he was deported to Germany.

Muck denied ever being disloyal to the United States but expressed relief at being back in Germany. He soon reestablished himself as a leading conductor of Wagner. He retired in 1933 and died seven years later.

Tim J. Watts

See also: Americanization Campaign (WWI); German Americans (WWI); Music (U.S., WWI)

REFERENCES

Baker-Carr, Janet. *Evening at Symphony: A Portrait of the Boston Symphony Orchestra.* Boston: Houghton Mifflin, 1977.

Ewen, David. *Man with the Baton: The Story of Conductors and Their Orchestras.* Freeport, NY: Books for Libraries Press, 1968, 1936.

Schonberg, Harold C. *The Great Conductors.* New York: Simon and Schuster, 1967.

O

Oliver, Joseph "King"

Joseph "King" Oliver (1885–1938), cornetist and bandleader, was born Joseph Oliver in or near New Orleans, Louisiana, the son of Jessie Jones, a cook. His father's identity is unknown. After completing elementary school, Oliver worked at a variety of menial jobs, including as a yard man for a clothing merchant. He began playing the cornet in early adulthood. From approximately 1905 to 1915, he played in a variety of brass and dance bands, and by 1915 he had achieved fame as a virtuoso on the streets of New Orleans. Between 1916 and 1918 Oliver worked as the cornetist in trombonist Edward "Kid" Ory's orchestra, which was one of the most highly regarded African American dance orchestras in New Orleans. During World War I, he developed many styles that became standard among jazz cornetists, in particular his use of straight and plunger mutes.

Oliver, who soon became co-leader of the orchestra with Ory, helped take the ensemble beyond its Storyville roots. (Storyville was New Orleans' red-light district in the late nineteenth and early twentieth centuries.) The band soon gained popularity among different races and across the city's various economic strata. The city's middle and upper class whites requested the band play at debutante balls; while working class New Orleans blacks could hear the band play at the many dance halls in the city's poorer neighborhoods.

Seeking to expand his fame and income, in 1919 Oliver joined the great migration of African Americans to the north and moved to Chicago. There he formed his own band, King Oliver's Creole Jazz Band, which was soon one of the most popular bands in the nightclubs of the South Side black entertainment district. Oliver mentored many of his band members, several of whom became major figures in American music, including Louis Armstrong (who credited Oliver as his primary influence), Johnny Dodds, Warren "Baby" Dodds, George "Pops" Foster, and Lester Young.

Many of the songs that Oliver wrote and performed in New Orleans and Chicago and recorded in 1923 and 1924, including "Sugar Foot Stomp" (later known as "Dipper Mouth Blues"), "West End Blues," "Chimes Blues," and "Doctor Jazz," became jazz classics. Oliver took his band to the East Coast in May 1927, but after little more than a month, it dispersed. For the next four years Oliver lived in New York City, touring occasionally and making records for the Victor Company at the head of a variety of ad hoc orchestras. Between 1931 and 1937 Oliver toured the Midwest and the Upper South. In 1937, he moved to Savannah, Georgia and supported himself by a variety of odd jobs. He died in Savannah of a cerebral hemorrhage in 1938.

Thaddeus Russell

See also: Jazz (WWI); Music (U.S., WWI)

REFERENCES

Wright, Laurie. *"King" Oliver* (1987, revised ed.); *Chicago Defender,* April 16, 1938.

P

Palmer, Alexander Mitchell

A U.S. representative and attorney general, A. Mitchell Palmer (1872–1936) orchestrated the mass arrest and deportation of suspected radicals during the red scare immediately following World War I. While serving in the House of Representatives, he helped secure Woodrow Wilson's 1912 and 1916 presidential nominations. From 1917 to 1919, he directed the administration of enemy-owned property within the United States. Appointed attorney general in 1919, Palmer addressed the growing threat of domestic terrorism and communist organizations. The Justice Department's Palmer Raids in 1920 resulted in thousands of alien arrests, many without warrants or probable cause. Following an unsuccessful presidential campaign, Palmer reemerged in national politics in 1932 to craft major portions of Franklin D. Roosevelt's New Deal program.

In 1908, Palmer won election to Congress from a steel and wool-producing district in Pennsylvania. As a prominent delegate to the National Democratic Convention in 1912, he organized the effort to nominate Wilson for president and later became one of Wilson's most trusted House members. Initially known for his pro-labor stance, Palmer lost the support of unions after he cowrote the 1913 Underwood-Simmons Tariff Act. The legislation reduced tariffs across the board, introducing competition to local industries, including steel and wool. In 1914, Palmer ran for a Senate seat, but was defeated due to the opposition of labor groups.

Wilson appointed Palmer alien property custodian in 1917. The position enabled Palmer to confiscate products of German-owned corporations operating within the country. He distributed German-made munitions and equipment to government agencies, took control of lumber and mining companies, and investigated German businessmen who appeared to be hiding assets.

After replacing Thomas W. Gregory as attorney general in 1919, Palmer used emergency war powers to halt nationwide railroad and mining strikes. In April, postal employees intercepted sixteen mail bombs addressed to Palmer and other public figures. Late in the spring, Palmer's home was partially destroyed by a bomb in a synchronized attack that included bombings in eight cities. Still, the attorney general was reluctant to initiate a full-scale investigation into radical behavior. In fact, he called for the early release of several prisoners charged with violating the 1917 Espionage Act.

By fall, however, public pressure persuaded him to take action against groups that advocated violence. In November, the Justice Department arrested and detained several members of the Union of Russian Workers.

The Palmer Raids began on January 2, 1920. Justice Department agents stormed into communist meeting places nationwide, arresting thousands of immigrants. Palmer and the head of his intelligence division, J. Edgar Hoover, launched the raids without consulting the Labor Department, the agency then responsible for issuing alien arrest warrants and deportations. The acting secretary of labor, Louis F. Post, eventually cancelled most of the arrests for lack of due process. Although House members considered impeaching Post, they generally applauded the Justice Department's actions. However, attorneys called the raids unconstitutional, a charge that dismantled Palmer's campaign for president that year. While he drafted Roosevelt's 1932 New Deal platform, Palmer remained associated with the red scare and the violation of civil rights in the post-war era.

Jane Armstrong Hudiburg

See also: Anarchists (WWI); Civil Liberties (WWI); Espionage Act (WWI); Palmer Raids (WWI); Red Scare (WWI); Biographies: Hoover, J. Edgar (WWI); Wilson, Woodrow (WWI)

REFERENCES

Braeman, John. "World War One and the Crisis of American Liberty." *American Quarterly* 16 (Spring 1964): 104–112.

Coben, Stanley A. *Mitchell Palmer: Politician.* New York: Columbia University Press, 1963.

Murray, Robert K. *Red Scare: A Study in National Hysteria, 1919–1920.* Minneapolis: University of Minnesota Press, 1955.

Paul, Alice

Alice Paul (1885–1977) was a militant suffragist who led the fight for a federal suffrage amendment, which was finally achieved in 1920. Paul earned her reputation as a dedicated suffragist from her arrests (and subsequent hunger strikes) as a member of the Women's Social and Political Union in Britain. Paul was directly responsible for transferring the militant tactics of British suffragists to the campaign in the United States. These tactics eventually led to the passage of the Nineteenth Amendment in 1919 and its ratification a year later.

In 1913, with the intervention of Jane Addams, Paul was named the head of the Congressional Committee of the National American Woman Suffrage Association (NAWSA). Paul promptly organized a suffrage parade down Pennsylvania Avenue for March 3, 1913, the day before Woodrow Wilson's inauguration. Hostile crowds turned the parade into a near riot, but Paul considered the parade a success because it diverted attention and people away from the inauguration, received national press coverage, and led to a marked increase in donations to the Congressional Committee. Paul quickly confronted the limits of the more conservative, state-by-state tactics of NAWSA and created the Congressional Union for Woman Suffrage, which separated from NAWSA in 1914. In 1916, Alice Paul founded a new political party for enfranchised women, the National Woman's Party (NWP). The NWP's single goal was to achieve the passage of the federal suffrage amendment.

Paul focused on blaming the party in power—the Democrats—for failure to support woman suffrage, lobbying to defeat as many Democratic candidates as possible in all full-suffrage states. In the elections of 1914 and the presidential elections of 1916, the Congressional Union was somewhat successful. During the first few months of 1917, after Woodrow Wilson's reelection, Paul tried a new tactic—members of the Congressional Union and the NWP picketed silently and continually in front of the White House carrying banners that asked questions such as, "Mr. President, what will you do for woman suffrage?"

After the United States entered the World War in early April, the public became hostile to the picketers, in part because Alice Paul and the NWP took no stand on the war, remaining a single-issue organization. Picketers often carried signs that emphasized the stark difference between Wilson's call for war to promote democracy abroad and the lack of democracy in the United States. One of their standard banners was lifted from Wilson's war message of April 2: "We shall fight for the things which we have always held nearest our hearts—for democracy, for the right of those who submit to authority to have a voice in their own governments. President Wilson's War Message, April 2, 1917." In the patriotic war fever that gripped the nation, the public responded with increasing violence to the picketers' messages, at times ripping signs away from the women or pushing or shoving demonstrators.

Authorities, while viewing the picketers as an embarrassment, did nothing to stop them until June, two days after what became known as the Russian Banner incident. Wilson, hoping to convince the new Russian Republic to stay in the war, sent a delegation to the country; in the course of a speech there, a delegate referred to the United States as a country where "universal, direct, equal, and secret suffrage obtained." Suffragists were outraged. When a delegation from Russia returned the visit to Washington, Paul positioned two picketers outside the White House with an enormous banner: "President Wilson and Envoy Root are deceiving Russia. They say 'We are a democracy. Help us to win the war so that democracies may survive.' We

women of America tell you that America is not a democracy. Twenty million women are denied the right to vote. President Wilson is the chief opponent of their national enfranchisement. Help us make this nation really free. Tell our government that it must liberate its people before it can claim free Russia as an ally." The crowd attacked the picketers and tore down the sign after the Russian delegation had entered the White House.

The Russian Banner incident made the front page around the country. After the disturbance, attacks by the public on White House picketers sometimes generated more publicity than the war itself. Police began to arrest picketers. The arrests and trials of "respectable," middle-class women created some controversy, even among people who disagreed with the picketing tactic. And confrontations between the picketers and crowds that gathered to witness their arrests were becoming more and more violent over the course of the summer. The daily negative publicity generated by the attacks and the arrests increased the pressure on the Wilson administration.

Paul orchestrated this pressure. Knowing that she too would be arrested, Paul led a protest in October 20, 1917. She was sentenced to seven months, the harshest sentence yet imposed. Paul began a hunger strike, a tactic she had learned in Great Britain, on October 30. After a few days, prison authorities began force-feeding Paul three times a day for three weeks, and took other measures to try to disrupt the hunger strike. Authorities separated Paul from the other prisoners, removed the door to her room, allowed her no mail or visitors, and woke her every hour throughout the night. Prison abuses of other suffragists were also becoming public. Pressure on the administration increased even further. Without explanation, authorities released all suffrage prisoners on November 27 and 28, 1917.

The militancy of the NWP spurred NAWSA, as the largest national suffrage organization, to launch a persistent lobbying campaign to put pressure on Congress to pass the federal suffrage amendment. The pressure created by Paul and the NWP also pushed Wilson to support the cooperative and less radical NAWSA. In mid-December, the House Rules Committee announced the suffrage amendment would come to a vote on January 10, 1918. With Wilson endorsing the measure at the last minute, the amendment passed the House with exactly a two-thirds vote. Wilson campaigned hard for the Senate to pass the amendment as well. The amendment failed at its first vote in the Senate, but after the signing of the Armistice on November 11, 1918, Wilson again urged the Senate to pass the federal suffrage amendment in a December address. Alice Paul and NWP members lobbied Congress heavily in the weeks before the scheduled June 4, 1919 vote. Finally, the Susan B. Anthony amendment passed the Senate by a vote of fifty-six to twenty-five. The amendment was ratified fifteen months later.

Melissa Doak

See also: Women (U.S., WWI); Biographies: Addams, Jane (WWI)

REFERENCES

Butler, Amy E. *Two Paths to Equality: Alice Paul and Ethel M. Smith in the ERA Debate, 1921–1929.* Albany: State University of New York Press, 2002.

Ford, Linda G. *Iron-Jawed Angels: The Suffrage Militancy of the National Woman's Party, 1912–1920.* Lantham, MD: University Press of America, 1991.

Irwin, Inez Hayes. *The Story of Alice Paul and the National Woman's Party.* Fairfax, VA: Denlinger's Publishers, 1964.

Lunardini, Christine A. *From Equal Suffrage to Equal Rights: Alice Paul and the National Woman's Party, 1910–1928.* New York: New York University Press, 1986.

Pershing, John J.

John Joseph "Black Jack" Pershing (1860–1948) was a U.S. Army officer who commanded the American Expeditionary Force (AEF) in Europe during World War I. A stubborn, strict man, Pershing nonetheless won the admiration of his men and the nation—an admiration he returned in kind. "Their deeds are immortal," Pershing declared of the Americans who had served in combat, "and they have earned the eternal gratitude of our country." Pershing was ultimately promoted to General of the Armies—the only American ever to hold that rank.

Pershing was born on September 13, 1860, in Leclede, Missouri, where he grew up with little interest in the military. (He attended West Point for the free education.) Pershing participated in the Indian Campaigns in the Southwest, earned a law degree, and served with the U.S. Tenth (Colored) Cavalry. This service, along with a reputation as a strict disciplinarian, earned Pershing (who was an outspoken defender of the courage of African American troops) the title of "Nigger Jack," later softened to "Black Jack," a name Pershing kept with pride.

During the Spanish-American War, Pershing and his African American troops came to the attention of Theodore Roosevelt during the charge up San Juan Hill. Pershing further impressed Roosevelt with his subsequent service in the Philippines. In 1906, largely because of his friendship with Roosevelt and his father-in-law (a U.S. senator), Pershing was promoted from captain to brigadier general over the heads of more than eight hundred fifty senior officers. Pershing served with distinction in Japan, in the Philippines, and in Europe, and then commanded the unsuccessful Punitive Expedition dispatched by President Woodrow Wilson in 1916 to pursue Mexican bandit Pancho Villa.

When Wilson's neutrality policy collapsed in 1917, he chose Pershing to form the AEF. As commander of the AEF, Pershing fought for permission to form an independent American army and for additional soldiers and material. Allied commanders had suggested that American units be sent piecemeal to reinforce exhausted European divisions. Pershing objected fiercely, and in the face of intense diplomatic pressure insisted on forming an American army. Pershing's stubbornness ensured the existence of an independent U.S. military force, thus increasing American prestige and power. While stubborn, Pershing was dedicated to Allied victory. When in 1918 the Germans launched a massive assault, Pershing announced that Americans would be honored to serve under French command. "At this moment," he declared, "there are no other questions but of fighting."

In September 1918, Pershing led his troops against the German's St. Mihiel salient, or section of the front, and then in the Meuse-Argonne offensive. Opinions differ on the effectiveness of this offensive: Some suggest that it was a complete success; others rightly argue that at least initially Pershing's doctrine of open warfare faltered in the face of the machine gun, and succeeded only after a reorganization of forces. Pressure applied by the AEF nonetheless helped bring about the Armistice (which Pershing opposed) on November 11.

After the war, Pershing returned to honor and promotion in the United States, and served as army chief of staff from 1921 to 1924. He remained involved in military affairs and, in the years leading to World War II, continued to speak out for military preparedness and for action against the Axis powers. "The enemies of liberty," Pershing declared, "if possible should be defeated." Pershing died on July 15, 1948.

Samuel Brenner

See also: Demobilization (WWI); Mobilization (U.S., WWI); Biographies: Roosevelt, Theodore (WWI); Villa, Pancho (WWI)

REFERENCES

Cooke, James J. *Pershing and His Generals: Command and Staff in the AEF.* Westport, CT: Praeger, 1997.

Goldhurst, Richard. *Pipe Clay and Drill: John J. Pershing, the Classic American Soldier.* New York: Reader's Digest Press, 1977.

Mason, Herbert Molloy, Jr. *The Great Pursuit: General John J. Pershing's Punitive Expedition across the Rio Grande to Destroy the Mexican Bandit Pancho Villa.* New York: Random House, 1970.

O'Connor, Richard. *Black Jack Pershing.* Garden City, NY: Doubleday, 1961.

Pershing, John J. *My Experiences in the War.* New York: Fredrick A. Stokes Company, 1931.

Smythe, Donald. *Pershing: General of the Armies.* Bloomington: Indiana University Press, 1986.

Trask, David F. *The AEF and Coalition Warmaking, 1917–1918.* Lawrence: University Press of Kansas, 1993.

Vandiver, Frank E. *Black Jack: The Life and Times of John J. Pershing.* College Station: Texas A&M University Press, 1977.

Pickford, Mary

Popular silent-film star Mary Pickford (1893–1979) was born Gladys Mary Smith in Toronto, Canada. Among the earliest of film's pioneer performers, she became "America's first sweetheart" and one of the first great legends of the screen. She was also one of the shrewdest businesswomen in Hollywood.

A stage actress since the age of five, she was hired as an extra for director D. W. Griffith in 1909. Her first breakthrough role was in 1914's *Tess of the Storm Country*. In 1915, she became the first female star to have her own corporation, establishing herself as an independent actor/producer. In 1919, she joined Charles Chaplin, Douglas Fairbanks, and D. W. Griffith in founding United Artists Corporation, which gave her the power to distribute her own movies.

Pickford became famous for playing strong, intelligent, perceptive women who were usually able to outwit the more powerful or pompous characters who challenged her. In films involving class struggle, she championed the poor over the rich. She was used to provoke popular anti-German sentiment in films produced during the Great War. In 1917's *The Little American*, Pickford's ship is torpedoed like the *Lusitania,* and her German-born husband becomes a mindless thug until he realizes she is about to be executed by the Kaiser's army. In 1918's *Johanna Enlists,* her sheltered character prays for romance and adventure and is visited by an entire regiment of eligible soldiers. An honorary colonel in the 143rd Field Artillery, Pickford arranged to have many of its members appear in the film.

Pickford's support of the war was not reserved to her roles on the screen. She traveled coast to coast for the Third Liberty Loan campaign, raising millions of dollars for the war effort. She made dozens of public appearances on behalf of war charities, including the American Red Cross, and often wrote personal letters of thanks to substantial donors.

In 1920, Pickford and Douglas Fairbanks shocked America by divorcing their spouses and marrying each other. They created their own private estate, dubbed "Pickfair," but the marriage dissolved in 1935. In 1933 Pickford retired from acting, having appeared in more than two hundred films.

Thaddeus Russell

See also: American Red Cross (WWI); Film (U.S., WWI); Biographies: Fairbanks Sr., Douglas (WWI)

REFERENCES

Brownlow, Kevin. *Mary Pickford Rediscovered.* New York: Harry N. Abrams, 1999.

May, Lary. *Screening Out the Past: The Birth of Mass Culture and the Motion Picture Industry.* New York: Oxford University Press, 1980.

Pinchot, Amos

At the turn of the century, sickness and poverty plagued the nation and many reformers saw this time as an opportune period to change the direction in which America was heading. These social reformers called themselves the Progressives. When World War I became a pressing issue in American politics, this group of reformers was split into two groups. One group, led by Theodore Roosevelt, pushed for social reform and greater military preparedness. The other more radical group, which was led by Amos Pinchot (1863–1944), argued that control over the country by the monopolies was to blame for poverty, a condition that would only be exacerbated by a war industry. When America declared war, Pinchot became even more active, shifting his energy from defending the working class to assisting the pacifists who had been caught in the American betrayal of civil liberties. He would spend the rest of his life working for these rights.

Pinchot, who was born in Paris, obtained his

college degree at Yale University in 1897. Shortly thereafter he enlisted in the New York Volunteer Cavalry to help the Cubans escape what he viewed as Spaniard exploitation in the Spanish-American War. When he returned to America, he finished his law degree at Columbia University and New York Law School. A year after he was admitted to the bar, however, he decided that his energies could be put to better use fighting the causes and effects of social illness. His efforts were first realized by the public when he helped his brother, Gifford Pinchot, fight the secretary of the interior's plans to exploit Alaskan land in the Pinchot-Ballinger controversy. A few years later, the experience and fame that he gained from this affair helped him rise to the top of the American Union, an organization that fought to stay out of the First World War.

Although he was a leader in the militant antiwar group, Amos Pinchot was not a pacifist; he disagreed with the war for social and economic reasons. Pinchot believed that American big business was using the preparedness campaign to not only reap profits but also to make the American working class think they needed the help of imperialistic powers to protect them. When America entered the war, the American Union lapsed into a state of inaction but Amos Pinchot's zeal did not. He redirected his attention to the other issue he believed strongly in: a citizen's rights, even in a time of war.

In addition to his opposition to the exploitation of the worker by monopolies, Pinchot was strongly opposed to any violation of civil liberties. He felt that the American government took advantage of World War I to take these rights away from its people. Pinchot believed that this was the worst casualty of the war, and he used his experience in the law to fight for pacifists who had been persecuted by the American government. Amos Pinchot took the energy that he had used before World War I fighting big business and redirected it toward big government.

Throughout World War I, Pinchot had performed this work with the Progressive Party, but because their power was greatly diminished by the war he founded his own organization. Until his death in 1944, he continued to fight against the violations to civil liberties in his group, the American Civil Liberties Union.

Rachel Bennett

See also: Civil Liberties (WWI); Progressivism (WWI)

REFERENCES

Kennedy, David. *Over Here: The First World War and American Society.* New York: Oxford University Press, 2004.

Marchand, C. Roland. *The American Peace Movement and Social Reform 1898–1918.* New Jersey: Princeton University Press, 1972.

Smith, Page. *America Enters the World: A People's History of the Progressive Era and World War I.* New York: McGraw-Hill Book Company, 1985.

R

Randolph, A. Philip

Born to a Methodist minister in Crescent City, Florida, African American union leader Asa Philip Randolph (1889–1979) moved to New York in 1911. He attended City College, New York, majoring in philosophy and economics. To support himself, he worked variously as a porter, a waiter, and an elevator operator. He married the widowed Lucille E. Green in 1914. They had no children. Her financial support freed him to express his socialist views, with which she agreed.

Randolph joined the Socialist Party and began speaking at Soapbox Corner (135th Street and Lenox Avenue, Harlem) about socialism and class consciousness. He quickly became known throughout Harlem.

Randolph was also a strong supporter of Marcus Garvey, at least initially. Randolph met Garvey in 1916 and introduced Garvey to Harlemites shortly after Garvey arrived there in the spring of 1917. By 1920 Randolph was among the black leaders who wondered about Garvey's motives and the practicality of Garvey's Back to Africa movement. When Garvey's United Negro Improvement Association (UNIA) fell afoul of the federal government in the 1920s, Randolph was among those calling for Garvey's deportation.

In January 1917 William White, president of the Headwaiters and Sidewaiters Society of Greater New York, asked Randolph and Chandler Owen to edit *The Hotel Messenger;* they agreed and renamed the publication *The Messenger.*

The first issue of *The Messenger* appeared in November 1917. *The Messenger* quickly acquired a reputation for quality. It gave an outlet for those opposed to Garvey's utopian populism and the NAACP's cautious elitism alike. While supporting civil rights, *The Messenger* (later *Black Worker*) criticized Woodrow Wilson, W. E. B. DuBois, and Booker T. Washington.

The Messenger advocated socialism. Socialism's focus on class rather than race made it less appealing to the black community, which preferred the racial emphasis of other black organizations such as the National Association for the Advancement of Black People (NAACP) and Garvey's UNIA.

With *The Messenger* giving them prominence, Randolph and Owen embarked on a speaking tour in 1918. They called on African Americans to refuse to join the army. The federal government arrested them for violating the Espionage Act. The judge, skeptical that two black men could write with such sophistication, assumed that they were tools of white socialists and dismissed the charges.

After World War I, Randolph remained active in labor, socialist, and black causes. He joined the newly organized Brotherhood of Sleeping Car Porters in 1925 (becoming its president in 1929) and made it the first significant national black union. He used his leadership in the civil rights movement in 1940 to threaten Franklin Roosevelt with a march on Washington for black equity in war jobs. Roosevelt barred discrimination in government contracts. Similar pressure against Truman in 1948 led to the desegregation of the armed forces. Randolph played major roles in both the CIO and the Second Reconstruction. He participated in the 1963 March on Washington. A. Philip Randolph died in New York City on May 16, 1979.

John Barnhill

See also: African Americans (WWI); National Association for the Advancement of Colored People (NAACP) (WWI); Socialist Party (WWI); Biographies: DuBois, W. E. B. (WWI); Garvey, Marcus (WWI); Randolph, A. Philip (WWII)

REFERENCES

Anderson, Jervis. *A. Philip Randolph.* Berkeley: University of California Press, 1987.

Kornweibel, Theodore, Jr. *Seeing Red.* Bloomington: Indiana University Press, 1998.

Patterson, Lillie *A. Philip Randolph.* New York: Facts on File, 1995.

Pfeffer, Paula. *A. Philip Randolph.* Baton Rouge: Louisiana State University Press, 1996.

Rankin, Jeannette

The only member of Congress to vote against U.S. entry into both World War I and World War II, Jeannette Rankin (1880–1973) also was the first woman to serve in Congress. Rankin was born near Missoula, Montana. She attended the Missoula public schools and graduated from Montana State University at Missoula in 1902 with a degree in biology. After seeing slums on a trip to Boston in 1904, Rankin enrolled in the New York School of Philanthropy. She then briefly practiced social work in Spokane, Washington. Finding that she did not like her new profession, she enrolled in the University of Washington, taking a wide range of courses. It was in Seattle that Rankin became active in the women's suffrage movement.

In 1910, she joined the state suffrage organization working to provide women with the right to vote. For the next five years, she campaigned for women's suffrage. Her efforts led to Montana extending the right to vote to women in 1914.

Finding politics enjoyable, Rankin decided to run for public office. In 1916, she was a Republican candidate for the U.S. House of Representatives from Montana. She was elected on a platform of women's suffrage, child protection legislation, and preparedness for peace. Rankin became the first woman elected to the U.S. Congress.

Four days after Rankin took her seat in 1917, she became involved in the debate about whether the United States should declare war on Germany. Her constituents knew she was a pacifist when they voted for her, and like most Americans, most Montanans desired that the United States remain neutral. By 1917 public opinion had shifted in favor of intervening in Europe. President Woodrow Wilson called a special session of Congress in April 1917, and the Senate passed a resolution to go to war. Despite recommendations from her advisors that she vote to go to war, Rankin was one of fifty-six members of Congress who voted against declaring war on Germany. She broke congressional tradition by prefacing her vote with an explanation that was published in the *Congressional Record.*

After war was declared, she joined the war effort at home. She promoted Liberty Bonds and voted for the military draft. She also continued her advocacy of women's rights. In 1918, Rankin unsuccessfully sought a seat in the U.S. Senate. For the next two decades, she worked as a lobbyist in Washington, D.C. She also established a residence in Athens, Georgia, where she founded the Georgia Peace Society.

She returned to Montana in 1939. Backed by her wealthy brother Wellington, she ran for a U.S. House seat in 1940. She ran a clearly antiwar campaign. She was elected and returned to Washington in 1941. After the bombing of Pearl Harbor on December 7, 1941, Rankin was the only member of Congress to vote against declaring war on Japan, stating, "As a woman I can't go to war, and I refuse to send anyone else." This vote ended her political career.

Rankin continued her peace activism for the rest of her life, even leading a number of protest marches during the Vietnam War. She died on May 18, 1973, in Carmel, California.

John David Rausch Jr.

See also: Pacifists (WWI); War Bonds (WWI); Women (U.S., WWI)

REFERENCES

Josephson, Hannah. *Jeannette Rankin, First Lady in Congress: A Biography.* Indianapolis: Bobbs-Merrill, 1974.

Kaptur, Marcy. *Women of Congress: A Twentieth-Century Odyssey.* Washington: Congressional Quarterly Press, 1996.

Redfield, William Cox

William Cox Redfield (1858–1932), the first secretary of commerce, was born in Albany, New York. He received his education in a public school in Pittsfield, Massachusetts. He worked in various jobs, including the post office, a paper company, a stationery business, and in the manufacture of iron forgings. Redfield also was involved in banking and life insurance. In 1896 he became interested in politics and was a delegate to the Gold Democrats National Convention held at Indianapolis. He was the commissioner of public works for Brooklyn Borough in 1902 and 1903. In the sixty-second Congress, he was the Democrat member from the Fifth District in New York. He tried unsuccessfully for vice-presidential nomination in 1912.

The Department of Commerce and Labor was separated by President William Howard Taft toward the end of his tenure. Redfield became the first secretary of commerce of the United States under President Woodrow Wilson. He remained in the office from March 4, 1913, to November 1, 1919, and was succeeded by Joshua Willis Alexander.

In *With Congress and Cabinet,* which was published in 1924, he outlined the workings of his department as well as the general functioning of the Congress. He had to face many statutes, official safeguards from law officers and the comptroller of the Treasury, and criticism on the floor of the House. But Redfield tackled all these with sincerity and vision. Although the department was not part of the military establishment, he cooperated with it fully.

Under Redfield, the Department of Commerce looked toward economic development by creating new jobs and improving the standard of living. It also collected population data, issued patents, and set up industrial norms.

One of the operating units of the department, the National Institute of Standards and Technology (NIST), set up in 1901, performed significant work in industry and science, such as research in metallurgy and electricity. Redfield visited the NIST in Washington, D.C., in 1918 and suggested improvements in its functioning. He was interested in the design and construction of the *Liberty* airplane motor, which was one of the important war assignments of the Commerce Department. Redfield was criticized for the failure of his department in the proper inspection of the steamboats. In September 1915, the sinking of the steamboat *Eastland,* with the loss of 2,500 people, was attributed to the faulty handling of inspection services of the Commerce Department by the Seamen's Unions.

Redfield remained as the secretary of commerce until 1919. Afterward he was involved in banking investment and insurance in New York City. He died in New York on June 13, 1932. He is best remembered as the first secretary of commerce of the United States.

Patit P. Mishra

See also: Business (U.S., WWI); Economy (U.S., WWI)

REFERENCES

Redfield, William C. *With Congress and Cabinet.* New York: Doubleday, Page and Co. 1924.
———. *We and the World.* New York: Silver Burdett and Company, 1927.

Reed, John

John Reed (1887–1920) was a noted left wing journalist who made his mark through eyewitness accounts of major historical events. Although not as well remembered as such, Reed was also a poet.

Reed was born in Portland, Oregon. Educated at Harvard, he participated in sports and wrote for the *Harvard Monthly* and the *Lampoon.* Upon graduation in 1910, Reed became a journalist, first for *American Magazine.* In 1912 he began writing for the famed radical magazine *The Masses,* along with other noted radicals such as Max Eastman and Floyd Dell. It was when writing for *The Masses* that he met Louise Bryant, the woman who would later become his wife.

From late 1913 through 1914, Reed covered the Mexican Revolution for *Metropolitan Magazine.* He met many revolutionary participants and leaders, including Pancho Villa. The wrote about his experiences in his first book, *Insurgent Mexico* (1914). Reed's book has been criticized for not being objective, but rather sympathetic to the revolution.

When World War I broke out in 1914, Reed traveled throughout several European nations, covering the war for both *The Masses* and *Metropolitan Magazine,* the latter of which often did not use his pieces due to their leftist leanings. As with his time in Mexico, his time in Europe resulted in another book, *The War in Eastern Europe* (1916). Health reasons prompted his return to the United States in 1916 to have a kidney removed. In 1917 he married Bryant, and in that same year they were both in Russia during the October Revolution. His experiences resulted in his most famous book, *Ten Days that Shook the World* (1919). Once again, Reed's reporting was not entirely objective, but his account provides vivid firsthand descriptions of people, events, and conversations.

In 1918, Reed and six other members of *The Masses* faced two trials for violating the U.S. Espionage and Sedition Acts, laws essentially aimed at suppressing antiwar dissent. The first trial in April, at which Reed was not present because he was in Europe, resulted in a mistrial. Reed was present for the second trial in June. This also resulted in a mistrial, and the government dropped the case.

In 1919, Reed was instrumental in the formation of the Communist Labor Party and served as a delegate to Communist International. He traveled and made numerous speeches on behalf of the revolution. But his health failed him and he came down with typhus; he died on October 19, 1920. Along with other Bolshevik heroes, he was buried in the Kremlin Wall.

His inspiration to many lived on through John Reed Clubs. In 1918, Warren Beatty's film *Reds* chronicled his life and work, especially through his relationship with Louise Bryant. Although the film was nominated for several Academy Awards, the idea of portraying Socialists in a sympathetic light was still taboo, and the film won but a single award for best supporting actress.

Mitchell Newton-Matza

See also: Journalism (U.S., WWI); Biographies: Eastman, Max Forester (WWI); Villa, Pancho (WWI)

REFERENCES

Fishbein, Leslie. *Rebels in Bohemia.* Chapel Hill: University of North Carolina Press, 1982.

O'Connor, Richard. *The Lost Revolutionary: A Biography of John Reed.* New York: Harcourt, Brace and World, 1967.

Rosenstone, Robert A. *Romantic Revolutionary: A Biography of John Reed.* New York: Knopf, 1975.

Rockefeller, John D.

Industrialist, "robber baron," and philanthropist, John Davison Rockefeller (1839–1937) was America's first billionaire. He was born in Tioga County, New York, the second of William and Eliza Rockefeller's six children. The family moved to Ohio in 1853, settling in Strongsville, near Cleveland. Rockefeller rented an apartment in Cleveland while attending school and became involved in the Erie Avenue (later Euclid Avenue) Baptist church. He became a church trustee at the age of twenty-one.

After completing six months' worth of classes at Folsom Mercantile College in only three months, Rockefeller went to work as an assistant bookkeeper for Hewitt and Tuttle, a small group of commission merchants and produce shippers. Rising quickly in the company, he managed to save one thousand dollars by 1859. Borrowing another thousand from his father, Rockefeller initiated a business partnership with Maurice Clark. In the same year the country's first oil well was drilled in Titusville, Pennsylvania. Cleveland, with strategic rail and shipping connections to western Pennsylvania oil fields, quickly emerged as a major refining center. Rockefeller and Clark hitched their fortunes to the rising star of the oil business in 1863. By 1865 their firm had five partners who so profoundly disagreed about the company's operation that they chose to sell it to the person or group who submitted the highest bid. Rockefeller and partner Samuel Andrews, who had practical experience in the refining business, bought the company for $72,500, forming Rockefeller & Andrews. By 1870, when Rockefeller and others established Standard Oil, the company was worth $1 million. Two years later Standard Oil Company controlled almost all the refining operations in Cleveland and even had its own barrel-making operation. In 1882,

While John D. Rockefeller's Standard Oil was broken up by the U.S. Supreme Court in 1911, the government promoted cooperation among oil companies during World War I. (Library of Congress)

when all of Standard Oil's assets were merged into a trust with forty-two owners, its assets were worth $70 million. Rockefeller also invested in timber, iron mining, railroads, manufacturing, and a variety of other enterprises.

Although an 1892 Ohio court decision dissolved the trust, Rockefeller and his partners reconstituted their operations as the Standard Oil Company of New Jersey, because New Jersey law allowed a parent company to hold stock in its subsidiaries. Throughout much of the 1890s, Standard Oil controlled up to 75 percent of the nation's petroleum. Rockefeller officially retired from Standard Oil in 1896, focusing his attention on philanthropy, but he retained the title of president until 1911 and

enjoyed substantial influence in the company well beyond that date.

Rockefeller's charitable activities were multifarious and significant. In Cleveland alone Rockefeller supported at least 118 agencies between 1860 and 1903. He helped establish many important institutions, including the University of Chicago, the Rockefeller Institute for Medical Research (now Rockefeller University), and the Rockefeller Foundation. Yet Rockefeller is also remembered as an archetypal "robber baron," subverting in the business world the very values he espoused in church. His practices were criticized by Henry Demarest Lloyd in 1894 and even more fiercely by Ida Tarbell in 1904.

In 1911, the U.S. Supreme Court found the Standard Oil Company in violation of antitrust laws and ordered its dismemberment. However, after the Great War broke out, the government reversed its antitrust policy and encouraged Standard Oil to pool its resources and coordinate its efforts to support the war. Rockefeller gloated, "the Government itself has adopted the views [that Standard Oil leaders] have held all these years, and notwithstanding the Sherman law and all the talk on the other side, the Government itself has gone further than any of these organizations dreamt of going." In February 1918 the Allies convened an Inter-Allied Petroleum Conference, hoping to efficiently coordinate oil production and supply. Putting aside its earlier hardball tactics, Standard Oil worked closely with its old rival, Royal Dutch/Shell Oil, to guarantee a steady supply of oil to the Allies. Eighty percent of all oil provided to the Allies came from the United States.

Rockefeller personally contributed $70 million to the war effort, including $22 million through the Rockefeller Foundation to rescue Belgians suffering from famine after the German invasion. His generosity in wartime did much to rehabilitate his battered public image. When Lord Curzon, a member of Great Britain's war cabinet, rose at a postwar banquet and proclaimed, "The Allied cause had floated to victory upon a wave of oil," Rockefeller felt vindicated. Surely, he believed, his experience and influence had contributed mightily to the Allied victory. Germany's defeat was, according to Ron Chernow, "the final sign of God's blessing on the Standard Oil Company." This triumph gave him the confidence to begin attacking Lloyd, Tarbell, and other of Standard's most vocal critics.

Although he fell short of his goal to live until his hundredth birthday, Rockefeller did manage to collect on his own life insurance, receiving $5 million on his ninety-sixth birthday. He died on May 23, 1937, at the age of ninety-seven.

Paul Hillmer

See also: Business (U.S., WWI); Economy (U.S., WWI)

REFERENCES

Chernow, Ron. *Titan: The Life of John D. Rockefeller, Sr.* New York: Random House, 1998.

Nevins, Allan. *Study in Power: John D. Rockefeller, Industrialist and Philanthropist.* Norwalk, CT: Easton Press, 1953.

Roosevelt, Theodore

One could argue that for Theodore Roosevelt (1858–1919), concerns regarding the home front began in 1897, when he became assistant secretary of the navy in the McKinley administration. During his year in office, he publicly argued for increased naval power and privately urged members of the administration to go to war with Spain. Roosevelt felt strongly about a vigorous United States projecting its power on the world stage; indeed, he resigned his navy post in 1898 and raised a volunteer army to fight in the Spanish-American War. His charge up San Juan Hill in Cuba made Roosevelt a war hero, and his actions emphasized his perspective that the United States was not doing enough to enhance its strength and position in the world. During the ten-year period following his presidential term and until his death (1909–1919), Roosevelt campaigned tirelessly for strong U.S. involvement in world affairs.

During his years as president (1901–1909), Roosevelt increased funding and training for all the armed services. Tensions rose in 1907 between the United States and Japan as the United States sought to restrict the number of Japanese immigrants coming to the United States. With sounds of war in the offing, Roosevelt commanded the entire U.S. naval fleet to circumnavigate the world, providing a display of power that was unmatched by any other nation. The sailing of the "Great White Fleet" was an impressive display of force. Sixteen battleships, numerous support craft, and more than eighteen thousand uniformed soldiers and sailors drove Roosevelt's point home that the United States could be the dominating world power if it so chose. While never reluctant to flex the power of the United States, Roosevelt was a skilled diplomat, and even though tensions were building throughout the world during his administration, he managed to defuse a volatile territorial dispute involving the Russians and the Japanese. His peace negotiations resulted in the Russo-Japanese Peace Treaty, for which he was awarded the 1906 Nobel Peace Prize (the first American so honored).

Essentially turning the presidency over to his hand-picked successor, William Howard Taft, in 1909, Roosevelt continued to stay extremely close to governmental action. Disappointed in Taft, Roosevelt ran in the 1912 presidential elections on the Progressive Party ticket, insuring a win by a man he hated more than Taft, Woodrow Wilson. Roosevelt regarded Wilson as weak and effete, in particular on foreign policy, and as tensions flared in Europe, Roosevelt agitated for American intervention. Although he had been out office for years, Roosevelt was still regarded as such a major figure that a week after WWI began with Germany invading Belgium in August 1914, Kaiser Wilhelm communicated to Roosevelt, expressing the pleasure he had experienced when Roosevelt had visited him after leaving the presidency in 1909. Roosevelt responded that he would long remember the Kaiser's hospitality—and perhaps even more so the hospitality of King Albert of Belgium, Roosevelt's next visit after Germany.

Roosevelt disagreed bitterly with Woodrow Wilson's early policies regarding WWI. As hostilities increased between the principal powers in Europe, Roosevelt, in *America and the World War* (1915), lobbied loudly and vigorously for the United States to intervene, if not militarily then at least in some forceful fashion that would lead the world back toward order. Roosevelt was clear in his repugnance for the "ultrapacifists," which he felt clearly described Wilson, adding that "Untried men who live at ease will do well to remember that there is a certain sublimity even in Milton's defeated archangel, but none whatever in the spirits who kept neutral, who remained at peace, and dared side neither with hell nor with heaven."

After Germany widened its belligerent activity to include more American concerns in 1917, Roosevelt, speaking of Wilson in a letter to his son Kermit, said, "Even the lily-livered skunk in the White House may not be able to prevent Germany from kicking us into war." At about this time, Roosevelt began pushing for permission to seek volunteers who would fight under him in Europe, which would have made him the first ex-President to lead troops in battle. When Wilson refused to grant permission, Roosevelt briefly went so far as to explore raising and training troops in Canada to take overseas. After the United States did declare war in April 1917, and finding himself still shut out from active duty by Wilson, Roosevelt did the next best thing: He had his four sons enlist in the armed services, and when the United States finally did become actively engaged in the battle, Roosevelt made sure that his sons saw action. Three were wounded and Roosevelt's favorite and youngest, Quentin, was killed in action when he was shot down over German-occupied France in July 1918. During this time, Roosevelt continued to rail against Wilson's strategies, arguing that not enough force was being applied to bring the conflict to a suitable resolution.

As the war ground down to its inevitable conclusion, Roosevelt protested as forcefully as he could in print and in speeches against Wilson's calls for moderation in dealing with a crushed Germany. His campaigning helped the Republicans capture control of both houses of Congress in the 1918 elections, further weakening Wilson's power base. The climate of massive and punitive retribution that a defeated Germany faced was a consequence to some extent of Roosevelt's influence. The Armistice was declared on November 11, 1918, and with that, Roosevelt began to turn his attention toward another possible run for the presidency in 1920. However, he had never fully recovered from the shock of losing his son, and he died only two months after the cessation of hostilities on January 6, 1919.

Brian Adler

See also: Republican Party (WWI); Biographies: Lodge, Henry Cabot; Wilson, Woodrow (WWI); Wood, Leonard (WWI)

REFERENCES

Brands, H. W. *TR: The Last Romantic.* New York: Basic Books, 1997.

Cadenhead, I. E. *Theodore Roosevelt: The Paradox of Progressivism.* New York: Barron's Educational Series, 1974.

Hagedorn, Hermann, ed. *The Works of Theodore Roosevelt.* National Edition, 20 vols. New York: Scribner's, 1926.

Harbaugh, William, ed. *The Writings of Theodore Roosevelt.* Indianapolis: Bobbs-Merrill, 1967.

Morris, Edmund. *The Rise of Theodore Roosevelt.* New York: Coward-McCann and Geoghegan, 1979.

———. *Theodore Rex.* New York: Random House, 2001.

Rosenwald, Julius

Julius Rosenwald (1862–1932) was an influential business figure in the United States during World War I. In his role as the president of Sears, Roebuck, and Company in Chicago, he used his wealth to support various causes in the United States (such as building schools for African Americans) as well as Jews in Russia. Born into a household of German Jews who immigrated to the United States in the early 1860s, young Julius worked his way up from a salesman in his family business in Springfield, Illinois to president of Sears and Roebuck in 1910.

During the first years of World War I, Rosenwald was an active supporter of a military buildup of the American armed forces, despite the official doctrine of neutrality espoused by Woodrow Wilson. Rosenwald, who was a Republican, supported Wilson's opponent, Charles Evans Hughes, during the 1916 election.

President of Sears and Roebuck department stores in the early twentieth century, Julius Rosenwald temporarilty gave up the daily running of the company to head the nation's Committee on Supplies during World War I. (Library of Congress)

Wilson held no animosity toward Rosenwald, despite their political differences, and in late 1916 appointed Rosenwald to the Advisory Council of National Defense. After the United States officially entered World War I in April 1917, he was made chairman of the Committee on Supplies, which was part of the Council of National Defense. Because of the demands of the job, he turned over day-to-day operations of Sears to Albert Loeb. His approach to supply acquisition was important for many of the businesses in the United States. He analyzed the costs of materials and labor for items such as shoes for the military and came up with the best possible solution so that the companies made a profit, yet the government paid a fixed price for shoes from all manufacturers.

In the summer of 1918, he made a trip to France to visit the front line troops and inspect the supply lines and material reaching the front. His compassion made him popular with the troops, especially Jewish troops, with whom he shared the same religion, and African American troops, whom he felt needed true equality back home in the United States. The Rosenwald Foundation was responsible for funding many schools for African Americans in the United States during and after World War I.

Following the cessation of hostilities in 1918, Rosenwald pledged $100,000 in aid so that the people of Germany could rebuild, and so that Germans, especially children, could eat. His generosity was noted on both sides of the Atlantic. He was recognized by the president of the Weimar Republic of Germany, Paul von Hindenburg, in 1930, with a letter of appreciation and a porcelain vase for his work on behalf of Germany. Rosenwald also continued with his philanthropical work in the United States, with support for more African American schools and donations for the construction of museums throughout the country. His crowning achievement for Chicago was the Museum of Science and Industry.

Cord A. Scott

See also: Business (U.S., WWI); Council of National Defense (WWI); Biographies: Hughes, Charles Evans (WWI)

REFERENCES

Ciccone, F. Richard. *Chicago and the American Century: The 100 Most Significant Chicagoans in the Twentieth Century.* New York: Contemporary Books, 1999.

Jarrette, Alfred Q. *Julius Rosenwald.* Greenville, SC: Southeastern University Press, 1975.

Joyce, Miriam. "Julius Rosenwald and World War I." *American Jewish Archives Journal* (Fall/Winter 1993), 207–217.

Werner, M. R. *Julius Rosenwald: The Life of a Practical Humanitarian.* New York: Harper and Brothers, 1939.

S

Sanger, Margaret

Feminist, social activist, and birth control movement pioneer, Margaret Sanger (1879–1966) opened the first American birth control clinic on October 16, 1916, in Brooklyn. A pacifist, Sanger was an outspoken critic of the American war effort.

Sanger was born into a large Irish Catholic family in Corning, New York. Her father was a freethinker and labor activist. Working as a nurse among the poor in New York City convinced Sanger that squalor and poverty could be mitigated by knowledge about "birth control" (a term she coined). In 1914, defying a federal law prohibiting the dissemination of information about contraception, Sanger started a magazine called *The Woman Rebel*, which avowed that "a woman's body belongs to herself alone" and that "Church, State, Big Business— will be struck such a blow that they will be able only to beg for mercy from the workers." For her efforts, Sanger faced criminal charges. Rather than stand trial, she fled to England for two years. Upon her return to the United States, Sanger opened the country's first birth control clinic, was arrested again, and spent thirty days in jail.

In print and in lectures, Sanger linked birth control to social reform and women's liberation. She advocated civil disobedience to promote social change. During the World War I years, she associated with such radical figures as the anarchist Emma Goldman and Socialist leader Eugene Debs. In January 1917, Sanger published the first issue of the *Birth Control Review*. In articles and cartoons the magazine derided the war effort, defended pacifism, and urged women to protest the military draft. In 1921, she founded the American Birth Control League, which became the Planned Parenthood Federation of America in 1942.

Tony Osborne

See also: Sexuality (WWI, WWII); Women (U.S., WWI); Biographies: Debs, Eugene V. (WWI); Goldman, Emma (WWI)

REFERENCES

Chesler, Ellen. *A Woman of Valor: Margaret Sanger and the Birth Control Movement in America.* New York: Simon and Schuster, 1992.

Jensen, Carl. *Stories that Changed America: Muckrakers of the 20th Century.* New York: Seven Stories Press, 2000.

Schneiderman, Rose

Rose Schneiderman (1882–1972) was a successful labor organizer and social reformer, fighting for the interests of women workers and women's suffrage, as the Great War began in 1914. Standing just four feet nine inches, Schneiderman was a powerful speaker and tireless organizer in New York City, the center of the nation's garment trade industry. As a representative and leader of the Women's Trade Union League (WTUL), both in New York and nationally, Rose fought with strikes, speeches, education, and legislation for many decades to improve the working conditions and lives of women.

Born in Russian Poland in 1882, Rose and her Jewish family made their way to the United States in 1890. Forced to leave school to work at age thirteen, Schneiderman worked in a department store before finding work in a cap factory in 1898. She helped organize the first female local of the United Cloth Hat and Cap Makers' Union and gained valuable experience during a 1905 strike. Massive strikes and unrest in the garment trades took place in the decade before WWI, during which Schneiderman primarily organized under the auspices of the New York WTUL, a group of allied working women trade unionists and middle- and upper-class supporters. During 1915–1916, Rose worked as a national organizer with the International Ladies Garment Worker's Union organizing shirtwaist workers in the Midwest and East.

After Schneiderman returned to the New York WTUL, she was elected president in 1918 and worked to protect previous gains and to prevent the suspension of labor laws protecting women workers during the war years. In addition to organizing, the WTUL began to focus more heavily on promoting protective legislation at the state level. Rose's devotion and service to the WTUL, which she called "the most important influence" of her life, continued until she retired in 1949. Schneiderman also served as president of the National WTUL from 1926 until her retirement.

Schneiderman cofounded the Industrial Section of the New York Woman Suffrage Party and in December 1914 represented working women at a suffragists' meeting at the White House with President Wilson. Already a notable labor leader and reformer, the New York State Labor Party nominated Schneiderman in an unsuccessful bid for U.S. Senate in 1920. Schneiderman was also nominated as one of two women in a delegation of trade unionists who traveled to Europe for the Paris Peace Conference.

Schneiderman's leadership of the New York WTUL brought her into contact with Eleanor Roosevelt and, eventually, Franklin Delano Roosevelt. Through discussions of the labor movement and women's struggles, her involvement with the Roosevelts grew and she was appointed by FDR as the only woman member of the National Recovery Administration Labor Advisory Board in 1933. Schneiderman served as the New York State secretary of labor from 1937–1943 and retired from the WTUL and public life in 1949. Rose remained active and published her memoirs in 1967. She passed away in 1972 at the age ninety in New York City.

Mark E. Speltz

See also: Trade Unions (U.S., WWI); Women (U.S., WWI)

REFERENCES

Dye, Nancy Schrom. *As Equals and As Sisters: Feminism, the Labor Movement, and the Women's Trade*

Union League of New York. Columbia: University of Missouri Press, 1980.

————. "Rose Schneiderman." 631–633 In *Notable American Women: The Modern Period,* eds. Barbara Sicherman, Carol Hurd Green, Ilene Kantrov, Harriette Walker. Cambridge, MA: Belknap Press of Harvard University, 1980.

Orleck, Annelise. *Common Sense and a Little Fire: Women and Working-Class Politics in the United States, 1900–1965.* Chapel Hill: University of North Carolina Press, 1995.

Schneiderman, Rose, with Lucy Goldthwaite. *All for One.* New York: Paul S. Eriksson, Inc., 1967.

Seeger, Alan

Alan Seeger (1888–1916), an American poet, was born in New York City and studied in the Horace Mann School. He graduated from Harvard in 1910. T. S. Eliot, the famous poet, was his classmate. He began to write poetry in Greenwich Village, where he lived for two years. In 1912, Seeger went to Paris, whose bohemian atmosphere suited his carefree attitude toward life. He traveled throughout the French countryside. When the First World War broke out in 1914, the young poet wanted to join what he viewed as the fight for freedom. But Seeger was an American citizen and the United States had not declared war against the Central powers, so he was not eligible for the French military. Instead, he joined the French Legion.

On July 1, 1916, French and German troops faced each other at the battle of Somme. The main motive was to draw the German army from the battle of Verdun. Casualities were heavy on both sides. The allied divisions attacked in regular waves to try to break through German lines. Seeger and his company marched toward the village of Belloy-en-Santerre to clear the Germans, and he rushed through in the first wave. One of the tallest men of his group, he died attacking with a bayonet amidst the fire of German machine guns.

Seeger became famous for a war poem aptly entitled, *I Have a Rendezvous with Death.* This apocalyptic poem is an expression of an anguished soul waiting for the inevitable end that is death. Seeger wrote: *I have a rendezvous with Death/At some disputed barricade,/When Spring comes back with rustling shade/And apple-blossoms fill the air—I have a rendezvous with Death.* His poems, published posthumously in 1917, are marked by high idealism, romance, solemnity, and sincerity. Some of Seeger's notable poems are *An Ode to Natural Beauty, The Deserted Garden, The Torture of Cuauhtemoc, The Nympholept, The Wanderer, The Need to Love, El Extraviado, La Nue, All That's Not Love, Paris, An Ode to Antares, Do You Remember Once, Champagne,* and *Ode in Memory of the American Volunteers Fallen for France.* The young American poet had met death voluntarily for the cause that he loved passionately. He wrote: *One crowded hour of glorious life/Is worth an age without a name.*

Patit P. Mishra

See also: Literature (U.S., WWI)

REFERENCES

Gardner, Brian, ed. *Up the Line to Death: The War Poets, 1914–1918; An Anthology.* London: Methuen, 1965.

Seeger, Alan. *Poems by Alan Seeger.* New York: Charles Scribner's Sons, 1918.

Sunday, Billy

Born William Ashley Sunday on November 19, 1862, popular Evangelist Billy Sunday grew up in an Iowa orphanage, where he developed a love of baseball and worked at various odd jobs to get himself through high school. In 1883 he moved to Chicago and became a member of the Chicago White Stockings baseball team. In 1886, he converted to Christianity, and in 1890 he retired from baseball to work for the Young Man's Christian Association as an assistant to evangelist Dr. J. Wilbur Chapman. In 1894, Sunday set out on his own as an evangelist. Joined by his wife, Nell, and their growing family, Sunday traveled around the Midwest and Plains speaking to ever-growing audiences as word of his theatrical, fiery sermons grew. Using simple language and employing metaphors from everyday life, including sports, Sunday could communicate with the common man through sermons that condemned the moral evils of the day, including alcohol, gambling, socialism, and political corruption.

Sunday reached the peak of his popularity during World War I. In 1917 he conducted a ten-week revival in New York City and a similar event in Chicago. He often appeared on the front page of newspapers, he dined with Presidents Theodore Roosevelt and Woodrow Wilson, and he held personal meetings with John Rockefeller Jr. and many movie stars. Sunday also fostered improvements in race relations when he insisted that a 1917 revival in Atlanta, Georgia be integrated.

Sunday supported the Wilson administration's decision to declare war on Germany. He encouraged his audiences to buy war bonds, and he regularly contributed money to war bond drives and the Red Cross. He spoke about saving food and fuel and encouraged young men to enlist in the army or navy. He spoke at

Evangelist Billy Sunday reached his peak of popularity and influence during World War I. The preacher supported American participation in the war. (Library of Congress)

military camps in America, but refused all invitations to journey to Europe to speak to soldiers at the front. Another area of concern for Sunday during this time was the battle over Prohibition. Viewing alcohol as a great threat to America's moral fiber, Sunday lent his name and his voice to Prohibition, first at the state level and later during the battles over the Eighteenth Amendment.

After the war, Sunday continued to preach to large crowds, but problems with his wife's health, his children's deaths, and investigations into his personal finances distracted him. He kept preaching until 1935, and died on November 6, 1935.

Jason Dikes

See also: Prohibition (WWI); Religion (U.S., WWI); Revivalism (WWI)

REFERENCES

Bruns, Roger. *Preacher: Billy Sunday and Big-Time American Evangelism.* New York: W. W. Norton, 1992.

Dorsett, Lyle W. *Billy Sunday and the Redemption of Urban America.* Grand Rapids, MI: W. B. Eerdmans Publishing Company, 1991.

T

Taylor, Frederick Winslow

A nineteenth century mechanical engineer and technological theorist, Fredrick Taylor (1856–1915) is best known for his book *Principles of Scientific Management,* published 1911, and for his ideas about the proper techniques of industrial production.

Taylor was born into an educated, professional upper-middle-class Philadelphia family on March 20, 1856. His father was a lawyer and his mother was an active abolitionist. After studying and traveling in Europe with his family for several years, Taylor entered the prestigious private school Phillips Exeter Academy. His parents hoped he would later attend Harvard Law School and have a career as a lawyer.

Despite his family's wishes, he did not go on to law school. In 1874, he was hired as an apprentice pattern maker and machinist in the Enterprise Hydraulic Works in Philadelphia. After several years, he moved on to the Midvale Steel Company, where he started as a manual laborer. It is important to note that Taylor did not work out of necessity; he was likely the only worker who went home to a house full of servants. Taylor saw these different jobs as educational and an invaluable way to see how work was really performed. In addition to his jobs he won the U.S. doubles championship in 1881, with his own specially designed racket, and received a degree in Mechanical Engineering from the Stevens Institute of Technology, in Hoboken, New Jersey.

In 1898, while working at the Bethlehem Steel Company, he developed the Taylor-White steel hardening technique with fellow engineer J. Maunsel White. This radical technique for the hardening of tool steel by a process of heating significantly improved the steel's cutting capabilities.

Due to continued resistance from management and workers toward his theories, he left the steel company and in 1901 began working as an independent corporate consultant for what he called Systematizing Shop Management.

Through close observation, measurement, and time and motion studies, he was able to see how sophisticated traditional skills could be reduced to a series of discrete tasks. Taylor sought to replace the skill and knowledge of preindustrial craftsmen by trying to systematize the process of fabrication into as many constituent parts as possible. He went as far as assessing the optimum quantity of a shovelful. These actions were simplified and put back together so they could be learned in a short time.

Taylor's principles were widely praised and, unfortunately, sometimes used to justify economic and professional dislocation caused by the process of industrialization. His theories and their application were always controversial. The implementation of some of Taylor's ideas at the government arsenal in Watertown, Massachusetts in 1911 led to a strike, which resulted in the House of Representatives authorizing a special committee to investigate the Taylor and other systems of shop management.

His detractors charged that his middle-class background blinded him to the social effects of his ideas and that his approach to work and the traditional dignity of labor was dismissive. His most vocal critics claimed that he saw workers only as objects to be sped up or fired.

Taylor was part of the first generation born after the introduction of the steam engine and the telegraph. During his lifetime, the technological progress of industrial capitalism was stu-

Frederick Winslow Taylor's theories on the scientific management of labor improved productivity in American factories, helping the country win World War I. (Library of Congress)

pendous, but society was also facing massive social dislocation and environmental transformation.

Like many nineteenth-century technologists, he saw himself improving human lives through greater systematization, automaton, and integration.

J. Ward Regan

See also: Business (U.S., WWI); Economy (U.S., WWI); Technology (WWI)

REFERENCES

Kanigel, Robert. *The One Best Way: Frederick Winslow Taylor and the Enigma of Efficiency.* Cambridge, MA: MIT Press, 2005.

Tucker, Sophie

Born Sonya Kalesh in the Hasidic shetl of Tulchin, Ukraine, vaudeville star Sophie Tucker (1886–1966) was the daughter of Charles Palteil Kalesh and his wife Jennie Linetsky. Shortly after her birth, the family immigrated to New York, changing their name to Abuza and settling in Hartford, Connecticut, where they ran a successful kosher restaurant. Sophie, although she eloped with Louis Tuck in 1903 and gave birth to a son, Albert, in 1905, desperately wanted to pursue a public singing career. Encouraged by restaurant patrons with contacts to New York vaudeville, Sophie left her husband and son in 1906 and began performing in beer gardens and cafes. She entered vaudeville as a blackface singer of "coon songs" and made a reputation as a "song plugger" for new material. Her beautiful rented gowns and brassy, exuberant personality caught the attention of Florenz Ziegfeld and agent William Morris, who arranged for her to move up to musical theater and phonograph recordings by 1910.

Sophie's material walked a thin line between rowdy and obscene, and she was arrested several times in conservative towns on the touring circuit. Encouraged by Jewish celebrities such as Al Jolson and Fanny Brice, she reduced her blackface material to add Yiddish songs and branch out into jazz and ragtime. Her personal life, including a divorce from Tuck in 1912 and brief marriages to musician Frank Westphal (1917–1921) and Al Lacky (1928–1934) added to her scandalous allure. During World War I, Sophie refused to sing nationalistic numbers and created a brief incident by criticizing an audience member noisily knitting for the troops, but participated enthusiastically in bond selling and morale visits to army camps, where she was a favorite entertainer.

A tireless promoter and networker, Sophie toured with a jazz band, the "Five Kings of Syncopation," often doubling by working both nightclubs and theaters while on tour. From records, she branched out to live radio performances and in 1922 made the first of many successful tours of Great Britain. Carefully cultivating composers, she established her signatures songs from Jack Yellin, "I'm the Last of the Red Hot Mammas" and "Yiddishe Mama," and Shelton Brooks's "Some of these Days." Sophie gained wide coverage for her beautiful clothes and worked steadily throughout the depression because of her ability to perform in theater, nightclubs, cabarets, and film (although she was disappointed by small showcase roles in films such as *Honky-Tonk* (1928) and *Broadway Melody of 1938.*

As honorary president of the American Federation of Actors (AFA), she insisted that theaters post bonds for performer's salaries and established a trust fund for sick and destitute members. The union collapsed through mismanagement, but Sophie emerged unscathed

Jewish immigrant and vaudeville star Sophie Tucker was opposed to U.S. participation in World War I, but nevertheless sold war bonds and went on morale tours to army camps. (Library of Congress)

to star in the Cole Porter/Samuel Spewack musical *Leave It to Me,* satirizing the Soviet Union and diplomacy. During World War II, Sophie was in great demand as a morale-building performer and was named "Woman of the Year" in 1951 by the Jewish American War Veterans for her tours.

In the 1950s, she became an outspoken supporter of Israel and sponsored many charities for Jews, Catholics, African Americans, and early cancer research, possibly more than $1 million by 1960 and funded by sales of her autobiography. Live television proved an uncomfortable fit for her uncensored style, but her tour performances continued unabated until ill health forced her to leave the stage in 1965. She died in New York City of lung cancer and kidney failure on February 9, 1966.

Margaret Sankey

See also: Jazz (WWI); Music (U.S., WWI); Theater (WWI)

REFERENCES

Fields, Armond. Sophie *Tucker: First Lady of Show Business.* Jefferson, NC: MacFarland and Company, 2000.

Lavitt, Pamela Brown. "First of the Red Hot Mamas: 'Coon Shouting' and the Jewish Ziegfeld Girl" *American Jewish History* 87, no. 4 (1999): 253–290.

Tucker, Sophie. *Some of These Days.* New York: Doubleday, 1945.

V

Veblen, Thorstein

An iconoclastic commentator on American economic and social conditions, Thorstein Veblen (1857–1929) was regarded by his contemporaries as a radical theorist with an unsparingly satiric point of view. After his death, when the unprecedented catastrophe of the Great Depression seemed to provide ample evidence of his prescience, he began to be regarded as a prophetic figure who was doubly tragic because his warnings had gone too long unheeded and because he had not lived quite long enough to see his theories confirmed.

Born in Cato, Wisconsin, and raised on a farm in Minnesota, Veblen was educated at Carleton College, Johns Hopkins University, and Yale University. After completing his Ph.D. at Yale, he returned to the family farm to write. Seven years later, he resumed his formal studies at Cornell University and the University of Chicago. As his writings began to be published and to attract some notoriety, he was offered a succession of positions at the University of Chicago, Stanford University, and the University of Missouri. But the controversies sparked by his economic theories, his own irascibility, and several indiscreet extramarital affairs turned him into an itinerant academic. In 1919, he became a founding faculty member of the New School for Social Research, and he taught there until his death.

Veblen's first and most significant work, *The Theory of the Leisure Class: An Economic Study in the Evolution of Institutions* (1899) defines the concept most associated with him, "conspicuous consumption." Veblen challenged the then prevailing notions that what profited the individual capitalist would ultimately benefit the broader capitalistic society and that economic competition, regardless of how ruthless it might seem in the short term, was ultimately the wellspring of economic and social progress. Instead, Veblen saw the conspicuous consumption of the wealthy class not only as an indicator of the corrupting effects of capitalism but also as a major diversion of resources and an obstacle to progress.

In addition to *The Theory of the Leisure Class,* Veblen's works include *The Theory of Business Enterprise* (1904), *The Instinct and Workmanship and the State of the Industrial Arts* (1914), *Imperial Germany and the Industrial Revolution* (1915), *An Inquiry into the Nature of Peace and the Terms of Its Perpetuation* (1917), *The Higher Learning in America: A Memorandum on the Conduct of Universities by Business Men* (1918), *The Place of Science in Modern Civilization* (1919), *The Vested Interests and the Common Man* (1920), and *Absentee Ownership and Business Enterprise in Recent Times: The Case of America* (1923).

Martin Kich

See also: Economy (U.S., WWI); Intellectuals (WWI)

REFERENCES

Blaug, Mark, ed. *Thorstein Veblen.* Aldershot, UK: Edward Elgar, 1992.

Dorfman, Joseph. *Thorstein Veblen and His America.* Fairfield, NJ: A. M. Kelley, 1934.

Griffin, Robert A. *Thorstein Veblen, Seer of American Socialism.* Hamden, CT: Advocate, 1982.

Jorgensen, Elizabeth. *Thorstein Veblen.* Armonk, NY: M. E. Sharpe, 1998.

Villa, Pancho

An effective, crude, and colorful Mexican guerilla leader who expanded a regional conflict by leading an attack upon the United States home front during World War I, Pancho Villa (1878–1923) was part of a whirlwind of shifting factions during the Mexican Revolution whose role changed as various strong men emerged. Upset by U.S. recognition of a regime established by President Venustiano Carranza, Villa led five hundred men across the U.S. border on March 9, 1916, in an attack upon Columbus, New Mexico. The Villistas set fire to buildings, fired weapons, and looted businesses until soldiers of the U.S. cavalry counterattacked and killed sixty-seven of Villa's men. The death of seventeen Americans in the terrorist strike precipitated a military expedition into Mexico led by General John Pershing to bring Villa and his followers to justice. Villa,

Mexican revolutionary Pancho Villa led a raid into the United States shortly before World War I, leading to U.S. military intervention south of the border. The head of that expedition, John J. Pershing, became head of U.S. forces in Europe in World War I. (Library of Congress)

however, managed to evade capture and enhanced his reputation as a folk hero to the common Mexican people.

Pancho Villa was born Doroteo Arango in San Juan del Río, Durango, Mexico, on June 5, 1878. He spent much of his life there until age sixteen, when he killed a man who had raped his younger sister. He fled to the mountains, where he joined a bandit gang who stole cattle from rich landowners. During this time he changed his name to Francisco "Pancho" Villa to evade the law and moved north to Chihuahua province. He added bank robbery to cattle rustling and murder on the list of crimes for which he was wanted by the Mexican government.

In 1910, Villa and his men joined Francisco Madero's revolutionary forces, marking his transition from bandit to revolutionary. Villa's charismatic leadership influenced thousands, including some Americans, to join the revolution and propel Madero to president of Mexico. After Madero was assassinated, Villa resisted the dictatorship of Victoriano Huerta by ruling over northern Mexico like a medieval warlord. He financed his army by stealing cattle and selling the animals to U.S. merchants for supplies of guns and ammunition. He gained a reputation as a Mexican "Robin Hood" by breaking up vast land holdings of hacienda owners and giving them to the widows and orphans of his fallen soldiers.

When the U.S. government openly supported a Carranza presidency, Villa retaliated by raiding Columbus, New Mexico. President Woodrow Wilson authorized General John J. Pershing to lead a punitive expedition of ten thousand into Mexico to kill or capture Villa and his army. Employing all the technology of war that could be mustered, including airplanes, motor vehicles, and radios, Pershing was unable to capture Villa, but he did manage to disrupt his organization. Villa still conducted some minor raids into U.S. territory until 1920, when the Huerta regime called for a truce and retired him with a general's stipend and a large ranch in Chihuahua. On July 20, 1923, Villa was assassinated along with seven of his bodyguards in Parral, Chihuahua.

Steven J. Rauch

See also: Mexico, U.S. Invasion of (WWI); Biographies: Pershing, John J. (WWI)

REFERENCES

Eisenhower, John S. D. *Intervention! The United States and the Mexican Revolution, 1913–1917*. New York: Norton, 1993.

Katz, Friedrich. *The Life and Times of Pancho Villa*. Stanford, CA: Stanford University Press, 1998.

Stout, Joseph A. *Border Conflict: Villisata, Carrancistas, and the Punitive Expeditionary Force, 1915–1920*. Fort Worth: Texas Christian University Press, 1999.

Villard, Oswald Garrison

Oswald Garrison Villard (1872–1949), grandson of abolitionist William Lloyd Garrison and son of railroad entrepreneur and newspaper publisher Henry Villard, was America's leading pacifist during World War I. Editor of the *New York Evening Post* since 1897, a liberal newspaper purchased by his father in 1881, he had gained recognition as a leading reformer by the time America entered the war. One of five founders of the National Association for the Advancement of Colored People (NAACP) in 1909, Villard promoted African American economic and social improvement, female emancipation and suffrage, birth control, and prison reform.

Villard's opposition to the war reflected his overall disappointment and disillusion with Woodrow Wilson, the president of the United States from 1913 to 1921. Believing that Wilson would promote policies to end racial segregation in the federal civil service system and legislation to end lynching, he endorsed Wilson's presidential candidacy in 1912. Villard lost confidence in Wilson's commitment to racial equality and integration after learning that black Treasury clerks had been separated from whites, that black federal officials were being replaced by whites throughout the government, and that whites had replaced the black ambassadors customarily assigned to Haiti and Santa Domingo.

In 1915 Villard worked as an *Evening Post* correspondent in Washington, D.C. He remained critical of Wilson, especially his unwillingness to censure Great Britain for preventing cargo ships leaving the United States from traveling without restriction to neutral ports. Villard interviewed Robert Lansing, a State Department official, who had written a diplomatic note, describing Britain's behavior as "unbearable." Publication of Lansing's remark in the *Evening Post* brought denials from both Secretary of State William Jennings Bryan and Lansing of the existence of the note but an apology from the British foreign office. Vindicated by the British response, Villard garnered much satisfaction from his report but disdain from Bryan, who told Villard privately that he did not understand the ethics of journalism particular to Washington. Villard, who founded the League to Limit Armaments, argued that Wilson permitted the United States to be drawn into the European conflict by failing to enforce the nation's neutrality.

Born in Wiesbaden, Germany, in 1872, Villard never lost his appreciation for German culture, history, language, and politics. In 1915, he published *Germany Embattled: An American Interpretation* to remind Americans of the contributions Germans had made to the nation. Combined with his opposition to the war, this publication suggested to most Americans that Villard was a traitor. Forced to sell the *Evening Post* due to declining readership during the war, Villard bought the *Nation,* another newspaper originally owned by his father. The Post Office attempted to block the September 14, 1918, publication of the *Nation* for an editorial criticizing labor leader Samuel Gompers for suppressing union discontent in support of American participation in the war. Villard complained directly to Wilson, who overruled the Post Office and permitted publication of the journal.

After the war, Villard covered the Paris peace talks leading to the Treaty of Versailles, which he described as very harsh on Germany. While in Europe, he visited postwar Germany, which was supposed to be off-limits to foreign journalists. Upon his return to the United States, the State Department invited him to Washington to report his observations. Through the 1920s, Villard wrote critically of government efforts to entrap and punish individuals suspected of being sympathetic to the Bolshevik Revolution.

Adam R. Hornbuckle

See also: Censorship (WWI); Journalism (U.S., WWI); National Association for the Advancement of Colored People (NAACP) (WWI); Biographies: Gompers, Samuel (WWI); Lansing, Robert (WWI)

REFERENCES

Humes, Dollena Joy. *Oswald Garrison Villard: Liberal of the 1920's*. Syracuse, NY: Syracuse University Press, 1960.

Wreszin, Michael. *Oswald Garrison Villard: Pacifist at War*. Bloomington, IN: Indiana University Press, 1965.

W

Wald, Lillian

Born to prosperous German immigrants, women's rights activist and pacifist Lillian Wald (1867–1940) grew up in Rochester, New York, was educated in private schools, and traveled widely. She attended New York Hospital School of Nursing, and in 1892, volunteered to teach a weekly home-nursing class for immigrant women on Manhattan's Lower East Side. Appalled by the poverty and desperation of the immigrant poor, Wald opened the Henry Street Settlement in 1893 with fellow nurse Mary Brewster. Her Visiting Nurse Society provided in-home health care and education for the poor and became a model for similar programs around the world.

Among her many accomplishments, Wald convinced legislators of the need for school nurses and lobbied for the creation of the U.S. Children's Bureau to restrict child labor. With Jane Addams and other activists, she formed the Women's Trade Union League in 1903 to protect women workers, and challenged major industries to implement health inspections in the workplace. At her urging, Columbia University appointed the first professor of nursing at an American university.

Through a network of female activists, Wald became involved in a variety of progressive causes. To circumvent New York's public segregation laws, Wald offered Henry Street Settlement for the 1909 meeting of the National Negro Conference that established the National Association for the Advancement of Colored People (NAACP). She served as honorary vice-president of the Women's City Convention for woman suffrage, marched for women's right to vote, and supported Margaret Sanger's birth control campaign.

Wald was an ardent peace activist. At the outbreak of World War I in 1914, she co-founded with Jane Addams and Florence Kelley the American Union Against Militarism (AUAM), which claimed six thousand members by 1915 and helped avert war with Mexico in 1916. When the United States declared war on Germany on April 6, 1917, Wald led protest marches and struggled to preserve civil liberties in the face of the Espionage and Sedition Acts of 1917–1918. She served as Chairman of the Committee on Community Nursing of the American Red Cross during the war, represented the United States at the International Red Cross, and battled the global influenza epidemic of 1918.

Hoping to influence the postwar settlement, Wald helped to establish the Foreign Policy

Association, which advocated American involvement in the League of Nations. She was active in the Women's Peace Party, which in 1921 adopted the name Women's International League for Peace and Freedom (WILPF). The WILPF demanded suffrage and equality for women, protested the harsh terms of the Treaty of Versailles toward Germany, and supported the League of Nations.

In the postwar years, Wald was accused of radicalism for continuing her work for peace and other progressive causes. The Henry Street Settlement suffered during the Great Depression, as sources of funding diminished while demand for health services increased. Wald supported Franklin Roosevelt's New Deal, but after suffering a heart attack and stroke in 1932, she was no longer politically active. Wald died of a cerebral hemorrhage on September 1, 1940.

Victoria Grieve

See also: Women (U.S., WWI); Women's International League for Peace and Freedom (WWI); Biographies: Addams, Jane (WWI); Kelley, Florence (WWI)

REFERENCES

Daniels, Doris Goshen. *Always a Sister: The Feminism of Lillian D. Wald.* New York: The Feminist Press at the City University of New York, 1989.

Weeks, John W.

John W. Weeks (1860–1926), an American politician, was born near Lancaster, New Hampshire. After graduating from the U.S. Naval Academy in 1881, he was a midshipman for two years. In the late 1880s, Weeks worked in banking and financial institutions, and from 1888 to 1914 he was in a brokerage business in Boston. He was a member of the Board of Visitors and the U.S. Naval Academy and also served as a lieutenant in the Volunteer Navy during the Spanish-American War. He became a member of the New Hampshire Society of the *Cincinnati* for serving the country with honor.

Weeks next turned his attention to politics, becoming alderman (1899–1902) and then mayor (1903–1904) of Newton, Massachusetts. He plunged into national-level politics as a member of the Republican Party. He became a member of the fifty-ninth Congress on March 4, 1905, and continued there until March 4, 1913. He held various posts including chairman of the Committee on Expenditures in the Department of State and member of the Committee on Post Office and Post Roads. He was a senator from March 4, 1913, to March 3, 1919.

In the war period, Weeks did commendable work in banking and conservation legislation. Although defeated in the reelection to the Senate in 1918, his involvement in the country's affairs continued. He was the secretary of war under President Warren Harding and President Calvin Coolidge. Week's resigned in 1925 due to failing health, and died on July 12 of the same year in Lancaster, New Hampshire.

Patit P. Mishra

See also: Republican Party (WWI); Biographies: Coolidge, Calvin (WWI); Harding, Warren Gamaliel (WWI)

REFERENCES

Garraty, John A., and Mark C. Carnes. *American National Biography.* Vol. 22: "Weeks, John Wingate." New York: Oxford University Press, 1999.

Washburn, Charles G. *The Life of John W. Weeks.* Boston: Houghton Mifflin Co., 1928.

Wells-Barnett, Ida Bell

Journalist, editor, lecturer, and activist Ida B. Wells-Barnett (1862–1931) is famous for her desegregation efforts, her pioneering 1890s anti-lynching work, and her continued defense of African Americans during and after World War I. Born to slaves in Mississippi, Wells-Barnett countered the standard explanation of lynching, that mobs were formed to punish men who raped white women, arguing that lynching was used against innocent blacks to thwart African American advancement. After her life was threatened, she moved North, eventually settling in Chicago. There she was active in many political organizations, including the three she founded: a black women's organization (later called the Ida B. Wells Club), a settlement house that provided aid and education to black men and served as a center for political organizing (Negro Fellowship League), and the first black female suffrage club in Illinois (Alpha Suffrage Club).

During World War I, Wells-Barnett actively supported the U.S. war effort by selling Liberty Bonds through the Ida B. Wells Club and distributing care packages to black soldiers, yet her primary concern remained violence against African Americans within the country. She worked in defense of accused black men in Chicago and made buttons commemorating the thirteen black soldiers hung by a military court following the 1917 Houston riot. She investigated the 1917 race riot in East St. Louis that killed thirty-nine African Americans and the 1919 race riots in Chicago and Arkansas. Her work drew the attention of federal agents, one of whom labeled her more dangerous than Marcus Garvey, an activist she supported. Nominated as a delegate to the Versailles peace talks by both the Equal Rights League and the Universal Negro Improvement Association, she was

Journalist and anti-lynching crusader Ida B. Wells-Barnett investigated the causes of anti-black race riots during World War I. Such activities got her investigated by the U.S. government. (Library of Congress)

denied a passport due to her reputation for militancy.

Lisa Schreibersdorf

See also: African Americans (WWI); Race Riots (WWI)

REFERENCES

Schechter, Patricia A. *Ida B. Wells-Barnett and American Reform 1880–1930*. Chapel Hill, NC: University of North Carolina Press, 2001.

Wharton, Edith

Born to a family of established social prestige and wealth, novelist Edith Jones Wharton (1862–1937) spent much of her childhood in Europe, where her parents traveled extensively in England, Germany, and Italy before returning to their Manhattan home. Because of the social conventions of the day, she was educated at home by a governess, and under family pressure, married Edward Robbins Wharton in 1885. The marriage, although a success by New York society standards, became increasingly unhappy for Edith because of Wharton's mental instability and intellectual dullness.

To escape her boredom, Edith retreated to Lennox, Massachusetts, where she built a country house and began to write, beginning with *The Decoration of Houses*, a collaboration with her architect, Ogden Codman, which criticized Victorian styles. Although her early short stories concerned the city poor, Edith's focus shifted to sharp and perceptive critiques of New York society and the social constraints placed on women, exemplified by her 1905 success, *The House of Mirth*. Edith moved permanently to Paris in 1907 and surrounded herself with an artistic circle, including Jean Cocteau, Henry James, and Henry Adams. In 1908, she began a short affair with journalist Morton Fullerton, and in 1913 she secured a divorce from Edward Wharton.

During World War I, Edith championed the cause of the Allies and encouraged America to enter the war by writing reports for American newspapers, editing a popular anthology of war writing, and criticizing America's delay in her novella *The Marne*. She also sheltered more than five hundred Belgian orphans at her estate and assisted those fleeing from northern France and Belgium through the American Hostel for Refugees.

Following the war, Edith's novel *A Son at the Front* (1923) described the anguish suffered on the American home front, while ironically noting that the glittering and socially restrictive world of her earlier novels had been destroyed in the cataclysm of the world war. Her later works dealt with the clash between American and European values and the experiences of wealthy American visitors, including the *Buccaneers* (1938) of her last, unfinished novel. In 1921, she was awarded the Pulitzer Prize for her work *The Age of Innocence,* an award that confirmed her status as the grand dame of American literature. Edith Wharton died at her home in suburban Paris on August 11, 1937, after a series of debilitating strokes.

Margaret Sankey

See also: Literature (U.S., WWI)

REFERENCES

Benstock, Shari. *No Gifts from Chance: A Biography of Edith Wharton.* New York: Scribner's, 1994.

Dwight, Eleanor. *Edith Wharton: An Extraordinary Life.* New York: Abrams, 1994.

Price, Alan. *The End of the Age of Innocence: Edith Wharton and the First World War.* New York: St. Martin's, 1996.

Willard, Daniel

Daniel Willard (1861–1942) was one of the most respected railroad men of the early twentieth century, having worked his way up from track crew to president of the B & O Railroad. During World War I, Willard served on the Council of National Defense and briefly headed the War Industries Board.

Willard was born on January 28, 1861, in North Hartland, Vermont. He had a lifelong love of learning but was unable to complete college. Instead, Willard became a track hand on the Vermont Central Railroad that ran past the family farm in 1879. Over the next three decades, Willard worked his way up through the railroad hierarchy. He was an engineer before he was twenty, and held the offices of conductor, agent, superintendent, and general manager. In January 1910, Willard became president of the B & O Railroad, a historic railroad that had fallen on hard times. Within six years, Willard's policy of modernizing equipment and increasing efficiency made the B & O one of the most profitable railroads in the United States. He also maintained good relations with the workers, thanks to his experiences as one of them. Unlike many operators, Willard supported the eight-hour day for railroad crews.

After World War I broke out in Europe, Willard was one of the proponents of American preparedness. He recognized that the war was an industrialized one unlike any earlier war. Because railroads were central to transporting men and equipment to places where they were needed, Willard believed they needed to work together. He had the opportunity to put his ideas to work when the National Defense Act of 1916 went into effect. It was the most comprehensive peacetime law preparing for war in American history. As a follow-up to the Act, the Army Appropriations Act was passed on August 29, 1916, with a rider calling for a Council of National Defense to plan America's industrial mobilization. An advisory committee of experts was authorized, to be appointed by the president. President Woodrow Wilson appointed seven men who were leaders in various industries. Willard was selected to represent transportation in general and the railroads in particular. The Advisory Committee was organized on October 11, 1916, and held its first meeting in Washington on December 6, 1916. Willard agreed to serve as chairman.

The Advisory Committee undertook a survey of industrial plants in the United States to determine what each could produce for the war effort. Each member headed a subcommittee that evaluated a particular industry. Willard worked with leaders of railroads and other forms of transportation. Five days after the United States declared war on Germany, leaders of the nation's railroads met in Washington under Willard's chairmanship. They formed a five-member Railroads' War Board, with Willard as ex-officio member. The Board oversaw a voluntary pooling of resources to supply equipment to where it was most needed. The organization was extra-legal and in violation of antitrust laws, but it was acceptable under the emergency situation. At first the system worked well, but by the winter of 1917–1918, the nation's railroad system faced collapse. The demands of wartime shipments, coupled with shortages of labor, threatened a complete breakdown.

Willard helped coordinate the railroads while remaining a member of the Advisory Board. In November 1917, he accepted an appointment by Wilson as chair of the War Industries Board (WIB). The WIB was intended to oversee all industries to prioritize which would receive raw materials and transportation to further the war effort and keep the civilian economy moving. Unfortunately, the WIB had no authority to compel industries to obey its directives. Frustrated, Willard resigned in January 1918. He remained chairman of the Advisory Board. In October 1918, Willard prepared to go to France to help direct the American Expeditionary Force's railroads, but the Armistice made his trip unnecessary..

After the war, Willard returned to the B & O. He remained one of the most labor-conscious railroad executives in America, encouraging workers to participate in management activities. Known as "Uncle Dan," Willard remained president of the B & O until 1941. He was chair of the Board of Directors until his death on July 6, 1942, in Baltimore, Maryland.

Tim J. Watts

See also: Council of National Defense (WWI); National Defense Act (U.S., WWI); War Industries Board (WWI)

REFERENCES

Hungerford, Edward. *Daniel Willard Rides the Line.* New York: G. P. Putnam's Sons, 1938.

Vrooman, David M. *Daniel Willard and Progressive Management on the Baltimore & Ohio Railroad.* Columbus, OH: Ohio State University Press, 1991.

Willard, Jess

Jess Willard (1881–1968) was the "Great White Hope" that brought the heavyweight boxing championship back to the white race in the early twentieth century. The world of boxing was turned upside down in 1908 when Jack Johnson became the first black heavyweight champion of the world. It was unpopular to be a black athlete, much less a black champion, in anything during this time in American history. Johnson added to this unpopularity with his arrogance and sexual relationships with white women.

The heavyweight crown symbolized athletic and physical superiority, and the boxing world was looking for someone to bring the championship back to the white race. The boxing world was looking for a "Great White Hope" and found it in Willard.

Willard, born in St. Clere, Kansas, in Pottawatomie County, stood at least six-foot, five-inches tall and weighed nearly 250 pounds, which led to the nickname of "Pottawatomie Giant." There is no absolute story describing how Willard got into boxing, but it probably started in December 1910 in Oklahoma City when he saw his first bout. Willard first entered into the ring in February 1911 for exhibition bouts at age twenty-nine. He was active in the ring the remainder of 1911 and continued to fight in 1912 and 1913. He fought at least once a month during this period of his career.

Johnson maintained his championship while Willard was rising to the top of the boxing world, and it was Willard who soon became the "Great White Hope" boxing sought.

A bout was arranged between Willard and Johnson to take place April 5, 1915, in Havana, Cuba. The fight was schedule for forty-five rounds, but Willard knocked Johnson out in the twenty-sixth round. It took place outdoors in simmering hundred-degree temperatures, and there was some conjecture after the fight that Johnson deliberately lost. Nonetheless, Willard was the new heavyweight champion of the world.

Willard capitalized on his newly found popularity by becoming a member of Buffalo Bill's Wild West Show. He eventually became a performer in the 101 Ranch Wild West Show, and he owned it from 1916 to 1918.

Willard's time spent on stage meant a decrease in the time he spent in the ring. He fought in some exhibition matches but defended his title only once in the four years he was champion. His income outside the ring — as much as $2,500 a day touring with the Wild West Shows —was more than he could make boxing. However, his income depended on remaining the heavyweight champion of the world, so he chose to risk his title as little as possible.

Jack Dempsey eventually took the title from Willard on July 4, 1919. Willard clearly had a size advantage over Dempsey, but Dempsey soundly beat Willard. The champion was knocked down several times in the first round and beaten badly in the second and third rounds. Willard was unable to answer the bell to start the fourth round, and Dempsey became the heavyweight champion.

Willard virtually vanished from the boxing scene after losing the championship. He eventually settled in the San Fernando Valley in California. He died December 15, 1968. Willard was elected to the Boxing Hall of Fame in 1977 and is also a charter member of the Kansas Sports Hall of Fame.

Robin Hardin

See also: Biographies: Dempsey, Jack (WWI)

REFERENCES

Jess Willard, Boxing Champion, Dies at 86. *New York Times*, December 16, 1968: 47.
Lipsyte, Robert. "Sports of the Times: The Great White Hope." *New York Times*, September, 21, 1968: 38.
Sugar, Bert R. *The Great Fights: A Pictorial History of Boxing's Greatest Bouts*. New York: Rutledge Press, 1981.

Wilson, William B.

America's first secretary of labor, William B. Wilson (1862–1934) was born in a small Scottish village. Shortly thereafter, Wilson's family immigrated to America and settled in Arnot, Pennsylvania. At nine years old, when his father became ill with lumbago, Wilson was forced to drop out of school and work in the coal mines. His enthusiasm for education, however, did not cease and he continued to educate himself and

his illiterate father on a variety of topics. Wilson's father was most interested in contemporary politics and philosophy, so one day when Wilson had saved a few extra dollars he brought home a second-hand edition of *Chamber's Information for the People*. This book would change the life of both father and son because they became more involved in the politics of their local union. William Wilson's reputation as an honest and dedicated worker helped him quickly rise to the top of his local unit.

Wilson was leader of the United Mine Workers from 1900 to 1908, after which he served in Congress until 1912. Then for a short period he was an intermediary for the American Federation of Labor (AFL) in the president's cabinet. In 1913, President Wilson created the Department of Labor and made Wilson the first American secretary of labor. Even though the Department of Labor was initially created only as a means for the president to find compromise among his union supporters and his advocates in big business, the inevitability of American involvement in World War I made it an important area of the administration. Secretary of Labor Wilson soon found himself in charge of the movement of millions of workers from nonessential industries to essential industries in very little time. His role became even more important as the Allies began to win and it looked like they would need to quickly move the workers back.

Secretary Wilson decided that he needed help, and he wanted it from his union friends. After a bitter fight with Secretary of the Navy Franklin D. Roosevelt, in 1918 Secretary Wilson convinced the president to expand his role in the Labor Department to cover the nation's labor policy. That same year, President Wilson created a War Labor Administration, also to be headed by Wilson. Secretary Wilson immediately got the AFL and the National Industrial Conference Board (NICB) involved by asking each group to nominate five people to sit on the War Labor Conference Board. By getting these groups involved, Wilson changed history. He had formed the first government-sponsored agency dedicated solely to issues of labor, and he did it by including union leaders instead of political bureaucrats.

Wilson resigned from his position in 1921 at the end of his term. He tried to continue a life in politics in 1926 with a bid for the Senate, but when he lost he retreated to local union work. He worked until his death in 1934 as an arbiter in the coal fields of Illinois.

Rachel Bennett

See also: American Federation of Labor (WWI, WWII); Economy (U.S., WWI); Trade Unions (U.S., WWI); War Labor Board (WWI)

REFERENCES

McCarin, Joseph A. *Labor's Great War: The Struggle for Industrial Democracy and the Origins of Modern American Labor Relations, 1912–1921.* Chapel Hill, NC: University of North Carolina Press, 1997.

Montgomery, David. *The Fall of the House of Labor: The Workplace, the State, and American Labor Activism, 1865–1925.* Cambridge: Cambridge University Press, 1987.

Wilson, Woodrow

President of the United States during World War I, Woodrow Wilson (1856–1924) was born in Staunton, Virginia. He was the son of Dr. Joseph Ruggles Wilson, a Presbyterian minister and director of the Augusta Female Seminary, and Janet Woodrow.

Wilson's heritage was Scotch-Irish and English. His childhood contained a mix of Calvinism and Southern values, along with a refined education he received at private schools. Wilson graduated from Princeton University in 1879, where he majored in history and politics. He next studied law at the University of Virginia, and went on to pass the Georgia bar examination in 1882. Wilson first practiced law in Atlanta, but he was not successful. Abandoning the legal profession, Wilson entered Johns Hopkins University to study constitutional and political history. On June 24, 1885, Wilson married Ellen Axson. He earned his Ph.D. from Johns Hopkins University in 1886. After teaching at a few schools, Wilson returned to Princeton University to join the faculty in 1890. In 1902, he was selected president of Princeton University. Wilson was eager to make drastic reforms to improve Princeton's academic reputation, but he could not win enough support so he resigned his position in 1910.

Wilson ran for governor of New Jersey, which he won in 1910. He acquired a reputation as a Progressive governor. Wilson's next big step in politics was to become the Democratic Party's presidential nominee, and then to become president in 1912 by beating William Howard Taft, the incumbent. Theodore Roosevelt (Progressive Party) and Eugene V. Debs (Socialist Party) also ran for the presidency. Wilson advocated "New Freedom," his concept of a government that should maintain freely competitive markets to encourage U.S. citizens to become successful by providing them with opportunities. Because the Republican Party was divided between Conservatives who supported Taft and Progressives who supported Roosevelt, this made it easier for Wilson to win the election. Wilson received 435 electoral votes to 88 for Roosevelt and 8 for Taft.

Wilson achieved three major reforms. First, he convinced Congress to pass the Underwood Tariff Act in 1913, which lowered import duties by about one-fourth and increased the number

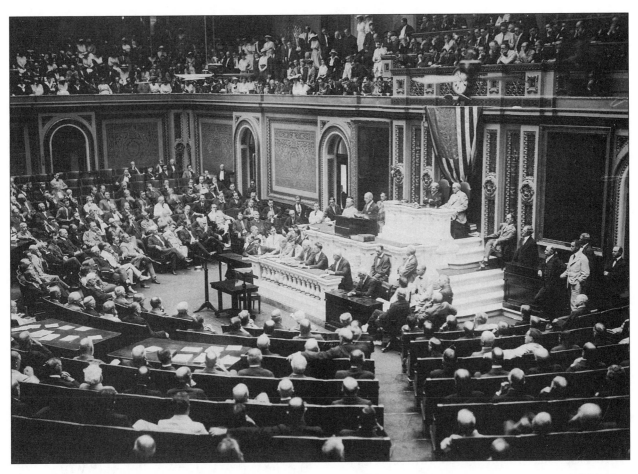

President Woodrow Wilson addresses Congress regarding severing U.S. relations with Germany before World War I. Congress was divided between those who supported America's entry into World War I and those who opposed it. (National Archives)

of duty-free items. To compensate for the expected loss of revenue, Wilson was successful in introducing the federal income tax. Second, based on a Wilsonian initiative, Congress enacted the Federal Reserve Act in 1913, which created twelve regional Federal Reserve banks, supervised by a Federal Reserve Board. The primary duty of the Board was to control the volume of money in circulation so as to maintain healthy monetary and credit conditions for the American economy. Third, Wilson pushed through Congress the Federal Trade Commission Act of 1914, which resulted in the birth of a new regulatory agency, the Federal Trade Commission (FTC), a government bureau with

substantial powers to check business concentration. Wilson also signed the Clayton Anti-Trust Act in 1914, which prevented interlocking company directorates and specified unacceptable kinds of monopolistic business practices. The Clayton Anti-Trust Act also declared that labor unions in and of themselves were not subject to injunction.

Wilson's foreign policies were not as successful as his domestic policies. Wilson believed in a dominant U.S. role in the western hemisphere. In support of this dominance, one of the first actions Wilson took was to promote Pan-Americanism, but Latin American countries rejected this for fear of establishing an

American hegemony over the region. To protect America's economic and strategic interests in the region, Wilson dispatched U.S. troops to occupy Haiti in 1915 and then the Dominican Republic in 1916. Wilson also intervened militarily in the Mexican Revolution, but this only increased the distrust of Mexicans toward the United States.

World War I broke out in July 1914. In August 1914, Wilson proclaimed the neutrality of the United States, a policy he made every effort to maintain over the next two years. Wilson made a series of attempts to mediate between the Allies and the Central Powers, but the result was that relations with Germany deteriorated. Finally, the Zimmermann Telegram incident and German resumption of unrestricted submarine warfare led to the U.S. entrance into World War I on April 6, 1917. Now the country's enormous financial, industrial, and military resources were brought to bear to assure the Allies of a victory.

In East Asia, Wilson agreed with Secretary of State Robert Lansing's idea that the United States should have a conciliatory relationship with Japan. Wilson tried to contain the Japanese program of expansion in China. The Lansing-Ishii Agreement was concluded in November 1917, which recognized Japanese "special interest" in Manchuria and Inner Mongolia, while embracing the American notion of "open door" principles for maintaining equal economic opportunity for all nations in the region and the preservation of China's territorial integrity.

On January 8, 1918, Wilson revealed his Fourteen Points, an idealistic vision of a peaceful and stable world based on self-determination, the League of Nations, and a liberal trade system. At the Paris Peace Conference, however, Wilson was forced to make a series of compromises to secure support for what he considered to be the most important clause of the Fourteen Points, the creation of a League of Nations. The peace conference resulted in the warring parties signing the Treaty of Versailles. Wilson returned to Washington to present the Treaty of Versailles to the U.S. Senate for ratification, but Republicans and even some Democrats tried to amend or attach strong reservations, which Wilson rejected. Wilson's uncompromising attitude failed to bridge the difference between himself and the Senate. The Senate rejected the treaty on November 19, 1919, and again on March 19, 1920, so the United States stayed out of the League of Nations.

Yoneyuki Sugita

See also: Democratic Party (WWI); Elections of 1916 (WWI); Federal Reserve (WWI); Fourteen Points (WWI); League of Nations (WWI); Mexico, U.S. Invasion of (WWI); Paris Peace Conference (WWI); Zimmermann Telegram (WWI); Biographies: Debs, Eugene V. (WWI); Lansing, Robert (WWI); Roosevelt, Theodore (WWI); Documents: On Neutrality, August 19, 1914; Democratic Party Platform, 1916; Declaration of War, April 2, 1917; "Do Your Bit," April 15, 1917; Proclamation of Conscription Policy, May 28, 1917; League of Nations Speech, September 26, 1919

REFERENCES

Knock, Thomas J. *To End All Wars: Woodrow Wilson and the Quest for a New World Order.* Princeton, NJ: Princeton University Press, 1995.

Nordholt, Jan Willem. *Woodrow Wilson: A Life for World Peace.* Berkeley: University of California Press, 1991.

Wood, Leonard

Born in Winchester, New Hampshire, American World War I commander Leonard Wood (1860–1927) spent his youth in New England and studied medicine at Harvard Medical School. For a short time he practiced medicine in Boston, but after performing operations without permission from his superiors, he was dismissed from his duties. After his dismissal, he entered the Army Medical Department in 1885 and headed west to serve on the frontier.

Early in his military career, Wood served as a surgeon in the U.S. Army's campaigns against the Apache along the border between Arizona and Mexico. His duties gradually expanded from medicine to include operational command as well. His most notable early military experience came in 1886, on the Army's expedition to capture the Apache leader Geronimo. There he displayed remarkable physical endurance, following the Indian leader for four months and traveling more than three thousand miles. He would later be awarded the Medal of Honor for his service in that campaign.

For the next twelve years, Wood served on garrison duty in a variety of posts around the United States. In 1898, with the outbreak of the Spanish American War, Wood sought a field command. He received it as commander of the First Volunteer Cavalry, popularly known as "The Rough Riders." Although Wood commanded the unit, he was overshadowed by his friend and second in command, Theodore Roosevelt. Wood led the Rough Riders in operations against Spanish forces defending Santiago, Cuba. After a sharp fight at Las Guasimas, in which Wood recklessly exposed himself to enemy fire, he was promoted to brigade command. He commanded that brigade in the disorganized fight on June 30 that led to the

Chief of staff of the U.S. Army from 1910 to 1914, Leonard Wood's efforts to reform and modernize smoothed the military's transition to a war footing after U.S. entry into World War I in April 1917. (Library of Congress)

American capture of the Spanish defenses on the San Juan heights.

After the fall of Santiago, Wood was made governor of the city, and he held that position until he was made military governor of Cuba, in which capacity he served until 1902. During his time in Cuba, Wood worked to feed the populace of the island, combat disease, address poor sanitation, and restore civil society. In 1903, the Army transferred Wood to the Philippines, to use his experience in civil affairs to help suppress the insurrection there. While there, he served as governor of the Moro Province, and later as commander of the Philippine Division.

From 1910 through 1914, Wood served as Chief of Staff of the Army, at a time when the Army was attempting to reform and become a more professional force. During this period Wood also stressed the military obligation of citizens in a democratic society, and he urged increased American military preparedness. He commanded the Department of the East from 1914 to 1917 but did not receive a European command in World War One. In 1920, Wood unsuccessfully sought the Republican nomination for president. His last assignment was as governor-general of the Philippines from 1921 until his death in 1927, as a result of complications from brain surgery.

Mitchell McNaylor

See also: Conscription (U.S., WWI)

REFERENCES

Lane, Jack C. *Armed Progressive: General Leonard Wood.* San Rafael, CA: Presidio Press, 1977.

Wood, Leonard. *The Military Obligation of Citizenship.* Princeton, NJ: Princeton University Press, 1915.

———. *America's Duty as Shown by Our Military History: Its Facts and Fallacies.* Chicago: Reilly and Lee, 1921.

———. *Leonard Wood on National Issues: The Many-Sided Mind of a Great Executive Shown by His Public Utterances.* Garden City, NY: Doubleday, Page and Company, 1920.

Z

Ziegfeld, Florenz

Born in Chicago to a show business family, theater impresario Florenz Ziegfeld (1867–1932) showed a talent for self-promotion from childhood when he charged neighborhood children to see his "invisible goldfish" which were, in reality, just an empty goldfish bowl. In 1893 he opened a music hall in Chicago promoting the strongman Eugene Sandow. For Sandow's debut, Ziegfeld staged a massive publicity campaign to help build anticipation and guarantee ticket sales. It was a technique he was to repeat throughout his career.

Relocating to New York City, Ziegfeld produced a series of musicals noted for their publicity as much as for their music. For his 1896 production of *A Parlor Match*, Ziegfeld stirred up publicity by claiming that the show's star, Anna Held, daily bathed in milk, and then sued a local dairy farm for selling her sour milk. After a brief run in New York, the show toured the rest of the country. Over the next dozen years, Ziegfeld repeated this process of promoting musicals before sending them on tour.

Anna Held provided Ziegfeld with the inspiration for his life's great work—the *Ziegfeld Follies*, based on the Parisian *Folies Bergère*. In July 1907, the first *Ziegfeld Follies* opened in the New York Theater's roof garden and became the first roof garden show to run a full summer. A combination of spectacular visual effects, topical comedy, and beautiful women kept the audiences coming back. The success of the 1908 *Follies* made it clear that the series would become an annual event as the mix of dancing, humor, and exotic sets attracted audiences night after night.

Although Ziegfeld continued to produce other musicals, it was the summer *Follies* that garnered his full attention. They continued to expand visual boundaries as Ziegfeld hired New York's best designers and set builders and encouraged them to come up with something new and spectacular on a yearly basis. They also introduced audiences to new, important performers, including Fanny Brice, Eddie Cantor, W. C. Fields, and Will Rogers.

Tired of seeing his audiences go out to spend their money elsewhere after attending one of his shows, Ziegfeld in 1914 produced the first of the *Ziegfeld Midnight Frolics* at the New Amsterdam Theater, featuring dance music between acts. Theatergoers reveled in the *Midnight Frolics* party-like atmosphere, and it was a tradition in New York until Prohibition forced its closure in 1923. The *Follies* ran strongly throughout the 1920s, and Ziegfeld

Impresario Florenz Ziegfield produced a string of hit Broadway shows during the World War I era. (Library of Congress)

continued to produce other musicals for his own Ziegfeld Theater. One musical, *Showboat,* dealt with themes rarely seen in musicals, such as racism and mixed marriages.

Ziegfeld always loved gambling both in casinos and on the stock market. When the market crashed in 1929, it damaged Ziegfeld's finances. He attempted to make movies, continued to stage musicals, and even tried to bring the *Follies* back, but to no avail. His health declined and he died on July 22, 1932.

Jason Dikes

See also: Music (U.S., WWI); Theater (WWI)

REFERENCES

Carter, Randolph. *The World of Flo Ziegfeld.* New York: Praeger, 1974.

Ziegfeld, Richard, and Paulette Ziegfeld. *The Ziegfeld Touch: The Life and Times of Florenz Ziegfeld, Jr.* New York: H. N. Abrams, 1993.

Zukor, Adolph

Adolph Zukor (1873–1976) was an up-and-coming movie executive when war broke out in Europe in 1915. He had merged his production company, Famous Players in Famous Plays, with the Paramount Company only a year earlier, and the war allowed Zukor to greatly expand his business. Paramount participated in governmental efforts to whip up public support for the war by making almost thirty war films, some of which were unabashedly patriotic and overtly anti-German.

Born in Risce, Hungary, in 1873 and orphaned at age seven, Zukor immigrated to America when he was sixteen. He immediately found work in a New York City fur shop and soon started his own business. In 1900, Zukor began investing in penny arcades, nickelodeons, and store shows. Zukor, however, dreamt of showing longer movies, and in 1913 he made history when he produced America's first feature-length film, *The Count of Monte Cristo.* He soon signed such rising stars as Mary Pickford and John Barrymore to his company. By 1914, Famous Players had churned out thirty feature pictures. Zukor signed with Paramount the same year to meld production with distribution.

During the war years, Zukor completed a series of mergers that allowed him to add exhibition to his production and distribution machine, thus giving him complete control of his films. Zukor joined several other filmmakers to form the War Cooperating Committee, which worked with the government to see how the industry might help the war effort. Although Zukor's native Hungary was allied with Germany, Paramount's films were decidedly pro-Ally, even before the company collaborated with the U.S. government on several "official films." Paramount agreed to undertake the production of movies for which the Committee of Public Information's Division of Films supplied the scenario, location, and permits. Paramount's various war films included patriotic epics such as *The Little American* (1917), recruitment propaganda such as *The Girl Who Stayed at Home* (1919), and anti-German melodramas such as *The Claws of the Hun* (1918). Paramount made between two and three pictures per week during the war, and Zukor looked to war-torn Europe to broaden the scope of his audiences. He showed films to U.S. servicemen and Allied nations, in addition to Americans on the home front.

The war also touched Zukor personally. He gave consent for his underage son Eugene to enlist in the navy. A number of the moviemaker's international family fought for the Allies, while others fought with the Central Powers.

Immediately after the war, Zukor traveled to devastated Risce to set up a relief fund for the town's most needy. He continued to expand Paramount by making films, adding theaters to his chain, and signing such talents as Greta Garbo, Mae West, Henry Fonda, and Bob Hope. Zukor became Paramount's board chairman in 1935 and continued his affiliation with the company until his death in 1976. Zukor shrewdly understood, well before most, the appeal and power of the motion picture to mass audiences.

Emilie Raymond

See also: Committee on Public Information (WWI); Film (U.S., WWI); Propaganda (U.S., WWI)

REFERENCES

Eames, John Douglas. *The Paramount Story.* New York: Crown, 1985.

Irwin, William Henry. *The House That Shadows Built.* Garden City, NY: Doubleday, Doran and Company, Incorporated, 1928.

Johnson, Winifred. *Memo on the Movies: War Propaganda, 1914–39.* Norman, OK: Cooperative Books, 1939.

Zukor, Adolph, and Dale Kramer. *The Public Is Never Wrong: The Autobiography of Adolph Zukor.* New York: Putnam, 1953.

WORLD WAR I:
TOPICS

———————— ◆ ————————

A

Adamson Act

The Adamson Act was a critical piece of federal labor legislation passed in 1916, limiting the workday for most railroad workers to eight hours.

By the spring of 1916, President Woodrow Wilson had overseen a program of domestic reform in labor and farming that had made him a favorite of social reform advocates and progressive politicians. As Wilson looked ahead to the presidential campaign of 1916, he and his campaign managers knew that he must retain both the support of the reformers while also capturing working class votes in the industrial Midwestern tier of Ohio, Illinois, and Indiana. At the same time, Wilson could not afford to antagonize corporations and industrialists. To avoid unnecessary controversy in foreign affairs, Wilson instructed the State Department to hold off on any diplomatic initiatives related to World War I until after the November election.

What neither Wilson nor his managers could handle or even predict were uncontrollable domestic events that exploded in late August 1916. Sensing a prime opportunity, frustrated railroad unions threatened a nationwide strike if their demands for an eight-hour work-day with time-and-a-half for overtime were not met. In an era before the development of an interstate highway system and a fleet of capable trucks, a railroad strike meant political and economic chaos and it would severely limit America's ability to provide needed war materials to Britain, France, and Russia.

In response, Wilson summoned union representatives and railroad owners to the White House. He urged the owners to accept the eight-hour workday and to allow a presidential commission to study the other demands. The owners refused. Wilson threatened to send the Army in to seize the railroads to keep them running. The owners still refused. Wilson's appeals to the unions to call off the strike also fell on deaf ears.

Acting quickly, Wilson appeared before a joint session of Congress asking for legislation allowing him to settle the dispute. Three days later, Congress presented Wilson with the Adamson Act, which he signed into law on September 2, 1916. The act established an eight-hour workday for railroad workers with no reduction in pay and created a commission to study the effects of the legislation.

Although the federal government had intervened in railroads before in order to promote competition, to outlaw rate setting, and to prevent monopolistic abuses, this marked the first time that the government intervened on behalf of the workers themselves. The Adamson Act was a political coup for Wilson as it pleased not only railroad workers but also the industrialists and corporations who depended upon the railroads for their business. In 1917, the Supreme Court, in a five-to-four decision, upheld the constitutionality of the Adamson Act.

Jason Dikes

See also: Economy (U.S., WWI); Supreme Court (WWI); Trade Unions (U.S., WWI); Biographies: Wilson, Woodrow (WWI)

REFERENCES

Saunders, Robert M. *In Search of Woodrow Wilson: Beliefs and Behavior.* Westport, CT: Greenwood Press, 1998.

Thompson, John A. *Woodrow Wilson.* New York: Longman, 2002.

Advertising

During World War I, the U.S. government collaborated with advertisers to promote the liberty loans, war stamps, income tax, and food campaigns within American society. This collaboration proved successful as most Americans donated to these campaigns and made numerous sacrifices throughout the war.

Following the U.S. declaration of war against Germany, advertising was used to generate support among the American public to enlist in the armed forces. Prior to the nation's involvement in the war, Americans expressed hostilities toward military service. Nevertheless, advertisers encouraged men between the ages of twenty-one and thirty to enroll in the army, navy, and marine corps on the basis of nationalism, loyalty, and patriotism. For example, one advertisement asserted that America's intervention into the war would spread democracy throughout the world, which would bring an end to Germany's autocratic system. Furthermore, another advertisement emphasized that registering for the armed forces personified manhood and American citizenship. These various advertisements were posted in movie theaters, industrial factories, local shops, office buildings, and churches. With all of these advertisements, the United States witnessed an increase in voluntary registration for military service during the war.

Advertising also represented a significant factor in the various Liberty Loan campaigns that occurred during World War I. On April 23, 1917, Congress approved legislation that established the first Liberty Loan. Federal officials noted that Americans could demonstrate their patriotism by purchasing these loans. They also maintained that these liberty loans served as an investment for the American public because these loans had an interest payment of nearly 3 percent. While the liberty loans were designed to finance America's involvement in World War I, some federal officials believed that if Americans failed to purchase loans, this would indicate to the Central Powers that the American population lacked dedication to the war effort. Thus, the U.S. government called upon advertisers to promote the various liberty loans campaigns. For example, one of the advertisements stated that if individuals purchased even small amounts of liberty loans, their actions would inspire others to participate in the campaign. Another advertisement emphasized that the purchase of loans would ultimately shorten the duration of the war. Thus, sons and husbands would be reunited with their families at home.

By late 1917, the federal government introduced additional financial measures to supplement the Liberty Loans. The establishment of war-savings certificates and the U.S. thrift cards was designed to provide additional funds for the war effort. Once again, federal officials called upon advertisers to promote these new measures. For example, one advertisement encouraged the American public to create war-saving societies, which would allow individuals to save their money on a joint basis. Additionally, the advertisements also targeted children. For instance, one advertisement maintained that young boys and girls could actively participate in the war effort by buying war stamps.

During the onset of World War I, some individuals supported the U.S. intervention in the war while others in American society regarded the conflict in Europe as a capitalists' war. These latter individuals remarked that bankers and merchants were benefiting from the war in Europe. One method by which these individuals expressed their discontent toward the war was to refuse to pay income taxes. While it probably had little effect on opponents of the war, advertisements encouraged nondissenting Americans to pay their income taxes on time because it would cost the government great sums of money in order to locate these delinquent individuals. Another advertisement asserted that merchants and bankers did not profit from the war because they had to pay a war profits tax. Thus, advertisers maintained that the burdens of the war impacted the rich as well as the middle-class and poor.

During the war, the Committee on Public Information collaborated with advertisers. Members of the committee encouraged advertisers to note the various violent actions that the German army inflicted upon the civilian population of Europe. For example, one advertisement remarked that German troops forced women and children to march in front of their regiments, causing the civilians to serve as a shield against enemy fire. The Committee on Public Information hoped that these advertisements would cause individuals to donate additional funds toward the war effort.

Following the establishment of the U.S. Food Administration in 1917, the federal government enlisted the assistance of advertisers to promote the various food campaigns during the war. The advertisements called upon farmers to increase agricultural production for the war in Europe. Another advertisement encouraged Americans to reduce their amount of food consumption and eliminate luxury items from their diets. For example, the advertisements discouraged Americans from eating meat, sugar, and wheat bread during the national crisis. Instead, individuals needed to substitute these items with fish, poultry, corn bread, and honey. Furthermore, advertisements encouraged Americans to plant home gardens and raise chickens to supplement their diets. By 1917, a majority of Americans adopted these measures, believing that their sacrifices would ultimately help win the war in Europe.

Prior to the outbreak of the war, advertising was regarded as a suspicious business venture and not a true profession. However, World War I improved the status of advertisers with the American public. Through advertisers' efforts during the war, the American public began to view these businessmen with more credibility.

Kevin M. Brady

See also: Business (U.S., WWI); Committee on Public Information (WWI); Food Administration (WWI); War Bonds (WWI)

REFERENCES

Cornebise, Alfred E. *War as Advertised: The Four Minute Men and America's Crusade, 1917–1918.* Philadelphia: American Philosophical Society, 1984.

Creel, George. *How We Advertised America: The First Telling of the Amazing Story of the Committee of Public Information That Carried the Gospel of Americanism to Every Corner of the Globe.* New York: Harper and Brothers, 1920.

Kennedy, David M. *Over Here: The First World War and American Society.* New York: Oxford University Press, 1980.

Mock, James R., and Cedric Larson. *Words That Won the War.* Princeton, NJ: Princeton University Press, 1939.

African Americans

African Americans during World War I experienced fundamental changes in daily life, and in other areas the persistence of discrimination continued seemingly unabated by global changes. The inequity of the front lines mirrored the home front experience for most African Americans. Over two million African American men registered for the draft and an estimated 370,000 served in the military. In segregated units, African American soldiers fought on the front lines, dug trenches, loaded ships, and served in nearly every capacity. But they were not allowed to rise through the ranks; the position of officer was off limits. Throughout the war, African American soldiers were over-represented in labor and service positions. African American women stepped forward in great numbers to serve in the nursing corps, but were not allowed to serve until the very end of the war. Despite these and other challenges to black civil rights, W. E. B. DuBois advocated African Americans to "close ranks" and support the war effort. DuBois argued that African Americans could demonstrate their patriotism, discipline, and loyalty, and prove to themselves and to the larger society that they shouldered the responsibilities of citizenship equally well.

Others argued that African Americans during the World War I period upheld their citizenship above and beyond the call of duty.

Demographics

The demographic changes in the African American community so fundamentally altered the urban landscape that the period between World War I and demobilization became known as the Great Migration. As industrial plants in the North and South raced to meet wartime demands in munitions, ships, and foodstuffs, African Americans left the rural South in even greater numbers than in any previous time. European immigration to the United States was curtailed for the duration and Northern industrialists scrambled to find another pool of cheap labor. Wages in the North were three to five times what Southern industries offered. Nearly one million African Americans left the South for destinations in the urban North and West. African American migrants made Southern cities their first but not necessarily their last step on their journey. Higher wages, access to skilled jobs, better schools for their children, a vibrant African American urban cultural scene, and the vote were all indeed distinguishing and beneficial features of life in the North and West. Though most African Americans would continue to live in the South, their move to Southern cities and ultimately Northern cities like Chicago, New York, and Detroit created new opportunities and challenges for African Americans throughout the United States.

African American migration out of the South started at the turn of the century and continued through World War I. White Americans also moved to the cities, but the most significant change occurred as African Americans created large communities within Southern and Northern cities. Many of the factors con-

Thousands of African American soldiers fought for the United States in World War I. But they did so in segregated units and faced the same racist discrimination upon their return to civilian life. (National Archives)

tributed to African American migration out of the rural South. The strengthening of "Jim Crow" laws—segregated and unequal services—was a critical issue: education, health services, public transportation, and public parks became increasingly segregated and unequal. Where African Americans could find good wages, they also found fewer places to spend it. Stores, theaters, and restaurants adhered to a strict racial code. Only a few generations removed from slavery, African Americans actively protested the encroachment upon their liberties. Disenfranchisement, through a series of laws and local practices, was the final

blow to citizenship. Some stayed in the South, but many left rather than continue to suffer daily humiliation and persecution.

On the railroad journey northward many African Americans, soldiers and civilians alike, experienced another—but not the final—humiliation of segregation: the segregated passenger railroad car. Segregation on the railroad meant that African American passengers were restricted to crowded dirty cars attached to the very end of the train. Jim Crow cars were sometimes complete cars or part of a car, usually the "smoker," where African Americans endured the fumes of white men's cigars.

World War I and the Great Migration created dramatic changes in the African American community, particularly in industrial work. The migration northward often occurred in stages, stopping first in a Southern or Mid-western "border" city before moving on to cities like Detroit, Chicago, and New York. African Americans maintained strong ties with their Southern roots through letter writing and visits, when feasible, back home. They brought back news of life in the North and encouraged, and occasionally discouraged, friends and family to join them. African American women were able to move out of domestic service work to a certain extent. African American communities in New York and Philadelphia were particularly attractive to women due to a preponderance of domestic jobs, but many men migrated there as well. Cleveland and Detroit held more industrial jobs for African American men than for women. However, African American women worked in some assembly-line jobs in munitions, glass manufacturing, and the garment industries. More often these women filled jobs in cleaning work, which were low wage and arduous, as well as in railroad cars, on factory floors, and in office buildings. Besides factory work, some African American women entered clerical and professional work. The industrial opportunities for African American men were greater, but no less riddled with challenges. In meatpacking, for example, African American men worked in semiskilled positions for the first time outside the South. Cities like Chicago and Detroit offered African American men low-wage and insecure common labor jobs; these were positions very much like the ones offered to European immigrant men in preceding years. Unlike immigrant workers, however, African American workers were barred from many jobs in meatpacking, automobile manufacturing, and steel industries. Promoting an African American worker to a supervisory position over whites, or even an integrated crew, was "unthinkable."

The growth of the African American working class developed in tandem with the growth of a small group of African American urban entrepreneurs. Concentrated housing patterns reflected the near impossibility of a separate residential area for middle-class African Americans. Money and education were insufficient to allow the African American professionals and entrepreneurs to foster the privileged suburban enclaves of white families. Instead, the growth of the African American community provided a means for these entrepreneurs to serve and profit from an African American-only clientele. Whereas before World War I, African American barbers, restaurant owners, and others might have catered to an exclusively white clientele, the shifting residential and industrial patterns encouraged a concentration of African American business within African American neighborhoods.

To sustain themselves and their families in the midst of arduous work and regular exploitation, African Americans created communities and institutions to ameliorate the harshness of urban life. Migrants formed social clubs, built churches, and established political organizations to ease the transition into urban life in the North. Many of these migrant institutions merged with established African American organizations, creating an amalgam of Southern and Northern tastes, styles of worship, and political perspectives. African American women played a central role in political organizing and social exchanges. Ida B. Wells, journalist and political activist, was at the forefront of the African American women's club movement. During the late nineteenth and early twentieth centuries, many highly educated African American women could not find work in their fields. As qualified teachers, nurses, and social workers, many like Wells used the club movement to promote positive images of African Americans and to provide instruction on education, health, and domestic science.

Women

American women's political activity gained new ground as they entered war work and demanded better wages, safer working conditions, and a voice in union affairs. However, not all of their efforts were successful. Wartime work brought white and African American working-class women in the North in more frequent contact with one another. Working side by side or just in the same factory started a process of cooperation and disagreement on several political issues. While middle-class women pushed for the right to vote, working-class women struggled in jobs with little or no union representation. Many women, African American as well as white, organized themselves through work and neighborhood clubs. African American women were struck by the impact of the Great Migration on themselves, their families, and their communities. While the war brought opportunity, it had also brought hardship. Urban life sometimes meant higher wages and better schools, but it also brought the deleterious effects of saloons, crime, and unsanitary residences. African American women in both the South and the North found allies in the white women's clubs and associations. However, Southern white women who crossed the color line to work for temperance, health services, and educational opportunities refused to stand with African American women on the right to vote, a right they viewed as exclusively white.

The shifting race and class relationship made within the African American community would have a profound effect on the music, art, and literature of the World War I period. Blues, ragtime, and the early days of jazz blurred the lines between country and city music, and introduced another generation of white aficionados to African American artistic expression. African American artists such as Louis Armstrong migrated out of the South and carried with them Southern African American traditions in music. The retention of customs and artistic expressions of the South eased homesickness and also provided a means to earn a living.

But earning a living was only one in a series of challenges in African American urban life. Housing discrimination thwarted many African Americans from participating equally in the industrial boom of World War I. African Americans gravitated to Northern neighborhoods where friends and family already resided. Often, African Americans were restricted in their choices of residences elsewhere. Chicago's "Black Belt" for example, became increasingly populated by African Americans as whites vacated neighborhoods rather than share the space with one African American family. White, middle-class homeowners rallied, organized, and set off nearly sixty bombings in the Chicago area to forestall an African American "invasion" into historically white, middle-class neighborhoods. Where restrictive covenants and harassment failed, whites simply moved out. Chicago was not alone in its racial tension as race riots fumed in East St. Louis and other cities as well.

Political debate on a variety of issues fueled political movements within the African American urban community. Marcus Garvey and the Universal Negro Improvement Association articulated the frustration of many African American women and men who migrated northward but found little to distinguish the North from the South. Emphasizing racial pride and separateness, Garveyites labored to build up African American-owned business and to eschew white notions of the "proper place" for African Americans in white society. Garvey's self-help ideology was not new or isolated: Booker T. Washington promoted a self-help ideology a generation before. Moreover, African American women's clubs continued a long tradition of using civic and church groups, along with these African American women's clubs, to educate and "uplift the race." Much of the political debate came out of the work experience of African American workers and soldiers. African American labor activists such as A. Philip Randolph joined in the celebration of black pride but faced the reality that most African American workers could not be employed solely by African American capital. Randolph, coeditor of the socialist newspaper *The Messenger,* organized one of the largest groups of African American workers, the Brotherhood of Sleeping Car Porters, and fought throughout the World War I period and into the 1920s for inclusion in the American Federation of Labor.

Rural-to-urban migration as well as a modicum of material gain by African Americans acted as catalyst for white militant racist organizations. The Ku Klux Klan formed in 1915 and proselytized throughout the United States for racial purity. The Klan acted as a grass-roots organization, preaching and demonstrating violence against Catholics, Jews, and African Americans. White racism could also take artistic but no less violent forms as in the case of the films *The Birth of a Nation,* directed by D. W. Griffith and *The Nigger.* Both films captivated audiences nationwide. The showing of these films also galvanized an African American response, and chapters of the National Association for the Advancement of Colored People registered their repugnance and horror with local theater operators and politicians from coast to coast. By the end of the war, militant white organizations and a plethora of African American civil rights organizations would spread throughout the United States. Having fought and won the war to end all wars, African American soldiers returned with a renewed commitment to exercising all the rights of citizenship, while African American workers and professionals continued to build the communities and institutions to pursue the promises of democracy.

Robin Dearmon Jenkins

See also: Agriculture (WWI); Jazz (WWI); Music (WWI); National Association for the Advancement of Colored People (NAACP, WWI); National Urban League (WWI); Race Riots (WWI); Biographies: DuBois, W. E. B. (WWI); Garvey, Marcus (WWI); Documents: Return Soldiers, May 1919

REFERENCES

Barrett, James R. *Work and Community in the Jungle.* Urbana: University of Illinois Press, 1987.

Foner, Philip S. *Organized Labor and the Black Worker, 1619–1973.* New York: International Publishers, 1974.

Gilmore, Glenda Elizabeth. *Gender and Jim Crow: Women and the Politics of White Supremacy in North Carolina, 1896–1920.* Chapel Hill: University of North Carolina Press, 1996.

Grossman, James R. *Land of Hope: Chicago, Black Southerners, and the Great Migration.* Chicago: University of Chicago Press, 1989.

Jones, Jacqueline. *Labor of Love, Labor of Sorrow: Black Women, Work and the Family, from Slavery to the Present.* New York: Vintage Books, 1985.

Kusmer, Kenneth L. *A Ghetto Takes Shape: Black Cleveland, 1870–1930.* Urbana: Univeristy of Illinois, 1978.

Spear, Allan H. *Black Chicago: The Making of a Negro Ghetto.* Chicago: University of Chicago Press, 1967.

Trotter, Joe William, Jr. *Black Milwaukee: The Making of an Industrial Proletariat, 1915–45.* Urbana: University of Illinois Press, 1985.

———. *The African American Experience.* Boston: Houghton Mifflin, 2001.

Agriculture

Though charged with the immense responsibility for supplying most of the necessary food and fiber for both the U.S. and Allied armed forces in World War I (not to mention domestic populations on both sides of the Atlantic), American farmers and the U.S. government managed to rise to the challenge. From Washington, the U.S. Food Administration—much like its counterpart, the War Industries Board—directed a successful nationwide campaign (under the motto "Food Will Win the War") to increase production, promote domestic conservation, and streamline distribution of those commodities essential for the war effort, in particular wheat, livestock, fats, and oils. The effort was not without its costs, however, as farmers overextended themselves to meet higher production goals only to find that when inflated wartime profits came to an abrupt end, they could no longer sustain their operations. In fact, the economic depression that would hit the entire nation in the 1930s arrived a decade earlier in much of the American countryside, in no small part due to the impact of World War I.

Farmers' "Golden Age"

Yet in the decades before American entry into the war, farmers in the United States had experienced what would subsequently be called their "golden age." Sustained domestic population growth, record levels of immigration, and then the outbreak of the European war itself all combined to increase demand for U.S. farm products. Farm productivity, however, had not kept pace with the demand over this same period and, as a result, both food and commodity prices rose steadily during the first decade-and-a-half of the twentieth century. Though this created a favorable situation for farmers themselves, the upturn in prices prompted complaints from manufacturing and laboring interests concerned with the rising cost of living, as well as anxiety in Washington about the potential damage to agricultural exports and even the future food security of the nation. In fact, experts warned that if productivity trends in agriculture remained flat, the United States might eventually have to import some essential foodstuffs. Moreover, in the prewar decades, the United States was still a "debtor" nation, and overseas agricultural sales were an important source of the capital inflows necessary to service that debt.

In response to these concerns, the nation's primary agricultural organization, the U.S. Department of Agriculture (USDA), urged farmers to expand production and increase their "efficiency" by adopting new technologies, crops, and "scientific" planting methods. To develop and disseminate these "improved" practices, Washington substantially increased both funding and personnel for the USDA and related state agricultural agencies in the decades before World War I. Between 1898 and 1913, for example, the USDA's funding increased eightfold while its staff of scientific personnel rose from 127 to over 2,000, a growth rate nearly matched at the experiment stations and agricultural colleges at the state. In the meantime, Washington expanded its efforts to better disseminate the research produced by this expanded professional staff. The Smith-Lever Agricultural Extension Act of 1914, for example, offered hundreds of thousands of dollars in federal funds to those states that promised to develop a system of county agents—farm "experts" who fanned out into the countryside to advise and educate farmers on the latest agricultural innovations and encourage their adoption.

Yet none of these efforts produced the desired result of increased productivity, as U.S. farmers proved wary of adopting innovations or investing in new machinery and land in order to expand output, even with the stimulus of higher commodity prices. Many American farmers remembered that in past boom times they had risen to the call for increased output only to find the subsequent period of overproduction and lower prices ruinous to their enterprise.

This cautious approach persisted until U.S. entry into the war in the spring of 1917, when Washington became much more aggressive in encouraging greater production and productivity from American farmers. Indeed, under the Emergency Food Production Act and the Food and Fuel Control Act (both passed in 1917), Congress gave the Wilson Administration wide-ranging powers to, among other things, "requisition foods, fuels and other supplies necessary to the support of the Army and Navy," control access to "farm implements and fertilizers" in order to maximize output of desired commodities, prohibit the utilization of "food materials" in the manufacture of alcoholic beverages, punish those who hoarded commodities, and "guarantee the price of wheat" in order "to stimulate production." To implement these measures, the previously voluntary county agent program was extended to every corner of the country, while the agents themselves took on added responsibilities, including helping the "Justice Department find seditionists and draft dodgers." In the meantime, the new federal wartime agency, the United States Food Administration, directed national production, distribution, and conservation from Washington.

Under the energetic leadership of future president Herbert Hoover (a wealthy mining engineer who had made an international reputation for himself by ably directing the food relief program for war-ravaged Belgium), the Food Administration achieved considerable success in both streamlining the nation's commodity processing and distribution systems and encouraging Americans to consume less of everything for the sake of the war effort. "Meatless Mondays" and "Wheatless Wednesdays" became the order of the day, while women were exhorted to adopt slimmer figures and use less material in their dresses (to save on food and fiber respectively), starting a trend that would continue in the postwar years. Meanwhile, the USDA and the Food Administration encouraged Americans to plant home gardens, can vegetables, and adopt food substitutes. While these measures had a negligible impact on increasing the availability of essential foodstuffs, their propaganda value was nonetheless useful.

Reorganizing Commodity Distribution

Of more practical importance, however, were Hoover's efforts to reorganize commodity distribution networks and price schedules to increase supplies of essential foods like wheat, fats, and sugar. For example, the Food Administration pursued agreements with grain millers (under the auspices of the Grain Corporation), sugar (the Sugar Equalization Board), and pork producers (lard from pork was then the major source of dietary fat in the United States), as well as foreign buyers (the Wheat Export Company) in order to stabilize both retail and producer prices at a level high enough to motivate domestic producers to increase output, but not so high as to overburden urban consumers. With some important exceptions—the 1917 wheat crop, for instance, came in well below expectations—the strategy worked well. Thus, after farmers were essentially guaranteed a price of at least $2.00 for a bushel of wheat in 1917, they responded by planting an additional twenty-seven million acres of the grain in the 1918–1919 season alone, yielding over 950 million bushels, of which 220 million were exported. In the final tally, American wheat farmers increased their acreage (mostly in winter wheat grown on the Great Plains) by over 50 percent and their output by 38 percent during the war years. The stimulus of guaranteed high prices had a similar effect on wartime pork and beef production, which increased 20 and 25 percent respectively, adding to an overall wartime increase in meat production of approximately 23 percent. In short, Hoover's Food Administration achieved its primary goal of increasing wartime production and export of the essential foodstuffs for the Allied effort.

But this goal was not achieved without considerable social and economic dislocation, both beneficial and otherwise. On the positive side, hundreds of thousands of African Americans left the burdens of Southern sharecropping for the industrial cities of the North during the war, starting a "Great Migration" that continued for the next half-century and steadily eroded the foundations of the white-supremacist regime in the Jim Crow South. At the same time, however, thousands of Mexican Americans were encouraged by wartime immigration policies to become temporary—and often poorly treated and paid—migrant workers on the giant fruit and vegetable farms of California's "industrial countryside."

At the same time, American farmers answered the patriotic call to increase production during the war by expanding their acreage and their equipment purchases—both at inflated wartime prices—only to find themselves in the postwar period struggling under a mountain of debt and higher taxes that could only be sup-

ported with the continuation of high commodity prices. Farm prices, however, fell sharply starting in 1920 (dropping by almost 50 percent between 1920 and 1921) as European farmers began to restore their own prewar production levels and as world trade regained momentum and with it the renewed competition of other commodity-exporting nations such as Argentina, Australia, and Canada. In the meantime, Washington suspended commodity price guarantees for American farmers, further depressing prices. Finally, in July of 1919, Washington ended the program of wartime credits for the Allied nations while still maintaining and even increasing tariff levels on European imports (the 1922 Fordney-McCumber tariff raised import duties to record highs), thereby reducing the ability of European countries to finance agricultural imports from the United States by selling more of their own manufactured goods stateside. The net effect of high debt, tumbling commodity prices, and the inevitable fall in land prices plunged U.S. farmers into a descending economic spiral that did not level out until the next World War.

J. Jacob Jones

See also: African Americans (WWI); Food Administration (WWI); Latinos and Latinas; Biographies: Hoover, Herbert Clark (WWI)

REFERENCES

Benedict, Murray B. *Farm Policies of the United States: A Study of Their Origins and Development.* New York: Twentieth Century Fund, 1953.

Danbom, David B. *Born in the Country: A History of Rural America.* Baltimore, MD: Johns Hopkins University Press, 1995.

Ferleger, Louis. "Arming American Agriculture for the Twentieth Century: How the USDA's Top Managers Promoted Agricultural Development." *Agricultural History* 74 (2000): 211–226.

Fitzgerald, Deborah. *Every Farm a Factory: The Industrial Ideal in American Agriculture.* New Haven, CT: Yale University Press, 2003.

Genung, A. B. "Agriculture in the World War Period." In *An Historical Survey of American Agriculture,* United States Department of Agriculture Yearbook Separate No. 1783, 277–296. Washington, DC: Government Printing Office, 1941.

Shideler, James H. *Farm Crisis, 1919–1923.* Berkeley: University of California Press, 1957.

Stoll, Steven. *The Fruits of Natural Advantage: Making the Industrial Countryside in California.* Berkeley: University of California Press, 1998.

Wilson, James. "Report of the Secretary." In *1912 Yearbook of the Department of Agriculture.* Washington, DC: Government Printing Office, 1913.

Alien Act

Under the Alien Act of 1918, for the first time, noncitizens who were members of associations that held or taught anarchical views could be expelled from the United States.

On October 16, 1918, reacting to public hysteria about the threat of communism, socialism, and radical labor, Congress passed Public Law 221, "An Act To exclude and expel from the United States aliens who are members of the anarchistic and similar classes." (The law excluded Native Americans and residents of islands or territories under U.S. jurisdiction.)

The Alien Act of 1918 expanded upon provisions of the Immigration Act of 1917. The 1917 law excluded from admission into the United States people who were Asians, illiterates, criminals, paupers, insane, alcoholic, ill with infectious diseases, of low moral standing, or anarchists. Anarchists were defined as persons who advocated the overthrow of the government by force or violence or the assassination of public officials, or who advocated and taught the unlawful destruction of property.

Several months prior to the passage of the Alien Act of 1918, President Woodrow Wilson issued a lengthy executive order (No. 2932) that specified rules and regulations for the exclusion, entrance, and deportation of aliens during wartime. Coupled with the executive order, the vague new law gave Attorney General A. Mitchell Palmer authority to conduct extensive raids, make mass arrests, and deport aliens without providing them the benefit of a proper hearing or trial. Palmer's abusive tactics, referred to as the Red Scare, generated admiration, scorn, and fear. Postmaster General Albert Burleson used the Alien Act as a tool to silence Socialist publications. On June 5, 1920, Congress passed an amendment to the Alien Act that enlarged the list of excluded persons to include saboteurs, aliens engaged in writing or publishing about subversive doctrine, and members of associations who circulated the anarchical doctrines.

The Alien Act of 1918 (as amended) was replaced by provisions of the Internal Security Act of 1950.

Diane M. T. North

See also: Immigration (U.S., WWI); Palmer Raids (WWI)

REFERENCES

Preston, William, Jr. *Aliens and Dissenters: Federal Suppression of Radicals, 1903–1933,* 2d ed. Urbana: University of Illinois Press, 1994.

Ambulance Drivers

American ambulance drivers appeared in France well before the American declaration of war against Germany and Austria. The first drivers were already in France at the outset of World War I, working in a philanthropic hospital outside Paris founded by American nationals in 1910. During the fighting near Paris in September 1914, the French Army permitted the hospital to treat French casualties, and in April 1915, the army agreed to allow American volunteers to enter combat zones to evacuate and treat the wounded. Volunteer ambulance units, each comprised of smaller ambulance sections, were formed as a result. Each ambulance section consisted of several motorized ambulances, driven by foreign volunteers and French medical officers, which would quickly transport battlefield casualties away from the fighting to surgical hospitals in the army's rear areas. By 1917, most of the ambulances themselves were manufactured by Henry Ford.

Many different ambulance units that aided the French and British armies in Europe accepted American volunteers. One unit named the American Field Service, organized by A. Piatt Andrew, was based at the American hospital outside Paris. H. Herman Harjes, senior partner of the Morgan-Harjes Bank in Paris, formed another ambulance unit called the Morgan-Harjes Section. The Morgan-Harjes Section later merged with a third ambulance unit called Richard Norton's Anglo-American Volunteer Motor-Ambulance Corps, to create the Norton-Harjes Section. Most American ambulance drivers volunteered to serve in these three units in the years prior to the American declaration of war in 1917.

It was the ambulance driver's duty to evacuate casualties from the battlefield and from field hospitals quickly and safely so that doctors away from the front could treat them. Successful treatment of wounded soldiers preserved their lives and allowed them not only to return to the war and fight, but also to eventually return home to their loved ones. Successfully aiding casualties also increased the army's morale generally, because men who saw that their wounded comrades were well cared for expected that they themselves would receive the same care should they be wounded. Allowing foreign volunteers to drive ambulances also freed more French and British soldiers for frontline service.

The conspicuous majority of the Americans who volunteered for service in these ambulance sections were college students. Most came from Ivy League schools such as Harvard, Yale, and Princeton, but many came from other universities across the country. Included in their ranks were several great authors and intellectuals of the twentieth century, such as John Dos Passos, William Seabrook, Malcolm Cowley, e.e. cummings, and Ernest Hemmingway. They were motivated by a desire to not only witness but also to participate in what they recognized as the great event of their time, World War I. After these initially starry-eyed and enthusiastic volunteers spent time on the battlefields of Europe, however, their motivations for serving in ambulance sections tended to change. Ambulance drivers became less enchanted with the idea of witnessing the war and more concerned with aiding the people and soldiers of the Allied nations.

Driving an ambulance is a difficult and dangerous activity. Ambulance drivers often must maneuver at ordinarily unsafe speeds in order to get medical attention for their patients as quickly as possible. On their journey they sometimes have to contend with poor weather conditions or mechanical failures in the ambulance itself. Ambulance drivers of World War I had to also compete with the dangers of the battlefield, such as bullets, artillery shells, and poisonous gas clouds. Flat tires and other mechanical problems in the ambulances were commonplace due to poor road conditions and frequent weapons fire.

Prior to official American entry into the war,

volunteer ambulance units and their drivers affiliated themselves with the Red Cross or the British or French armies. Once war was declared, however, the American Expeditionary Force appropriated these units for its own use and enlisted the drivers into the U.S. Army. Some ambulance sections were permitted to continue aiding the French, but under American command. At the time of the American declaration of war, over 3,500 American volunteers had served as ambulance drivers. Their importance to American culture and society far outweighed their numbers. Volunteer drivers viewed the war from the cabins of their ambulances. Their observations and feelings crossed the Atlantic Ocean through newspapers and letters, allowing ambulance drivers to influence the way America viewed the war in Europe. Ambulance drivers came to influence the many Americans who saw the war as a terrible tragedy, yet believed it their duty to aid the suffering English, French, Russian, and Italian soldiers and civilians in their struggle.

Thomas I. Faith

See also: American Red Cross (WWI); Biographies: cummings, e.e. (WWI); Dos Passos, John (WWI); Hemingway, Ernest (WWI)

REFERENCES

Haller, John S. *Farmcarts to Fords: A History of the Military Ambulance, 1790–1925.* Carbondale: Southern Illinois University Press, 1992.

Hansen, Arlen J. *Gentleman Volunteers: The Story of American Ambulance Drivers in the Great War, August 1914–September 1918.* New York: Arcade, 1996.

American Federation of Labor

During World War I, the American Federation of Labor (AFL) sought to demonstrate the patriotism of its members while simultaneously endeavoring to improve the condition of the workers for whom the organization existed. Formed in 1897 to protect the interests of craft laborers, by 1917, the AFL represented approximately 2.3 million workers in the United States. Under the leadership of Samuel Gompers, the years of World War I saw the AFL reach an unprecedented level of cooperation with the federal government and also experienced a dramatic increase in both membership and national profile.

Prior to World War I, many of the AFL's constituent unions were avowedly pacifistic. Concerned that this stance might appear unpatriotic, the AFL undertook a "loyalty campaign" following the U.S. entry into the war in April 1917. Gompers firmly believed that working with the government through supporting the war would improve labor's position more so than opposing American participation in the conflict. He therefore designed the campaign to mute the pacifistic elements within the AFL itself and to counter efforts by more left-leaning unions to leverage an increase in their membership through an antiwar platform at the expense of the Federation. The AFL initially began the loyalty campaign in the New York area, but with Gompers's assistance on August 16, 1917, the American Alliance for Labor and Democracy was created to extend the loyalty campaign to a national scale. During the war, the Alliance organized patriotic rallies and issued approximately 450 weekly and daily publications. Although it at times engendered resentment from members of the AFL itself who felt that such demonstrations of their loyalty were unnecessary, the Alliance remained active until 1919 promoting the message that organized labor enthusiastically supported America and the war.

A much greater challenge for the AFL than demonstrating the patriotism of its members lay in the organization's attempts to establish representation within the federal government, facilitate the contribution made by organized labor to the war effort, and ensure that American workers would not be exploited by the exceptional circumstances created by the conflict. To that end, Gompers and the AFL met with mixed success.

Determined to maintain a voice in the control of labor, the AFL secured membership on the three main labor organizations established by the Wilson administration. In late 1916, Wilson created the Council of National Defence to oversee preparations for mobilization. Gompers was named to the labor committee of the Council, which reported to the Secretary of War. After the American entry into the war, the War Labor Policies Board was created with the mandate to establish a series of overarching regulations under which labor would operate. Dissatisfaction with the Polices Board led to the convening of a War Labor Conference Board out of which the War Labor Board emerged. The AFL maintained significant membership on these boards, which ultimately reached a number of agreements pertaining to the rights of organized labor.

Out of negotiations between the AFL representatives, other members of organized labor, and federal representatives several key policies were established: Workers were permitted to keep the right to organize and bargain collectively; fixed wages, minimum rates of pay, and maximum working hours were established; and employers were compelled not to relax health and safety conditions of laborers despite increased rates of production. In return, labor issued a no-strike pledge for the duration of the war, assisted in the distribution and training of new workers necessary for mobilization, and offered to play a role in mediating disputes that did arise between unions and the federal government.

However, the AFL's efforts to secure these rights did not meet with the complete approval of the federation's constituent unions. There were many who saw the war as an opportunity for organized labor to extract greater concessions from the federal government. More radical elements within the AFL deemed the approach taken by its representatives in Washington as too conciliatory, and at times put great pressure upon committee and board members to advocate more actively for craft workers' rights.

Regardless of whether or not the AFL played too conciliatory a role in its relationship with the federal government, the federation clearly was amongst the most prominent representatives of labor during World War I. The organization itself grew dramatically to almost three million members by the end of 1918. Its numbers and influence, within organized labor and without, would continue to increase briefly and immediately after the end of the conflict, but following that would not attain similar heights until World War II.

Brendan Dominick

See also: Council of National Defence (WWI); Economy (U.S., WWI); Mobilization (U.S., WWI); Trade Unions (U.S., WWI); War Industries Board (WWI); War Labor Board (WWI); Biographies: Gompers, Samuel (WWI)

REFERENCES

Livesay, Harold C. *Samuel Gompers and Organized Labor in America.* Boston: Little, Brown, 1978.

Lorwin, Lewis L. *The American Federation of Labor: History, Policies and Prospects.* New York: AMS Press, 1970.

Taft, Philip. *The A.F. of L. in the Time of Gompers.* New York: Octagon Books, 1970.

American Legion

The American Legion was launched in 1919 (shortly after the Armistice ending World War I) as a patriotic, wartime veterans organization by U.S. military officers anxious to boost American morale and to ensure that veterans of the American Expeditionary Force (AEF) would receive pensions. In addition to seeking benefits for veterans, in the period after the war the Legion dedicated itself to defense preparedness, anticommunism, and, what the organization called, "one hundred per cent Americanism," and helped fuel the anticommunist hysteria that led to the Red Scare of 1919–1920.

After the 1919 Armistice ended hostilities in Europe, American soldiers wanted to go home immediately, but because it took time to demobilize, many were left in Europe for months with no war to fight and no job to do. As a result, more Americans were going AWOL (absent without leave) and morale among American troops was plummeting. At the same time, American officers were deeply worried by what they viewed as the dangers posed by "Bolshevism." The AEF's own experience with communism was entirely negative: After the Russian Revolution of 1917, the Russians had deserted the Allies to make a separate peace with Germany in the Treaty of Brest-Litovsk, and had thus freed one million German troops from the eastern front for combat against the Allies in the west.

On February 17, 1919, twenty officers met and drafted plans for the creation of a veterans' organization that they hoped would encourage veterans to work together in order to wield political power, stand firmly for military preparedness, and recognize and oppose the spread of radicalism within the United States. In recognition of these goals, in the preamble to their constitution the members of the American Legion declared that they would work to provide mutual support, maintain law and order, "foster and perpetuate a one hundred per cent Americanism," and "combat the autocracy of both the classes and the masses." Before long, the Legion, which by 1931 had over one million members, dwarfed the Veterans of Foreign Wars (VFW), the existent veterans' organization in the United States.

The Legion's first priority was to seek benefits for veterans as well as pensions and health care for disabled veterans and their dependents. In August 1921, the Legion achieved success in its efforts to promote the establishment of a permanent government department designed to help veterans with the creation of the United States Veterans Bureau, which was the forerunner to the United States Veterans Association. In May 1924, it similarly achieved success in its efforts to demand additional payments to veterans.

During the war, the question rose of whether or not veterans should be paid additional funds once they returned home, and after the creation of the Legion, the organization's spokesmen argued that veterans should be paid "adjusted compensation" to make up for the difference between military pay and the relatively high civilian wages of the World War I period. Despite the successful efforts of opponents to label payments as "bonuses" and the opposition of Presidents Harding and Coolidge, in 1924 Congress passed (over Coolidge's veto) the World War Adjusted Compensation Act, which was popularly known as the "Soldier's Bonus Act." This act provided veterans with $1 for every day of domestic service and $1.25 for every day of service abroad. These funds would be used to create a twenty-year endowment, though in the short term, veterans were entitled to borrow up to 22.5 percent of the value of the fund. Members of the Legion were not entirely satisfied, as they wanted immediate cash payments, and during the Great Depression they joined the "Bonus Army" as it marched on Washington, D.C., to demand early distribution of the funds.

The Legion's secondary priorities were to seek a strong national defense program, to oppose immigration (which brought undesirable radicals into the country), to encourage patriotism and patriotic expression, and to fight communism. Given these priorities, it is no surprise that Legionnaires were among those at the forefront during the Red Scare and the Palmer Raids of 1919–1920. While many in the Legion distributed anticommunist pamphlets and marched in anticommunist parades, others volunteered to assist police as they arrested suspected radicals during the Palmer Raids, and still others joined mobs that attacked communist and socialist organizations directly.

The American Legion remained active in American politics, veteran affairs, and anticommunism, and increased hugely in size as a result of World War II. By the end of the twentieth century, the organization had over three million men and women as members, with posts throughout the United States as well as in Mexico, France, and the Philippines.

Samuel Brenner

See also: Demobilization (WWI); Immigration (U.S., WWI); Palmer Raids (WWI); Red Scare (WWI)

REFERENCES

Baker, Roscoe. *The American Legion and American Foreign Policy.* New York: Bookman Associates, 1954.

Moley, Raymond. *The American Legion Story.* New York: Duell, Sloan, and Pearce, 1966.

Pencak, William. *For God and Country: The American Legion, 1919–1941.* Boston: Northeastern University Press, 1989.

Rumer, Thomas A. *The American Legion: An Official History, 1919–1989.* New York: M. Evans, 1990.

American Protective League

The American Protective League (APL) was a national private association of volunteer spies authorized to assist the Justice Department. In February 1917, a Chicago advertising executive, Albert M. Briggs, volunteered to support local Justice Department officials investigate the activities of Germans suspected of disloyalty. He supplied automobiles and drivers who helped agents track suspects in Chicago, New York, and Washington, D.C. By March, the chief of the federal Bureau of Investigation, A. Bruce Bielaski, agreed to Briggs's domestic security plan whereby a national army composed largely of middle- and upper-class white male volunteers would work as intelligence operatives alongside government agents. Briggs selected leaders who, in turn, chose volunteers for a network of state, county, and metropolitan units. These citizen spies reported directly to APL headquarters in Washington, D.C., and to local Bureau agents who tried unsuccessfully to control APL activities. Because the League functioned as an unpaid voluntary organization, it was not subject to congressional oversight.

As Congress passed new wartime mandates, the power of the Justice Department and the APL grew. The League regarded itself as the country's second line of defense, stretching the boundaries of the law even as its members used the rhetoric of democracy and the legitimate tools of the state. The APL held Germans and German Americans in contempt and blamed them for nefarious plots. It targeted socialists, pacifists, Mexican Americans, and members of the Industrial Workers of the World. The APL attacked free speech, press, assembly, and association rights and violated due process. Its members illegally entered and searched homes and offices, read mail, wiretapped conversations, and seized property. League volunteers relied on reckless undocumented accusations, public opinion, and hearsay. Based upon faulty APL recommendations, loyal citizens were denied jobs and detained by authorities.

By the end of the war, the APL boasted a quarter of a million members. It had absorbed the Minute Men, a hyper-patriotic spy organization that operated largely in the Pacific Northwest, and had taken over the work of State Councils of Defense loyalty committees investigations. In December 1918, Briggs announced that the League would cease operation and requested that branches submit their final reports. The APL received both praise and condemnation for its work.

Diane M. T. North

See also: Federal Bureau of Investigation (WWI); Industrial Workers of the World (WWI); Slackers (WWI); Vigilantism (WWI)

REFERENCES

Jensen, Joan M. *The Price of Vigilance.* Chicago: Rand McNally, 1968.

American Red Cross

Clara Barton, Civil War nurse and humanitarian reformer, originally founded the American Red Cross in 1881 as the American Association of the Red Cross. It was intended to act in concert with the international medical community and governments of the world to provide care and comfort to war casualties and disaster victims. Barton's organization became part of the International Red Cross, founded by Jean Henri Dunant in 1882 with the belated ratification of the 1864 Geneva Convention by the U.S. Senate.

Prior to direct American military involvement in World War I, the American Red Cross provided its services to belligerent European powers. In September 1914, funds were raised to purchase, equip, and dispatch the *Red Cross,* a trans-Atlantic ship that transported medical personnel and equipment to each of the nations engaged in the war. After establishing sixteen hospitals for the treatment of the war wounded throughout Europe, however, the American Red Cross judged its resources insufficient to continue such direct aid and it recalled its doctors and nurses in October 1915. After this unfortunate setback, the American Red Cross largely confined its humanitarian efforts to contributing as many medical supplies as it was able amid the British blockade.

America's entry into the war against Germany and Austria in 1917 was a major turning point for the American Red Cross. Official participation in the Great War transformed the relatively small, ineffective, and internationalist organization into a well-funded, -organized and -supplied extension of the Federal government's war effort. The American Red Cross reluctantly shelved its commitment to aiding all soldiers regardless of nationality to expressly aiding the American war effort. With the urging of Woodrow Wilson's administration, the

While the American Red Cross offered aid to all belligerents before U.S. entry into World War I, America's 1917 declaration of war saw the humanitarian organization enlarge its mission enormously. (Library of Congress)

American Red Cross created a new administrative body called the War Council. Henry P. Davidson, a very successful banker and member of the J. P. Morgan firm, was appointed the first War Council chairman. Under his capable leadership, the American Red Cross appealed to American patriotism using newspapers, magazines, motion pictures, posters, billboards, parades, and pageants to publicize funding drives and encourage volunteers to lend their support. These appeals were extremely effective and, by 1919, the American Red Cross had raised over $400 million and its membership had peaked at 20,832,000 men and women. Its leadership also realized that, in addition to traditional medical service, the Red Cross's mostly

female volunteers could provide a wide variety of hospitality services to American soldiers as well.

War mobilization sent men into military field service away from their homes and families in unprecedented numbers, and the Red Cross worked to make separation as bearable as possible for them. Smiling volunteers distributed creature comforts such as coffee, doughnuts, sandwiches, cigarettes, clothing, and chocolate to soldiers who were being transported to military bases, training facilities, and ports of embarkation throughout the United States. The American Red Cross created canteens across the country, which served food and refreshments to forty million members of the armed forces throughout the course of the war. Home Service volunteers in the Red Cross helped families locate and stay in contact with loved ones who were fighting overseas or who were recuperating in hospitals after being wounded. They also helped servicemen obtain furloughs and secure government benefits when possible. Additionally, the Red Cross provided important medical services in the United States. The organization purchased medical supplies such as gauze masks, surgical dressings, and hospital gowns for the armed forces, and Red Cross volunteers worked alongside army hospital physicians during the nationwide influenza outbreak in 1918.

In Europe, the American Red Cross Foreign Service provided hospitality services to Allied soldiers and refugees, and acted as official auxiliaries to the military's medical services. Following the declaration of war in 1917, Red Cross volunteers arrived in France in strength before the American Expeditionary Force. The Red Cross opened and operated canteens and restaurants behind the front lines throughout France for American, French, and British soldiers as well as civilian refugees. Ambulance units, hospitals, and aid stations created and

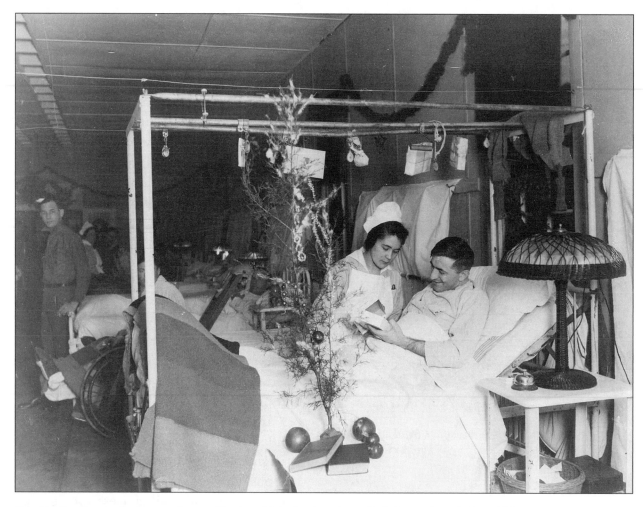

World War I was the first major conflict in which the American Red Cross, founded in 1881, did its humanitarian work. Here, Red Cross nurses treat a wounded soldier. (Library of Congress)

staffed by Red Cross volunteers were in many cases absorbed by the Army Medical Department outright once the members of the American Expeditionary Force began to arrive in Europe, but others were operated by the Red Cross for the duration of the war. Red Cross medical personnel worked in concert with the Army Medical Department to provide care to wounded soldiers in military recovery hospitals in France and England, in Army rear areas, and on the battlefield. At home and in France, the American Red Cross and its members rendered valuable service to the war effort.

Thomas I. Faith

See also: Ambulance Drivers (WWI); Influenza Epidemic of 1918 (WWI); Women (U.S., WWI)

REFERENCES

Davidson, Henry P. *The American Red Cross in the Great War.* New York: MacMillan, 1919.

Dulles, Foster Rhea. *The American Red Cross: A History.* New York: Harper and Brothers, 1950.

Haug, Hans, et al. *Humanity for All: The International Red Cross and Red Crescent Movement.* Berne: P. Haupt, 1993.

Hutchinson, John F. *Champions of Charity: War and the Rise of the Red Cross.* Boulder, CO: Westview Press, 1996.

American Union against Militarism

In the decade before World War I, the European situation seemed worrisome as nations there fought for empire, engaged in an arms race, and participated in several proxy wars in succession. Complacency among the American populace and in the corridors of Congress that peace would last forever, gave way to worry about the possibility of war. Existing peace groups attracted new members, and many new peace organizations came into being. Some peace advocates wanted to create an international world court. In 1911, Andrew Carnegie established a group called the Carnegie Endowment for International Peace in order to research peaceful solutions to world conflicts.

When the war began anyway, the older and more conservative groups—including Carnegie's—suspended their work and supported the Allies under the assumption that defeat of Germany would be the first step in establishing the international system. Conservatives joined together into the Association for a League to Enforce Peace, which sought a postwar coalition for peace.

Some progressive peace advocates and other reformers felt that the older groups were not really working to end the war, but were instead helping to arm the allies. Progressives, socialists, and pacifists organized to stop war preparations. These people formed new groups including the Women's Peace Party (later the Women's International League for Peace and Freedom) and other short-lived organizations. Among the new groups was the American Union Against Militarism. The AUAM lobbied, published, lectured, and set up the Civil Liberties Bureau that later became the National Civil Liberties Bureau, later yet the American Civil Liberties Union.

In November 1915 in New York City, the AUAM came into being as a reaction to groups such as the National Security League, which were working to expand the U.S. army and navy. The organization was initially the "Antimilitarism Committee." In January 1916, in reaction to Woodrow Wilson's preparedness speech, it became the "Anti-preparedness Committee," and the Washington lobby was established. Later in 1916, it became the AUAM. Other names included the American Union for a Democratic Peace and the League for an American Peace.

The AUAM leadership were progressives, socialists, pacifists, or near-pacifists. Among them were the social worker Jane Addams, *The Nation*'s Oswald Garrison Villard, the labor lawyer Crystal Eastman, and the reform-oriented Rabbi Stephen Wise. Other active members included Emily Greene Balch, Charles Hallinan,

One of the largest organizations protesting U.S. entry into World War I, the American Union against Militarism is parodied in this cartoon as yapping dachsunds, a German breed of dog. (Library of Congress)

Paul Kellogg, Amos Pinchot, Henry R. Mussey, Alice Lewisohn, Zona Gale, and Florence Kelley. The Socialist influence of Scott Nearing and others created tension for the liberals.

The AUAM's leaders had good connections in Washington, D.C., due to their experience in progressive causes. In Washington, D.C., they lobbied to keep the United States truly neutral and tried to shape public opinion against the draft and preparedness. The AUAM's "Truth About Preparedness" campaign of 1915 exposed the way America was shifting toward war.

Increased publicity increased membership. Within a year the AUAM had twenty-two chapters and a mailing list of fifty-six thousand. It kept a lobbyist in Washington, D.C., sent mass mailings, and had access to President Woodrow Wilson. It worked against military expansion.

When she was an AUAM member, Eastman founded the Woman's Peace Party, the oldest extant women's peace organization. As AUAM executive director, Eastman lobbied against American involvement in Europe and Mexico. The AUAM also tried to stop arms profiteering, imperialism, and conscription.

In 1916, Roger Baldwin, a pacifist who previously had been one of the founders of the Fellowship of Reconciliation at the war's onset, became executive director of AUAM. He, Eastman, and Norman Thomas, Socialist Party leader and its candidate for President in several elections, established the National Civil Liberties Bureau (NCLB).

The NCLB's primary purpose was to protect conscientious objectors and preserve basic American civil rights despite the tendency of war to weaken them. American entry into the war brought government repression, dissent became equated with disloyalty, and conscientious objectors were prosecuted and hounded by vigilantes. An antiwar speaker faced assault, jail, or worse, especially if he was foreign-born. Some in the AUAM wanted the organization to silence antiwar speech in support of national unity, but Baldwin and Eastman led the faction that maintained that freedom of speech was too vital to sacrifice for any cause. In order to preserve that freedom of protest and conscientious objection, they founded the NCLB.

The AUAM was able to keep Wilson from war with Mexico in 1916, and it managed to keep a peacetime draft from occurring after the war. It could not stop repression of dissenters or conscientious objectors during the war. Still, although occasionally the government raided AUAM offices or the post office stopped its publications, throughout World War I it remained a voice critical of government warmaking and vigilante patriotism.

John H. Barnhill

See also: Civil liberties (WWI); Pacifists (WWI); Women's International League for Peace and Freedom (WWI); Biographies: Addams, Jane (WWI); Eastman, Crystal (WWI); Kelley, Florence (WWI); Pinchot, Amos (WWI); Villard, Oswald Garrison (WWI)

REFERENCES

Cottrell, Robert C. "Roger Nash Baldwin, the National Civil Liberties Bureau, and Military Intelligence during World War I." *Historian* (Fall 1997): 87–106.

Walker, Samuel. *In Defense of American Liberties*, 2d ed. Carbondale: Southern Illinois University Press, 1999.

Americanization Campaign

A loosely coordinated attempt by governmental and private agencies, educational institutions, patriotic organizations, and business groups to ensure the loyalty of immigrants during the World War I and the postwar Red Scare, the Americanization Campaign encouraged citizenship and rapid assimilation, and promoted American ideals and institutions among various ethnic communities.

In the 1880s, so-called "new immigration" to the United States from Southern and Eastern Europe displaced an earlier trend in which the majority of immigrants came from the northern and western—or Anglo-Saxon—regions of the continent. Established Americans of "old-stock" origins perceived the arrival of so many non-Protestant, non-English-speaking, impoverished representatives of seemingly inferior races as a serious threat to the nation's social cohesiveness and political stability. War in Europe and the possibility that the United States might become involved in that conflict aggravated the fear of social disunity. Prominent politicians like Theodore Roosevelt and Woodrow Wilson legitimated this fear in the 1916 presidential election with their calls to replace hyphenated ethnicity with "100 percent" Americanism. Although immigration effectively ceased when the United States entered the war, appeals for unity among the nation's multi-ethnic population coalesced in the Americanization Campaign, which was an array of programs that aimed to transform millions of potentially disloyal foreigners into patriotic American citizens.

One of the largest social and political movements in American history, the Americanization Campaign involved over one hundred public and private agencies, and the total number of programs available for immigrants numbered in the thousands. The array of programs that were implemented by various organizations suggests that Americanization provided a convenient rationale for addressing a whole host of social problems related to immigration. Thus, for example, the North American Civic League for Immigrants and other business or-ganizations addressed problems of labor unrest and high turnover rates by training unskilled immigrants to become more efficient workers. Settlement and social workers developed programs for the children of immigrants stuck between the "Old World" of their parents and the "New World" of their peers in an attempt to minimize juvenile crime and delinquency. Public school programs targeted civics and English language classes primarily to working-class, adult men whose votes might otherwise fuel urban, ethnic political machines. The Young Women's Christian Association taught domestic and childcare skills to immigrant women, on the assumption that Americanized homes were the only way to ensure Americanized children.

In an attempt to maintain support for the war effort among immigrants, the Committee on Public Information, through its Division of Work with the Foreign Born, headed by Josephine Roche, inundated various ethnic groups with pro-American propaganda translated into the appropriate language, including a message explaining President Wilson's special interest in their respective homelands. Frances Kellor and the National Americanization Committee had perhaps the most eclectic program. This carefully orchestrated "scientific" approach involved, among other things, mixing immigrant and American workers to minimize the influence of foreign propaganda in the factories, political and legal education for foreign-born men, and domestic training for immigrant women. For their part, immigrants resisted Americanization initiatives they found too intrusive or offensive. At the same time, however, ethnic organizations supported Americanization in various ways, including promoting Liberty Loan drives in the name of "100 percent" Americanism and encouraging community members to participate in patriotic displays, such as the "I Am an American Day" parades on July 4, 1918.

Historians have distinguished between Americanizers on the basis of their approach to culture: *Cultural pluralists* encouraged immigrants to retain their own customs and traditions and argued that "immigrant gifts" would enrich the larger American cultural mosaic; *cultural conformists*, on the other hand, clung to an Anglo-Saxon American ideal, unpolluted by foreign influences. Despite their diverse views on immigrant and American cultures, all Americanizers ultimately sought common goals of social stability and political conformity. Because of its associations with forced conformity, the expression "Americanization" began to assume negative connotations after the war. Nonetheless, the Americanization Campaign continued into the 1920s as immigration resumed. Concerned citizens searching for an antidote to the revolutionary fever that had swept from Europe into Russia saw Americanization as a way to innoculate immigrants against radical ideologies like socialism and communism. The Americanization Campaign effectively ended in 1924 with the implementation of the Quota and National Origins Acts, laws that severely restricted immigration from regions outside Northern and Western Europe.

Critics of the Americanization Campaign have contended that the very idea of foisting patriotism, citizenship, and political conformity on immigrants is contradictory to American democracy, but the campaign can be credited for presenting immigrants with useful information, educational opportunities, and social services that might otherwise not have been available at the time.

Mary Anne Trasciatti

See also: Committee on Public Information (WWI); Daughters of the American Revolution (WWI); Immigration (U.S., WWI); Palmer Raids (WWI); Red Scare (WWI)

REFERENCES

Carlson, Robert A. The Americanization Syndrome: A Quest for Conformity. London: Croom Helm, 1987.

Hartmann, Edward George. *The Movement to Americanize the Immigrant.* New York: Columbia University Press, 1948.

Higham, John. *Strangers in the Land: Patterns of American Nativism, 1860–1925,* 2d ed. New York: Atheneum, 1971.

McClymer, John F. "Gender and the 'American Way of Life': Women in the Americanization Movement." *Journal of American Ethnic History* (Spring 1991): 3–20.

Anarchists

The assassins of Austrian Archduke Francis Ferdinand and his wife were Serbian anarchists. In France, anarchists had entered the labor movement by the 1890s and soon began agitating for the general strike and the separation of syndicalist organizations from parliamentary labor parties. Anarchists in German states and cities after the war shared power with socialists.

Anarchists believe that all governments interfere with liberty and are unnecessary because truly free individuals will cooperate for mutual benefit. The anarchist movement was important for workers' organizations until Haymarket, a union laborer demonstration in Chicago where a bomb was thrown for which anarchists were implicated. After that, its influence was restricted to immigrants, and the fringe labor movements such as the Industrial Workers of the World incorporated anarcho-syndicalism.

Because anarchists tend to be anti-authority, they also tend to be targets of the authorities, especially if they talk of either violent or peace-

Anarchists vociferously opposed American capitalism and saw World War I as a rich man's war and a poor man's fight. Sometimes their protests pitted them against law enforcement. (Library of Congress)

ful opposition to the state, which many anarchists and anarcho-syndicalists did during World War I.

American anarchism became conspicuous in 1886 during the McCormick Reaper labor dispute in Chicago. Someone threw a bomb at Haymarket Square where union laborers were demonstrating. Eight anarchists were implicated, four of which were hanged. No evidence linked them to the bombing. They were the first anarchist victims of the state. McKinley's assassin was an anarchist. The New York anti-anarchist law of 1902 served as the model for criminal syndicalism laws on state and federal levels. In 1903, for the first time since the Alien and Sedition acts of 1798, Congress criminalized the belief in or advocacy of overthrowing the government by force or violence. Immigrants who had anarchist beliefs were barred from admission.

In 1917, one third of the inhabitants of the United States were first- or second-generation immigrants. The Irish had good reason to be anti-British and unsympathetic to the Allied cause. The millions who were born in Germany and the millions more of German descent were particularly worrisome to the anti-anarchist American public. Then the Bolsheviks took Russia out of the war. Additionally, a lot of recent American immigrants from eastern Europe looked and talked differently, enforcing the stereotypical image of the bearded anarchist with a bomb in his hand. An anarchist was easily categorized as pro-Bolshevik or antiwar or something other than purely American.

World War I only intensified the federal government's efforts against labor, antiwar, and anarchist elements. Tom Mooney and Warren Billings, antiwar labor leaders, went to jail for a Preparedness Day parade bombing in San

Francisco in 1916. The Espionage and Sedition Acts sent thousands of people to jail, including anarchists such as Ricardo Flores Magon.

One of the most prominent of agitators was Emma Goldman. She was not a pacifist, but she was against war as something that exceeds state power. She also believed that the capitalists waged the wars but the workers were the cannon fodder. She used *Mother Earth* to oppose the draft as illegitimate coercion. *Mother Earth* was banned along with other antiwar periodicals. Deportation of foreign-born radicals followed. Goldman formed the No-Conscription League shortly after America entered the war. She spoke against the draft, supported conscientious objection, and was arrested with Alexander Berkman on June 15, 1917. Sentenced to two years in prison, she appealed, failed, served her term, was released, then arrested again in 1919 by J. Edgar Hoover, whose crusade to get her citizenship revoked led to her deportation to the Soviet Union in 1919.

The most visible anarchist organization was the IWW, which opposed war, militarism, conscription, and government. It was anarcho-syndicalist, seeking one big umbrella union encompassing smaller unions that work together in place of a government. It had no problem with using violence and sabotage, having come from the west where violence was integral to labor disputes. The IWW's interference with recruitment, its public disclosure of military information, and its antiwar activities in general led to a public perception that the German government was financing it. The government charged 166 Wobblie leaders, destroying the organization. But it was an anarchist case that began the process of reversing the decisions against socialist speech in Debs and Schenck. Jacob Abrams and other anarchists distributed leaflets opposing the U.S. involvement in the Russian civil war. Although the Supreme Court ruled that their Espionage Act convictions for conspiracy were valid, Justices Holmes and Brandeis dissented. Holmes, notably, enunciated the concept of the clear and present danger and reminded his colleagues that the free marketplace of ideas was superior to censorship.

The 1919 Red Scare essentially ended anarchism along with other American radicalisms.

John H. Barnhill

See also: Immigration (U.S., WWI); Industrial Workers of the World (WWI); Red Scare (WWI); Biographies: Goldman, Emma (WWI); Mooney, Tom (WWI)

REFERENCES

Avrich, Paul. *Anarchist Voices: An Oral History of Anarchism in America.* Princeton, NJ: Princeton University Press, 1995.

Berkman, Alexander, and Gene Fellner. *Life of an Anarchist: The Alexander Berkman Reader.* New York: Seven Stories Press, 1992.

Chalberg, John C. *Emma Goldman.* London: Longman, 1997.

Renshaw, Patrick. *The Wobblies.* Chicago: Ivan R. Dee, 1999.

Anti-Prostitution Campaign

The Anti-Prostitution Campaign was the largely successful effort by social and moral reformers to close down legalized and segregated vice districts in American cities during the Progressive Era. Throughout the Gilded Age, prostitution was viewed as a necessary evil. As long as it remained remote from the avenues that the respectable middle class traveled, the sale of sex was tolerated. By 1910, however, the mood had changed. A growing sense of civic pride and concern over public health led social reformers to view prostitution as a threat to the moral and physical well-being of society. Sensationalistic muckraking journals spread the horrors of prostitution into the homes of the middle class. In 1907, *McClure's* magazine created the enduring myth of the "white slave trade." Although there was little truth in the fabrication, millions believed that decent, self-respecting girls were being drugged, kidnaped, and sold into sexual slavery. In response, the federal government passed the Mann Act (1910), which forbade the transportation of a nonconsenting female across state lines.

Believing that the environment shaped behavior, vice crusaders felt the best solution was to close down the brothels. One by one, scores of cities large and small cleaned up their red-light districts. Generally, the efforts were coordinated by the American Social Hygiene Association (ASHA), founded by John D. Rockefeller in 1914. ASHA provided investigators who discreetly collected information and published reports. While written for and aimed at government agencies and private philanthropies, these reports were then used by indignant citizens to motivate reluctant politicians to close the brothels. ASHA and local organizations vigilantly patrolled the city to ensure that a red-light district did not return. During World War I, vice crusaders then turned their attention to military bases. With the vigorous assistance of Newton Baker, Secretary of War, prostitution was kept a safe distance from the camps. In the 1920s, social reformers then turned their attention to other issues, such as prohibition. The vice crusade was quite successful in closing down the brothels, but virtually ineffectual in eliminating street-walking.

Gregory Dehler

See also: Muckrakers (WWI); Women (U.S., WWI)

REFERENCES

Connelly, Mark Thomas. *The Response to Prostitution in the Progressive Era.* Chapel Hill: University of North Carolina Press, 1980.
Gilfoyle, Thomas J. *City of Eros: New York City, Prostitution, and the Commercialization of Sex, 1790–1920.* New York: W. W. Norton, 1992.

Anti-Semitism (UK)

During World War I, the Anglo-Jewish minority faced both recurring anti-Jewish violence in the course of riots in immigrant quarters as well as racist anti-Semitism, which was widely voiced in the press and public.

Between 1914 and 1918, anti-alien violence directed against persons and property was ripe and its main victims were the some sixty thousand German nationals that resided in Britain. Eastern European Jews, sharing with the Germans the same areas of residence and their status as foreigners or resident aliens were repeatedly caught up in these outbreaks of violence, which began in October 1914. These came to a climax in the course of the *Lusitania* riots, which took place in the wake of the ship's sinking by German submarines in May 1915. Whereas these earlier incidences had concentrated on Germans, in 1917, a series of violent riots occurred that were specifically directed against Jews. These outbreaks were triggered by the reluctance of the majority of Russian Jews as "friendly aliens" to stand by flag and country voluntarily. In June and September 1917, violence took place in Leeds and London in those districts that were mainly inhabited by East European Jews. The street fights and ransacking involved mobs of several thousands and continued in both towns for several days. These incidents can be misleading as to the focus of the anti-Semitism: During World War I, the enemies of the Jewish minority did not direct their attacks against the recent immigrants from Eastern Europe, but rather against the assimilated British Jews who, thanks to their success in industry, finance, and politics, were visible in Parliament, the City, London's financial district, and the London Society.

In these years, anti-Semitism in most cases went along with Germanophobia: Jews faced a spectrum of stereotypes that construed a political nearness of Jews in Britain to Germany. The accusations ranged from vague allegations of pro-German sympathies to the simple equating of Jews with Germans. The most notorious was the journalist and editor James Leopold Maxse with his monthly "The National Review." Almost every war issue contained articles exploring the alleged "pro-German machinations of the International Jew" or, alternatively, attacks on "German Jews" who resided in London and who, according to Maxse, had "undermined the City as well as Parliament to the detriment of England and for the benefit of Germany." But Leo Maxse's venom only mirrored those stereotypes that could be found elsewhere in the press. The Jewish weekly *The Jewish World* took up the task to fight back against anti-Semitism during World War I, and thus provided ample insight into the prevalent accusations. Indeed, the most frequent variants of prejudices taken up by *The Jewish World* were either attacks on "German Jews," who were without distinction portrayed as extraordinarily "bad"—in contrast to the "good" British or French Jews—and the identifications of Jews with Germans. When, in May 1915, Jews were amongst the victims of the mob in the course of the Lusitania riots, *The Jewish World* was convinced that this had been the case because in Britain Jews were generally supposed to be Germans, since "Jew" and "German" were being used by many as synonymous terms. It is certainly hard to establish whether this had been the main reason, but still *The Jewish World,* the second largest Jewish weekly in Britain, deemed as a contemporary observer the prejudices that construed a nearness of Jews to Germany and even an identity of Jews with Germans to be strong enough to lead to this violence.

Many of the anglicized Jews could trace their roots back to German lands from where their ancestors had immigrated into England in the last decades of the eighteenth century and the first half of the nineteenth century. In addition, some five thousand German Jews had come to Britain in the second half of the nineteenth century, and many out of the latter group were amongst the Anglo-Jewish elite who had made careers in politics, the industry, and finance. But, by 1914, all of them were either naturalized British subjects for at least several decades, if they had not been actually born in Britain. Still, these British subjects were considered and attacked as "German Jews," which clearly indicates major shifts in the general attitude toward naturalization that was in all of these cases judged null and void.

The Bolshevik revolution in the fall of 1917 combined with the comparatively high percentage of Jews—or Russians with a Jewish background—in the Russian revolutionary movement as well as the Bolshevik rank and file after November 1917 inspired anti-Semites to the new prejudices, and the arsenal of anti-Semitic stereotypes grew with the identification of Jews with Bolsheviks, violence, and destruction.

Obviously in reaction to the widespread Germanophobia in general as well as the anti-Semitic stereotypes outlined above, many Jewish families anglicized their German names. It has been widely noted that the wish to demonstrate Jewish loyalty to the national cause was extraordinary during World War I, and this has been attributed to a heightened sense of unease in the reaction to the general nationalism and to anti-Semitism: Public Jewish criticism of Tsarist Russia for the treatment of Jews there was practically silent in Britain beginning from August 1914. Moreover, the leadership of the Jewish minority, the Board of Deputies of British Jews, declined to intervene on behalf of foreign Jews who had been interned as "enemy aliens."

The question of the political implications and consequences of any prejudice should be approached with care. Still, research has shown that the assumption of strong pro-German sympathies among Jews was prevalent in the Foreign Office and played a significant role in the prehistory as well as the eventual announcement of the Balfour-Declaration in 1917: Jews were considered to be connected internationally, united by one political will and politically powerful enough to help change the course of the war, if their sympathies could be secured for the British and Allied side. Since the conviction of Jewish pro-German sympathies was deeply ingrained into the perception of Jews by leading Foreign Office officials as well as in the government, London felt it was necessary to take this step in order to draw "Jewish sympathies" away from Germany.

Susanne Terwey

See also: German Americans (WWI); Immigration (U.S., WWI)

REFERENCES

Almog, Shmuel. "Antisemitism as a Dynamic Phenomenon: The 'Jewish Question' in England at the End of the First World War." *Pattern of Prejudice* 21 (1987): 3–18.

Bryan, Cheyette. *Constructions of "The Jew" in English Literature and Society: Racial Representations, 1875–1945.* Cambridge: Cambridge University Press, 1993.

Levene, Mark. "The Balfour Declaration: A Case of Mistaken Identity." *English Historical Review* 107 (1992): 54–77.

Terwey, Susanne. "Juden sind keine Deutschen! Ueber antisemitische Stereotype um Juden und Deutschland in Grossbritannien vor und waehrend des Ersten Weltkrieges und die juedischen Abwehr." *Sachor* 11 (2001): 41–62.

Armaments Industry

World War I revealed the ambivalent relationship between the privately owned armaments industry, the government, and the public. Both the government and the public acknowledged that private armaments were necessary to conduct the war, but President Wilson, concerned that the country remain neutral "in thought as well as deed," refused to order armaments purchases that would have assisted with provisioning Allied troops once the United States entered the war. The public worried about the "war profits" of private arms manufacturers. The ambivalent attitude of the government and the public would manifest itself again in the interwar years in the form of disarmament debates and, in particular, the Senate investigation into the role of private armament makers in World War I.

Outbreak of War

At the outbreak of World War I, the United States possessed a substantial navy but only a very small professional army. It possessed a modest array of field artillery and a stock of rifles, carbines, and pistols manufactured at leisure and stored in armories until a time when units were ready to use them. An American expeditionary force capable of making an effective contribution to the war in Europe would need large numbers of modern field medium and heavy guns, and still larger numbers of mortars and machine guns. Such weapons could not be produced in useful quantities in just a few weeks, or even a few months. Some of them could not be produced at all until designs were approved, prototypes tested, and factories built or enlarged and provided with tools and plants. The military authorities could not hope to have them ready for use in an emergency unless crucial decisions were made long before the emergency arose.

The United States was a highly industrialized nation, and it was also a peace-loving democracy in which the army was kept firmly in its place. Companies and corporations whose arms-producing potential were commensurate with the army's needs were not lacking, but their relations with the military authorities were very different from those subsisting between arms manufacturers and ordnance departments in European countries. They received no contributions from the Department of the Army to the cost of maintaining research and development departments and little or no indirect support in the shape of reliable indications of the nature of the weapons it might be worth their while to develop as private ventures in the hope that, if they were successful, the army would adopt them. An American inventor of a weapon with a purely military application could not expect to receive a penny from his own government until he perfected his design and the prototype was tested and approved. He might then be awarded a contract if he could find a manufacturer able and willing to undertake quantity production on acceptable terms. Not surprisingly, such pioneers of the automatic weapon as Hiram Maxim, John Browning, Isaac Lewis, and Benjamin Hotchkiss made arrangements for their inventions to be manufactured and marketed by foreign firms. New

field medium and heavy guns were still less likely to be developed for the U.S. Army by private ventures.

The army did, of course, possess facilities of its own for research and development, but at best these could not do much more than enable experts to keep track of current trends: There is a substantial difference between knowledge of the kind of equipment that may be useful in a future war and the ability to produce it in large quantities at short notices. Executive decisions and productive capacity are needed to translate theory into practice.

A number of attempts were made between the end of the Civil War and 1914 to persuade federal authorities to put the national defenses on a sounder footing. Soon after the outbreak of the war in Europe, advocates of military preparedness suggested to President Woodrow Wilson that an attitude of strict neutrality toward the conflict need not preclude the United States from equipping itself by producing the artillery and other heavy equipment that might be needed by an expeditionary force. President Wilson refused to sanction measures that might imply the United States was preparing to enter the war.

Arms manufacturers, it was clear, could not expect to do much business with the Department of the Army while the country was at peace. On the other hand, there was nothing to prevent them and other manufacturers from selling their products to overseas buyers who were able to pay for them and to take delivery. Industrial firms, some of them with little or no experience in the arms trade, accepted large orders from foreign governments for a wide range of military equipment. American manufacturers equipped themselves on a massive scale for the production of weapons and ammunition of European caliber and pattern.

In 1916, the President sanctioned an ambitious program of naval expansion. No ships of the 1916 program had been completed when, in the spring of 1917, the German government's refusal to call off unrestricted U-boat warfare gave him no choice but to ask Congress to recognize that a state of war existed between the United States and Germany. During the debate over entry into the war in April, 1917, Senator George E. Norris of Nebraska charged that vast propaganda was forcing America into war to guarantee "the enormous profits of munitions manufacturers, stockbrokers, and bond dealers." He thus revealed the uneasiness with private armament manufacture.

Toward the end of the war, American-made machine guns began to meet the demand; but the artillery problem was solved by adopting the French 75 (as well as their 155 Howitzer) because the French could provide them in numbers and also because they simplified the matter of ammunition supply. A great effort was made to produce airplanes in quantity at the expense of the then-enormous sum of about a billion dollars. It was an almost complete failure: Even with the primitive designs of the period, a volume aircraft industry simply could not be set up in the time available. In spite of such shortcomings, the mobilization of 1917–1918 served the needs.

Criticism of War Profiteering

As the war dragged on, the charge that politicians extended the war for the profit of the arms industry attracted a good deal of support. The flaw in this argument was the absence of any evidence either that arms manufacturers as a class expected to profit by continuance of the struggle or that their influence was decisive.

The Paris Peace Conference of 1919 revealed this same uneasiness about the private manufacture of arms. The League of Nations Covenant called for control of the munitions trade and stated that members would entrust to the League supervision of the arms trade with countries in which control of the trade was necessary to the common interest. Throughout the 1920s, the disarmament movement gathered steam in the United States. Then, in the year 1934, a special committee of the U.S. Senate undertook an investigation to determine whether or not those people who had profited from war—armament manufacturers, shipbuilders, financiers—also bore responsibility for World War I.

The munitions investigation had an enthusiastic newspaper press, and even obtained large support from distinguished scholars. Many Americans believed that munitions makers had organized an international combine or ring. The ring included Vickers-Armstrong of Great Britain, S. A. Bofors of Sweden, Schneider-Creusot of France, Skoda of Czechoslovakia, Krupp of Germany, and E. I. du Pont de Nemours and Company of the United States. These munitions makers, according to many Americans, were the root of all the world's problems.

By providing very little evidence for these assertions, the Senate committee debunked this thesis. During deliberations, the committee discussed the possibility of regulating or nationalizing the private arms industry. A result of this inquiry was the creation of a National Munitions Controls Board. The board maintained watch over the munitions industry and arms trade, facilitated military aid to the Allies after 1939, and helped mobilization when the United States entered a new World War in 1941.

The 1934 Senate investigation revealed that both the American people and the U.S. Congress struggled in both times of war as well as peace over the appropriate relationship between private armament manufacturers and the government.

Michael McGregor

See also: Business (U.S., WWI); Economy (U.S., WWI); League of Nations (WWI); Paris Peace Conference (WWI)

REFERENCES

Baldwin, Hanson W. *The Great Arms Race.* New York: Praeger, 1958.

Crosby, J. R. *Disarmament and Peace in British Politics, 1914–1919.* Cambridge: Harvard University Press, 1957.

Sampson, Anthony. *The Arms Bazaar.* London: Hodder and Stoughton, 1977.

Armistice

The Armistice officially ended World War I on November 11, 1918. Leading up to the Armistice, the activities of two countries exercised considerable influence on the course of the war as it began to shift toward conclusion: the United States and Russia. While the United States was neutral at the beginning of the war, it broke off relations with Germany in February 1917 after Germany resumed unrestricted submarine warfare in the Atlantic Ocean at the end of 1916. On April 6, 1917, the United States formally entered the war.

Meanwhile in Russia, in March 1917 the February Revolution broke out and Czar Nicholas II was forced to abdicate and Prince Georgi Lvov then became head of a provisional government that commanded little popular support. In April 1917, Vladimir Lenin, along with other revolutionary Bolsheviks, returned to Russia. The Bolsheviks, led by Lenin, resorted to a military revolution (the October Revolution), seizing supreme power in Russia in November 1917. The new Soviet Russia and the Central Powers concluded the Treaty of Brest-Litovsk on March 3, 1918, which then brought Soviet Russia's participation in World War I to an end.

The U.S. participation in and the Russian withdrawal from World War I greatly influenced the course of the war. The United States provided the Allied powers with almost unlimited industrial and manpower resources; Washington sent approximately two million soldiers to the war. The Treaty of Brest-Litovsk then released German armies from the eastern front, which moved to the Western Front where they engaged in extremely bloody battles with the Allied powers.

However, seven months of fighting after Brest-Litovsk eventually exhausted German resources and caused morale to collapse, although the German government was not yet ready to concede military defeat. German troops were still occupying territory from France to the Crimea, although there was no single truly decisive battle having been fought. But in the beginning of October 1918, Prince Maximilian of Baden, the German imperial chancellor, sent a request to U.S. President Woodrow Wilson via Switzerland for an immediate armistice and the opening of peace negotiations upon the basis of the Fourteen Points, a set of ideals the United States proposed to Germany to govern a peace settlement if the war could be ended.

World War I did great damage to all participants. The total amount of war expenditure reached $186 billion and more than 37 million people died or were wounded in battle. The Paris Peace Conference was held in order to establish a permanent peaceful world. The so-called Big Four led the conference: Woodrow Wilson for the United States, Georges Clemenceau for France, David Lloyd George for Great Britain, and Vittorio Emanuele Orlando for Italy. The idealistic premises of the Fourteen Points were the basis of peace negotiations, but the European powers eventually sacrificed most of them, with the exception of the establishment of the League of Nations. The Treaty of Versailles, the result of the peace conference, placed all responsibility for the war on the shoulders of Germany and its allies, and imposed upon Germany the burden of the reparations payments. The treaty also forced Germany to forfeit its overseas colonies. Germany was allowed to have a maximum of 100,000 soldiers and the German navy was also severely reduced. In addition, Germany was forbidden to build major weapons of aggression. Germans felt betrayed when the Treaty of Versailles nullified the ideals of the Fourteen Points and imposed harsh terms and conditions upon Germany. After futile protests to the Allies, the country grudgingly accepted the treaty, which took effect in January 1920.

The Armistice and the Treaty of Versailles completely changed the structure of international relations. The collapse of the Central Powers and the Russian Empire laid the groundwork for what later became known as Eastern Europe. Not only the defeated nations but also the victorious traditional great powers—Great Britain and France—saw their power and influence decline as a result of the exhaustion caused by such a long war. Encouraged by the ideal of national self-determination contained in the Fourteen Points proposal, anticolonialist political movements began in Asia and Africa, and two new axes of international relations then rose to the surface: The rise of the United States as the most productive nation in the world and the birth of the Soviet Union as the world's first prominent socialist country.

Yoneyuki Sugita

See also: Fourteen Points (WWI); League of Nations (WWI); Paris Peace Conference (WWI); Biographies: Clemenceau, Georges; Emanuele, Vittorio; George, David Lloyd (WWI); Wilson, Woodrow (WWI)

REFERENCES

Coffman, Edward M., ed. *The War to End All Wars: The American Military Experience in World War I.* New York: Oxford University Press, 1968.
Walworth, Arthur. *America's Moment, 1918: American Diplomacy at the End of World War I.* New York: Norton, 1977.

Arts, Visual

Visual artists in the United States, Great Britain, and Canada responded to World War I in unprecedented numbers. The war evoked a range of responses, including conservative patriotism and avant-garde critique. Artists expressed these views through a variety of mediums, from mass-media illustrations to high-end painting. One of the remarkable developments that emerged during World War I was the development and implementation of official governmental propaganda operations that employed the visual arts. Pictorial propaganda was utilized in an attempt to win over audiences both at the home front and abroad, and it played an important role as a form of persuasion from the onset of the war.

Posters

The most prevalent form of visual art displayed at the home fronts during World War I was the poster. Incorporating picture and text, posters transmitted powerful and emblematic images while calling for a wide range of wartime needs—from recruitment to fundraising, glorification of the Allies to demonization of the "Hun." Several advantages made the poster a popular choice to convey the propaganda needs of each country. Along with affordability and speed of production, the colorful lithographic process of the poster allowed the artist to achieve a strong visual impact that was intended to grab the viewer's attention quickly and leaving an emotional punch. Printed in large runs and displayed in an array of public places, posters proved to be remarkably effective in persuading people to be sparing with supplies, to donate money, or to defend their country.

Posters produced in all three countries were quite similar both thematically as well as visually. In Great Britain, the most famous poster was Alfred Leete's (1882–1933) 1914 recruitment notice portraying War Minister Lord Horatio Herbert Kitchener gravely pointing his right forefinger out to the viewer while large, bold text explains his charge: "Britons, Kitchener 'Wants You' [to] Join Your Country's Army!" Inspired by Leete's illustration, American magazine illustrator James Montgomery Flagg (1877–1980) created his iconic 1917 image of a pointing Uncle Sam looming above the slogan "I want you for the U.S. Army." World War I posters promoted other home-front concerns and efforts as well. In "Remember, We Must Feed Daddy Too," a 1918 poster commissioned by the Canadian Food Board, artist Robert Edwin Johnson (1885–1933) depicted a woman feeding a small child at a table while an image of her uniformed husband holding a rifle flashes in the background. Posters reiterating the importance for those at home to conserve food, fuel, and other resources similarly reinforced traditional gender roles. Regardless that many women entered the domestic workforce during the war, posters tended to represent women in more traditional roles, such as wives and mothers in need of pro-

tection or beautiful, patriotic cheerleaders, as pictured in Howard Chandler Christy's (1873–1952) Navy recruitment posters.

In addition to posters, cartoons were another visual medium that was utilized at home to aid the war effort. In the United States, the Committee on Public Information (CPI) established a Cartoon Bureau that contracted and distributed cartoonists' works. The majority of these drawings were published in newspapers, though some were reproduced as large-scale posters. The subjects varied from expressing disapproval of the war to government-sanctioned works that clearly supported the campaign. The latter could be found in publications, such as a 1918 book of cartoons—appropriately named *The Cartoon Book*—that was issued to raise money for the third Liberty Loan appeal.

Fine Art

Fine art painters responded to the war as well. Many, drawing from traditional modes of depicting war, composed grand and idealized battle scenes popular amongst home-front audiences. These highlighted the bravery and heroism of the soldiers engaged in combat. Works like *The Taking of Vimy Ridge, Easter Monday,* and *1917* (1919) by the Canadian painter Richard Jack (1866–1952) avoided the harrowing casualties that accompanied this assault, concentrating instead on the brawny figures of the cannon loaders instead. Other artists, like the English painter James Clark, avoided the effects of modern technological warfare. His representation of a dead soldier in his 1914 painting, *The Great Sacrifice,* is unblemished by any disturbing wounds that commonly caused death on the battlefield.

The governments of all three nations also recruited artists to produce large-scale paintings intended to function as records and memorials of each respective nation's war effort in the combat zone and at home. The first official art program was established in Canada in November 1916 under the direction of Canadian native and wealthy newspaper owner Sir Max Aitken (1879–1964). The Canadian War Memorials Committee (CWMC) employed artists from both Canada and Great Britain, and for many artists, their service shaped their artistic development. This is exemplified in the work of A. Y. Jackson (1882–1974), whose oil painting *A Copse, Evening* (1918) captures the ravaged landscape of the frontline. His focus on the topography, with its blasted trees silhouetted against a pale sky, foreshadows his work as one of Canada's leading landscape painters as a member of the Group of Seven. Female artists contributed to the CWMC as well. The painter Mabel May (1877–1971) relays the physical exertion of the women filling shells in a munitions factory in her 1919 painting *Women Making Shells*. Works like this and others by artists including Albert Robinson (1881–1956), Arthur Lismer (1885–1969), and Manly MacDonald (1898–1971) documented the contributions made by those remaining at home in farming, shipping, and industry.

Government Recruitment of Artists

The government of Great Britain first enlisted artists in 1916. Early recruits, like the first official war artist Muirhead Bone (1876–1953), created conventional representations that avoided the dire realities of trench life. But the visual arts were not given much attention until 1917, when the Department of Information (DoI) was established. This organization stressed visual propaganda and hired many young artists to produce works based upon their experiences on the frontline. Artists like C. R. W. Nevinson (1889–1942), who had been

a medic in France, offered a critical interpretation of the war that contrasted with the more prevalent sanitized depictions. Nevinson's painting *Paths of Glory* (1917) was famously censored by the army for graphically showing two dead British soldiers lying face down in the mud. The British War Office prohibited artists from representing such realistic and disturbing scenes; they also forbade disputes over censorship, a rule that Nevinson boldly challenged by exhibiting in London his painting covered in brown paper that was inscribed with the word "CENSORED."

In early 1918, the DoI was replaced with the Ministry of Information (MoI). Prime Minster Lloyd George appointed Canadian-born Max Aitken, now Lord Beaverbrook, as his minister of information. Following the example of the extremely successful CWMC, Beaverbrook set out to do the same for Britain, forming the British Memorials War Committee (BMWC). The BMWC enlisted artists of various styles and temperaments. The well-known American expatriate painter John Singer Sargent (1856–1925) was commissioned to represent the cooperation between the British and American troops. He was moved, however, to paint the epic he titled *Gassed,* a work showing a line of blindfolded victims of mustard gas at a casualty clearing station. It became one of the most celebrated representations of the war. Practitioners of more modern artistic styles, like Wyndham Lewis (1882–1957), produced abstracted works such as *A Battery Shelled* (1919), in which soldiers are turned into robot-like figures inhabiting an industrialized combat zone.

In the United States, the idea to appoint official war artists was formulated by the CPI three months after America declared war upon Germany in 1917, although the American program was much smaller in scale and production than its British and Canadian counterparts. Eight artists, including Harvey Thomas

Dunn (1884–1952) and Ernest Clifford Peixotto (1869–1940) were sent to the warfront to document the Army's participation in the conflict. After the war, in 1920, the U.S. Army transferred the art produced by its war artists to the Smithsonian Institution, now in the Museum of American History.

Following the end of the war, exhibitions highlighting works by official war artists were held in major cities in all three countries, including New York, London, and Ottawa. But these shows were temporary, and the postwar years were spent securing permanent homes for the tremendous creative output generated by artists. In Great Britain, these works were incorporated into the collection of the Imperial War Museum in London, an institution founded in March 1917. Although by the end of the war there were two competing plans to build an art gallery in Ottawa to house the Canadian art collection, neither were ever realized. Art created for the CWMC remained in the possession of the National Gallery of Canada until 1971, when the works were transferred to the Canadian War Museum in Ottawa. Posters, due to their more ephemeral nature, were not viewed as collectible art; yet the large numbers of posters printed over the course of the war has meant that many examples have survived to the present day, often in private collections. What has proved more lasting, perhaps, is the iconic nature of some of the images produced for the home front during World War I. Images, like Leete's Kitchener or Flagg's Uncle Sam, were adapted by artists during World War II and are familiar to viewers even to this day.

Mary-Kate O'Hare

See also: Committee on Public Information; Propaganda (Canada, WWI); Propaganda (UK, WWI); Propaganda (U.S., WWI)

REFERENCES

Cornesbise, Alfred E. *Art from the Trenches: American Uniformed Artists.* College Station: Texas A&M Press, 1991.

Darracott, Joseph. *The First World War in Posters.* New York: Dover, 1974.

Harries, Meiron, and Susie Harries. *The War Artists: British Official War Art of the Twentieth Century.* London: Michael Joseph in association with the Imperial War Museum and the Tate Gallery, 1983.

Olivier, Dean F., and Laura Brandon. *Canvas of War: Painting the Canadian Experience.* Ottawa: Canadian War Museum, 2000.

Robb, George. *British Culture and the First World War.* New York: Palgrave, 2002.

Tippett, Maria. *Art at the Service of War: Canada, Art and the Great War.* Toronto: University of Toronto Press, 1984.

B

Banking and Finance

Commercial banks occupy a key position in the program of Treasury borrowing. They are by far the largest purchasers of government obligations to the public. Moreover, their smooth functioning depends upon the possibility that the tremendous shifting about of funds may be accomplished without disruption. Finally, the needs of private customers may be served where consistent with war objectives, and their interests are safeguarded in both the immediate and more distant future.

At the start of World War I, it was decided that the Treasury and the Federal Reserve Banks should not participate in the actual sale of bonds to the public; their activities were directed, instead, toward problems of organization and administration. Accordingly, the sale of bonds to the public devolved upon local committees and banks.

One of the initial steps in preparing for the First Liberty Loan was to set up an organization to conduct the selling program. This organization, which was divided into twelve groups corresponding to the twelve Federal Reserve Districts, was largely under the supervision and direction of bankers. The most important of the regional groups—important particularly in terms of total sale—had its center in New York. Under the supervision of this central group in New York, volunteer committees were formed in different occupations to assist in the sale of securities, and teams of bond salesmen conducted a house-to-house canvass. Representatives from investment banking played a particularly active role in the selling organization. Subcommittees carried the campaign into all parts of the Reserve District.

One of the basic features of the bond-selling program was the reliance upon quotas. A quota committee was appointed by the Federal Reserve Bank of each district to allocate quotas among the states in the District. State committees made allocations among the counties, and county chairmen apportioned quotas among towns and communities. Local committees composed chiefly of bankers—whose names were not made public—decided upon the quotas of individuals.

Although there were frequent complaints that individual and community quotas were unfair, on the whole the system seems to have functioned surprising well. One of the chief criticisms was that the method served to discourage subscriptions in excess of the quota: It had been hoped the quota would be viewed as a minimum amount to be subscribed, but was more frequently looked upon as a maximum. Furthermore, if an individual subscribed more than his quota, it often happened that the quota was raised the next time; this higher quota then might be excessive, but at any rate the individual would lose recognition and satisfaction he might otherwise have received from exceeding his quota.

The direct purchase of government securities by commercial banks was a minor, though by no means unimportant, lender to the government. Government borrowing was based chiefly upon Treasury obligations in the form of short-term certification of indebtedness and the longer-term bonds and notes. The former, which constituted the bulk of the flouting debt, consisted mainly of loan certificates or tax anticipation certificates, issued in anticipation of income to be obtained later from the sale of bonds or from taxation. The other group of obligations included long-term bonds offered in four successive Liberty Loan issues at different dates during 1917 and 1918, and Victory Notes, having a maturity of four years, which were offered some months after the Armistice.

Because of their short maturities and satisfactory yield, the loan certificates were appealing to banks. Prior to the Third Liberty Loan, a system of quotas for the purchase certificates was introduced, and the Secretary of the Treasury sent a telegram to every bank and trust company in the country urging it to subscribe. Before the Fourth Liberty Loan campaign, the banks were virtually ordered to subscribe to certificates at a monthly rate equivalent to 5 percent of gross resources. This provided a wider and more even distribution of certificates among the banks of the country. Commercial bank holdings of government securities, both short-term and long-term, reached a peak of more than $5 billion in the middle of 1919.

The bank's part in financing a war may involve considerably more than supplying the Treasury with the necessary funds. It ordinarily entails the financing of enterprises engaged in war production, and may include lending to individuals in order that they, in turn, may lend to the government. Between the outbreak of war in Europe in 1914 and our entry into the war in 1917, loans and discounts of national banks rose to 36 percent. The total continued to rise thereafter at about the same rate until 1919, when the rate of increase became more rapid. A considerable proportion of the increase in loans by national banks between 1917 and 1919 was in the form of loans on the collateral of government bonds. Loans of this type, which were popularized under the slogan "Borrow and Buy," constituted one of the distinctive features of financial policy during World War I. A customer of a bank was allowed to buy a government bond and pay for it with the proceeds of a loan secured by the bond itself. Since the loan was repaid either currently or out of a deposit that had been accumulated gradually, the effect was similar to the purchase of a bond on the installment plan. While these loans were technically of a private nature, their effect was to make bank credit indirectly available to the government. There can be little doubt that the action of the banks in lending to their customers on the security government bonds contributed materially to the success of the Liberty and Victory Loan drives. On the other hand, considerable dissatisfaction was expressed at the time and subsequently with respect to the operation of the policy of borrow-and-buy. Banks experienced some difficulty with the loans, and their general effect was held to be inflationary.

Michael McGregor

See also: Federal Reserve (WWI); War Bonds (WWI)

REFERENCES

Abrahams, Paul P. "American Bankers and the Economic Tactics of Peace: 1919," *Journal of American History* 56 (1969): 572–583.

Anderson, Benjamin M. *Economics and the Public Welfare: Financial and Economic History of the United States, 1914–1946.* New York: D. Van Nostrand, 1949.

Gilbert, Charles. *American Financing of World War I.* Westport, CT: Greenwood Press, 1970.

Baseball

By the time of American entry into World War I, baseball had established itself as the national pastime. During the 1917 season, owners displayed their fidelity to the great national crusade by ordering their players to practice military drills before each game. Eventually this was dropped, but the leagues and owners encouraged fans and players to buy Liberty Bonds and donate to the Red Cross. Admission to ball games was free to members of the armed services.

Several weeks into the 1918 season, Secretary of War Newton Baker issued his "work or fight" order. After much lobbying by the owners, major league baseball was exempted until September 1, 1918, but the season had to be shortened to get the World Series in before the deadline. Attendance dropped by more than two million fans in 1918. Over 220 major league players were drafted or volunteered for the armed services, causing the owners to employ overaged and inexperienced players. The minor and the semiprofessional leagues were decimated and unable to continue play. Several hundred more players went to work in factories where they spent much of their time playing for company teams, inviting the anger of the league owners and the charge of being slackers.

In 1919, the owners cut the season to 140 games, which was a poor decision since the war was over and attendance skyrocketed to six million fans. The nation was rocked by the "Black" Sox scandal of 1919. Although the eight Chicago White Sox players were acquitted in federal court for throwing the 1919 World Series to the Cincinnati Reds, Baseball Commissioner Judge Kenesaw Mountain Landis banned the eight men from baseball. The following year George Herman "Babe" Ruth belted fifty-nine homeruns for the New York Yankees, thereby restoring the fans' devotion to the game and ushering in a new era of baseball.

Gregory Dehler

See also: Biographies: Cobb, Ty (WWI); Jackson, "Shoeless" Joe (WWI)

REFERENCES

Asinof, Elliott. *Eight Men Out: The Black Sox and the 1919 World Series.* New York: Holt, Rinehart and Winston, 1963.

Burk, Robert F. *Never Just a Game: Players, Owners, and American Baseball to 1920.* Chapel Hill: University of North Carolina, 1994.

Reiss, Steven A. *Touching Base: Professional Baseball and American Culture in the Progressive Era.* Westport, CT: Greenwood Press, 1980.

Boston Police Strike

The roots of the Boston Police strike of 1919 can be traced to a convergence of two trends that stretched beyond the city itself: progressive era efforts to reform municipal police and broad postwar labor unrest. Likewise, the strike's consequences can be charted nationally: for Calvin Coolidge, a career boost that carried him from the State House to the White House; and for rank-and-file police, a half-century freeze on unionization.

Contemporary observers and subsequent historians concur that Boston's police had much to complain about: War-induced inflation eroded their already low wages, while unsanitary conditions flourished in their station houses. In these bread-and-butter grievances, the patrolmen had much in common with the one-fifth of the nation's workforce that struck that year. But it was Police Commissioner Edwin Curtis's refusal to recognize the policemen's affiliation with the American Federation of Labor that triggered the walkout and also subsequently revealed the ethnic and class struggles underlying the widespread efforts to professionalize police departments.

Since the 1880s, the movement for police reform—initiated by Protestant business and civic interests—had sought to wrest control of police forces from political machines and their ethnic power bases. Thus, under the banner of good government, the Massachusetts legislature had in 1885, amid Irish Catholics' growing power in Boston, transferred authority over the capital's police from the frequently Democratic mayor's office to that of the reliably Republican governor's. In Boston, as in other cities, these reforms often produced bureaucratized departments with autocratic management practices that empowered chiefs at the patrolmens' expense.

Curtis, a Brahmin with more inherited wealth than political acumen, after his 1918 appointment, exploited such reforms in order to strengthen his hand over the predominantly Irish and already disgruntled police force. Not strictly bound by civil service lists, he promoted favorites. Similarly, he refused to negotiate with the Boston Social Club—formed in 1906 by patrolmen as a bargaining agency—and established in its stead a docile Grievance Committee. Nationwide, similar management tactics had led police to the AFL in order to defend the traditional workplace autonomy targeted by reformers. Police hoped the Federation—which began issuing charters to police unions in June—could establish fair complaint mechanisms and provide legal and political muscle to discontented officers. Indeed, when Boston's officers applied for their charter on August 15th, thirty-seven city police forces had already affiliated with the Federation—a burst of unionizing that, according to the organization's president, Samuel Gompers, outpaced all other industries.

If the AFL and police cheered the news, neither Boston's mayor, Andrew Peters, nor its commissioner did the same—if to different degrees and for different reasons. Curtis, interpreting affiliation as a challenge to his authority, not only promptly added a rule to the department's regulations forbidding association with outside organizations but also had the new union's leaders tried for violating it. Peters, although sympathetic to the patrolmen's grievances and the Federation's aims, feared AFL-affiliated officers might lack impartiality if called to suppress violent strikes. Having defused a threatened firemen's walkout the previous year, Peters sought a similar compromise before a strike left Boston unprotected. And indeed the crises seemed averted when the citizens' committee Peters had established swiftly produced a "basis of settlement"—drafted by the policemen's lawyers, amended by the committee, and endorsed by most newspapers—providing for an unaffiliated union. Curtis, however, claimed the agreement ignored his obligation to punish the violators of his new regulation and suspended the offending officers. The patrolmen responded by voting to strike the next evening, September 9. Governor Coolidge met with Peters and Curtis, but refused to intervene.

When three-quarters of the force walked out, the city slipped into a looting frenzy. At dawn, Peters, invoking public order statutes, assumed police control from Curtis, called out the city's one thousand guardsmen and requested more. Their arrival restored order by afternoon, but only after the untrained troops killed three Bostonians. Having dithered at the crisis's beginning, Coolidge announced on its third day he was assuming command of both guardsmen and police alike. Although Coolidge knew the police had little sympathy for radicalism, he nevertheless seized upon the media attention Boston's chaos produced (the *Los Angeles Times* warned, "no man's wife (would) be safe" if police followed the "orders of the Red Unionite bosses") to present himself as a law-and-order leader checking a Bolshevik menace in the wake of Russia's revolution, giving national significance to his actions. His pronouncement, "There is no right to strike against the public safety by anybody, anywhere, anytime" echoed profitably for him throughout his 1920 vice-presidential campaign to become enshrined in public memory.

Gregory Fritz Umbach

See also: American Federation of Labor (WWI); Strikes, Labor (WWI); Biographies: Coolidge, Calvin (WWI); Curtis, Edwin Upton (WWI)

REFERENCES

Lyons, Richard L. "The Boston Police Strike of 1919," *New England Quarterly* 20, no. 2 (1947): 147–168.

Russell, Francis. *A City in Terror.* New York: Viking Press, 1975.

Business (U.S.)

Business leaders, serving as administrators of the War Industries Board (WIB), directed one of the most ambitious attempts at institutional coordination in American history. Sophisticated in their ideology and skilled in their managerial ability, they set out to mobilize the country's economic resources for war and to protect its industrial economy for peace. They achieved a great deal in the short time available to them and built up a fund of experience and knowledge for the crisis managers of the future. In the end, however, the institutional realities of Progressive America overcame the rhetoric of integration and synthesis. The imperatives of modern war forced significant shifts in traditional institutional patterns, but the WIB business leaders were unable to assert complete control over this process.

War Industries Board

The WIB was the major civilian agency for industrial mobilization. Established as a subordinate part of the Council of National Defense at the end of July 1917—almost four months after America entered the war. The original members of the board were: Frank A Scott, a Cleveland manufacturer, chairman; Bernard M. Baruch, a Wall Street speculator, commissioner of raw materials; Robert S. Lovett, chairman of the Union Pacific Railroad, commissioner of priorities; Robert S. Brookings, a retired millionaire and former president of Washington University in St. Louis, commissioner of finished products; Hugh A. Frayne, an American Federation of Labor organizer, commission of labor; and Colonel Palmer E. Pierce from the army and Rear Admiral F. F. Fletcher from the navy. The board's duties included acting as a clearinghouse for the war industry needs of the government and determining the most effective ways of meeting the government's needs as well as the best means and methods for increasing production.

To gain legitimacy in the eyes of the American public, the WIB had to prove that it could harness the nation's economic units to a mobilization program designed to serve the national interest. There were major obstacles to convincing the public of its administration: After all, it drew its staff and administrative resources largely from the very economic groups it promised to regulate and it encouraged organizational trends that were antithetical to long-standing popular suspicions toward concentrations of private political and economic power. As with most regulatory activity, the WIB's relationships with its business clientele in practice assumed the nature of a gaming process marked by loose, informal understandings, ad hoc arrangements, calculated risks of infringement, and persuasive bargaining. Yet the WIB had to assure the public that the national interest received adequate protection and that, in the last analysis, business interests yielded to the public need. WIB administrators wanted to promote this image so that industry would emerge from the conflict in public favor. Non-cooperation, speculation, and reckless business behavior bothered them not just as wartime administrators trying to get a job done, but as business leaders anxious to prove that industry deserved the public's respect and trust. They felt responsible for proving that American business did indeed harbor the spirit of service and community conscience its publicists had so often claimed for it. They also wanted to prove that industry could achieve a degree of mobilization through voluntary cooperation that wartime critics argued could come only through extensive government takeovers. They set out to show that, with proper treatment by Washington agencies, American business could

plan for a nation at war without disturbing in any fundamental way the basic structure of the corporate capitalist state.

Wilson did not simply abdicate to big business in the evolution of the WIB. His caution in delegating authority, especially over prices, his reluctance to yield to business demands for a munitions ministry, and his refusal to undermine the traditional role of military institutions suggest that abdication is too easy an answer to explain Wilson's relationship with big business. Wilson possessed only a small and inexperienced peacetime bureaucracy with which to mobilize the country's major economic institutions. While Wilson might go so far as to advise and coordinate private economic decision making, he had no wish to supplant it. So, given a commitment to the basic structure and prerogatives of corporate capitalism and an aversion to the growth of an extensive and powerful state bureaucracy, even when faced with the institutional requirements of modern war, it was largely inevitable that mobilization went forward by means of a voluntary expert staff and the private administration of public policy.

Bernard Baruch was the perfect choice as institutional middleman. Baruch, the self-made millionaire who had beaten the money moguls at their own game, brought the traditional habits and values of individualism to an emerging bureaucratic system. Baruch was able to reconcile American individualism with scientific control. Baruch's style, personality, and values matched perfectly the informal, fragmented system of American industrial mobilization.

As one of the organizational pioneers of American preparedness, Baruch showed an early awareness of the institutional requirements of mobilization for modern war. But he possessed no clearer conception of the detailed complexities of the process than many other businessmen drawn into public life in 1915 and 1916. Baruch cultivated strategically placed individuals in business and politics. Moreover, unlike some businessmen in government, Baruch gave himself over completely to public life. A sweeping usurpation of traditional prerogatives and responsibilities was out of the question in the early stages of the war, but Baruch's chances improved as the crisis deepened, and his mandate finally came in March 1918. It is through the symbol of Bernard Baruch that the vision of a stable, cooperative system of industrial mobilization finally found the kind of fulfillment denied to it during World War I.

Interest group politics, corporate ideology, and structural imperatives of the economy and the state are among the major processes that defined business-government relations in the WIB. Interest group politics criss-crossed the business community. The pull of region, for instance, is exemplified very well by the resources and conversion section of the WIB's commodity organization. Likewise, a corporate ideology characterized key WIB administrators. The antidemocratic tendency of the business-sponsored administrative reform also finds many parallels during the war, and is certainly true in the case of the WIB. And finally, some American industries called for state intervention to obtain the rationalization and stability they could not guarantee on their own. No single one of them can be disregarded for a comprehensive account of the problem for the war years. They operated side by side throughout the conflict, and their interactions provides one of the central determinants of the WIB's evolution and operation.

Accelerated Growth

Because the war so accelerated the growth of business organizations, state agencies like the WIB had to take them into account as never be-

fore. In terms of comparative influence, however, there is no doubt about the crucial significance of giant corporations. Negotiations between the WIB and the corset manufacturers' association were of almost no consequence to the mobilization program compared to the outcome of discussions with big steel over prices, or with General Motors over automobile curtailments. The exigencies of war favored industrial consolidation and placed a premium upon the managerial and productive capacities of major American corporations. Even when the WIB struck up a continuing relationship with a business association, such as the U.S. Chamber of Commerce, it did so largely to satisfy public demand for regularized, democratic procedures while maintaining easy access to big business interests.

The WIB was staffed by a special group of men. They were business politicians rather than economic entrepreneurs, and they should not be confused with the actual owners and managers of the giant enterprises. Indeed, it was their very separation from centers of private economic power that made men like Baruch so attractive to the Wilson Administration.

A thoroughgoing pragmatism far more than ideological commitment to the ideal of business-government cooperation characterized private industry leaders who negotiated with the WIB in Washington. Judge Elbert Gary, for instance, hesitated over private agreements in the spring and summer of 1917 lest they reduce his prerogatives and profits, but in December 1918, he was the first in line for an agreement with the state as a way to guarantee price stability and profits during an anticipated market decline. The cooperative ideal did become systematized further, but it would be misleading to call it a guiding force of big-business action. Moreover, given the trend toward institutional coordination generated by the war itself, there was every reason to expect cooperation among institutional blocs such as business and government.

Structural Dimensions of the Economy

The structural dimensions of the economy and the state proved an important influence on business-government relations under the WIB. The structure of an industry largely determined the nature of its interest group representation, just as it set real limits on the practicality of realizing corporate ideals. The state bureaucracy itself reflected characteristics of the country's underlying economic structure. The search for coordination and control through the WIB, for instance, stemmed in part from the American industry's need for a stable administrative environment conducive to private corporate planning, and reorganization of the army's purchasing system was undertaken to match a national economy organized along commodity lines. However, the bureaucracy is a dependent variable of the country's economic structure, for that would overlook the significant ways in which the state influenced its relationship with specific business groups. For instance, bureaucratic disorganization and inadequate administration were contributing factors to business-government tension in the early months of the war. When state bureaus fought amongst themselves over jurisdiction and policy, business firms suffered the consequences. And further, the relationships between industry and government improved as the state rationalized its administrative procedures and substituted business volunteers for its regular civilian and military personnel. However, conflict between state advisors and private businessmen did not entirely disappear. While they all agreed they should do everything possible to protect America's industrial structure, they argued over the best means of doing this. Values and structure interacted at this point. Men who considered the needs of the whole system, as members of an agency of coordination, clashed with private managers whose interest-conscious views were appropriate to those in command of particular parts of the national economy.

In a situation tending by its very nature toward centralization and integration, the trends toward the growth of economic interest groups, giant corporations, corporate ideology, and intimate alliances between businessmen and the state all received widespread encouragement. The rhetoric of war itself reflected this organizational impulse as "cooperation" and "consolidation" replaced "individualism" and "competition" as rhetorical ideals.

It is possible to recognize the important acceleration of centralizing, consolidating, and integrating trends, however, without ignoring or underestimating the strength of those forces within the state, the economy, and the society that opposed them.

The degree of close, continuing integration implied by phrases like the "New Nationalism," "political capitalism," or "corporate liberalism" varied in practice during the war according to the segments of the economy and state involved and the issues on which they joined. The better organized an industry in peacetime, the smoother the adjustment was likely to be in war, although clashes over particular policy decisions could quickly cancel structural advantages. Much depended on the kinds of issues involved: It is fairly easy, for example, to compose a glowing portrait of business-government cooperation based upon the interaction of business interests and the WIB's conservation division. Throughout its work, the division relied exclusively upon voluntary adoption of conservation programs designed by the industries themselves. Such reforms could hardly become an occasion for conflict between businessmen and the state because they were obviously aimed at helping industry through the war and strengthening its competitive position for peace. Moreover, they raised substantive questions of power and control, and in these issue areas relations could be ambiguous, tense, and sometimes bitter. In most cases, the agreements that ultimately followed the threats and counterthreats of negotiations were remarkably mild. But even so, the outcome was not determined by the prewar structure of business thought and business-government relations alone. The process of the role definition between businessmen and the state evolved partly out of the war crisis itself.

Michael McGregor

See also: American Federation of Labor (WWI); Armaments Industry (WWI); Council of National Defense (WWI); War Industries Board (WWI); Biographies: Baruch, Bernard (WWI)

REFERENCES

Bogart, Ernest Ludlow. *War Costs and Their Financing.* New York: D. Appleton-Century, 1921.

Clark, John Maurice. *The Costs of the World War to the American People.* New Haven, CT: Yale University Press, 1931.

Clarkson, Grosvenor B. *Industrial America in the World War.* Boston: Houghton Mifflin, 1923.

Kuznets, Simon. *National Product in Wartime.* New York: National Bureau of Economic Research, 1945.

Paxson, Frederic Logan, *American Democracy and the World War.* Boston: Houghton Mifflin, 1939.

C

Cabarets

Cabarets in the United States during World War I were influenced by their European counterparts that offered song, dance, booze, and close mingling between the sexes. In America, cabarets sprang from lower-class establishments to become popular, pricey clubs. Prior to prohibition, cabarets were most often found in restaurants and cafes in larger cities.

Cabarets were not family entertainment centers; they were places where adults could drink, dance, and entertain themselves. During World War I, cabarets provided an outlet where people could forget about the conflict. The clubs often featured elaborate, suggestive chorus productions with scantily clad young women. Most cabarets did not have a stage. Performers used the floor of the club to mingle with the crowds.

Prohibition in 1920 brought changes to the cabarets. Alcohol was the mainstay of the clubs, and most could not survive without it. The few that did survive had famous reputations, such as the Cotton Club in New York. During Prohibition, the cabaret was replaced by speakeasies—illegal clubs where one could obtain alcohol. These establishments were often found in the basements and backrooms of other businesses. The alcohol was supplied by the mob, which also controlled the clubs. Live entertainment at these venues continued to be popular, with jazz and other performers as their mainstays.

Dancing in America underwent radical changes, thanks to the cabaret. Formal dancing, where partners followed a strict code of limited body contact was replaced by movements that enabled more bodily expression and physical interaction with partners. Cabarets also had an influence on music in America. Early jazz artists worked in the clubs and there they helped develop its unique sound. Cabarets were where many famous musicians got their early start. This was also the case for other entertainers and performers, such as comedy acts or chorus girls who later went on to film careers in Hollywood.

Kelly M. Jordan

See also: Jazz (WWI); Music (WWI); Prohibition (WWI)

REFERENCES

Erenberg, Lewis. *Steppin Out: New York Nightlife and the Transformation of American Culture.* Westport, CT: Greenwood Press, 1991.

Gavin, James. *Intimate Nights: The Golden Age of New York Cabaret.* New York: Grove Weidenfeld, 1991.

Campaign for Social Purity

The Progressive movement that erupted in America at the turn of the century was a combination of forces working to better the life of the working-class family. One component of this movement was a group of primarily middle-class women who wanted to rid society of corruption and vice, which mainly referred to prostitution and alcohol. By the outbreak of World War I, it was clear that the moral education and volunteer work of these women had become increasingly powerful, but reformers feared that the social degradation that war brought to Europe would take its turn on American society. Thus, as America prepared itself for war, purity campaigners also readied themselves for a fight inside their own camps.

Historically, America had not promoted chastity amongst its soldiers. During the War for Filipino independence, the armed forces had outraged reformers by encouraging prostitution with a state-run brothel for the soldiers. To prevent this from recurring, women from groups like the Women's Christian Temperance Union and the American Social Hygiene Association went directly to the leaders of the army to voice their protest. By arguing that the once-innocent soldiers would pollute American society by bringing back European morals and diseases, they got through to the army and won their cooperation.

The armed forces created an entire committee to address this problem, forming the widely successful Committee on Training Camp Activities (CTCA). In just over a year, the CTCA eliminated all of the red-light districts that existed in America. Then, with pamphlets, photographs, and movies, they began to address prostitution overseas. They encouraged soldiers to avoid things that led to sexual excitement, such as pornographic conversations, pictures, and magazines. Propaganda also criticized the patriotism of anyone who brought back sexually transmitted diseases and questioned the commitment of soldiers who could be distracted by the promise of sexual gratification. Other groups also rallied to the purists' cause by hosting events where the soldiers could meet young respectable women.

The CTCA joined the Young Men's and Women's Christian Associations to organize activities like athletic programs, community socials, and small gatherings for the troops. While these alternatives were very successful with the young soldiers, government officials and reformers alike began to fear the adverse effects the fraternizing had on the young ladies involved. Prostitution had been reduced greatly, but a new source of sexual vice emerged: the "khaki-mad girls." These young ladies, traditionally from working-class families, were often chastised for their alleged loose morals. They were labeled as delinquents and blamed for the spreading of venereal disease within the camps. The armed forces responded to this threat by once again creating a committee; they formed the Committee on Protective Work for Girls.

The Committee on the Protective Work for Girls joined middle-class progressive women in trying to help these "fallen" girls. The government and the reformers, however, did not agree upon issues concerning the girls, and soon the organizations split. The Committee tried to prevent sexual misconduct by sending officers to follow young couples outside of the events, making sure that young women did not sneak into the camps, and forcing all women who lived near the camps to be tested for diseases and undergo physical examinations. The Progressive reformers, on the other hand, offered a more preventative solution.

The progressive campaign to promote purity in working-class neighborhoods focused on the delinquent girl and what social factors led to her behavior. After years of social analysis on working-class families, progressive reformers decided that the neglect that these girls experienced when both parents worked often caused their behavior. The solutions that progressive women presented were intended to focus on the problems that led up to delinquency. They did this by going into the neighborhoods and educating families on the dangers of loose morals. When these methods failed, the social purists sent the "fallen" girls into reformatories.

Although it is difficult for historians to measure the success of these purity campaigns in the army, their immediate effects on postwar American society are very clear. In 1919, purity campaigners were rewarded for their concern with the Eighteenth Amendment, which banned the production, consumption, and sale of all alcohol.

Rachel Bennett

See also: Progressivism (WWI); Prohibition (WWI); Women (U.S., WWI)

REFERENCES

Kennedy, David M. *Over Here: The First World War and American Society.* New York: Oxford University Press, 2004.

Odem, Mary E. *Delinquent Daughters: Protecting and Policing Adolescent Female Sexuality in the United States, 1885–1920.* Chapel Hill: University of North Carolina Press, 1995.

Schaffer, Ronald. *America in the Great War: The Rise of the War Welfare State.* New York: Oxford University Press, 1991.

Censorship

Britain did it for its citizens at home and abroad. The United States got quite zealous about it. Germany censored to motivate, maintain morale, and keep its citizens focused in the right direction. When over 300,000 Germans poured through Belgium and into France in August 1914, French generals and politicians applied the tightest press censorship of any participant, exceeding even Germany. Censors suppressed or delayed publication of news, features, and even advertising, which virtually disappeared until the front stabilized.

The British censored their troops' letters too, including those from the empire. Once a week, the chief censor reported his findings. Canada censored reports on the war and the mails.

When the United States declared neutrality at the onset of World War I in 1914, President Woodrow Wilson authorized the navy to censor international telegraph and radio messages. When the United States entered the war, the military took over almost all commercial and amateur radio. Journalists switched from the wireless telegraph to the cable telegraph.

America's security bureaucracy was initially quite small, but when the war was fully under way, there were three dozen agencies involved—slowly at first, but more readily with time, they became comfortable with censoring telephones, the telegraph, the mails, and publications. Censorship had the support of both the Congress and the Courts. Loyal citizens, already spying on their neighbors, had no problem with censorship. Claiming national interest, the Federal Censorship Board oversaw the process.

In June 1917, distrustful of the millions of immigrants in the United States, Congress passed the Espionage Act, which prohibited obstructing the draft or promoting disloyalty by writing or speaking. It also led to the removal of "subversive" books from bookstores and libraries. In the year after its enactment, more than seventy-five newspapers lost their mailing privileges or changed their editorial positions to keep the privilege.

In 1918, the Sedition Act outlawed the publication of writing disrespectfully of the government, the flag, the Constitution, or military uniforms.

The wartime legislation of the United States provided for censorship of the foreign-language press, which was often supportive of socialism and anarchism and critical of the war. Two thousand people were prosecuted, among them Charles Schenck. He served ten years in prison for writing and distributing a pamphlet that declared the draft illegal.

To promote the war, Wilson created the Committee on Public Information headed by former journalist George Creel, who oddly was a critic of government censorship. Aside from propaganda on behalf of Allied war efforts (and demonization of the Central powers and home dissenters), the CPI established a "voluntary" code of censorship for journalists. Violators were cut off from access to government information, so reporters conformed to official guidelines. The CPI issued over six thousand press releases guiding the newspapers as to the correct position to take. Creel backed the Espionage and Sedition acts. The CPI also asked newspapers to send photos for CPI approval before publishing them. Frontline reporters relied on military photos at first, but eventually were able to take their own. Still, they were subject to censorship to prevent publication of anything harmful to morale or of benefit to the enemy. Newspapers critical of the war or radical, such as the socialist *Appeal to Reason* were silenced for the duration of the war.

Zealous censors barred the playing of German symphonies and other music. And U.S. soldiers were subject to censorship, too (for the first time). Censors looked for information that might be of value to the enemy, troop strength for instance, and checked morale. When immigrant or second-generation doughboys wrote home in their native languages, the censors, unable to read the letters, prohibited their delivery.

John H. Barnhill

See also: Civil Liberties (WWI); Committee on Public Information (WWI); Espionage Act (WWI); Journalism (U.S., WWI); Sedition Act (WWI); Documents: Assert Your Rights, 1917; *Schecnk v. U.S.,* 1919; Sedition Act, May 16, 1918

REFERENCES

Keshen, Jeffrey. *Propaganda and Censorship during Canada's Great War.* Edmonton, Canada: University of Alberta Press, 1996.

Smith, Jeffrey. *War and Press Freedom: The Problem of Prerogative Power.* New York: Oxford University Press, 1999.

Watkins, Glenn. *Proof through the Night: Music and the Great War.* Berkeley: University of California Press, 2003.

Welch, David. *Germany, Propaganda and Total War, 1914–1918.* New Brunswick, NJ: Rutgers University Press, 2002.

Civil Liberties

World War I marked a watershed in the history of civil liberties in the United States. The years 1917 and 1918 witnessed some of the most severe and systematic violations of civil liberties in American history. State and and local governments worked to suppress antiwar sentiments, and the war saw the emergence of a permanent federal bureaucracy to counter subversion. Patriotic-minded vigilantes sought to enforce support for the war through threats and violence. At the same time, the war experience laid the groundwork for an expanded notion of individual freedom of expression. Some Americans, repelled by the ferocity of the attack on dissenters, began to place a higher value on dissent. The war also saw the emergence of a new organization, the National Civil Liberties Bureau (NCLB), for contesting the violation of freedom of expression.

Precedents

The repression during World War I was not without some precedent. Since the creation of the Constitution until 1917, the federal government had engaged in suppression of expression, although such efforts were either fleeting in nature or limited in scope. For example, in 1798, during a war scare with France, the Federalist party authored the Sedition Act, which outlawed intentionally defamatory criticism of a "false, scandalous, and malicious" nature aimed at the government; a number of individuals were prosecuted for speaking harshly of President John Adams. During the Civil War, the Lincoln administration oversaw the arrests of a number of Northerners who spoke out against the war. In 1873, Congress passed legislation that became known as the "Comstock Law," after its chief enforcer, Anthony Comstock of the Post Office Department. Comstock targeted for prosecution materials of a sexual nature, which in practice included literature critical of the institution of marriage. Before World War I, however, perhaps the most frequent abusers of the freedom of speech were

local governments, which often saw nothing wrong with arresting or harassing labor or radical speakers. For example, orators from a radical labor union, the Industrial Workers of the World (IWW), were frequently detained by local authorities as they tried to speak on streets and in public places. These arrests were so pervasive that the IWW embarked on its "Free Speech Fights" campaign in which their speakers deliberately courted arrest by the police in an effort to demonstrate their lack of freedom. The judicial tradition before 1917 was far less solicitous of first amendment rights than it would become in subsequent decades. As historian David M. Rabban notes, judges often subscribed to the "bad tendency" doctrine—the notion that the state had the right to curb speech that fostered harmful behaviors among the public.

The intensity of the campaign against dissent during World War I owes much to the escalating fear of foreign subversion during the period from 1915 to early 1917. In 1915, it was disclosed that the Central Powers had tried to subsidize propaganda in the United States. In 1915 and 1916, the Justice Department charged several individuals with having tried to sabotage cargo shipments to the Allies. Revelations such as these helped to shape the public rhetoric toward a less tolerant stance toward immigrants and dissent. Before the end of 1915, President Woodrow Wilson was bewailing the lack of loyalty of certain elements in the United States, while former President Theodore Roosevelt criticized what he termed "hyphenated Americanism." Wilson's message of April 2, 1917, to Congress calling for a declaration of war alleged that Germany's government "has filled our unsuspecting communities and even our offices of government with spies and set criminal intrigues everywhere afoot against our national unity of counsel . . ." and warned that "[i]f there should be disloyalty, it will be dealt with with a firm hand of stern repression." Such messages about the prevalence of German conspiracies were reinforced by the Committee on Public Information, a federal agency established in 1917 to encourage popular support for the war. One print advertisement from 1918 asserted that "German agents are everywhere . . ."

The vehemence of the wartime attack on dissent also reflects the fact that America was truly divided about the wisdom and morality of military intervention. Shortly before the congressional vote on the war, for example, one Wisconsin community held a referendum on the war question—and by a 9-to-1 ratio, voters opposed entering the conflict. After the congressional declaration of war, the Socialist party in an emergency meeting voted to roundly condemn the decision to intervene in the conflict. The decision to impose the draft, too, met with a good deal of resistance. The Socialist party's declaration against the war turned it into an electoral vehicle for antiwar sentiment, for the party's share of the vote in numerous cities and towns jumped dramatically in 1917. Targets of wartime intolerance included pacifists, Socialists, and German Americans, and the radical labor union, the Industrial Workers of the World (IWW), likewise came under attack. Although the IWW, for the most part, did not directly challenge the decision to go to war, its anticapitalist and antimilitarist ideology, as well as its leadership of wartime strikes, led to its being targeted by government prosecutors.

Much of the coercion and punishment aimed at dissenters was carried out by private citizens who enthusiastically supported the war. The homes or property of disloyalists were smeared with yellow paint. Mobs tarred and feathered dissenters, or forced them to pay homage to the flag in public ceremonies. A minister deemed insufficiently patriotic was subjected to a whipping in Kentucky, while a German immigrant living in Collinsville, Illi-

nois, was lynched by a mob that believed him to be dangerous. This climate of fear naturally encouraged many Americans to take drastic steps to combat antiwar sentiments.

Local and state governments often demonstrated little concern for civil liberties. During an IWW-led strike in Bisbee, Arizona, a vigilante mob, guided by the local sheriff, rounded up more than a thousand workers and shipped them out of town on railroad cars. A number of states also passed sedition laws: A Wisconsin man was found guilty of violating his state's sedition law when he denounced war as barbaric and senseless. South Dakota's State Council of Defense barred the use of the German language in public groups of more than two individuals, save in certain situations.

Espionage Act

At the federal level, the legislative centerpiece of the campaign against dissent was the Espionage Act of June 1917. The Act made it illegal to try to hinder military enlistments or the draft, to deliberately make untrue statements that impeded the operation of the armed forces, or to foster disobedience in the armed forces. Under the act, critics of the war faced prosecution, as their comments supposedly posed a threat to the nation's armed forces. An even more severe amendment to the Espionage Act passed in May 1918, known as the Sedition Act, made it illegal to express any "disloyal, profane, scurrilous, or abusive language" with the intention of besmirching "the form of government of the United States, or the Constitution, or the flag." Federal attorneys, assisted by investigators from the Justice Department and its Bureau of Investigation, secured the conviction of hundreds of defendants under the original Espionage Act and under its amended version.

The Espionage Act also enabled the Post Office to play a critical role in suppressing dissent. The Act asserted that treasonous materials, as well as material that violated the act, could be denied use of the mails. Postmaster General Albert Burleson thus began withholding mailing privileges from pacifist, Socialist, and radical journals. The powers of the Postmaster General were further bolstered by the Trading with the Enemy Act of October 1917, which mandated that foreign-language newspapers provide the Post Office with English-language versions of items dealing with the government or how the war was being conducted. The Postmaster General could also issue permits exempting newspapers from such obligations. The onerous cost of such translations, noted the historian Carl Wittke, helps explain why German-language newspapers scaled back their war-related coverage.

In addition, the U.S. Department of Justice embarked upon a campaign to intimidate people suspected of speaking out against the war. In countless cases, Justice Department investigators paid visits on supposed critics of the war, and warned them to remain silent on the issue. A volunteer auxiliary, the American Protective League, assisted the Justice Department in its investigative duties. The U.S. Army, too, engaged in repression, as its military intelligence operatives monitored radical labor unions, and as Army units arrested members of the IWW and staged raids on the union's offices in Washington state and Montana.

Indeed, few institutions of American society were able to escape the demand for total loyalty to the war effort. Academia embraced the call for muffling dissent, and professors allegedly lacking in support for the war lost their jobs at the universities of Oregon, Michigan, Minnesota, Virginia, and Wisconsin. Churches came under federal surveillance: Justice Department informants attended religious meetings to assess their degree of disloyalty. The leadership of the Russellites (later known as the Jehovah's Witnesses), a sect that disapproved of earthly wars, was convicted of violating wartime sedition statutes, although their convictions were later overturned on appeal.

The judiciary provided little protection from this onslaught against dissent. Federal judges, for example, rarely interpreted the Espionage Act or its Sedition Act amendment in a way that would guard the free speech rights of defendants. In March 1919, after the end of the war, the Supreme Court upheld four cases involving convictions under the Espionage Act.

Post–World War I Impact

At the same time, the war laid the groundwork for the future expansion of civil liberties. Even before World War I, some legal scholars had begun to advocate a more libertarian approach to issues of freedom of expression. Additionally, the systematic nature of the campaign against dissent, and the often inhumane treatment meted out to dissenters led many, especially on the left, to put a higher value on the freedom of expression. The writer Theodore Schroeder had criticized the "bad tendency" test as unnecessarily restrictive of speech, and had been a guiding light of the Free Speech League, which had waged lonely battles in the courts against limitations on freedom of expression. The repression of World War I galvanized some Americans into taking up the cause of freedom of speech for unpopular groups. Thus, the year 1917 saw the birth of a new organization dedicated to preserving first amendment rights—the National Civil Liberties Bureau. (The NCLB was the further development of the Civil Liberties Bureau, which had originated as a wing of a pacifist organization, the American Union Against Militarism, in 1917). The NCLB lent legal assistance to defendants being prosecuted by the government, and authored publicity materials condemning the widespread crackdown on first amendment freedoms. However, the NCLB had little success in transforming civil liberties into a central political issue during the war.

The war experience had two especially important consequences. First, it helped to transform the Justice Department and its Bureau of Investigation into the nation's premier countersubversive bureaucracy. In the postwar "red scare" of 1919–1920, the Department and BI rounded up and secured the deportation of allegedly radical unnaturalized immigrants, and in subsequent years, the BI would monitor and harass individuals and groups it deemed subversive. Second, the NCLB (which, in 1920, became the American Civil Liberties Union, or ACLU), helped draw attention to the excesses of the postwar deportation campaign, and would go on to play a leading role in contesting future governmental infringements of civil liberties.

William H. Thomas, Jr.

See also: American Protective League (WWI); American Union against Militarism (WWI); Censorship (WWI); Civil Liberties Bureau (WWI); Espionage Act (WWI); Federal Bureau of Investigation (WWI); German Americans (WWI); Industrial Workers of the World (WWI); Sedition Act (WWI); Socialist Party (WWI); Biographies: Burleson, Albert Sidney (WWI); Documents: Assert Your Rights, 1917; Espionage Act, June 15, 1917; *Schenck v. U.S.,* 1919; Sedition Act, May 16, 1918

REFERENCES

Gruber, Carol S. *Mars and Minerva: World War I and the Uses of Higher Learning in America.* Baton Rouge: Louisiana State University Press, 1975.

Murphy, Paul L. *World War I and the Origin of Civil Liberties in the United States.* New York: Norton, 1979.

Preston, William, Jr. *Aliens and Dissenters: Federal Suppression of Radicals, 1903–1933,* 2d ed. Urbana: University of Illinois Press, 1994.

Rabban, David M. *Free Speech in Its Forgotten Years.* New York: Cambridge University Press, 1997.

Ross, William G. *Forging New Freedoms: Nativism, Education, and the Constitution, 1917–1927.* Lincoln: University of Nebraska Press, 1994.

Scheiber, Harry N. *The Wilson Administration and Civil Liberties, 1917–1921.* Ithaca, NY: Cornell University Press, 1960.

Stevens, John Dean. "Suppression of Expression in Wisconsin during World War I." Ph.D. dissertation, University of Wisconsin, 1967.

Thomas, William H., Jr. "The Department of Justice and Dissent during the First World War." Ph.D. dissertation, University of Iowa, 2002.

Wittke, Carl. *The German-Language Press in America.* Lexington: University of Kentucky Press, 1957.

Civil Liberties Bureau

Initially a component of the American Union Against Militarism during World War I, the Civil Liberties Bureau became the American Civil Liberties Union in 1920.

World War I was unpopular with a large segment of the American people, including isolationists and pacifists. Conspicuous objection came from radical leftist unionists, anarchists, and socialists. To build support for the war and to quiet dissent, the federal government established prowar propaganda programs and enacted laws to repress dissent and dissenters. Measures such as the Espionage, Sedition, and Selective Service acts provoked opposition from pacifists and near pacifists, who disliked the martial spirit the war generated.

In 1915, even before the American entry

into the war, New York antiwar activists united into the Anti-militarism Committee. In January 1916, the organization became the Anti-preparedness Committee and established a lobbying program in Washington, D.C. Other names the group went by included the American Union for a Democratic Peace and the League for an American Peace. Late in 1916, the committee became the American Union Against Militarism (AUAM), with a focus on opposition to military training in schools and universities.

The most important political freedom during the war was the right to oppose the war. The Civil Liberties Bureau defended the Constitutional rights of war objectors and pacifists during a time of war fever. Roger Baldwin of the AUAM thought he could use his connections with high-ranking members of the Wilson administration to safeguard the Industrial Workers of the World (IWW) as well as others accused of antiwar behavior. He failed. But he showed his solidarity with the war resisters by intentionally violating the Selective Service Act and going to jail.

The AUAM lobbied, published, and lectured against war. The AUAM helped to keep the United States from war with Mexico in 1916, but it failed to stop American entry into World War I. Its opposition to peacetime conscription after World War I and other activities against the repressive federal government of 1919 and 1920 resulted in government raids of its offices and suppression of its publications by the postal service. Late in the war, the AUAM effort against selective service and ROTC became less important than the CLB efforts on behalf of free speech. The CLB became the independent National Civil Liberties Bureau, precursor to the American Civil Liberties Union.

The NCLB had roots in the freethought movement, which opposed all efforts to restrict freedom of expression, but NCLB membership was more progressive middle class than the freethought movement, which appealed to more liberal fringe elements. The NCLB emphasized political freedom but had no qualms about suppressing pornography and other forms of expression. For Baldwin and many progressives, social well-being was more important than individual expression, so pornography as a social ill was legitimately suppressed while political speech was essential to the well-being of the nation and had to be protected fully. Still the NCLB under Baldwin incorporated much from the Free Speech League, including publications and expertise the FSL gained fighting Comstockery (blue nose censorship/prudery) and the Espionage Act. In the area of political freedom, the NCLB was as radical as the anarchists, abolitionists, and freethinkers that were its intellectual precursors. However, Baldwin could not bring the NCLB to true freethought or anarchism. He defended the political rights of the Industrial Workers of the World (IWW) and other radical groups, although he disapproved of their views.

As the war ended and objectors were released from prison, the NCLB's attention shifted from war resisters' rights to broader civil rights. The NCLB in 1920 became the American Civil Liberties Bureau, then the American Civil Liberties Union (ACLU.)

Founders of the ACLU were a who's who of progressivism. They included lawyers such as Clarence Darrow and Felix Frankfurter, the social reformers Jane Addams and John Dewey, and socialist Norman Thomas. Women's rights activists and leftist reformers on the board included Crystal Eastman, Florence Kelley, Lillian Wald, Oswald Garrison Villard, Paul Kellogg, Charles Beard, Abraham Muste, Elizabeth Gurley Flynn, and Upton Sinclair. Roger Baldwin served as Director of the ACLU for nearly thirty years.

The ACLU became nationally prominent by

supporting the Constitutional rights of the poor, minorities, immigrants, homosexuals, and other oppressed groups. Celebrated cases included the Scopes "Monkey" Trial (1925), the *Ulysses* censorship case (1933), the Jehovah's Witnesses cases (1940s), *Brown v. Board of Education* (1954), the Nazis in Skokie, IL (1977–1978), and *Roe v. Wade* (1973). The legacy of Roger Baldwin and the NCLB persists, as the ACLU remains vigilant to this day against efforts by government and others to trample Americans' Constitutional rights.

John Barnhill

See also: American Union against Militarism (WWI); Anarchists (WWI); Civil Liberties (WWI); Committee on Public Information (WWI); Conscientious Objectors (WWI); Conscription (U.S., WWI); Espionage Act (WWI); Federal Bureau of Investigation (WWI); Industrial Workers of the World (WWI); Isolationism (WWI); Pacifists (WWI); Palmer Raids (WWI); Progressivism (WWI); Red Scare (WWI); Sedition Act (WWI); Socialist Party (WWI)

REFERENCES

Cottrell, Robert. *Roger Nash Baldwin and the American Civil Liberties Union.* New York: Columbia University Press, 2000.
Rabban, David M. *Free Speech in Its Forgotten Years.* New York: Cambridge University Press, 1997.

Comics

Comics, a series of drawings in panels that tell a narrative, had become a part of everyday life well before the onset of World War I in 1914, with newspapers running multiple daily strips and full Sunday pages by 1910. Comics were inexorably tied to the newspaper industry at this point, as the comic book did not come about until the 1930s, and they were almost always humorous in nature. On the American home front, the war seems to have had little impact on how these comics were produced or the topics they covered. There were, of course, many politically concerned posters, postcards, and individual cartoons regarding the war. Nevertheless, looking at the daily comic series of the era, one would hardly realize what was happening on the international stage.

Comics came and went during this time, unlike the lasting series developed in later comic books, but there were always a few that stood the test of time. Rudolph Dirks's "Katzenjammer Kids" started long before the war and continued well after it. Dirks himself was born in Germany and had immigrated to America as a child. The majority of comic strip artists at the time shared a similar story, being immigrants or first-generation citizens. The dialog between his comic strip characters, Hans and Fritz, was even written with a German dialect indicated and this never changed, though he did change the name of the strip to "Captain and the Kids" due to the anti-German sentiment that the war had generated. Comic strips such as this as well as "Little Jimmy," "The Happy Hooligan," and "Alphonse and Gaston" carried on the prewar feelings of comfort and contentedness that they always had. There were a few that focused on more serious and mature issues, like "Abie the Agent," which dealt with the pressures of the business world, but for the most part, comic strips during WWI presented the nation with an absurd and humorous world to escape into.

If cartoonists had any agenda regarding the war at all, it was simply to distract their audiences from thinking about the war through humor and trite concerns rather than national security. There was a genre of strips that derived their plots from popular movies of the day.

Hairbreadth Harry's adventures began before the war, with him as the unlikely short and silly savior of Beautiful Belinda, who often needed to be rescued from the Ruthless Rudolph, whose top hat and sinisterly curved moustache became the archetypical symbols for villainy. By the time the war was in full swing, Harry had grown into a dashing hero, just like his counterparts in the movies. This comic strip, in which good always triumphed over evil, provided reassurance and comfort on a slightly more serious level than most did. Returning to the lighthearted side, Charlie Chaplin's movie adventures, which provided great comic relief to his audience, were converted into a comic strip during the war.

Many strips, such as the widely popular "Buster Brown," devoted their last panel to explaining the moral of the story to their readers, giving the comics a didactic dimension as well. These comics extolled American virtues and sought to foster them in young readers. But it should always be remembered that the primary audience of these strips were adults, as they were the ones buying the papers.

Crystal Yates

See also: Arts, Visual (WWI); Journalism (U.S., WWI)

REFERENCES

Goulart, Ron. *The Adventurous Decade.* New Rochelle, NY: Arlington House, 1975.

Robinson, Jerry. *The Comics: An Illustrated History of Comic Strip Art.* New York: G. P. Putnam's Sons, 1974.

Wright, Bradford W. *Comic Book Nation: The Transformation of Youth Culture in America.* Baltimore, MD: Johns Hopkins University Press, 2001.

Committee on Public Information

Created by President Woodrow Wilson's advisors at the start of World War I, the Committee on Public Information (CPI) was a vast federal information agency that churned out millions of stories and images favorable to the war effort aimed at shaping public opinion.

The CPI was created April 14, 1917, one week after war was declared. It became the most far-reaching propaganda apparatus ever created. Some 150,000 people were involved in executing its mission: persuading the public to support the war. The CPI mobilized every conceivable communication channel—especially the cutting edge technologies of radio and movies. Although it lasted merely two years, the techniques that the CPI pioneered shaped twentieth-century advertising and public relations. Walter Lippmann had advised Wilson to create an official government news bureau that would advertise the war as necessary "to make the world safe for democracy." In effect, the CPI used the American public as a test audience for techniques of persuasion. The CPI proved that ideas could be sold like soap.

Wilson needed to sell the American public on the war because vast numbers were vehemently opposed to entering the war. In 1916, he had campaigned on the slogan "He Kept Us Out of War." Wilson considered public opinion volatile, and middle-class America tended to be isolationist. The country's enormous immigrant population was also cause for concern: Many Irish Americans reviled the British; and to whom would German-born citizens be loyal? The foreign born could not be counted upon to support the war without an "advertising" campaign to promote loyalty. There was also criticism from pacifists, anarchists, and socialists that World War I was "a rich man's war" designed to save France and England from defeat so they would not default on Wall Street loans. To stifle criticism that World War I was a "capitalists' war," Wilson appointed George Creel to head the CPI. Creel had won renown as a muckraking journalist by exposing government and corporate corruption and would therefore give the CPI credibility.

Creel said the CPI "was a plain publicity proposition, a vast enterprise in salesmanship, the world's greatest adventure in advertising." However, Creel claimed the CPI's job was not censorship. He called this vast communication network a "medium of expression" and dubbed the CPI the "house of truth."

Creel enlisted some of the country's top journalists to man the CPI's Division of News, which flooded the mails and telegraph wires with thousands of war news press releases day and night. The CPI also published its own newspaper, the *Official Bulletin* (circulation 115,000), which targeted public officials and newspaper editors. To bolster loyalty among the immigrant population, the CPI created links with some six hundred foreign language papers in the United States that were published in nineteen languages. The CPI also monitored the foreign press abroad to capture distortions that might hurt American morale. The CPI maintained offices in over thirty countries, and used U.S. Navy radio transmitters to broadcast a steady stream of pro-American stories.

In addition to radio and newspapers, the CPI used the telegraph, posters, signs, and motion pictures; and in a bold and innovative move, Creel asked the advertising industry for help. The CPI's work "was so distinctly in the nature of an ad campaign that we turned almost instinctively to the advertising profession for advice and assistance," said Creel. "If ads could sell face cream and soap, why not a war?" The professionals who ran the CPI's Advertising Division leaned on newspapers around the country to donate free space, which they filled with the hundreds of advertisements they designed. The CPI also produced 200,000 slides and photographs that were exhibited in schools and churches. The country's top commercial artist, Charles Dana Gibson, ran the CPI's Division of Pictorial Publicity, to which artists volunteered their services. The CPI's Bureau of Cartoons published the *Weekly Bulletin for Cartoonists,* which contained ideas and captions that the 750 newspaper cartoonists who received the *Bulletin* were urged to draw from. The CPI's Division of Films created story plots and passed them along to movie producers, who in turn distributed the CPI movies along with their regular Hollywood fare. Hollywood producers agreed not to sell any movies to any foreign theater that refused to show the CPI's war movies. And no movies were sold to any theater showing any type of German movie.

Crucial to the CPI's success in shaping attitudes were 75,000 volunteer public speakers, called the "Four-Minute Men," after the length of their speeches. Speeches were delivered anywhere crowds gathered; movie theaters were typical venues. Once a week the CPI mailed each speaker a sort of "how-to" manual called the *Four-Minute Man Bulletin* that contained outlines of speeches such as "Why We Are Fighting," "Unmasking German Propaganda," and "The Danger to Democracy." The Four-Minute Men also had a Negro Division and held speaking contests for children to select members for their Junior Division.

The CPI was disbanded one day after the Armistice, November 11, 1918.

Tony Osborne

See also: Advertising (WWI); Propaganda (U.S., WWI); Documents: Four Minute Man Speech, October 8, 1917

REFERENCES

Ewen, Stuart. *PR!* New York: Basic Books, 1996.

Mott, Frank L. *American Journalism.* New York: Macmillan, 1962.

Schudson, Michael. *Discovering the News.* New York: Basic Books, 1978.

Communist Party (U.S.)

Like Communist parties throughout the world, the Communist Party, USA (CPUSA) grew out of World War I and the Russian Empire socialist revolution. Communist parties everywhere developed out of deep divisions in the Socialist movement over such questions on the nature of imperialism, strategies for establishing socialism, and responses to nationalism and war. World War I turned these divisions into a schism.

Left-wing socialists everywhere saw World War I as a capitalist war for expanded profits and economic empires and sought to transform the war into an international class war for socialism. Right-wing socialists supported their national governments in the war and sought to transform the war into campaigns to advance socialist-oriented reforms.

Unlike the socialist parties of the major belligerent powers who supported the war when it broke out in 1914, the Socialist Party of America (SPA) opposed U.S. entry in April 1917. By then, the war had cost millions of lives in Europe and had led to widespread repression of socialists and other progressive forces by conservative nationalist governments.

The Bolshevik revolution of November 1917, the first successful Socialist revolution in history, brought revolutionary socialists to power in the large Eurasian-Russian empire, and became the rallying point and great hope for left-wing socialists, anti-imperialists in the colonial regions, and other revolutionaries throughout the world. In Europe and North America, these groupings split from existing Socialist parties and established Communist parties. In Asia and to a lesser extent Africa, where Socialist parties did not for the most part exist, they established where possible Communist parties under various names.

On two central questions, the organization of a revolutionary party and the forces to be organized internationally in the fight for socialism, Communists adopted the theories of Vladimir Lenin, leader of the Bolsheviks, who advocated a "vanguard party" of "professional revolutionaries"—committed activists rather than passive party members discussing issues—to coordinate and lead all social struggles. Lenin also saw the struggle against imperialism and the organization of the masses of Africa, Asia, and Latin America in the struggle for their liberation against imperialist powers as central to the victory of socialism over capitalism. As political parties representing these principles began to come into existence at the end of the war, a new international of revolutionary parties, called the Third or Communist International (Comintern) to distinguish it from the so-called Second or Socialist International, was founded at Moscow in 1919.

In the United States, the principal support for what later became the Communist party came from left-wing socialists, members of foreign language federations of immigrants with roots in the Czarist Russian empire, and activists of the Industrial Workers of the World, a revolutionary Syndicalist labor organization. All of these groups faced heightened repression in the United States in 1917–1918.

Socialist Louis Fraina's early work, *The Proletarian Revolution in Russia* (1918), served as an important rallying point for these groups, as did the Friends of the Russian Revolution and the American Bolshevik Information Bureau, formed in 1917 and 1918 by left-wing socialists and others to challenge the anti-Bolshevik hysteria of the press and to resist U.S. intervention in the Russian Civil War, which followed the revolution.

Wartime and postwar repression strengthened left-wing socialists in the SPA, who elected a majority of delegates to the party's coming convention in Chicago in 1919. In response, the SPA's right-wing dominated National Executive Committee, fearing correctly that it would be ousted by the left wing, launched mass purges of the foreign language federations and others, expelling nearly two-thirds of the party membership.

The left-wing socialists themselves then split between a group based in the foreign languages federations calling itself the Communist party, with Louis Fraina as its most important leader, and a smaller, predominantly English-speaking group, including the revolutionary socialist journalist, John Reed, author of the best known U.S. account of the Russian revolution, *Ten Days that Shook the World*, calling itself the Communist Labor Party. Initially, the differences between the two parties were less centered on questions of theory than on relations with the Socialist party, differences that lost their meaning when members of the Communist Labor party, who supported continued work in the Socialist party, were expelled at the Socialists rump Chicago convention.

The two Communist parties were rapidly driven underground by the Red Scare and the Palmer raids, the latter directed by the young Justice Department attorney, J. Edgar Hoover. By 1922, the two parties had formed a United Communist Party and, as was true in other countries where Communists were denied the right to organize openly as Communists, a Workers Party, which Communists hoped would attract workers and trade unionists and then become a mass party. Such figures as Jay Lovestone, William Z. Foster, and Earl Browder, all of whom were to be influential in the decades ahead in both Communist and anti-Communist political activities in the United States and internationally, were already active in the new party.

Although much smaller than the prewar Socialists(most of its initial followers had been driven away by the Red Scare), the CPUSA sought to learn from the mistakes of the Socialists and apply lessons learned from the Russian revolution by establishing the Trade Union Educational League(TUEL) to organize outreach and a strategy for labor, develop specific appeals and organizations, and mobilize African Americans as a colonized people with the intention of fighting racism as essential to the battle for socialism.

Developing out of the World War I era, the CPUSA constituted in the 1920s a new left with greater zeal, breadth, and focus than its predecessors. These factors, and its association with a global movement that had triumphed in the creation of the Soviet Union, would be valuable assets in its future struggles.

Norman Markowitz

See also: Industrial Workers of the World (WWI); Palmer Raids (WWI); Red Scare (WWI); Socialist Party (WWI); Trade Unions (U.S., WWI)

REFERENCES

Bart, Philip, and Arthur Zipser, eds. *Highlights of a Fighting History*. New York: International Publishers, 1979.

Draper, Theodore. *Roots of American Communism*. New York: Viking Press, 1966.

Fraina, Louis C., ed. *The Proletarian Revolution in Russia*. New York: The Communist Press, 1918.

Murray, Robert. *Red Scare: A Study in National Hyste-*

ria, 1919–1920. Minneapolis: University of Minnesota Press, 1955.

Schmidt, Regin. *The FBI and the Origins of Anti-Communism in the United States, 1919–1943.* Copenhagen: University of Copenhagen Press, 2000.

Conscientious Objectors

Once America declared war against Germany and its allies, the nation's political and military leaders became apprehensive about its ability to meet the manpower requirements of a modern war. In order to provide the Armed Forces with the men that the fighting in France would require, they enacted the Selective Service Act on May 18, 1917, which made it possible for the government to compel healthy male adults to perform military service. Conscientious objectors were people who were unable to perform such service due to a moral or religious opposition to war. The law's authors knew that an appreciable number of the nation's population would oppose compulsory service on spiritual and moral grounds, so they included a provision designed to excuse conscientious objectors from fighting in Europe.

A conscientious objector under the Selective Service regulation of 1917 was excused from combat service if he belonged to a recognized peace sect, or in other words, a religious sect whose members and institutional principles opposed war. While the law itself failed to list the names of peace sects whose members were entitled to claim exception as a conscientious objector, these sects in practice included Quakers, Mennonites, members of the Church of the Brethren, and other smaller groups. A member of one of these groups who became classified as a conscientious objector would be inducted into the army with the restriction that he was only to perform noncombatant service.

This usually meant that he would serve in the Medical, Quartermaster, or Engineer Corps.

Over the course of the war, 64,693 men claimed to be conscientious objectors under the law, and draft boards approved 56,830 of these claims. Only 20,783 of those men whose conscientious objector claim was approved by their draft board were actually ordered to serve and inducted into the Armed Forces, and the overwhelming majority of those inductees abandoned their objections and consented to combat duty. One of the most celebrated American heroes of the war, Sergeant Alvin C. York, was a draftee who changed his mind after declaring himself a conscientious objector and submitted to combat service. Over the course of World War I, the War Department had to support fewer than 4,000 draftees who remained opposed to combat service.

While the principle behind the conscientious objector combat exemption in the Selective Service Act of 1917 was sound, the law sometimes fell short of its intentions in practice. Under the wording of the Act, a person with a firm religious opposition to war who was a member of a religious organization other than a historic peace sect could be compelled to serve in combat. Draftees whose objection to military service was based upon ideological or political—rather than spiritual—grounds, such as socialists and anarchists, could also be held to military service. Members of recognized peace sects who successfully obtained conscientious objector status, moreover, were still inducted into the Armed Forces and subject to military authority. This created problems for those conscientious objectors whose beliefs prohibited any cooperation with the Armed Forces. Members of groups such as the International Bible Students and the Christadelphians, who believed that noncombatant work performed for the military still aided the war effort, sometimes refused to do any work at all.

Mennonites whose faith prohibited them from wearing buttons had difficulty complying with orders to wear uniforms. Conscientious objectors who disobeyed orders to perform noncombatant work or act according to military decorum were subject to military arrest.

Treatment of conscientious objectors who refused to obey orders on the grounds of their beliefs varied from place to place. In some locations, conscientious objectors were treated with tolerance and consideration, but in others they were treated as slackers, cowards, or traitors. Some conscientious objectors were intimidated and abused by soldiers and officers in order to force their submission to military authority. Contemporaries charged that some draftees whose conscientious objector claims had been approved by their local draft boards were illegally bullied into combat service. Draftees whose objection to combat service was not recognized by the draft board were usually arrested and imprisoned by military authorities if they refused to perform whatever service they were assigned. Seventeen arrested conscientious objectors were sentenced to death by courts martial, but none of their sentences were carried out. Others convicted of disobeying orders were sentenced to lengthy prison terms, including life imprisonment, but no World War I conscientious objector remained incarcerated after 1933. Military authorities in the United States studied the positive and negative experiences they had with conscientious objectors during World War I, and applied the lessons they learned to future draft legislation.

Thomas I. Faith

See also: American Union Against Militarism (WWI); Anarchists (WWI); Conscription (U.S., WWI); Pacifists (WWI); Mobilization (U.S., WWI); Religion (U.S., WWI); Socialist Party (WWI); Biographies: Goldman, Emma (WWI); Documents: Proclamation of Conscription Policy, May 28, 1917

REFERENCES

Brock, Peter, and Nigel Young. *Pacifism in the Twentieth Century.* Syracuse, NY: Syracuse University Press, 1999.

Chambers, John Whiteclay. *To Raise an Army: The Draft Comes to Modern America.* New York: Macmillan, 1987.

Keim, Albert N., and Grant M. Stoltzfus. *Politics of Conscience: The Historic Peace Churches and America at War, 1917–1955.* Scottdale, PA: Herald Press, 1988.

Kohn, Stephen M. *Jailed for Peace: The History of American Draft Law Violators, 1658–1985.* Westport, CT: Greenwood Press, 1986.

Peterson, H. C., and Gilbert C. Fite. *Opponents of War, 1917–1918.* Madison: University of Wisconsin Press, 1957.

Schlissel, Lillian. *Conscience in America: A Documentary History of Conscientious Objection in America, 1757–1967.* New York: E. P. Dutton, 1968.

Conscription (Canada)

Prime Minister Robert Borden's promise in August 1914 that Canadian participation in World War I would be voluntary in nature ensured general public support despite misgivings in some quarters. Borden was undoubtedly sincere when he made that commitment because, like so many others, he thought the war would be relatively brief and Canadian participation modest, albeit significant. He also knew that there was widespread enthusiasm for participation, a fact that was reflected in the ease with which the government raised its initial call-up of 25,000 men, as well as the second 25,000 a few months later.

For a country whose prewar army comprised fewer than 3,000 men, recruiting 50,000 men for overseas service was an impressive achievement. The war quickly demonstrated, however, not only that it was not going to be brief but also that it was going to destroy manpower at an unprecedented—and previously unimagined—rate. As the Flanders slaughterhouse consumed men by the hundreds of thousands, the British appealed repeatedly to Canada and the other Dominions for more men. At the same time, British propaganda increasingly portrayed the war not as a conflict among rival European empires but as a moral crusade to protect civilization from the forces of barbarism. The Canadian government clearly accepted this interpretation of the situation and committed itself to raising five divisions at a time when enlistments were beginning to fall off, due no doubt to the lengthening lists of obituaries appearing daily in newspapers across the country.

Having carried out a national assessment of available manpower, Borden concluded in the spring of 1917 that the only way Canada could maintain its commitments was to introduce conscription. Accordingly, he invited proconscription Liberals to join his government, introduced conscription, and called an election to seek a mandate. This divided the country sharply, most notably between English-speaking Protestants who generally supported conscription (in the belief that it was largely French Canadians who would be conscripted), and French-speaking Catholics who generally did not. The situation was more complex than this, however, a fact that Borden clearly recognized when he rewrote the electoral laws to ensure victory. Immigrants from what were now enemy countries were disfranchised, while female relatives of soldiers were enfranchised. The votes of soldiers serving overseas could be distributed to constituencies throughout the country if the soldiers did not specifically stipulate their home constituency and the soldiers in Europe were heavily pressured to vote for conscription, which they did by an overwhelming majority.

Despite this extraordinary manipulation of the system, the government won only 53 percent of the popular vote, and even this was only achieved after it announced, just weeks before the balloting, that the sons of farmers would be exempt from conscription. Farmers were, of course, the majority of the population in 1917.

The popular uproar following the introduction of conscription was profound, not merely in Quebec but in rural regions throughout the country, especially after the exemption for farmers' sons was cancelled. The fact was that the great initial enthusiasm for enlisting had been dominated by young men who had immigrated in recent years from Britain. Of the 36,267 men who went overseas in the first contingent in October 1914, 72 percent were British-born. It was when that pool of young men dried up that the enlistment problem began to emerge. Despite the popular view, encouraged by the government, that the growing shortfall in enlistments reflected a lack of patriotism in Quebec, 94 percent of the men conscripted across Canada sought exemption and conscription ended up raising 64,745 English-speaking but Canadian-born men compared to only 27,557 French Canadians.

The conscription crisis fractured the fragile national unity that had been built up in the prewar years and also provoked the first debate in Quebec's legislative assembly on a resolution calling for that province's separation from Canada. Additionally, it destroyed the Conservative party in both Quebec and the Prairie province, ensuring Liberal Party domination of Canadian federal politics through the rest of the twentieth century.

Brian Tennyson

See also: Mobilization (Canada, WWI); Biographies: Borden, Robert Laird (WWI); Documents: Appeal for National Service, October 23, 1916

REFERENCES

Armstrong, Elizabeth. *The Crisis of Quebec, 1914–1918*. Toronto: McClelland and Stewart, 1937.

Brown, Robert Craig. *Robert Laird Borden*. 2 vols. Toronto: Macmillan, 1975–1980.

Granatstein, J. L., and J. M. Hitsman. *Broken Promises: A History of Conscription in Canada*. Toronto: Oxford University Press, 1977.

Morton, Desmond, and J. L. Granatstein. *Marching to Armageddon: Canada and the Great War, 1914–1919*. Toronto: Lester and Orpen Dennys, 1989.

Wade, Mason. *The French Canadians, 1760–1945*. Toronto: Macmillan, 1955.

Conscription (UK)

Conscription was one of the most controversial issues in Great Britain during World War I. Alone among the major combatants in 1914, Britain relied on voluntary enlistment. Despite considerable prewar agitation for compulsory military service, the British public as well as both Conservative and Liberal governments remained opposed to it. It would take the all-consuming impact of total war to force Britain into accepting conscription. Even then, there would be limits to how far Britain would go. Although the story of conscription is usually presented by British historians as a betrayal of Britain's liberal freedoms, it actually reveals their strength.

Before 1914, most Britons would not stand for conscription. As an island nation with a widespread empire, the Royal Navy was the most respected branch of the British armed forces. After the Crimean War, Victorian Britons thought of the British Army primarily as a force that would expand and police its empire with a minimum of fuss or expense. The disastrous performance of the British Army during the South African War of 1899–1902 created considerable soul searching. During this conflict, Britain's army only avoided defeat by sending massive reinforcements. The weakness of Britain's recruiting methods was revealed when up to one in three men who volunteered was rejected as medically unfit. In the aftermath of the Boer War, a new organization called the National Service League was formed. Eventually led by Boer War hero, Lord Frederick Roberts, the League unsuccessfully attempted to convince the British public of the necessity for compulsory military service. Despite building up an active membership of 100,000, the National Service League was mostly scorned or ignored.

When Britain entered World War I in August 1914, it did so with a very small professional voluntary army. Several divisions of the army, named the British Expeditionary Force (BEF) were rapidly sent over to the continent after Germany invaded Belgium. Though decimated by losses, the BEF played a vital role in stopping the German advance. At first, these losses seemed to be compensated by voluntary recruitment. Lord Horatio Herbert Kitchener, an old imperial war hero, was appointed by the Liberal Government as the Secretary of State for War. Filled with wartime enthusiasm and a sense of adventure, nearly 750,000 men volunteered to join Kitchener's "New Armies" by the end of September 1914. By 1915, recruitment numbers had begun to lag and, with large-scale losses accumulating on the Western Front, various initiatives were undertaken. Eventually, these efforts would fail and Britain would be forced to adopt conscription in stages.

Restrictions

The traditional British support for liberal freedoms is best shown by the stages that Britain went through and later the limitations placed on conscription once it was implemented. The first stages were the creation of the National Registration Act in August 1915 and the Derby Scheme of October-December 1915. The National Registration Act attempted to get an accurate estimate of the nation's manpower situation. Under it, all citizens of working age had to report personal information to canvassers, including their current employment and skills they had that would be useful to war work. After getting an idea of the number of potential recruits available, the Derby Scheme attempted to give voluntary enlistment one last chance. Under the Derby Scheme, men of recruiting age were asked to either volunteer immediately or attest to their willingness to enlist in the military if called. Many married men attested their willingness to serve with the understanding that single men without family responsibilities would be called up first.

The canvass of the Derby Scheme was completed in December 1915. By this time, the pressure for conscription was mounting. The Liberal government of H. H. Asquith had been forced to form a coalition with Conservatives in May 1915. Conservative cabinet ministers in the new coalition such as Walter Long, Lord Nathaniel Curzon, Austen Chamberlain, and Andrew Bonar Law all supported conscription. The Derby Scheme and National Registration were Asquith's way to avoid or delay the inevitable. By January 1916, conscription could not be avoided. Even then, a remarkable number of safeguards and exemptions were retained. The first British conscription act of January 1916 applied only to unmarried men and widowers without dependents from ages eighteen to forty-one. It allowed exclusions for those engaged in vital war work and exemptions for unmarried men who were the sole supporters of dependents. It also had provisions for medical disabilities and conscientious objectors. Ireland was entirely excluded from the scheme. Although conscription had been conceded, the British regard for personal liberties remained. Nevertheless, this act still was too much for some. John Simon, the Liberal Home Secretary resigned from the Cabinet and both the Labour Party and Labour movement expressed their opposition. Trade unionists feared that military conscription would be followed by industrial conscription.

As losses mounted on the Western Front, pressure soon came to extend conscription in Britain. Asquith's first instinct was to support a compromise plan that included measures such as encouraging enlistment of married men with the threat of a partial extension of conscription if it failed. This limited gesture led to fierce Conservative opposition and the government eventually passed a second Military Service Act in May 1916. The second conscription act was more wide-ranging than the first, but still had paid some respect to personal liberties. This act extended the first act to married men and withdrew the previous exemptions for unmarried men with dependents. Exemptions for conscientious objectors and medical disabilities remained but were tightened. Amongst Liberals, Lloyd George argued strongly in favor of the new act. Labour figures, such as Arthur Henderson, Chairman of the parliamentary Labour Party, continued to speak out against it. Labour uneasily accepted the second act. For Asquith, the second act was a betrayal of traditional Liberal principles and, after its passage, his days as wartime Prime Minister were numbered.

Universal Military Conscription

After May 1916, universal military conscription was an established fact. Therefore, the debate shifted from the principle of conscription to the terms of its implementation. Despite increased manpower in the army, the war continued to go badly for the Allies. In 1916, Britain suffered its greatest losses yet in the murderous Battle of the Somme. Pressure mounted for fresh leadership at the top. In December 1916, Asquith was maneuvered into resigning and a new coalition was created under the dynamic Liberal David Lloyd George. Lloyd George had been open to conscription and he presided over a coalition that consisted predominantly of like-minded Conservatives. This new government attempted to implement conscription in an even wider fashion. Controversies arose in the latter part of the war over exclusions from conscription as well as the possibility of industrial conscription.

The fear of industrial conscription remained until late into the war. Despite the two conscription acts of 1916, the military made fresh demands on the Lloyd George government to free up more men for military service. Responding to these demands, the government undertook new initiatives that led to large-scale industrial protest. In March 1917, the government attempted to regain its power from the trade unions to control which individuals among skilled tradesmen should be protected from military service. While the amended "Schedule of Protected Occupations" led to major protests, ultimately it stayed in place until March 1918. Another initiative from March 1917 failed. Dr. Christopher Addison, the minister of munitions, attempted to introduce dilution of labor in privately operated factories and was forced to retreat. Dilution was the introduction of semiskilled workers (usually women) into industry to free up men for military service. It had been widespread in government-operated munitions plants since 1915. These gestures would be followed by further efforts in 1918. The final major revision to conscription occurred due to the pressures of the German spring 1918 offensive. This offensive, unlike previous German attacks, broke through the Allied lines and put the Germans within sixty miles of Paris. In the crisis atmosphere of the period, drastic new measures were undertaken. A Military Service Act of April 1918 raised the liability for conscription to age fifty, strengthened the ability of the government to eliminate exemptions, and helped the government "comb out" fit young men working in the munitions industry, Admiralty workshops, coal mines, and agriculture. Most controversially, it also unsuccessfully attempted to introduce industrial conscription and apply conscription to Ireland. In spite of the crisis, the last two measures failed. Due to trade union protests, the government decided it would only encourage skilled male workers to enroll as War Munitions Volunteers (who could be relocated to factories chosen by the Ministry of National Service). The application of military conscription to Ireland became unworkable. Despite the efforts of Lloyd George to tie the imposition of conscription to the introduction of Irish Home Rule, the government met with a united front of opposition and was effectively withdrawn.

In the end, conscription came to Britain in installments and with considerable safeguards. Even in the worst crisis of the war, there were still practical and political limits to how far conscription could be applied. In some ways, the continuance of exemptions for conscientious objectors and the realistic assessment of the Lloyd George government toward conscription for Ireland and industrial conscription reveals that Britain retained some of its liberal freedoms. Perhaps the best proof of all is shown in the postwar fate of conscription in Britain. After his victory in the general election of 1918, Lloyd George moved quickly to end conscription. Although the bulk of the Army could not be immediately disbanded due to postwar manpower needs, conscription was wound down. By 1920, demobilization was complete and the

Army was raised solely by voluntary enlistment. Despite the problems this development caused for the Army, conscription would not be undertaken again until April 1939. At this time, the potential threat of Hitler's Germany and the generally successful experience with the gradual introduction of conscription in World War I made the reimposition of universal military service uncontroversial.

Matthew Hendley

See also: Mobilization (UK, WWI); Biographies: George, David Lloyd (WWI); Kitchener, Horatio Herbert (WWI)

REFERENCES

Adams, R. J. Q., and Philip Poirier. *Conscription Controversy in Great Britain, 1900–1918.* Columbus: Ohio State University Press, 1987.

Hayes, Denis. *Conscription Conflict: The Conflict of Ideas in the Struggle For and Against Military Conscription in Britain between 1901–1939.* Reprint, New York: Garland, 1973.

Hendley, Matthew. "The Conscription Movement in Great Britain, 1899–1914." Master's thesis, McGill University, 1991.

———. "Patriotic Leagues and the Evolution of Popular Patriotism and Imperialism in Great Britain, 1914–1932." Ph.D. dissertation, University of Toronto, 1998.

Conscription (U.S.)

When World War I began, the United States was militarily unprepared. After the Civil War, the army had shrunk markedly. For the most part, the military's efforts had been small-scale—Indian Wars and interventions in the Caribbean and Latin America, most recently the pursuit of Pancho Villa through northern Mexico. Army strength in 1917 was 200,000—80,000 of whom were national guard. The European battles routinely killed more than that.

In anticipation of the war, the national Defense Act of 1916 provided for army expansion through voluntary accessions to the army and reserves. The idea was good, but the reality was that volunteers were insufficient for the army envisioned. Over the course of the entire war, only 300,000 volunteers came forth.

After the United States entered World War I in April 1917, it became apparent that conscription would be necessary, and Congress approved the draft on May 18, 1917. The policy required all men between twenty-one and thirty (inclusive) to register for the draft. Because of previous experience in the Civil War, when draft riots occurred, many anticipated that civil disturbances would follow implementation, but the draft had wide approval, and implementation occurred without significant incident.

One factor leading to the acceptance of the draft was the civilian-dominated "preparedness" movement, which had made the case that conscription was the most efficient and equitable method of raising an army in an industrial society. Agrarians, isolationists, and other Southerners and Westerners shared the views of antiwar Northerners that a draft was wrong.

The Selective Service Act of 1917 required all men in the age group to register—with exceptions. Exemptions from call-up went to men with families, indispensable duties, or physical disabilities. Essential work deferments applied to industry and farms. Members of pacifist religious organizations could receive conscientious objector (CO) status, but they were required to perform alternative service within the military. War objectors without religious bases went to prison—some died there. The law outlawed enlistment bounties and hiring of substitutes that had generated much of the opposition to the

Civil War draft. Under Selective Service in 1917 and 1918, 23.9 million men between eighteen and forty-five registered. The 3.5 million-man army included 2.8 million draftees, 72 percent of the force.

The Selective Service System headquarters was home to a major general. The system included about 4,000 local draft boards staffed by volunteer civilians who had the power to interpret broad national guidelines in determining who was inducted and who was deferred.

The Civil War draft riots did not recur, but there were occasional episodes of violence and antidraft demonstrations. Most opposition occurred through public or written criticism and draft evasion. Somewhere between two and three million eligibles failed to register, and 12 percent of draftees (338,000) failed to report or deserted from camp. Requests for CO status were approximately 64,700. Of those, 20,900 were drafted, and 4,000 of the draftees refused to do anything "military." Hard core "absolutists" went to prison—450 of them.

The federal government had the responsibility for enforcement of the conscription laws, but its Bureau of Investigation agents were overstretched by the pursuit of more serious offenses—sabotage, espionage, and violations of the Sedition and Espionage acts. Into the gap sprang local law enforcement, the local postman, and the American Protective League. Bounty hunters worked for the $50 per deserter the government offered.

There were abuses of due process and occasional use of excessive force. When government agents pursued violators of the conscription laws, they generally exercised restraint while the local amateurs succumbed to the wartime hysteria.

The draft did not go unchallenged. The U.S. Supreme Court decided a series of cases in Arver v. United States (245 U.S. 366) in January 1918, ruling that conscription was not involuntary servitude as defined by the Thirteenth Amendment.

The war made doughboys of over four million Americans. Half of them went overseas with the AEF. Military service was the shared experience of over a fourth of the American population between eighteen and thirty-one. They and the American people were familiar with Belleau Wood, Saint Mihiel, and Meuse-Argonne, major battles in which American forces fought, and the 100,000 American dead in the war. And they did it although the United States in 1917 was as unprepared for war as it had been at any time since the Civil War.

John H. Barnhill

See also: American Protective League (WWI); Mobilization (U.S., WWI); Documents: On U.S. Conscription Policy, 1917; Proclamation of Conscription Policy, May 28, 1917

REFERENCES

Henry, Mark. *The US Army of World War I.* Buffalo, MN: Osprey, 2003.

Keene, Jennifer D. *Doughboys, the Great War, and the Remaking of America.* Baltimore, MD: Johns Hopkins University Press, 2001.

Conservative Party (Canada)

Among the many Canadian casualties of World War I was the Conservative party. Created in 1854, the Liberal Conservative Party—to give it its official name—had ruled Canada until the 1890s when the new moderate Reform (Liberal) Party led by Wilfrid Laurier replaced it as the dominant centrist party in national politics.

Losing its Quebec base in 1896 had the unfortunate result of accelerating the growing dominance of the Conservative Party by English-speaking Protestants who were developing a form of nationalism that combined Canadian patriotism with close kinship to Britain and its empire. This enabled it to rally English Canadian opposition to the Laurier government's decisions to establish an independent navy rather than contribute directly to the expenses of the Royal Navy and to sign a reciprocity (free trade) agreement with the United States. At the same time, it formed a highly problematic alliance with the Nationalist Party in Quebec, and together they succeeded in bringing down the Laurier government.

The Conservative Party that took control of the government and led Canada through World War I was a very complex organization. While it was dominated by English-speaking Protestants whose views on most issues were fairly predictable, there was a French-speaking Catholic wing, admittedly weak, whose views were quite nationalistic in the Quebecois sense. Also, there were many, including Robert Laird Borden, the party's leader, who were strongly influenced by the progressive thinking of the time in regard to the need to address the rapid socioeconomic changes taking place as a result of industrialization, urbanization, and immigration. Indeed, despite the strength of business and financial interests in the party, some, such as Borden, were very open to the idea of a stronger role for government in regulating and directing society, and even hoped to persuade people of the need to set aside partyism in favor of the pursuit of the common good.

When World War I broke out, Borden quickly came to see it as the ultimate moral crusade, in which the forces of good were struggling against the forces of evil, and he expected Canadians to do whatever was necessary in order to achieve victory. From an initial commitment of 50,000 men, Borden ultimately promised 500,000 men, in addition to Canada's financial and economic contribution. By 1917, he was prepared to introduce conscription and invited Liberals and independent men of influence to join the government, even offering to give up the prime ministership if necessary. Many did not agree, however, that World War I was a moral crusade and therefore did not support the idea of unlimited sacrifices, which led to the implication that their loyalty or patriotism was questionable.

In this crisis, the Conservative Party—now calling itself the Conservative and Union Party—did whatever it had to do to stay in office, not for partisan advantage but because it believed that a vote for Laurier was a vote for the kaiser. Thus, the government sought and seemed to achieve a popular mandate in the 1917 election, but only after rewriting the electoral laws in order to disenfranchise large numbers of recent immigrants who it thought would vote for Laurier, enfranchising female relatives of men serving in the armed forces who it was assumed would vote for the government, and seriously manipulating the overseas soldiers' votes.

After the war, the Conservative and Union Party sought reelection in 1921 only to be wiped out by a tidal wave of hostility from Quebec, the Prairies, urban industrial workers, and rural Canada generally. Canada elected its first minority government in 1921, but the Liberal era—which has continued to the present day—had begun.

Although the Conservative Party—which later changed its name again to the Progressive Conservative Party—did hold office in 1930–1935, 1957–1965, and 1984–1994, the overwhelming fact is that the Liberal party has been in office for all but nineteen years since World War I. It would be simplistic to attribute this entirely to the Conservative Party's leadership, policies, and general attitudes during

World War I, but there can be no doubt that this was the root of the problem. Its policies during World War II, particularly on the conscription issue, only served to reinforce the public view that it had learned nothing from its experience. The result has been to effectively make Canada, on the national level, a one-party state.

Brian Tennyson

See also: Conscription (Canada, WWI); Liberal Party (Canada, WWI); Biographies: Borden, Robert Laird (WWI); Laurier, Sir Wilfrid (WWI)

REFERENCES

Borden, Robert Laird. *Robert Laird Borden: His Memoirs.* 2 vols. Edited by Henry Borden. Toronto: Macmillan, 1938.

Brown, Robert Craig. *Robert Laird Borden.* 2 vols. Toronto: Macmillan, 1975–1980.

Brown, Robert Craig, and Ramsay Cook. *Canada 1896–1921: A Nation Transformed.* Toronto: McClelland and Stewart, 1974.

Dafoe, J. W. *Clifford Sifton in Relation to His Times.* Toronto: Macmillan, 1931.

English, John. *The Decline of Politics: The Conservatives and the Decline of the Party System, 1901–1920.* Toronto: University of Toronto Press, 1977.

Conservative Party (UK)

World War I transformed British politics. While there is an enormous amount of historical literature on the impact of the war on the Liberal and Labour parties, there is significantly less on the Conservatives. This is unfortunate because of the substantial impact of the war on the Conservative Party. From 1906 to 1914, the Conservatives lost three successive general elections—their worst series of defeats in the twentieth century. However, once the war ended in 1918, the party dominated the interwar period. In World War I, although their leadership was often neglected or submerged in various coalitions, the Conservatives never neglected to remember their party's interests. Furthermore, the war also moved public opinion in directions beneficial to the party.

Onset of World War I

When Britain entered the war in August 1914, politics was at a boiling point. Edwardian Britain had been subject to an increasingly bitter debate over Irish Home Rule. The Conservatives, led by the abrasive Andrew Bonar Law after 1911, seemed to be willing to do anything to prevent Irish Home Rule—including threatening civil war and military mutiny. The coming of war seemed to dampen the partisan ardor of the Conservatives, and in the opening months of the war, Conservatives made a number of efforts to put nation before party. Bonar Law offered a political truce in August 1914 and the parties agreed not to contest by-elections as well as to cooperate in aiding voluntary recruitment through the Parliamentary Recruiting Committee.

Conservative leaders were not publicly prominent during the World War I. Until May 1915, many Conservatives felt disempowered; Conservatives were not part of the government but felt constrained due to the party truce. In particular, Bonar Law refrained from outright attacks on the Asquith government. Backbench Conservatives were able to voice criticisms through the Unionist Business Committee, which was founded in January 1915. It consisted of about forty Conservative MPs and combined criticism of the Liberals with traditionally Conservative protariff policies. Conservatives were reassured by the creation of a coalition government in May 1915 but, unfortunately, this was no coalition of equals and the Conservatives were given minor positions. Even Bonar Law was only made Colonial Secretary, a second-rate post in wartime. Conservative backbench anger at Liberal arrogance led to the formation of a stronger Conservative opposition group called the Unionist War Committee, led by the Irish Unionist leader, Edward Carson. The Unionist War Committee was outside of the control of the Conservative leadership and had the support of over one hundred Conservative MPs. It represented a threat to both Bonar Law and Asquith. In November 1916, the Unionist War Committee transformed the obscure issue of the confiscation of enemy businesses in Nigeria into a confidence vote in the Asquith coalition. Bonar Law rallied a narrow majority of Conservative MPs into supporting the government, but Conservative discontent was clear.

Unease over the Asquith coalition government led to the creation of a new coalition government under David Lloyd George in December 1916. Previously hated by Conservatives as a leading Liberal radical, Lloyd George had shown considerable administrative skill as minister of munitions and ability in patriotic speech making. Once again, the Conservative Party's official leaders were put into the background. Although Bonar Law played a crucial role in the formation and operation of the second coalition, it was always behind the scenes. He served as Chancellor of the Exchequer and government leader in the House of Commons. Lloyd George took a more presidential approach and was the public face of the government. Other leading Conservatives in Lloyd George's War Cabinet, such as Lord Nathaniel Curzon and Lord Alfred Milner, were not originally part of the mainstream Conservative leadership. The Conservative leadership suffered

another blow when Lord Henry Lansdowne, the former Conservative leader in the House of Lords, wrote his famous letter to the British press in November 1917 calling for a negotiated peace and was instantly disowned by the party.

Although the main Conservative leadership was not prominent with the public during the war, its membership remained active and its party organization did not deteriorate to nearly the level it would during World War II. The Conservative membership responded patriotically to the war: About one-third of all Conservative MPs and party employees actively served in the armed forces. Furthermore, the party organization was used for voluntary recruitment drives and continued to assist the army with enlistment after conscription became law in 1916. The party also served as a vehicle for wartime propaganda campaigns such as the War Savings and War Aims movements. Despite all of this national service, the party organization never lost sight of the need to defend its own interests. The Representation of the People Act of 1918 threatened to submerge the Conservative Party by tripling the franchise and propelling Britain into an age of mass democracy. Although Conservative activists could not prevent it from becoming law, they did work successfully to limit its impact. As the bill worked its way through parliamentary committees and debate, Conservatives intervened to ensure that measures traditionally beneficial to Conservatives, such as plural voting, university, and agricultural constituencies, remained. John Ramsden has argued that Conservative attention to detail in amendments to the 1918 Act may have helped "deny Labour a parliamentary majority in 1929 and may have even been sufficient to make the Conservatives the largest rather than the second party in 1923–24."

Along with the continued partisanship of the Conservative organization, the other significant wartime factor that helped the Conservative Party was the overall shift of the political climate. Although the Conservatives did not alter many of their political opinions, the British public became more receptive to their message, and circumstances dampened many anti-Conservative arguments. The only prewar issue that remained troublesome for Conservatives were tariffs. The two issues that inflamed Conservatives before 1914 were Irish Home Rule and conscription. Fervent Conservative opposition to the former and general support for the latter was not generally replicated by British voters before 1914. With the force of war, the political atmosphere changed. Although the Liberals did push through Irish Home Rule legislation after war was declared (while suspending it for the duration), the prewar terms of the Home Rule argument quickly became irrelevant. The Easter rebellion of 1916 in Ireland and the brutal British response led to the radicalization of Ireland. The Irish Nationalist Party's dream of Home Rule was swept aside by the more radical call of the political party Sinn Fein for outright independence. By 1918, Home Rule as originally conceived was essentially unworkable. The Conservatives had begun to shift from opposition to Home Rule to a call to exclude Ulster, the northern part of Ireland in which Protestants were demographically dominant, before 1914. With the changes wrought by war, Conservatives were able to stick to the Ulster exclusion. The Irish Free State Treaty signed by the Lloyd George coalition in 1921 after years of guerilla war granted a *de facto* partition that the Conservatives and most Britons found acceptable.

On the issue of conscription, events also worked in the Conservatives' favor. Although the Party had shied away from unequivocal support of conscription in peacetime, Conservatives clearly felt more comfortable with the idea than Liberals. Once war was declared, Conservatives were the ones who pressed hardest for conscription. By 1916, increasing losses on the Western Front and falling rates of voluntary recruitment made conscription politically workable. Asquith's coalition government passed conscription in two acts. This action helped divide Liberals but unite Conservatives.

Tariffs

Tariffs were an issue on which the war had a less decisive effect. Before the war, the Conservatives argued unsuccessfully for the need for tariff reform in three general elections. The war showed that free trade finance did not work: In 1915, the armor of free trade was pierced by the McKenna duties that were placed on luxury goods to raise revenue and reduce demand on unessential goods. Increasing government involvement in wartime regulations as well as arms production showed again that prewar economic certainties no longer held. However, by 1918, the issue was far from settled. Although Lloyd George's postwar government did embrace some measures of protectionism, it did not turn its back on free trade. Instead it spoke of selective tariffs (so-called "safeguarding"). When the Conservatives fought the general election of 1923 on a wide-ranging tariff platform, it ended in their worst interwar disaster and defeat. Tariffs would only become politically acceptable in the midst of the Depression in 1932.

The Conservative Party was not swept aside by World War I. Although Conservative leaders were often less obviously visible than they might have been, the Party did quite well by the war. The Conservative membership and organization remained engaged in the war without losing its partisanship. Although the party tied itself to two Liberal prime ministers in coalitions, it never lost its sense of identity. On a number of issues, including Irish Home Rule and conscription, the changed circumstances of war helped the Conservatives; it was only on the divisive issue of tariffs was there no wartime dividend to Conservative political fortunes. On balance, the Conservative Party had a good war and would emerge as a major force in the interwar era. Compared from the perspective of the party's disastrous showing in the 1945 general election, World War I was a storm the Conservatives endured far better than World War II.

Matthew Hendley

See also: Easter Rising (WWI); Liberal Party (UK, WWI); Biographies: Asquith, Herbert (WWI); George, David Lloyd (WWI); Law, Andrew Bonar (WWI)

REFERENCES

Blake, Robert. *The Conservative Party from Peel to Churchill.* New York: St. Martin's Press, 1968.

Ramsden, John. *The Age of Balfour and Baldwin, 1902–1940.* New York: Longman, 1978.

———. *An Appetite for Power: A History of the Conservative Party since 1830.* London: HarperCollins, 1998.

Taylor, A. J. P. *English History, 1914–1945.* New York: Oxford University Press, 1965.

Corporatism (U.S.)

Corporatism refers both to a distinctive institutional structure and a body of political thought. Its central characteristic is a system of governance exercised through an established set of private associations linking business, labor, agriculture, and other functional groups with each other and with the state for purposes of achieving political stability and harmonious economic and social development. In most versions of corporatism, business, labor, agriculture, and professional societies have representation in joint councils that share power with public agencies and theoretically serve all legitimate interests. During World War I, corporatist ideas gained a wide following in both Great Britain and the United States, proving important for the U.S. economy's transition from one based upon individual competition to a more collectivist economy based upon groups or associations.

America and Britain both shared a longstanding faith in the ideals of competitive individualism and limited government, but by the early years of the twentieth century, both nations had developed political economies in which there was a significant degree of collective organization and in which the state was beginning to take on new responsibilities.

For both the United States and Britain, the requirements of national mobilization during World War I greatly accelerated prewar trends toward collective organization and centralized economic planning and coordination. Lacking the tradition of centralized state authority characteristic of the other major belligerents, and being dependent upon the virtual monopoly of industrial expertise possessed by their nations' private sectors, the governments of both the United States and Britain had to pursue the economic objectives of war mobilization largely by fostering a system of voluntarism.

In both nations, this meant government cooperation with, and in some cases promotion of, trade associations and organizations representing employer groups from a variety of industries. In the United States, the principal government agency responsible for industrial mobilization, the War Industries Board (WIB), worked closely with existing trade associations so that rationalization and planning might be undertaken primarily on a voluntary basis. In

Britain, too, the war spurred the growth of trade associations and also led to the formation of the nationwide Federation of British industries. As in the United States, a pattern of government-business collaboration unlike any previously contemplated had emerged by war's end.

An efficient mobilization of national resources also required the cooperation of labor. The British and U.S. governments both came to the realization that the effective implementation of a rational and systematic labor policy required dealing directly with responsible organizations of workers. The demands of war thus contributed to the adoption of government policies that gave added legitimacy to organized labor. This was especially important for unions in the United States. Even before the United States entered the war, Woodrow Wilson had established a more prolabor record than any previous president, but it was not until the creation of the National War Labor Board (NWLB) that the government explicitly affirmed the right of workers to organize in trade unions and to bargain collectively through chosen representatives. In large part as a result of government policy, union membership in the United States increased by 85 percent between 1913 and 1920. In Britain, too, the government need for the cooperation of organized labor, as well as the existence of tight labor markets, contributed to a doubling in union membership in the same period.

During the war years, a surge of strike activity focusing on issues of workers' control occurred that was unprecedented in American history. The establishment of shop committees, or works councils, open to all grades of workers emerged as one response to the demands of workers for a greater voice in industry.

A movement for workers' control erupted in Britain during the war that paralleled in many ways the movement taking place in the United States. The British movement, however, was far more powerful and was led by an insurgent group of shop stewards whose ideological perspective was much clearer than that of their U.S. counterparts. The wartime shop stewards' movement, which flourished mainly in Britain's engineering industry, was largely inspired by the doctrines of industrial unionism, revolutionary syndicalism, and guild socialism. All three shared the common goal of creating a nonbureaucratic system of socialized industry based upon actual workers' control rather than state ownership and cooperation. Wartime conditions made it possible for a radical conception of workers' control to have an important impact on British labor.

The U.S. political economy of the 1920s came to be increasingly characterized by "a form of American corporatism" based upon an "associational ideology" emphasizing the need for "stability, planning, and orderly growth." Although the government was not as directly or extensively involved in industrial relations during these years as it had been during the war, the associationalism of the postwar decade continued to be based upon a conception of political economy that stressed the importance of group organization and functional integration and that assumed the possibility of a harmony of interests between labor and management.

Michael McGregor

See also: Business (U.S., WWI); War Industries Board; War Labor Board (WWI)

REFERENCES

Cuff, Robert D. "We Band of Brothers—Woodrow Wilson's War Managers," *Canadian Review of American Studies* 2 (1974): 135-148.

Hawley, Ellis W. *The Great War and the Search for a Modern Order: A History of the American People and*

Their Institutions, 1917–1933. New York: St. Martin's Press, 1979.

Himmelberg, Robert F. "Government and Business, 1917–1932: The Triumph of 'Corporate Liberalism?'" In *Business and Government,* ed. Joseph R. Frese and Jacob Judd. Tarrytown, NY: Sleepy Hollow Press, 1985.

McQuaid, Kim. "Corporate Liberalism in the American Business Community, 1920–1940," *Business History Review* 52 (Autumn 1978): 342–368.

Weinstein, James. *The Corporate Ideal in the Liberal State, 1900–1918.* Boston: Beacon Press, 1968.

Council of National Defense

Prior to 1917, U.S. business leaders thought that the situation in Europe would force the United States to intervene in World War I. These capitalists also believed that the U.S. involvement in the war would lead to greater prosperity within the nation's economy, so they favored cooperation between the federal government and industry as the country prepared for war. In August 1916, Congress created the Council of National Defense (CND), which consisted of the secretaries of war, navy, agriculture, commerce, labor, and interior. The federal government asserted that military officials and members of the State Department had been excluded from the council because they did not create the CND to engage in diplomatic relations or wage war, but rather it had been established as a liaison between the government and the various war industries. One of the main components of the CND was the Advisory Commission, which enabled business owners, union leaders, engineers, academic professors, and medical doctors to supervise the mobilization of U.S. industry during World War I. Thus, the CND represented a mutual collaboration among business leaders, professionals, and the federal government during the war.

In September 1916, members of the CND maintained that every state needed to establish a council of defense. They believed that the formation of these councils at the state level would encourage Americans to also create them at the county level within each state. Furthermore, the members remarked that the county councils would foster the establishment of community councils of defense within the various school districts. Therefore, the organization of the Council of National Defense was designed to reach every section of American society.

By October 1916, the CND conducted a detailed inventory of the nation's scientific and industrial resources. The information collected from this inventory allowed the federal government to determine the availability of supplies and the cost of production within the war industries. Additionally, the CND provided government officials with information relating to how the nation needed to utilize railroads during the war. Furthermore, the council offered industrialists data regarding governmental needs for national defense.

In February 1917, members of the CND believed that they would serve national interests by dividing the Advisory Commission into seven committees, which included medicine; labor; transportation and communication; science and research; raw materials, minerals, and metals; munitions and manufacturing; and supplies. The CND rationalized this measure by asserting that each committee could focus on a specific aspect of the U.S. economy as the nation prepared for war.

Although the CND created councils on both the state and local levels in order to supervise industrial mobilization, the elaborate organization of the council actually hindered the federal government's efforts to coordinate with the war industries. Therefore, government officials viewed the council as an inadequate measure for industrial mobilization. This ineffectiveness of the CND led, then, to the creation of the War Industries Board (WIB).

Kevin M. Brady

See also: Business (U.S., WWI); Mobilization (U.S., WWI); War Industries Board (WWI)

REFERENCES

Clarkson, Grosvenor B. *Industrial America in the World War: The Strategy behind the Line, 1917–1918.* Boston: Houghton Mifflin, 1923.

Cuff, Robert D. *The War Industries Board: Business-Government Relations during World War I.* Baltimore, MD: Johns Hopkins University Press, 1973.

Kennedy, David M. *Over Here: The First World War and American Society.* New York: Oxford University Press, 1980.

D

Daughters of the American Revolution

The hereditary organization Daughters of the American Revolution (DAR), was founded amidst a wave of similar groups in the 1890s as a way for Americans with ties to the founding generation to distinguish themselves from the thousands of new immigrants who had swarmed into the country in the previous decades. At its conception and still today, this patriotic club of women prides itself on maintaining the most members of any other hereditary club in U.S. history. Initially, the DAR limited their efforts to historical preservation and restoration; however, the significance and impact of their efforts in World War I created a new role for the organization.

In the beginning of World War I, the DAR wanted to preserve the ideology of the forefathers by staying out of the war, which they considered to be solely a foreign affair. Soon though, their ardor for the politics of George Washington turned them against Wilson's policy of isolation, and they began encouraging the United States to become more involved in protecting its own shores. They believed that the different movements against war were too apathetic as to whether the United States could defend itself or not. The DAR policy that emerged from this disenchantment in the early stages of World War I focused on militant patriotism, a change that would represent their role not only in World War I but also in all national politics since.

The women of the DAR, even while they still lacked the power of the vote, used their organization to voice their political views. They did this by allying themselves with politicians such as Theodore Roosevelt and financiers like J. P. Morgan and John D. Rockefeller—support that forced the public to take them seriously. These powerful friends and the DAR's efforts to advocate patriotic involvement in World War I was so successful that it could not be overlooked by the contemporary male organizations. At a time when most women's political action was disregarded, the DAR was rewarded with national recognition.

After the German sinking of the *Lusitania*, the American Defense Society and the National Security League stepped up their efforts to get the United States involved in the war. In January 1916, the National Security League, which was based in New York, staged a three-day convention in Washington, D.C., to gain support from their political allies, concluding the meeting with a major rally at the DAR headquarters. Most women's organizations at this time were fighting for international peace and many were not taken seriously on a political level. The League's inclusion of the DAR was not taken lightly by these women; they were honored. The League and the American Defense Society continued to win over the women of the DAR by having distinguished speakers appear in the drawing rooms of the clubs all across the nation.

In early 1917, President Wilson announced that the United States was going to join the Allied Powers in the war in Europe. The DAR celebrated their victory by unanimously passing a resolution favoring a democratic and universal system of military service and training. They also began their hard work for the war effort on the home front. The contributions of the DAR were astounding: Members purchased over $100 million in Liberty war bonds, donated land to the Food Administration and the National Council of Defense, urged conservation through the publication of recipes and food drives, and donated millions of dollars worth of gifts to the armed forces. But their work for the war effort did not stop there: The DAR was also active in the effort to punish the Americans who lacked their zeal. They compiled lists of people who stood in the way of the war machine, including those they felt were German sympathizers, "suspicious characters," socialists, labor union leaders, and anyone else they viewed as unpatriotic.

As peace descended upon the nation, the DAR once again viewed their president's policies with caution. This time, however, Wilson did not underestimate the value of their opinion and he vied for their support by sending them a message: "Daughters of the American Revolution, we need you!" The DAR agreed unanimously to accept the League of Nations.

World War I proved to be a defining moment in the history of the Daughters of the American Revolution. Since their contributions to World War I, their duties as defenders of national patriotism have been taken very seriously, both internally and externally.

Rachel Bennett

See also: Council of National Defense (WWI); Food Administration (WWI); League of Nations (WWI); War Bonds (WWI); Women (U.S., WWI); Biographies: Morgan, J. P. (WWI); Rockefeller, John D. (WWI); Roosevelt, Theodore (WWI)

REFERENCES

Anderson, Peggy. *The Daughters: An Unconventional Look at America's Fan Club—The DAR.* New York: St. Martin's Press, 1974.
Gibbs, Margaret. *The DAR.* New York: Holt, Rinehart and Winston, 1969.

Demobilization

The United States has historically never been a stranger to military demobilization. Until the Cold War Era, strong-standing armies were considered by the U.S. citizenry and political leaders to be a potential threat to liberty, republican style government, and an unwanted expense. Consequently, the end of World War I—the first total war—witnessed an immediate U.S. military demobilization that, within eighteen months of the war's end, drastically altered the military's size and effectiveness.

During World War I, the U.S. Army consisted of nearly five million men. Shortly after the signing of the Armistice on November 11, 1918, the U.S. War Department ordered the immediate halt to further mobilization. Colonel Casper H. Conrad's (U.S. Army War Plans Division) study was adopted and soldiers were ordered discharged by units rather than as individuals. In all, the Army discharged 818,532 of its wartime strength of 3,703,273 men, with a further 2.7 million discharged by June 1919. Within one year of the Armistice, the Army had demobilized fifty-five of its sixty-two (15,000 man strong) divisions. Furthermore, the National Defense Act of 1920 set the authorized Army total at 296,000 men, with a National Guard of 435,000 men, and also an Organized Reserve. Congress followed these reductions with even more in 1922, cutting the Army's size down to just 136,000 men. Put into context, by 1940, post-World War I demobilization had reduced the Army's size to nineteenth largest in the world, one behind Portugal.

During World War I, the U.S. Navy consisted of 81,000 sailors and nurses. The German submarine threat had caused the United States to produce a great number of destroyers and other smaller warships. Combined with a widespread desire to reduce military expenditures and ensure that such a war never occurred again, the decommissioning of many battleships was pressed forward. After World War I, progressive idealism and reform failed to gain a worldwide audience, and as a result the American people were determined to avoid military entanglements overseas and a powerful navy was seen by many as an unwarranted luxury. In addition, many air power advocates believed that airplanes had made navies obsolete.

Traditionally one of the smallest branches of the military, the Marine Corps grew substantially during World War I and was deployed to multiple fronts and duties. However, after the Armistice, demobilization was carried out swiftly. Beginning with "duration-of-war men" and reservists, the Marine Corps rapidly demobilized its ground forces, naval ship detachments, and its growing aero-corps. Within one year of the war's end, due to demobilization, the Marine Corps saw its ranks plummet back to their prewar totals of less than 15,000 men. As a result, the Marine Corps had to fight to justify its continued existence.

After World War I, the military air pioneers of all three branches of service fought in vain to grow their departments, particularly the Army. In 1918, 150,000 officers and men constituted the air-arm of the Army, and by 1920 that number fell to 1,000 officers and 10,000 enlisted men. Compounding the effects of demobilization, Congress further cut the Army's already trim aero-budget in the early 1920s, and hundreds of excess military planes were sold off.

African Americans, Native Americans, women, and other minorities all served with honor in the American Expeditionary Force. While they comprised less than 20 percent of the total force, they nonetheless fought to make the world safe for democracy. Unfortunately, during demobilization many minority groups and women returned to the United States to face the same racial discrimination and Victorian-Era holdovers that they had left behind when they enlisted.

To many Cold War Era and present-day Americans, the notion is difficult to contemplate that, until World War II, rapid and sometimes dangerously excessive demobilization occurred after every major war America fought in. Yet, after World War I, demobilization was encouraged because Americans believed that they were safely guarded by two large oceans and bordered by two weak neighbors. Moreover, Britain and France were strong allies, the Versailles Treaty significantly weakened Germany, and the 1922 Washington Conference had resulted in a treaty that significantly limited Japan's naval abilities. Should a threat arise, the Navy would serve as a buffer until American industrial mobilization could forge the armies, ships, and planes needed to confront any future enemy. However, well before the Great Depression, American attitudes and Congressional views on military spending were not a priority; a course of action that failed to prevent future crises and ended up costing the American people dearly in the early months of World War II.

William McWhorter

See also: Mobilization (U.S., WWI); National Defense Act (U.S., WWI)

REFERENCES

Arbon, Lee. *They Also Flew.* Washington, DC: Smithsonian Institution Press, 1992.

Britten, Thomas A. *American Indians in World War I: At War and at Home.* Albuquerque: University of New Mexico Press, 1999.

Buckley, Thomas H. *The United States and the Washington Conference, 1921–1922.* Knoxville: University of Tennessee Press, 1970.

Coffman, Edward M. *The War to End All Wars: The American Military Experience in World War I.* New York: Oxford University Press, 1968.

Cooper, Jerry. *The Rise of the National Guard.* Lincoln: University of Nebraska Press, 1997.

Harris, Stephen L. *Harlem's Hell Fighters: The African-American 369th Infantry in WWI.* Washington, DC: Potomac Books, 2003.

Huelfer, Evan Andrew. *The "Casualty Issue" in American Military Practice: The Impact of World War I.* Westport, CT: Praeger, 2003.

McClellan, Edwin N. *The United States Marine Corps in the World War I.* Washington, DC: U.S. Marine Corps, Historical Branch G-3 Division Headquarters, 1920.

Urwin, Gregory J. W. *The United States Infantry.* New York: Sterling, 1988.

Wilson, John B. *Maneuver and Firepower: The Evolution of Divisions and Separate Brigades.* Washington, DC: U.S. Army, Center of Military History, 1998.

Democratic Party

Although the Democratic Party controlled the White House and the Senate when the United States entered World War I in 1917, public support for the Democrats had begun to slip as the party's liberal coalition started to crumble under both domestic and international pressures. Woodrow Wilson, a scholar, former president of Princeton University, and the Progressive governor of New Jersey, won the 1912 presidential election against the incumbent William Howard Taft, a Republican whose party was divided between its conservative and progressive factions. By the time of the election, most progressive Republicans had split from the party and sided with Theodore Roosevelt, who had served as president from 1900 to 1908, and had campaigned for president under the Progressive "Bull Moose" banner in 1912. Even though Wilson captured 435 Electoral College votes (82 percent), he claimed only 42 percent of the popular vote, while Roosevelt garnered 27.5 percent, and Taft collected 23 percent.

Wilson won because he promised a "New Freedom" for Americans. Political historian William N. Chambers defined Wilson's New Freedom as "a latter-day Jeffersonian effort to reestablish an open, competitive economy in an age of business combinations," which precisely distinguished him from Taft and Roosevelt. Wilson's New Freedom appealed to a liberal coalition of Americans interested in continuing the Progressive-era achievements of Theodore Roosevelt but not under the Republican party, which seemed by then to have abandoned progressive ideals. The liberal democratic coalition included African Americans, Catholics, Jews, immigrants, and labor interests concentrated in Northeastern urban areas. The coalition also included Southern and Western populists, who supported Wilson through the campaigning efforts of longtime democratic presidential candidate William

Jennings Bryan, the chief spokesman of populism since the late nineteenth century.

Under Wilson's leadership, in 1913, the Democrats quickly passed legislation to establish a fair and regulated business environment. This legislation established the Federal Reserve System to regulate the money supply and the Federal Trade Commission to promote fair business practices. The Underwood Tariff-Reduction Act promoted equitable international trade, while the Clayton Anti-Trust Act strengthened existing regulations against monopolies, exempted unions from anti-trust laws, and discouraged court involvement in labor disputes. Legislation passed in 1914 established farm-extension services and other credit procedures to help farmers finance their crops. Additional legislation created federal boards to assist railroad workers and empower the Interstate Commerce Commission to regulate railroad rates and practices. Measures to bar the products of child labor from interstate commerce, however, were ruled unconstitutional by the Supreme Court. Wilson's New Freedom, in effect, moved the Democratic Party away from the states-rights and laissez-faire views of the eighteenth and nineteenth centuries to the industrial outlook of the twentieth century.

Just as the Democratic Party completed passage of its New Freedom reform legislation, the outbreak of World War I caused Wilson to focus more attention on foreign affairs. Proclaiming American neutrality, Wilson called for the nation to prepare for war and tempered his zeal for reform. On May 7, 1915, Germany's submarine attack upon the *Lusitania,* a British ocean liner, killed 1,201 people, including 128 Americans. In response, Wilson urged the Germans to stop attacking passenger vessels, which it did until 1917. World War I became a major campaign issue in the 1916 elections as Charles Evans Hughes, the Republican presidential candidate, assailed Wilson for not preparing the nation for war, but the incumbent campaigned on the success of his domestic agenda and the fact that he had kept the nation out of the war. Wilson narrowly won presidential re-election and the Democrats maintained their majority in the Senate despite losing two seats to the Republicans, who had gained a single seat advantage over the Democrats in the House of Representatives.

Democratic reform conceded to military priorities on April 6, 1917, when the United States declared war on Germany. New organizations, such as the War Industries Board and the War Labor Board, directed the nation's economy toward the war, a Committee on Public Information generated patriotic fervor, and the Espionage and Sedition Acts quelled dissent. Despite Wilson's vigorous promotion of the Fourteen Points as the United States' moral purpose for entering the war, he was unable to hold the liberal coalition together that had elected him to the presidency and the Democratic Party to legislative majorities in 1912. Voters across the board resented the draft, while Northeastern labor interests opposed higher taxes and anti-trust legislation. But perhaps more than anything else, including the war, voters begrudged the apparent Southern domination of the Democratic Party, with its zeal for prohibition and racial segregation.

The Democrats of the Wilson era concentrated on developing the top rather than the bottom of the party, where its structure had changed little from what it had been during the late nineteenth century. Without the leadership of Wilson, the Democrats suffered a disastrous defeat to the Republicans in 1920, but not before Wilson experienced the bitter humiliation of having twenty-one Democrats in the Senate join the Republicans in rejecting the Treaty of Versailles that ended World War I and established the League of Nations.

Adam Revere Hornbuckle

See also: Elections of 1916 (WWI); Elections of 1920 (WWI); Progressivism (WWI); Biographies: Wilson, Woodrow (WWI); Documents: Democratic Party Platform, 1916

REFERENCES

Burner, David. *The Politics of Provincialism: The Democratic Party in Transition, 1918–1932.* Cambridge: Harvard University Press, 1968.

Chambers, William Nisbet. *The Democrats, 1789–1964: A Short History of a Popular Party.* New York: D. Van Nostrand, 1964.

Rutland, Robert Allen. *The Democrats: From Jefferson to Clinton.* Columbia: University of Missouri Press, 1995.

E

Easter Rising

From April 24 to 29, 1916, there occurred a suicidal military rebellion of Irish nationalists in Dublin, staged with the intention to achieve independence from British rule. The Easter Rising, as it came to be called, had little popular support from the Irish public.

This rising had been planned in 1915 because the Home Rule Bill had been postponed in British Parliament. Ultimately two opposing groups, the Irish Volunteers, a national defense body established in 1913 and headed by the scholarly Padraig Pearse (1879–1916), who initiated a cult of peasant mysticism, and the Irish Citizen Army commanded by the Marxist-oriented Republican James Connolly (1868–1916), carried out the plans. Both men romanticized the contemporary cult of violence and blood sacrifice in the name of Irish Nationalism. The IRB (Irish Republican Brotherhood) had been established in 1913 and usurped power from the Irish Volunteers. Many IRB members had been elevated to officer ranks in the Irish military. The Volunteer contingent, all solid Republicans, favored physical force. However, the Catholic Chief of Staff, historian Eoin MacNeil (1867–1945), cofounder of the Gealic Leagus, wished to bargain with Britain at the end of World War I; he strongly opposed rebellion.

A Doomed Rebellion

The Rising, according to most historians, was problematic from its inception and doomed to fail. Connolly, as commander of the Socialist Labor Union, organized the illegal 200-member Irish Citizen Army founded by Jim Larkin and endangered the secret plans when he attempted to start a rebellion on his own. But, to prevent a fiasco and to prevent undermining the chances of the Rising, Connolly joined forces with the IRB. Together they planned to attack the following Easter Sunday. The political activities of the groups were financially supported in large part by contributions from Irish Americans.

To confuse informers, the Volunteers planned three days of military exercises for the Easter weekend. While the British would deem it at face value, the rebels realized it was preparation for the Rising. MacNeil found out the plans and threatened to inform the British at their headquarters in Dublin Castle. However, when MacNeil, who had not been included in the planning, was informed about a shipment carrying 20,000 German rifles and ten machine guns being brought from Germany to support the Rising, having been organized by the esteemed Irish consular agent, Sir Roger Casement (1864–1916), he briefly acquiesced. However, he reverted his decision and canceled any actions for Sunday when he discovered that the German ship *Aud* that was carrying the shipment was scuttled by the British and Casement was arrested at Tralee in County Kerry. MacNeil's order to call off the Rising was countermanded by IRB officers. Confusion reigned. Consequently, only 1,800 out of 10,000 men, and 300 Citizen Army members reported for duty. The paucity of arms and men would prove disastrous for the rebels; the Rising was doomed before it began.

The Rising officially began at noon on Easter Monday when Pearse, a fierce nationalist Catholic who strongly desired martyrdom, read the Proclamation of Irish Independence, declared an Irish Republic, declared a provisional government, and announced his presidency of the Irish Republic. The document was signed by himself; the Fenian ex-convict, Thomas J. Clarke (1858–1916); rebel commander Eamonn Ceannt (1881–1916); Sean (MacDiarmada) MacDermott (1884–1916); Joseph Plunkett (1887–1916); Connelly; and Thomas MacDonagh (1878–1916). The unenthusiastic Dubliners present were completely unaware of the intention of the rebels; they were bewildered. Additionally, the women, dependent on a British war allowance, were angry because their money was now negated by the Proclamation. It was the problems created by World War I, rather than independence, that were the citizens' paramount concern.

Plunkett had devised a plan to seize strategically important buildings: five north of the River Liffey and nine south, as well as railway stations, in a ring around Dublin. Consequently, the rebels were divided into four battalions and a fifth combined from remnants of the first four. The Fifth Battalion included Pearse, Connolly, Augustine Joseph Clarke (1896–1974), MacDermott, Plunkett, and the highly intelligent organizer Michael Collins (1890–1922). Together they seized the indefensible General Post Office on Sackville Street and made it their headquarters.

The Four Courts was seized by the First Battalion under Ned Daly while the Second Battalion, headed by MacDonagh, seized Jacob's Factory. St. Stephen's Green, under Constance Gore-Booth the Countess Markiewicz (1868–1927) and Michael Mallin (1874–1916), effectively barred British access from the Portobello Barracks and the Harcourt Street Station. The Third Battalion at Bolan's Bakery, under Eamon de Valera (1882–1975), would oversee the routes that would be taken by British reinforcements while the Fourth Battalion seized the South Dublin Union Workhouse under Ceannt. In order to transport troops from Liberty Hall to the GPO, a public bus was commandeered at gunpoint and taken to the site; all fares were paid. The Rising was also supported by a Youth Organization, the *Fianna* (armed with pikes), and the women's organization *Cumann na Mban*.

Although some police guarding Dublin Castle were shot, the seizure of the Castle failed as did the capture of the arsenal at Phoenix Point. However, the rebels did cut the Castle's telephone lines. They were surprised by the reaction they received from the workers at Jacob's Factory, who opposed the Rising.

The British, meanwhile, had no idea about the size of the rebel group. They only had 400 troops themselves because at least 75 percent were on leave for the Bank holiday, leaving them critically undermanned. The British therefore relied heavily on the Royal Irish Constabulary, the 10,000-strong armed police force that was completely loyal to the Crown.

British Counteroffensive

The British counteroffensive began on Tuesday when martial law was declared for all of Ireland. The 1,600 reinforcements from the Third Cavalry Brigade appeared from Athlone and were supplemented by the two infantry brigades of the 59th Northland Division. More British reinforcements formed at Kingstown Harbour; they were greeted by tea cakes and biscuits from the local Irish women, who had no idea what was going on. The Fifth and Sixth Battalions of the Sherwood Foresters faced no opposition upon arrival. The British military cordoned slowly, and soon methodically squeezed Dublin.

Some Foresters were confronted at Boland's Flour Mill. Two expert Irish marksmen at 25 Northumberland Road opened fire and killed or wounded dozens of British troops. However, they did manage to continue their march. The British retaliated by starting fires throughout Dublin. A lack of water allowed the fires to burn out of control, causing unbelievable damage. Some Dubliners resorted to looting from various stores but mostly from the upscale department store named Clerey's. Fur coats, tweeds, dress suits, golf clubs, and sacks full of a variety of goods provided unimaginable opportunities for the poor of Dublin. Some looters were shot. The rebels at St. Stephen's Green had moved into the Royal College of Surgeons, making it their strong point.

On Wednesday, the British attacked an empty Liberty Hall. The inexact firing resulted in severe damage to surrounding buildings.

Meanwhile, Dubliners were feeling the effects of the Rising, as they could not access food; they were the victims of a conflict they had neither supported nor understood.

Sir General John Maxwell (1859–1929), who had recently returned to England from India, arrived on Thursday under orders from Prime Minister Herbert Asquith (1852–1928) to quash the rebellion. By this time, British reinforcements started killing civilians because they could not differentiate the rebels since the rebels did not wear uniforms.

On Thursday, the British won the skirmish at Boland's Mill. The rebels at the South Dublin Union also lost their battle. The GPO was shelled so severely that it began burning from its roof. The fires in Dublin now posed a threat.

On Friday, Connelly ordered the women in the GPO to leave. The British continued to shell the GPO, so Pearse, Connolly, and others evacuated it and Connelly was carried out on a stretcher due to several disabling wounds. Meanwhile, the British bayoneted and shot Dubliners hiding in various cellars because the British thought they were rebels. At North King's Street, 200 rebels controlled by the Four Courts garrison fought 5,000 British troops who used artillery and armored cars. The twenty-hour-hour battle yielded the British only 150 yards.

By Saturday, Dublin had been shelled to ruins. The rebels were eventually crushed into submission. The reaction against the rebels became bitter as many lives were needlessly lost and Dublin has suffered some 2.5 million pounds in damage. Some 500 Irish were killed, of which 300 were civilians. Of the 2,500 Irish that were injured, 200 of which were civilians. The rebels unconditionally surrendered to Maxwell on Saturday, ostensibly to prevent further bloodshed. The next day the rebels were marched across the city and faced the heckles of angry Dubliners.

Some 3,600 men and 80 women were jailed and interned in British camps, and about 170 were court-martialed in a private military court. Pearse and the fourteen other leaders agreed to executions to spare the lives of the internees. Connelly, due to his injuries, was executed while tied to a chair, which enraged the Irish. They were also furious at the callous murder of the popular pacifist Francis Sheehy-Skeffington (1878–1916), who was shot by a deranged British officer. It was because of these final executions that the Irish populace ultimately turned against the British.

Annette Richardson

See also: Biographies: Asquith, Herbert Henry (WWI)

REFERENCES

Boyd, Neil. *Rebels: The Irish Rising of 1916*. London: Bantam Press, 1990.

Kee, Robert. *Ireland: A History*. London: Weidenfeld and Nicolson, 1981.

Lydon, James. *The Making of Ireland: From Ancient Times to the Present*. London: Routledge, 1998.

Moran, Sean Farrell. *Patrick Pearse and the Politics of Redemption: The Mind of the Easter Rising 1916*. Washington, DC: Catholic University of America Press, 1994.

O'Connor, Ulick. *The Troubles: The Struggle for Irish Freedom, 1912–1922*. London: Mandarin Paperbacks, 1989.

Purdon, Edward. *The 1916 Easter Rising*. Dublin: Mercier Press, 1999.

Taillon, Ruth. *The Women of 1916: When History Was Made*. Belfast: Beyond the Pale, 1996.

Tierney, Michael. *Eion MacNeill, Scholar and Man of Action, 1867–1945*. Oxford: Clarendon Press, 1980.

Economic Policy

When the United States entered World War I, the global conflict had been underway for more than two-and-a-half years. Europe's existing alliance structure pitted the Central Powers (Germany, Austria-Hungary, and Italy) against the Triple Entente (France, Britain, and Russia). After provocation from Germany, whose naval fleets had begun to sink American merchant ships in British waters, President Woodrow Wilson (1913–1921) made the decision to mobilize U.S. troops.

Wilson did much to encourage the United State's changing role in the world economy. In his view, free trade promoted both universal prosperity and universal peace and democracy. International commerce led to a strong domestic economy and exports were essential for continued U.S. economic growth. Wilson felt that restrictions on trade, such as tariffs and trade agreements, hindered efficiency and denied the natural cycle of the international economy.

The president's decision had immediate economic repercussions as the U.S. government faced the task of raising money for the war effort. Analysts determined that the country would need upward of $33.5 billion to finance its participation in the war, plus money for loans to European allies. With the War Loan Act (1917), Congress proposed that the United States provide $3 billion in such loans, though the sum was later increased. Now it fell upon President Wilson and Congress to determine where the necessary money would come from. They offered a solution by passing the War Revenue Act (1917), which stated that 74 percent of funding for the war would come from taxation imposed on the highest individual and corporate incomes. With this legislation, Wilson and Congress demonstrated an intent to place the financial burden on the wealthy and to give a break to middle- and lower-income individuals and families. A year later Congress passed another revenue act, which increased this burden on the nation's wealthiest, who were now called upon to provide 80 percent of funding for the war.

In 1917, few people had any idea about the impact the war would have on the economy and public policy. World War I brought the federal government into the economy in ways that had been unimaginable only a few years before. Congress passed the Lever Act of 1917 and the Overman Act of 1918, giving the president absolute authority over farm production, commodity prices, and the uses and prices of industrial raw materials. Wilson created the U.S. Railroad Administration and assumed virtually complete control over American railroads in order to guarantee the uninterrupted shipment of goods. The Food Administration supervised rationing programs and helped augment U.S. food production, while the Fuel Administration stimulated coal production by bringing marginal mines into service. To prevent debilitating labor strikes, Wilson created the National War Labor Board to arbitrate management-labor problems, and his War Labor Policies Board guaranteed labor's right to bargain collectively and set minimum wages and maximum hours.

War Industries

U.S. participation in World War I required not only the mobilization of people but also of materials in the United States. The war effort demanded that industry join with the federal government to ensure an adequate flow of supplies to the front and to keep things moving smoothly at home. Wilson declared that "it is not an army that we must shape and train for war, it is a nation." Of all the committees and agencies that were established to advise and oversee the production and movement of materials, raw and finished, the most important was the War Industries Board (WIB), which, for the duration of the war, ran the nation's economy. It was formed in July 1917 and was given broad authority over industrial prices, allocation of raw materials, and production priorities in order to guarantee sufficient war production and to meet domestic economic needs. The working relationship between the federal government and the private sector, which would later come to characterize much of the American political economy, had its beginnings during World War I.

The war was also enormously profitable to the United States. Because the United States was protected from the physical ravages of war by the Atlantic Ocean, the U.S. economy boomed between 1914 and 1918, becoming the largest in the world in terms of gross national product (GNP) and the world's financial center shifted from London to Wall Street. The war almost instantly reversed the credit standing of the United States. The nation, by the war's end, held billions of dollars in European debt obligations and it became the globe's greatest creditor as well as its greatest economic power. By forcing the Europeans to accept goods instead of loans, the Wilson administration guaranteed that the country would be banker, arsenal, and breadbasket to the Allies. World War I set the foundation for the prosperity of the 1920s and, as some economists argue, the background for the Great Depression (1929–1939) as well.

In another move designed to raise money, the U.S. Treasury Department issued a series of bonds called Liberty Loans. These were long-term bonds that promised to earn the holder 3.5 to 4.25 percent in interest. The campaign to sell the bonds was massive in scope. Liberty loan committees formed in all regions of the country and spokespersons appeared in theaters, hotels, restaurants, and other public gathering places while banks stepped forward to lend money for the liberty loans at rates lower than the interest on the bonds. The campaign was a tremendous success.

War Debts

During the war, the United States lent more than $7 billion to the Allied nations in order to assist them in fighting the war. Then after the war, to assist in reconstruction, the United States expanded those loans by $3.3 billion, bringing the total to $10,350,479,075. Although more than 90 percent of the money had been used to purchase U.S. agricultural and manufactured goods, creating unprecedented prosperity, the American public expected repayment in full, at 5 percent interest. At first, the debtor nations, who expected to receive large reparations payments from Germany, which was held chiefly responsible for the war, were willing to pay, but when the German economy collapsed (1921) and reparations were scaled down in the Dawes Plan (1924) and the Young Plan (1929), the Allied nations claimed that they would be unable to repay the debt. American officials, such as President Calvin Coolidge, demanded payment but the Europeans countered with a demand that the United States should cancel the debts in the name of world prosperity. Between 1923 and 1925, the United States reached agreements with its debtor nations, mostly by scaling down the size of the debt, but this changed when the depression struck the world in 1929, ending any chance of paying the war debts. On December 15, 1932, six nations, including Belgium and France, formally defaulted on their debts, and on June 15, 1934, the rest of them did so as well, with the exception of Finland, which paid its debt.

Martin J. Manning

See also: Council of National Defense (WWI); Economy (U.S., WWI); Federal Reserve (WWI); Mobilization (U.S., WWI); Taxation; War Bonds (WWI); War Industries Board (WWI); War Labor Board (WWI)

REFERENCES

Beaver, Daniel R. *Newton D. Baker and the American War Effort, 1917–1919*. Lincoln: University of Nebraska, 1966.

Carson, Thomas, ed. *Gale Encyclopedia of U.S. Economic History*. Detroit, MI: Gale Group, 1999.

Curzon, Gerard. *Multilateral Commercial Diplomacy*. New York: Praeger, 1965.

Rosenberg, Emily S. *Financial Missionaries to the World: The Politics and Culture of Dollar Diplomacy, 1900–1930*. Cambridge: Harvard University, 1999.

U.S. Department of State, *Papers relating to the Foreign Relations of the United States: 1917, Supplement 2: The World War, part 2*. Washington, DC: Government Printing Office, 1932.

Economy (Canada)

World War I had a very significant impact on the Canadian economy, not just because of the increased demands for goods and services that war always brings, but also because it accelerated the maturation and industrialization of the economy. The impact of these trends was delayed somewhat by a profound postwar recession, but the structural changes were permanent.

Canada entered World War I in August 1914 in the midst of a recession, which was in some ways worsened by the war. The first impact of the war was a reduction in availability of foreign capital, a traditional mainstay of Canadian economic development ever since the transportation boom of the nineteenth century. Net capital imports, almost 18 percent of GNP before the war, fell to only about 1 percent by 1916. Borrowers, however—most notably the federal government—found domestic sources of capital and, by the end of the war, Canada was a net capital exporter.

In the early months of the war, transportation and construction declined sharply, largely because of the shortage of capital; similarly, unemployment increased into 1915. This trend was reversed, however, as the demands of war called on labor, as well as with the virtual end of immigration. Annual immigrant arrivals, which totaled over 400,000 in 1913, fell to only 50,000 in 1916.

While the labor supply decreased, production was increasing, particularly of exports. In 1913, exports represented only 20 percent of the GNP; by 1917, this figure had more than doubled. Similarly, the government's role in the economy grew: Spending by all levels of government increased from about 10 percent of the GNP in 1913 to almost 15 percent by midwar. In absolute dollars, this represented a tripling of spending by the federal government alone, which had to pay not only the soldiers' wages, but for their food, uniforms, and arms as well.

The government determined to finance this spending with debt rather than by increasing taxation, not only because Conservative Prime Minister Robert Borden, as well as his Finance Minister Thomas White, believed in minimal taxation, but also because they believed that the ultimate beneficiaries of the war effort would be the next generation, who rightly could pay for it. However, Canadians' traditional foreign sources of borrowing, particularly the London bond market, were not available; the British government was itself borrowing as much as the world market could provide. Ottawa first turned to New York—in the still neutral United States—but ultimately White turned to domestic sources. Despite initial skepticism about the capacity of Canadian public savings to finance the war, by 1918, Ottawa had raised over $2 billion in war bonds within Canada.

During the latter stages of the war, the government did introduce a novel new tax when it unveiled the 1917 Dominion Income War Tax, the first tax on incomes in Canadian history. Up to this point, two-thirds of the federal government's revenue came from customs duties, and the income tax—along with the Business Profits Tax Act of 1916—was introduced largely as a political measure, intended more to answer demands that it tax war profiteers than raise revenues. Income tax was symbolic only in hindsight. It was not onerous, and it was not—despite promises when it was introduced—temporary. Unlike other measures intended to last only for the duration of the war, Ottawa found that it needed every revenue source available in peacetime, both to service the war debt and to fund military pensions, which when combined represented more than all total prewar government expenditures.

While the Canadian economy grew dramatically during the war years, perhaps more significantly, it saw major changes to the distribution of production. Manufacturing, not surprisingly, played an increasingly important role. Since the introduction of a comprehensive protective tariff policy under Prime Minister John A. Macdonald in the 1880s, Canadian manufacturing was considered to be in an "infant" stage, producing almost exclusively for the small domestic market. It was neither competitive nor efficient, and there were legitimate questions as to whether it could supply the war needs. Consequently, despite protests from ambitious—and profit-eager—Canadian producers, as the war began, Imperial munitions buyers placed their orders with the United States. By 1916, however, Canadian arms manufacturers were receiving the bulk of these orders, largely because of the creation of the Imperial Munitions Board, headed by the Canadian meat-packing magnate Sir Joseph Flavelle. The resultant growth in manufacturing for export was evident not just in munitions, but also across a wide range of goods. While only 7 percent of Canadian manufactured goods sold outside Canada in 1913, by 1918 that figure was over 40 percent.

Agriculture was also greatly affected by the war. Farmers felt the greatest impact of the pre-war recession, particularly in the western prairie provinces. There, mostly on land only opened to settlement late in the nineteenth century, farmers were still carrying heavy start-up debt. Moreover, low grain prices and low yields made 1914 a very difficult year for western wheat farmers, who represented the vast majority of Canadian farmers. Within a year, however, they saw a dramatic turn-around. By 1915, the demand created by the war, particularly the disruption of supplies from Russia and other affected areas of Europe—combined with record yields caused by good weather—brought prosperity. This trend continued throughout the war, as demand continued to grow—especially in 1917 when the Imperial government announced it would buy all that Canada could produce.

The boom in demand for wheat brought even more farmers into wheat production—and inflated not only the price of what they produced but the value of their land as well. It would take two decades—and another world war—to bring prices of both back to the same level. The war also changed the grain market itself, which had been long subject to the whims of world markets and resultant price fluctuations. In 1915, the Canadian government began to buy grain directly, and in 1917, in an effort to stabilize the market while meeting the British demand, it established a Board of Grain Supervisors—with the power to set grain prices while coordinating all overseas sales. In 1919, shortly after hostilities ended, Ottawa replaced it with the Canadian Wheat Board, the even broader mandate of which included all marketing of the grain. When the government decided a year later to end what it considered a temporary measure, western farmers, who wanted the price stability that the free market could not offer, protested. This political discontent contributed to the defeat of the Conservative government in Ottawa in the first postwar election in 1921.

The long-term impact of the war on the Canadian economy was somewhat mixed. It clearly had an accelerating effect on development of industry: The total production of the manufacturing sector, as well as its proportion of the national economy, grew during the war years. However, the immediate postwar recession brought both back to prewar levels, and the same was true of industrial employment. Nevertheless, the economy certainly had increased capacity, most notably in the newly developing automotive industry. It would see the benefits of this growth in capacity in the mid-1920s, following the end of the recession, but much more so only after it survived the depression of the 1930s—when another world war began.

Curtis J. Cole

See also: Mobilization (Canada, WWI); Biographies: Borden, Robert Laird (WWI)

REFERENCES

Brown, Robert Craig, and G. Ramsay Cook. *Canada, 1896–1921: A Nation Transformed.* Toronto: McClelland and Stewart, 1974.

Deutsch, J. "War Finance and the Canadian Economy." *Canadian Journal of Economics and Political Science* 6, no. 4 (1940): 525–542.

Norrie, Kenneth, and Douglas Owram. *A History of the Canadian Economy,* 2d ed. Toronto: Harcourt Brace Canada, 1996.

Thompson, John Herd. *The Harvests of War: The Prairie West, 1914–1918.* Toronto: McClelland and Stewart, 1978.

Urquhart, M. C. "New Estimates of Gross National Product, Canada, 1870–1926: Some Implications for Canadian Development." In *Long-Term Factors in American Economic Growth,* ed. Stanley L. Engerman and Robert E. Gallman. Chicago: University of Chicago Press, 1986.

Economy (UK)

In the beginning of the twentieth century, the United Kingdom was one of the strongest economic powers, having commercial and industrial leadership of the world. Its share in the world GDP had increased from 5 to 8 percent and the United Kingdom's own GDP increased by six times from the earlier century. World War I resulted in a considerable shrinkage of the economic clout of the United Kingdom. Its economy had been one of relative prosperity, notwithstanding the fact that its industrial production was less than that of the United States and Germany. On the eve of the war, its labor force from agriculture comprised about 12 percent of the total UK labor force, distribution and services 32 percent, while manufacturing and construction contributed 38 percent. It was the most industrialized country of the world. With a life expectancy of fifty-three years and a literacy rate of 96 percent, the United Kingdom was an advanced country.

War Declared

War was declared against Germany on August 4, 1914, after Germany's violation of Belgian neutrality. The United Kingdom was for the first time fighting a large-scale global war that required major economic readjustments. Its economy was influenced greatly in temporal and spatial dimensions, and the political instability, decline in capital movements, hampering of international trade, and global protectionism created adverse conditions. Before 1914, an ordinary Briton was hardly feeling the existence of a state apart from paying a reasonable amount of tax, getting benefits of insurance and old-age pensions, and adhering to the law. The primary job of the citizen was now to serve the state. His food was rationed, work conditions regulated, freedom of movement curtailed, daytime extended by an hour, even lights on the street became dim and five million joined the armed forces.

The third ministry of Herbert Henry Asquith (1852–1928) (February 1911–May 1915) received a credit of 100 million pounds on August 6, 1914, in Parliament. Speculation in the London Stock exchange had resulted in it having been closed with transactions conducted in cash only. Bank rates were raised to 10 percent. The exchange rate with the U.S. dollar increased from $4.86 to $7. The Chancellor of Exchequer, David Lloyd George (1863–1945), issued paper notes of one pound and ten shillings denominations. The note circulation increased from 34 million to 299 million pounds at the end of war. But the gold standard was not abandoned. The income tax rate was doubled, giving the government an additional 1 million pounds per week in revenue, whereas the expenditure was the same amount per day. With the takeover of the Railways, there was a revamping of the transport system, covering 23,387 miles. Additionally, the merchant ships were requisitioned to carry army personnel. The government guaranteed the dividends and partially met the expenses, contributing 95 million pounds.

A coalition ministry was formed under Asquith in May 1915, after a scandal over the shortage of explosive shells, which had led to losses on the battlefield. It was recognized that the whole economy, along with manufacturing and support services, were to be focused toward war. Under Lloyd George, the Ministry of Munitions came into existence for the purpose of reorganizing the country's industrial resources. The Munitions Act of July 2, 1915, tightened governmental control over factories and limited the profits of the owners. Strikes were banned. The ministry had set up 218 national factories and 2,000 small factories to meet wartime needs. Steel, leather, and wool were requisitioned by the government for various industries. By July 1915, 594 million pounds were received as war loans with an interest rate of 4.5 percent taken out by private investors or foreign governments like the United States and Canada. The cost of the war had increased to 5 million pounds per year and, in 1915, there was a deficit of 1.285 billion pounds. Taxes on profit and income were further raised, and now cars, watches, matches, and mineral waters also came under the tax net. There was then an increase in prices due to inflationary finance. The government failed to control food and pension disbursal satisfactorily.

On December 5, 1916, Asquith resigned and Lloyd George was appointed as Premier. New departments were established to address the problems arising from the war economy. In February 1917, the war loans had brought in 1 billion pounds. By April 1917, the cost of the

war had risen to 7.8 million pounds per day, and the tax on excess profit was a staggering 80 percent. Taxation from different sources covered the interest payments of the unlimited government borrowing. Interest rates for the loans were kept high—around 5 percent—so that foreign money would remain inside the country. A situation had developed by which the government was paying interest on money it had itself minted. Because of the lending, the wealthier class generally had money to spend; it was the poor that primarily carried the burden of the rising prices. One could purchase only one-third of goods with one pound in 1918–1919 that one could have purchased compared to the year 1914.

The problem of food supply was becoming difficult. The supply of sugar had been cut off and, due to long queues at butcher and grocery shops, there was panic in the public mind about food shortages. The rise in prices greatly affected fixed-salary groups and people who had invested money in real estate. Food rationing was introduced, and restrictions were imposed upon meals and drinks taken in restaurants. A standard bread was adopted and the 261 flour mills came under governmental control in April 1917. There was voluntary rationing and individual garden products were encouraged. The United Kingdom was able to produce all the potatoes it needed in 1918. The new Food Controller was a survivor of *Lusitania;* David Alfred Thomas (1856–1918), who rationed about 85 percent of the food consumed by the civilians in June 1917 except milk, vegetables, and fish. Ration cards were issued, maximum prices were fixed for 94 percent of the food and drink, and from February 1918, items like meat, butter, and margarine were rationed. Adequate food supplies were ensured and prices were fixed during the winter of 1917–1918. However, the United Kingdom had to purchase food from the United States and, from October 1917 to February 1919, it received about two million tons of meat, grains, and other supplies by paying 276 million pounds, and an additional supply of 75 million bushels of wheat came in early 1918.

The economy of the United Kingdom was tied with that of the United States in a major way. Not only was the United Kingdom borrowing from the United States so as to buy essential war materials, it also had received loans amounting to 1 billion pounds. There was no increase of export to the United States, but supply imports became more due to a shortage of U.S. funds to aid Britain. Huge amounts of loan capital was borrowed from the U.S. market and the British citizens sold securities that invested in the United States with a loss of 207 million pounds. But the British investment in other countries increased by 250 million pounds during the war period and exports brought increased profit due to the price escalation. The shipping industry also contributed to the profit. Except for the year 1918, the international balance of payments remained favorable. It was 200, 101, 101, and 107 million pounds in 1915, 1916, 1917, and 1918 respectively. With the British pound comparatively strong in the international market, there was no exchange control or export of capital. The government had given loans to the Allies that totaled 1,825 million pounds, and a major share of that came directly from the U.S. loans that it had received.

Women in the Labor Force

The war had a substantial impact on women and the labor force. The militant suffragettes demanded the right to serve the nation, and women joined in Voluntary Aid Detachments as nurses and worked as tram and bus conductors, post women, and chauffeurs. Two hundred thousand women worked in various departments of the government, half a million began clerical work in private offices, and 800,000 were employed in engineering shops. The emancipation of women was taking effect in the UK. The excellent work done by the women made it possible for the grant of the franchise to women of not less than thirty years by the Act of 1918. All single men and childless widowers between the ages of eighteen and forty-one were drafted for military services in February 1916, and this age was subsequently raised to fifty-one in 1918, substantially affecting the labor force. The members of engineering unions were no longer exempted from military services, and this helped set off engineering strikes in May 1917. There was a severe shortage of labor, resulting in an average annual net loss of labor during the war period of 1.6 million pounds.

World War I ended after the signing of the Armistice in November 1918. It was a time of disillusionment and difficulty for the victorious nation, which had been drained of manpower and wealth. A million people from the United Kingdom and its colonies had died, and those returning faced a decline in wages, industrial profits, and export industries. Strikes were frequent and unemployment figures surpassed two million people. The government owed 850 million pounds to the United States, but the internal debt was even more alarming. With the war cost amounting to 9 billion pounds, only 28 percent could be met from taxes. The pound sterling was replaced by the dollar as the global leading currency and New York became the financial capital of the world. By the time another world war had started, the hegemony of the United Kingdom had become a thing of the past.

Patit P. Mishra

See also: Mobilization (UK, WWI); Trade Unions (UK, WWI); Biographies: Asquith, Herbert Henry (WWI); George, David Lloyd (WWI)

REFERENCES

Churchill, Winston. *The World Crisis.* New York: Scribner, 1931.

Constantine, Stephen, Maurice W. Kirby, and Mary B. Rose, eds. *The First World War in British History.* London: Edward Arnold, 1995.

Dewey, Peter. *War and Progress: Britain 1914–1945.* London: Longman, 1996.

Dintenfass, Michael. *The Decline of Industrial Britain, 1870–1980.* Independence, KY: Routledge, 1993.

Floud, Roderick, and Donald McCloskey, eds. *The Economic History of Britain since 1700,* 2d ed. Vol. 2: *1860–1939.* Cambridge: Cambridge University Press, 1994.

Groot, Gerard J. de. *Blighty, British Society in the Era of the Great War.* London: Longman, 1996.

Marwick, Arthur. *A History of the Modern British Isles, 1914–1999: Circumstances, Events, and Outcomes.* Malden, MA: Blackwell, 2000.

Mathias, Peter. *The First Industrial Nation: An Economic History of Britain, 1700–1914,* 2d rev. ed. London: Methuen, 1983.

May, Trevor. *An Economic and Social History of Britain, 1760–1970.* Harlow, UK: Longman, 1994.

More, Charles. *The Industrial Age: Economy and Society in Britain, 1750–1985.* London: Longman, 1989.

Pollard, Sidney. *The Development of the British Economy, 1914–1950.* London: Edward Arnold, 1962.

Seaman, L. C. B. *Post-Victorian Britain: 1902–1951.* London: Methuen, 1966.

Economy (U.S.)

For the U.S. economy, the period from 1901 to 1914 was one of relatively stable prosperity except for the two brief financial crises of 1903 and 1907. Possessing a third of the global industrial product, the United States was the largest economy of the world one year before the outbreak of World War I. It led the world in the usage of internal combustion engine vehicles, and U.S. railways carried 35 billion passengers in 1913 alone. The beginning of World War I transformed the U.S. economy even before it joined the war in April 1917. U.S. President Woodrow Wilson had declared neutrality in war that broke out in Europe. But an industrial boom occurred that not only resulted in prosperity in the subsequent years, it also heralded an imminent U.S. depression in 1914, which was averted through the U.S. entry into World War I.

The earlier Progressive Era had tried to change the market-oriented American society into a government-controlled regime. There were major changes in various arenas in the United States, and the economic system after 1914 almost became a period of "war socialism," which left a clear imprint after the war. Major institutional changes occurred before the United States became a belligerent power. An economic policy was initiated that aimed at promoting national interests and international stability, which brought changes in the role of government, internal economy, and U.S. positioning in the world economy. The government undertook measures to prepare for wartime and massive mobilization in various fields.

The U.S. anticipated that the war would cost the United States a substantial sum of money. Capital would need to be raised in order to fund massive loans to the Allies as well as the United States' own war efforts. Production of both agricultural and manufactured goods needed to be increased in order to be sold to the Allied forces. Taxes on income, corporate profits, and inheritances contributed to about one-third of war finances, totaling about $10 billion. There was a steep rise in income tax, including a tax on income over $1 million that was assessed at 77 percent, which contrasted sharply with the 7 percent tax from 1913 —a tax that, at the time, seemed high. For some, the inheritance tax rose to as high as 70 percent. On December 23, 1913, the Federal Reserve System, serving as the country's central bank, was created by an act of Congress. Its tasks were regulating money supply, issuing national currency, checking bank runs, and fighting inflation. The Federal Reserve System satisfied the government's need for money and credit. The inflationary money creation and borrowing helped finance a major segment of the cost of war. On the whole, the burden of the war finance was spread widely and the spending was done without economic chaos.

The United States was following a policy of benevolent neutrality toward the Allied countries like Great Britain and France. It had extended loans to them totaling $2.3 billion, whereas Germany had received only $27 million. The future of U.S. economic prosperity was undeniably interwoven with the success of the Allied forces. In order to buy essential war materials, the Allied powers were borrowing heavily from the United States, and many of these goods, such as those needed to maintain British naval supremacy, were purchased from the U.S. manufacturers by using U.S. bank credits. A German victory would have meant disaster for the U.S. economy, so it was in the best commercial interest for the United States to favor the Allies. There was an appreciable fall of trade with Germany, whereas commerce with Britain increased. But even then, the United States did not join the war. The unrestricted submarine warfare by Germany, causing the sinking of passenger ships on which American citizens were traveling, resulted in its official entry in April 1917.

The U.S. federal government spread its scope and size enormously after its entry into the war. It expanded its power immensely by the way in which it took control of its own economy. Earlier, when U.S. expenditures were not even 2 percent of the country's Gross National Product (GNP), agricultural production, labor relations, security markets, and other economic spheres had not been regulated by the U.S. government. Now the warfare state of the U.S. government set up agencies for controlling production, regulating prices, producing war materials, and streamlining vital sectors like railways, telephone, telegraph, and ocean shipping. Armed with almost absolute power by the Congress, the president created five hundred new agencies and the Council of National Defense outlined areas of the economy that were vital for the war effort.

The War Industries Board created in July 1917 under financier and stock speculator Bernard Baruch (1870–1965) was one of the most important wartime mobilization agencies, regulating U.S. industrial production, determining priorities, purchasing military supplies, and standardizing various products. Baruch became the virtual tsar of U.S. industry. Under his guidance, U.S. industries saw a threefold increase in profits between 1914 and 1919. There was a mutually beneficial alliance between the government and the private sector that supervised production of 30,000 different types of products and commodities. In fact, years later, the methods used for the mobilization of these industrial and agricultural resources served as a model for Franklin Roosevelt's New Deal. The Food Administration, set up under the Lever Act in August 1917 under Herbert Hoover (1874–1964), supervised the distribution of U.S. agricultural products both to the United States as well as its Allies. Voluntary conservation was encouraged by the Hoover administration with slogans like: "Meatless Mondays," "Wheatless Wednesdays," "Porkless Thursdays" and "Food will win the war." Production of basic foodstuffs like wheat was encouraged, and its acreage increased to 75 million in 1919 from just 45 million in 1917. The nation exported three times more meat, bread, and sugar in 1918 than it had before the war. Voluntary price control and rationing paid off well for the rational distribution of edibles, enabling Hoover to become an admirable figure in U.S. politics.

The pragmatic Secretary of Treasury William Gibbs McAdoo took charge of the railway system as Director General in December 1917. His "Liberty Bonds" and "Victory Bonds" had raised $21 billion between May 1917 and 1919. With a half-billion-dollar budget, the Railway War Board expedited both an efficient system of wartime supplies for the U.S. army as well as the transport of goods to the East coast for further shipment to Europe. From May to July in 1917, 75,682,028 bushels of wheat, corn, barley, oats, and other grains were shipped to the Allies. A satisfactory and unified continental system of transport was feasible due to the voluntarily merger of what had been the competitive operation of 693 railroads within the United States, bringing railroads to the peak of efficiency. Many agencies of transport and communication, such as express companies, elevators, warehouses, telephone, cable lines, and telegraph, soon also came under the control of the government.

The National War Labor Board created in April 1918 under William Howard Taft compelled the industries to give the workers an eight-hour day, equal pay for women doing equal work, and a minimal living standard. In return, the workers were not to resort to strikes during this crucial wartime. The president of the American Federation of Labor and a member of the National War Labor Board, Samuel Gompers, watched with satisfaction as the labor unions increased in membership by about 1.5

million between 1917 an 1919, and this credited to the wartime prosperity and full employment. About four million workers were employed in jobs related to war industries by the U.S. Employment Service. Felix Frankfurter (1882–1965) was the director of War Labor Policies Board standardizing wages and hours. The War Labor Policies Board's policy, along with declining immigration and an increase in male military enlistments, had created opportunity for marginalized sections of the society to fill the demands of the labor shortage caused by the drop-off in immigration and war mobilization. About 500,000 African Americans migrated north from the South between 1916 and 1918 for wartime jobs. Mexican Americans moved from the Southwest to the North, and Hispanics were employed as agricultural workers in California. Employment opportunities became available for about a million women in the wartime industries out of an already working female workforce of eight million. Many women volunteered for war-related jobs. The Fuel Board, under Harry A. Garfield, started daylight savings, introduced "Fuelless Mondays," banned displays that used excessive electricity, and closed nonessential factories. The agencies like the Shipping Administration, Aircraft Production Board, Emergency Fleet Corporation, and others also contributed to the war economy in their respective spheres. Despite some blunders and not always achieving full conservation and production goals, the country succeeded in having a regulated economy with production working at full capacity.

The U.S. government also had to find capital for the Allied countries. The Inter-Allied Purchasing Commission was established in 1917 for the purpose of procuring wartime Allied requirements. About $10 billion in treasury loans were extended to Britain, France, and Italy during the two years after the United States entered the war, which, in turn, was primarily spent in the United States itself. By 1919, the total war expenditure was about 25 percent of the U.S. GNP. The direct cost of the war amounted to $36 billion for the nation and the sum increased by $6 billion more after the war due to indirect costs like interest on national debt, veterans' benefits, pensions, and bonuses for the soldiers.

After the end of the war, the United States had replaced Britain as the chief financier in the world economy. It became a creditor nation, New York emerged as the financial capital of the world, and the dollar became the most important currency in the international money market. Exports were more than the imports and Americans received more investment income from other countries than they paid to foreigners. The end of World War I saw the country made prosperous as it entered the 1920s and established precedents for future developments.

Patit P. Mishra

See also: Banking and Finance (WWI); Council of National Defense (WWI); Economic Policy (WWI); Mobilization (U.S., WWI); Trade Unions (U.S., WWI); War Industries Board (WWI); War Labor Board (WWI)

REFERENCES

Atack, Jeremy, and Peter Passell. *A New Economic View of American History: From Colonial Times to 1940.* New York: Norton, 1994.

Farwell, Byron. *Over There: The United States in the Great War, 1917–18.* New York: W. W. Norton, 1999.

Ferrell, Robert H. *Woodrow Wilson and World War I, 1917–1921.* New York: Harper and Row, 1985.

Goldstein, Donald M., and Harry J. Maihafer, eds. *America in World War I.* Washington, DC: Brassey's, 2004.

Heckscher, August. *Woodrow Wilson.* New York: Collier Books, Macmillian, 1991.

Kennedy, David M. *Over Here: The First World War and American Society.* New York: Oxford University Press, 1982.

McMaster, John B. *The United States in the World War (1918–1920).* New York: Appleton, 1920.

Schaffer, Ronald. *America in the Great War: The Rise of the War Welfare State.* New York: Oxford University Press, 1991.

Welsh, Douglas. *The USA in World War I (Americans at War).* New York: Galahad Books, 1982.

Elections of 1916

War in Europe was a crucial issue in the 1916 national elections in the United States. Following the sinking of the *S.S. Lusitania* the year before (and the loss of 128 American lives, mostly women and children), some Americans called for U.S. entry into the war. For many Americans, especially in cities where Germans congregated, the call for intervention was far less prevalent. Many Americans wanted the United States to remain neutral: Europe's war should stay in Europe, was the cry from the isolationists.

For the Democrats who controlled the White House, the goal was to retain power. Woodrow Wilson had called for neutrality in the war, since the war would benefit no one in the United States, where many immigrants from the warring countries lived in close proximity to one another. For industrial firms, the war would mean more profits, but the sales of weaponry were already being conducted with the European powers. As many of the industrial powers (who were Wilson's power base) pushed for war, Wilson was placed in a difficult decision. For the opposition to Wilson, it was a time of rebuilding their image as a foil to the president.

The Republicans met in Chicago to repair their fractured party in July of that year. Theodore Roosevelt broke from the Republican Party and had run in 1912 as the Progressive ("Bull Moose") Party candidate, and his showing had siphoned off enough votes to give Wilson the victory. Roosevelt withdrew from the 1916 race and endorsed Charles Evans Hughes, the Republican candidate. This act reunited the Republican Party for the 1916 election.

Other candidates ran on varied platforms. Among the various minor party candidates were Allan Benson of the Socialist Party ticket, James Hanly of the Prohibition Party, and Arthur Reimer of the Socialist Labor Party. One of the most vocal candidates was Jeanette Rankin, who ran for the seat of Representative to Congress from Montana on the Pacifist Party platform. Despite the fears of U.S. entry into the Great War, the U.S. punitive expedition into Mexico also created concern among some people who saw Wilson's intervention as little different from the war overseas.

During the final weeks of campaigning, Hughes and Wilson sparred over what national policy should be concerning U.S. policy in Europe. Given the massive propaganda that had permeated the United States, Republicans, led by Hughes, called for greater mobilization and military preparedness. Wilson insisted that the United States remain neutral.

In the election results, Wilson won on both the electoral and popular votes, but barely on both counts (9.1 million versus 8.5 million for Hughes; 277 electoral votes to 254). Benson and Hanly both had vote tallies in the low six figures, and Reimer barely eked out 15,000 votes. Rankin became the first woman elected to Congress. She also carried out her campaign promise, voting against U.S. entry into World War I on April 6, 1917. As the ranks closed once the United States entered the war, Rankin was voted out in the 1918 Congressional elections. For Wilson, the promise of neutrality did not hold.

Cord A. Scott

See also: Democratic Party (WWI); Republican Party (WWI); Socialist Party (WWI); Biographies: Hughes, Charles Evans (WWI); Wilson, Woodrow (WWI); Documents: Democratic Party platform, 1916; Republican Party Platform, 1916

REFERENCES

Keene, Jennifer. *The United States and the First World War.* Essex, England: Pearson Education, 2000.

Rosebloom, Eugen Holloway. *A History of Presidential Elections.* New York: Macmillian, 1957.

Wiebe, Robert. *The Search for Order: 1877–1920.* New York: Hill and Wang, 1967.

Elections of 1920

The election of 1920 was the first presidential election following World War I and one in which the Republicans won an historic victory. The election also marked a stinging rebuke of former president Woodrow Wilson and his League of Nations.

The Election of 1920 took place during one of the most turbulent times in U.S. history. When the United States emerged from World War I with no plan for reconversion to peacetime, the economy went into recession and unemployment mounted. Massive strikes and police raids throughout 1919 and into early 1920, known as the Red Scare, created an atmosphere of nervousness and tension. Many blamed immigrants from Eastern Europe who they believed imported socialist doctrines into the United States for starting the trouble, creating a tension between native-born Americans and the newcomers. Americans were further divided over the issue of prohibition. During this time, President Woodrow Wilson, a Democrat, attempted to rally the United States to enter the League of Nations. He tried to make U.S. entry a great moral crusade and refused to allow Senate Democrats to accept revisions in the treaty. After Wilson was stricken by a stroke in the summer of 1919, the federal government was left rudderless.

Republicans

When the Republican convention met in Chicago on June 8, 1920, no candidate had collected enough delegates in the primaries to secure the nomination. The leading candidates were General Leonard Wood, claiming the support of law-and-order types and Eastern conservatives; Illinois Governor Frank Lowden, the champion of mid-Westerners, moderates, and fiscal conservatives; and U.S. Senator Hiram Johnson of California, the choice of progressives and civil libertarians. Trailing behind were several dark horse candidates, including Massachusetts Governor Calvin Coolidge, Pennsylvania Governor William Sproul, and U.S. Senator Warren G. Harding of Ohio. Throughout the first day of balloting, no candidate could gain enough delegates to capture the nomination. In the evening, party managers held meetings at the Blackstone Hotel. Here is where the myth of the "smoked-filled room" arose to suggest that Harding was foisted upon the party by the old guard political bosses of the Senate. Harding's candidacy, however, had several im-

portant advantages. First, he had always been a conciliator among factions and had no real enemies within the party. Second, he came from Ohio, a traditionally Republican state that went Democratic in 1912 and 1916. Finally, Harding's campaign manager Harry Daugherty was very skillful in building temporary alliances to build up his candidate's delegate count. The balloting resumed the following day, and on the tenth roll call, Harding gained the nomination. Despite a weak attempt by the mid-Western progressives to give the vice presidential nomination to U.S. Senator Irvine Lenroot of Wisconsin, Calvin Coolidge was overwhelmingly selected by the delegates. The platform supported at Chicago was conservative in nature, anti-League of Nations (but mildly international), and a decisive rebuke of Wilson's polices.

Democrats

The Democrats were divided along two axes. First, a Northern, predominantly Catholic, immigrant and urban wing was pitted against one that was Southern, Protestant, nativist, and agrarian. The former tended to be "wet" and the latter "dry" on the issue of prohibition. Second, the controversial policies and patronage appointments of Woodrow Wilson had polarized the Democratic party into decidedly pro- and anti-administration wings. Like the Republicans, no Democratic candidate had a decisive number of delegates when the convention convened in San Francisco on June 28, 1920. Former Secretary of the Treasury William Gibbs McAdoo and Attorney General A. Mitchell Palmer split the vote of pro-administration, "dry," Southern delegates, while Ohio Governor James Cox and New York Governor Alfred Smith divided the anti-administration, "wet," and Northern delegates. The balloting was further confused by numerous favorite-son candidacies and the failure of Woodrow Wilson to equivocally state that he was not a choice. It took the Democrats a week and forty-three ballots before they declared James Cox the nominee. To balance the ticket geographically and soothe the administration, Assistant Secretary of the Navy Franklin D. Roosevelt of New York was chosen as Vice President.

Harding and the Republicans did not pursue a vigorous campaign. In addition to their overwhelming sense of confidence, the paramount reason for this was that Harding firmly believed the United States wanted serenity and peace in a time of emotional unrest and upheaval, and the best way to provide this was to conduct a relaxed "front porch" campaign. He seldom ventured from his home in Marion, Ohio, where he could best display his affability and emotional stability. Harding and Coolidge campaigned on the slogan of "Normalcy," a promise to return to the days before Theodore Roosevelt and Woodrow Wilson had charged the air with moralistic crusades, expanding federal government, and war.

The Democratic candidates conducted a more lively campaign. Cox traveled over 22,000 miles and Roosevelt 18,000 miles. After promising Wilson to support U.S. entry into the League without reservations, Cox emphasized the importance of the issue to voters. Cox and Roosevelt lambasted the Republican Party for its close proximity to big business and the millions of dollars it received from corporate contributors. But they were fighting an uphill battle. The devastating losses the Democrats had suffered in the 1918 midterm elections greatly weakened the party's structure in key areas. Financially, the Republicans enjoyed a three-to-one superiority in funds. When it came to judging the mood of the electorate, Harding had

Promising a return to "normalcy" at home and an end to internationalism abroad, Republican Warren Harding was overwhelmingly elected president in the 1920 election, the first following World War I. (Library of Congress)

been right. The emotional appeals of Cox and Roosevelt and their excessive progressive language did not strike a resonate cord with voters.

On November 2, 1920, Americans went to the polls. It was the first presidential election in which women could vote. Warren Harding won a decisive victory, gaining over sixteen million popular and thirty-seven electoral votes in one of the largest landslides in American history. The Republicans broke the solid Democratic South by taking Tennessee and Oklahoma. The Democrats won nine million popular and 127 electoral votes. They failed to carry a single state outside the South. Minor candidates, including Socialist Eugene Debs running from federal prison where he was serving a sentence for violating the Sedition Act, claimed 1.5 million votes nationwide, but these were indecisive to the outcome.

Gregory Dehler

See also: Democratic Party (WWI); League of Nations (WWI); Republican Party (WWI); Biographies: Coolidge, Calvin (WWI); Harding, Warren G. (WWI); Wilson, Woodrow (WWI); Documents: On Normalcy, May 14, 1920

REFERENCES

Bagby, Wesley M. *The Road to Normalcy: The Presidential Campaign and Election of 1920.* Baltimore, MD: Johns Hopkins University Press, 1962.

McCoy, Donald R. "Election of 1920." In *History of American Presidential Elections,* vol. 3, ed. Arthur Schlessinger Jr., 2349–2458. New York: Chelsea, 1971.

Morello, John A. *Selling the President, 1920: Albert D. Lasker, Advertising, and the Election of Warren G. Harding.* Westport, CT: Praeger, 2001.

Murray, Robert K. *The Harding Era: Warren G. Harding and His Administration.* Minneapolis: University of Minnesota Press, 1969.

Noggle, Burl. *Into the Twenties: The United States from the Armistice to Normalcy.* Urbana: University of Illinois Press, 1974.

Scammon, Edward, comp. and ed. *America at the Polls: A Handbook of American Presidential Election Statistics, 1920–1964.* New York: Arno Press, 1976.

Trani, Eugene P., and David L. Wilson. *The Presidency of Warren G. Harding.* Lawrence: University of Kansas Press, 1977.

Espionage Act

As the United States entered World War I, the U.S. government took steps to ensure that all Americans rallied to the cause of victory against Germany and the Central Powers. Sometimes that was done by way of patriotic propaganda and appeals for voluntary sacrifice, and sometimes that was done by warning Americans of the legal consequences of defiance.

The Espionage Act of 1917 was an example of the latter. Actually, the Espionage Act was written before the United States entered the war. It had been drafted by the Justice Department and introduced to Congress prior to April 6, 1917, when war was officially declared. When the law was passed on June 15, 1917, it promised harsh punishment for any American who would:

> . . . willfully make or convey false reports or statements with intent to interfere with the operation or success of the military or naval forces of the United States, or to promote the success of its enemies . . . or to willfully cause . . . or incite . . . insubordination, disloyalty, mutiny, refusal of duty, in the military or naval forces of the United States, or shall willfully obstruct . . . the recruiting or enlistment service of the United States . . . and shall willfully utter, print, write or publish any disloyal, profane, scurrilous, or abusive language about the form of government of the United States or the Constitution of the United States, or the military or naval forces of the United States, or the flag . . . or the uniform of the Army or Navy of the United States, or any language intended to bring the form of government . . . or the Constitution . . . or the military or naval forces . . . or the flag . . . of the United States into . . . disrepute.

Furthermore, persons who tried to defend anyone advocating any action mentioned in the law could also be prosecuted. The law also gave the U.S. Government the right to prosecute people if they obstructed the sale of Liberty Bonds or tried to prevent the U.S. from loaning money to or receiving money from other nations. Punishments included a fine of not more than $10,000 or imprisonment for not more than twenty years, or both.

Once it became law, the Espionage Act was broadly interpreted by various government agencies. Postmaster General Albert Burleson used the law to ban a wide range of materials from the nation's mails, while Attorney General Thomas Gregory used it to conduct a round-up of people he considered to be traitors, pacifists, war critics, and radicals. More than two thousand indictments were filed during the war. Perhaps the most notable was the one filed against Eugene Debs. In a speech given in Canton, Ohio, Debs called the war a capitalist exercise and a violation of the First Amendment. He was convicted and sentenced to ten years in jail. That episode, as well as others, raised the level of criticism about the Espionage Act and its impact on the civil liberties of Americans. One Idaho senator called the Espionage Act "omnipotently comprehensive. No man can foresee what it might be in its consequences." But it seems clear the intention of the law was to limit dissent and criticism, an intention the U.S. Supreme Court later affirmed. In 1919, the Court ruled in the case of *Schenck v. United States* that the Espionage Act was properly used in the conviction of a Socialist party officer who had mailed antidraft leaflets to members of the armed forces. The case appeared to focus on free speech as guaranteed under the First Amendment. However, the Court ruled that free speech had its limits, especially in times of war, and that the materials distributed represented "a clear and present danger" to the nation.

After World War I, the Espionage Act lay dormant until 1940, when it was revived in anticipation of World War II. A form of the earlier law still exists today.

John Morello

See also: Sabotage and Spies (WWI); Biographies: Debs, Eugene V. (WWI); Burleson, Albert Sydney (WWI); Documents: Espionage Act, June 15, 1917; *Schenck v. U.S.*, 1919

REFERENCES

Goldfield, David. *The American Journey: A History of the United States.* Vol. 2. Englewood Cliffs, NJ: Prentice Hall, 1998.

Knock, Thomas. *To End All Wars: Woodrow Wilson and the Quest for a New World Order.* New York: Oxford University Press, 1992.

Tindall, George Brown. *America: A Narrative History,* 2d ed., New York: W. W. Norton, 1988.

Europe, American Attitudes Toward

July 28, 1914, marks the start of World War I. U.S. president Woodrow Wilson proclaimed the neutrality of the United States in August 1914, and made every effort to maintain that policy for the next two years. In May 1915, a German submarine sank the *Lusitania,* a British passenger liner, which resulted in the deaths of 128 Americans. This incident aroused protest against Germany in the United States. When a German submarine sank the *Sussex,* an American vessel, on March 24, 1916, Wilson issued an ultimatum to Germany. In response, Germany pledged to cease its unrestricted submarine attacks. Wilson dispatched Colonel Edward M. House, Wilson's confidant in foreign policy, to Europe in January 1915 and again in January

1916 to explore the possibility of the United States mediating between the warring parties. House believed that the United States should work through the British to achieve peace. House's negotiations with British Foreign Secretary Sir Edward Grey resulted in the so-called House-Grey Memorandum of February 1916, which established that if Germany rejected U.S. mediation, the United States would enter the war against Germany. This policy represented a radical turning away from the official U.S. policy of neutrality. Moreover, House did not obtain Wilson's preapproval for this memorandum. Luckily, the British government vetoed this memorandum, which spared House from being humiliated back in Washington.

On December 18, 1916, Wilson invited both the Allies and the Central Powers to state their "war aims." Suspecting that Wilson had ulterior motives, Germany decided that Wilson should not play any official role in any armistice negotiation. By mid-January 1917, it was clear that Wilson's mediation effort had failed. On January 22, 1917, Wilson delivered his "Peace Without Victory" speech to the U.S. Senate, calling for international conciliation and outlining his ideal vision of a postwar future. However, on January 9, 1917, Germany had already decided to declare its intention to resume unrestricted submarine warfare. On February 3, 1917, the United States severed diplomatic relations with Germany. The American people, however, still supported a policy of neutrality with respect to the war. In addition, Germany wisely refrained from attacking U.S. shipping.

Then, suddenly, the Zimmermann Telegram incident took place, which inflamed U.S. public opinion and led to demands to declare war on Germany. On January 16, 1917, Germany's Secretary of State for Foreign Affairs, Arthur Zimmermann, sent a telegram to the German ambassador in Mexico to be submitted to the Mexican government. In this telegram, Zimmermann asked the Mexican government to ally with Germany if the United States declared war against Germany. In return, the telegram said, Germany would support efforts by Mexico to recover Texas, New Mexico, and Arizona from the United States. Intelligence officials working at the British Admiralty intercepted and decoded this secret telegram, and transmitted it to the United States on March 1, 1917.

On March 9, 1917, Wilson ordered the arming of U.S. merchant ships. German submarines sank three U.S. merchant ships between March 16 and March 18. Now backed by strong support from a large segment of the American people, President Wilson finally submitted a war resolution to a special session of Congress on April 2. The Senate approved the resolution on April 3, followed by the House of Representatives on April 6. Thus, the United States officially declared war on Germany on April 6, 1917.

The U.S. entry into World War I constituted a turning point. The United States provided the Allied powers with almost unlimited financial and industrial resources. By April 1, 1917, the Allies had exhausted their means of paying for war supplies from the United States. Between 1917 and the end of the war, the United States provided its European Allies with $7 billion in loans. American industry ran at full power to produce necessary war goods. The enormous financial and industrial power of the United States maintained a constant flow of arms and supplies across the Atlantic.

The United States also contributed troops during the war. The Selective Service Act of May 18, 1917, introduced a conscription system, but it took many months to train soldiers and send them to Europe. Only 85,000 U.S. troops were stationed in France in March 1918, but this number jumped to 1.2 million by September 1918. By the end of the war, more than 380 U.S. naval crafts were based overseas. Before the war ended, the United States ended up sending some two million soldiers to the war.

On January 8, 1918, President Wilson, speaking before a joint session of the U.S. Congress, presented his Fourteen Points, a collection of idealistic proposals grouped under fourteen separate headings that spelled out the essential elements for a peaceful settlement of World War I. Wilson sought to use the Fourteen Points to undermine the morale of the Central Powers and their will to continue fighting by guaranteeing national sovereignty and self-determination for the peoples of all nations participating in the war. Moreover, Wilson's ideal vision of a peaceful and stable world based upon self-determination contained a proposal to form a League of Nations as well as a liberal trading system that stood in sharp contrast to the revolutionary appeals Soviet Russia was making to areas of the world that were suffering from oppression. At the beginning of October 1918, Prince Maximilian of Baden, the German imperial chancellor, sent a request to Wilson via Switzerland for an immediate armistice and the opening of peace negotiations on the basis of the Fourteen Points. This led to the convening of the Paris Peace Conference, where Wilson was forced to make a series of compromises to secure support for the creation of the League, which he believed was the most important proposal among the Fourteen Points. The warring parties signed the Treaty of Versailles, which both created the League of Nations and also settled the terms of the postwar peace.

Yoneyuki Sugita

See also: German Americans (WWI); League of Nations (WWI); *Lusitania,* Sinking of (WWI); Paris Peace Conference (WWI); Zimmermann Telegram (WWI)

REFERENCES

Floto, Inga. *Colonel House in Paris: A Study of American Policy at the Paris Peace Conference 1919.* Princeton, NJ: Princeton University Press, 1980.

Keene, Jennifer D. *The United States and the First World War.* New York: Longman, 2000.

F

Fashion

Although the trend toward informality in fashion began before World War I, the experience of war encouraged Americans' desires for simple clothing. Cut off from Europe, American fashion designers and manufacturers were given the opportunity to gain prominence within the domestic market, but were limited by the military's need for considerable amounts of textile resources. While clothing was never rationed, civilians were encouraged to restrict their textile usage and manufacturers were asked to conserve resources for the war effort. Meanwhile, the growing number of employed women popularized a tailored style that seemed more appropriate to their changing social roles.

The formation of a distinctly twentieth-century style began before the war. By 1913, the characteristic Edwardian female silhouette, with its tightly corseted body and long skirts, had given way to a straight, high-waisted look that was thought to be more "natural" than previous styles. As the decade progressed, women's fashions grew less restrictive, and flared skirts, loose jackets, and less-confining foundation garments became the norm. Men's fashions grew similarly relaxed during this period; although the suit remained the essential male outfit, versions that were originally worn only for casual or sportswear became acceptable street and office wear.

While there were efforts to promote American fashion designers and to create a distinct American style in the decade before the war, Paris had long been the center of the fashion world and most American couturiers and department stores sold either copies of French designs or used French labels to sell what were in truth American designs. The growth in popularity of ready-made clothing meant that even items sold to middle- and lower-class Americans were derived from Parisian designs. However, the outbreak of war threw the French fashion industry into disarray. Shipping of both supplies and finished goods became exceedingly difficult, and U.S. store buyers increasingly came to rely upon overtly American designs. The domestic fashion media quickly began to promote these styles and designers, and competitions and exhibitions were organized in order to inspire designers and create publicity.

One of the most important influences on U.S. designers and clothing manufacturers was the military's need for textile supplies. Before the war, natural fiber (wool, linen, cotton, and silk) fabrics were used for virtually all clothing. Once the United States entered the war, however, most of these textiles were appropriated by the military, and fabric for civilian usage became extremely scarce. In order to meet civilian demand and to free up valuable resources for the war effort, manufacturers experimented with alternatives such as remanufacturing wool, substituting cotton in place of wool, and also experimenting with artificial fiber fabrics as a replacement for silk.

Civilians were encouraged to conserve personal textile use by repairing and remodeling existing garments. The Commercial Economy Board, part of the Conservation Department of the War Industries Board, made a series of style recommendations in an effort to limit the amount of materials used for civilian clothing and to reduce the need for new clothing purchases. Manufacturers were asked to maintain basic styles and silhouettes, design standard fabrics, and avoid details that wasted fabric. Fashion magazines and pattern companies promoted mending and remodeling as a patriotic duty. Women increasingly substituted simple "all day" one-piece dresses or suits for the occasion-specific prewar styles, and men's jackets became shorter, sleeves and trouser legs narrower, and decorative touches such as belts, pleats, and patch pockets disappeared.

Women's widespread entry into the workplace, taking over jobs vacated by enlisted men, affected prevailing fashions as well. Working women needed simpler, less restrictive clothing, and the relatively shorter and wider skirts popularized during the war allowed greater range of movement. In addition, the notion that women were taking on traditionally male tasks made tailored styles such as the suit seem more appropriate to women's new responsibilities.

The restrictions of the war years and women's changing social roles caused many Americans to prefer simpler clothing long after the end of World War I. While Paris reasserted itself as the center of the fashion industry, the war's brief break from international competition laid the groundwork for American designers and manufacturers to claim a share of the fashion market. Meanwhile, the focus turned to those designers who successfully captured Americans' desire for "modern," practical, but still fashionable clothing. Furthermore, manufacturer's experiments with new production techniques and materials during the war years laid the groundwork for innovations in the postwar era.

Kendra Van Cleave

See also: Advertising (WWI); War Industries Board (WWI); Women (U.S., WWI)

REFERENCES

Ewing, Elizabeth. *Twentieth-Century Fashion.* New York: Costume and Fashion Press, 2001.

Field, Jacqueline. "Dyes, Chemistry and Clothing: The Influence of World War I on Fabrics, Fashions and Silk." *Dress* 28 (2001): 77–91.

Lab, Susan Voso. "'War' drobe and World War I." In *Dress in American Culture,* ed. Patricia A. Cunningham and Susan Voso Lab, 200–219. Bowling Green, OH: Bowling Green State University Popular Press, 1993.

Milbank, Caroline Reynolds. *New York Fashion: The Evolution of American Style.* New York: Harry N. Abrams, 1989.

Federal Bureau of Investigation

In 1908, Attorney General Charles J. Bonaparte created a force of special agents within the Department of Justice, staffed it with thirty-one investigators, and placed it under the Office of Chief Examiner Stanley W. Finch. In March

1909, Attorney General George W. Wickersham named the organization the Bureau of Investigation (BOI). Thus, the FBI was born.

The BOI investigated violations of national bankruptcy, banking, naturalization, peonage, land fraud, and antitrust laws. Agents received no special training, so the BOI sought recruits with previous law enforcement or law experience.

Passage in 1910 of the Mann (White Slave) Act, which prohibited the transportation of women across state lines for immoral purposes, expanded the BOI's jurisdiction. The bureau used the Mann Act to pursue criminals violating state but not federal laws. The agency grew to more than 300 agents and 300 support personnel with field offices in major cities and on the Mexican border. The latter focused on smuggling, violations of neutrality, and collection of intelligence, often tied to the Mexican Revolution.

World War I saw a major enlargement of the agency as it became responsible for assisting the Department of Labor in investigating enemy aliens and enforcing the wartime Espionage, Sabotage, and Selective Service acts. In 1919, Congress passed the National Motor Vehicle Theft Act, and the bureau now had another tool for pursuing criminals who dodged state laws by crossing state lines. The bureau also abetted the aggressive pursuit by illegal means of aliens and radicals by Attorney General A. Mitchell Palmer during the Red Scare of 1919.

An assistant to the attorney general, J. Edgar Hoover (1895–1972), observed the Red Scare and learned that all was fair in the ongoing struggle between Americanism and the Red Menace. Hoover began keeping files on peace activists such as the social worker Jane Addams and African American leaders such as W. E. B. DuBois and foreigners such as the German novelist Thomas Mann. Hoover used illegal wiretaps, spies, and assorted abuses of due process to pad his dossiers on the allegedly un-American left. His service to Palmer was the springboard to Hoover's becoming BOI director in 1924.

Under Hoover the BOI professionalized. The bureau had become lax to downright sloppy in the years after the war. Hoover fired the misfits, molded the rest. He preferred law and accounting experience to a background in law enforcement. Agents were trained and expected to abide by a code of conduct and dress appropriately. Hoover set up a national fingerprint database and a crime lab that law enforcement agencies throughout the nation relied upon. He used his bureaucratic skills and his media connections to ensure a favorable press for the G-men as they brought to justice such gangsters as Pretty Boy Floyd and John Dillinger.

The Bureau of Investigation became the Federal Bureau of Investigation (FBI) in 1935.

In the 1930s, fascist Germany, Japan, and Italy began their aggressions against the world and communist Russia took the opportunity to enhance its world position. The United States responded by enacting neutrality into law. The United States was in the middle of the Great Depression, which spawned groups sympathetic to the fascists and the communists as well as homegrown radicals crying for a change in the system. In 1936, Secretary of State Cordell Hull authorized the FBI to watch these groups. Additional authority came from Franklin Roosevelt's 1939 presidential directive and the Smith Act (1940), which outlawed advocacy of violent overthrow of the government.

The Bureau watched the American Communist Party, the German-American Bund, the Silver Shirts, and Huey Long and Father Caughlin.

John H. Barnhill

See also: Americanization Campaign (WWI); Communist Party (U.S., WWI); Palmer Raids

(WWI); Red Scare (WWI); Sabotage and Spies (WWI); Biographies: Palmer, A. Mitchell (WWI); Hoover, J. Edgar (WWI)

REFERENCES

Gentry, Curt. *J. Edgar Hoover: The Man and the Secrets.* New York: Norton, 2001.

Powers, Richard Gid. *Secrecy and Power: The Life of J. Edgar Hoover.* New York: Free Press, 1987.

Federal Reserve

During World War I, the newly created Federal Reserve, the central bank of the United States, adopted monetary policies that assisted the U.S. Treasury Department in financing the war. By loaning money to banks at a cheap rate, the Federal Reserve encouraged banks to make loans to individual investors for the purchase of Treasury bonds. After the war, the Federal Reserve would establish policies independent of the Treasury Department.

The Federal Reserve came into existence only months before the onslaught of the Great War in August 1914. The Federal Reserve System was an attempt to gain the benefits of central banking—mobilizing reserves and providing greater stability for the country's banks. The banking system was to be removed from Treasury control. The country was divided into twelve regions, and a federal reserve bank was set up in each district. A Federal Reserve Board was established to supervise the whole system. By this means, it was hoped to regionalize the central banking function as well as to separate what was supposed to be the needs of sound credit policy from the fiscal activities of the U.S. Treasury, which in former years had often dominated the money market.

The Federal Reserve's main wartime activity was selling Treasury bonds. The governors of the reserve banks served as chairmen of the committees organized in each district to sell Treasury bonds to the nonbank public. Since the amount being borrowed was large—relative to the size of the country or previous credit demands—the System ensured the success of the four wartime Liberty Loans by making two types of loans. Short-term loans at preferential discount rates encouraged banks to buy short-term Treasury certificates during the interval between bond drives. Initially, the discount rate on these loans in New York was 3 percent for fifteen days and 3.5 percent for sixteen to ninety days. Rates rose to 3.5 and 4 percent in December 1917 and to 4 and 4.5 percent in April 1918, where they remained until November 1919. Loans were also made to encourage banks to stretch out the public's payments for purchases of Liberty Loan bonds over $1,000. The latter was known as the "borrow and buy" policy. Its original intent was to avoid a short-term contractive effect on the money stock and interest rates as buyers drew down their balances to make payments to the Treasury. Later it became a marketing device for the bonds, since buyers could defer payments for as much as a year from the time of purchase.

The Treasury's borrowing tested the system's ability to pool reserves. By far the largest part of the Treasury's short-term borrowing was in New York, so the New York bank was under pressure to finance the purchases. The Federal Reserve Board urged other reserve banks to buy acceptances from New York to relieve the strain on its reserve position, and New York renewed the request at the November Governors Conference. All banks except Kansas City, Chicago, and Atlanta agreed to buy acceptances to earn interest for their banks and thereby supply additional gold reserves to New York.

By offering discounts at a preferential rate on Treasury certificates, the Federal Reserve abandoned the penalty rate, one of the main principles on which it was founded. Member banks could borrow at a preferential rate below the rate paid on the Treasury certificates or Liberty bonds, so borrowing became profitable. Penalty rates for other types of borrowing remained, but most borrowing was at the preferential rate, so higher rates had no effect.

The Federal Reserve's wartime policy achieved the Treasury's objective of marketing an extraordinary increase in debt at a relatively low direct cost to the Treasury. The public bought most of the debt, but between 1916 and 1919, commercial banks bought almost $5 billion, approximately 20 percent of the total issued. The banks financed their purchases in part by borrowing $2 billion from the Federal Reserve.

The history of the early postwar years is principally the story of the Federal Reserve's struggle for independence from the Treasury and the deflationary consequences of the policies after it obtained independence. This was the System's first opportunity to take independent policy action.

Michael McGregor

See also: Banking and Finance (WWI); Economic Policy (WWI); War Bonds (WWI)

REFERENCES

Beckhart, Benjamin Haggott. *Federal Reserve System.* Washington, DC: American Institute of Banking, 1972.

Gilbert, Charles. *American Financing of World War I.* Westport, CT: Greenwood Press, 1970.

Whittlesey, C. R. *The Banking System and War Finance.* New York: National Bureau of Economic Research, 1943.

Film (UK)

Many breakthroughs and transformations took place within Great Britain's film industry during World War I. The war became the subject of most motion pictures shown, and realistic battle scenes captivated British audiences. The cinema was still in its infancy as an instrument of both information and entertainment in 1914, yet the use of film as a medium for wartime propaganda helped to shape the public's understanding of the war. The cinema was predominantly a working-class form of recreation in Great Britain during the early 1900s. Since it was less expensive than a concert or the theatre, usually three pence per seat, nearly 20 million people attended the 3,000 movie houses across the country each week during the war. The typical British cinema was congested and noisy. Audiences often talked throughout the films and openly expressed their satisfaction or discontent. Projectors were sometimes placed on trucks called "cinemotors" so that films could be shown on the sides of buildings to large groups of spectators. Motion pictures from the United States, featuring stars such as Charlie Chaplin, Douglas Fairbanks, and Mary Pickford, were favorites in Great Britain during the war. These films provided a temporary escape from the harsh realities of total war.

The War Office believed that propaganda films would be wasted on the pedestrian masses that attended the cinema. The British government maintained a negative opinion of cinema audiences, and attributed working-class maladies like juvenile delinquency to the motion picture industry. It was believed that uneducated spectators stole the money that was needed for admission into movie houses, and that they were likely to mimic any violence that was portrayed onscreen. Charles Masterman, the head of Wellington House, an organization that conducted propaganda in Great Britain until it was taken over by the Department of Information in 1917 and later became the Ministry of Information in 1918, was persistent in convincing the government that films from the front would be effective in winning over neutral countries to the Allied cause, motivating the British working class, and generating revenue. The British public, especially newspaper editors such as George Geoffrey Robinson of the *London Times,* were also calling for more realistic depictions of the war. The War Office finally yielded to the pressure, and began planning an official war film in January 1915. Lieutenant Geoffrey Malins was commissioned to film sailors on the H.M.S. *Queen Elizabeth* and soldiers in France. The finished product was released in December 1915; a feature-length motion picture entitled *Britain Prepared. Britain Prepared* primarily contained footage of training maneuvers aboard the massive dreadnought, as its main objective was to combat rumors that Great Britain's ability to wage war was weakening. *Britain Prepared* was received by the public with great enthusiasm, and it paved the way for more official war films.

The War Office formed the Cinematograph Committee, which sent Malins along with Captain J. B. McDowell to France in June 1916 to film the Allied push along the Somme River. A massive British bombardment of the German trenches was already underway when the cameramen arrived at the front. Malins and McDowell were with General Henry Rawlinson's Fourth Army on July 1, the first day of the Somme Offensive. The British Army suffered nearly 60,000 casualties, the bloodiest single day in its history. The two cameramen continued to work until July 10, often filming under dangerous conditions. McDowell was decorated for the risks that he took while working on the film. The material was sent back to Great Britain and censored by the War Office. They decided not to break down the footage into short newsreels,

but to release it as another feature-length film entitled *Battle of the Somme.* The one-hour-and-fifteen-minute production was screened on August 7, and opened to the public on August 21 in thirty-four theatres, grossing approximately 30,000 pounds in two months.

Prior to *Battle of the Somme,* the War Office prohibited cameramen from filming the front due to fear that the material would fall into enemy hands and be used by German intelligence. Filmmakers worked around these limitations by piecing together stock military footage, filming soldiers training, and staging reenactments to satisfy the public demand for war films. These techniques were first employed during the Boer War, and resulted in biweekly newsreels that averaged about ten to fifteen minutes in length. About 152 of these brief newsreels were released in Great Britain during World War I. *Battle of the Somme* proved to be the most influential and provocative British film of the war because it was the first motion picture to display actual footage from the battlefield. The opening scenes of *Battle of the Somme* featured the preparation for the offensive and the preliminary bombardment. This portion of the film was targeted directly at the British working class. The contribution of munitions workers to the war effort is illustrated by images of shells being unpacked from crates, loaded into artillery pieces of various sizes, and fired across no man's land. This is accompanied by a caption commending the British munitions industry. The climax of the film arrives in the attack sequences. The battleground riddled with shell holes, the wounded being carried to safety, sheepish German prisoners being ushered to the rear, and dead soldiers being buried in mass graves are all featured here. The most controversial moments unfold during this portion of *Battle of the Somme.* In one scene, several soldiers emerge out of a trench, and two of them tumble to the ground and lie motionless. Two more soldiers fall while crossing no man's land in the very next sequence. Crowds sat uncharacteristically quiet, some audience members to burst into tears, and others stormed out of movie houses as these images passed before their eyes. Ironically, these segments were staged, but they provided a sobering contrast to the scenes of British soldiers smiling and waving at the camera that were commonly shown in newsreels. Those with "Victorian" sensitivities felt that *Battle of the Somme* was in poor taste; they believed that the film had gone beyond the boundaries of what a motion picture should be: entertainment. Those who had lost loved ones in the war came to the film's defense, and claimed that it helped them to understand the sacrifices made by those close to them.

After the controversy caused by *Battle of the Somme,* the War Office removed scenes showing dead and wounded soldiers from future official war films prior to their release. This caused the British public to lose interest in the films by 1917. *The Battle of Ancre and the Advance of the Tanks* opened in January 1917. Initially, audiences flocked to movie houses to see the British Army's newest weapon in action, but the novelty of the tank and attendance figures soon declined. *The German Retreat and the Battle of Arras,* released in June 1917, was a financial disaster. With official war films no longer drawing audiences or money, the War Office Cinematograph Committee, then chaired by William Maxwell Aitken, Lord Beaverbrook, decided to return to producing newsreels. By that time, however, the cinema had played its role in bringing the realities of World War I across the English Channel to the British people, and the potential of the motion picture as an instrument of propaganda was realized.

Jeffrey LaMonica

See also: Propaganda (UK, WWI)

REFERENCES

Brownlow, Kevin. *The War, the West, and the Wilderness.* New York: Alfred A. Knopf, 1979.

Hynes, Samuel. *A War Imagined: The First World War and English Culture.* New York: Antheneum, 1991.

Marwick, Arthur. *The Deluge: British Society and the First World War.* New York: W. W. Norton, 1965.

Reeves, Nicholas. "Cinema, Spectatorship, and Propaganda: *Battle of the Somme* 1916 and Its Contemporary Audience." *Historical Journal of Film, Radio, and Television* 17, no. 1 (1997): 11.

———. "Official British Film Propaganda." In *The First World War and Popular Cinema: 1914 to the Present,* ed. Michael Paris, 27. New Brunswick, NJ: Rutgers University Press, 1999.

———. *The Power of Film Propaganda: Myth or Reality?* New York: Cassell, 1999.

Sillars, Stuart. *Art and Survival in First World War Britain.* New York: St. Martin's Press, 1987.

Sorlin, Pierre. "Cinema and the Memory of the Great War." In *The First World War and Popular Cinema: 1914 to the Present,* ed. Michael Paris, 12. New Brunswick, NJ: Rutgers University Press, 1999.

Steed, Andrew. "British Propaganda and the First World War." In *War, Culture, and the Media: Representations of the Military in 20th Century Britain,* ed. Susan L. Carruthers and Ian Stewart, 32. Madison, WI: Fairleigh Dickinson Press, 1996.

Film (U.S.)

Motion pictures have long enjoyed a symbiotic relationship with American culture. During World War I, film became a mirror of America's hopes, fears, and concerns about the conflict. Motion pictures became increasingly popular and influential in the years between the beginning of the European conflict and the Armistice. Audiences paid to see movies about and related to the conflict and, in 1917, Hollywood itself became part of the U.S. propaganda machine.

The motion picture industry had its start in 1894 with the appearance of the Edison Kinetoscope, an invention capable of showing short lengths of film. Within a few years, nickel theaters, or "nickelodeons," showed longer films to enthusiastic audiences. As demand for films increased, the business expanded from the east coast to the west with Hollywood, California, emerging as the industry's unofficial capitol. Motion pictures could be fictional (westerns, romances, adventures, etc.) but educational and informational films were also produced and distributed across the country.

The advent of the war in Europe in 1914 provided a further boon to Hollywood. France and Germany, the former leaders in the film industry, produced few motion pictures during the war. This allowed the United States to take the lead in production. War, particularly past European wars, became a popular subject matter with American audiences, as did footage of American volunteers fighting in Europe. The average three-to-six month production process allowed filmmakers to respond to national and international events in a timely manner. By 1916, motion pictures had begun to reflect the societal debate about a possible U.S. entry into the conflict. As many Americans began to advocate U.S. preparedness for war, films such as *The Battle Cry of Peace* (1915) and *The Nation's Peril* (1915) reflected these concerns by playing out tales of a United States invaded by foreign enemies. Other films, such as Thomas Ince's *Civilization* (1916), took firm antiwar stances with plots conveying the carnage and futility of battle.

As soon as the United States entered the war in the spring of 1917, the film industry and filmgoers became the most enthusiastic of patriots. The film industry, fearing it might be deemed nonessential and shut down for the duration, made itself an indispensable part of the war effort. Its trade association, the National Associa-

tion of the Motion Pictures Industry (NAMPI) assigned experienced industry personnel to the War Department, Navy Department, Department of Agriculture, and other government offices through its new War Cooperation Committee. Motion picture houses ensured their own survival by putting up pro-American displays, featuring the singing of patriotic songs before shows and seeking out films appropriate to the public's new prowar sentiment. German documentary films on the conflict all but disappeared, but official French and British documentaries such as *Fighting for France* (1916) and *The Battle of the Somme* (1916) drew huge crowds. Hollywood stars such as Mary Pickford, Douglas Fairbanks, Charlie Chaplin, and William S. Hart did their part for the war effort by appearing in pro-American feature films, participating in Liberty Loan drives, and raising money for the Red Cross.

The U.S. government recognized the increasing influence of movies on American life and culture and incorporated film directly into the war effort. The Committee on Public Information (CPI), created in 1917 as a propaganda agency, had a special Division of Films. The CPI used the photographic division of the Army Signal Corps to obtain photographs from Europe. When the results proved disappointing, professional film photographers were drafted into the cause. The Red Cross helped distribute this footage, which made its way into the newsreels that were shown before the feature films. The CPI kept its costs down by utilizing a production facility belonging to the French film company Pathé. It contracted out some of the production to commercial filmmakers, but the CPI also produced its own feature films. Some of these, such as the documentaries *Pershing's Crusaders* (1918) and *Our Colored Fighters* (1918), presented a positive view of American troops. Meanwhile fictional features, such as *The Prussian Cur* (1918) and *The Kaiser, the Beast of Berlin* (1918), were designed to inflame audiences with tales of alleged German atrocities. While Hollywood resented being cut out of some of the profits of filmmaking during the war, it maintained a relatively civil relationship with the CPI's Division of Films.

Censorship also became a key issue in wartime filmmaking. In 1917, the Division of Films insisted that the government censor movies that presented Allied nations in an unfriendly light. With the passage of the Espionage Act of 1917 and the Sedition Act in 1918, restrictions on free speech, including film, grew even tighter. The CPI also decided which films could be exported to audiences in other countries. It refused to export films that might damage the image of the United States or her allies abroad.

The outbreak of influenza in the fall of 1918 dealt a blow to the motion picture business as well as the larger war effort. In an attempt to halt the spread of the deadly disease, many movie houses shut down, and the industry ground to a halt for several months.

After the Armistice, the CPI continued to produce official war documentaries, including the eight-episode *Made in America* (1919) series. As Americans struggled to come to terms with the meaning of the conflict, audiences lost interest in prowar films. By the 1920s, the war itself became a popular source for fictionalized film plots. These movies stressed realism—and often ambivalence—over blind patriotism. As World War II approached, however, filmmakers rediscovered themes of redemption and valor in war pictures. These themes became prominent in films following the U.S. entry into that conflict.

The American film industry emerged from World War I as a major business, its nickelodeon past firmly behind it. A trip to the movies was now a respectable form of entertainment for millions of Americans. Perhaps most significant of all, it was now American films, American actors, and American production companies that dominated the industry, a trend that has continued to the present day.

Eileen V. Wallis

See also: Censorship (WWI); Committee on Public Information (WWI); Propaganda (U.S., WWI); Biographies: Bara, Theda (WWI); Chaplin, Charlie (WWI); Fairbanks Sr., Douglas (WWI); Griffith, D. W. (WWI); Hart, William S. (WWI); Keaton, Buster (WWI); Lloyd, Harold (WWI); Pickford, Mary (WWI)

REFERENCES

Campbell, Craig W. *Reel America and World War I: A Comprehensive Filmography and History of Motion Pictures in the United States, 1914–1920.* Jefferson, NC: McFarland, 1985.

DeBauche, Leslie Midkiff. *Reel Patriotism: The Movies and World War One.* Madison: University of Wisconsin Press, 1997.

Kennedy, David M. *Over Here: The First World War and American Society.* New York: Oxford University Press, 1980.

Paris, Michael, ed. *The First World War and Popular Cinema, 1914 to the Present.* New Brunswick, NJ: Rutgers University Press, 1999.

Food Administration

The U.S. Food Administration was one of the most important agencies established by the Wilson administration during World War I. It marked a major extension of federal authority, and encouraging and controlling food production made a significant contribution to the war effort.

In 1917, the problem of food supplies and prices in the United States reached crisis proportions. Poor harvests in 1916 and again in

1917, coupled with the huge demand for exports to Britain and France, created shortages and rapidly increasing prices. Between 1914 and 1917, food prices had risen by 82 percent. Wheat, sugar, and pork were particularly badly affected. In response to this situation, President Wilson presented Congress with legislation to implement regulation through a new agency rather than increase the powers of the Agriculture Department. Initially Congress delayed passage of the bill and Wilson used his authority under the Army Appropriations Act to appoint Herbert Hoover as food administrator in May 1917. The Lever Food and Fuel Act, finally passed on August 10, 1917, established

the Food Administration to ensure adequate production and control the price and supply of food and feeds in the United States during the war. The act also prohibited the use of food in the production of "distilled spirits for beverage purposes."

According to the *New York Tribune* (August 9, 1917), the Food Act marked "the longest step toward socialism ever taken by the American Congress." Appointed head of the Administration, Hoover stimulated production by setting "fair" prices and purchasing entire crops of certain commodities, such as wheat, sugar, and hogs through government corporations like the Grain Corporation. However, he refused to

The Food Administration helped coordinate food production and supply during World War I. Here an administration worker lectures on food conservation in Newark, New Jersey. (National Archives)

introduce rationing, which he regarded as "Prussianization." Rather than "dictatorship," the Food Administration relied upon voluntary cooperation mobilized by a massive program of exhortation and propaganda urging self-denial and self-sacrifice. Using the slogan "Food will win the war," the population was urged to conserve food supplies and observe "wheatless, meatless and porkless" days. Hoover's team, working through state committees, enlisted the aid of 750,000 volunteers, particularly women, in local committees and organizations behind this effort. Consumers were urged to utilize scraps and use substitutes for wheat flour such as buckwheat and corn flour. As a result, consumption of sugar and wheat fell and food exports rose by more than 50 percent.

Abolished in 1919, the Food Administration was regarded as one of the great successes of the war and it helped to make Hoover a household name. However, in encouraging an expansion of food production, the wartime policies also contributed to the creation of surpluses. High prices could not be maintained after the war and, with the withdrawal of government controls, many farmers were plunged into a ruinous situation.

Neil Alan Wynn

See also: Agriculture (WWI); Fuel Administration (WWI); Biographies: Hoover, Herbert (WWI)

REFERENCES

Cuff, Robert D. "Herbert Hoover, the Ideology of Voluntarism and War Organization during the Great War." *Journal of American History* 44 (September 1977): 358–372.

Eisner, Marc Allen. *From Warfare State to Welfare State: World War I, Compensatory State Building, and the Limits of the Modern Order.* University Park: Pennsylvania State University Press, 2000.

Hibbard, Benjamin. *Effects of the Great War upon Agriculture in the United States and Great Britain.* Carnegie Endowment for International Peace, Preliminary Economic Studies of the War, no. 11. New York: Oxford University Press, 1919.

Hoover, Herbert C. *The Memoirs of Herbert Hoover: The Years of Adventure, 1874–1920.* New York: Macmillan, 1952.

Kennedy, David M. *Over Here: The First World War and American Society.* New York: Oxford University Press, 1980.

Mullendore, William Clinton. *A History of the United States Food Administration, 1917–1919.* Stanford, CA: Stanford University Press, 1941.

Soule, George. *Prosperity Decade: A Chapter from American Economic History, 1917–1929.* London: Pilot Press, 1947.

Wynn, Neil A. *From Progressivism to Prosperity: World War I and American Society.* New York: Holmes and Meier, 1986.

Fourteen Points

The Fourteen Points were a set of ideal proposals grouped under fourteen separate headings that spelled out the essential elements for a peaceful settlement of World War I that President Woodrow Wilson presented during a speech to a joint session of the U.S. Congress on January 8, 1918.

The essence of the Fourteen Points was: (1) Open covenants of peace openly arrived at, with no secret diplomatic agreements in the future; (2) Absolute freedom of navigation upon the sea; (3) The removal of all economic barriers and the establishment of an equality of trade conditions; (4) Adequate guarantees that national armaments would be reduced to the lowest point; (5) A free, open-minded, and absolutely impartial adjustment of all colonial claims; (6) The evacuation of German troops from all Russian territory and such a settlement of all questions affecting Russia; (7) The evacuation of German troops from Belgium and the country should be restored without any attempt to limit the sovereignty; (8) All French territory should be freed from German troops and the invaded portions restored; (9) A readjustment of the frontiers of Italy should be effected along clearly recognizable lines of nationality; (10) The peoples of Austria-Hungary should be accorded the freest opportunity of autonomous development; (11) The evacuation of German troops from Rumania, Serbia, and Montenegro, and occupied territories should be restored; (12) The Turkish portions of the present Ottoman Empire should be assured a secure sovereignty while other nationalities must have autonomous development, and the Dardanelles should be permanently opened as a free passage; (13) An independent Polish state should be erected with the territories inhabited by indisputably Polish populations; and (14) A general association of nations must be formed.

The Fourteen Points primarily consists of three parts: first, a set of general ideal principles to manage postwar international relations as outlined in points One through Five; second, a series of concrete recommendations for adjusting postwar boundaries and for establishing new nations as described in points Six through Thirteen; third, as insisted by Wilson, establishment of a League of Nations that Wilson felt would be indispensable for implementing the other proposals and building a new world order in the post-World War I period.

The United States entered World War I in April 1917. By publicly articulating the Fourteen Points, Wilson tried to undermine the morale of the Central Powers to continue fighting by guaranteeing national independence and self-determination for the people of all nations fighting throughout all of the war. At the same time, Wilson's lofty vision of a peaceful and stable world based upon self-determina-tion, the League of Nations, and a liberal trade system stood in sharp contrast to the revolutionary appeals Soviet Russia was making to exploited peoples.

At the beginning of October 1918, Prince Maximilian of Baden, the German imperial chancellor, sent a request to Wilson via Switzerland for an immediate armistice and the opening of peace negotiations on the basis of the Fourteen Points. The Paris Peace Conference was held in order to establish a permanent peaceful world. The so-called Big Four led the conference: Woodrow Wilson for the United States, Georges Clemenceau for France, David Lloyd George for Great Britain, and Vittorio Emanuele Orlando for Italy. The idealistic principles contained in the Fourteen Points constituted the basis for peace negotiations, but the European powers were strongly opposed to the Fourteen Points because they were primarily interested in gaining territory and war reparations from Germany. The Treaty of Versailles, the result of the peace conference, placed all responsibility for the war on the shoulders of Germany and its allies, and imposed the burden of reparations payments on Germany. The treaty also made Germany forfeit its overseas colonies. Germany was allowed to have a maximum of 100,000 soldiers and the German navy was severely reduced. In addition, Germany was forbidden to build major weapons of aggression. In order to secure support for the most important clause of the Fourteen Points, the creation of a League of Nations, Wilson was forced to make compromises during negotiations that led up to the agreement on the Treaty of Versailles. Germans felt betrayed when the treaty nullified the ideals of the Fourteen Points and imposed harsh terms and conditions on Germany. After futile protests to the Allies, Germany grudgingly accepted the treaty, which took effect in January 1920.

Yoneyuki Sugita

See also: League of Nations (WWI); Paris Peace Conference (WWI); Biographies: Lloyd George, David (WWI); Wilson, Woodrow (WWI)

REFERENCES

Howard, Michael Eliot. *The First World War.* New York: Oxford University Press, 2002.

Macmillan, Margaret Olwen. *Paris 1919: Six Months That Changed the World.* New York: Random House, 2002.

Fuel Administration

The Fuel Administration was one of the many emergency agencies formed to handle the crisis of World War I. It may have been the most successful in creating stability in prices and in promoting cooperation between fuel producers, workers, and government regulators. The Fuel Administration's policies and structure influenced later federal agencies designed to ensure a steady flow of fuel to consumers.

The Fuel Administration was created by President Woodrow Wilson on August 23, 1917, under the authority granted him by the Lever Act. Wilson selected fellow historian and college president Harry A. Garfield to head up the new agency. Garfield was the son of assassinated president James Garfield and had maintained relations with Washington insiders most of his life. He faced a daunting task, since Wilson had charged the Fuel Administration with five major tasks. These included encouraging the maximum possible production of coal and oil; restricting the consumption of fuel by civilians and industries that did not contribute to the war effort; promoting the voluntary conservation of fuels; regulating the distribution of coal by dividing the country into different zones; and, regulating fuel prices to curb inflation and prevent shortages and speculation. Garfield used a combination of methods to achieve his goal. The Fuel Administration educated the public about the need to conserve, while also encouraging the voluntary cooperation between producers in order to maximize production. Garfield rarely used the power to close down inefficient producers, but he reminded industry leaders of his ability to do so.

Garfield devoted most of his efforts to bituminous coal, the most commonly used fuel in the World War I-era United States. His agency issued posters and press releases urging Americans to use less coal by keeping their houses cooler than usual. He also instituted the idea of Heatless Thursdays, on which no coal would be used to heat their homes. Other posters encouraged miners to work harder to produce more coal. Garfield met with industry leaders and tried to get them to pool their resources for greater efficiency, even though this action may have violated antitrust laws.

Before Garfield took office, Wilson had personally set a maximum price for coal. Under pressure from both workers and producers, Garfield gradually allowed coal prices to inch upward. He was careful, however, not to allow producers to make overly large profits or to keep wages from increasing as profits increased. Garfield's administration of the coal industry created a stability that owners and workers had never enjoyed before. While other industries were hampered by unrest, the coal sector remained peaceful during the war.

The greatest crisis Garfield faced as the Fuel Administration director was in the winter of 1917–1918. The winter was the coldest in history, and the demand for fuel was greater than usual. Wartime demands added to the strains on the U.S. railroads, causing them to break down. A shortage of cars suitable to carry coal also existed. The head of the Railroad Administration assigned other products higher priority on the railroads than coal enjoyed and, as a result, by Christmas 1917, many cities in the Northeast were nearly out of coal for power and heat. Terrified Americans in Ohio tore up the tracks to keep trains from taking coal to other cities so they could use it. Ice on the east coast prevented shipments of coal by water. Garfield recognized action had to be taken by the beginning of 1918. He convinced Wilson to give coal a higher priority than any other goods on the railroads. He also devised an extreme plan to conserve the supplies available. Using his power under the Lever Act, Garfield issued an order on January 17, 1918, closing all industries east of the Mississippi that used bituminous coal and were not essential to the war effort. The plants were closed for five days. Garfield also ordered that the plants be closed every Monday for the next two months. By issuing this order, Garfield reduced the amount of coal needed, and he also reduced the backlog of manufactured goods that needed to be moved, freeing up railroad cars. He asked manufacturers to pay workers their normal wages, but most did not. Although many Americans had their wages reduced, most accepted the necessity with good humor.

While Garfield spent most of his time with the coal industry, he also recognized the growing importance of oil as a fuel. He convinced Wilson to create an Oil Division within the Fuel Administration. On January 11, 1918, Wilson appointed Mark Requa as the director. Requa worked with oil corporation executives to devise a fair schedule of prices and to plan for increased production. He also used his power under the Lever Act to cancel purchase contracts with individuals and to divert additional oil to government use. Requa encouraged research on increasing production and improved distribution of existing stores. Programs to encourage the conservation of oil were conducted, similar to those for coal.

The Fuel Administration ceased to exist on June 30, 1919. Although not spectacular, the Administration had achieved a high degree of success. Improved cooperation and integration in the coal and oil industries had ensured adequate supplies for both private and military consumers. The model established by the Fuel Administration influenced later government efforts to regulate fuels. President Calvin Coolidge created the Federal Oil Conservation Board in 1924, based upon the Fuel Administration. The Oil Code of the National Recovery Administration in 1933 owed much to Garfield's work. During the next wars, agencies similar to the Fuel Administration were created. The Petroleum Administration for War during World War II and the Petroleum Defense Administration during the Korean War were based upon the Fuel Administration.

Tim J. Watts

See also: Economic Policy (WWI); Mobilization (U.S., WWI); Biographies: Garfield, Harry (WWI)

REFERENCES

Cuff, Robert. "Harry Garfield, the Fuel Administration, and the Search for a Cooperative Order during World War I." *American Quarterly* 30 (Spring 1978): 39–53.

Johnson, James P. *The Politics of Soft Coal: The Bituminous Industry from World War I through the New Deal.* Urbana: University of Illinois Press, 1979.

Nash, Gerald D. *U.S. Oil Policy, 1890–1964.* Pittsburgh, PA: University of Pittsburgh Press, 1968.

G

German Americans

On the eve of World War I, German Americans were one quarter of all first- and second-generation Americans and almost 9 percent of the entire U.S. population. Germans had been migrating to the United States since the colonial period, and the diversity of the German American population in the beginning of the twentieth century reflected the variety of motivations they had for immigrating as well as the different times of immigration and parts of Germany from which they had come. World War I was a time of intense scrutiny of German American identity and pressure to assimilate.

In the early twentieth century, many German Americans maintained their group identification through German American organizations including churches, singing groups, and clubs, and there was a strong tradition of German-language publication. The National German-American Alliance, established as an umbrella organization in 1907 to promote cultural interests, had a membership of more than two million in 1914. When German American voters unified, it was often to fight nativism, support German-language education, and oppose prohibition and Sunday observance laws.

Between 1914 and 1917, before the U.S. declaration of war, German-language publications sought to increase public sympathy for Germany and campaigned against what they saw as an U.S. pro-British stance masquerading as neutrality. The German-American Alliance lobbied against policies favoring England, organized demonstrations, promoted Imperial war bonds, and collected for German relief funds. However, increasing anxiety about German American loyalty as the war wore on made such efforts unacceptable to many Americans.

The phrase "hyphenated Americans" came into popular use in the 1910s and, by 1915, it was largely a disparaging synonym for German Americans that connoted political divisiveness. In the presidential election campaign of 1916, both Hughes and Wilson attempted to distance themselves from "the hyphen vote." Wilson did so more consistently and Hughes was labeled the German candidate. Roosevelt spoke most strongly against the un-American hyphenates and railed against the disloyalty of "professional German-Americans." Election results show that German Americans did not vote as a bloc and that local issues played a larger factor in their preferences.

Upon the declaration of war against Germany, many Americans feared that U.S. citizens of German birth or ancestry maintained connections to the German government and schemed against the United States. Fall 1917 to spring 1918 saw the height of anti-German American activity. Although the targets of investigations by the American Protective League, the National Security League, and state councils of defense included people of all backgrounds, German Americans felt particular pressure to demonstrate their loyalty. Politicians made distinctions between Americans of German origins and immigrants of divided loyalties; however, the distinction was vague and remarks were often seen as an attack on anyone who retained ties with German culture. Cartoons, articles, and sermons against "the hyphen" proliferated.

Suspicions of German Americans led to mob violence against them, including beatings, tar-and-feathering parties, and at least one lynching—the April 1918 lynching of Robert Prager in Collinsville, Illinois. There are reports from across the country of German Americans physically forced to display their loyalty through public acts of patriotism, such as saluting or kissing the U.S. flag. For the most part, attacks against "the hyphen" were focused on the cultural elements: German musical instruments and books were destroyed, sauerkraut was renamed "liberty cabbage," towns and organizations were renamed, German music was prohibited, schools refused to teach the German language, and German-language publications were banned or failed. There were even some short-lived prohibitions against speaking German in public. In response, organizations made efforts to demonstrate patriotism or to remain inconspicuous, and many German societies ceased holding public meetings. Most German-language publications had been shifting from strong pro-German positions to support for U.S. involvement on the Allied side since the U.S. declaration of war. Despite re-

peated pledges of war support from national and local chapters, a 1918 act of Congress repealed the charter of the once-powerful German-American Alliance.

The anti-German sentiment of World War I accelerated the assimilation of most German American groups, intensifying a process that had already begun by the end of the nineteenth century. Many churches stopped giving services in German during the war and did not restart after 1918. German American clubs never regained prewar membership and the number of German-language publications was never as high. However, Germans were favored by postwar nativist immigration restrictions that set quotas based upon historical immigration patterns.

Lisa Schreibersdorf

See also: American Protective League (WWI); Americanization Campaign; Immigration (U.S., WWI); National Security League (WWI)

REFERENCES

Luebke, Frederick C. *Bonds of Loyalty: German Americans and World War I.* De Kalb: Northern Illinois University Press, 1974.

Wittke, Carl. *German-Americans and the World War: With Special Emphasis on Ohio's German-Language Press.* Columbus: Ohio State Archaeological and Historical Society, 1934.

Great Migration

The "Great Migration" was the description given to the large-scale movement of African Americans from Southern states to Northern industrial centers during World War I. Although small in comparison to the movement that occurred during World War II, this migration brought a shift in focus for African American social and political organizations and is often regarded as a watershed in African American history. However, it also resulted in social and economic conflict leading to rioting and violence in the "Red Summer" of 1919.

Demographics

When the war in Europe broke out in 1914, over 90 percent of the African American population lived in the former Confederate states of the South, mainly engaged in agricultural production, generally as sharecroppers or tenant farmers. Although theoretically guaranteed the vote and equal rights as citizens under the Fourteenth and Fifteenth Amendments, in reality African Americans in the South experienced economic, political, and social discrimination. Laws requiring racial segregation in all places of public accommodation (transport, schools, hospitals, places of entertainment, etc.), introduced throughout the South from the 1880s onward, established a system of separation know as "Jim Crow." At the same time, legislation introducing literacy tests, "grandfather" clauses, and poll taxes were passed to exclude African Americans from the polling stations. These legal devices were reinforced with violence and intimidation: Between 1880 and 1917 more than 3,000 African Americans were lynched. In the years just before World War I, the poverty and economic hardship of the Southern African American population also increased as a consequence of natural disaster, floods, and the ravishes of the boll weevil that destroyed cotton crops.

As war industries boomed in the United States during World War I and the traditional sources of immigrant factory labor fell from a prewar level of over a million to 100,000, new employment opportunities opened up for African Americans. Faced with the increased labor shortages in the North, industrial labor agents set out to recruit African American workers from the South. Equally influential was the African American press, particularly the *Chicago Defender* and the *Crisis* (the journal of the National Association for the Advancement of Colored People [NAACP]), which called upon the African American population to escape Southern discrimination and segregation for a better life in the North. The National Urban League (NUL) also provided assistance in finding jobs and homes, especially in Chicago.

Earlier African American migrants also wrote letters home telling of the opportunities in the North where one could earn five dollars in only a day compared to the five dollars a week in the South. They also wrote of the greater social freedom and opportunities. As a consequence, many African American families and communities organized themselves and moved en masse to the "Promised Land" in response to the new possibilities and in protest against the poverty and hardship of Southern life. In the process of movement, the African American migrants rejected the accommodationist position of the late-nineteenth century black leader Booker T. Washington, who had famously urged African Americans to make their life in the South. Approximately 400,000 African Americans, about 5 percent of the African American Southern population—many of them now from the Deep South rather than just the border states—migrated to Northern industrial centers between 1915 and 1920, compared to the normal average of 67,000 per decade between 1870 and 1910. In total, thirteen Southern states suffered a net loss in population, the biggest in Mississippi of 75,000. Over 65,000 moved to Chicago alone. New York City, Detroit, and Philadelphia also attracted huge numbers as "northern fever" gripped the South. At one point, it was estimated that 1,000 African American migrants were arriving in Detroit per month, and in total the African American population of that city increased by over 600 percent between 1910 and 1920.

Racial Violence

The North proved to be far from a "promised land," as the new workers crowded into already congested ghettos such as Harlem in New York or the Southside in Chicago, leading to problems of overcrowding and competition for jobs. While white Southerners, fearful of the loss of their labor force and anxious that migration might disturb existing racial patterns, tried to halt migration, Northerners too often responded negatively to the influx. Many white workers saw African Americans as strike breakers, or as a possible cause of reduced wages, or even a direct threat to their jobs. Residential and social segregation, although not sanctioned by law as in the South, increased as a result of restrictive housing covenants as well as custom and practice. Attempts to move into new areas was often met with an aggressive response. The resultant tensions led to an increase in race violence. In 1917, more than forty African Americans and eleven whites were killed in a race riot that swept East St. Louis, a major rail terminus that had witnessed an increase of 10,000 in its African American population. Worse was to follow when riots broke out in Chicago, Washington, D.C., and more than a dozen other towns ranging from Charleston, South Carolina, to Longview, Texas, in the "Red Summer" of 1919. In Chicago, twenty-three African American and fifteen white people were killed in the week-long riot that broke out on July 27 after an

African American youth was stoned by white men and drowned at the lakeside. Nine African Americans were killed the previous week in the riot that disrupted the nation's capital. More than eighty African Americans, some still in military uniform, were lynched in 1919.

The wartime and postwar racial conflict was part of a wider response to the social and economic upheavals brought by the war and reflected the struggle to redefine relations between the different races. However, the migration did lead to greater job opportunities and higher earnings, and marked the development of an African American industrial working class. The number of African Americans in industrial occupations almost doubled, from 550,000 to 901,000, between 1910 and 1920. In Chicago, the proportion of African American workers employed in domestic service was very nearly halved as more and more found work in meatpacking, the steel industry, and also in automobile manufacturing. Out of the violence, too, grew a mood of defiance and resistance articulated in the new urban centers by the "New Negro." This was reflected in increased membership of the NAACP, the rise of the African American separatist movement led by Marcus Garvey, (the UNIA), and a celebration of African American culture and race pride in the literary and artistic movement known as the Harlem Renaissance in the 1920s. The movement of African Americans continued as the economy continued to expand and immigration controls were introduced in 1921 and 1924. Between 800,000 and 1 million left the South in the 1920s and, by 1930, the percentage of African Americans living in the South had fallen to about 75 percent.

By 1930, the African American urban population numbered more than 5 million, and the proportion of the African American population classified as urban had risen from 27 percent in 1910 to 34 percent in 1920 and 43 percent in 1930. This African American urban population was to have an increasingly significant impact on politics, particularly in Northern cities. In 1920, approximately 40 percent of the African American northern population was concentrated in three cities—New York, Chicago, and Philadelphia. Their influence was to be reflected during the 1930s in the changing policies of the Democratic Party under Franklin Roosevelt's "New Deal." More than this, the vibrant lifestyle and culture of the African American ghetto often appealed to white Americans who were disillusioned with postwar materialism. It was for this reason that the 1920s was sometimes described as the "Jazz Age."

Neil Alan Wynn

See also: African Americans (WWI); Jazz (WWI); National Association for the Advancement of Colored People (WWI); National Urban League (WWI)

REFERENCES

Gottlieb, Peter. *Making Their Own Way: Southern Blacks' Migration to Pittsburgh, 1916–1930.* Urbana: University of Illinois Press, 1987.

Griffin, Farah Jasmine. *"Who Set You Flowin'":: The African-American Migration Narrative.* New York: Oxford University Press, 1995.

Grossman, James R. *Land of Hope: Chicago, Black Southerners, and the Great Migration.* Chicago: University of Chicago Press, 1989.

Harrison, Alferteen, ed. *Black Exodus: The Great Migration from the American South.* Jackson: University Press of Mississippi, 1991.

Henri, Florette. *Black Migration: Movement North, 1900–1920.* Garden City, NY: Doubleday/Anchor, 1975.

Lemann, Nicholas. *The Promised Land: The Great Black Migration and How It Changed America.* New York: Alfred A. Knopf, 1991.

Marks, Carole. *Farewell—We're Good and Gone: The Great Black Migration.* Bloomington: Indiana University Press, 1989.

Phillips, Kimberely L. *Alabama North: African-American Migrants, Community, and Working-Class Activism in Cleveland, 1915–45.* Urbana: University of Illinois Press, 1999.

Sernett, Milton C. *Bound for the Promised Land: African American Religion and the Great Migration.* Durham, NC: Duke University Press, 1997.

Spear, Allan H. *Black Chicago: The Making of a Negro Ghetto, 1890–1920.* Chicago: University of Chicago Press, 1967.

Trotter, Joe W., Jr. *Black Milwaukee: The Making of an Industrial Proletariat, 1915–45.* Urbana: University of Illinois Press, 1985.

I

Immigration (U.S.)

World War I significantly reduced immigration into the United States from over one million in 1913 to just over 100,000 in 1917. In the wake of the U.S. entry into the war, many Americans focused on the need for national solidarity. Some Americans questioned whether immigrants, particularly German American immigrants, would sympathize with their home country and threaten the national unity necessary for winning the war. This aggravated nationalism that characterized the war years enhanced the United States' prewar nativist sentiments, and efforts to assimilate, or "Americanize," immigrants increased. It also heightened the feeling that legislation was needed to restrict immigration by establishing nationality quotas.

Before the War

Before the war, the United States was a country that accepted millions of immigrants to its shores every year. From 1900 to 1920, the United States admitted over 14.5 million immigrants, the greatest number since the nation's founding. The source of these immigrants shifted from Northwestern to Southeastern Europe. Americans had always assumed that immigrants would easily and effortlessly Americanize or assimilate into American society, but many Americans expressed concern that the new immigrants were not assimilating. In the prewar years, some Americans lobbied for immigration restrictions.

Only on the eve of the U.S. entry into World War I did the restrictionists manage to swing enough congressional support to override a second Wilsonian veto. The Immigration Law enacted in February 1917 was a comprehensive measure that codified existing legislation, doubled the head tax to $8.00, and added chronic alcoholics, vagrants, and "persons of constitutional psychopathic inferiority" to the list of excluded classes. The statute also established a "barred zone" in the southwest Pacific, thus excluding virtually all Asian immigrants not already debarred by the Chinese Exclusion Act and the Gentlemen's Agreement of 1907. Finally, the law provided for the exclusion of adult aliens unable to read a short passage in English or some other language or dialect. This requirement was not, however, to apply to aliens fleeing from religious persecution, nor was it to prevent admissible aliens from bringing in illiterate members of their immediate families.

Though the demand for the literacy test originated in prewar conditions, its enactment in 1917 was essentially due to the added strength of restrictionism that was derived from the anxieties provoked by the European war. World War I was a major turning point in the history of American nativism. By making Americans aware as never before of the persistence of Old World ties, and thus of their own disunity, the conflict bred a strident demand for a type of loyalty involving complete conformity to the existing national pattern. This manifestation of the nationalist spirit, which came to be generally referred to as "100 percent Americanism," proved to be more than a mere wartime phenomenon. Persisting into the 1920s, it became an essential ingredient of the movement that carried the restrictionists to final victory.

A new insistence upon national solidarity was apparent almost from the start of the European conflict. The German American campaign of 1914–1915 for an embargo on U.S. exports of arms to the belligerents was widely interpreted as a German-inspired attempt to overthrow U.S. neutrality. Complaints of the divided loyalty of the German element developed into a widespread agitation against hyphenated Americans with Theodore Roosevelt and Woodrow Wilson as its leading spokesmen. Although German "tools of the Kaiser" remained the main target for criticism, Irish Americans also incurred a great deal of hostility on account of their rabid pro-Germanism.

It was the Germans, however, who were the main victims of the fresh wave of xenophobia that came in the wake of the U.S. entry into the war. The belligerent nationalism that had earlier characterized the preparedness campaign now erupted in a wave of hysterical anti-Germanism. Despite the fact that the great mass of German Americans loyally supported the declaration of war on Germany, wild rumors circulated of their involvement in spying and sabotage. Excited patriots, now thoroughly infected by the intolerant, coercive spirit of 100 percent Americanism, proclaimed that loyalty demanded the complete eradication of German culture. Accordingly, the teaching of German was in many places prohibited; German music and opera were shunned; the charter of the German-American Alliance was withdrawn; towns, streets, and buildings with German names were rechristened; even sauerkraut became "liberty cabbage," while hamburgers turned into Salisbury steaks.

The concentration of antiforeign sentiment upon the Germans afforded the rest of the foreign-born population a welcome immunity from criticism. Yet doubts remained concerning the loyalty of immigrants generally were demonstrated by the new direction and emphasis given by the war to the Americanization movement. The organized efforts to Americanize the immigrants, which began in the first decade of the twentieth century, originated in a common concern for social unity on the part of a number of divergent groups. A program of immigrant education and assimilation appealed equally to social workers anxious to alleviate the conditions of immigrant life, to employers' associations desirous of improving the economic efficiency of newcomers and of safeguarding against labor unrest, and to patriotic societies worried about the threat to American institutions posed by immigrant ignorance. In the decade before the war, therefore, widespread efforts were made, both by these voluntary groups and by state agencies, to promote immigrant welfare and education by means of pamphlets, lectures, and evening classes.

Americanization Movement Changes

With the rise of wartime nationalism, the Americanization Movement underwent a rapid metamorphosis. From 1915 onward, the Americanization of the immigrant became a patriotic duty, absorbing the energies of thousands of schools, churches, fraternal orders, patriotic societies, and civic and business organizations. In their anxiety to promote national unity, zealous patriots subjected immigrant groups to a high-pressure sales campaign designed to promote naturalization and the learning of English and to inculcate knowledge of and respect for American institutions and ideals. These had been among the aims of the prewar Americanizers, too, but it was not until American nationalists began to demand a completely conformist loyalty that the effort to teach immigrants things like personal hygiene and industrial safety was jettisoned in favor of persuading them to forget their Old World heritage. Many immigrants reacted bitterly. They felt humiliated at the suggestion that their cherished ways of life were proof of their inferiority. Having evolved from an instrument of social welfare into one of social solidarity, the Americanization movement did survive briefly into the postwar era to play its part in the crusade against Bolshevism. During the course of the war, the movement had become increasingly frenzied and intolerant and, with the arrival of the Red Scare, it fell completely under the domination of the superpatriots.

Michael McGregor

See also: Alien Act (WWI); Americanization Campaign (WWI); German Americans (WWI); Latinos and Latinas (WWI)

REFERENCES

Archdeacon, Thomas J. *Becoming American: An Ethnic History.* New York: Free Press, 1983.

Daniels, Roger. *Coming to America: A History of Immigration and Ethnicity in American Life,* New York: Harper Collins, 1991.

Highams, John. *Strangers in the Land.* New Brunswick, NJ: Rutgers University Press, 1988.

Kennedy, David. M. *Over Here: The First World War and American Society.* New York: Oxford University Press, 1980.

Industrial Workers of the World

The Industrial Workers of the World (IWW) was a radical national labor union for unskilled workers—often unorganized and ignored by the traditional trade unions of the early twentieth century—that was founded in 1905 but faded into obscurity in the early 1920s.

The main federation of those trade unions, the American Federation of Labor, was committed to craft unionism working within a capitalist system. Many of the craft unions refused membership to immigrant workers, and the AFL in general rejected the idea of one big union of the skilled and the unskilled workers alike. In 1905, the Western Federation of Miners, along with forty-two other organizations, opposed to the AFL's approach combined into the radical Industrial Workers of the World, which became known as the IWW or, as it was more popularly known, the "Wobblies."

The IWW was a union of the unskilled workers. Its membership included lumber workers in the Northwest, dockworkers in port cities, and wheat harvesters in the central states. It also attracted miners and textile workers. Additionally, it was open to immigrant workers. Many of the IWW leaders were first- and second-generation immigrants. Among them were the Irish-born union organizer and United Mine Workers official Mary "Mother" Jones (1830-1930); the Virgin Islands–born socialist intellectual, writer, and black nationalist Hubert Harrison (1883-1927); Italian-born editor of an antifascist newspaper Carlo Tresca (1879-

1943); Italian-born socialist Arturo Giovannitti (1882-1959); and Swedish-born socialist, union organizer, and songwriter Joe Haaglund Hill (1882-1915). The three most important leaders were William Haywood (1869-1928), the Dutch-born Daniel De Leon (1852-1914), and Eugene V. Debs (1855-1926).

From their inception, the Wobblies combined two contradictory impulses. Socialists such as Debs and De Leon (representing two separate socialist parties) supported political action through trade unionism, collective bargaining, and the Socialist Party's goal of a workers' state. William Haywood led the syndicalist group that rejected the legitimacy of the state in any form. This faction supported the boycott, general strike, and—opponents charged—sabotage as tools to change the system. In 1908, the socialists lost the battle for control of the IWW and left the organization.

The IWW advocated direct action. Over its life, it engaged in approximately 150 strikes. It supported miners at Goldfield, Nevada, in 1906–1907, textile workers in Lawrence, Massachusetts, in 1912, and silk workers at Paterson, New Jersey, in 1913. Other strikes were of iron miners in the Mesabi Range of Minnesota in 1916, lumbermen in the northwest in 1917, the Seattle general strike of 1919, and a strike of miners in Colorado in 1927–1928. Membership before World War I ranged between 30,000 and 100,000.

The IWW and its opponents were sometimes violent. In 1914, Joe Haaglund Hill was convicted of murdering a Salt Lake City businessman. The evidence was circumstantial, but mass protests failed to prevent Hill's execution by firing squad on November 19, 1915. Frank Little, another IWW leader, was lynched in Butte, Montana, in 1917, either for his union-organizing activities or his antiwar views.

Because of its position against war and militarism, the IWW opposed the entry of the United States into World War I. Opponents accused members of evading the draft, and the IWW itself was charged with being in the pay of the Germans to start strikes to aid the enemy by crippling war industries. Sabotage and criminal syndicalism were illegal activities that opponents alleged the IWW engaged in. Under the 1917 Espionage Act, which mandated fines of up to $10,000 and imprisonment of up to twenty years for interference with military recruitment or the disclosing of defense information to the enemy and that had additional penalties for refusal of military service, William Haywood and other IWW leaders (a total of 166 Wobblies) were subject to prison for speaking against the war. Convicted and facing a $30,000 fine and twenty years in prison, Haywood appealed. On bail pending appeal, Haywood fled to Russia, where he stayed until he died and received burial in Red Square.

The war's end and the Russian Revolution of 1917, which brought a communist government to that country, shifted the hyper-American patriotism from the wartime enemy to the older socialist bogeyman. During the Red Scare of 1919, police and legal authorities harassed IWW members. Lynching, deportation, and widespread persecution forced the IWW onto the defensive. In 1924, the eastern and western arms of the IWW split over the issue of centralization and, by 1925, membership was small. The IWW does persist, although as a faint shadow of what it was before World War I.

The IWW failed—aside from the repression of the war and postwar years—because most of its members were casual laborers, migratory and hard to hold together as a cohesive effective labor organization. By 1930, it had fewer than 10,000 members, and, in the mid 1990s, its membership was below 1,000.

John H. Barnhill

See also: Anarchists (WWI); Civil Liberties Bureau (WWI); Espionage Act (WWI); Red Scare (WWI); Seattle General Strike (WWI); Sedition Act (WWI); Socialist Party (WWI); Strikes, Labor (WWI); Trade Unions, (U.S., WWI); Vigilantism (WWI); Biographies: Heywood, William "Big Bill" (WWI)

REFERENCES

Dubofsky, Melvyn A. *We Shall Be All: A History of the Industrial Workers of the World,* 2d ed. Urbana: University of Illinois Press, 1988.

Renshaw, Patrick. *The Wobblies: The Story of Syndicalism in the United States.* Garden City, NY: Doubleday, 1967.

Thompson, Fred. *The I.W.W.: Its First Fifty Years.* Chicago: Industrial Workers of the World, 1955.

Influenza Epidemic of 1918

Beginning in the 1880s, the influenza virus was a regular visitor to the United States and Europe, proving deadly to the weakest demographic segments of the population, the elderly, and the very young. In 1918, however, a new form of the disease appeared, possibly resulting from a mutation in China, which combined the virus with the bacteria causing pneumonia. Early outbreaks in Spain led to the name "Spanish Flu" or "the Spanish Lady," but the most serious pandemic outbreaks surfaced in U.S. army training bases in the Midwest. Tragically, this flu attacked a different demographic, proving most deadly to young adults aged twenty to forty, whose own immune systems' reactions to the flu caused their deaths through hemorrhaging, suffocation, and fever.

U.S. soldiers transmitted the flu to the European battlefields, where poor hygiene and crowded conditions encouraged its spread, eventually infecting more than half of all World War I participants. Thought to be a biological agent unleashed by the Germans, the flu caused panic in the ranks of the Allied armies up until the Armistice. With a mortality rate of 50 in every 1,000 infected, the disease seriously hampered demobilization, spreading quickly as soldiers returned home and civilians gathered for parades and homecomings. With little prevention except gauze masks, health providers around the world converted public buildings into makeshift hospitals, and public services like police and fire protection shut down for months during the fall and winter of 1918. Since the deaths occurred most frequently among adolescents and young adults, families faced the tragedy of losing children to both the war and the flu, while fear amongst school children led to chilling nursery rhymes and songs about the flu.

The economic consequences of the flu were enormous as U.S. and European businesses released workers to nurse the sick, and money was diverted to public health services. In the infant nations of Poland, Czechoslovakia, and independent Hungary, the health crisis crippled early attempts to organize politically and financially. The flu even interfered with the Versailles Conference, as Woodrow Wilson's illness during the treaty negotiations may have been an attack of the disease. Perhaps fortunately, Western Europe and the United States, already on war footing, were in a position to impose curfews, implement public health standards, and restrict freedom of movement. In other parts of the world, particularly urban areas of China and India, the flu ran wild, infecting far more than the 28 percent of Americans who caught the flu (approximately 675,000 died in the United States, including 43,000 military servicemen) and accounting for the bulk of the

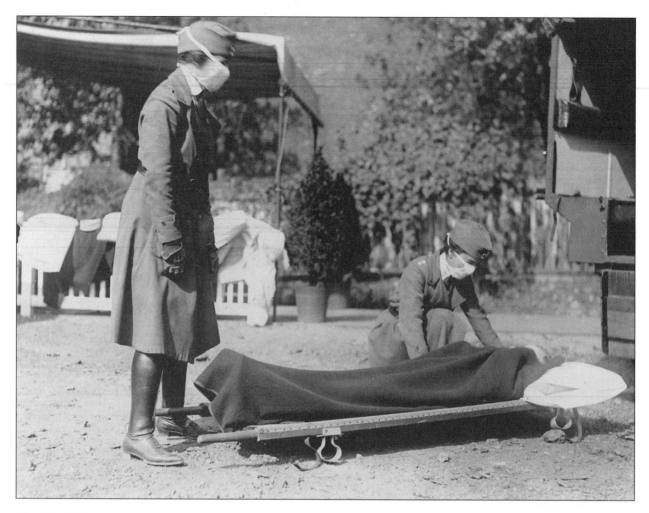

Two Red Cross nurses practice emergency procedures in Washington, D.C., during the post–World War I influenza epidemic. Millions died of the flu in the United States and around the world before the epidemic died out in the early 1920s. (Library of Congress)

20–40 million dead. A year later, this deadly strain of influenza had run its course and disappeared, except in the samples kept by doctors and scientists for further study and the live viruses buried with victims in the frozen ground of Alaska and the Soviet Union.

The intense trauma of the pandemic demographically contributed to the losses suffered in World War I, while also leaving economic problems and deep psychological scars behind. In the United States, the prospect of death through war or disease heightened the sense of urgency fueling the Roaring Twenties, while in Europe, it seemed yet another devastating fallout of the "War to End All Wars."

Margaret Sankey

See also: Demobilization (WWI)

REFERENCES

Beveridge, W. I. B. *Influenza: The Last Great Plague.* New York: Prodist, 1977.

Collier, Richard. *The Plague of the Spanish Lady: The Influenza Pandemic of 1918–1919.* New York: Atheneum, 1974.

Crosby, Alfred W. *Epidemic and Peace, 1918.* West-port, CT: Greenwood Press, 1976.

Intellectuals (U.S.)

World War I was a divisive and disillusioning event for U.S. intellectuals. The decades prior to the war were characterized by progressive movements to address social, economic, and political problems caused by industrialization and immigration. The Progressive era's emphasis on rational planning and education created new roles and responsibilities for intellectuals in education, journalism, and government: Pragmatism emerged as an experimental philosophy to solve modern problems through human action; muckrakers exposed corruption through the new journalism; and intellectuals began to see themselves as important leaders in a changing society, especially with the election of Democrat Woodrow Wilson, the president of Princeton University, to the U.S. presidency in 1912.

When war broke out in Europe in 1914, most American intellectuals remained committed to neutrality. Although President Wilson urged Americans to remain "impartial in thought as well as in action," such neutrality proved difficult to maintain as political and economic circumstances gradually drew the United States into the war. Many recent immigrants retained strong ties to European combatants and economic ties to the Allies proved a serious obstacle to neutrality. With the British blockade of Germany, the United States traded almost exclusively with Britain and France, making the United States neutral in name only. Public support for war rose with the sinking of the British liner *Lusitania* in 1915 and the French *Sussex* in 1916, as well as the release of the Zimmermann Telegram in 1917.

The rhetoric of the Progressive era was used to support the war. Progressive intellectuals such as John Dewey and Walter Lippmann viewed the government as a source of authority in solving social and economic problems, and many saw World War I as an opportunity for the federal government to increase its influence in business regulation, labor disputes, and political efficiency and also to spread political democracy around the world. The editors and writers of the *New Republic,* founded in 1914, Herbert Croly, Walter Weyl, and Walter Lippman, initially opposed the war but, after the sinking of the *Lusitania,* urged U.S. involvement. On April 6, 1917, President Wilson declared war on Germany in order to make the world "safe for democracy," and then set to work, with the assistance of liberal policy makers, creating his Fourteen Points.

But other intellectuals remained adamantly opposed to the war. Randolph Bourne's scathing essay, "The War and Intellectuals," castigated intellectuals for succumbing to political pressure to support the war. Editor Max Eastman and most contributors to the socialist journal *The Masses* believed that imperialism and corporate greed were responsible for the war. When the journal maintained its support for U.S. neutrality, it lost its mailing privileges. Similarly, the outspoken opposition of editors Waldo Frank, Louis Untermeyer, James Oppenheim, and Paul Rosenfeld to the war resulted in a loss of funding for their literary magazine, *The Seven Arts.*

In 1916, pacifists formed the American Union Against Militarism to lobby against the preparedness campaign. A strong peace movement led primarily by women remained active throughout the war. Progressive reformers such as Jane Addams and Lillian Wald spoke out against war, and a group of Democratic congressmen opposed U.S. involvement.

Shortly after declaring war, Wilson created the Committee on Public Information (CPI) to sell the war to the American public. The CPI produced pamphlets, books, posters, and articles that defined the war as a moral crusade. Newspapers, advertisements, and films starring Charlie Chaplin, Mary Pickford, and Douglas Fairbanks helped to sell war bonds. Journalists Ida Tarbell and artist Charles Dana Gibson used their talents to support the war. The idealistic message of this propaganda and its push for conformity gradually weakened dissent.

Despite Wilson's progressive goals, power politics took precedence at the Versailles peace conference in 1919, and the idealistic aims outlined in the Fourteen Points were defeated. The destruction and pointless slaughter of World War I shattered the optimism of liberal intellectuals in the ability of humans to intelligently shape society. Pessimism, irony, and doubt replaced the faith in progress that characterized prewar U.S. intellectual life. Increasingly repressive restrictions on civil liberties under the Espionage Act of 1917 and the Sedition Act of 1918 muzzled socialists, pacifists, labor unions, and other social critics, bringing more than 2,100 cases to court. Postwar fears of radicalism incited a Red Scare from 1919 through 1921, resulting in arrests, deportations, and other repressive measures against radicals of all stripes. Finally, the harsh terms of the Versailles Peace Treaty disappointed hopes for a more liberal postwar world. The promises of a new world order that U.S. leaders had popularized in order to increase support for the war had the unintended result of intensifying postwar disappointment. All of these developments ended the Progressive era by 1919 and brought a mood of cynicism and disenchantment to American intellectuals that lasted throughout the 1920s.

Meanwhile, new scientific concepts, some of them developed before World War I, began to have a wider impact. Scientists were organized in the National Research Council to put science to wartime use, resulting in new developments in surgery and psychological testing. Albert Einstein's theories displaced fundamental assumptions of Newtonian physics that had prevailed for two centuries. The relativistic implications of Einstein's theories also encouraged philosophers and artists to experiment, resulting in the modern paintings of artists like Pablo Picasso and the psychological theories of Sigmund Freud.

Rejecting the values of U.S. materialism and disillusioned with the United States' postwar return to normalcy, a number of intellectuals, poets, artists, and writers fled to France in the post-World War I years. This "Lost Generation," a term coined by poet Gertrude Stein, included Ernest Hemingway, John Dos Passos, and F. Scott Fitzgerald, among others. T. S. Eliot's *The Waste Land* was a study of passive nihilism, and Hemingway's *The Sun Also Rises* (1926) and his bitter *A Farewell to Arms* (1929) illustrated the pointlessness of war. F. Scott Fitzgerald's *The Great Gatsby* (1933) displayed the self-absorption of the Jazz Age. These disaffected intellectuals expressed the themes of spiritual alienation, self-exile, and cultural criticism. Their literary innovations challenged traditional assumptions about writing and expression, and paved the way for subsequent generations of avant-garde writers.

Victoria Grieve

See also: Literature (U.S., WWI); Biographies: Croly, Herbert (WWI); Lippmann, Walter (WWI); Wilson, Woodrow (WWI)

REFERENCES

Dolan, Marc. *Modern Lives: A Cultural Re-reading of the "Lost Generation."* West Lafayette, IN: Purdue University Press, 1996.

Pells, Richard H. *Radical Visions and American Dreams: Culture and Social Thought in the Depression Years.* Middletown, CT: Wesleyan University Press, 1973.

Isolationism

Isolationism can be broadly defined as a government's intention to steer clear of political and military involvement with other nations. Individual isolationists, however, may have narrower geographic or topical concerns than a complete rejection of all foreign entanglements. For example, some isolationists might oppose formal membership in international governmental organizations; others could reject the use of economic resources to assist countries in turmoil or distress; while still others could support close relations with neighboring nations, but not nations in a different hemisphere. Despite these various viewpoints, isolationists remain united in their concern that certain international alliances or connections could constrain national interests and have undesirable domestic consequences.

In the early 1900s, most Americans equated isolationism with keeping the United States protected from European balance-of-power politics. This association between isolationism and separation from Europe has a long history. Many of the earliest colonists settled in North America out of a desire to isolate themselves from powerful European monarchies and established state religions. After the United States became an independent nation, George Washington's Farewell Address, perhaps the most famous foreign policy statement in U.S. history, argued that the nation should avoid entangling alliances with Europe, whose different interests and concerns could jeopardize U.S. peace. Even those policies and events that appeared nonisolationist, like the Monroe Doctrine that promised U.S. intervention in independent Latin American nations threatened by Europe and the Spanish-American War, linked the United States more to the Caribbean and Asia than they did in Europe. Moreover, the United States' desire to isolate itself from the wars and rivalries that seemed to dominate continental diplomacy did not mean that foreign policy decision makers also wanted to cut economic ties to Europe. Most Americans believed that a strong trading relationship with European nations was essential to U.S. prosperity.

When war broke out in Europe in 1914, Americans were not only shocked and dismayed by the slaughter, but also glad that an ocean separated the United States from the fighting. At the beginning of the conflict, President Woodrow Wilson spoke to the United States' isolationist tradition by urging U.S. citizens to remain neutral in their thoughts as well as their actions. The American public responded sympathetically to Wilson's plea, since most believed that the United States had no stake in the war's outcome. Strict neutrality was difficult to maintain during the war, however, because of the administration's desire to continue normal trading relationships with the belligerents. Both the British and the Central Powers violated U.S. rights by expanding the contraband list, mining the seas, and harassing U.S. merchant ships. Eventually, Wilson advocated a "preparedness" program to expand the U.S. military establishment in case U.S. sovereignty was threatened by the violence overseas.

The strength of the United States' isolationist sentiment can be seen in the difficulty Wilson's preparedness plans encountered in Congress. Progressive politicians, such as Robert La Follette, argued that the administration's proposed military buildup would pull the government's focus away from domestic reforms and push the United States into the war. This reaction nearly succeeded in reducing one of the president's military appropriations bills and did force a revision of his plan to increase the size of the military. In the spring of 1917, however, the sinking of three unarmed U.S. merchant ships by German submarines persuaded Wilson to ask Congress for a declaration of war. While congressional isolationists voted against the resolution, suggesting that the United States had no duty to save England and that protecting the profits of munitions makers lay behind the president's decision, they were outnumbered in the Senate by 82-6 and in the House by 373-50. Following the war declaration, U.S. industry quickly converted to war production, Congress passed military expenditure bills, and the government instituted a national draft. By June 1917, the first U.S. troops arrived in France. A little over a year later, Germany requested an armistice.

U.S. participation and victory in the war failed to undermine isolationist attitudes. Prior to the end of the war, Wilson had proposed establishing an international governmental body that would ensure world peace through collective security measures. During peace negotiations, the Allies created the League of Nations to fulfill this intergovernmental role. The Senate, however, refused to join the League of Nations because the League's Covenant required all members to come to the aid of any other member nation threatened by "external aggression." Many congressional members believed that this commitment would constrain U.S. national interests and make it more difficult for the United States to avoid getting involved in future European conflicts. The Senate's eventual rejection of the League of Nation membership, as well as its later refusal to join other international governmental organizations like the World Court, illustrates the continuing influence of isolationism in the United States.

Although U.S. involvement in World War II and the challenges posed by the Cold War weakened isolationist sentiment in the United States, strains of the philosophy continued to be seen in the early twenty-first century. Calls for the United States to withdraw from the United Nations, to cut or eliminate foreign aid, and to reject free trade agreements all acquired some measure of legitimacy due to the United States' foreign policy tradition of isolation.

Christy Jo Snider

See also: Conscientious Objectors (WWI); Europe, American Attitudes Toward (WWI); League of Nations (WWI); Pacifists (WWI); Biographies: La Follette, Robert (WWI)

REFERENCES

Cooper, John Milton. *The Vanity of Power: American Isolationism and the First World War, 1914–1917.* New York: Greenwood Press, 1969.

Doenecke, Justus D. "The Literature of Isolationism, 1972–1983: A Bibliographical Guide." *Journal of Libertarian Studies* 7 (Spring 1983): 157–184.

Gladwin, Lee A. "Hollywood Propaganda, Isolationism, and Protectors of the Public Mind, 1917–1941." *Prologue* 26 (1994): 234–247.

May, Ernest R. *The World War & American Isolation, 1914–1917.* Cambridge: Harvard University Press, 1959.

Powaski, Ronald E. *Toward an Entangling Alliance: American Isolationism, Internationalism, and Europe, 1901–1950.* New York: Greenwood Press, 1991.

Rieselbach, Leroy N. *The Roots of Isolationism: Congressional Voting and Presidential Leadership in Foreign Policy.* Indianapolis, IN: Bobbs-Merrill Company, 1966.

Italian Immigrants

As the unionization of U.S. workers escalated toward the end of the nineteenth century, industrial leaders looked to Europe for cheap labor in order to keep their factories running. Immigrants from southern and eastern Europe were heavily recruited. In southern Italy, where jobs were scarce, men were willing to take the difficult and often temporary jobs available in the United States. From 1901 through 1910, almost 2.5 million Italians immigrated to the United States, although many Italians who immigrated during this time period stayed only an average of two to five years. Most Italians gravitated toward urban areas, with tight-knit communities being formed in the largest cities such as New York, Boston, and Chicago. There was no shortage of work for the Italians in the most back-breaking jobs necessary for building a nation. In Chicago, for example, most Italian men worked in a railroad gang where they laid and maintained 2,000 miles of track within the city limits and averaged $1.50 per day.

The entry of the Italians, along with Jewish and Slavic immigrants from Eastern Europe, sowed the seeds of the most nativist period in U.S. history. The violent unrest in Europe accompanied by the presence of immigrants from these volatile areas only fed this nativism. The Italians, as well as most of the Slavic immigrants, were Catholic, and their strange languages, customs, and even stranger religion presented a threat to the established Anglo-Americans. Out of this nativist movement came derogatory terms like "wop" and "dago," epithets that were to become painfully familiar to Italian Americans. Although crime statistics did not support it, Italians as a race were believed to be lawless, immoral, and illiterate.

Despite the rampant racism and anti-Catholicism, by the start of World War I many Italian Americans, especially those in the larger cities, had established themselves as respectable tradesmen, such as tailors, electricians, and shoemakers, and had even made inroads into banking and running retail grocers and Italian restaurants. Woodrow Wilson's "peace with honor" platform attracted the Italians, who strongly supported his election in 1916. Some Italians, however, suspicious of President Wilson's war intentions, joined with other immigrant groups in a movement called America First to protest in favor of the Axis nations. But with the entry of the United States into the war, Italian Americans proved their allegiance to their new country. More than 300,000 Italian Americans served in the U.S. armed forces, and others left the United States to fight with the Italian army as part of the Allied forces. Thousands died, and 103 Italian Americans were awarded the Distinguished Service Cross at the end of the war.

On the home front, nativism reached its peak during the war years. With the astonishing success of the Bolshevik communists in Russia in 1917, anyone who opposed the war was branded a "Red." The attorney general, A. Mitchell Palmer, led raids into the homes of suspected criminal radicals—who were mostly immigrant workers. Those with radical leanings were labeled anarchists and became the most vulnerable of Palmer's targets. The most renowned of those targeted were Nicola Sacco and Bartolomeo Vanzetti, who were arrested in Boston in 1920, tried, and found guilty of murder. They declared their innocence until they were executed in 1927. It is still unclear whether they were guilty of the crime, and the two men remain martyrs in Italian American history.

In the election of 1920, Italian Americans deserted Wilson, mostly because of his failure to support Italy's claims to portions of Yugoslavia at the Paris Peace Conference. Nativism remained high after the war, and this led to historic changes in immigration law. In 1924, the Reed-Johnson Immigration Act ended the previously liberal admission of immigrants from southern and eastern Europe. Despite restrictions, by the end of the 1920s nearly five million Italians had arrived in the United States.

Donna M. Abruzzese

See also: Immigration (U.S., WWI); Palmer Raids (WWI); Red Scare (WWI); Sacco and Vanzetti Case (WWI)

REFERENCES

Duff, John B. "The Italians." *The Immigrants' Influence on Wilson's Peace Policies,* ed. Joseph P. O'Grady. Lexington: University of Kentucky Press, 1967.

Fuchs, Lawrence H. *The American Kaleidoscope.* Hanover, NH: Wesleyan University Press, 1990.

Gambino, Richard. *Blood of My Blood.* Garden City, NY: Doubleday, 1974.

Iorizzo, Luciano J., and Salvatore Mondello. *The Italian-Americans.* New York: Twayne, 1971.

Linkh, Richard M. *American Catholicism and European Immigrants, 1900–1924.* Staten Island, NY: Center for Migration Studies, 1975.

Mangione, Jerre Gerlando. *Five Centuries of the Italian American Experience, 1492–1992.* New York: Harper Collins, 1992.

Takaki, Ronald T. *Strangers from a Different Shore.* Boston: Little, Brown, 1998.

J

Jazz

The Great War in Europe (1914–1919) coincided with the birth of jazz in the United States. Jazz, as a musical language, was the unique invention of African Americans, evolving out of the spiritual travails of the Deep South's slave culture from two centuries of work songs, prison songs, and the assimilation of Christian religious music. Since the turn of the century, African American musicians in the South, especially in the bars and back alleys of New Orleans, had been performing a kind of improvised counterpoint called "Dixieland," which was played by ensembles of five to eight instruments (usually including cornet, clarinet, violin, and trombone, plus a rhythm section of bass, drums, and piano, or guitar or banjo). This new type of music, however, had remained underground—the private intellectual property of a disenfranchised minority. The war created social changes that brought this unique idiomatic musical expression to the attention of the dominant European American society. In Europe, the presence of men from hitherto separate classes all fighting and dying together in the same trenches helped break down the traditional class distinctions that had governed European social structure for centuries; like-

wise, jazz became a prime signifier of major changes taking place in the American social consciousness.

Great Migration

The single most important event responsible for initiating these changes was the so-called "Great Migration of 1914-1919." The Great Migration was an exodus of African Americans moving in several massive waves from the South, up the Mississippi River to Memphis and Chicago, and finally to New York. Several factors are responsible for the coincidence of the Great Migration with World War I. The advent of war in Europe had slowed the flow of European immigrants who had been flooding U.S. shores for the past forty years down to a trickle. At the same time, intensified industrialization in the North had opened up a host of factory jobs to urban dwellers. The lack of foreign immigrants to fill these new jobs created a vacuum that African Americans were able and anxious to fill. Also, there was a climate of change in the air, a mood articulated by newly created, socially conscious publications; *The Chicago Defender*, the first African American periodical, actually declared the date of the "Great Northern

343

Drive" as May 15, 1917. African American jazz musicians flowed north with the tide and, in their new urban setting, enjoyed the support of an audience larger and more enthusiastic than they had ever known in the rural South.

In order to follow how jazz developed from its primitive roots to become the first great indigenous American Music, it is not only necessary to understand the relationship of jazz music to prejazz music, but it is also important to understand the position of jazz in a period of rampant social change. If it were necessary to make a single essential distinction between European music and American music in the year 1900, it might be this: European music had evolved for some five hundred years under the sheltering umbrella of the aristocratic patronage system, a system where commissioned music was produced for a specific occasion by an enlightened patron whose taste was well understood, and whose approval was largely a foregone conclusion. In contrast, American music was born of the middle class and began its infant career as more of a business than as art for art's sake. The presence of a tangible motivating force (money) behind the creation of American music helped pinpoint its reason for being with forceful clarity in the minds of its creators; moreover, the challenge of satisfying a fickle buying public's insatiable appetite for novelty inspired ingeniously original creative efforts.

Another difference between European and American music of this time was that the European tradition was based on a massive body of *written* material, whereas a truly American music unexpectedly erupts into being from a wellspring of *recorded* material.

The first jazz music had its roots in ragtime, which in turn had its roots in the imported music of European operetta; the million solo piano copies sold of the sheet music to Scott Joplin's "Maple Leaf Rag," in 1899 bespeak a solid foundation in the written tradition. But jazz history does not really begin with the published rags of Scott Joplin as much as it does with the recording of "Livery Street Rag" by Nick La Rocca's Dixieland Jass Band in 1917. The living reality of jazz was beyond music notation's ability to reproduce it. The ever-changing, ever-surprising vicissitudes of jazz improvisation perfectly reflected the excitement and insecurity of a period of intense, radical social change.

The acceptance of African American music into the dominant white culture of the North is what heightened its profile from an obscure rural folk expression into a vivid, telling urban language. In fact, the assimilation of African American artists into a largely European American milieu was more rapid than most of these musicians might have hoped for. Urban whites may not have wanted to sit side-by-side on a bus with African Americans, but they had no trouble being entertained by an African American man on a stage. And, although the first jazz recording was made by a white band (because African Americans were not allowed to record), the barriers of racial prejudice were soon blown wide open, and a wealth of African American recorded material became available to a society craving distraction from the madness taking place overseas.

In 1917, when the United States entered the war, the tempo of the northern migration increased as more and more factory workers were siphoned off to serve in weapons and munitions factories, as well as at the front. Segregated African American units, crudely nicknamed Jazzboes after "jazzbo"—a kind of slapstick physical comedy popular in vaudeville—served in the trenches, behind the lines in menial support capacities, and as musicians whose military function was to boost the morale of the white majority. African American regimental bands were formed by people like

James Reese Europe, who is largely responsible not only for proclaiming jazz to be the music of choice of his people, but for bringing jazz music, at its insemination, to the European continent, where it was eagerly embraced by a public just as hungry for musical distraction as their American brothers. Ironically, African Americans did not face the same type of discrimination in Europe that they suffered at home, and not only their music, but also themselves were welcomed. Bands like Will Marion Cook's New York Syncopated Orchestra toured extensively in Europe in 1918. Consequently, there has been a tradition of jazz-playing in France almost as old as the history of jazz in America.

Some of the African American jazz musicians who spearheaded the migration to Chicago, Memphis, and New York were: Bill Johnson, founder of the Original Creole Orchestra, one of the first African American bands to venture outside the Deep South; "Jelly Roll" Morton, the great jazz piano stylist who, early on, toured with minstrel shows and vaudeville troupes; W. C. Handy, composer of the *St. Louis Blues,* one of the most recorded songs in music history; and Joe "King" Oliver, who gave the great Louis Armstrong his start in 1922.

Relations among Musicians

The early chronicles of jazz history read more like family history than music history: All the musicians knew each other, played with each other, competed with each other, and fought with each other. It is significant that, whereas European musicology is very much about comparing various published texts of established masterworks of the written tradition, jazz musicology has largely to do with who moved where, and who played and/or recorded with whom, in what band, and in what city—true social history. This is so because the discussion of the printed text of a jazz tune (most often a highly abbreviated affair at best) has seemed an exercise in futility—it is the recorded performances that are the true music. Thus, the popular media, including radio, phonograph, and silent movies, became the channel through which African American artists proclaimed their legitimacy as artists and their social presence to a white society.

World War I was followed, hard on its heels, by the roaring twenties, when the linking in the American mind of illegal booze and gangsters with jazz wrote another complicated chapter in the continuing saga of the quest of jazz artists for acceptance and support. White musicians rapidly assimilated the jazz spirit and, during this next period, became worthy competitors for positions in the jazz hall of fame; but 99 percent of the credit for this World War I period of transition and initiation belongs to the African American immigrants who brought forth an anomalous cultural artifact from the bayous of Louisiana to the ears of an entire world.

Richard Freeman-Toole

See also: Cabarets (WWI); Music (WWI); Theater; Biographies: Armstrong, Louis (WWI); Berlin, Irving (WWI); Cohan, George M. (WWI); Morton, "Jelly Roll" (WWI); Oliver, Joe "King" (WWI)

REFERENCES

Hennessey, Thomas J. *From Jazz to Swing: African-American Jazz Musicians and Their Music, 1890–1935.* Detroit, MI: Wayne State University Press, 1994.

Mancuso, Chuck, Dave Lampe, and Reg Gilbert, eds. *Popular Music and the Underground: Foundations of Jazz, Blues, Country, and Rock, 1900–1950.* Dubuque, IA: Kendall/Hunt, 1996.

Morris, Ronald L. *Wait until Dark : Jazz and the Under-*

world, 1880–1940. Bowling Green, OH: Bowling Green University Popular Press, 1980.

Schuller, Gunther. *Early Jazz: Its Roots and Musical Development.* New York: Oxford University Press, 1968.

Jews (UK)

By 1914, more than 250,000 Jews were living in Great Britain, most of whom resided in London (180,000), Manchester (30,000), and Leeds (20,000). At the onset of the Great War, more than two-thirds of the Jewish population were either immigrants or descendants of immigrants from Eastern Europe who had fled destitution, discrimination, and violence in Tsarist Russia since the 1880s.

Thus, the Jewish community was roughly divided into two groups: the largely middle-class anglicized minority with a background of residence on the British Isles for several generations, out of which the representatives and the leadership of the Anglo-Jewry were recruited; and the Yiddish-speaking and religiously more traditionally living Russians, whose process of acculturation and assimilation was in the earlier stages, and whose occupational structure was working-class and artisanal. With the beginning of the war and as a consequence of the military alliances, the Jewish minority was split up into three groups with respect to their legal status: first, British subjects, including the descendants of Russian immigrants who were born in Britain; second, the Russians, who were categorized as "friendly aliens"; and third, German nationals and East Europeans who had immigrated from Austria-Hungary, turned into "enemy aliens" and were subjected to the same restrictions and control procedures as every other "enemy national." This latter group is hard to quantify but was certainly very small, numbering no more than a few hundreds.

As soon as the war had begun, the leaders of Anglo-Jewry strove to demonstrate Jewish loyalty to the national cause. They found themselves in a dilemma that was rooted in the different socialization and degrees of integration into British society of Jews in the country: Whereas the young generation of anglicized and assimilated British Jews volunteered for the army while their parents demonstrated their patriotism with special prayers in synagogues, many of the Russian Jews were very reluctant to enlist and, as "friendly aliens," they were not obliged to do so, even after the introduction of conscription in 1916. Apart from their patchy assimilation into British society, there was one other crucial motive for Russian Jews to shy away from military service: Jews in Russia had suffered immensely at the hands of the Russian military and, once they had conscripted themselves, often fell victims to abuse and discrimination. As a result, many Jewish men had fled Russia in order to escape Russian military service. Hence, instinctively aping their fathers, the young men, now in Britain, kept distance from the army. This reluctance triggered anti-Jewish violence in 1917. In addition, the British government, with the support of the Anglo-Jewish leadership, began to devise a system—that ultimately was never seriously implemented—under which those Russian Jews who refused to serve in the British forces should be deported to Russia; but this only after the overthrow of the Tsar in March 1917: It was through these major political changes on the European continent that brought the emancipation of Russia's Jews, a major concern of British Jews—and Western Jews in general—during the preceding decades. With the beginning of World War I in August 1914, the Anglo-Jewish leadership and press had muted their open criticism of now-allied Russia, though continued to lobby the British government on behalf of the Tsar's Jewish subjects.

The year 1917 was a turning point in Anglo-Jewish and indeed Jewish history in general: It saw the publication of the Balfour Declaration by the British Government (November 2, 1917) and the promise to establish a national home for Jews in Palestine. The successful military advance of British troops under the command of General Edmund Allenby in the region and the occupation of Jerusalem in December 1917 fueled hopes that Jewish national aspirations could materialize. From then on, with Zionism being official policy, it also began to take hold amongst a growing number of British Jews, who until then were rather sceptical and worried that the endorsement of Jewish nationalism might undermine their status as British subjects of Jewish persuasion and would cast doubt on their patriotism and loyalty to the national cause.

Several changes were brought about by World War I for Jews in Britain. Overall, the military service as well as economic changes helped to precipitate the acculturation of the Eastern European immigrants and their children, but these changes also furthered a loosening of religious observance. Until 1914, the majority of Jews in Britain lived in neighborhoods (most of them in London's East End) that were overwhelmingly "Jewish" and had hardly any contact, whether professional or social, with non-Jews. All in all, more than 40,000 young Jewish men fought with the British forces, with many of them born in Britain but with an Eastern European immigrant background. Their military service brought them into close contact with gentiles for the first time in their lives, and these contacts then intensified after the war. In the wake of World War I, the Jewish occupational structure began to change: Both men and women increasingly took up white-collar jobs, and whereas more and more men opted for higher education, women chose to train as teachers and secretaries. These changes mirrored the Jewish upward mobility as a consequence of the war: The demand for uniforms and boots during the war had brought modest affluence to Jewish workshops specializing in the garment industry well before 1914, and thus enabled many families to leave the densely populated immigrant neighborhoods. This Jewish population movement also led to an increase of contact with gentiles. Thus, World War I worked as a catalyst toward assimilation and integration for the East Europeans, but also forced Jews to face and counter prejudice. For the years of 1914–1918, the most important English-speaking weeklies of British Jews were *The Jewish Chronicle* and *The Jewish World,* both edited by Leopold Greenberg (1862-1931). The two papers constitute prime sources for Jewish concerns during World War I.

Susanne Terwey

See also: Anti-Semitism (UK, WWI); Immigration (U.S., WWI)

REFERENCES

Endelman, Todd M. *The Jews of Britain, 1656–2000.* Berkeley: University of California Press, 2002.

Levene, Mark. "Going against the Grain: The Jewish Memoirs of War and Anti-War, 1914–1918" in *Jewish Culture and History* 2 (1999): 66–95.

Levene, Mark. *War, Jews, and the New Europe. The Diplomacy of Lucien Wolf, 1914–1919.* Oxford: Oxford University Press, 1992.

Rubinstein, William D. *A History of the Jews in the English-Speaking World: Great Britain.* Basingstoke: Macmillan, 1996.

Journalism (UK)

Journalism in Britain had flourished during the Boer War, and in World War I, it rose to its position of greatest prominence and influence. The buildup to August 1914, the decision to go to war, the conduct of the war, and the terms of the peace all exercised press and public opinion as no other event had in the twentieth century to date, and just as the war served to consolidate and empower many sections of society, it also elevated the position of newspapers and, most visibly, of editors and proprietors. In a new period of mass literacy, cheap newsprint, and great events, journalists became participants in affairs of state, and some assumed greater importance than politicians or generals.

Britain was—and remained—an unusually competitive market for journalism, and war conferred political purpose to even the mass-circulation popular papers. Partly in consequence of the South African War at the turn of the century and mirroring the rise of Pulitzer and Hearst in America, there had been the marked development of the "yellow press": sensational, nationalist, populist reporting on poor quality paper that could be said to have democratized or coarsened public debate, or both. The more strident tone characterized the period immediately before World War I and contributed to various naval scares and diplomatic tensions. A bloody war nourished extremists and demagogues, most notably Pemberton Billing, who became an MP, while Leo Maxse's *National Review,* and Horatio Bottomley's *John Bull* were pungent examples in print. A general sensationalism was evident in those sensational times: Fictitious stories of violated Belgian nuns and German spies contributed to the general hysteria, while the German-speaking R. B. Haldane and Prince Louis of Batten-

berg were driven out of the government by the press. Some journalists even turned on themselves: Ralph Blumenfeld, editor of the *Daily Express,* felt it necessary to publish a front-page assurance that he was not, and had never been, German.

The often speculative and aggressive nature of wartime journalism was in part because newspapers were not the large, corporate concerns they later became. Personified as never before or since, the "great editors" included Sir Robert Donald (*Daily Chronicle*), J. A. Spender (*Westminster Gazette*), J. L. Garvin (*The Observer*), H. A. Gwynne (*Morning Post*), F. W. Hirst (*The Economist*), H. W. Massingham (*The Nation*), A. G. Gardiner (*Daily News*), and Joseph St. Loe Strachey (*The Spectator*); the "great proprietors" included Lord Edward Burnham (*Daily Telegraph*), Lord Riddell (*News of the World*), Lord William Maxwell Beaverbrook (*Daily Express*), Sir Edward Hulton (*Daily Sketch*), and, most importantly, Alfred and Harold Harmsworth, who became Viscounts Northcliffe and Rothermere respectively (*Daily Mail* and *The Times*). The ratio of proprietors being knighted or ennobled illustrated the value that politicians—particularly conservative politicians—placed on them, and the "Press Lords" shared this high opinion of themselves. While there was also at this time a particularly vibrant provincial press, it irritated provincial editors that they tended to be eclipsed by their national counterparts—another trend that was further accelerated by the war.

A parliamentary truce and the absence of official opposition meant that the role of the press had never been so important in Britain and, in the age before other forms of media, never was again. Though part of the three Defence of the Realm Acts bore comparison with restrictions in other countries, actual censorship was nominal; disapproval—official or popular—was muted, and the Official Press Bureau proved to be just as toothless as every other regulatory body for journalism had been. Overseas distribution of the *Nation* was banned, but there was no antiwar journalism significant in terms of circulation and, indeed, the vast majority of the coverage called for an acceleration in the war effort. To that end, politicians and soldiers furthered their particular causes by leaking stories and gossip to their particular contacts in the press, and editors and proprietors were happy to assume the role of actors in the unfolding drama: Northcliffe and Rothermere undertook work for the government, Charles Masterman of the *Daily News* ran the War Propaganda Bureau for the Foreign Office, and Beaverbrook was actually made minister of information.

It was certainly the case that the distinction between journalism and propaganda had become blurred, though the extent to which the press sought to lead news or actively to misrepresent political leaders tended to be in relation to the success of the war effort at the time. Perceived inefficiency invited heightened attacks and, as in May 1915 and December 1916, could have direct political consequences. Newspapermen who had been anxious to secure the inclusion of Field Marshal Kitchener into what many regarded as an unwarlike Cabinet, for instance, were soon to berate his subsequent failures and distance themselves from their role in his appointment. Asquith's experiences reinforced his own low opinion of journalists, but the consequences of a bad press were such that, at the end of the war, several senior politicians could be found scrambling for ownership or control of several titles.

Progressive papers were outnumbered by conservative journals, and anti-Germanism was soon replaced by anti-Bolshevism. Not only did the preoccupations of the age lend themselves to reactionary opinion, reactionary opinion lent itself to popular journalism. Lloyd George was the only Liberal who realized the importance of good relations with the press. The changes of government, and the tenor of the 1918 general election, were defined in large part by journalism, with Lloyd George the beneficiary in every case. Northcliffe and Beaverbrook, in particular, might be said to have achieved for journalism what Rudyard Kipling would soon describe as "power without responsibility—the prerogative of the harlot throughout the ages."

Martin Farr

See also: Propaganda (UK, WWI); Biographies: Asquith, Herbert Henry (WWI); Lloyd George, David (WWI); Kitchener, Horatio Herbert (WWI)

REFERENCES

Havighurst, A. F. *Radical Journalist: H. W. Massingham.* London: Cambridge University Press, 1974.

Jones, Kennedy. *Fleet Street and Downing Street.* London: Hutchinson, 1919.

Koss, Stephen. *Fleet Street Radical: A. G. Gardiner and the Daily News.* London: Allen Lane, 1973.

Koss, Stephen. *The Rise and Fall of the Political Press in Britain,* Vol. 2. London: Hamish Hamilton, 1984.

Riddell, George. *Lord Riddell's War Diary 1914–1918.* London: Nicolson and Watson, 1933.

Smith, Adrian. *The "New Statesman": Portrait of a Political Weekly, 1913–31.* London: Frank Cass, 1996.

Spender, J. A. *Life, Journalism and Politics.* London: Cassell, 1927.

Taylor, Sally J. *The Great Outsiders: Northcliffe, Rothermere and the Daily Mail.* London: Weidenfeld and Nicolson, 1996.

Wilson, Trevor, ed. *The Political Diaries of C. P. Scott, 1911–1928.* London: Collins, 1966.

Journalism (U.S.)

Journalists from the United States covering World War I faced red tape and censorship in getting to the front lines. The trenches provided human-interest stories, but no journalist could present a direct, intelligible account of the big picture—which required the cooperation and candor of military leaders. Lacking access to the top brass, reporters became adept at cultivating sources and mining press releases, and newspapers such as the *New York Times* printed government reports, speeches, and treaties to help readers make sense of the conflict. During the war and directly after, public relations emerged to challenge the stature and prestige of journalists: Individual enterprise counted for less as reporters were fed press releases. Such routines begat pack journalism. The very concepts of "facts," "news," and newspapers' role in a democratic society were questioned. Journalists then fought back by putting more interpretation and less "objectivity" into their stories.

Foreign Propaganda

In the fall of 1914, aiming to veer U.S. neutrality, Britain and Germany bombarded the U.S. with public relations messages. At the outset, most U.S. newspapers were neutral, numbering at 240, compared with 105 pro-Ally or pro-British, and only 20 pro-German. The *New York World* and the *New York Times* were the leading pro-British papers. The country's leading anti-British papers were the *Washington Post,* the *Chicago Tribune,* the *Los Angeles Times,* William Jennings Bryan's weekly, the *Commoner,* and William Randolph Hearst's influential *New York Journal.* To tilt the picture, German agents secretly purchased the *New York Tribune;* they were soon exposed. From the start, the Germans suffered a bad image owing to the unpopularity of Kaiser Wilhelm II. Then, on May 7, 1915, a German submarine torpedoed the British liner *Lusitania,* killing some 1,200 passengers, including 128 Americans. This caused U.S. newspapers to blanch on neutrality.

The British won the "press agents' war" because they knew the culture and mindset of their direct descendents: the Americans. This knowledge fashioned the messages in the British public relations campaign, which utilized public lectures, pamphlets, and personal contact. The British also censored all war news sent to the United States. Reports of German atrocities, many of which appear to have been false—figured in the British accounts and inflamed Americans. Seven American journalists who covered the German army's march through Belgium, reporters from the *New York World,* the *Chicago Daily News,* the *Chicago Tribune,* the *Associated Press,* and the muckraking magazine *Collier's,* all signed a statement saying they did not witness any atrocities.

It took more than one year after the United States declared war in April 1917 for the U.S. press corps to fully deploy. About forty journalists covered the front. The *New York Herald Tribune* of June 6, 1918, contained a reporter's eye-witness account of the fighting at Chateau Thierry: A bridge was blown up and "German bodies went hurtling through the air with the debris" and "machine guns spat precise streams of lead at the enemy troops." Several hundred journalists manned European cities. In Paris in February 1918, Harold Ross—later the distinguished editor of the *New Yorker* magazine—became chief editor of a new military newspaper, the eight-page *Stars and Stripes,* which lasted eighteen months and carried news, editorials, features, cartoons, and advertisements. The great New York sports writer Grantland Rice lent his talent to the *Stars and Stripes.* Other professional journalists in the army, of all ranks, staffed the army camp weekly papers. These papers, including a syndicated "chain" serving thirty-eight camps, were distributed free to soldiers. The *Chicago Tribune* published an Army edition daily for seventeen months to bring news of the home front to Europe.

All stories went through military censors. The mails and cables were censored in a heavy-handed manner at the beginning of the war. A vast propaganda apparatus was in charge of censorship, the Committee on Public Information (CPI), which was created by President Woodrow Wilson April 14, 1917, one week after the United States entered the war. (The CPI was disbanded a day after the Armistice signing on November 11, 1918.) Placed in charge of the CPI was the muckraking journalist George Creel, who was respected by both newspaper and magazine editors. When he asked them to voluntarily censor news of troop movements and ship sailings, they did so and went much further to aid the war effort by emphasizing positive war news and downplaying the negative.

On June 15, 1917, the Espionage Act was enacted, imposing heavy penalties for inciting disloyalty among the armed forces and the obstruction of recruiting. The Postmaster-General barred from the mails anything he thought treasonous. Seventy-five newspapers—fifty-five of which were socialist—were denied mailing privileges during the Espionage Act's first year. The Sedition Act of May 16, 1918, amplified the Espionage Act: To bring the U.S. government, the Constitution, the flag, or the military or naval forces into "contempt, scorn" or "disrepute" was a crime.

The CPI enlisted an army of journalists who gladly supported the U.S. war effort. However, they took note of how easily advertising and public relations techniques succeeded in swaying public opinion. Doubt crept in about U.S. institutions and ideals, including the press and democracy. The CPI's campaigns succeeded by stressing images over words, and emotion over reason. The muckraking journalists who, prior to the war, had taken big business and government to task, now worked for the government. After the war, they would be taking "handouts"—press releases—from big business and the government. (Woodrow Wilson was the first U.S. president to hold regular press conferences.) Public relations agents gained importance. They claimed they did more than filter information, rather they "created" news; they also questioned the sanctity of facts, saying there were no "facts," only opinions and interpretations, which they, as public relations practitioners, created. Thus public relations challenged the status of journalists. Muckraking journalists had served as the vanguard of the Progressive movement, believing that the road to progress lay in uncovering the "facts" for an educated reading audience. The leading columnist and editor Walter Lippmann—who had helped conceive the CPI—said democracy would suffer because opinion and emotionally charged images were replacing fact-based reporting. "Where all news comes at second-hand, where all testimony is uncertain, men cease to respond to truths, and respond simply to opinions," wrote Lippmann.

Public Relations

Journalists responded to the ascent of public relations and the attack on facts and objectivity by becoming more interpretive. When Henry Luce founded *Time* magazine in 1923 he said: "Show me a man who thinks he's objective and I'll show you a man who's deluding himself." Luce disavowed the "old" rules of journalism, of reporting both sides of an issue without comment. Instead, *Time* gave both sides of the story, but indicated which side was right.

Journalists also became specialists. By developing expertise in medicine, law, science, or finance, for example, the journalist would be less dependent on public relations handouts. In 1920, E. W. Scripps, who started the first newspaper chain in 1893, funded a special press association, the Science Service.

The war created conditions that spurred chain ownership and the attendant era of merger and consolidation. Because of the five-hour time difference between Paris and New York, evening newspapers, with fresher news, flourished during the war. At the same time, escalating production costs drove hundreds of daily and weekly newspapers out of business or into consolidation: 2,435 newspapers disappeared between 1914 and 1919. During the war, the press magnate Frank A. Munsey, owner of newspapers in Boston, New York, Philadelphia, Baltimore, and Washington D.C., said: "Small units in any line are no longer competitive factors in industry, in transportation, in commerce, in merchandising and banking." The small newspaper competitor must be absorbed and the field cleaned up.

After World War I, the syndicated opinion column emerged. With Henry Luce and *Time* magazine's style leading the way, newspapers and radio news interpreted the news and offered analysis. "*Time*-style" used colorful adjectives to influence point-of-view: The magazine described New York City Mayor Fiorello La Guardia as "fat, rancid" and "garlic-smelling."

The big newspapers permitted their best reporters to interpret the news. Leading the way was Walter Lippmann, whose thrice-weekly column of news analysis for the *New York Herald Tribune* in 1931 was the first of its kind. By 1939, 160 newspapers carried Lippmann's column.

Tony Osborne

See also: Advertising (WWI); Censorship (WWI); Committee on Public Information (WWI); Muckrakers (WWI); Propaganda (U.S., WWI); Biographies: Lippmann, Walter (WWI)

REFERENCES

Baughman, James L. *Henry R. Luce.* Boston: G.K. Hall, 1987.

Cray, Ed, Jonathan Kotler, and Miles Beller. *American Datelines.* New York: Facts On File, 1990.

Mott, Frank L. *American Journalism.* New York: Macmillan, 1962.

Schudson, Michael. *Discovering the News.* New York Basic Books, 1978.

Journalism (Canada)

The spread of literacy combined with the dramatic developments in communications technologies in the late nineteenth century meant that increasing numbers of people received news of domestic and foreign events more or less as they happened. However, at the start of World War I, the role of the war correspondent was almost nonexistent. British Secretary of War, H. H. Kitchener, established policies and decisions that shaped and defined the role of journalists during the early part of the hostilities. All prospective war correspondents, Canadian or otherwise, required approval by the Army Council before being granted a licence that recognized them in the official registry of war correspondents. Consequently, war correspondents were subject to military law and the Chief Field censor attached to General Headquarters became their commanding officer. Initially, Kitchener banned all journalists from entering military zones where the British Expeditionary Forces served. Kitchener also demonstrated his distrust for war correspondents in other ways. Through the War Office, daily reports on what the military leadership deemed suitable for publication trickled down to the various newspaper and media representatives. Furthermore, the War Office scrutinized and censored all dispatches from France before releasing the information to the general press.

Censorship

The main civilian apparatus for censorship and the dissemination of news, the Press Bureau, was organized immediately upon the outbreak of the war. The Bureau was to issue official war communiqués and to provide information and answers to the press about the progress of the war. However, military services also dominated and controlled the activities of this agency. Through the Press Bureau, either the government or the military command could issue so-called "D-Notices" to the press, requesting that certain items be withheld from publication "in the national interest." Political motives combined with structural features, as well as the ensuing regulations and other measures designed to control the flow of information to journalists and to the wider world, derived from the British government and military authorities' need to maintain public support for the war effort as well as the need to control news for obvious security reasons. Given these stringent guidelines, civilian newspapers concentrated their reporting on the enthusiasm and patriotism that characterized the population's mobilization and training for the war. Canadian newspapers that were without the financial resources to underwrite the expenses associated with supporting a journalist in Europe usually relied upon copy that was written by other wire services. Consequently, many weekly or small-town Canadian newspapers recycled articles written by the accredited war correspondents in order to fulfill the public demand for news of the war.

As the British Commonwealth forces increased their war contributions, they began to pressure the War Office for approval to create their own organizations to deal with news, propaganda material, and, by extension, photographic records of events. Max Aitken, a Canadian journalist and entrepreneur who later earned a peerage, was the driving force behind the creation of an office devoted to disseminating information about the activities of Canadian forces overseas. In January 1915, Aitken learned of the newly established post dubbed "Canadian Eye Witness." By navigating through the British bureaucracy and "proper channels," Aitken received his appointment to this post. In the early months of 1915, Aitken traveled to the front lines and wrote first-hand accounts of battles and the Canadian troops' movements.

With the sanction of Canadian Prime Minister Borden and the British War Office, Aitken's role expanded to include taking "charge of the work connected with records generally appertaining to the Canadian Overseas Expeditionary Force, and particularly the reporting of casualties." At his own expense, Aitken set up a London office, declaring from the outset that he was determined to compile proper records. In France, he rented a house and provided his own transport and staff for forays into the battlefields. Throughout 1915 and 1916, Aitken wrote dispatches about Canadian exploits for the press and also sent daily cables in code to the Canadian Prime Minister to inform Canadian government authorities about the progress of the war.

Soon, the War Office named Aitken as head of the Canadian War Records Office (CWRO). Relying on his own resources, Aitken expanded his London offices to accommodate the CWRO, which opened officially on January 1,

1916. Aitken announced that the goals of the CWRO included the gathering and dissemination of publicity material, procedures, and facilities to build up the written and visual records of the war for Canada.

Aitken used his rank as head of the Canadian War Records Office to grant Canadian commissions and to increase his influence in the organization of British propaganda generally. He also started a newspaper for Canadian troops entitled *The Canadian Daily Record*. In April 1916, he succeeded in securing the appointment of a Canadian-serving soldier, Harry Knobel, to act as the official photographer on the Western Front. When Knobel left this position due to illness, Ivor Castle, a former *British Daily Mirror* professional photographer, took his place. Later William Rider-Rider, another British photographer, joined the ranks of the Canadian War Records Office. Of the 40,000 official photographs sanctioned by the War Office, 4,000 were taken by the Canadian contingent.

After Kitchener died at sea in 1916, David Lloyd George replaced him as Secretary of War. Under Lloyd George's leadership, the number of accredited war correspondents increased dramatically. Cinematographic and photographic sections received more funding, and writers and journalists for magazines joined the corps of accredited war journalists.

By November 1916, Aitken had accepted the chairmanship of the War Office Committee for Propaganda, and he also chaired the Pictorial Propaganda Committee, a subsidiary of the Department of Information and the War Office Cinematograph Committee. In February 1918, Aitken achieved even greater influence through his appointment as Britain's first minister of information. Many high-ranking British officials recognized that Aitken's incredible success as a propagandist and active supporter of the Canadian Expeditionary Forces accounted for his dominant role in developing the form and delivery of wartime journalism.

Overseas Press Centre

During his tenure as minister of information, Aitken created an Overseas Press Centre, arranged tours for overseas journalists, and generally exploited every conceivable opportunity "to report and glorify the exploits of the Canadians, and to keep the public as fully informed as possible." Privately, Aitken revealed his political motives, stating that: "The more the British were reminded of their debt to Canada, the better for Canada's post-war status and for the great cause of Empire unity."

Many journalists, referred to as neutrals or "outlaw" correspondents, operated outside the jurisdiction of the War Office. Some reported from Belgium or from the fields of France. Others defied the War Office and were able to use the telephone to send in their reports. For a short time, a special courier system was maintained, but the War Office acted quickly to dismantle these forms of "unaccredited" communications. Overall, the costs associated with providing news coverage rose. Some newspapers located within the combat zones were either forced to suspend their operations or to take new forms. News exchanges between countries was interrupted and subject to censorship. Basic materials and the delivery of newsprint also posed production problems for newspapers in Canada and other countries involved in this major political crisis. Demand for news of the war strained the resources of Canadian newspapers and communications agencies. In 1917, regional news services in Canada joined to form The Canadian Press Ltd., an organization that the Canadian government transformed by Dominion Charter into a national association. This formal reorganization provided the association with a government subsidy of $50,000 that helped to defray the costs of leased wire services.

Max Aitken's entrepreneurialship and the financial support of the Canadian government ensured that civilians on the home front remained informed about wartime events. Max Aitken, by this time rewarded with his peerage and known as Lord Beaverbrook, left a considerable legacy to historians and researchers of World War I. His partisan book, *Canada in Flanders,* was widely distributed. Most significantly, through his efforts, Aitken was directly responsible for the thousands of feet of film, the paintings and drawings, the millions of pages of text, and the thousands of photographs that have helped later generations understand and analyze the Canadian perspective of the war.

Inge V. Sanmiya

See also: Propaganda (Canada, WWI)

REFERENCES

Kesterton, W. H. *A History of Journalism in Canada.* Toronto: McClelland and Stewart, 1967.

Wilson, C. Edward. *300 Years of Vigorous Journalism.* London, ON: University of Western Ontario, School of Journalism, 1976.

L

Labour Party (UK)

The Labour Party was brought to prominence by the conditions and requirements of the war. As the parliamentary section of the organized labor movement, the Labour Party was necessarily central to the unlimited, industrial, and "total" war that the conflict became for Britain. Through the conscription of men into military service and the compulsion of men and women into the productive sectors of the economy, the war required the consent of the still-recently enfranchised working-class electorate, and in so doing empowered it. By 1918, the Labour Party—which was still only twelve years old—had replaced the Liberals as Britain's second party of government.

Where the Liberals went into the war united and then split under its pressure, Labour went into the war divided, but was forged into a stronger and more coherent organization as the fighting went on. In 1914, Keir Hardie, spiritual leader of the Labour movement but an internationalist and pacifist, opposed the war and its attendant chauvinism. Though Hardie's was an unpopular position in the country, it nevertheless reflected an important strand of opinion in the party. On the left, the Independent Labour Party (ILP) was joined by the Union of

Democratic Control (UDC) in opposition to the war, and it was in the Labour Party leader, Ramsay MacDonald, that the Party had a visible and eloquent figurehead. It was not, however, a sustainable position.

When the parliamentary party voted for war credits in August 1914, MacDonald resigned and was replaced by Arthur Henderson. The change was significant: "The boneless wonder" represented a vague utopian socialism while "Uncle Arthur" was the solid pragmatic parliamentarianism of organized labor. The right had overcome the left, and not for the last time. The war had revealed an essential truth, but one uncomfortable to radicals: The British Labour movement was fundamentally conservative, and while hostile to the Conservative Party, was as equally animated by nationalism and wartime militarism. The ILP may have published a manifesto entitled *German Workers are our Comrades,* but an international brotherhood was less a reality than the recruitment offices overwhelmed with British workers queuing to kill their German comrades in the name of the Crown.

With an industrial and a political truce in place, Henderson was active on the Parliamentary Recruiting Committee, was made a Privy Councillor in January 1915, and became the

Keir Hardie, intellectual leader of the British labor movement and Labour Party, was a pacifist who opposed British entry into World War I. (Library of Congress)

first Labour minister when Asquith appointed him to the cabinet in May. Acting much as Labour Minister Ernest Bevin would do in the second war, Henderson was promoted to the small War Cabinet when Lloyd George became Prime Minister, and became a central figure in the government. Nevertheless, Henderson's advocacy of an international socialist conference in Stockholm in 1917, upon returning from a trip to Russia, aroused anti-Bolshevik suspicions in the press and parliament, and he was forced to resign, being replaced by George Barnes, minister of labor and former party leader.

In January 1916, the Labour Party Conference both supported participation in the Asquith Coalition and rejected conscription by

similar margins; a year later, it supported participation in the Lloyd George Coalition, as had the Conservatives, and with it universal conscription. The decision demonstrated the desire of the party not only to win the war, but also to benefit from it. John Clynes, Frank Hodges, and George Roberts took other ministerial positions, while the War Emergency Workers' National Committee, constituted by representatives of the party and trade unions, monitored the concessions that had been conceded—such as the Treasury Agreement and the Munitions of War Act—and further argued for state control of mines and of shipping as well as a Ministry of Labour. Similarly, though Barnes had replaced Henderson as Labour's principal representative in the government, he had not replaced him as party leader. As in 1939–1945, Labour paid more attention than its opponents to planning for the reconstruction. In November 1917, the party newspaper, *The Daily Herald,* demanded: "Let Labour Try Its Hand," and the process culminated with the abandonment of electoral agreements and the adoption of the new party constitution by the Conference held the following January. Written by Henderson and Sidney Webb, its ultimately infamous Clause IV committed the party to "common ownership of the means of production, distribution, and exchange."

Thus Labour was transformed from a loose federation of affiliated associations into a fully independent, nationwide, political organization, bringing together individual members, trade councils and unions, and socialist societies, all subject to central discipline and committed to contesting all elections against all opponents. Additionally, 1918 was the year of the Representation of the People Act, which dramatically increased the electorate, further to Labour's advantage. The progress could be measured: The number of constituency parties rose from 179 in 1914 to 418 in 1919, and total party membership rose from 1.6 million to 3.5 million; in the 1910 general election, the party received 371,802 votes, just 6 percent of the total cast, while in 1918 the number had risen to 2,245,777, totaling now 21 percent.

Though still supportive of the war effort, the party became increasingly critical of the government, and by the general election of 1918, the war had effectively resolved the prewar issue of independent Labour representation in Parliament. The breakthrough had not yet been made electorally, but the simultaneous internal fracturing of the Liberal Party as the organizational development of Labour meant it was simply a matter of time: The Labour Party now had a revised structure and broad appeal, and its leading figures had experienced government office. With the Liberal Party split and Labour emboldened, the British electoral system could only produce one result. The Liberal government of 1914 was the last, and within six years after the end of the war, a Labour government was elected for the first time.

Martin Farr

See also: Conscription (UK, WWI); Conservative Party (UK, WWI); Liberal Party (UK, WWI); Trade Unions (UK, WWI); Biographies: Bevin, Ernest (WWII); Lloyd George, David (WWI)

REFERENCES

Briggs, A., and J. Saville, eds. *Essays in Labour History, 1886–1923.* London: Macmillan, 1971.

Leventhal, F. M. *Arthur Henderson.* Manchester: Manchester University Press, 1989.

Marquand, David. *Ramsay MacDonald.* London: Jonathan Cape, 1977.

McKibbin, Ross. *The Evolution of the Labour Party 1910–1924.* Oxford: Oxford University Press, 1974.

Swartz, M. *The Union of Democratic Control in British Politics during the First World War.* Oxford: Clarendon Press, 1971.

Tanner, Duncan. *Political Change and the Labour Party.* Cambridge: Cambridge University Press, 1990.

Turner, John. *British Politics and the Great War: Coalition and Conflict.* New Haven, CT: Yale University Press, 1992.

Winter, J. M. *Socialism and the Challenge of War: Ideas and Politics in Britain 1912–18.* London: Routledge and Kegan Paul, 1974.

Wrigley, C. J. *Lloyd George and the British Labour Movement: Peace and War.* Hassocks: Harvester Press, 1976.

Latinos and Latinas

World War I marked a turning point in the history of Latino/as in the United States. In 1910, the U.S. born Latino/a population stood at 330,000, roughly three times the immigrant population of Latino/as. By 1920, the Latino/a immigrant population would exceed the U.S.-born population as social, economic, and political changes in both Mexico and the United States would increase Latino/a migration. Mexican Industrialization and urbanization propelled many rural dwellers into the United States, increasing the migrant laborer population throughout the southwest. The commercialization of U.S. southwestern agriculture, especially in California and Texas, encouraged the migration of unskilled farm labor from Mexico. In California, especially, Latino/a immigrant labor replaced Asian immigrant labor, which California had seen significantly reduced or eliminated by the Chinese Exclusion Acts of 1882, 1892, and 1902, as well as the Gentlemen's Agreements with Japan of 1900 and 1907. In addition to agriculture, Latino/as worked in factories and mines, highway and railroad construction, urban infrastructure construction, and lumbering.

Latino/a immigrant labor ameliorated the labor shortage in the United States during World War I. However, America's entry into World War I coincided with the implementation of the Immigration Act 1917. This immigration statute included a literacy test and an $8 head tax. In 1917, as a result of the immigration law, European immigration dropped to 300,000 from 1.2 million in 1914. After 1917, the $8 head tax was a major obstacle to poor Latino/as, who had no choice but to remain in Mexico or enter the United States without proper documentation. U.S. agricultural and industrial leaders pressured federal authorities to waive the literacy and head tax requirements to permit the unrestricted flow of Latino/a labor. In response to the concerns of U.S. agricultural and industrial interests, federal immigration authorities exempted illiterate contract workers from the literacy requirement, and seasonal laborers from the head tax.

During World War I, the United States relaxed efforts to control immigration from Mexico and simultaneously developed dependency on Mexican labor. Federal labor officials assured Congressional leaders that relaxed immigration, especially from Mexico, was only a stopgap measure to alleviate the labor shortages brought about by the war, but government permitted the measures to remain in effect until October 1, 1921, long after a surplus of labor had again developed in the United States. Unlike during the Mexican Revolution, the U.S. military did not patrol its border with Mexico and, from 1917 to 1921, when exemptions to immigration laws were in force, 72,862 Mexicans entered the United States with documents, while hundreds of thousands crossed the border without documents. As long as jobs were plentiful in the United States, undocumented workers continued to flow across the border, and as the U.S. government looked the other way.

Many war-related industries located in South California attracted many Latino/as. In Los Angeles, especially, the influx of Latino/as and African Americans created new social and economic pressures, exacerbating already overcrowded housing conditions. The social and racial integration of Latino/as was a slow process, aggravated by language and skin color, as darker Latino/as faced extreme discrimination. By the end of the war, Latino/as comprised 5 percent of the Los Angeles population, which had topped a million. The largest concentration of Latino/a-working families lived in the Central Plaza district of Los Angeles, and the Southern Pacific Railroad employed nearly half of these residents. In an area of less than 5,000 square feet of living space, twenty families lived in dilapidated housing courts, 79 percent lived in houses without indoor baths, and 28 percent had no sinks at all. Violence characterized the community, as Latino/as constituted 11 percent of the deaths in Los Angeles. White Angelinos blamed the conditions suffered by Latinos/as on the Latinos/as themselves, saying that the foreigners contributed to the a precipitous decline in the nation's traditional values.

Improving economic, social, and political conditions in Mexico lured many immigrants back to their homeland. Additionally, the fear of being drafted into the U.S. armed forces and sent to fight overseas encouraged many Latinos to return to Mexico. Because of the labor shortage during the war, the federal government enlisted Roman Catholic clergy to assure Latinos that they would not be drafted, but some boards drafted them anyway. For many Latinos, military services highlighted the contradictions of living in the United States, because when they returned home from the war, they still continued to have limited access to the rights and privileges that they fought to defend. But serving the country made Latinos feel truly like Americans, thereby raising their political consciousness.

Adam Revere Hornbuckle

See also: Immigration (U.S., WWI)

REFERENCES

Acuna, Rodolfo. *Occupied American: A History of Chicanos,* 5th ed. New York: Pearson Longman, 2004.

Anderson, David T. *Mexican Americans: The Roots of Identity.* Torrance, CA: F. Schauffer, 1995.

Reisler, Mark. *By the Sweat of Their Brow: Mexican Immigrant Labor, 1900–1940.* Westport, CT: Greenwood Press, 1976.

League of Nations

The League of Nations was an international organization established after World War I to achieve cooperation, peace, and security among the countries of the world. The League began operation in 1920 and was dissolved in 1946. The League had its headquarters in Geneva, Switzerland.

On January 8, 1918, President Woodrow Wilson presented his Fourteen Points during a speech to a joint session of the U.S. Congress. Wilson's fourteenth point proposed that a general association of nations be formed. Wilson was convinced that the establishment of an international assembly of nations would be indispensable for implementing the other proposals contained in the Fourteen Points as well as for building a new world order in the post-World War I period.

At the Paris Peace Conference held to conclude World War I, Wilson was forced to make a series of compromises to secure support for creation of the League, which he believed was the most important proposal among the Fourteen Points. The agreement that eventually emerged from the conference was the Treaty of Versailles.

The Treaty of Versailles adopted the Covenant of the League of Nations on April 28, 1919, and the Covenant went into force on January 10, 1920. Although Wilson strongly emphasized the importance of the League of Nations, he could not convince the U. S. Senate to ratify the Treaty of Versailles. Consequently, the United States never became an official member of the League. On November 15, 1920, the League of Nations held its first meeting involving forty-two nations in Geneva. Germany joined the League in 1926 and the Soviet Union joined in 1934. Eventually, sixty-three governments became members. Before the dissolution of the League, however, Japan, Italy, Germany, and fourteen other states had withdrawn and, in 1939, the League expelled the Soviet Union. The total membership at any one point never exceeded fifty-eight, and the peak year was 1934.

The Covenant contained twenty-six articles. Articles one to seven primarily dealt with methods to achieve and maintain peace. Articles eight to seventeen were devoted to the maintenance of peace, emphasizing the importance of arbitration, judicial settlement, and international law. Article fourteen was concerned with the establishment of the Permanent Court of International Justice. Articles eighteen to twenty-one required that all treaties be registered with the Secretariat of the League of Nations. Article twenty-two dealt with territories that had been confiscated from Germany and Turkey. Article twenty-three was concerned with humanitarian goals. Article twenty-four established several international agencies under

Established in the wake of World War I, the League of Nations' mission was to use international diplomacy and pressure to prevent conflict between nations. Here delegates meet at the 1920 opening session in Geneva, Switzerland. (Corel)

the umbrella of the League of Nations, including the International Labor Organization. Article twenty-five encouraged the development of national Red Cross societies. Finally, Article twenty-six spelled out the procedures for amending the Covenant.

An Assembly and a Council constituted the primary executive organs of the League of Nations. Both bodies were assisted by a permanent Secretariat. All members of the League constituted the members of the Assembly, which meant that each nation was entitled to one vote. The Assembly was responsible for the budget and membership. The Assembly held at least one session a year. The Council was to consist of five permanent members—the United States, Britain, France, Italy, and Japan—and four nonpermanent members (eventually increased to eleven) elected by the Assembly. The United States, however, never participated in the League. When Germany and the Soviet Union joined the League, they became permanent members. The Council was responsible for the political work and the settlement of international disputes. The Council met several times a year or when necessary. The Secretariat consisted of an international staff of several hundred officials. They were responsible for the practical day-to-day administration of the League.

The League of Nations made important contributions to building and maintaining a peaceful, stable, and healthy world. From 1920 to 1940, it handled about forty international disputes, playing an important problem-solving role in some cases. Successful interventions include the Aaland Islands controversy between Sweden and Finland, the boundary dispute between Bulgaria and Greece, and the confrontation between Peru and Colombia over Leticia. The League also successfully carried out an international administration of Danzig from 1920 to 1939 and the Saar from 1920 to 1935. When Japan invaded Manchuria in September 1931, the Council dispatched its first-ever international commission, the Lytton Commission, to investigate Japanese actions. After a careful study, the Lytton Commission issued a report that condemned Japan as an aggressor. Based on the report, the League of Nations recommended that its members refuse to recognize Manchuko as an independent sovereign country. The League also saw great achievements in another area: public health. In 1920, the Council established the Epidemics Commission, which successfully prevented cholera and typhus from spreading westward from Russia and Poland.

The League, however, was full of shortcomings. The global economic depression in the 1930s precipitated a series of international crises that the League could not handle. Because of a lack of enforcement capabilities, the League was unable to force Japan to pull out of Manchuria, and it only managed to impose nominal economic sanctions on Italy after it invaded Ethiopia, leaving Italy's vital oil supplies in tact and its access to the Suez Canal unimpeded. Moreover, it could not prevent Japan, Germany, or Italy from withdrawing from the League and, finally, it had absolutely no power in the late 1930s to prevent the outbreak of World War II. On April 8, 1946, the League of Nations held its last meeting, thus bringing its twenty-six-year history to a close. A bitter lesson from its shortcomings was learned, with the result that the United Nations, which superseded the League of Nations, was founded as a more powerful international organization.

Yoneyuki Sugita

See also: Fourteen Points (WWI); Isolationism (WWI); Paris Peace Conference (WWI); United Nations (WWII); Biographies: Lloyd George, David (WWI); Wilson, Woodrow (WWI); Documents: Fourteen Points, January 8, 1918; Against League of Nations, August 12, 1919; League of Nations Speech, September 26, 1919

REFERENCES

Cooper, John Milton, Jr. *Breaking the Heart of the World: Woodrow Wilson and the Fight for the League of Nations.* New York: Cambridge University Press, 2001.

Kuehl, Warren F., and Lynne K. Dunn. *Keeping the Covenant: American Internationalists and the League of American Internationalists and the League of Nations.* Kent, OH: Kent State University Press, 1997.

Liberal Party (Canada)

The Liberal Party of Canada evolved out of the Reformers of the nineteenth century who advocated responsible government and equality as opposed to the ruling-class-based elitism of the Conservatives who composed Canada's business and professional elite. The Reformers worked in various groups throughout present-day Ontario and Quebec to establish the British constitutional system, thereby obliterating the tyrannical privileges accorded the elite at the expense of the rising middle class and the working class.

By 1896, the Reformers, now named Liberals, were elected under Wilfrid Laurier. He opposed imperialism, favored free trade with the United States, and had strong connections to Quebec. Laurier believed Canada should be responsible for her own foreign policy and established the Department of External Affairs in 1905 and the Canadian Navy in 1910. By creating a Canadian ambassadorship to the United States, Laurier established Canada's independence from British control over Canada/U.S. relations.

The Liberals lost the 1911 election, and so Sir Robert Borden was Prime Minister when World War I broke out. In 1914, Canada contributed 30,000 volunteers, most of whom were recent British immigrants loyal to the British Empire. However, Quebecers were not enthused about enlisting in a military they saw as excessively pro-British, nor were they expecting a warm welcome being French-speaking and Catholic; they anticipated being badly treated. Only adventurers, tired of farm life, joined the Les Fusilier Mont Royal. The general staff in Ottawa exacerbated the problem even more by rejecting many recruits from Quebec. By 1915, some 150,000 men were expected to volunteer, but volunteer figures had plummeted. Borden had promised 500,000 recruits to the Allied Forces. Canada endured 3,000 killed and 7,000 wounded at Vimy Ridge and was in desperate need of more troops. Borden passed the Military Conscription Act allowing conscription, which resulted in a grave crisis that split the country: English Canada agreed with Borden while French Canada vehemently opposed conscription.

During the December 17, 1917 election, Borden granted the vote to soldiers serving overseas. Women were also granted the franchise. The Conservative and many pro-conscription Liberals, who had abandoned Laurier's antiproscription faction, joined Borden's Unionist party in a coalition and won a seventy-one-seat majority. The ambiguous Military Service Act, enforced on January 1, 1918, called up 40,000 men but contained numerous exemptions. Riots ensued in Quebec and four people not involved in the event were shot. After an amendment eliminating the exemptions, some 125,000 men were conscripted, however only 25,000 saw action. The conscription issue was not solved when Borden retired in 1920. The Conscription Crisis proved a boon for the Liberals as Quebec never voted Conservative for many decades thereafter.

Annette Richardson

See also: Conscription (Canada, WWI); Conservative Party (Canada, WWI); Biographies: Borden, Robert Laird (WWI); Laurier, Wilfrid (WWI)

REFERENCES

Cook, Ramsay, Craig Brown, and Carl Berger. *Conscription.* Toronto: University of Toronto Press, 1969.

Dawson, R. MacGregor. *The Conscription Crisis of 1944.* Toronto: University of Toronto Press, 1961.

Granatstein, J. L., and J. M. Hitsman. *Broken Promises: A History of Conscription in Canada.* Toronto: Oxford University Press, 1977.

Haydon, Andrew. *Mackenzie King and the Liberal Party.* Toronto: T. Allen, 1930.

Heppe, Paul H. *The Liberal Party of Canada.* Ann Arbor, MI: University Microfilms, 1957.

Morton, Desmond. *A Military History of Canada.* Edmonton: Hurtig Publishers, 1990.

Liberal Party (UK)

The British Liberal Party, although it took Britain into World War I, was ultimately broken by that very experience. The Liberals were elected in 1906, and then reelected in 1910, but in 1916 split when Lloyd George replaced Asquith as Prime Minister, and the party was never to return to power. The reasons for the decline of the Liberal Party constitute one of the central questions of British history, and the war was a central issue. "Classical" Liberalism was essentially libertarian, but in the years before the war the party adopted a "New" interventionist approach required by mass democracy in an industrial society. These differing attitudes could be accommodated in peacetime, but the requirements of "total" war and coalition government exacerbated ideological and personal differences characterized by its leading men, Asquith and Lloyd George. By the end of the war, the Liberals found themselves replaced in government by Conservatives, and in opposition by the Labour Party.

Going to War

That a progressive and internationalist party managed to go to war intact remains one of the Liberal Party's greatest feats. Defending Belgium's neutrality against German violation was a moral cause for many, just as it was a practical concern for others, but the waging of the war was harder for some to bear. The central paradox for Liberals was the need to defeat Prussianism by Prussian methods: order, control, militarism—at times, almost martial law, with populist reactions ranging from patriotism through jingoism to xenophobia. These issues collectively would much better serve Labour on the left, and the Conservatives on the right. Many Liberals felt that as soon as the country had gone to war, Liberalism was "dead."

The terms often applied to the party's approach to the war were "laissez-faire," "business as usual," and "limited liability," phrases taken

from the normal operation of the free market. Their application is generally misleading, but it nevertheless followed that the broad theme under which many of the controversial measures can be grouped was "compulsion." The erosion and, in some cases, the absolute rejection, of the voluntary principle represented not only a philosophical problem, in that liberty and free will were being impeded, but also a practical one, in that many felt the market was actually the best way of allocating resources. The first indication that "business as usual" had been abandoned came with the 1914 Defence of the Realm Act and the 1915 Munitions of War Act, both of which expanded the remit of the state into new areas. Suppression of the press, mail censorship, and the interning of enemy aliens may be regarded as inevitable wartime requirements, or could also be viewed as a profound rejection of the principles upon which not just Liberal, but British values had been based. While many Liberals were unhappy with such measures, it must be remembered in light of its historical reputation that it was the Liberal Party that enacted them.

Growing criticism of indecision and a series of embarrassments in the running of the war, combined with the desire to avoid a "khaki" general election (which usually only benefited the Conservative Party), led Asquith to reform the government as a coalition in May 1915. The move, although necessary, was unpopular with Liberals, not only for the admission of enemy politicians being inherently painful, but also because it would mean even more illiberal measures. Asquith's achievement in ensuring that Liberals retained the principal offices was largely only tactical, and within a month the National Registration Bill prepared for the introduction of the Military Service Acts of January and May 1916, when men were summarily forced to enlist for the first time in British history. In September 1915, the McKenna Duties—named after the Chancellor of the Exchequer, Reginald McKenna—introduced tariffs on luxury goods and, in doing so, contravened the central liberal principle for many Liberals (himself included): free trade. McKenna and others felt the approach of Lloyd George and the Conservatives was reckless in that it risked British industry at home and credit overseas. It was a harder argument to make than that which called for "victory at all costs," and in making it, personal relations became so bad that the government could not continue. Lloyd George and his Conservative associates increasingly believed the Prime Minister was no longer capable, an impression Asquith reinforced by tactically resigning in December 1916, expecting no one to be able to replace him.

Asquith had overestimated his importance, and Lloyd George very easily organized a largely Conservative coalition to support him in power for the rest of the war, with the added assistance of the press and the Labour leadership. This was largely a political rather than an ideological development, however. The main evidence that the Liberal Party was not thrown from office through a refusal to rise to the challenge of war is that the change in government saw no real difference in policy: The Lloyd George coalition marked a change of men, not measures. The problem for the party was that most of the men were not Liberals. Most Liberals remained loyal to Asquith but, for a number of obvious reasons, declined officially to oppose or to seek to organize a new radical party. Issues such as conscription in Ireland or the prospects for a negotiated peace passed without concerted action until Asquith formally challenged Lloyd George in the Maurice Debate of May 1918, in which ninety-eight Liberals joined him, and seventy-two supported Lloyd George, though Conservative MPs en-

sured a safe government majority. Nevertheless, on several occasions in the last eighteen months of the war, Lloyd George made overtures to his former chief, and with Asquith's rejection of the position of Lord Chancellor in October 1918 went the last hope of reunion.

Election of 1918

When an election was called immediately after the end of the war in November 1918, Lloyd George stood as the leader of a "national" government, forced by his Conservative partners to give official blessing—in the form of a coupon—only to Liberals who supported the government. Though they had retained control of party finances as well as the support of the National Liberal Federation, Asquith, Grey, McKenna, Simon, and the others could not cope with a "khaki" campaign, and lost their seats. The party was reduced to fewer than thirty MPs (from 272 in 1910), the government was elected with a huge majority, and it was largely a government of Conservative MPs. Lloyd George would forever be a hate figure for those around Asquith, which meant that the split would be of a long duration. Meanwhile the left had reorganized with a newly expanded franchise: The independent Liberals won fewer votes than Labour, while the Irish had voted decisively for independence. Two of the pillars of Liberal government had been removed, while the party itself had become divided. In the British electoral system, governments realistically come only from the leading two parties; from being the first, in four years the Liberals had become the third.

Martin Farr

See also: Conscription (UK, WWI); Conservative Party (UK, WWI); Labour Party (UK, WWI);

Biographies: Asquith, Herbert Henry (WWI); Lloyd George, David (WWI); McKenna, Reginald (WWI)

REFERENCES

Bentley, Michael. *The Liberal Mind 1914–1929.* Cambridge: Cambridge University Press, 1977.

Cook, Chris. *A Short History of the Liberal Party 1900–1984.* London: Macmillan, 1984.

David, Edward. "The Liberal Party Divided 1916–1918." *Historical Journal* XIII (1970): 509–533.

David, Edward, ed. *Inside Asquith's Cabinet: From the Diaries of Charles Hobhouse.* London: John Murray, 1977.

Douglas, Roy. *The History of the Liberal Party 1895–1970.* London: Sidgwick & Jackson, 1971.

Dutton, David. *A History of the Liberal Party in the Twentieth Century.* Basingstoke: Palgrave, 2004.

Fraser, Peter. "British War Policy and the Crisis of Liberalism in May 1915." *Journal of Modern History* 54 (March 1982): 1–26.

Hazlehurst, Cameron. *Politicians at War: July 1914 to May 1915. A Prologue to the Triumph of Lloyd George.* London: Johnathan Cape, 1971.

Koss, Stephen. "The Destruction of Britain's Last Liberal Government." *Journal of Modern History* XL, 2 (1968): 257–277

Searle, G. R. *The Liberal Party: Triumph and Disintegration, 1886–1929.* London: Macmillan, 1992.

Wilson, Trevor. *The Downfall of the Liberal Party 1914–1935.* London: Collins, 1966.

Liberalism

Liberalism is a political philosophy based upon individual freedom, the essential goodness of mankind, and the value of rational thought. Prior to World War I, liberalism was used in Europe and North America to support the protection of individual freedoms and limited roles for a representative government. Acceptable government duties included the enforcement of civil order, the provision and maintenance of a stable currency, and the protection of citizens from foreign invasion. Liberalism included a belief in laissez-faire economics, which suggests governments should not interfere with the operation of markets. The social miseries created by free-market capitalism and the devastation of World War I led to the postwar rejection of liberal ideas, an increase in the size and scope of government, and the rise of authoritarianism.

Liberalism is derived from two distinct sources. One source, which traces back to classical antiquity, views the primary purpose of government as the protection of individual liberty. This tradition is represented by the political doctrines of the English Whigs in the seventeenth and eighteenth centuries. Whigs favored severe restrictions on the power of the monarchy. The other source, which developed on the European continent, favored a reconstruction of society in accordance with the principles of reason. This tradition is represented by the Enlightenment philosophies of Rene Descartes, Voltaire, and Jean-Jacques Rousseau. These ideas assume that people are able to recognize problems and take active steps to improve the human condition. These two sources combined in the nineteenth century to become liberalism. Liberal beliefs include government by democracy, equality of men, and the individual freedoms of thought, speech, and the press. Liberalism stands in contrast to conservative and authoritarian philosophies, which favor the restriction of individual liberty by established religious and political authorities.

Liberalism's popularity in the nineteenth century gave rise to powerful political parties in the United Kingdom and Canada. The British Liberal Party, which was influential from 1832 to 1922, supported free trade and individual liberties, but opposed imperialism and government interference in the economy. Notable leaders include William E. Gladstone, Herbert Henry Asquith, and David Lloyd George. In Canada, Wilfrid Laurier led the Liberal Party to power as the prime minister from 1896 to 1911.

The liberal movement in the United States never reached the magnitude of that in Europe, primarily because many goals of liberalism, such as the establishment of individual freedoms, were already embodied in the U.S. Constitution and Bill of Rights.

By the end of the nineteenth century, the unregulated industrialization and development of business resulted in huge inequalities of wealth and power. Other undesirable outcomes were widespread pollution, famines, unsafe working conditions, and the use of child labor. Liberalism and its support of free-market capitalism seemed to promote exploitation, colonialism, imperialism, war, inequality, and poverty.

The negative consequences of industrialization led many people, especially poor workers, to question the liberal philosophy. Liberal thinkers developed new interpretations of individual freedom. These included movements to protect workers' rights through the creation of trade unions. Thus, in the early twentieth century, liberalism began to advocate an active role for the government in the promotion of social progress and the provision of a minimum level of individual welfare. This sentiment was also the foundation of the Progressive movement, which shared liberalism's belief in the ability to improve living and working conditions and advocated change over the maintenance of the status quo. In Great Britain, Liberals successfully implemented national insurance, welfare programs, and laws regulating conditions for workers. In Canada, Prime Minister Laurier's continued support for traditional liberal ideas, such as the promotion of free trade with the United States, led voters to replace him in 1911 with a Conservative Party candidate.

The promotion of a more active social role for government was a distinct departure from classical liberal thought and is now known as social liberalism. An alternative branch of liberalism, which prefers the classical interpretation of minimal government, is now known as libertarianism.

The justification for social liberalism is the belief that in order for people to be free, society needs to provide them with basic education, protections, and opportunities. Thus many liberal thinkers advocated laws that mandated minimum standards for wages and working conditions and against the employment of children. Laissez-faire liberals viewed such laws as unnecessary impediments to free-market capitalism.

World War I dealt a severe blow to the popular support of liberalism. There was a perception that liberalism contributed to the conditions that led to World War I. Disillusionment with the duration of the war and the huge loss of life created a backlash against liberal thought. Citizens encouraged governments to play a more active role in managing their economies and societies. Some nations even adopted socialism or Fascism as better alternatives to liberalism. This rise of authoritarianism, including the subsequent rise of Nazism in Germany, became a factor leading to World War II.

World War I had a profound effect on societies. It led to the expansion of governmental power and authority in many countries, including the United States, Great Britain, and France. World War I helped destroy the strong belief in liberalism that had prevailed in Europe since the Enlightenment. Liberalism returned to popularity after World War II with the belief that democratically elected governments would better serve societies than the authoritarian regimes that had emerged in the early twentieth century.

John B. Buck

See also: Democratic Party (WWI); Economic Policy (WWI); Economy (Canada, WWI); Economy (UK, WWI); Economy (U.S., WWI); Liberal Party (Canada, WWI); Liberal Party (UK, WWI)

REFERENCES

Brinkley, Alan. *The End of Reform: New Deal Liberalism in Recession and War.* New York: Alfred A. Knopf, 1995.

Dewey, John. *Liberalism and Social Action.* New York: G. P. Putnam's Sons, 1935.

Hayek, Friedrich A. *New Studies in Philosophy, Politics, Economics and the History of Ideas.* London: Routledge & Keagan Paul, 1982.

Hobhouse, L. T. *Liberalism.* London: Williams and Norgate, 1911.

Mansfield, Harvey. *The Spirit of Liberalism.* Cambridge: Harvard University Press, 1978.

Schapiro, J. Salwyn. *Liberalism: Its Meaning and History.* Princeton, NJ: D. Van Nostrand Company, 1958.

Sykes, Alan. *The Rise and Fall of British Liberalism 1776–1988.* London: Longman, 1997.

Literature (Canada)

Before World War I, Canadians were searching for a sense of identity, and this search was reflected in their literature. By the end of the conflict, Canada's 60,000 war dead had earned the nation a seat at the Paris peace talks, and Canadian authors had gained a greater sense of confidence and purpose.

The 1867 Constitution and the 1885 completion of the transcontinental railway had sparked pride and patriotism in the country, but there was still a great deal of uncertainty about what it meant to be "Canadian." The nation's literature struggled to define itself as sep-arate from the colonial traditions of "Mother England" and the overwhelming force and vigor of "Uncle Sam" to the south. Popular writing at the time was regional, rather than national, in outlook. The "Confederation Poets" Charles G. D. Roberts, Bliss Carman, William Wilfred Campbell, Duncan Campbell Scott, Frederick George Scott, and Archibald Lampman inspired their compatriots with rapturous odes to the rugged landscape of central and Atlantic Canada. Novelists Stephen Leacock and Lucy Maud Montgomery exposed the foibles of the small town in such books as *Sunshine Sketches* and *Anne of Green Gables.* Robert Service vividly illustrated life in the far North, with poems like "The Cremation of Sam McGee." Ralph Connor penned sensational novels such as *Corporal Cameron of the North West Mounted Police* to dramatize the settling of the Canadian West. All of these popular works concentrated on rural existence and tended to sentimentalize, satirize, or sensationalize Canadian life. The new literary developments that were beginning to stir in other parts of the world barely touched Canada's shores. Indeed, the development of the Modernist movement was as foreign and poorly understood in Edwardian Canada as the clouds of war gathering over Europe at the time.

English Canadian writers, like the English-speaking public, were quick to embrace the war as an adventure and a chance for Canada to prove itself in an international arena. Not everyone was eager to lay down their lives for "Mother England," however. Canada's Francophone population felt little connection to the European war, and no need to partake in the battle. French Canadian writing reflects this disinterest: With few exceptions, French Canadians wrote little literature about the war. Indeed, World War I, and the bitter Conscription Crisis of 1917, served to reinforce linguistic and cultural divisions between English and French Canada.

Censorship

From the moment war was declared, the secret propaganda unit of the Allied forces, located at Wellington House in London, swung into action. Canadian authors were fed tales of German atrocities and encouraged to glorify the Allied cause. The stories disseminated by Wellington House vilified the Germans as mechanized war mongers, sanctified the Belgians as innocent victims, and glorified the Allies as heroic soldiers. Canadian authors were not only encouraged to toe the party line; they were actively recruited for the job. Indeed, popular Canadian-born novelist Sir Gilbert Parker was appointed to Wellington House in 1914 with the sole mission of influencing American neutrality on the war. Sir Max Aiken, "the Canadian Eye Witness," published two volumes of *Canada in Flanders,* which were patriotic chronicles of the Canadian battles in Belgium and France. These works held a thinly disguised propagandist motive: To give the Canadian government a right to make decisions in the conduct of the conflict. Eventually, Wellington House had no need to promulgate the propaganda, as patriotic Canadians began publishing the Allied messages themselves. Such works included volumes like 1918's *Out There (Somewhere in France)* and 1919's *The Great War in Verse and Prose,* which contained such blatantly propagandist poems as "The Debt Unpayble" and "The Canadian Twilight."

Canadian soldiers did not often record their true experiences of trench life in civilian literature: "In order to be quickly published, authors had to be careful not to name individuals or regiments, to be vague about place, to be un-

critical, not reveal any information that would in any way disclose information to the enemy, and to be full of praise for Allied efforts and aims," notes scholar Peter Buitenhuis. One exception to soldier writing was Robert Service's dispatches to the newspaper the *Ottawa Journal.* Service was an ambulance driver in France during the war. His poems frankly documented the horrors he saw in the field. But even Service's popularity was not enough to spare him from the censor, however. In 1916, the *Journal's* editor was reprimanded for printing his poems.

Major John McRae is Canada's most famous soldier poet of World War I. Born in Guelph, Ontario, in 1872, he was a medical doctor with the 1st Brigade Canadian Field Artillery when he penned the most popular poem of the war. He wrote "In Flanders Fields" after witnessing the carnage of the 2nd battle of Ypres. Published anonymously in the British magazine *Punch* in 1915, the poem was quickly reprinted all over the world. The force of the poem lies partly with the haunting power of its opening lines:

> In Flanders fields the poppies blow
> Between the crosses, row on row
> That mark our place; and in the sky
> The larks, still bravely singing, fly.

The true popularity of the poem may well reside with its effectiveness at rallying perceived "shirkers" to the glorious cause. From a literary standpoint, the poem has been sniffed at as "recruiting poster rhetoric," says historian Paul Fussell. Nevertheless, its impact cannot be denied. Countless school children have recited its plaintive lament for the dead, and the poem's poppy motif inspired the Commonwealth tradition of wearing a memorial poppy on Remembrance Day (November 11).

One exception to the sometimes painfully patriotic literature of the time can be found in the writing of the various soldier newspapers and military publications issued by the battalions comprising the Canadian Expeditionary Force. These newspapers exposed a more honest version of life in the trenches. While never allowed to outwardly question the value of the conflict, the publications were able to critique military bureaucracy, dull training, and army regulations. Mostly fed by soldier contributions, these newspapers were as close as the Canadian soldier could come to seeing their experiences reflected in print: "In their pages servicemen acknowledged, as far as possible under the guidance of military editors, that once exposed to the desolation of No Man's Land, shell fire, or perhaps the death of a comrade, idealism frequently waned in favour of cynicism and despair," says historian Jeffrey Keshen. While censors certainly reviewed the publications, they allowed all but the most bitter of the satire and black humour. Still, newspapers like *The Shell Hole Advance* and the *Lethbridge Highlander* had only a limited audience. Often no more than a thousand copies were printed and it was sometimes years before civilians were able to read them.

Women Writers

Home front literature, especially that written by women, was also an important part of Canadian World War I writing. Female authors like L. M. Montgomery and Nelly McClung reflected a different experience of the war. Their writing illustrated how fundamentally this first "total war" in Canadian history affected not only the soldiers at the front, but also those who stayed behind. Most female authors sought to illustrate the courage, strength, and heroism that Canadian women demonstrated while their men-folk were away: Whether it was acquiring new skills and trades, learning to speak up for themselves, or even nobly sacrificing brothers, husbands, and sweethearts to the Great Cause, the women of home front literature were as courageous as the boys in the trenches.

Only a few wartime soldier publications, such as Robert Service's *Rhymes of a Red Cross Man* and Edgar W. McGinnis's *Poems Written at the Front,* expressed even mild antiwar sentiment. Most Canadian writers who had fought in the war took about a decade to question the conflict that shattered their lives. Thus, in the 1930s, a whole spate of memoirs and novels were published dissecting the war and analyzing its effectiveness. Peregrine Acland's *All Else Is Folly* (1929), Philip Child's *God's Sparrow* (1937), and Charles Yale Harrison's *Generals Die in Bed* (1930) all critiqued the Allied war effort. *Generals Die in Bed* is an excoriating look at the corruption, inefficiencies, hypocrisy, and horror of life on the front, which reflects Harrison's own experiences as a machine gunner for the Royal Montreal Regiment. The novel, like many of the works published at the time, offers a savage critique of war that was supposed to save civilization, but instead destroyed it.

By the end of the war, Canadian society had irrevocably changed: Women were enfranchised; income tax had been introduced, and the mud of France and Belgium had become the burial ground for thousands of Canadians. The values of humanism, the belief in the essential progress of civilization, and a sense of security had been ripped away from a generation who then faced the bitter realities of the Depression. Canadian literature could not go back to the rural idylls and high sentiment of the past. After World War I, there was rampant disillusionment at the waste and uselessness of the conflict and intense anger with the older generation who were perceived as having caused the war. Satire was one of the most successful genres in the 1920s. The romance, earnestness, and morality of prewar literature was ridiculed and rebelled against.

World War I continues to hold a place in the Canadian imagination. Perhaps it's the myth that the nation was forged at the decisive Battle of Vimy Ridge that has caused Canadian writers to hearken back to World War I so often. Novels, poems, and plays, such as Timothy Findley's *The Wars,* Jane Urquhart's *The Stone Carvers,* Roch Carrier's *La Guerre, yes sir!,* John Gray and Eric Peterson's play *Billy Bishop Goes to War,* Alden Nowlan's poem "Ypres: 1915," Marilyn Bowering's *Grandfather was a Soldier,* Donald Jack's *The Bandy Papers,* Hugh McClennan's *Barometer Rising,* and Robertson Davies's *Fifth Business,* portray one of the bloodiest periods of Canada's history in order to understand the nation.

Amy Margaret Tector

See also: Journalism (Canada, WWI); Propaganda (Canada, WWI); Biographies: McClung, Nellie (WWI)

REFERENCES

Buitenhuis, Peter. *The Great War of Words: British, American and Canadian Propaganda and Fiction. 1914–1933.* Vancouver: University of British Columbia Press, 1987.

Coates, Donna. "The Best Soldiers of All: Unsung Heroines in Canadian Women's Great War Fictions." *Canadian Literature* 151 (Winter 1996): 66–99.

Colombo, John Robert, and Michael Richardson. *We Stand on Guard: Poems and Songs of Canadians in Battle.* Doubleday: Toronto, 1985.

Fussell, Paul. *The Great War and Modern Memory.* Oxford: Oxford University Press, 1975.

Keshen, Jeffrey A. *Propaganda and Censorship During Canada's Great War.* Edmonton, AB: University of Alberta Press, 1996.

Vance, Jonathan. *Death So Noble: Memory, Meaning and the First World War.* Vancouver: University of British Columbia Press, 1997.

Wetherell, J. E., ed. *The Great War in Verse and Prose.* Toronto: A. T. Wilgress, 1919.

Literature (UK)

Poetry

British poetry about World War I began to appear shortly after the beginning of the conflict and, to some extent, serves as a gauge of gradually shifting literary attitudes toward the war. In 1914, the anthology *Des Imagistes, Songs and Sonnets for England in War Time* appeared, showcasing the work of eleven contributors, including Richard Aldington, H. D. (Hilda Doolittle), Ford Madox Ford, James Joyce, Amy Lowell, Ezra Pound, and William Carlos Williams. T. E. Hulme provided much of the theoretical focus among those writers whose loose association produced the Imagist movement, and his approval of the war (he ultimately died in a bombardment in 1917) influenced the content of the volume. Hulme's own contribution, "Trenches: St. Eloi," describes the stark realities of trench life against the backdrop of night and emphasizes the necessity of perseverance. The first collection by a single author focusing on the war was Maurice Hewlett's *Singsongs of the War.*

In 1915, more than a half-dozen noteworthy collections by individual authors were published, including volumes entitled *Battle* by both W. W. Gibson and Julian Grenfell, Richard Aldington's *Images, 1910–1915,* Robert Nichols's *Invocation: War Poems and Others,* Jesse Pope's *War Poems,* Frank Sidwick's *Some Verse,* and Katharine Tynan's *Flower of Youth.* But the most remembered collection published in this year was Rupert Brooke's *1914 and Other Poems.*

The collection includes the often anthologized poems "Peace," "Safety," and "The Soldier," which drew on the poet's battle experience in Belgium. Brooke died in April 1915 of blood poisoning while en route to Gallipoli.

In 1916, more than a dozen significant collections by individual authors appeared, including Gilbert Frankau's *The Guns,* F. W. Harvey's *A Gloucestershire Lad at Home and Abroad,* W. N. Hodgson's *Verse and Prose in Peace and War,* Patrick MacGill's *Soldier Songs,* E. A. Mackintosh's *A Highland Regiment,* John Masefield's *Gallipoli,* H. Smalley Sarson's *From Field and Hospital,* Cicely Fox Smith's *Fighting Men,* Charles Hamilton Dorley's *Marlborough and Other Poems,* J. C. Squire's *Survival of the Fittest,* W. J. Turner's *The Hunter and Other Poems,* and Willoughby Weaving's *the Star Fields and Other Poems.* Robert Graves's collection *Over the Brazier* includes poems written while he was convalescing from a wound and offers juxtapositions of his conviction about the necessity of the war and his deepening sense of the absurdities in how the war was being conducted.

In 1917, as the British war effort reached its crescendo, there was a corresponding crest in the outpouring of war-related poetry from the British presses. The notable volumes by individual poets included Herbert Asquith's *the Volunteer and Other Poems,* Laurence Binyon's *The Cause: Poems of the War* and *For the Fallen,* Leslie Coulson's *From an Outpost and Other Poems,* W. N. Ewer's *Five Souls and Other Wartime Verses,* Gilbert Frankau's *The City of Fear and Other Poems,* Lord Gorell's *Days of Destiny: War Poems at Home and Abroad,* Ivor Gurney's *Severn and Somne,* F. W. Harvey's *Gloucestershire Friends: Poems from a German Prison Camp,* Francis Ledwidge's *Last Poems,* Henry Newbolt's *Poems: New and Old,* Robert Nichols's *Ardours and Endurances,* John W. Streets's *The Undying Splendour,* R. E. Vernede's *War Poems and Other Verses,* and Francis Brett Young's *Five Degrees South.*

Robert Graves's second collection about the war, *Fairies and Fusiliers,* was a more mature effort than *Over the Brazier,* emphasizing the camaraderie among frontline troops, the continuous discomforts of trench life, the terrors of combat, and the agonies of wounded and dying men. Graves's own war service had ended after he had been badly wounded and had experienced severe shell shock. Closely associated with Graves, Siegfried Sassoon also initially supported the war and yet knew firsthand how it had degenerated into an unprecedented spectacle of carnage that no one in command seemed to understand. His first collection of poems about the war was *The Old Huntsman and Other Poems.* The title refers sardonically to his romantic naïveté about his physical and psychological readiness for war at the time of his enlistment.

In 1918, the new collections by individual poets included Paul Bewsher's *Bombing of Bruges,* Vera Brittain's *Verses of a VAD,* Ford Madox Ford's *On Heaven and Poems Written on Active Service,* Gilbert Frankau's *The Judgment of Valhalla,* P. H. B. Lyon's *Songs of Youth and War,* E. A. Mackintosh's *War the Liberator and Other Pieces,* Edward Thomas's *Last Poems,* Katharine Tynan's *Herb o' Grace,* and Alec Waugh's *Resentment.* But the most significant collection published during the final year of the war—and one of the most significant collections ever published about the war—was Siegfried Sassoon's *Counter-Attack and Other Poems.* It provides his readers with an unsparingly, and often a very brutally, honest depiction of what the war in the trenches was doing to a whole generation of British men. Near the end of the war, Sassoon was sent to a psychological hospital after he refused to continue to lead his men in what he saw as completely purposeless and essentially suicidal attacks on the German lines.

Among the more important volumes of poetry about the war published since the armistice have been Richard Aldington's *Images of War* (1919), Wilfred Owen's *Poems* (1920), Ezra Pound's *Hugh Selwyn Mauberley* (1920), T. S. Eliot's *The Waste Land* (1925), David Jones's *In Parentheses* (1937), and Isaac Rosenberg's *Collected Works* (1937).

Fiction

During the war, relatively little notable British fiction about the war was published—especially in comparison to the large outpouring of poetry about the war. Of course, it was relatively easy, if only in a strictly comparative sense, for combatants to compose short poems in the lulls between combat, but it would have been next to impossible to sustain the writing of a novel under those conditions. In addition, the strict censorship of all publications during the war meant that any novels that depicted the war with any sort of ambivalence—never mind any that pointedly criticized the war—would have been held from publication.

Ian Hay's *The First Hundred Thousand*, published in 1915, is remembered for being the first British novel about the war, but little else about it has been especially memorable. Initially published anonymously in *Blackwood's Magazine,* the novel presents a fictional version of Hay's experiences with the initial contingent of the British Expeditionary Force in Belgium. Also published in 1915 were William Le-Queux's *At the Sign of the Sword,* Patrick MacGill's *The Amateur Army,* Arthur Machen's *The Angels of Mons,* and Evelyn Sharp's *The War of All the Ages.*

Published in 1916, H. G. Wells's *Mr. Britling Sees It Through* presents a satiric portrait of a superficial and self-absorbed British gentleman who gradually comes to recognize that the war is more than a personal inconvenience and to understand that it is a truly terrible cataclysm

beyond his comprehension. Other war-related novels and books of short fiction published in 1916 included Bruce Bairnsfather's *Bullets and Billets,* Donald Hankey's *A Student in Arms,* Henry Newbolt's *Tales of the Great War,* and Hugh Walpole's *The Dark Forest.* In 1917, John Snaith's *The Coming* was published and, in 1918, Lord Sunsany's *Tales of War* appeared.

A number of British novelists produced largely forgotten series of war-related novels during the war. F. S. Brereton provided what amounted to a running survey of the battle-fronts in *With French at the Front* (1915), *Under French's Command* (1915), *With Joffre at Verdun* (1916), *Armoured Car Scouts* (1917), *Under Haig in Flanders* (1917), and *With the Allies to the Rhine* (1919). Joseph Hocking wrote *All for a Scrap of Paper* (1915), *Dearer than Life* (1915), *Tommy* (1916), and *The Path of Glory* (1917). R. W. Campbell presented a sort of "everyman" soldier in *Private Spud Tamson* (1915) and *Sergt. Spud Tamson* (1918). Several novelists authored series under pseudonyms. Writing as Boyd Cable, E. W. Ewart produced *Between the Lines* (1915), *Action Front* (1916), and *Front Lines* (1918). As Escott Lynn, Jack Spur authored *In Khaki for the King* (1915), *Oliver Hastings, V. C.* (1916), *Knights of the Air* (1918), and *Lads of the Lothians* (1920). And, as "Sapper," H. C. McNeille wrote *The Lieutenant and Others* (1916), *Sgt. Michael Cassidy, R. E.* (1918), and *War Stories* (1930).

Among the more important novels about the war published since the armistice have been Richard Aldington's *Death of a Hero* (1929) and *Roads to Glory* (1930), Frederic Mannings's *The Middle Parts of Fortune* (1929) and *Her Privates We* (1930), Harold Brighouse's *Once a Hero* (1922), and R. H. Mottram's *The Spanish Farm Trilogy 1914–1918* (1927). Acclaimed series of novels about the war have been subsequently produced by Ford Madox Ford in his tetralogy *Some Do Not* (1924), *No*

More Parades (1925), *A Man Could Stand Up* (1926), and *Last Post* (1928), and by Pat Barker in her trilogy, *Regeneration* (1991), *The Eye in the Door* (1994), and *The Ghost Road* (1995).

Nonfiction

Shortly after war was declared, the War Propaganda Bureau recruited two dozen prominent British authors to produce materials in support of the war effort. The novelist Arnold Bennett produced the pamphlets *Liberty: A Statement of the British Case* (1915) and *Over There: War Scenes on the Western Front* (1915). The latter was a recruiting tool that he wrote after a visit to the front lines that left him physically and psychologically sickened by the conditions in the trenches, but that also left him convinced that such terrible sacrifice had to be rewarded with victory.

Having served as a doctor during the Boer War, the acclaimed mystery novelist Arthur Conan Doyle had argued in *The War in South Africa* (1902) that the British aims and tactics during that war had been entirely justified. During World War I, he worked, like Bennett, for the War Propaganda Bureau, producing the pamphlets *To Arms!* (1914) and *A Visit to the Three Fronts* (1916). A commentator on war news for the *Daily Chronicle,* Doyle eventually wrote the six-volume history, *The British Campaign in France and Flanders.*

After participating in the Dardanelles campaign, the novelist Compton Mackenzie was appointed to direct the Aegean Intelligence Service headquartered in Syria. In 1932, his memoir of that period, *Greek Memories,* was withdrawn from publication after the government claimed that some of the details that Mackenzie had included violated the Official Secrets Act. Mackenzie himself believed that the British intelligence service was actually more bothered by his unflattering recollections about its operations and about the personalities of some of its operatives.

Martin Kich

See also: Journalism (UK, WWI); Propaganda (UK, WWI); Biographies: Asquith, Herbert Henry (WWI)

REFERENCES

Bergonzi, Bernard. *Heroes' Twilight: A Study of the Literature of the Great War.* London: Constable, 1965.

Blunden, Edmund. *War Poets, 1914–1918.* London: Longmans, Green, 1958.

Crawford, Fred D. *British Poets of the Great War.* Selingsgrove, PA: Susquehanna University Press, 1988.

Fussell, Paul. *The Great War and Modern Memory.* London: Oxford University Press, 1975.

Greicus, M. S. *Prose Writers of the Great War.* London: Longman, 1973.

Hibberd, Dominic, ed. *Poetry of the First World War: A Casebook.* London: Macmillan, 1981.

Johnston, John H. *English Poetry of the First World War: A Study in the Evolution of Lyric and Narrative Form.* Princeton, NJ: Princeton University Press, 1964.

Moore, T. Sturge. *Some Soldier Poets.* London: Grant Richards, 1919.

Onions, John. *English Fiction and Drama of the Great War, 1918–1939.* New York: St. Martin's, 1990.

Silkin, Jon. *Out of Battle: The Poetry of the Great War.* London: Oxford University Press, 1972.

Literature (U.S.)

Most of the American literature about World War I was written on Allied home fronts rather than on the battlefields themselves. Literature published during the war included major works by Carl Sandburg, T. S. Eliot, and Willa Cather.

However, it was in the years immediately following the war that American writers like Ernest Hemingway and F. Scott Fitzgerald began fully to process and respond to the war experience. Literary modernism, the preeminent artistic movement of the period, reached its apex in its response to the experience of World War I, though not all successful writers in the interwar period joined in the modernist claim to abandon traditional literary structures. For decades after World War I, Americans continued to write about the war experience, and the literary legacy of the war extends to the present day.

American literature flourished during the World War I era. During the mid–1910s, the Chicago-based journal *Poetry* published work by some writers who became major American poets, including Wallace Stevens, Marianne Moore, and Hilda Doolittle (H. D.). In 1916, the year before the United States entered the war, Carl Sandburg published *Chicago Poems,* Robert Frost published a collection of poems called *Mountain Interval,* which included "The Road Not Taken," and Amy Lowell published *Men, Women and Ghosts,* which contained her poem "Patterns," among others. In 1917, T. S. Eliot published *Prufrock and Other Observations,* which included one of his best-known poems, "The Love Song of J. Alfred Prufrock." In the same year, Sinclair Lewis published his novels *The Job* and *The Innocents,* William Carlos Williams published a collection of poems called *Al Que Quiere!,* and Edith Wharton published her novel *Summer.* In 1918, Wharton published another novel called *The Marne,* Willa Cather published the now-classic novel *My Ántonia,* and Theodore Dreiser published *Free and Other Stories.*

Some American literature responded to the war through well-established literary forms and a reiteration of established moral codes. Writers who experienced combat firsthand often sought familiar literary structures, including Alan Seeger, who wrote his brief poem "I Have a Rendezvous with Death" shortly before his death in France in 1916. If Seeger's opening stanza reveals his technical traditionalism, it also reveals a startling fatalism:

> I have a rendezvous with Death
> At some disputed barricade,
> When Spring comes back with rustling shade
> And apple-blossoms fill the air—
> I have a rendezvous with Death
> When Spring brings back blue days and fair.

Authors like Willa Cather, whose 1922 novel, *One of Ours,* won the Pulitzer Prize the next year, gained broad popularity by describing World War I as an affirmation of older visions of honor and bravery.

Literary Modernism

One of the most important intellectual responses to the war was the development of new forms of literary modernism. Characterized by the fracturing of linear temporality and the erosion of narrative structures, literary modernism mimicked the uncertainties felt by those who experienced the war both from the battlefront and from the home front. Earlier in the twentieth century, when inventors and entrepreneurs like Thomas Edison, the Wright Brothers, and Henry Ford became household names, technological advancement seemed to many Americans an unequivocal tool for social progress. During World War I, however, the horrors wrought by new weapons like machine guns, poison gas, tanks, and fighter planes made people less certain about the benign nature of technology. Moreover, the anonymity and static nature of trench warfare made it harder to think of the war in terms of courage and individual glory.

The American literature that emerged during and after the war reflected the ambiguity and multiplicity of modernism. While various definitions of modernism abound, literary modernists never spelled out a unified program. Modernism was at once a movement that rejected urbanism and technology by taking refuge in primitivism and ancient mythologies and also a movement enamored of speed, machines, and newness at all costs. Much of the best American literature about the experience of the war itself appeared well after the war ended, often written by American expatriates living in Europe. During and after the war, some of the most talented and influential American writers lived in London and Paris, including Ezra Pound, T. S. Eliot, Ernest Hemingway, H. D., Gertrude Stein, F. Scott Fitzgerald, and others. In 1922, Eliot published his masterpiece, the long poem *The Waste Land*. Early on, he demands answers about the desolation around him, only to cast doubt on the existence of meaningful certainties:

> What are the roots that clutch, what branches
>   grow
> Out of this stony rubbish? Son of man,
> You cannot say, or guess, for you know only
> A heap of broken images, where the sun beats,
> And the dead tree gives no shelter, the cricket
>   no relief,
> And the dry stone no sound of water. Only
> There is shadow under this red rock,
> (Come in under the shadow of this red rock),
> And I will show you something different from
>   either
> Your shadow at morning striding behind you
> Or your shadow at evening rising to meet you;
> I will show you fear in a handful of dust.

In 1926, Hemingway published *The Sun Also Rises,* whose protagonist, a young veteran made impotent by a battle injury, epitomizes the post-war sense of futility, disorientation, and diminishing hope among veterans and their contemporaries, sentiments that echoed the mood of Fitzgerald's 1925 *The Great Gatsby.* Hemingway, who volunteered for the Red Cross as an ambulance driver in the war, based his 1929 *A Farewell to Arms* on his war experience, an authority that made his debunking of easy notions of honor all the more powerful. Although Fitzgerald himself never fought in the war, he provided one of the most vivid descriptions of the meaning of World War I in his 1934 *Tender is the Night* through the words of a veteran visiting the trenches years later with friends:

> See that little stream—we could walk to it in two minutes. It took the British a month to walk to it—a whole empire walking very slowly, dying in front and pushing forward behind. And another empire walked very slowly backward a few inches a day, leaving the dead like a million bloody rugs. No Europeans will ever do that again in this generation . . .
>
> This western-front business couldn't be done again, not for a long time. The young men think they could do it but they couldn't . . .This took religion and years of plenty and tremendous sureties and the exact relation that existed between the classes . . . You had to have a whole-souled sentimental equipment going back further than you could remember. You had to remember Christmas, and postcards of the Crown Prince and his fiancée, and little cafés in Valence and beer gardens in Unter den Linden and weddings at the mairie, and going to the Derby, and your grandfather's whiskers . . .
>
> Why, this was a love battle—there was a century of middle-class love spent here. This was the last love battle.

In their novels, Hemingway and Fitzgerald described the fragility of older moral codes and their subsequent destruction, but even as their characters express feelings of apathy and willful isolation they often mourn the shattering of old sureties in spite of themselves. The authors' articulation of this specific postwar mentality made them the most visible members of an artistic coterie that Gertrude Stein dubbed "The Lost Generation," a group that also included Stein herself, John Dos Passos, Henry Miller, and Ford Madox Ford.

Helen Zoë Veit

See also: Censorship (WWI); Committee on Public Information (WWI); Journalism (U.S., WWI); Muckrakers (WWI); Biographies: Anderson, Sherwood (WWI); Cather, Willa (WWI); cummings, e.e. (WWI); Dos Passos, John (WWI); Dreiser, Theodore (WWI); Grey, Zane (WWI); Hemingway, Ernest (WWI); Wharton, Edith (WWI)

REFERENCES

Cross, Tim, ed. *The Lost Voices of World War I: An International Anthology of Writers, Poets & Playwrights.* London: Bloomsbury Publishing, 1988.

Dawes, James. *The Language of War: Literature and Culture in the U.S. from the Civil War through World War II.* Cambridge: Harvard University Press, 2002.

Eliot, T. S. *The Waste Land.* San Diego: Harcourt Brace & Company, 1997.

Fitzgerald, F. Scott. *Tender Is the Night: A Romance,* ed. Arnold Goldman. London: Penguin, 2000.

Glover, Jon, and Jon Silkin, eds. *The Penguin Book of First World War Prose.* London: Viking Penguin, 1989.

Kennedy, David M. *Over Here: The First World War and American Society.* New York: Oxford University Press, 1980.

Norris, Margaret. *Writing War in the Twentieth Century.* Charlottesville: University Press of Virginia, 2000.

Seeger, Alan. "I Have a Rendezvous with Death." Bartleby.com. Online Resource. Accessed at: http://www.bartleby.com/104/121.html.

Lusitania, Sinking of

The Cunard passenger liner the *Lusitania* was torpedoed and sunk by a German U-boat on May 7, 1915, off the south coast of Ireland, en route from New York to Liverpool, with the loss of 1,200 lives, 128 of them American. Allegations of a conspiracy to sink the *Lusitania* center upon the claim that the then-First Lord of the British Admiralty, Winston Churchill, colluded with the First Sea Lord, Admiral Jack Fisher, and other senior leaders of the Royal Navy, to place the liner in peril, anticipating that heavy loss of American lives would hasten the intervention of the United States in World War I. While it is accepted that part of the *Lusitania*'s cargo comprised munitions for the Allied war effort, there have also been suggestions of a conspiracy to conceal both the precise nature of these war supplies and the military capacity of the ship itself.

The emergence of a conspiracy to sink the *Lusitania* is usually traced to a conference hosted by the British Admiralty in Whitehall on May 5, two days before the liner was sunk, where a decision was made to withdraw the *Lusitania*'s naval escort without notifying the ship, in waters where U-boats were known to be active. Among others summoned to attend the meeting was Joseph M. Kenworthy, a Lieutenant Commander who worked for Naval Intelligence, and whose only prior association with Churchill had been when Kenworthy submitted a report, commissioned by Churchill, assessing the political outcomes should a passenger liner carrying American citizens be attacked and sunk by the German navy. But the suggestion that Churchill and other senior

While the 1915 sinking of the British liner Lusitania cost 128 American lives, it failed to draw the United States into World War I, though it did tilt public opinion further away from support for Germany, which had torpedoed the ship. (Bettmann/Corbis)

members of the Admiralty conspired to sink the *Lusitania* is problematic. Records from the Admiralty conference on May 5 indicate that British naval forces stationed in Ireland were instructed to protect the ship. It is also a matter of record that at least eight, and possibly more, warnings of U-boat activity off southern Ireland were communicated to the *Lusitania* on May 6 and May 7. Notwithstanding the urgency of these warnings, and the Admiralty's awareness of the U-boat threat, a more prosaic explanation for why the liner found itself unguarded in dangerous waters, may lie in the complacency of the British military. In April 1915, Churchill had written that Britain "enjoyed a supremacy at sea the like of which had never been seen even in the days of Nelson." Assured, they assumed, of naval supremacy, and with their attention focused on the ongoing campaign in the Dardanelles, the men responsible for

British naval policy may simply have paid insufficient attention to the dangers of U-boat activity closer to home. The notional desertion of *Lusitania* by her naval escort, the *Juno,* has been described, even by those who see a conspiracy, as following the standard pattern for rotation of patrol ships in the area.

Secret Military Cargo

Suspicions regarding the exact nature of the *Lusitania*'s cargo have been aroused by discrepancies in the two separate cargo manifests Cunard lodged with U.S. customs, one before and one after the ship's departure from New York. In order to keep cargoes secret from German informers operating on the New York docks, it was standard practice for British shipping companies during World War I to file conflicting or incomplete manifests before sailing, and nobody has yet demonstrated convincingly that Cunard actively misled either the U.S. authorities or the public as to the contents of the ship's hold. The day after the *Lusitania* was torpedoed, for example, the *New York Times* published full details of the liner's military cargo in its edition of May 8. The civilian status of the *Lusitania* has also been challenged, with allegations that the liner carried a hidden arsenal that could be rapidly mobilized for use as necessary; and a conspiracy to conceal the *Lusitania*'s military capacity has even been linked with an unidentified relative of an unidentified future American president. But none of the 109 passengers who eventually testified to the two public enquiries into the disaster recalled seeing guns mounted on the liner.

More intriguing is the debate about what caused the fateful "second explosion" on board the ship. Although the Admiralty maintained for some years that U-boat U-20 had hit the ship with two torpedoes, it is now widely accepted that the submarine fired only one torpedo at the *Lusitania,* and that the second catastrophic detonation, the one that sank the liner so quickly with such a huge loss of life, was caused by an unknown object or substance the ship was carrying in its cargo. The second explosion has been explained in a number of ways, ranging from the lurid (the *Lusitania* was carrying a cargo of secret explosive powder) to the banal (the ship was sunk by a detonation of highly flammable coal dust following the impact of the torpedo). But no comprehensive explanation for the second explosion has ever been offered, and the Admiralty's initial insistence on the "two torpedo" scenario has kept alive the theory of a high-level cover-up regarding the contents of the *Lusitania*'s holds.

In addition to the cause of the second explosion, one further aspect of the *Lusitania* conspiracy remains unresolved. In the aftermath of the sinking, early accounts estimated that the liner had taken to the bottom of the sea several thousand dollars in cash. By 1922, these estimates had been revised, with some commentators valuing the ship's cargo at $5 to 6 million, much of it in gold. During the 1950s, the activities of the salvage company Rizdon Beezley around the wreck revived suspicions of Churchill's involvement in the disaster, with allegations that Churchill had commissioned the company to remove evidence of contraband from the wreck. To this day, no convincing explanation has been offered as to why the *Lusitania* would have been carrying millions of dollars of gold into a war zone.

Lance Janda

See also: Armaments Industry (WWI); Shipping (WWI); Submarine Warfare (WWI); Zimmermann Telegram (WWI)

REFERENCES

Bailey, Thomas A., and Paul B. Ryan. *The Lusitania Disaster: An Episode in Modern Warfare and Diplomacy.* New York: Free Press, 1975.

Churchill, Winston. *Thoughts and Adventures.* New York: Scribners, 1932.

Preston, Diana. *Lusitania: An Epic Tragedy.* New York: Walker & Co., 2002.

Simpson, Colin. *Lusitania.* New York: Penguin, 1983.

M

Mexico, U.S. Invasion of

After the Mexican Revolution in 1910, there was a growing concern in the United States over the safety and security of the U.S.-Mexican border. After an incident between U.S. sailors and Mexican authorities led to an U.S. landing and occupation of Vera Cruz in 1914, both sides were wary of an escalation of hostilities. The United States also expressed concern over the growing influence of Imperial Germany on Mexico.

On March 9, 1916, perhaps upset at the loss of U.S. support, or just desperate to once again be a player in Mexican politics, Francisco "Pancho" Villa launched an attack on the town of Columbus, New Mexico. When Villa and his mounted raiders withdrew, eighteen U.S. citizens lay dead and the town center had been burned to the ground. The attack provoked a fire storm of protest in the United States, and President Woodrow Wilson sent General John "Blackjack" Pershing in "hot pursuit" of Villa. It took time to assemble a force, and Pershing did not cross into Mexico until March 15, 1916.

What was to ensue was an eleven-month-long incursion by U.S. troops hundreds of miles into the Mexican state of Chihuahua. While a military failure, it did provide the U.S. Army with much-needed field experience and a chance to develop the staff skills needed to run and support a large army in Europe. In particular, Pershing pioneered the use of the aircraft in the U.S. Army to serve in a reconnaissance role.

U.S. and Constitutionalist forces went out of their way to avoid each other, and U.S. forces were forbidden to enter any towns. Mexican president Venustiano Carranza at first simply wanted to contain the penetration of U.S. forces, and then get them out of Mexico as fast as possible. Pershing wanted only to capture Villa and cared little for a military confrontation with Constitutionalist forces. What evolved was a situation that was not quite war and was not quite peace.

The Mexicans demanded that first the Americans leave, and then they could jointly resolve the problem of cross-border raids. The United States countered by offering to work out a plan after they captured Villa. Both sides tirelessly avoided open confrontation, but the political strain started to show as each side was unwilling to concede to the other.

To resolve this impasse, both sides formed the Joint Commission to find a solution. The Commission met many times in New London, Connecticut, between September 1916 and

Government soldiers pose for the camera in the midst of the Mexican Revolution. The chaos in Mexico led to a U.S. military intervention in that country on the eve of U.S. entry into World War I. (National Archives)

January 1917. While the commission met often, it never reached an accord. The Expedition would end only when Woodrow Wilson chose to end the expedition unilaterally. The one sticking point was whether the United States would withdraw before or after an accord was reached on dealing with border raids.

Militarily, Constitutionalist and U.S. forces did clash twice in the towns of Parral and Carrizal. While there were some losses (at Carrizal, both sides suffered 25 percent casualties), commanders on both sides moved to keep the conflict from escalating from skirmishes to full-scale battles. That could have then escalated into a full war, which was something that neither Wilson nor Carranza wanted or could easily afford.

By January 1917, Wilson saw that the threat from Germany was greater than the threat posed by Mexico, and he ordered Pershing to return with his command to the United States.

The "hot pursuit" never came close to catching Villa, and it had served only to degrade an already strained relationship between the United States and Mexico. The worry of German influence would come to the forefront with the famous Zimmermann Telegram of 1917, in which Germany offered Mexico the return of the Southwest United States in return for Mexican support in a war between the United States and Germany.

Interestingly, the revelations of the Zimmermann Telegram in March 1917 did not lead to renewed calls for action against Mexico, but only for war with Germany. As the United States became more involved in World War I, Mexico faded from the scene, and while there was talk in 1919 of invading Mexico (where the specter of Bolshevism had replaced the fear of German Imperialism), nothing came of it. By the 1920s, the United States and Mexico had found a peaceful (if imperfect) resolution to their differences with the Bucareli Agreement of 1923.

Drew Philip Halévy

See also: Zimmermann Telegram (WWI); Biographies: Pershing, John J. (WWI); Villa, Pancho (WWI)

REFERENCES

Camin, Hector, and Lorenzo Meyer. *In the Shadow of the Mexican Revolution*. Austin: University of Texas Press, 1993.

Gilderhus, Mark T. *Diplomacy and Revolution: U.S.-Mexican Relations under Wilson and Carranza*. Tucson: University of Arizona Press, 1977.

Haley, P. Edward. *Revolution and Intervention: The Diplomacy of Taft and Wilson with Mexico, 1910–1917*. Cambridge: MIT Press, 1970.

Riding, Alan. *Distant Neighbors A Portrait of the Mexicans*. New York: Vintage Books, 1986.

Mobilization (Canada)

When Britain was at war, Canada, as a Dominion that did not control its foreign policy, was also automatically at war. Yet Canadians chose the level and extent of their commitment. English Canadians embraced the war and stood firmly by Britain's side. With a population of not yet eight million, more than a million Canadian males tried to enlist, 600,000 were accepted, and 424,000 served overseas. At home, Canadians raised hundreds of millions of dollars to pay for the war, created a massive munitions industry, and played an essential role in supplying Great Britain with enormous supplies of food and raw staples. While Canada suffered a crippling 60,000 dead overseas, the war provided a strong impetus for modernizing Canada, creating social and economic change, and increasing the role of government in the lives of all Canadians.

Canadians marched proudly to war in August 1914. While there had been cheering in the streets and a rush to enlist for King and country, Canada was wholly unprepared for war. Canada had a permanent army of only 3,000, but a larger cadre of militia-men, almost 80,000 strong, from which to draw on to form a larger army. The Canadian economy and government were no better prepared to support an unlimited war. To mobilize the nation for the struggle that was to unfold over the next five years would require men and war supplies in unprecedented numbers.

In the heady days of August, the government passed orders—in council to activate home defense units, establish censorship laws, and shore up the credit of banks to guard against anticipated runs against their funds—and crafted new legislation like the War Measures Act to give it powers to fully prosecute the war effort. While the First Contingent of 30,000 men sailed overseas in September, the government passed legislation for $50 million to meet new expenses. It was not nearly enough, and so began a continual struggle to finance the war.

Sam Hughes

Sam Hughes, the minister of militia, and the figurehead of the war effort for the first three years of the war, cared little about costs. He was a man of action and he immediately established new committees to purchase war material and to facilitate shell contracts. However, Hughes's decisiveness was undercut by damaging patronage politics and scandals. Canada's heads of industry, on the other hand, were delighted, as the nation was still mired in the effects of the devastating prewar depression. At the start of the war, industry was moribund, working at less than half production and having had to fire tens of thousands of workers. Many of those men were the first to enlist, but the companies, receiving new contracts and injections of capital, retooled themselves to produce necessary war weapons and supplies.

The most important industry was shell production. Sam Hughes established a Shell Committee in early 1915 to act as a purchasing and distribution agent for British munitions contracts. Staffed with Conservative politicians and cronies, it was rife with corruption. By the summer of 1915, $170 million worth of shell contracts had been placed, but Canada had only delivered $5.5 million worth. The British were outraged, investigated, and established the Imperial Munitions Board, headed by a Canadian, Joseph Flavelle, a respected and wealthy Toronto businessman. Flavelle modernized, cajoled, and threatened the heads of the new munitions factories to meet the necessary contracts, and when that did not always work, he nationalized the companies and made them Crown-corporations. At its high peak in 1917, Canada's munitions industry would employ 250,000 workers, of which some 30,000 were women, and manufactured more than 60 million shells during the war. That same year, one quarter of all shells fired by British artillery had been manufactured in Canada.

The excitement of 1914 carried into 1915 and Canadians continued to enlist in enormous numbers. That was good because the Conservative government of Sir Robert Borden continued to raise total force levels: 150,000 by July, to 250,000 in October, and finally to half a million by January 1, 1916. While Canadian men were enticed to enlist with notions of duty and adventure, there was subtle and then force-ful pressure put on them to support the war effort. When enlistment figures began to dry up by mid–1916, Canadian recruiting agents and patriotic citizens commenced campaigns to force young men into uniform. The pressure was enormous. Everywhere one turned there was a patriotic poster or a speech from a politician or clergyman endorsing the war and the need for more men. But by 1916, the reality of war had come home and many young men were already "doing their bit" by working on farms or in factories. They were not easily persuaded to serve in the rat-infested trenches of the Western Front to become one more name on the already sickenly long casualty lists.

Up to 1916, then, Canada relied on patriotic citizens to support the war. Men were encouraged and pressured to serve overseas and women were expected to back them. And they did. Communities across the country devoted enormous energy to raising money for the "boys" overseas. Women engaged in unpaid labor as they knitted socks and sweaters and pulled together millions of care packages of tobacco, writing material, and food. The link between the home front and the firing line was a strong one, and was continually reinforced by the letters and packages that passed across the Atlantic.

This community patriotism also extended to financing the war. After loans from London and New York became harder to secure, the federal government, with much trepidation, turned to its own citizens. Bonds were issued and the response was remarkable: A series of Victory loans would yield hundreds of millions of dollars for the government. But it was not enough. In 1916, an income tax was levied against businesses, and a year later against wealthy Canadians. These temporary taxes soon became permanent.

The fourth year of the war, 1917, was a hard

one for Canadians. Recruitment had almost entirely dried up and pressure from the government did little to encourage farmers to release their sons, as they were having prosperous crops that year, and nor did it have an impact in Quebec or the Maritimes, where a foreign war had little attraction for more established Canadians with weaker bonds to the British Empire. But Canada now had four divisions in the field and needed more men to fill the ranks caused by the attritional fighting. Despite impressive battlefield victories like Vimy Ridge in April 1917 that became a symbol of what the young nation could accomplish together, the home front was being pushed toward crisis.

The federal government, with its new powers that extended to all parts of society, passed legislation to conscript able-bodied men from across the country. The bitter 1917 federal election was fought over the conscription issue and was barely won by the proconscription government, but only with the help of women who had been enfranchised for their patriotic war work. The extremity of the war effort was pitting English against French, farmers against urbanites, and labor against business. With inflation and imposed rationing, the country was split as never before in its history.

End of the War

Canada limped to victory in the last year of the war. Greater government intervention into the lives of all Canadians allowed for a more controlled war effort, but the poisonous conscription debates had nearly torn the country apart. When the sojourning Canadian soldiers returned from overseas in 1919, they found a country very different than the one they left behind. Industrialization and unions had radically changed the work environment; farmers

had enjoyed larger crops, but many of their sons and daughters had moved to the cities for higher-paying factory jobs, and that led to greater urbanization; the government, in all spheres, had become stronger and gained more intrusive powers into the lives of all Canadians, powers that it was slow to relinquish; and even the social fabric of the country had changed with women's enfranchisement and a new medical system structured to care for wounded veterans. Canada could look proudly upon its mobilization of men and resources for the British Empire, but there were also deep and bitter divisions throughout the country due to the extremity of the war effort. The country would never be the same.

Timothy Cook

See also: Armaments Industry (WWI); Conscription (Canada, WWI); Economy (Canada, WWI); Economy (UK, WWI); Propaganda (Canada, WWI); War Bonds (WWI); Women (Canada, (WWI); Biographies: Borden, Robert Laird (WWI); Hughes, Sir Sam (WWI); Documents: Appeal for National Service, October 23, 1916

REFERENCES

Brown, Robert Craig, and Ramsay Cook. *Canada, 1896–1921: A Nation Transformed*. Toronto: McClelland and Stewart, 1974.

Morton, Desmond, and J. L. Granatstein. *Marching to Armageddon: Canadians and the Great War 1914–1919*. Toronto: Lester & Orpen Dennys, 1989.

Miller, Ian Hugh Maclean. *Our Glory and Our Grief: Torontonians and the Great War*. Toronto: University of Toronto Press, 2002.

Bliss, Michael. *A Canadian Millionaire: The Life and Business Times of Sir Joseph Flavelle, Bart., 1859–1939*. Toronto: Macmillan, 1978.

Mobilization (UK)

Mobilization for World War I came late to Britain, as British diplomats struggled to devise a means of getting Serbia and Austria to resolve their outstanding differences without going to war. As late as the end of July 1914, Britain had yet to take a public position regarding the impending war, and held out hope that a peaceful resolution could be found to avert full-scale war.

As the assassination of the Archduke Ferdinand in Sarajevo led to the July crisis, the British by and large sat on the side lines. As late as the end of July, when Germany started mobilization, Britain had not taken a definitive stand on the impending crisis. Both France and Germany pushed Britain to clearly state its position, and what action it would take if war broke out in Europe. At the end of July, Britain proposed to all sides a conference to defuse the crisis and get each side to back down from war.

This approach was not without historical precedent, as the nations of Europe had successfully avoided conflict over the Moroccan Crisis of 1911, and had worked to contain the spread of a regional war in the first and second Balkan Wars in 1912–1913.

British Exceptionalism

The mobilization in Britain also differed from other countries in the fact that the Royal Army was a small but very professional force to be deployed as an Expeditionary Force in times of crisis, with the Territorial Forces (as second-line troops) were to serve to defend Britain in case of an invasion.

The other nations depended upon much larger conscript armies that spent a short time serving in active service, and then went into a long-term reserve status. This gave nations like France and Germany both large-standing armies as well as a pool of second-line troops who had some prior military training and could be called into service and sent to the field quickly.

The driving force behind the need to call up their troops in late July 1914 was that each nation felt that it had to mobilize before its enemy did, or it would be at a great military disadvantage. Compounding this was the problem that once partial mobilization started, each side felt that it could not back down, lest the enemy escalates the crisis and then carry through with full mobilization of their military.

Mobilization on both sides had become a complex process that consumed more and more time of the General Staffs of each army. Mobilizations involved not only the calling up of troops, but also full control of the railroads to move these troops to the front as quickly as possible, as well as the creation of large-scale supply depots to outfit the troops when they arrived. These timetables were calculated down to the second, and any change or delay could have a ripple effect, greatly effecting the ability to get troops to the front.

Once started, military leaders were loathed to interfere or postpone the process, and the technical necessities of mobilizing millions of troops started to overtake diplomatic efforts to resolve the crisis. No longer were the merits of the case based on diplomatic rationale or military necessity, but simply the need to beat the enemy to the front.

As the military men may have wanted war, or desired a war now rather than later, the diplomatic corps grew increasingly impotent. Diplomats from each side tried to stop the march to war, but were having a hard time being heard by the political leaders. Just before the war broke out, the German Kaiser even sent his cousin, the Russian Czar, a series of personal letters requesting that he not mobilize his troops, and asking that a way be found to keep the peace.

While Britain also faced a mobilization crisis, it did not face the direct threat of an enemy on its border, as did the Continental Powers. British mobilization would be smaller due to the size of its army and would be dispatching troops to help France defend herself, rather than to defend its own frontier.

On August 4, 1914, when England declared war on Germany, the British could field only about 975,000 men, while Germany could call upon 4.5 million. In both cases, of course, not all of those would serve as front-line combat troops. However, the smaller size of the Royal Army meant that, internally, the impact upon the home front was not as severe as Germany, France, or Russia.

Britain was also unique in that she was an island nation and depended heavily on her navy for defense. In 1914, the Royal Navy was the largest in the world, with more than 200,000 officers and men, and dozens of capital ships and scores of smaller ships. With a worldwide empire of 400 million to protect, the Royal Navy absorbed not only large numbers of men, but much of the defense spending, as Britain and Germany had been engaged in a naval arms race for the decade preceding 1914.

The declaration of war by Britain was driven not by Austria's attack on Serbia (July 29, 1914), or even Germany's declaration of war on Russia (August 1, 1914) or France (August 3, 1914). Rather, England chose to go to war over Germany's declaration of war on and violation of the neutrality of Belgium on August 4, 1914.

Britain felt a moral and legal obligation to Belgium since it, along with many of the other Continental Powers, had guaranteed Belgium's neutrality in case of an invasion since 1839 in the Treaty of London. When Germany invaded Belgium, that served as a trigger, and Britain declared war on Germany the same day.

Full Mobilization

With the British government now ordering a full mobilization, troops gathered from across England to prepare to go to France to stop the German invasion. Some of the troops were able to arrive as soon as the next day. By that time, however, Germany had already made great gains on the Western Front, having pushed deep into Belgium.

The British took time to get into the line, and it would be ten days before the first contingent fully landed in France, and it would be a few more days before the Royal Army took part in large-scale fighting.

While England was able to rely on its professional Army for a while, it became clear that more men were needed. Britain sent 160,000 troops to France in August 1914. The British also planned on sending over the Territorial Troops as a second wave, and then to raise a third wave of troops, known as the New Army. The leadership of Lord Horatio Herbert Kitchener, hero of Khartoum, who was made minister of war by Prime Minister Herbert Asquith on the outbreak of hostilities, was crucial in this planning.

Kitchener realized almost immediately that many more men would have to be called up, trained, and sent to the front to fight in a war of this scale. Although widely criticized at the time, Kitchener's public calls that the war would require millions of men in uniform would prove to be prophetic in the end.

To achieve this, Kitchener called for volunteers in August 1914. The response to this call for troops was overwhelming, as hundreds of thousands answered the call to enlist. Public support for the war was high, as patriotic men and women flocked to serve in the military or to support the war effort by some other means. It would take time, however, to get these men trained, outfitted, and sent to the front.

One of the interesting aspects of Kitchener's New Army was the "Pal's Battalions," where men in a community, sports team, or workplace could sign up and be guaranteed to serve together in combat. This had the effect of bringing to the unit built-in cohesion and a sense of comradeship that is not normally found in newly formed military units. It appealed to the British, and some units were quite large, such as factory workers from Liverpool.

The drawback was that, after a heavy engagement of battle, small communities that may have sent their fire department or workers from the local factory were hard hit, with dozens or hundreds of deaths and wounded from the same area. The impact on the home front of this kind of loss was debilitating, and discouraged others from joining.

Mobilizing Civilians

Mobilization also had a major impact on the civilian economy, as millions of working men were called away from civilian jobs to serve in the army and the entire civilian train system was taken over for the needs of the military. Although not in the levels that would be seen in World War II, increasing numbers of women started to work in industry in order to fill the labor shortage created by men leaving for the front. By 1917, over a quarter of a million women were working on farms in Britain to help ease the labor shortage.

As women started to work in larger numbers and also suffer their own privations on the home front in the form of rationing and sporadic air attacks by the Germans, they began to claim a role in the war. Although not to the scale of air attacks in World War II, there were dozens of attacks, both by airplane and airship, with hundreds killed. All of this combined to put women in the position to demand more social equality. One of the arguments for women's voting rights that was made was the role that women played in the war.

Britain also took steps to keep up morale and prevent dissent. In August 1914, the Defense of the Realm Act was passed, giving broad powers to protect the war effort. Among the powers granted was to the military to take control of factories in war industries. Britain also developed a very effective propaganda program to maintain support for the war. In particular, this propaganda was effective in getting U.S. support for the war effort, and later helping to bring the United States into the war.

Within the first few months of the war, the peacetime British Army had ceased to exist as a fighting force. At Ypres, the British suffered 24,000 dead, with little strategic gain to show for it. By the end of 1914, more than half of the 160,000 men sent to France could be counted as casualties, missing, or prisoners.

As the number of casualties started to mount, few people came forward to volunteer. From the beginning, Kitchener privately advocated for conscription, but did not speak out publicly since the Prime Minister did not feel the public was as yet ready for such a move. Kitchener was killed in 1916 when the ship he was sailing to a meeting in Russia was sunk by a German sea mine.

When he died, the government was just starting to implement the first of five "Military Service Acts" that were passed in January 1916. These acts provided for conscription to provide the troops that Britain needed to prosecute the war. Each revision of the act expanded the pool of people eligible to be drafted, and the fifth and final version all but did away with exemptions from service. Between 1914 and 1918, roughly 3 million men would volunteer for military service, with another 2.3 million being called through the various Military Service Acts.

Drew Philip Halévy

See also: Conscription (UK, WWI); Economy (UK, WWI); Trade Unions (UK, (WWI); Biographies: Asquith, Herbert Henry (WWI); Kitchener, Horatio Herbert (WWI)

REFERENCES

Dewey, Peter. *War and Progress: Britain, 1914–1945.* New York: Longman, 1997.

Gilbert, Martin. *The First World War: A Complete History.* New York: Henry Holt, 1996.

Horne, John, ed. *State, Society, and Mobilization in Europe during the First World War.* New York: Cambridge University Press, 1997.

Keegan, John. *The First World War.* New York: Vintage, 2000.

Lafore, Laurence. *The Long Fuse: An Interpretation of the Origins of World War I.* Long Grove, IL: Waveland, 1997.

Mombauer, Annika. *The Origins of the First World War: Controversies and Consensus.* London, New York: Longman, 2002.

Robb, George. *British Culture and the First World War.* New York: Palgrave Macmillan, 2002.

Steiner, Zara S. *Britain and the Origins of the First World War.* New York: Palgrave Macmillan, 2003.

Stevenson, David. *The Outbreak of the First World War: 1914 in Perspective.* New York: St. Martin's, 1997.

Mobilization (U.S.)

Mobilization came very late to the United States when, in 1917, three years after all the other major combatants, the United States entered the war. Unique among all the combatants in World War I, the United States was still in the process of mobilizing for a full deployment to Europe while simultaneously engaged in fighting Germany. The war ended before the United States could completely mobilize all the divisions it planned on sending to Europe, with only some of them seeing combat in France.

Neutrality

On the outbreak of war in 1914, President Wilson immediately declared U.S. neutrality, considering the war a European issue. At the time, the United States was already deeply involved with the occupation of the port Vera Cruz in Mexico. What had started as a diplomatic spat over proper courtesies had evolved into a landing and a year-long occupation of the City of Vera Cruz.

In 1915, the United States came very close to breaking off diplomatic relations with Germany over the sinking of the ocean liner *Lusitania,* which killed 1,198 people, among them 128 Americans. Only by the extraction of a promise from Imperial Germany to suspend unrestricted submarine warfare (attacking ships without warning and not rescuing survivors in the water) was the United States kept from entering the war in 1915.

In 1916, U.S. attention was again focused on Mexico when, in March the Mexican rebel leader Francisco "Pancho" Villa launched an attack on the town of Columbus, New Mexico. When the attack was over, eighteen U.S. citizens lay dead and the town center was left in ruins. The attack provoked a firestorm of protest in the United States, and President Woodrow Wilson sent General John "Blackjack" Pershing in "hot pursuit" of Villa. It took time to assemble a force and formulate a plan, and Pershing did not cross into Mexico until a few days later.

What was to ensue was an eleven-month-long incursion by the United States hundreds of miles into the Mexican state of Chihuahua. This was neither war nor peace, but the situation was very tense on both sides of the border. Pershing never came close to capturing Villa, and the U.S. and Mexican governments spent most of their time trying to keep the hunt for Villa from turning into a full-scale war.

While a military failure, the chase of Villa did provide the U.S. Army with much-needed field experience, as well as a chance to develop the staff skills that would be needed to run and support a large field army in Europe. Many young officers who would later prove themselves in World War I and World War II, such as George Patton and William Donovan, gained priceless experience in Mexico.

Increasing Aid to Allies

While the United States remained neutral between 1914 and 1917, it increasingly supplied material to the Allied side, and public opinion was strongly in favor of the Allied cause. Trade with the Allies grew from $825 million in 1914 to $3.2 billion in 1916. British propaganda proved very successful in turning U.S. public opinion against the Central Powers. Additionally, actions like the sinking of the *Lusitania* also served to turn public opinion against Germany.

In 1916, Wilson issued a Peace Note to all belligerents, requesting that both sides in the conflict state their conditions for peace, but got an unsatisfactory response from the Central Powers and a noncommittal response from the Allies. Wilson then addressed the U.S. Senate, calling for Peace without Victory, and for both sides to cease hostilities.

In January 1917, the Germans announced that they were going to resume unrestricted submarine warfare at the beginning of February. When Germany followed through with this threat, Wilson severed diplomatic relations on February 3, 1917. Wilson then attempted to get the U.S. Congress to authorize the arming of U.S. merchant ships, but was unable to win approval. He later brought about the arming of merchant ships by executive order.

The final event that pushed the United States to war was the Zimmermann Telegram, named after the German Foreign Minister, Arthur Zimmermann. In this telegram to the German Minister in Mexico City, he was instructed to offer Mexico the return of a large part of the western United States in exchange for Mexico going to war against the United States in conjunction with Germany. In addition, the telegram requested that the Mexicans approach the Japanese about joining the Central Powers.

The Zimmermann Telegram was intercepted by the British in January 1917, but they shrewdly held onto it until the end of February, when they could maximize the impact of the telegram when they presented it to the United States. When the telegram became public in March (and the Germans admitted its authenticity) it caused an outrage in the United States, as Mexico and Japan quickly disavowed anything to do with the plan. At the same time, three U.S. ships were sunk on the same day by German U-boats. Based on these events, the United States formally declared war on Germany on April 6, 1917.

Unprepared for War

Considering that the United States had more than two years to learn the lessons of World War I and adopt them accordingly, the entry into the war found the U.S. military woefully unprepared for war in Europe. In the beginning of 1917, the active U.S. Army numbered just more than 100,000 men, then the seventeenth largest military in the world. Considering the British Army suffered 60,000 casualties on the first day of the Battle of the Somme in 1916, an army of 100,000 was not going to last long in the large-scale combat raging on the Western Front.

Based on his handling of the troops in the Villa Expedition, General Pershing was given command of the U.S. troops that were going to be deployed to Europe. In May 1917, the United States decided that the only way to rapidly expand the military in time was through a draft. Twenty-four million men were eligible, and 2.8 million would be called up to serve in 1917. The question that would effect the outcome of the war was if the United States could get troops to Europe faster than the Germans could disengage from the Eastern Front (where the Russian Army had all but collapsed in the wake of the Russian Revolution).

As the United States mobilized, it took many men out of the workforce, and women increasingly started to get to work in order to deal with the labor shortage. Not only did they work in traditional peacetime industries, but they also worked in the growing munitions industry needed to support the war effort.

Much of the work was dangerous, and women faced discrimination in the workplace, often being paid much less than the men they had replaced. They also faced opposition from some labor unions who did not want women working in factories. After, the women seeking the vote used the participation of women in industry or military auxiliary roles in World War I to demand the vote. However, a greater emancipation of women and a redefining of their role in U.S. society would have to wait until World War II.

The home front also had to endure food shortages early on. However, under Herbert Hoover, control of the food supply in the United States was noncoercive, depending upon food conservation, as opposed to direction rationing. With themes like "meatless days" and housewives signing pledge cards delivered door-to-door, the government used the same method to conserve food as it did to sell war bonds, and both proved successful.

Early on, Wilson also sought to build up public support for the war. He appointed George Creel to oversee the Committee on Public Information, which was a vast organization to propagandize for the war. It was effective, (perhaps too effective) promoting support for the war through concepts of Americanism and of demonizing the enemy.

In June 1917, the Espionage Act was passed, which essentially silenced any criticism of the war or the war effort. The lingering effects of this propagandizing and suppression of dissent would be seen in the Red Scare that took place just after the war, where radical alien residents were rounded up and deported during the Palmer Raids.

General Pershing arrived in Europe in June 1917, and started to lay the groundwork for bringing U.S. troops into France, giving them more training, and then bringing them into combat. From the beginning, Pershing had fought both the French and British to keep them from using U.S troops as piecemeal to fill in holes in the line. Pershing stood his ground and demanded that the Americans would fight as a U.S. Army, and demanded a U.S. sector on the front line. While reluctant at first, the Allies gave in and, as Pershing built a mass of troops, he started planning for the U.S. entry into combat.

One of the barriers to fighting in Europe is that everything, from men to material, has to be shipped across the Atlantic, unloaded, and then moved to the front line. Unlike World War II, the United States used very little of its own military equipment in World War I. Most of the aircrafts, tanks, and artillery were lent to the United States from the French and the British. Much of U.S. industry was instead dedicated to producing armaments, fuels, and ships. U.S. shipyards designed and built a new class of ships in order to provide escorts for U.S. troops being shipped to Europe.

By March 1918, more than 300,000 U.S. troops were in France, training and getting ready to move into the line. Although Pershing did resist calls to put the Americans into the line as filler for the French and British units, he did lend out some U.S. units to help out in a crisis. In late May, the 2nd and 3rd Infantry Divisions (with elements of the U.S. Marine Corp) fought in and around Belleau Wood and Chateau-Thierry.

By this time, 250,000 U.S. troops were arriving in France each month, and there were twenty-five divisions in France, with another fifty-five divisions being formed in the United States. In July 1918, the French launched a counterattack against the German lines at Villers-Cotterêts with eighteen divisions, five of which were American.

By August, Pershing was tired of parceling out divisions and was ready for the U.S. military to take its place on the front. The Americans were sent to reduce the St. Mihiel salient. In an operation led by Pershing, the Germans were pushed back from the salient. While German forces had planned on withdrawing from the area, the U.S. attack was unexpected, and heavy losses were inflicted on the Germans. What is more important, it was now clear that the weight of U.S. military would be felt more and more each month, as the Germans (along with the French and British) had exhausted their supply of manpower and could not fight much longer.

The United States, while not fully mobilized and deployed to Europe, still played a major role in the defeat of the Central Powers. As much as for conduct in battle, the specter of an ever-larger U.S. army, planning to be fully deployed to France in 1919, helped to bring an end to the war. Sadly, domestic policies in the United States were to prevent the United States from playing a larger role in postwar diplomacy.

Drew Philip Halévy

See also: Conscription (U.S., WWI); Economic Policy (WWI); Economy (U.S., WWI); Documents: U.S. War Readiness, 1917; Proclamation of Conscription Policy, May 28, 1917

REFERENCES

Gilbert, Martin. *The First World War: A Complete History.* New York: Henry Holt, 1996.

Gilderhus, Mark T. *Diplomacy and Revolution: U.S.-Mexican Relations under Wilson and Carranza.* Tucson: University of Arizona Press, 1977.

Gregory, Ross. *The Origins of American Intervention in the First World War.* New York: W. W. Norton, 1972.

Keegan, John. *The First World War.* New York: Vintage, 2000.

Kennedy, David M. *Over Here: The First World War and American Society.* New York: Oxford University Press, 1982.

Lafore, Laurence. *The Long Fuse: An Interpretation of the Origins of World War I.* Long Grove, IL: Waveland, 1997.

Marrin, Albert. *The Yanks Are Coming: The United States in the First World War.* New York: Atheneum, 1987.

Tuchman, Barbara W. *The Zimmermann Telegram.* New York: Ballantine, 1985.

Muckrakers

Between 1890 and World War I, a reform impulse arose in the United States in response to the social and economic challenges arising from industrialization. Although not united by any single goal or methods, Progressives shared a fundamental belief that Americans needed to challenge political corruption, urban social problems, dishonest business practices, and poverty. Progressives believed if the public was educated about social ills, citizens would mobilize to reform and improve their society.

Changes in journalism helped spur the progressive movement by drawing public attention to social problems. In the 1890s, the rise of inexpensive, popular mass-market magazines such as *McClure's* and *Munsey's* gave the "new journalists" a forum for their reporting and access to millions of middle-class readers. In 1893, S. S. McClure launched America's first mass-market magazine, combining an engaging format including fiction and articles on science, art, and history with an affordable price that attracted millions of readers. A host of new magazines such as *Cosmopolitan, Collier's, Everybody's*, and the *Saturday Evening Post* soon joined *McClure's* in attracting readers away from the more sedate *Atlantic Monthly* and *Harper's* magazines.

Known as muckrakers, the new journalists of the Progressive era believed that exposure and public education would motivate activism and correct social problems. Efforts at reform in government, politics, and business were not new, but the arrival of national mass-circulation magazines such as *McClure's* provided muckrakers with both sufficient funds for in-depth investigations and an audience large enough to arouse nationwide concern. The muckrakers wrote about child labor, prisons, religion, corporations, insurance companies, and, most often, political corruption.

One of the earliest muckraking books, *How the Other Half Lives,* was written by a *New York Tribune* police reporter, Jacob A. Riis. The 1890 exposé about urban slums and the poverty of their immigrant residents attracted much attention, including that of New York Police Commissioner, Theodore Roosevelt. Modern technological advances in photography, including the invention of flash powder, allowed Riis to take nighttime photographs of filthy conditions in tenements, sweatshops, and saloons.

Exposés of political corruption and corporate scandals required reporters to substantiate their stories. Magazines and newspapers hired talented young journalists who completed meticulous research and saw themselves as objective reporters of social issues. In 1903, Lincoln Steffens documented local political corruption in "The Shame of Minneapolis," and in 1904, published a collection of his articles in the book *The Shame of the Cities*. His investigation of state politicians, *The Struggle for Self-Government,* was published in 1906. Another journalist, Ida Tarbell, uncovered John Rockefeller's unfair business practices in a series of articles in *McClure's* between 1902 and 1904. She published the series in her 1904 book, *History of the Standard Oil Company.*

Muckraking journalism was popular with readers and lucrative for magazine owners. The middle-class readers responded to calls for social activism, and muckraking reached a peak between 1902 and 1908. Perhaps the most famous muckraking novel was published by a young socialist in 1906. Upton Sinclair's *The Jungle* exposed the filthy and dangerous working conditions in Chicago's meatpacking factories. The public outrage inspired by the book led to regulatory legislation, the Meat Inspection Act of 1906.

President Theodore Roosevelt coined the term muckraker in 1906. Irritated by a story by David Graham Phillips entitled "The Treason

Muckraking journalists, like Lincoln Steffens, provided a major impetus for Progressive era reforms. World War I blunted the progressive cause and ended an era of government activism. (Library of Congress)

in the Senate," which accused congressmen of political corruption, Roosevelt compared investigative journalists with the muckraker in John Bunyan's *The Pilgrim's Progress:* "the man who could look no way but downward with the muck-rake in his hands; who would neither look up nor regard the crown he was offered, but continued to rake to himself the filth on the floor."

The investigative journalism of the muckrakers lent public support for many of the programs of the Progressive movement. At the state level, their accomplishments included abolition of many convict systems, prison reform, and child labor laws. At the federal level, the Pure Food and Drug Act and the Meat In-

spection Act were passed in 1906, conservation measures preserved forest lands and reclaimed millions more acres, and the Sixteenth Amendment authorizing the income tax and the Twentieth Amendment guaranteeing women the right to vote were passed. Finally, large trusts in the oil, beef, and tobacco industries were dissolved. Muckraking declined after President Roosevelt's attack and as public interest in social reform began to wane.

Victoria Grieve

See also: Journalism (U.S., WWI)

REFERENCES

Chalmers, David Mark. *The Muckrake Years.* Huntington, NY: R. E. Krieger, 1980.

Schveirov, Matthew. *The Dream of a New Social Order: Popular Magazines in America, 1893–1914.* New York: Columbia University Press, 1994.

Serrin, Judith, and William Serrin, eds. *Muckraking! The Journalism that Changed America.* New York: New Press, 2002.

Tichi, Cecelia. *Exposes and Excess: Muckraking in America, 1900–2000.* Philadelphia: University of Pennsylvania Press, 2004.

Music (U.S.)

Americans during World War I had no shortage of music to entertain, promote national unity, and express the collective sentiments of a nation at war. The music produced during the war years was appreciated and consumed by a wide spectrum of audiences: Modern classical music appealed to the taste of audiences with prior exposure to the avant-garde; roots, country, and ethnic music appealed to largely working-class tastes; and the vast number of popular songs coming out of Tin Pan Alley were consumed by a broad audience drawn from all so-cial classes. Each genre of music responded to the U.S. entry into combat in a different way, but no music was unchanged by the advent of war.

The invention of the phonograph in the years before the war put a great deal of music at the disposal of ordinary Americans. Where one might have previously been required to trek out to a symphony hall to enjoy a piece of classical music, the phonograph brought famous performers like Enrico Caruso right into audience's parlors. Though records were a popular way to enjoy music in private, other options were still available, most notably the Pianola (commonly known as a player piano), which performed songs that had been previously recorded onto piano rolls. The player piano was common by the onset of World War I and allowed music fans to sing along to popular songs even if they lacked a sophisticated talent for playing piano. Piano rolls were printed with lyrics on their margins beginning in 1916, making their appeal that much stronger. Still, sheet music remained the most common way music was consumed at home. Families and parties would gather around a piano in a parlor to sing the latest songs from Tin Pan Alley, which were readily available for ten cents at Woolworth's five-and-dime department stores.

Musical Venues

Although there was no shortage of venues for musical performances outside the home, the beginning of the war drastically reduced the number of dancehalls, nightclubs, and vaude-ville stages remaining open for business. Many of these establishments were just beginning to find widespread acceptance and popularity as the United States entered the war. The cost of fuel and power to keep such places open, how-ever, was prohibitive during the years of active combat, and many performers enlisted over-seas; as a result, music was largely limited to home consumption. The greatest exception to this rule was the movie theaters, many of which accommodated both films and more tradi-tional vaudeville performances. It was not un-common to find the accompanist performing a new popular song while film reels were changed. Slides of the sheet music's cover were often projected during such performances, en-couraging those in attendance to purchase the songs for their own enjoyment at home.

Popular music was dominated by the six largest publishers of Tin Pan Alley, a stretch of 28th Street between 5th Avenue and Broadway in Manhattan that housed many songwriting companies. These publishers responded to the war by producing songs related to the new con-cerns of life during wartime: nostalgia for peace, yearning for home, losing a loved one, taunting enemies, promoting patriotism, and strengthening the bonds of nationhood. These producers also altered the format of sheet mu-sic production, reducing the dimensions of songs and eliminating a center page to use less valuable wartime materials. Additionally, the U.S. government did some of the work to pro-mote popular songs. Convinced that singing cultivated national unity that could win the war, George Creel's Committee for Public Informa-tion actively promoted Tin Pan Alley's songs as a vital part of the war effort, even going so far as to publish songbooks. Leo Feist, one of the major publishers of popular songs, reflected these sentiments in a typically exuberant adver-tising campaign that boasted: "Songs are to a nation's spirit what ammunition is to a nation's army."

The style of music from Tin Pan Alley var-ied: Some songs incorporated the popular syn-copation and musical structure of ragtime; oth-ers echoed the sentimentalism of musical theater; still others strived to replicate the energy and excitement of the blues, popular in the South and made more so by new exposure among the troops. The songs quickly changed their themes as the national mood changed. A song expressing pacifist sentiment, called "I Didn't Raise My Boy to Be a Soldier," was rejoined, when the predominant sentiment shifted from isolation to belligerence, with one entitled, "I Did Not Raise My Boy to Be a Coward." The most famous songs of Tin Pan Alley were "Over There," by George M. Cohan, which sold two million copies of sheet music and one million recordings, and "Till We Meet Again," by Richard Whiting and Ray Eggan, which sold 3.5 million copies of sheet music. Each of these songs expressed support for the soldiers engaged in combat and channeled U.S. support for the war.

Though Tin Pan Alley's producers were extraordinarily influential during the war, they did not entirely corner the market on popular music. Musical theater continued to be successful with audiences throughout the United States, many of which adopted war themes. Sigmund Romberg's *Over the Top* and Ivan Caryll's *The Girl Behind the Gun* are two notable examples, and Captain Bruce Bairns wrote *The Better 'Ole* about his own experiences overseas. Even *Ziegfeld Follies* included content relating to the war in its bawdy performances. Perhaps most famously, Irving Berlin, called to war in 1917, produced a musical called *Yip, Yip, Yaphank*, which was performed by his fellow recruits in Camp Upton, New York. Berlin's famous performance of "Oh, How I Hate to Get Up in the Morning" was rehashed in his World War II musical, *This Is the Army*.

The constant reports of news from overseas did not serve only to spark U.S. pride; many first- and second-generation immigrants were also reminded of the countries of their heritage or birth. Though the songs of foreign na-

tions might not have been readily available at the Woolworth's sheet-music counter, recordings of folk and popular songs from countries around the world were still widely distributed. The Pathé Frères Phonograph Company advertised their records as "The Real *Heart Music* of Foreign Peoples," and invited listeners to "see mental pictures of gay-ribboned peasants dancing 'neath sunny skies; of dusky-skinned mothers crooning lullabies over swinging cradles." Including recordings in Hebrew, Russian, German, Hungarian, and other languages, the Pathé Frères series countered the propagandistic jingoism of many popular songwriters with an attention to the pluralistic identity of so many Americans and the conflicted affiliations aggravated by the war.

Country music would not be named for another twenty years, but the conventions of the genre were already being mapped out during World War I. The push for a strong national identity during these years yielded a fresh attention to Southern rural music, incorporating white folk and African American music stylings into a new form. Musicians who played white Southern music tended to be promoted as nostalgic curiosities and were romanticized as authentically American, offering a vision of both a national past and a tradition to build on for the future. Fiddlers, bagpipe players, yodelers, and banjo or guitar pickers became national heroes and emblematic of the quest for freedom and tradition that marked the optimism of the days of war.

If country music carved out a new space for poor white performers, African Americans were still limited by the vexing popularity of blackface performance. An antebellum form that featured white men portraying caricatured black people, blackface minstrelsy remained a common convention for the performance of racial difference. Well-received singers like Al Jolson and Eddie Cantor often performed in blackface, and African American performers like Mamie Smith were often assumed to be white as a result. The persistence of blackface performance reveals the troubling dimensions of racism that continued well beyond the war. George O'Connor served as a blackface performer to presidents McKinley all the way through Truman and became famous for introducing the blues to white audiences in 1916. Still, in spite of the obstacles erected by a white institutional establishment loathe to acknowledge black innovations, contributions, and origins, artists such as James Reese Europe and Louis Armstrong were exploring the exciting possibilities of new jazz styles.

Classical Music

Although classical music could not be produced so rapidly, and was therefore delayed in its response to war, it was not immune to the effects of World War I. Perhaps the most famous American composer of the time was Charles Ives, an unabashed modernist whose songs strove for a democratic aesthetic that could incorporate both high and low within the conventions of serious music. Ives did not receive wide recognition until much later. In addition to composing, and after initially opposing U.S. entry into the war, Ives dedicated himself to the war effort by campaigning vigorously for war bonds. His hectic schedule and determination resulted in a heart attack in 1918 that did not kill him but did leave him forever changed. His experience of the World War I home front left an indelible mark on his Fourth Symphony and his famous songs, "In Flanders Field," and "He is there!"

With the conclusion of World War I, popular songwriters immediately returned to their old themes, cautioning performers to avoid songs that remembered the stressful days of war. New songs bore little imprint of the war, save for the new physical dimensions of sheet music that remained reduced as a cost-saving device. The ascendance of the phonograph and the slow decline of the parlor piano led to the eventual death of Tin Pan Alley, but not before many of the techniques of songwriting and mobilizing national sentiment were revisited in the context of the next big thing, World War II. American musicians would never again be unprepared for the challenges of meeting audience demands during a time of war.

Aaron Lecklider

See also: Cabarets (WWI); Jazz (WWI); Theater (WWI); Biographies: Armstrong, Louis (WWI); Berlin, Irving (WWI); Cohan, George M. (WWI); Morton, "Jelly Roll" (WWI); Oliver, Joe "King" (WWI); Ziegfeld, Florenz (WWI); Documents: Over There, 1917

REFERENCES

Ewen, David. *All the Years of American Popular Music.* Englewood Cliffs, NJ: Prentice-Hall, 1977.

Furia, Philip. *The Poets of Tin Pan Alley: A History of America's Great Lyricists.* New York: Oxford University Press, 1992.

Hamm, Charles. *Yesterdays: Popular Song in America.* New York: W. W. Norton, 1979.

Malone, Bill. *Singing Cowboys and Musical Mountaineers: Southern Culture and the Roots of Country Music.* Athens: University of Georgia, 1993.

Sanjek, Russell. *American Popular Music and Its Business: The First Four Hundred Years,* vol. 3: *From 1900 to 1984.* New York: Oxford University Press, 1988.

Tawa, Nicholas. *The Way to Tin Pan Alley: American Popular Song, 1866–1910.* New York: Schirmer, 1990.

N

National Association for the Advancement of Colored People (NAACP)

The National Association for the Advancement of Colored People (NAACP) is the longest surviving African American civil rights organization in the United States. It was formed following a race riot in Springfield, Illinois, in August 1908, which provoked white journalists and reformers Oswald Garrison Villard, Mary White Ovington, and William Walling to call a meeting for action on February 12, 1909, the centennial of Abraham Lincoln's birth. The new organization was officially established in 1910. The NAACP rejected the accommodationist approach adopted earlier by the African American leader Booker T. Washington, and called instead for the end to segregation, the complete enfranchisement of African Americans, and the enforcement of the Fourteenth and Fifteenth Amendments. Early members included leading Progressive reformers such as Jane Addams, Ray Stannard Baker, Mary McLeod Bethune, Sophonisba Breckinridge, Clarence Darrow, John Dewey, Florence Kelley, Lincoln Steffens, Lillian Wald, and Ida Wells-Barnett. Its monthly journal, *The Crisis,* which began in November 1910, was edited by the inspirational African American writer, academic, and spokesman, W. E. B. DuBois, and quickly established the NAACP as the voice of African American protest. In 1915, the NAACP was prominent in opposing the showing of D. W. Griffith's movie *The Birth of a Nation* because of its negative portrayal of African Americans and its defense of the Ku Klux Klan.

The African American writer and diplomat James Weldon Johnson succeeded Mary White Ovington as national secretary in May 1917, with another African American, Walter Francis White, as field secretary. Together they helped to expand the membership to 43,994 members and 165 branches by 1918. During World War I, the NAACP organized a silent protest along Fifth Avenue in New York City, following the East St. Louis riot in July 1917 in which at least forty-seven people died. Among their banners was one that read "Mr President, why not make America safe for Democracy?" Although the NAACP successfully campaigned for the establishment of an officers' training camp for African Americans, they were unable to affect any change in the policy of segregation in the military or do much about discrimination and violence in the country as a whole. DuBois attracted some criticism from the African American press when he wrote an editorial in *The Crisis* in July 1918 calling upon African Americans to "Close Ranks" with their white countrymen during the war, but after the war, he and the NAACP were once more at the forefront of the campaign for equality.

The NAACP led protests against the wave of race violence that erupted in the "Red Summer" in 1919 with an increase in lynching and riots in several cities including Chicago and Washington, D.C. The protests and writing in *The Crisis* reflected the mood of the "New Negro" and saw the membership of the NAACP rise to 90,000 in 1919. During the 1920s, the NAACP led the campaign against lynching, beginning with the publication of *Thirty Years of Lynching in the United States: 1889-1918* (1919). In 1920, it held its annual conference in Atlanta, Georgia, to show it would not be intimidated by the Ku Klux Klan or race violence. In 1921, the NAACP successfully persuaded congressman L. C. Dyer to introduce an antilynching bill in the House of Representatives, but it failed to pass in the Senate. Similar measures failed again in 1935 and 1940. Walter White personally investigated many lynchings and published reports of them in his book *Rope and Faggott* (1929). He became executive secretary of the NAACP in 1929. During the 1930s, the NAACP took part in the defense of the nine young Scottsboro boys charged with rape, and helped to save them from execution. In 1935, the organization established a legal department under the leadership of Charles Houston that initiated the legal challenges to segregation, which ultimately culminated in the *Brown v. Topeka Board of Education* decision in 1954.

During World War II, the association supported A. Philip Randolph's call for executive action to end discrimination in defense industries and campaigned for the wider inclusion of African Americans in the armed forces. Later, the NAACP was one of the organizing groups involved in the march on Washington in 1963 and, with the Southern Christian Leadership Conference, Congress on Racial Equality, and Student Non-Violent Co-ordinating Committee, was an active campaigner for civil rights legislation and voter registration. The NAACP continues to be active to this day.

Neil Alan Wynn

See also: African Americans (WWI); Race Riots (WWI); Biographies: DuBois, W. E. B. (WWI); Randolph, A. Philip (WWI)

REFERENCES

Ellis, Mark. *Race War and Surveillance: African Americans and the United States Government During World War I.* Bloomington and Indianapolis: Indiana University Press, 2001.

Franklin, John Hope, and Alfred A. Moss. *From Slavery to Freedom: A History of African Americans,* 7th ed. New York: McGraw Hill, 1994.

Janken, Kenneth. *White: The Biography of Walter White.* New York: New Press, 2003.

Kellogg, Charles Flint. *NAACP: A History of the National Association for the Advancement of Colored People,* Vol. 1: *1909–1920.* Baltimore, MD: Johns Hopkins University Press, 1967.

Levy, Eugene D. *James Weldon Johnson: Black Leader, Black Voice.* Chicago: University of Chicago Press, 1973.

Lewis, David Levering. *W. E. B. Du Bois: Biography of a Race, 1868–1919.* New York: Henry Holt, 1993.

Zangrando, Robert L. *The NAACP Crusade Against Lynching, 1909–1950.* Philadelphia, PA: Temple University Press, 1980.

National Urban League

The National Urban League (NUL) was a voluntary service organization founded in 1910 during the Great Migration in order to provide social services to African American migrants living in urban environments following World War I. It was started as a result of the combination of three major African American activist groups: the Committee for Improving Conditions Among Negroes in New York, the League for the Protection of Colored Women, and the Committee on Urban Conditions among Negroes. The three organizations pooled their social and financial resources to help Southern African Americans adapt to their new urban environment.

The onset of World War I increased the number of industrial jobs available in Northern cities. Increases in arms production and the enlistment of white soldiers created a large opening for an influx of African American laborers looking to escape the harsh realities of the Jim Crow South. While racism was still present in a majority of Northern cities during World War I, the opportunity for greater financial freedom was far more inviting to thousands of African American migrants.

The NUL offered its social services to the growing African American community in order to ease the transition from rural to urban life. The organization was already dedicated to the elimination of racial segregation and discrimination; however, they expanded their services even further during World War I. Members of the NUL began lobbying businesses, labor unions, and the government for better vocational opportunities for African American workers, as well as providing basic social services to the rest of the African American population.

The NUL based its model of social service on that of white charitable organizations at the turn of the century. Members counseled African American migrants on proper behavior and dress in an effort to ease their social transition and accommodate white notions of morality. The NUL used sociological research to help dispel rumors of African American inferiority and promoted a general message of self-improvement. They helped train social workers and brought new educational and employment opportunities to the African American community.

Historians claim that it was the NUL's research into the many problems faced by the African American urban community that led to the organization's rapid growth. The Great Migration increased the demands placed upon the organization. It began offering vocational training to migrants, urging businesses to hire African Americans and attempting to persuade unions such as the American Federation of Labor to accept African American members. By the end of World War I, the NUL had eighty-one staff members working in over thirty cities across the country. However, the organization's gains were temporary. The end of the war brought thousands of soldiers home, many of whom forced African American laborers out of work.

Catherine D. Griffis

See also: African Americans (WWI); American Federation of Labor (WWI); Race Riots (WWI); Trade Unions (U.S., WWI)

REFERENCES

Moore, Jesse Thomas. *A Search for Equality: The National Urban League, 1910–1961.* University Park: Pennsylvania State University Press, 1981.

Parris, Guichard. *Blacks in the City: A History of the National Urban League.* Boston: Little Brown, 1971.

Native Americans

The Native American experience during World War I was characterized by two events: their contribution to the war effort and difficult relations with the federal government. Native Americans on the home front were active contributors to the conflict abroad. They purchased war bonds, contributed money to the Red Cross, worked in defense industries, grew food and harvested raw materials. These were all activities that the federal government encouraged. What the government also hoped was that the involvement of Native Americans in the war would help to hasten their acculturation. Under the Bureau of Indian Affairs (BIA), the government sought to increase the agricultural production of the Indians and eventually discontinue federal guardianship over them. It was the belief that hard work through self-supporting agricultural production would foster assimilation.

The 1917 Declaration of Policy was used to encourage this assimilation of the tribes. Fee patents (land grants) were issued to Native Americans deemed competent (those literate and self-sufficient), thus allowing the BIA to focus on those who needed to achieve competency. Through the fee patents, a large number of Native Americans raised crops and livestock. Problems occurred immediately with the program; poor weather and old cultivation methods hindered crop production, as well as insufficient money directed to the program and general resistance from the Native Americans. This was exacerbated by taxes on the properties owned by the already poverty-stricken tribes. Many of them lost their lands through loans they could not pay off; as a result, their property fell into the ownership of non-Native Americans.

The fee patent program was not successful in the BIA's attempt to acculturate Native Americans. The agency was plagued by the inability to maintain a cohesive policy toward the tribes, calling for self-sufficiency yet still maintaining tight control. They were also unprepared for the renewal of Native traditions and tribal pride that emerged through Native American participation in World War I. While tribal pride was a byproduct of Native American participation on the home front as well as the battlefield, their participation also signaled their inclusion in the national American identity. This would be further evidenced in their participation and great contributions made during the next world conflict—World War II.

Kelly M. Jordan

See also: Agriculture (WWI)

REFERENCES

Barsh, Russel. "American Indians in the Great War," *Ethnohistory* 38, no. 3 (1991): 276–303.

Britten, Thomas A. *American Indians in World War I: At Home and At War.* Albuquerque: University of New Mexico Press, 1997.

Wood, David L. "American Indian Farmland and the Great War," *Agricultural History* 55, no. 3 (1981): 249–265.

National Consumers' League

Founded in 1899 to protect the welfare of workers and consumers, the National Consumers' League (NCL) participated in the U.S. war effort during World War I by helping establish minimum labor standards for goods produced under government contract. It also supported restrictive legislation to keep women out of certain forms of employment.

Working conditions for Americans before the war were often appalling. Workers were underpaid and safety and health protections were lax or even nonexistent. Members of the NCL hoped to encourage humane and equitable working conditions by educating consumers. By the turn of the century, branches of the NCL could soon be found all over the country. These were female-dominated from the very beginning, and most members were educated, urban, white women interested in Progressive reform. Its most able leader was social reformer and settlement house veteran Florence Kelley, hired in 1899.

The NCL was concerned with the wages and working conditions of women and children, both of whom were considered uniquely vulnerable to exploitation. Its best tool in this campaign was its "white label," issued to employers whose wages and working conditions met NCL standards. Consumers were urged to look for the white label before buying manufactured goods and to boycott employers and products that did not have it. The NCL also supported minimum wage laws and restrictive legislation to keep women and children out of certain occupations.

World War I opened some new opportunities to women workers. About a million women took up some form of war work, and women hoped that the war would signal a new day of better pay and more opportunities. During the war, NCL members focused on preventing the production of uniforms from women's homes and the entry of women into new professions considered dangerous or inappropriate.

Home work, the production of garments at home, had long been a major concern of the NCL because such work was often underpaid and performed in squalid tenement houses.

The Quartermaster Corp, charged with supplying uniforms to the armed services, had long relied on such labor. Before the war, no state or organization had been able to legally prohibit such work. But in the spring of 1917, recognizing that the Quartermaster Corps would now be scrambling to find enough uniforms to outfit U.S. troops, the NCL took a stand. On May 11, 1917, it adopted a resolution that the Secretary of Labor should try to minimize the granting of government contracts and subcontracts to companies using tenement house labor. In August 1917, the Amalgamated Clothing Workers of America (ACWA) joined with the NCL to convince Secretary of War (and newly installed NCL president) Newton D. Baker to form the Board of Control of Labor Standards for Army Clothing. The Board then successfully pressured the Quartermaster to stop putting out contracts to any company having parts of uniforms made in tenement homes. Florence Kelley was one of the four individuals serving on the Board. In November 1917, the Secretary of War issued "General Orders, No. 13." This established daily hours, wage standards, and a ban on tenement home work for women in all businesses working under government contract. Progressives had long dreamed of such legislation, but it was only under the extraordinary conditions of a world war that the Wilsonian government felt it could act on such matters.

The NCL also worried that some of the new professions women had adopted during the war would either make them too vulnerable to sexual exploitation or force them to work inappropriate hours. In 1918, the National Consumer's League supported restrictive legislation to prevent the employment of women under twenty-one years of age in professions such as letter carriers, messengers, and elevator and street railroad employees. Even without these restrictions, the employment gains women made during the war years proved to be short-lived. Following the Armistice, most women either left or were fired from their wartime jobs so their positions could go to returning soldiers.

In the years after the war, the NCL continued to focus on protective labor legislation but faced growing challenges. In the 1920s, it actively opposed the passage of the Equal Rights Amendment on the grounds that it would wipe out protective legislation for wage-earning women. It also dropped the use of its label after a prolonged and often bitter battle with representatives of the International League of Garment Workers Union (ILGWU). The NCL's influence began to decline in the 1950s, but it continues to exist today as a broad-based consumer protection and advocacy organization.

Eileen V. Wallis

See also: Progressivism; Women (U.S., WWI); Biographies: Kelley, Florence (WWI)

REFERENCES

Boris, Eileen. *Home to Work: Motherhood and the Politics of Industrial Homework in the United States.* Cambridge: Cambridge University Press, 1994.

Boris, Eileen. "Tenement Homework on Army Uniforms: The Gendering of Industrial Democracy During World War I." *Labor History* 32, no. 2 (1991): 231–252.

Kessler-Harris, Alice. *Out to Work: A History of Wage-Earning Women in the United States.* New York: Oxford University Press, 1982.

Muncy, Robyn. *Creating a Female Dominion in American Reform, 1890–1935.* New York: Oxford University Press, 1991.

Wolfe, Allis Rosenberg. "Women, Consumerism, and the National Consumers' League in the Progressive Era, 1900–1923." *Labor History* 16, no. 3 (1976): 378–392.

National Defense Act (U.S.)

On June 3, 1916, Congress passed the National Defense Act, one of the most important pieces of military legislation in U.S. history. It provided for increases in the Army, Navy, Merchant Marines, and National Guard; established the nationwide Senior and Junior ROTC programs; and stipulated the governance, organization, and administration of the War Department.

At the beginning of 1916, Europe was deeply embroiled in a terrible global conflict—more destructive than ever seen before. At the outbreak of the war, President Woodrow Wilson had declared the U.S. government's intention of maintaining a policy of strict neutrality, which at first was interpreted to mean impartiality between and among the warring coalitions. However, while the subsequent U.S. decision to allow private sales and loans to states engaged in the war was meant to reinforce this stance of impartiality, in practice, most of this assistance benefited the British and their allies, not the Central Powers. As merchant ships steamed across the Atlantic—transporting goods from the U.S. to primarily Britain and France—the Germans responded by declaring a blockade of the British Isles, which it planned to enforce through its submarines, called U-boats.

On May 7, 1915, a German U-boat torpedoed the British passenger liner *Lusitania,* which sank so quickly that few passengers survived—1,198 died, including 128 Americans. In March 1916, a U-boat attacked the *Sussex,* a French vessel crossing the English channel, injuring four Americans. These incidents contributed to an already mounting public outrage against Germany's submarine warfare, and President Woodrow Wilson demanded that Berlin stop the marauding submarines or the

United States would sever diplomatic relations. However, harsher words—including a threat of military action—were not politically feasible for Wilson at that time because of a strong pacifist movement in the United States.

Led by coalitions of antiwar politicians and prominent social figures, the pacifist movement dominated much of the public discourse and demanded that President Wilson keep the nation out of the conflict. In the United States, 1916 was an election year, and Wilson responded to this public sentiment by campaigning for reelection on a peace platform in what became a very close presidential race against Supreme Court Justice Charles Evans Hughes of the Progressive Party. Further, on several occasions Wilson tried to bring the warring nations to a conference table, urging them to end the war and resolve the main issues peacefully. For example, early in 1916 Wilson sent his personal advisor Colonel Edward M. House to Berlin and London in an effort to arrange peace, disarmament, and the establishment of a "league of nations" to maintain peace in the future. However, receiving no encouragement from either the Germans or the British, House returned to Washington and reported to Wilson that neither side appeared to desire a negotiated end to the conflict.

Repeated failures to secure the peace, coupled with the increasingly active naval warfare—and the toll it was taking on U.S. exports—led to growing support of another political movement in the nation, focused on strengthening the homeland defense. Prominent advocacy groups—including the National Security League and the Navy League—joined forces with former U.S. President Theodore Roosevelt and U.S. Senator Henry Cabot Lodge in demanding that the Wilson administration beef up the military in case the situation in Europe eventually necessitated U.S. involve-

ment. At the very least, they argued, the nation should increase its preparedness. After considerable debate in Congress, the National Defense Act was passed in the summer of 1916.

Among the major provisions of this legislation, the most significant impact was seen in three areas: increases in the military; the establishment of ROTC programs; and new regulations for the governance, organization, and administration of the War Department. To begin with, the National Defense Act doubled the size of the Army, appropriated the largest naval expenditures in the country's peacetime history, and enlarged the nation's merchant marine corps. The Act also called for the establishment of summer training camps, modeled on a camp in Plattsburg, New York, where "citizen soldiers" had trained in 1915 to support the state militia. Further, this legislation guaranteed the state militias as the primary reserve force of the nation, which would now be called the National Guard, and gave the president the authority to mobilize the guard during war or national emergency.

The National Defense Act also called for the training of civilians as reserve military officers in the event that the United States entered World War I. Military training had been taking place at civilian colleges and universities as early as 1819, and the Act brought this training under a single, federally controlled entity: the Reserve Officers' Training Corps (ROTC). In the autumn of 1916, nearly 40,000 students were enrolled in the first ROTC programs at forty-six schools throughout the country (including the Citadel, St. John's College, and the Universities of Maine, Arkansas, and Texas A & M). Army ROTC is now the U.S. military's largest officer-generating organization, having commissioned more than a half-million second lieutenants.

Finally, the Act called for a drastic reduction in the numbers of General Staff of the War Department and restricted them to advisory roles. The provisions of this legislation pertaining to the governance, organization, and administration of the War Department were revised through a major reorganization in 1950. In its entirety, the National Defense Act has had a dramatic impact on the nation's military preparedness for every major conflict in which the United States has engaged in since World War I.

James J. F. Forest

See also: Conscription (U.S., WWI); Mobilization (U.S., WWI); *Lusitania,* Sinking of (WWI)

REFERENCES

Boyer, Paul S., ed., et. al. *The Oxford Companion to United States History.* New York: Oxford University Press, 2001.

Chambers II, John Whiteclay, ed., et. al. *The Oxford Companion to American Military History.* New York: Oxford University Press, 2000.

Cooper, Jerry M. *The Rise of the National Guard: The Evolution of the American Militia, 1865–1920 (Studies in War, Society, and the Military, Vol. 1).* Lincoln: University of Nebraska Press, 1997.

Doubler, Michael D., and John W. Vessey Jr. *I Am the Guard: A History of the Army National Guard, 1636–2000.* Collingdale, PA: Diane, 2003.

Neiberg, Michael S. *Making Citizen-Soldiers: ROTC and the Ideology of American Military Service.* Cambridge: Harvard University Press, 2001.

Smith, Daniel M. *Great Departure: United States and World War I.* New York: Wiley, 1965.

Wright, Robert K., Jr. *A Brief History of the Militia and the Army National Guard.* Washington, DC: Departments of the Army and Air Force Historical Services Branch, 1986.

National Security League

The National Security League (NSL) was originally organized to promote military preparedness for war and universal military training. It evolved into a super-patriotic group after the United States entered World War I, demanding conformity by all Americans to its standards. Eventually, the NSL's extreme conservatism and involvement in partisan politics caused its downfall.

The NSL was founded by S. Stanwood Menken, a prominent New York attorney. He was on a business trip in Great Britain in August 1914 when that country declared war on Germany. Temporarily stranded in the country, Menken spent his days in the House of Commons, watching Parliament debate appropriations for the armed services and make other preparations for war. Menken was appalled by how unprepared Great Britain was. He feared the United States would fare even worse if it was drawn into the war. When he managed to return to the United States, Menken made military preparedness his chief concern.

Menken found many Americans who shared his views. The men with whom he consulted included Theodore Roosevelt, former Secretary of War Henry Stimson, international lawyer Frederic R. Coudert, publisher George Haven Putnam and inventor Henry Alexander Wise Wood. With their support, Menken incorporated his organization as a New York corporation in January 1915. Its purpose was to promote education and national sentiment among the public and to promote the idea that the obligation of universal military service required universal military training. The NSL was openly biased toward the Allies and portrayed Germany as the most likely enemy. Menken organized committees to investigate the conditions and readiness of the army, navy, militia, National Guard, and Congress. The information found was used to lobby for larger appropriations for the Army and the Navy.

The NSL's educational efforts were very successful. The central office turned out many pamphlets and stories about German atrocities. Warnings about German invasion and occupation of the United States were spread by "flying squads" of speakers, organized by the NSL. These speakers traveled across the country, speaking to chambers of commerce, rallies, civic groups, and at school assemblies. During 1916, the NSL expanded enormously. Over seventy branch organizations were created in twenty-two states, and membership grew to 100,000. Financial support was provided by Menken's friends and acquaintances, but small donations flowed in from around the country.

The NSL's call for universal military service helped inspire a series of camps offering basic military training for interested men. The organization gave financial support to the Plattsburg training camp, organized by General Leonard Wood. Menken was disappointed when the National Defense Act of 1916 did not include compulsory military service, but he continued to campaign for its adoption. He was thrilled when President Wilson proposed conscription soon after his declaration of war.

After the United States declared war on April 6, 1917, the NSL's focus changed from military preparedness to support for the war. Gradually, the measure of whether one supported the war effort was based upon the attitudes of the local organizations. Emphasis was placed on conformity, especially among German Americans who were suspected of treasonable attitudes. Local NSL members intimidated German-born Americans and helped pressure them to abandon any shred of German culture and heritage. Even native-born Americans came under scrutiny. NSL members organized

"slacker" raids to round up young men who did not register for the draft or refused to serve.

The Committee on Patriotism through Education continued the educational mission of the NSL. Under the directorship of Robert McNutt McElroy, a history professor from Princeton, the Committee pressured college and university faculty to downplay German contributions to society and to stress U.S. links with the Allies. Faculty who were suspected of German sympathies were attacked, and university administrators were urged to fire them. McElroy often operated at odds with Menken and the central office of the NSL, but he refused to be reined in. The differences between the two finally came to a crisis in June 1918, and Menken was forced to resign as director of his organization.

Menken was replaced by Charles E. Lydecker, a conservative Republican. Under Lydecker, the NSL moved farther to the right. The original founders of the NSL, who had been concerned with military preparedness, were largely replaced by conservative businessmen more interested in forcing their attitudes on American society. Under Lydecker, the NSL continued to attack those who held different views. It also actively campaigned against candidates in the 1918 congressional elections that the leadership believed were not "100 percent American." As a result, a special committee was appointed by the House of Representatives to investigate the NSL. They found it was guilty of violations of the Corrupt Practices Act, which required organizations involved in politics to file a report of their expenditures with Congress.

With the end of the war, anti-German passions cooled. Increased tolerance among Americans as well as government supervision of the NSL's activities led to a decline in membership. The NSL's concerns about communists and socialists were not important to most Americans during the 1920s. The NSL continued in existence until 1942, when it ceased to exist as a corporation.

Tim J. Watts

See also: National Defense Act (WWI); Biographies: Wood, Leonard (WWI)

REFERENCES

Blakey, George T. *Historians on the Homefront: American Propagandists for the Great War.* Lexington: University Press of Kentucky, 1970.

Edwards, John Carter. *Patriots in Pinstripe: Men of the National Security League.* Washington, DC: University Press of America, 1982.

P

Pacifists

On the eve of World War I, many people believed that peace between the great powers of the world could be maintained. There had not been a major war between them since the Napoleonic Wars at the beginning of the nineteenth century. The scale and duration of the relatively small wars that had occurred since then seemed to most observers to be getting smaller with each decade. Governments seemed to favor increasingly liberal international trading policies, which suggested that there would be more cooperation and fewer disagreements among nations. Peace enthusiasts around the world were confident that within a short time, minor wars would cease to begin, just as major wars had, and some were optimistic about a future without war altogether. Most ignored signs that indicated a destructive world war was possible, even probable. Despite lip service to the cause of international peace, most world leaders continued militaristic policies domestically and engaged in entangling mutual defense agreements internationally. The destructive power that weapons were capable of inflicting also continued to increase unabated in the years preceding the war.

The members of a number of diverse and disparate groups were pacifists at the beginning of the twentieth century. Religious groups who opposed war, such as the Society of Friends, the International Bible Students, and the Mennonites, comprised an important percentage of pacifists. Many political societies that opposed war also existed, such as the American Peace Society and the New York Peace Society. Although socialist organizations never formed a firm opposition to war, an appreciable number of socialists also opposed war because they believed it caused the members of the working classes of the nations to fight each other at the behest of ruling elites. The prewar peace movement enjoyed ample respectability and social prestige. Its members included lawyers, businessmen, educators, clergy, wealthy socialites, and political elites. Individuals such as Jane Addams, William Jennings Bryan, Elihu Root, and Andrew Carnegie were ardent pacifists whose commitment to the cause and public visibility lent credence and support to the movement. While the respectability and amount of support for pacifism declined sharply during World War I, the movement's core constituency remained largely the same.

The outbreak of World War I in 1914 shocked and disillusioned those who believed that a major war among the nations of Europe

American pacifist and social reformer Emily Greene Balch was dismissed from Wellesley College in 1918 for advocating the cause of conscientious objectors. Balch became a cofounder of the Women's International League for Peace and Freedom. (Library of Congress)

would never again occur, and that war itself was nearing end. Some held on to hope that the war would be a short one, but after peace still eluded the belligerent nations in the spring of 1915, a fast end to the fighting seemed unlikely. American pacifists began to focus on mediation schemes designed to end the fighting and on maintaining U.S. neutrality. In December 1915, Henry Ford financed the voyage of a peace ship across the Atlantic Ocean that would carry mediators to Europe in order to begin negotiations and end the war. The enterprise was somewhat overoptimistic, and the warring governments ignored the mediators once they arrived in Stockholm, Sweden, and established the Neutral Conference for Contin-

uous Mediation. Ford's peace ship was nevertheless an important cause for celebration for American pacifists, who saw the endeavor as an unprecedented attempt by ordinary citizens to mediate peace between nations.

Pacifists' efforts met with little support from Woodrow Wilson and the U.S. Congress. Wilson embarked on a preparedness campaign designed to increase the strength of the U.S. Army and Navy for use in the event of participation in the war. He also sent troops into northern Mexico under General John J. Pershing in pursuit of Mexican General Francisco Villa and his men, following the massacre of U.S. civilians along the border. Despite Wilson's dubious commitment to pacifism, most pacifists supported his reelection in 1916 given that he had, as his campaign slogan advertised, kept us out of war. Yet in April 1917, Wilson asked Congress for, and received, a declaration of war against Germany and Austria-Hungary.

The U.S. declaration of war badly splintered prewar peace associations. Many pacifists who had opposed war while the United States remained neutral now felt obligated to support the war effort. Once the United States became involved in World War I, pacifist denunciations of the war struck an unpatriotic chord for many Americans. Pacifists who continued to speak against war began to be portrayed in the press as disloyal, and were accused of actively working for Germany against America. Pacifists were persecuted in communities across the United States, sometimes violently. The Espionage Act of 1917 and the Sedition Act of 1918 sanctioned the arrest and prosecution of pacifists under federal law. Restrictions were placed on the principle of free speech, so that dissenters could be jailed for publicly denouncing the U.S. military or the war effort.

Some remained committed to pacifism, however. It was apparent to those who remained that the peace movement had failed in its primary goal: the maintenance of international peace. With that in mind, pacifists largely used their remaining influence to advocate an end to the war to the extent possible, and the establishment of a permanent peace once the fighting subsided. Peace organizations supported Wilson's plan for a lenient peace, self-determination for the nations of the world, free trade, and the establishment of the League of Nations. They hoped for the most part that Wilson's proposals would provide a framework through which future conflicts between nations could be resolved peacefully. Even though it rapidly became clear that postwar reality would fall far short of the hopes of treaty supporters, pacifist organizations gained strength following World War I.

In the 1920s and 1930s, pacifists formed societies that would work for disarmament, international economic and political cooperation, and the resolution of conflicts between nations through diplomatic means. The experience of the war instilled a new sense of urgency in many pacifists that did not exist in the prewar period. Pacifists had witnessed the consequences of modern war on the battlefields of Europe and on civil liberties at home, and wanted to work to try to prevent such a war from occurring again.

Thomas I. Faith

See also: American Union Against Militarism (WWI); Conscientious Objectors (WWI); Socialist Party (WWI); Women's International League for Peace and Freedom (WWI); Biographies: Addams, Jane (WWI); Ford, Henry (WWI); La Follette, Robert (WWI)

REFERENCES

Alonso, Harriet Hyman. *Peace as a Woman's Issue: A History of the U.S. Movement for World Peace and Women's Rights.* Syracuse, NY: Syracuse University Press, 1993.

Brock, Peter, and Nigel Young. *Pacifism in the Twentieth Century.* Syracuse, NY: Syracuse University Press, 1999.

Chambers, John Whiteclay, ed. *Eagle and the Dove: The American Peace Movement and United States Foreign Policy, 1900–1922,* 2d ed. Syracuse, NY: Syracuse University Press, 1991.

Chatfield, Charles. *For Peace and Justice: Pacifism in America 1914–1941.* Knoxville: University of Tennessee Press, 1971.

Chatfield, Charles, and Robert Kleidman. *The American Peace Movement: Ideals and Activism.* New York: Twayne Publishers, 1992.

DeBenedetti, Charles. *The Peace Reform in American History.* Bloomington: Indiana University Press, 1980.

Marchand, C. Roland. *The American Peace Movement and Social Reform, 1898–1918.* Princeton, NJ: Princeton University Press, 1972.

Peterson, H. C., and Gilbert C. Fite. *Opponents of War, 1917–1918.* Madison: University of Wisconsin Press, 1957.

Palmer Raids

The Palmer Raids were a series of law enforcement raids on communists and suspected radicals conducted between 1919 and 1920 under the aegis of A. Mitchell Palmer, Woodrow Wilson's Attorney General and the symbol of the first "Red Scare." Palmer warned Americans about a communist plot to seize control of the United States and argued that communism was "eating its way into the homes of the American workman." Ultimately, Palmer's fears proved groundless, and the raids stopped as Americans began to question whether Palmer had exaggerated the threats posed by communists in the United States in order to try to win the Democratic presidential nomination in 1920.

Alexander Mitchell Palmer, who was born in Moosehead, Pennsylvania, on May 4, 1873, was a congressman who endeared himself to Progressives and civil libertarians by campaigning for Wilson and by supporting tariff reform, women's suffrage, and the abolition of child labor. When, in 1919, he was appointed Attorney General by Wilson, it seemed that he would continue to be a champion of Progressive reform. Soon after he took up the post, however, Palmer changed his stance on civil liberties, cracked down on communists and radicals, and had Americans arrested and illegally held without trial.

Nativism

The Red Scare and the Palmer Raids would probably not have been possible had the nation not recently emerged from World War I. Security concerns brought on by the war had sensitized Americans to the presence of immigrants and radicals in the nation's cities, and the 1917 Communist Revolution in Russia had convinced Americans that these radicals might try to launch a revolution in the United States. At first, Attorney General Palmer paid no heed to the country's rising nativist feelings. His views changed radically, however, after a series of riots and bomb attacks in May and June 1919.

On May 1, 1919, unknown mail bombers attempted to assassinate thirty-six government officials, Supreme Court justices, and business leaders. Palmer's Justice Department suggested that the bombs were intended to signal a May Day reign of terror, and enraged anticommunist mobs responded by attacking radicals in cities including Chicago, Boston, and Cleveland. On June 2, 1919, more bombs—this time accompanied by pamphlets urging communist revolution—exploded in eight cities. One bomber even attempted to assassinate Palmer

himself, but succeeded only in damaging Palmer's house. In response to this obvious conspiracy, and fearful of what seemed clearly would be more violence, Palmer appointed J. Edgar Hoover to gather information on radical organizations. Among the materials collected by Hoover's General Intelligence Division (later the FBI) were numerous communist pamphlets calling for immediate revolution. Although it now seems clear that there was no real chance of such a revolution occurring, Palmer interpreted these documents to mean that there was an imminent threat to the United States.

In June 1919, Palmer's analysts reported that the communists were planning widespread attacks on July 4, and Palmer decided to round up and deport alien radicals. Even though the promised violence failed to materialize, Palmer continued to suggest that the country was in peril and, as the summer progressed, Americans became increasingly concerned. Race riots in Washington and Chicago, newspaper reports of Bolshevik plots, and the formation of the American Communist Party late in the summer all contributed to the tension. The Boston Police Strike, which began on September 9 and that observers blamed on radical agitation, further exacerbated the situation.

On November 7, 1919, the second anniversary of the Russian Revolution, Palmer's agents arrested hundreds of suspected radicals. Many of these arrests were illegal, and some suspects were severely beaten by the police. Numerous smaller raids continued through the end of the year and, while many suspects were released due to lack of evidence, in December, Palmer had 249 anarchists (among them the feminist writer Emma Goldman) deported to Russia aboard the *Buford*, which was nicknamed the "Soviet Ark."

The largest and most spectacular of the Palmer Raids came on January 2, 1920. Between the beginning of January and the middle of February, over 3,000 suspected radicals were arrested and over 3,000 others were detained without being arrested. During the raids, police and civilian volunteers (usually members of private patriotic organizations, including the American Legion)—again operating without warrants—broke down doors, confiscated possessions, and, in a number of cases, threatened and beat suspects to obtain confessions.

Despite these illegal tactics, Americans at first generally approved of these raids and of taking dangerous radicals off the streets. Eventually, however, various people (led by disaffected Justice Department officials and concerned newspaper editors) began to speak out against Palmer's actions. In January, New York's state legislature had refused to seat five duly elected Socialist legislators. This violation of democratic ideals, combined with the dangers posed to civil liberties by the draconian peacetime sedition bills Palmer was supporting, began to give some Americans doubts about the entire Red Scare.

Overturning the Arrests

In March 1920, Acting Labor Secretary Louis F. Post, who had jurisdiction over all deportation matters, began reviewing and rejecting the great majority of Palmer's arrests as illegal. A furious Palmer argued that Post was releasing dangerous radicals, and predicted that communists were planning a national revolution and bloodbath for May 1, 1920. When May Day passed without violence of any sort, Palmer's reputation was irreparably damaged. On May 2, many newspapers printed comments suggesting that Palmer was subject to hallucinations, and his doomsday predictions were laughed off as ridiculous. As policemen began admitting during trials that they had operated illegally

and without warrants, Americans became increasingly disillusioned with Palmer's actions. Palmer himself continued to insist that only a strong Justice Department could prevent widespread radical violence.

Despite increasing criticism, Palmer nonetheless remained a strong candidate for the 1920 Democratic presidential nomination. In the campaign, Palmer continued to speak out against the threat posed by communists and radicals. At the nominating convention, both Palmer and fellow front-runner William McAdoo ultimately lost to dark-horse candidate James M. Cox. This loss ended Palmer's political career. Over the next few years, Palmer was slowed by a series of heart attacks. Although he did help Franklin Roosevelt craft the 1932 Democratic Platform, he grew disenchanted with Roosevelt's New Deal. Palmer died on May 11, 1936.

Samuel Brenner

See also: Alien Act (WWI); American Legion (WWI); Communist Party (WWI); Federal Bureau of Investigation (WWI); Red Scare (WWI); Sabotage and Spies (WWI); Sedition Act (WWI); Biographies: Goldman, Emma (WWI); Hoover, J. Edgar (WWI); Palmer, A. Mitchell (WWI)

REFERENCES

Braeman, John. "World War One and the Crisis of American Liberty." *American Quarterly* 16, no. 1 (1964): 104–112.

Coben, Stanley. *A. Mitchell Palmer: Politician.* New York: Columbia University Press, 1963.

Coben, Stanley. "A Study in Nativism: The American Red Scare of 1919–20." *Political Science Quarterly* 79.1 (March 1964): 52–75.

Feuerlicht, Roberta Strauss. *America's Reign of Terror: World War I, the Red Scare, and the Palmer Raids.* New York: Random House, 1971.

Murray, Robert K. *Red Scare: A Study in National Hysteria, 1919–1920.* New York: McGraw-Hill, 1964.

Nielsen, Kim E. *Un-American Womanhood: Antiradicalism, Antifeminism, and the First Red Scare.* Columbus: Ohio State University Press, 2001.

Schmidt, Regin. *Red Scare: FBI and the Origins of Anticommunism in the United States, 1919–1943.* Copenhagen: Museum Tusculanum Press, University of Copenhagen, 2000.

Williams, David. "The Bureau of Investigation and Its Critics, 1919–1921: The Origins of Federal Political Surveillance." *The Journal of American History* 68, no. 3 (December 1981): 560–579.

Paris Peace Conference

The most important assembly of national leaders since the Congress of Vienna in 1815, the Paris Peace Conference opened on January 12, 1919. Its purpose was to enable the victorious powers of World War I to replace the Armistice with a permanent diplomatic settlement between the belligerents. Dominated by Britain, France, and the United States, it was remarkable in many ways, not least in that representatives of the defeated nations—Germany, Austria-Hungary, and Turkey—were explicitly excluded, and the new, rising power in the east—the Soviet Union—refused to send a delegation. The conference, which closed on January 20, 1920, produced treaties named after the Paris suburbs in which they were negotiated and concluded: Versailles (Germany), St. Germain (Austria), Trianon (Hungary), Sèvres (Turkey), and Neuilly (Bulgaria). All of these agreements were unsatisfactory compromises and ultimately failed, for however punitive they appeared to the Central Powers, they were never severe enough to satisfy Allied public opinion. They were, however, more than sufficiently painful to leave a deep sense of bitterness amongst the vanquished, particularly the Germans.

Over thirty victorious nations sent delegations and, in many cases, national leaders to the conference. Yet while such states represented a large proportion of the world's population, the critical negotiations were, according to a long tradition in Great Power diplomacy, conducted by the principal victors, in this case the so-called "Big Five": Britain, France, the United States, Italy, and Japan. Even then, the French, British, U.S., and Italian leaders regularly met in private, and were thus free to discuss quietly the most important issues. Lesser nations were left to squabble amongst themselves.

Early in this highly complex political process, it became apparent that the nations had diverging objectives. President Woodrow Wilson in particular found himself at odds with the French premier, Georges Clemenceau. This put the British Prime Minister, David Lloyd George, in the position of mediator. Vittorio Orlando of Italy was concerned exclusively with issues bearing on his own country. Wilson had managed to persuade the Germans to sign an armistice agreement on the basis of his "Fourteen Points," but early in the conference, it was revealed that often these could not be reconciled with the war aims of the various Allied powers, especially those of France. Whereas Wilson sought a relatively lenient settlement, the French and, to a lesser extent, British representatives sought to satisfy domestic public opinion, which demanded harsh terms for Germany.

The process was further complicated by the conclusion, during the war itself, of various diplomatic agreements between the Allied governments, many of which had agreed to terms that could not then be reconciled with the "just" peace that Wilson sought, much less the punitive one that the French vociferously de-

Delegates in Versailles' Hall of Mirrors draft the peace treaty between the Allies and Germany in 1919. The United States would refuse to ratify the treaty, signing its own agreement with Germany and other belligerent powers. Wallace, Duncan-Clark, and Plewman, Canada in the Great War, 1919.

manded. Russia's absence further complicated matters, for it left the other delegates in the uncertain position of trying to revise the borders of eastern Europe, including those of the newly created Poland.

The Treaty of Versailles, concluded between the Allies and Germany on June 28, 1919, inevitably served as the main focus of the proceedings. Presented to the German delegates for their signature, the 440 clauses were condemned by the German government and public as a "diktat"; the Allies had rejected nearly all of the German delegation's numerous objections and calls for revision. Significantly, the treaty failed to reflect the terms of the Four-

teen Points and imposed severe punishment. Germany was stripped of approximately 15 percent of its prewar territory, an equal proportion of its economic resources, about seven million people, and all her overseas territories. Alsace and Lorraine, taken by Germany after the Franco-Prussian War in 1871, were restored to France, who came close to achieving permanent occupation of the Rhineland and the Saar—both rich mining areas—but was prevented from doing so by British objections. Instead, these areas came under Allied occupation for a period of fifteen years.

Belgium received Eupen and Malmédy, while in the east, Lithuania received part of

East Prussia, Czechoslovakia annexed the Sudetenland, and Poland was granted a strip of land running through East Prussia in order to provide her with access to the sea: the "Polish corridor." The German port of Danzig became a "free city" to be administered by the League of Nations, a forerunner of the United Nations. The German Army was subject to severe restrictions in terms of size and the types of weapons available to it. The Navy, in turn, was banned from maintaining submarines and large capital ships. Future political union between Germany and Austria was explicitly prohibited. Most severe (and controversial) of all, the so-called "war guilt" clause, Article 231, laid responsibility for the war on Germany, on the strength of which she was made liable for the full financial cost of the conflict in the form of reparations.

If the Germans were disappointed, Allied representatives were not entirely satisfied themselves. Whereas Wilson had come to Paris with high hopes for the establishment of a lasting and just peace, he ultimately found elements of his extensive agenda modified—sometimes out of all recognition—or rejected outright. He successfully proposed the establishment of the League of Nations, but only after considerable compromise over other cherished objectives. Opinion on the treaty in the United States was divided, with hostility from isolationists and those generally opposed to Wilson's liberal agenda. Congress ultimately rejected the treaty, and thus Versailles failed to provide the safeguards it might have done had the League included the United States. The other Allies, apart from China, ratified the agreement in January 1920, but subsequent years witnessed British attempts to lessen its more punitive features. The French remained determined that Germany should fulfill all her commitments.

The peace treaties concluded at Paris laid a poor foundation for future European security. Throughout Europe and North America a sense of dissatisfaction persisted. Peace was to last less than two decades, during which time the victors were never entirely able or willing to enforce the Versailles terms. Vanquished nations tirelessly campaigned for revision. A vengeful Germany, in particular, engaged in outright noncompliance and, eventually, during the early Hitler years, scrapped the hated agreement altogether.

Gregory Fremont-Barnes

See also: Fourteen Points (WWI); Isolationism (WWI); League of Nations (WWI); Biographies: Wilson, Woodrow (WWI); Documents: League of Nations Speech, September 26, 1919

REFERENCES

Boemeke, M., Gerald Feldman, and Elizabeth Glaser. *The Treaty of Versailles: A Reassessment after 75 Years.* New York: Cambridge University Press, 1998.

Dockrill, Michael, and John Fisher. *The Paris Peace Conference, 1919: Peace without Victory?* New York: Palgrave, 2001.

Macmillan, Margaret. *Peacemakers: The Paris Conference of 1919 and Its Attempt to End the War.* London: J. Murray, 2001.

Sharp, Alan. *The Versailles Settlement: Peacemaking in Paris, 1919.* New York: St. Martin's Press, 1991.

Progressivism

The "Progressive Era" was the period from about 1890 to World War I in which Americans from different backgrounds and parties responded to the problems produced by the rapid industrialization and urbanization of the United States. Progressivism was a diverse movement that almost defies definition. Histo-

Needing big business' help in the war effort, the federal government backed off its Progressive Era antitrust action during World War I. (Library of Congress)

rians continue to debate the sources of the reform movement with some arguing that it was driven by motives of self-preservation among business interests and the middle classes and others pointing to genuine altruistic and humane concerns. If there was a common element, it was that, while the reformers believed in progress, they did not think it should be left to go unchecked. But while some wanted to regulate industry to allow for fairer competition and to protect workers and consumers, others wished to democratize the political processes and make government more accountable. They also attempted to tackle urban problems such as poor housing, sanitation, and public transport, and many reformers worked in the settlement houses among the immigrant communities. Some reformers were more concerned with moral issues such as prohibition or prostitution, while others emphasized "Ameri-

canization" and other issues related to immigration. While Progressivism thus took on many forms at both the local and the state levels, it reached its height with the presidencies of Theodore Roosevelt (1901–1909), William Howard Taft (1909–1913), and Woodrow Wilson (1913–1921). However, many observers, and subsequently several historians, believed that World War I brought the movement to an end.

During the last thirty years of the nineteenth century, the United States was transformed. Rapid industrialization saw manufacturing outstrip agriculture by 1890 and, by 1900, the United States rivaled Great Britain and Germany in terms of industrial production. With this growth went the rise of mass production, the growth of huge national corporations, and increased urbanization. Into the expanding cities poured millions of "new" immigrants from eastern and southeastern Europe who were to constitute 60 percent of the industrial workforce. This changing environment was one of enormous inequality. While it was estimated that there were 4,000 millionaires in 1890, there were also ten million people living in poverty. Many cities lacked proper regulation and suffered from inadequate sanitation, poor housing, and insufficient health care provisions that led, in turn, to high mortality rates. The city was also often associated with crime and political corruption. Regularly high unemployment, low wages, and frightening levels of death and injury through industrial accidents led to the rise of class-based movements—trade unions, the Industrial Workers of the World (IWW), and the Socialist Party of America—that to some observers threatened the very fabric of society. Labor relations in the late nineteenth and early twentieth centuries were often marked by high levels violence. These were the problems that produced Progressivism.

Origins

Although urban-based, the origins of the Progressive movement lay in the earlier agrarian Populist movement and abolitionism. It also reflected a religious revival with the rise of the "Social Gospel" and development of groups like the Young Men's Christian Association (YMCA) (1851) and the Salvation Army (1880), which hoped to arrest the decline in religion through social action. The rise in big business brought with it an increase in the number of college-educated professional and clerical workers. Many of these were influenced by the new social sciences and the emphasis on the application of knowledge to social problems. Also influential were the "human interest" stories written in the latest popular jour-

nals such as *Harper's* and *McClure's* by journalists (described by Theodore Roosevelt as "Muckrakers"), such as Lincoln Steffens and Ida Tarbell, criticizing urban government and industrial mismanagement. Significant too was the rise in the number of college-educated women, many of whom, like Jane Addams, found an outlet for their skills in the settlement houses, working to improve the lot of urban immigrant or African American communities. Women were also prominent in the temperance movement, the call to protect consumers, and the demand for child labor and welfare reform. The increased employment of women in industry brought calls for regulation and reform, and many women contributed to the growing demand for women's suffrage articulated by National American Woman Suffrage Association led from 1900 by Carrie Chapman Catt.

As the Progressive movement spread from the city to state to national level, it influenced both major parties and spawned new ones such as the Progressive Party and Prohibition Party. While city mayors, such as Samuel Jones in Toledo, Ohio, and Tom Johnson in Cleveland, tackled issues of public utilities, urban transportation, and local government, governors like Hiram Johnson in California tackled corruption and graft in state government. Robert La Follette turned Wisconsin into a "laboratory of reform" with the introduction of railway regulation, income tax, civil service reform, public health laws, workmen's compensation legislation, and direct elections, among other things.

Reform reached the federal level when Theodore Roosevelt became President after the assassination of William McKinley in 1901. Roosevelt brought an energy and exuberance to the White House that made the presidency the center of national attention. He initiated the regulation of monopolies and railroads, established the Department of Commerce and

Labor, backed the Pure Food and Drug Act and Meat Inspection Act, and supported land conservation. His successor, William Howard Taft, continued many of these policies and established a separate Department of Labor and the Children's Bureau. However, Taft increasingly sided with the more conservative elements in the Republican Party and alienated the reform element, particularly over the issue of conservation. This insurgent group formed a Progressive Republican League and, when the party nominated Taft once more, they broke away to form a separate Progressive Party. Initially their support was for La Follette, but switched to Roosevelt when he returned to political life. The 1912 presidential election was contested by Taft (Republican), Roosevelt (Progressive), Eugene V. Debs (Socialist Party), and Woodrow Wilson (Democrat), all of whom claimed to be progressive. In the election, Roosevelt was ahead of Taft with over four million votes, but the split in the Republican Party gave victory to the Democrats and Woodrow Wilson.

Wilson had promised a "New Freedom" as opposed to Roosevelt's "New Nationalism." This meant using the power of the federal government, and particularly the president, to restore a free, competitive society that would reward self-reliance and individualism with upward mobility. He was, as he said in his inaugural, "for the man on the make, not the man who had made it." He maintained the attack on business monopoly through antitrust suits and strengthened the government's power to regulate business through the Clayton Anti-trust Act (1914). In 1913, he drastically reduced the tariffs protecting U.S. industry. An element of federal bank regulation began with the creation of the Federal Reserve system in 1913 and easier credit was made available to farmers through the Farm Loan Act (1916). In 1916, Wilson appeared to shift position, probably to lessen the Progressive challenge in the elections, when he

supported the passage of the Child Labor and Workmen's Compensation Acts as well as legislation introducing the eight-hour workday on interstate railways. These measures helped secure his reelection in 1916 but, increasingly, his administration was dominated by the war in Europe.

Progressivism and Peace

For many American Progressives, the cause of international peace was an important issue. Forty-five different peace organizations were established between 1900 and 1914 alone. Thus, the outbreak of war in Europe in 1914 was regarded as a shocking and retrograde development that only served to confirm European backwardness. It was a catastrophe Americans should stay out of and, as evident in the Women's Peace Parade in New York City on August 29, 1914, an event to be mourned. President Wilson's immediate response was to call upon citizens of the United States to remain impartial in thought as well as action. The policy of neutrality also no doubt reflected the diversity of background of the immigrant population in the country, with almost half the population of British or French descent, a fifth of German origin, and others from Russia, Italy, and Austria. Jane Addams and the Women's Peace Party (formed in 1915), attracted a considerable membership and tried to exert an influence on European statesmen through the International Peace Congress in the Hague in 1915 as well as supporting Henry Ford's peace campaign later that year.

Although these attempts by concerned individuals and their organizations came to nothing, Woodrow Wilson himself began to work for a U.S.-mediated peace settlement in 1915 and again in 1916. On January 22, 1917, the president called upon the belligerents to accept "peace without victory," but his call fell upon deaf ears. The German government announced the resumption of unrestricted submarine warfare on January 31, 1917, and this issue, coupled with the publication of the Zimmermann Telegram, led Wilson to call for a declaration of war on April 2, 1917. Only six Senators, one of them Robert M. La Follette, voted against the declaration.

Civil Liberties

Some opponents of war concentrated on civil liberties and the protection of conscientious objectors after 1917. A few groups, particularly those associated with the Socialist Party, continued to speak out against both the war and the draft. Many reformers, however, were persuaded by Wilson's idealistic call to fight in order that "the world must be safe for democracy." He further articulated his vision of a liberal peace in his "Fourteen Points" address to Congress in January 1918. They included self-determination and national autonomy for new nations to emerge from the Austro-Hungarian and Ottoman Empires, freedom of the seas, free trade, open agreements openly arrived at between nations, and the peaceful settlement of disputes through "a general association of nations." However, many of these high hopes were to be dashed during the Versailles Peace Conference, and large numbers of Progressives felt betrayed by the tarnished peace, the allied intervention in Russia, and the treatment of antiwar groups and radicals at home during the war and in the "Red Scare" that followed.

The wartime clampdown on civil liberties under the Espionage and Sedition Acts and the power of propaganda to incite war hysteria caused many of those formerly in the Progressive camp to lose their optimistic faith in government and even in popular democracy. However, the war had also provided reformers with opportunities to enact elements of their program. Many Progressives were involved in the nationalizing activities of the Committee on Public Information (CPI), others were active in the American Red Cross, the War Camp Community Services programs, and some played a part in the housing developments initiated by the U.S. Housing Association. Progressives were also evident in the War Labor Board and War Labor Policies Board, and in the Women in Industry Service that later became the Women's Bureau. Concern for the health and welfare of the nation during the war was manifest in the work of the Children's Bureau. The war also sped up the acceptance of the Nineteenth Amendment recognizing women's right to vote, the Eighteenth Amendment introducing Prohibition, and the implementation of controls on immigration. Thus, by the war's end, the Progressives had achieved a number of their major objectives. However, with the war's end and the debacle that followed Versailles, a conservative mood swept the country in a desire to return to what the new Republican President-elect, Warren Harding, called "normalcy."

Although the prevailing mood of the 1920s was opposed to reform, Progressivism did not totally disappear. In 1924, Republicans disillusioned with the return to conservatism in the postwar era, joined forces with elements of the "farm bloc," members of the American Federation of Labor and Socialists to endorse the third party candidature of Robert M. La Follette. The party platform called for further legislation against monopolies, greater farm relief, and the public ownership of utilities and the railroads. La Follette won almost five million votes and carried his own state of Wisconsin but trailed in third behind Calvin Coolidge and

John W. Davis. Despite this defeat, Progressives continued to play a role in Congress and at the state level, and many reappeared in the early New Deal years of the 1930s.

Neil Alan Wynn

See also: Adamson Act (WWI); American Union Against Militarism (WWI); Civil Liberties (WWI); Intellectuals (WWI); Muckrakers (WWI); Pacifists (WWI); Biographies: Bourne, Randolph (WWI); Croly, Herbert (WWI); Fosdick, Raymond (WWI); Frankfurter, Felix (WWI); Kelley, Florence (WWI); La Follette, Robert (WWI); Lippmann, Walter (WWI); Wald, Lillian (WWI)

REFERENCES

Chambers, John W., III. *The Tyranny of Change: Americans in the Progressive Era, 1890–1920.* New York: St. Martin's Press, 1971.

Cooper, John Milton, Jr. *Pivotal Decades: The United States, 1900–1920.* New York: W. W. Norton, 1990.

Davis, Allen F. *Spearheads for Reform: The Social Settlements and the Progressive Movement, 1890–1914.* New York: Oxford University Press, 1967.

Diner, Steven J. *A Very Different Age: Americans of the Progressive Era.* New York: Hill & Wang, 1998.

Ekirch, Arthur A., Jr. *Progressivism in America: A Study of the Era from Theodore Roosevelt to Woodrow Wilson.* New York: New Viewpoints, 1974.

Hofstadter, Richard. *The Age of Reform: From Bryan to F. D. R.* New York: Knopf, 1955.

Link, Arthur, and Richard L. McCormick. *Progressivism.* Arlington Heights, IL: Harlan Davidson, 1983.

Marchand, C. Roland. *The American Peace Movement and Social Reform.* Princeton, NJ: Princeton University Press, 1973.

Wiebe, Robert H. *The Search for Order, 1877–1920.* New York: Hill & Wang, 1967.

Wynn, Neil A. *From Progressivism to Prosperity: World War I and American Society.* New York: Holmes & Meier, 1986.

Prohibition

In the second half of the nineteenth century, the latent Puritanism in the American character and the increasing political radicalism among the farm communities of the plains states combined to produce a number of not entirely coherent social, economic, and political movements, one of which was the temperance movement. Rapid growth in industrialization, urbanization, and immigration fed the deepening conviction that traditional American values were threatened by the erosion of the agrarian ideal, the devaluation of the Protestant ethic, and the undermining of the primacy of the family in the social structure. In particular, the great shift to unskilled and semiskilled labor in factories was linked to increased rates of alcoholism and all of the attendant consequences on family life. Among temperance groups, alcoholism was not just a conspicuous negative consequence of the stresses of modern life, but *the* evil from which most—if not all—other social ills could be traced. What clergy denounced for its moral consequences, corporate leaders decried for its impact on productivity. In this manner, fundamentalist religion and big business thus found common ground, despite the fact that the only things demonized as much as alcohol in rural America were the railroads, the banks, and the "tycoons."

Pre-War Years

In the early decades of the nineteenth century, some states had enacted temperance laws prohibiting the manufacture, sale, and consumption of alcoholic beverages, but within a relatively short time, most of these laws were repealed because they were unpopular, impos-

Prohibition officers pour liquor down the drain after a raid on a Washington restaurant. Efforts to keep soldiers sober during World War I helped usher in the Prohibition Amendment banning alcohol in America from 1920 to 1933. (Bettmann/Corbis)

sible to enforce, or politically volatile. In particular, it was difficult to stigmatize drinkers in a nation in which the rough frontier ethos remained an immediate influence and in which masculinity was defined in manifold ways by the consumption of alcoholic beverages. In 1846, however, Maine passed temperance legislation that quickly became a widely imitated model. In this legislation, the emphasis shifted from stigmatizing and penalizing the consumption of alcohol to criminalizing its manufacture and sale. In this way, consumption of alcoholic beverages would be discouraged by reducing the availability of the beverages and by concentrating the blame for the problem on the distillers and saloon-keepers. An unintended, ironic consequence of this legislation would be, of course, that it allowed heavy drinkers to rationalize that they were not, after all, ultimately responsible for their addictions. (Ultimately, this sort of unintended irony would undermine the national enthusiasm for and commitment to Prohibition.)

War Years

In 1869, victories by temperance candidates in local and state elections convinced leaders in the movement to develop a national party. Starting in 1872, this Prohibition Party has fielded candidates in every subsequent presidential election, but its influence peaked in 1888 when Clinton B. Fisk won almost 250,000 votes and in 1892 when John Bidwell won just under 265,000 votes. Thereafter, the unanimity on the temperance issue has not carried over to other issues of interest to agrarian America, such as the shift to a silver standard, and, for the first few decades of the twentieth century, the party inspired much less commitment than its central issue. Interestingly, the sense of crusade that characterized the U.S. entry into World War I fueled the fervor of the temperance movement on the home front, even as the doughboys in France were being exposed to a much more relaxed European attitude toward drinking alcoholic beverages. Whether or not the Great War would indeed be "the war to end all wars," the temperance movement was determined that it would spell the end of the consumption of alcohol in the United States. They were determined that the doughboys would return from Europe spiritually galvanized by the survival of their great test of courage and they would return to an America soberly rededicated to its fundamental ideals.

On the heels of the Armistice, the Eighteenth Amendment to the U.S. Constitution was approved, outlawing the manufacture, sale, import, or export of alcoholic beverages within the United States and its territories. In 1919, the Volstead Act was passed, empowering federal officers to enforce the provisions of the Eighteenth Amendment and authorizing federal prosecutors to bring charges against the violators. It quickly became apparent that Prohibition was much easier to enforce in rural communities where there was already a great antipathy toward drinking alcohol. Paradoxically, however, the federal powers of enforcement did make the most fervent supporters of Prohibition uneasy, since many of them were committed to states' rights and every bit as skeptical of big government as they were of big business.

Post-War Years

In urban areas, however, Prohibition was almost impossible to enforce. The proliferation of speakeasies and the lack of legal penalties for patronizing them transformed drinking into a sort of "daring" social activity in which ostensibly risky behavior actually carried little risk. The speakeasy made the jazz age possible, and the popularity of jazz legitimized the speakeasy. Although it is impossible to prove the oxymoronic paradox that Prohibition actually increased the consumption of alcoholic beverages across much of the United States, it is indisputable that among certain segments of U.S. society, consumption increased dramatically and ebulliently. The demand became so great that illicit producers of spirits inevitably filled the void created by the end of production by most legitimate brewers.

It is not at all an exaggeration to say that Prohibition made possible the development of "organized" crime in the United States. In every large city, the ethnic neighborhoods had been dominated by criminal gangs specializing in such "rackets" as gambling, prostitution, loan-sharking, extortion, and protection. But control of liquor distribution suddenly meant millions of dollars in an age when a million dollars still represented tremendous wealth, and the ensuing "wars" among the gangs led to the establishment of criminal hierarchies locally, then regionally, and finally nationally. The creation of a syndicate of five New York "families" by Charles "Lucky" Luciano eventually led to the creation of a national syndicate. On both levels, the aim was to define the "territories" of each "family" and to reduce the violence between them. (These "territories" were less geographical than economic. Several families could control different enterprises within a given section of a city, especially in New York.)

Although Chicago became most strongly identified with bootlegging during Prohibition, the development of organized crime in Chicago was in many ways anomalous. The South Side gangs eventually were dominated by the Sicilian Americans under Johnny Torrio and then Al Capone. The North Side gangs were dominated by the Irish and Germans under Dion O'Bannion, Earl "Hymie" Weiss, and George "Bugs" Moran (Weiss and Moran were actually Polish Americans who changed their birth names for "professional" reasons). The escalating "wars" between these two gangs made headlines throughout the 1920s. They became part of the national folklore, but when a never-identified group of Capone's men slaughtered a group of Moran's intimates in what became known as the St. Valentine's Day Massacre, the bloodshed in Chicago became a "national shame." Violating one of Luciano's tenets for mob leadership, Capone had sought out celebrity and became an underworld equivalent to Rudolph Valentino, Jack Dempsey, and Babe Ruth. After the St. Valentine's Day Massacre, Capone became the target of multiple investigations and was eventually imprisoned for tax evasion at roughly the same time that Prohibition was being repealed. The consolidation of the Chicago gangs actually occurred in the aftermath of Prohibition, when the "big money" made from bootlegging was no longer available. Although the New York families were closely allied to Jewish gangs and included "associates" of other ethnicities, the Chicago "Outfit" became the United States' first truly multi-ethnic mob.

In the end, the horrific bloodletting caused by the criminal efforts to profit from the illicit manufacture, distribution, and sale of alcoholic beverages created public pressure for the repeal of Prohibition. But, in a more pernicious way, the failure to penalize the consumption of alcohol made much of the public complicit in the criminality that made drinking possible.

Clearly, most Americans were not being guided toward an acceptance of temperance and, eventually, the hypocrisy was too close to the surface of American life to ignore. The failure of the "Great Experiment" was inevitably acknowledged with the calamitous collapse of the stock market and the U.S. economy in the Great Depression. When a third of the nation's workforce suddenly became unemployed and a third was underemployed, taking a stiff drink suddenly seemed less a sin than a necessity.

Martin Kich

See also: Anti-Prostitution Campaign (WWI); Cabarets (WWI)

REFERENCES

Altman, Linda Jacobs. *The Decade That Roared: America during Prohibition.* New York: Twenty-First Century, 1997.

Ashbury, Herbert. *Carry Nation.* New York: Knopf, 1929.

Hill, Jeff. *Prohibition.* Detroit, MI: Omnigraphics, 2004.

Lieurance, Suzanne. *The Prohibition Era in American History.* Berkeley Heights, NJ: Enslow, 2003.

Propaganda (Canada)

Propaganda, the manipulation of information to influence public opinion, was utilized in Canada to ensure a total commitment to Canada's participation in World War I and to unify opinions of the diverse Canadian public during the war. Canada's geographic distance from the war enabled the government to maintain tight controls of the news media; propaganda became the means through which Canadian citizens learned of the war in Europe. In pamphlets, posters, and papers, Canadians heard simplified and romanticized versions of battle that lured men to the front in search of glory, encouraged the purchase of victory bonds, and separated Canadian citizens from the harsh reality of World War I.

On August 14, 1914, Britain declared war on Germany; Canada, the eldest sister of the British Empire, was automatically entered into history's first world war. Canada was strategically situated as the closest English-speaking colony to Britain, and yet far enough away from battle to provide a relatively safe place to train British troops. With its vast expanses of land and natural resources, the fledgling nation could also offer lumber, metals, coal, and various other raw materials to Mother Britain in order to support the war effort.

In response to the declaration of war, the Canadian government did indeed pledge troops, supplies, and training grounds to Britain, and, although Canada's entry into the war was mandatory, many segments of Canada's diverse population supported Canadian participation, and consequently little propaganda was needed to garner support for the war. Both the Germans and the British believed that the war would be over by Christmas, and the persisting notion that war was a noble affair led many Canadians to war in search of a short-term military adventure. On the eve of war, even French Canadian Nationalist Henri Bourassa pledged support for the war effort.

The propagandistic techniques used in Canada in World War I were not highly developed or controlled. Early on in the war, however, fear of negative news reports lowering the national moral and suspicion that troop movements and other intelligence would be leaked to the enemy led to the establishment of the Chief Press Censor's Office on June 10, 1915. From that date forward, newspapers were regulated under the watchful eye of Canada's chief

censor, Ernest J. Chambers, whose powers over communications and the Canadian press increased exponentially over the course of the war.

Additionally, at the beginning of the war, there was no central government agency to regulate the production of posters. Posters were the most recognizable form of propaganda produced during the war, and the lack of regulation resulted in a wide range of quality and content. Propagandistic posters were produced by private companies as well as the government. Often targeting specific ethnic groups, early recruiting posters displayed jovial men marching down country roads to battle, or

This recruiting poster from World War I encouraged Canadian men to sign up for military service. (Library of Congress)

standing in front of the Union Jack. English posters were often modified versions of British war posters. French posters were frequently translated English posters, or played on ties between France and French Canadians. Some also targeted Scottish and Irish communities. Recruitment posters also advertised specific battalions, so soldiers knew that they would be fighting with their own ethnicity and religion.

Propaganda, however, was not only directed toward recruitment. World War I propagandistic pamphlets were written on a variety of topics, including recruitment, but generally targeted women on the home front, and were concerned with food and meal preparation. The pamphlets, produced by the Department of Agriculture, encouraged, among other things, canning, limiting meat intake, and recipe suggestions to stretch food resources. The pamphlets stressed that the relatively small sacrifices made in Canadian homes had a major impact on the war. The department of Agriculture and the food board also produced posters that discouraged food hoarding and encouraged buying fish to save meat for "our soldiers and allies." A large proportion of propagandistic posters also promoted the purchase of victory bonds. Victory bonds were touted in posters as a means through which women, children, and men on the home front could contribute to the war effort.

By the beginning of 1916, more than 300,000 men had enlisted. As the war dragged on and casualties mounted, support for the war waned as the demand for men increased. Propaganda then held increasing importance. In 1916, the federal government established the War Poster Service, and Prime Minister Robert Borden tried in vain to keep his election promise not to enforce conscription. French Canadians, Canada's largest and most powerful minority group, supported Canada's participation in the war as long as they would not be required to fight in it. In 1917, dwindling military recruits and increased demands from Britain led Borden to enact a Military Service Bill that resulted in the conscription crisis, and the defeat of his government in the November election.

Concurrently, reports from the European front were slowly leaking back to Canada, and the calls for men to enlist became more desperate. The idyllic country backdrops were replaced by bombs and battles. Posters increasingly depicted wounded soldiers asking for assistance on the front and played on peer pressure with sayings like: "Your chums are fighting, why aren't you?" "Send more men, won't you answer the call?" and "Who's absent? Is it you?"

At the end of the war, over 600,000 Canadians had served in the army, 20,000 in the British Flying Service, and 10,000 in the navy. Additionally, more than 3,000 nursing sisters had contributed to the war effort. In their absence, Canada had gone from colony to nation, and the censorship and propagandistic techniques that kept Canadians motivated during the war created a reality foreign to those who had experienced it.

Dawn Berry

See also: Conscription (Canada, WWI); Journalism (Canada, WWI); Mobilization (Canada, WWI); Biographies: Borden, Robert Laird (WWI)

REFERENCES

Buitenhuis, Peter. *The Great War of Words: British, American, and Canadian Propaganda and Fiction, 1914–1933.* Vancouver: University of British Columbia Press, 1987.

Choiko, Mark H. *Canadian War Posters: 1914–1919, 1939–1945.* Laval, QU: Meridian, 1994.

Coutard, Jérôme. "Presse, censure et propagande en 1914–1918: la construction d'une culture de guerre." *Bulletin d'histoire politique* 8, no. 2–3 (hiver/printemps 2000): 150–171.

Keshen, Jeffery A. *Propaganda and Censorship During Canada's Great War.* Edmonton: University of Alberta Press, 1996.

Tippett, Maria. *Art at the Service of War: Canada, Art, and the Great War.* Toronto: University of Toronto Press, 1984.

Propaganda (UK)

Great Britain entered World War I with little preparation to wage an effective propaganda war. It was widely believed that secrecy was more important than mobilizing public opinion. British propaganda targeted four chief constituencies: domestic public opinion, Britain's wartime Allies, neutral opinion, and the morale of the enemy. Heavy reliance was placed on the use of private organizations rather than direct government involvement. These private bodies included prowar committees and the press. It was not until late into the war that the British government moved to direct oversight of domestic propaganda.

The British and Canadian governments dispatched popular Canadian novelist Gilbert Parker to the United States to help influence popular opinion in favor of the Allied war effort in the early months of World War I. (Library of Congress)

Agencies

British propaganda efforts were marked by a number of competing and overlapping agencies that included the War Propaganda Bureau (known as Wellington House), the News Department that operated out of the Foreign Office, and the Neutral Press Committee at the Home Office. By 1917, Prime Minister David Lloyd George ordered the creation of a Department of Information to concentrate propaganda efforts. Finally, in March 1918, propaganda operations were centralized in the Ministry of Information headed by the Canadian newspaper magnate Max Aitken (Lord Beaverbrook). The Enemy Propaganda Department, known as Crewe House, came into being under the British newspaper editor and proprietor Alfred Charles William Harmsworth, 1st Viscount Northcliffe. Crewe House handled propaganda directed at enemy countries, while the National War Aims Committee (NWAC) oversaw domestic propaganda. Wellington House had responsibility for all other operations.

From the beginning of World War I, Britain instituted measures designed to mobilize public opinion and to repudiate German propaganda. Censorship was imposed upon the press. British propaganda stressed the heroism of the British soldiers, which was contrasted with those who decided to remain safely at home, and the barbarism of the Germans. The Parliamentary Recruiting Committee (PRC) operated the earliest propaganda campaign in the war in order to raise volunteers for the British Army. Leaflets, mass rallies, and posters were further used to encourage enlistment. Military bands and speakers toured the country to rally support for the war. Britain entered the war with a small professional army. By the end of the war, however, 2.5 million men had volunteered for army service.

Films played a significant role in the propaganda war. Mobile cinema vans employed by the PRC traveled around Britain showing patriotic films such as *Our Navy* and *With the Royal Flying Corps in France*. *Britain Prepared* (1915) and *Battle of the Somme* (1916) proved effective propaganda films for domestic and overseas use. Wellington House distributed postcards, cigarette cards, and photographs. Posters served as a highly effective medium, and millions were printed and displayed. A cadre of artists made valuable contributions through their war paintings and exhibits.

German actions provided an abundance of material for British propagandists. Atrocity stories played a significant role in the propaganda war. The invasion of Belgium at the beginning of the war placed Germany on the moral low ground from the outset. The German violation of international law and treaty obligations further outraged public opinion. Stories of German atrocities in Belgium surfaced soon after the invasion: stories of civilians either being shot or deported as forced labor back to Germany, looting and destruction of innocent villages, the raping of women and young girls, bayoneting babies, and torture. While many of

these atrocity stories were fabricated or exaggerated, Germany's disregard of international law and the brutal treatment of Belgian civilians provided ample fodder for propaganda. The NWAC published a calendar of German atrocities listed by each month. With the publication of the Brice committee report in 1915, titled Report of the Committee on Alleged German Outrages, the charge appeared that German crimes could not be accounted for by accident or the lack of discipline among soldiers, but rather as part of German planning for the invasion of Belgian. The lengthy report proved a popular bestseller.

Atrocity stories encouraged anti-German feeling and hate aimed at Germans living in Britain. Stories circulated of Germans putting poison in food, building bombs, and German barbers cutting the throats of customers. Patriotic newspapers, such as the *Daily Mail* and *John Bull,* encouraged fears of German agents on the home front. Politicians with German sounding names or prewar business contacts found themselves targets of newspaper attacks or hounded out of public life. Following the sinking of the *Lusitania* in 1915, seven individuals were killed and hundreds of buildings destroyed. Mob violence against perceived domestic enemies proved all too frequent in wartime Britain. By 1918, Metropolitan Police launched an investigation into the charge that the Germans aimed to destroy British morals.

From the start of the war, the British government laid great stress on the volunteer spirit. The British public needed little encouragement to take up such spirit. Overall, the public proved to be inclined to believe the most lurid atrocity stories and remained steadfast in support of the war effort as their patriotic duty. Uncertain about the value of direct intervention, the government left much of the shaping of public support for the war to private organizations, and Britain had no shortage of prowar, patriotic bodies: The Victoria League, the United Workers, the Atlantic Union, the Cobden Club, and other private bodies. The Fight for the Right Movement issued a manifesto reaffirming the rightness of Britain's cause. Churches joined in with jingoistic sermons delivered from the pulpit. One newspaper proprietor moved to stage a mock trial of the Kaiser. All of these efforts stressed the need for sacrifice in the cause of a just war.

Early in the war, the most important private organizations were the Central Committee for National Patriotic Organizations (CCNPO) and the Parliamentary Recruiting Committee. Organized in August 1914, the CCNPO functioned as an educational body. While chartered as a private body, the CCNPO had many important political figures as members. Prime Minister Asquith served as honorary president and A. J. Balfour, British foreign secretary, held the post of vice president. The PRC functioned as a quasi-governmental body. It received advice from the War Office and worked in cooperation with other government ministries.

Department of Information

After several years of bad news from the front, in December 1917, Prime Minister David Lloyd George moved to form the Department of Information. The creation of the department led to a more direct role of the British government in the home front propaganda campaign. The National War Aims Committee (NWAC) was formed by the Department of Information. It absorbed the private CCNPO and adopted many of its methods. The NWAC and the CCNPO shared the same administrative head, Sir Edward Carson, and received the largest amount of government home front propaganda funding. By the last year of the war, the NWAC had control of all home front propaganda. It organized public meetings as well as the production of posters and pamphlets.

The British Press played a central role in home front propaganda. From the time of the German invasion of Belgium, the British Press proved to be patriotic and supportive of the war. Newspapers had wide readership and a keen understanding of how to reach a large audience. Early in the war, the Press Bureau was established with the goal of providing filtered information on the conduct of the war from the War Office and Admiralty to the press. Many government ministers had close relationships with the press lords. The government often feared that the press would leak sensitive information to the enemy, such as weather reports or have a negative impact on public morale, so the government continued the prewar practice of press self-censorship. The Press Bureau issued notices to editors on what topics they could not cover, although these guidelines were often far from clear.

In 1915, however, Lord Robert Cecil, Parliamentary Under Secretary at the Foreign Office, argued that government efforts to control the flow of new information undermined the usefulness of the press to the war effort. New codirectors of the Press Bureau moved to improve relationships with the press, and weekly press conferences were arranged. Up until 1915, correspondents were barred from the front lines. But thereafter, senior naval and army officers gave weekly briefings presenting the official view of the war. Any criticism of the government or the conduct of the war was considered unpatriotic, but the government had little reason to fear a lack of public backing for the war. Private and public efforts to convince the British public to support the war and make needed sacrifices simply reinforced established attitudes.

Van Michael Leslie

See also: Conscription (UK, WWI); Film (UK, WWI); Journalism (UK, WWI); *Lusitania,* Sinking of (WWI); Mobilization (UK, WWI); Biographies: Asquith, Herbert Henry (WWI); Lloyd George, David (WWI)

REFERENCES

Bourne, J. M. *Britain and the Great War, 1914–1918.* London: Edward Arnold, 1989.

DeGroat, Gerard J. *Blighty: British Society in the Era of the Great War.* London: Longman, 1996.

Douglas, R. "Voluntary Enlistment in the First World War and the Work of the Parliamentary Recruiting Committee." *Journal of Contemporary History* 42 (1970): 564–585.

Sanders, M. L., and Philip M. Taylor. *British Propaganda during the First World War.* London: Macmillan, 1982.

Wilson, Trevor. "Lord Bryce's Investigation into Alleged German Atrocities in Belgium, 1914–1915." *Journal of Contemporary History* 14 (1979): 369–381.

———. *The Myriad Face of War: Britain and the Great War, 1914–1918.* Cambridge: Polity, 1986.

Propaganda (U.S.)

As World War I began in 1914, the United States was placed in a unique position. Many Americans saw the war in Europe as just that: a European war, which was to be avoided by Americans who immigrated to get away from such problems. Because of the ties to the home world, and the volatile mix of ethnicities in major U.S. cities, however, persuasive imagery and stereotypes quickly arose. Often the newspapers were of mixed opinion as well. For those newspapers owned by William Randolph Hearst, the war was to be avoided by Americans, as European problems had always existed, regardless of U.S. intervention. The papers also often questioned first- and second-generation Americans, especially those with ancestry of what was considered to be

Propaganda posters, such as this one, were used to urge Americans to join in the fight against Germany during World War I. This particular poster plays off of fraudulent news reports that German soldiers were bayoneting babies in neutral Belgium. (Library of Congress)

the belligerent nations—Germany, the Austro-Hungarian Empire, and the Ottoman Empire—of the Great War.

For example, in Chicago, where the population of the city (in 1914) was approximately 25 percent German heritage, the stereotypes quickly arose following the German invasion of Belgium in August 1914. The image of the German as the "Hun" bent on torture, rape, and pillage filtered through even the newspapers that talked of neutrality, and spread to the point that many people of German heritage downplayed or even denied their heritage. In cities where former citizens of the warring powers lived in close proximity to one another, German titles were changed quickly to reflect a disconnection from Germany and its deeds. Frankfurters became hot dogs, hamburgers became Salisbury steak, German Shepherds became Alsatian Shepherds, and Sauerkraut became Liberty Cabbage. All of these attempts to show a disconnect from Europe became more pronounced after the events of 1915–1916.

Sinking of *Lusitania*

Some Americans became more vocal in their call for U.S. entry into the war following the sinking of the *S.S. Lusitania* (with over 125 American deaths) in 1915. Rumors spread that the German U-Boat crews had intentionally targeted a passenger ship, in clear violation of the rules of "civilized" warfare. It was reported that the crew of the German submarine was commended for this act, further showing contempt for the neutrality of any nation. Surrounding the Zimmermann Telegraph of early 1917 (in which the United States received a translation of a telegram from German Ambassador Arthur Zimmermann to the Mexican government stating that if Mexico declared war on the United States, Mexico would receive the states of Texas, New Mexico, Arizona, and California as a reward), members of the U.S. government realized that public opinion needed to change, and that affronts to the American ideal of life had to stop. To that end, the U.S. government created the Committee for Public Information (CPI), led by George Creel, who was a reporter and publisher. The Creel Commission, as the CPI became publicly known, was divided into two parts: the Domestic office, which was responsible for all propaganda in the United States, and the Foreign division, which was further subdivided into the Foreign Press Bureau, the Wireless and Cable Services, and the Foreign Film Service.

For the domestic division, media was limited, yet effective. Creel gathered a group of public speakers who were able to talk to people at public gatherings and stir up emotions for either recruitment or purchases of war bonds. Dubbed the "four-minute men" because of their timed four-minute speeches in places like movie theaters, the speakers could command an audience that a movie or newspaper article could not. The speakers, many of which had experience in the advertising field before the war, served as a direct sales staff as well. In fact, Creel later wrote a book that discussed how the propaganda worked, entitled *How We Sold America: The First Telling of the Amazing Story of the Committee on Public Information 1917-1919*. These speeches would later be emulated when radio broadcasts became widespread in the 1930s.

The oration aspect was only one arena of propaganda to the masses. The most symbolic form of propaganda from World War I was the famous recruitment poster for the U.S. army. Painted by James Montgomery Flagg, "Uncle Sam Wants You" was a great image of the need for the war recruiting effort, as well as an effective poster. The image of "Uncle Sam" looking and pointing directly at the viewer was striking in its appeal to the patriotic nature of Americans. The poster itself was not original in nature, however. The image of Uncle Sam had been around for some eighty years previously, and the poster format was based off of a 1915 British Poster "Your Country Needs You," featuring the British minister of war, Lord Alfred Kitchener.

These posters also aimed to appeal to a sense of masculinity in American men of military age. Many of the images in the posters relied upon the physical form or the virility of youth. For example, one recruitment poster noted "Gee! I wish that I could be a man, so that I could join the Navy." Another poster used wordage that questioned manhood by stating: "It takes a man to fill it (the uniform of

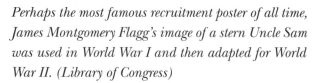

The U.S. military, including the Marines, adopted the bold imagery and simple messages of commercial advertising to promote recruitment during World War I. (Library of Congress)

Perhaps the most famous recruitment poster of all time, James Montgomery Flagg's image of a stern Uncle Sam was used in World War I and then adapted for World War II. (Library of Congress)

the U.S. Navy)." Other posters noted exotic locations or adventures that would be encountered. The Marines used posters that featured leopards, for example. Other posters looked at the total war effort of the population. Lady Liberty and the female representation of Columbia were often used to symbolize the state. One poster noted "Lady Liberty" being handed a sword of democracy presented by a Boy Scout (first formed in 1910, and seen by many as either a premilitary organization or a refining tool for masculinity). Finally, the portrayal of enemy forces, particularly German forces, were seen in the pickelhaub (spiked helmet) often either carrying a club or a half-dressed woman,

signifying the rape of common decency. Often depicted as a brute or a beast, the images were the visual connection to the wartime atrocities that were either committed (or perceived to have been committed) by German forces.

Creel's Committee was also effective in incorporating new media into the propaganda effort. Using famous directors and movies stars of the day, such as director Cecil B. De Mille and actress Mary Pickford, promilitary movies such as *the Little American* and *The Great Liberty Bond Hold-up,* appealed directly to the sense of morality of Americans and the vicious nature of the Germans. *The Little American* was loosely based on the *Lusitania* incident—in which a German submarine sinks a defenseless passenger liner and witnesses numerous atrocities before being saved by the Allies—stoking the fires of patriotism and hatred of the Germans.

The Foreign Division was responsible for sending the movies as well as other forms of propaganda toward U.S. allies or enemies. The foreign division was also involved in creating pamphlets that were spread by dirigible, airplane, or even specially designed munitions that could deliver the pamphlets into enemy territories. While the majority of the CPI's work was based on domestic propaganda, the foreign division was also responsible for overseeing film distribution, news information, and wireless and cable messages. As with most effective propaganda, the CPI utilized actual events as well as stereotypes that had at least some superficial truth to them, and then exaggerated the issues for maximum effectiveness.

War Opponents

Those who opposed the war were often branded as enemies or coconspirators against the United States. For instance, when Jeannette Rankin ran for the office of Representative to the U.S. congress from Montana on a Pacifist platform, she was branded as an opponent of U.S. values after war was declared by Congress (she was not only the first woman elected to Congress, but has the distinction of being the only person to vote against U.S. entry into both World Wars). For socialists like Eugene Debs, the propaganda of Communists wanting to destroy American values led to his arrest and ten-year conviction for violating the Sedition Act of 1918. Propaganda supported the war effort as an allied front to make the world safe for democracy, as envisioned by President Woodrow Wilson's Fourteen Points, but at the same time, Wilson, and many Americans, would not support equal rights for African Americans or other minorities, as they were stereotyped as not being equal to others (meaning whites) when it came to governance and the rule of law. It was issues like this unfair treatment of minorities that plagued returning soldiers by 1919.

As the events following U.S. entry into World War I changed the nature of the war—the various French mutinies and the Communist revolution in late 1917—the CPI began to alter their propaganda to not only show the fear of the Hun, but to keep the U.S. citizen on the alert against the forces of communism or other forms of subversion. The CPI also influenced the movie industry by incorporating a moral code by which to censor the movies being produced, or the depiction of certain groups. Ironically, many scholars of the Creel Commission felt that Creel himself and the CPI were far more judicious in reporting the facts and getting out the information than later organizations in the United States, such as the Office of War Information or the U.S. Information Agency of the Cold War Era.

Cord A. Scott

See also: Committee of Public Information (WWI); Conscription (U.S., WWI); Journalism (U.S., WWI); Mobilization (U.S., WWI)

REFERENCES

Keene, Jennifer. *The United States and the First World War.* Harlow, England: Pearson Education, 2000.

Paret, Peter, Beth Irwin Lewis, and Paul Paret. *Persuasive Images.* Princeton, NJ: Princeton University Press, 1992.

Rawls, Walton. *Wake Up America! World War I and the American Poster.* New York: Abbeville Press, 1988.

Taylor, Phillip. *Munitions of the Mind,* 3d ed. Manchester, England: Manchester University Press, 2003.

Winkler, Allan. *The Politics of Propaganda: The Office of War Information 1942–1945.* New Haven, CT: Yale University Press, 1978.

R

Race Riots

The years of the Great War in Europe saw the worst outbreak of race rioting in U.S. history to that time. Although there had been notable riots in recent years prior to the war, such as those in Springfield, Illinois; Atlanta, Georgia; and Brownsville, Texas, all previous riots had been isolated in time, place, and cause. The fact that in the three years from 1917 to 1919, at least thirty-one riots erupted between African Americans and whites—not counting those involving various white ethnic groups—sets these war years apart from any other prior to the late 1960s.

Several factors that had nothing to do with the war contributed to the causes of the riots. These factors had everything to do with creating an atmosphere of unusually intensified racist sentiment during an age when racism was basically accepted by the public at large as normal. Among the factors were the revival of the Ku Klux Klan, the release of the ultraracist motion picture *Birth of a Nation,* and the death of African American accommodationist Booker T. Washington all in 1915, the publication of Madison Grant's Anglo-Saxon supremacist book, *The Passing of the Great Race,* in 1916, the racist tenor of Woodrow Wilson's presidential administration, the rise of African American nationalist agitator Marcus Garvey and his UNIA, the development of the quasi-science of I.Q. testing, the advent of the "New Negro" and the jazz music craze, and, finally, articles written by W. E. B. DuBois in the NAACP's *Crisis* and by A. Philip Randolph in his socialist newspaper the *Messenger* openly advocating African American armed resistance to white outrages.

"Great Migration"

Undoubtedly the most important of all the factors contributing to the riots was the "Great Migration" of African Americans from the rural South to the urban North in the years before and during the war. Many northern cities found themselves ill-equipped to handle the tremendous growth of their African American populations. Between 1910 and 1920, the African American population of Chicago more than doubled, while Cleveland noticed a fourfold increase, Pittsburgh a fivefold, and Detroit an eightfold increase. Historians commonly hold that the war created new job opportunities for African Americans in such northern industrial centers, but that explanation of the pull factor of northern cities fails to account for several push factors in the South. In 1914–1915, the South suffered an agricultural depression, which was partly caused and partly exacerbated by devastating floods hitting Alabama and Mississippi and the boll weevil simultaneously making his unwelcome appearance on the stage of history.

The first of the tragic race riots of World War I occurred in East St. Louis, Illinois, resulting in forty-seven confirmed deaths and perhaps more unconfirmed. The city was an ugly, squalid, working-class, industrial town in which the African American population had doubled between 1910 and 1917. It was caused by union recruiters' propaganda, which told white workers that they should join the union to protect themselves from African Americans who would work cheaper and thus steal their jobs. Not only did white workers respond positively to the union message, they reacted harshly toward their potential replacements. Eight whites and thirty-nine blacks died in the riot. One hundred African Americans were wounded and six thousand were left homeless after the burning of their community. Nothing less than the arrival of the Illinois militia could put down the riot.

One month after the East St. Louis riot, the town of Chester, Pennsylvania had one as well. Soon after that, Pittsburgh and Homestead, Pennsylvania, also had riots. In between these last two Keystone State outbreaks, there was a riot in Weehauken, New Jersey. More important than any of these, however, was one that broke out in August among the all-black 3rd Battalion, 24th Infantry, and local white policemen at Camp Logan near Houston, Texas. A combination of police brutality, white civilians' and white policemen's repeated use of the term "nigger," and general distrust and suspicion among both the blacks and whites precipitated the riot. In the end, two black soldiers, five white policemen, and thirteen white civil-

ians lay dead. Afterward, 118 African American soldiers were thereafter court-martialed, 110 were convicted, 28 received death sentences, and 13 were actually executed. The rest had their sentences commuted by President Wilson, and all remaining served life sentences in Leavenworth Federal Penitentiary in Kansas.

A similar disaster was averted in another army camp town, Spartanburg, South Carolina, in 1917. This near miss of a racial explosion was precipitated by the infamous Noble Sissle incident. Sissle was a black soldier who, as a prewar civilian, had been a prominent jazz musician. As such, he was what many whites in that day called "uppity." When he entered a local hotel without removing his hat, the white owner knocked it off his head. When Sissle bent down to pick it up, the man clubbed him, which provoked fellow African American soldiers to plan a retaliatory riot. The army headed off the impending riot by deploying the African American troops to Europe sooner than originally planned.

Although the United States declared war in April 1917 and sent troops to Europe thereafter, 1918 was the main year of U.S. involvement in the Great War. Curiously, no major racial altercations occurred on the home front, despite the fact that the lynching count increased to fifty-eight in that year. On the Western Front, however, at least one serious disturbance was reported. At Camp Romagne in the Argonne Forest, approximately a thousand African American soldiers were ordered to collect bodies from the battlefield, place them in coffins, and load them onto trucks. Some three-hundred whites had the easier job of driving the trucks to the camp cemetery, where another thousand blacks would unload the coffins and bury them.

Midway through the task, word reached the soldiers that General Pershing would make a ceremonial visit to Camp Romagne on Decoration Day. To make the cemetery more presentable for the general, the African American soldiers were ordered to postpone the burial duty and fill in all the predug graves, placing a cross on top of each. Once Pershing had come and gone, they were to continue the burial process, redigging the graves and moving the rest of the bodies. The African American soldiers resented the extra work but carried out their orders nonetheless.

Upon finally completing the assignment, blacks and whites alike simultaneously filed into the same Knights of Columbus and YMCA huts for rest and recreation. Being outnumbered nearly seven to one, feeling cramped and uncomfortable in more ways than one, and wanting segregated space, the whites complained to camp officers, who then erected separate facilities for the small group of white soldiers. When the blacks tried to enter the new hut as well, the whites denied them admission. The black soldiers, already angry for having to do so much more work than the white truck drivers, threatened to kill all of the whites. A group of indignant African Americans laid siege on the white barracks. For the next two days, the two sides exchanged sporadic gunfire in the standoff, until military police finally arrived to quell the disturbance.

After the armistice of November 1918, the United States began demobilizing. Sending black and white veterans alike home to face an uncertain job market could only lead to more racial tension. In 1919, the number of lynchings rose to seventy-six, which represented the highest body count in more than a decade. Included among the victims were ten African American veterans still in uniform who had gone to France and become enlightened about their race's rightful place in the world and their nation. Consequently, they had grown indignant and insistent in their demand for equal treatment, which made them appear "uppity" to white racists.

1919

In 1919, seven major race riots erupted in addition to several lesser ones. Chicago, Washington, D.C., and rural Phillips County, Arkansas, all hosted riots with multiple deaths and widespread destruction, as did Charleston, South Carolina; Longview, Texas; Knoxville, Tennessee; and Omaha, Nebraska. In addition to these, there were at least fifteen other minor racial conflagrations scattered around the nation. They included episodes in Berkeley, Millen, Dublin, and Ocmulgee, Georgia; Coatesville and Philadelphia, Pennsylvania; New London, Connecticut; Bisbee, Arizona; Port Arthur, Texas; Norfolk, Virginia; Bogalusa and New Orleans, Louisiana; Syracuse, New York; Baltimore, Maryland; and Wilmington, Delaware. No section of the country was spared—New England, the Eastern Seaboard, the Southeast, the Southwest, the Great Plains, or the Mountain West. Virtually everywhere an African American population of any size existed, racial tension increased, and in several places it reached the breaking point.

The first of the 1919 riots occurred in Charleston in May, when white sailors roamed the city streets at night, entertaining themselves by harassing local African Americans and vandalizing their property. Ironically, one branch of the U.S. armed forces, the Marines, were called in to put a stop to the violence that was started by members of another branch, the Navy. From July to September, three very similar riots broke out, all of which involved white lynch mobs seeking the death of an African American alleged rapist while African Americans tried to either prevent it and/or attain retribution for it—first in Longview and later in Knoxville and Omaha. Meanwhile, in July in the nation's capitol, a combination of factors, including blacks and whites competing for jobs, another alleged rape and attempted lynching, and sailors with too much time on their hands, resulted in a four-day riot that required federal troops to stop it.

Among these summertime riots, the Knoxville incident seems particularly odd. It involved a city that claimed to have the most progressive race relations in the entire South prior to 1919. Unlike in most other southern cities, whites in Knoxville afforded African Americans the full panoply of their civil rights. Yet, within the year immediately preceding the riot, both the Ku Klux Klan and the NAACP started chapters in the city, causing the previously quiescent population to stir with racial animosity. As tensions began to flare, dozens of African Americans could be seen entering white-owned hardware stores buying bullets and shotgun shells—a strange spectacle indeed! Soon enough, the white owners stopped the practice, but it was too late. Both sides were by then equally armed for the conflict to come. After the bloodletting ended, a white veteran who had just returned from the Western Front remarked that he found the trenches of France and Flanders to be more hospitable than the streets of Knoxville during the riot. The Tennessee authorities deliberately avoided making an official body count, but the best estimates place the number killed around thirty, with less serious casualties in the hundreds.

At the end of July, the worst riot of the bloody "Red Summer" (so named by African American Harlem Renaissance writer James Weldon Johnson) erupted in Chicago over the most seemingly trivial thing—an African American swimmer crossed the imaginary line in Lake Michigan separating the black side of the beach from the white. Whites threw rocks at the swimmer until he drowned. African Americans called for the police to arrest the whites but the officers arrested several African Americans instead. African American Chicagoans then began rioting, which led to a white backlash that lasted for two weeks. In the end, twenty-three whites and twenty-five blacks lay dead, more than five hundred people were seriously injured, and much of the African American section of Chicago smoldered.

In September, the last of the major race riots of 1919 occurred, this one in Arkansas. The so-called "Elaine" Riot, named for the town in Phillips County that served as ground zero, was different from any other in the Red Summer because it was not urban and did not involve a lynching or any of the other aforementioned causes. Instead, a socialistic African American farmers' union sought to disrupt the local sharecropping system—which placed blacks at the mercy of white landowners and creditors—and local whites resisted their attempt at economic independence. Nothing less than federal troops was required to put down the riot.

After 1919, the nation's race problems seemed to fade into the background as Americans by and large began focusing on the issues that would characterize the 1920s as a decade of peace, prosperity, prohibition, and partying. Yet, there arose sporadic, isolated racial conflagrations in Tulsa, Oklahoma, in 1921; Rosewood, Florida, in 1923; and Detroit, Michigan, in 1925, which, although not connected to the riots of the war years, were certainly influenced by them. In general, all of the race riots of the World War I years have one thing in common: White actions led to black reactions. This is a pattern that would not hold true in the wave of riots to come in the 1960s.

Thomas Adams Upchurch

See also: African Americans (WWI); Great Migration; National Association for the Advancement of Colored People (NAACP) (WWI); Biographies: Randolph, A. Philip (WWI); Documents: Speech on East St. Louis Riot, July 8, 1917

REFERENCES

DeChenne, David. "Recipe for Violence: War Attitudes, the Black Hundred Riot, and Superpatriotism in an Illinois Coalfield, 1917–1918." *Illinois Historical Journal* 85 (1992): 221–238.

Doreski, C. K. "Chicago, Race, and the Rhetoric of the 1919 Riot," *Prospects* 18 (1993): 283–309.

Henri, Florette. *Black Migration: Movement North, 1900–1920.* Garden City, NY: Anchor Press, 1975.

Lakin, Matthew. "A Dark Night: The Knoxville Race Riot of 1919." *Journal of East Tennessee History* 72 (2000): 1–29.

Meier, August, and Elliott Rudwick. *From Plantation to Ghetto,* 3d ed. New York: Hill and Wang, 1976.

Smith, C. Calvin. "The Houston Riot of 1917, Revisited." *Houston Review* 13 (1991): 85–102.

Waskow, Arthur I. *From Race Riot to Sit-In: 1919 and the 1960s.* Garden City, NY: Doubleday, 1966.

Red Scare

The Red Scare of 1919–1920 had its roots in World War I. George Creel's Committee on Public Information roused the American people to a fevered patriotism that encouraged vigilantism against conscientious objectors, slackers, draft dodgers, immigrants, communists, German Americans, anarchists, socialists, and anyone who wasn't "100 percent American." This vigilante patriotism shifted readily after the war to support Attorney General A. Mitchell Palmer's Red Scare.

When the war ended, the Creel-inspired hatred of the enemy did not. It transferred from the "Huns" to the communists, anarchists, and immigrants. After the Bolshevik Revolution of 1917, communists had tried to foment revolution in Europe and the United States, and consequently, anticommunist feeling wasn't totally irrational. Additionally, because Woodrow Wilson was busy establishing world peace at the Versailles Peace Conference in France, presidential leadership in the transition from war to peace was absent in the United States.

Tensions at Home

Compounding the situation, the United States' domestic scene was ugly. The end of the war released nearly nine million workers in war industry and four million in uniform. The end of the war ended war contracts. There was no government plan for a transition from a wartime economy with wage controls to a peacetime one capable of absorbing wage demands and the millions dislocated by peace. Workers and the unemployed alike had economic complaints.

Then the strikes began. In 1919, four million workers struck in 3,600 separate incidents. A dock strike in Seattle in January led to the intervention of the U.S. Marines. The IWW was blamed, wrongly, for the 35,000 man strike in Seattle that turned into a 60,000 man general strike. As far as authorities were concerned, the strike was clearly the work of Reds trying to foment revolution. Mayor Ole Hansen called for federal help. The strikers backed off, and Hansen took credit. Months later a bomb plot was revealed—one of the targets was Hansen.

The summer of 1919 saw race riots in dozens of cities—with death and injury. The Boston police strike occurred in September.

A wave of anticommunist hysteria swept through the United States in the wake of World War I. Here Boston police pose with literature and pamphlets sezied from the Communist Party Headquarters in that city in November 1919. (Topical Press Agency/Getty Images)

The fall brought a steelworkers' strike demanding an eight-hour workday. In November, vigilantes in Centralia, Washington, castrated and hanged an IWW labor organizer. The Industrial Workers of the World (IWW) was already under suspicion—or worse—because of its antiwar attitudes and actions, encouraging strikes and draft resistance and speaking against the war.

Americans disliked not only the IWW but also the socialists. Socialism was not something that arose new with the Bolshevik Revolution. It had been around since the nineteenth century,

primarily in the form imported at mid-century by German immigrants, and before the war, enjoyed a respectable audience of followers. The immigrant socialist Victor Berger served as mayor of Milwaukee, Wisconsin, and was in Congress for three terms. The socialist Eugene V. Debs got nearly 900,000 votes for the U.S. presidency in 1912. As late as 1914, socialists held city and state positions. However, socialists, like Protestants, split often and usually over minute details that only a true believer could appreciate. But the one thing socialists agreed on was that the war was a bad idea. And in voicing that opinion, they violated the Espionage and Sedition Acts. Berger and Charles Schenck were convicted in the Socialist Cases, and Debs went to jail for speaking against the war. Then the Bolshevik Revolution of 1917 and the subsequent withdrawal of Russia from the war tarred U.S. socialists with the brush of betrayal of America.

Overseas, the communists were making inroads in Germany, Hungary, Italy, and Poland. Red hunters at home started after Red professors and public school teachers. These groups were built upon the wartime American Defense Society, National Security League, and American Protective League, and used the same coercive vigilante methods to force patriotism as they defined it. The American Legion was founded on May 19, 1919, to work for "100 percent Americanism" and law and order. By the fall, it had 650,000 members and, at year's end, it was over a million. The Ku Klux Klan revitalized during this time as well.

Wilson appointed a new attorney general in 1919, A. Mitchell Palmer of Pennsylvania, who had a good liberal progressive background. Once in office, his support for labor and women's suffrage gave way to the repression of radicalism.

In April, the Postal Service let it be known that thirty-eight letter bombs had gone through the mails to leading businessmen and politicians, punctuated by a bomb and the anarchist wielding blowing up outside Palmer's home. Then, May Day rallies in 1919 turned into riots. In June, another bomb plot was revealed. Adding to all of this, there were the Boston and steel strikes, sending the message to the American people that, indeed, anarchists and communists were everywhere. Palmer was convinced that he had a radical plot to deal with.

Palmer was not alone in his crusade. He asked J. Edgar Hoover to help. Palmer was impressed with Hoover's use of the Espionage and Sedition Acts during the war, and as Palmer's newly appointed assistant, Hoover used those Acts effectively against postwar radicals. Hoover's antiradical division compiled 200,000 cards on radical organizations and individuals.

The radicals Palmer tracked included more than communists and anarchists: Jane Addams, a social worker, supported conscientious objection and opposed the draft and the historian Charles A. Beard was under scrutiny for writing that the founding fathers had economic motives for much of what they did. Others who failed to toe Palmer's orthodox line included reformers Lillian Wald and Oswald Garrison Villard. Surveillance of these individuals wasn't new; they had been under the government's eye for years. Civil rights activists, more vocal than ever after the return of the "New Negro" veterans who were committed to immediate equality, were under watch as well.

Local and state governments outlawed radicals and radical activity to one extent or another. The communist flag was outlawed in thirty-two states. Congressmen introduced seventy antisedition bills but failed to enact any. Lee Overman's Judiciary Subcommittee held hearings and heard witnesses say that some leaders of the Russian Revolution were New York Jews. In New York, State Senator Clayton R. Lusk alleged that the United States harbored half a million Reds, all preparing for an imminent revolution. The Lusk Committee raided Russian, socialist, and IWW offices.

Palmer Raids

On November 7, 1919, the first of the Palmer Raids occurred—on the second anniversary of Russia's October Revolution (due to the calendar change instituted by the new Bolshevik government, the October Revolution actually occurred in November). Palmer's agents rounded up more than ten thousand communists and anarchists, detaining many for extended periods of time without pressing charges. Despite their best efforts, Hoover and Palmer could find no evidence of a plot. Most were released eventually, but 248 alien detainees were placed aboard the "Soviet Ark," the *Buford,* in December and deported to Russia by way of Finland. Among them were Emma Goldman, anarchist opponent of the draft and advocate of birth control.

In January 1920, although lacking credible evidence of a communist plot, Palmer and local law enforcement again raided throughout the United States, nabbing six thousand suspects. Again, while there was no evidence of a plot to overthrow the government, a substantial number of Wobblies (IWW members) were taken and held without trial.

Palmer's undoing came on May Day, 1920. Palmer claimed that the socialists would foment huge demonstrations to encourage the revolution. Among other public responses to this prediction, New York's legislature expelled its five socialist legislators. Regardless of the alarm that Palmer caused the public, the day passed with little occurring out of the ordinary. Palmer's credibility had already been in decline, and critics began pointing out that he had conducted searches without warrants and kept detainees indefinitely without legal counsel. Some charged that he had created the Red Scare to boost his reputation and gain the Democratic presidential nomination in 1920.

In May 1920, a group of attorneys, including Harvard professor Felix Frankfurter who later became a Supreme Court justice, listed the Department of Justice's abuses of civil liberties. National newspapers and politicians (including Senator Warren G. Harding and A. Mitchell Palmer, who didn't want socialists lumped with communists) protested New York's removal of its socialist assemblymen. Antisedition bills met with newspaper objections, and anticommunist bills aroused businessmen who were worried that their laborers might be deported. The tide had turned.

The states kept their antisyndicalism laws and restrictions on the display of the Soviet flag as well as other forms of free speech. The communist impulse slowed and then reversed in Europe. Cooler heads prevailed as Democrats and Republicans came to realize that a system that allowed the outlaw of socialists could outlaw Democrats and Republicans just as easily. Palmer backed off. The federal government removed from its deportation rules much that was arbitrary or left to the discretion of the individual agent, and court rulings began favoring the victims instead of the government. By June 1920, even communists were tolerated as long as they abided by other U.S. laws. When a bomb exploded on Wall Street on September 16, 1920, killing thirty-three and wounding more than two hundred, the nation took it in stride.

When it was done, six hundred people were deported. The raiders had used five thousand warrants to take over sixteen thousand people into custody.

John H. Barnhill

See also: Alien Act (WWI); Anarchists (WWI); Civil Liberties (WWI); Espionage Act (WWI); Industrial Workers of the World (WWI); Palmer Raids (WWI); Sedition Act (WWI); Biographies: Goldman, Emma (WWI); Hoover, J. Edgar (WWI); Palmer, A. Mitchell (WWI)

REFERENCES

Bennett, David. *The Party of Fear: From Nativist Movements to the New Right in American History.* Chapel Hill: University of North Carolina Press, 1988.

Hoyt, Edwin P. *The Palmer Raids 1919–1920: An Attempt to Suppress Dissent.* New York: Seabury Press, 1969.

Murray, Robert. *Red Scare: A Study in National Hysteria, 1919–1920.* New York: McGraw-Hill, 1964.

Preston, William, Jr. *Aliens and Dissenters: Federal Suppression of Radicals,* 2d ed. Chicago: University of Illinois Press, 1995.

Religion (U.S.)

Organized religion in the United States—including most Protestant, Catholic, and Jewish institutions as well as their leaders—supported U.S. participation in World War I on the side of the Allies and worked actively to bolster the war effort. Mainstream clerical and lay figures viewed patriotism and religion as irrevocably linked and saw the war as a crusade to make the world safe for democracy and (by implication) for religious freedom.

This almost universal prowar and pro-Allied sentiment during World War I is deeply rooted in American religious tradition and culture. The sense that God had endowed the United States with a divine civilizing mission (which is particularly strong among the Protestant churches) predated the American Revolution going back to the Puritans. During the era of U.S. expansionism, it fused with nationalistic ambitions embodied in the concept of "Manifest Destiny," which was used to justify the Mexican War and annexation of Texas, California, and other territories in the 1840s. After the Civil War, it carried over into support for overseas imperialism and for the war with Spain in 1898.

Nevertheless, there was no consensus among U.S. religions for intervention on the Allied side. Traditional distrust of "entangling alliances" initially influenced many Americans against involvement. German philosophy and theology had exercised predominate influence in U.S. academic circles for over a century. Moreover, many churches served large European immigrant communities who brought their prejudices with them from their native lands. Irish Catholics who remembered oppression by Great Britain and Jewish immigrants fleeing persecution by Tsarist Russia hardly sympathized with the Allies. England's suppression of the Easter Rebellion in Ireland in the spring of 1916 further strengthened anti-British sentiment among Irish-Americans and Irish-Catholic leaders. Isolationism among Catholics was further strengthened by the attitude of the leadership in Rome. Under Pope Benedict XV, the Vatican was officially neutral but sympathized with the Central Powers, particularly Catholic Austria-Hungary.

Running against isolationist sentiment, however, was widespread pro-Allied feeling among denominations with clear British origins—Presbyterians, Congregationalists, Methodists, and, most outspokenly, Episcopalians. The steady pro-Allied pressure from these Protestant elements undoubtedly encouraged President Woodrow Wilson, despite obvious risks, to follow a course that tolerated Great Britain's sea blockade of the Central Powers while taking far stronger issue with German submarine warfare against neutral shipping. Growing anti-German sentiment among Protestant churches fed on incidents such as the sinking of the British passenger liner *Lusitania* by a U-boat in May 1915 and reports of German atrocities in Belgium. Continuing reports of German barbarism from Allied propaganda sources fed growing chauvinism and increasingly violent anti-German outbursts in religious circles in the United States. The image of the Allied cause as a crusade for democracy was further strengthened by the February 1917 revolution in Russia that overthrew the Tsarist regime and swept a sup-

Pope Benedict XV emphasized the need for neutrality and peace during World War I. But many Catholics on both sides of the conflict failed to heed his advice and supported their respective government's war efforts. (Library of Congress)

posedly democratic Provisional Government into power.

The nation's religious organizations, as a result of growing patriotic pressure, almost unanimously supported President Wilson when he asked Congress to declare war on Germany in April 1917. Religious leaders across all denominations fell into line. The antiwar opposition was reduced to the core of Quakers, Mennonites, and other conscientious objectors.

Almost all pronouncements by Christian and Jewish organizations supported the notion that the war was now a crusade ordained by God against the unholy German militarist autocracy to safeguard democracy and ensure its

spread to all nations. Church spokesmen and publications accepted the most hideous images of bloodthirsty German soldiers from Allied and U.S. propaganda organizations. Personal attacks on the German Kaiser, Wilhelm II, as well as on German society in general, grew more strident and violent as the war went on and U.S. troops, arriving in France in increasing numbers, became more involved in the fighting.

Predictably, given the patriotic intensity of their rhetoric, U.S. religious organizations did all they could to aid the military effort. Their work led them into two different campaigns: a ministry to bases and camps in the United States and among the forces overseas and participation in numerous tasks aimed at bolstering the "home front."

U.S. belligerency caught the nation's churches unprepared. There was a severe shortage of military chaplains, and civilian religious services to the armed forces were virtually nonexistent. In May 1917, the Protestant-oriented Federal Council of Churches organized the General Wartime Commission, a coordinating agency with representatives from thirty-five different religious organizations. The Commission took responsibility for the religious needs of the military services including the recruitment and training of chaplains; the provision of Bibles and other reading materials; and the creation of recreation and rest centers at home and abroad. Likewise, the National Catholic War Council and the Jewish Welfare Board performed the same tasks of recruiting clergy and providing for the religious needs for Catholic and Jewish servicemen.

U.S. religious institutions also involved themselves directly in war work. Local ministers labored to recruit young men into military service by encouraging enlistments and urging compliance with the draft. Churchmen conducted liberty loan drives and incorporated government propaganda into their sermons. In addition, the war years witnessed a radical expansion of social services by religious organizations to bolster home front morale.

With most religious organizations so closely involved in support for the war, the comment by one observer that "at least for the period of World War I the separation of church and state was suspended" cannot be disputed. The long-term consequences of their support for their government's war policies were considerable. The unprecedented interfaith cooperation among Protestant, Catholic, and Jewish organizations carried over into the postwar years, as did their new social activism. On the other hand, the disillusionment over the peace discredited the basic premise of their support for the war—which came out of the belief that a more just and democratic international system would result from the defeat of German militarism. Over the next two decades, particularly during the Great Depression of the 1930s, this factor would lead many religious groups into a doctrinaire pacifism that blinded them to the threat posed by Hitler's Germany. The next war would find organized religion in the United States pursuing a much more low-profile support for their country's war effort.

Walter F. Bell

See also: Anti-Semitism (WWI); Revivalism (WWI); Biographies: Sunday, Billy (WWI)

REFERENCES

Abrams, Ray H. *Preachers Present Arms: The Role of American Churches and Clergy in World War I.* New York: Round Table, 1933.

Ahlstrom, Sydney E. *A Religious History of the American People.* 2d ed. New Haven, CT: Yale University Press, 2004.

Piper, John F., Jr. *The American Churches in World War I.* Athens: Ohio University Press, 1985.

Republican Party

By the end of World War I, the Republicans had overcome the divisions that, in 1912, had threatened the party's survival, retook Congress from the Democrats, and put themselves in a position to frustrate President Woodrow Wilson's agenda for the postwar world. Despite continuing divisions between various wings and along sectional lines, the wartime GOP achieved a modicum of consensus in criticizing Wilson's uncertain handling of the international crisis and his attempts to strengthen the executive branch's control over the economy. The Republican platform during the war years emphasized higher tariffs, lower taxes, and a profound skepticism of Wilson for both his handling of U.S. foreign relations and his mobilization of the country for war. With the end of the war, the ascendant Republicans took aim at Wilson's project for a League of Nations, which they managed to defeat in the Senate in 1920.

Out of Power

With Wilson in the White House and the Democrats in control of Congress until 1919, the Republicans were largely forced to react to their adversaries' initiatives. Despite the hostility between Wilson and many Republican leaders, the President often relied on GOP support in Congress, particularly after the Democrats' dominance of Congress was reduced by the 1916 elections. It was Republican votes, for example, that allowed Wilson's proposal to institute conscription to become law. Republican support was also instrumental in the passage of the Nineteenth Amendment, granting suffrage to women, which Wilson promoted against the wishes of many Congressional Democrats. The GOP itself never united around a single platform, however. On questions of preparedness and neutrality, Eastern internationalists vied with Western isolationists. On domestic issues, the party's progressive wing clashed with the "old guard," which was committed to the socioeconomic status quo.

The GOP's recovery from the disaster of 1912 was due in large part to the reintegration of Theodore Roosevelt and his followers, who, in 1912, had mounted a third-party presidential campaign under the banner of the Progressive, or Bull Moose, Party. By 1916, the Progressive Party was a shadow. Roosevelt had rejoined the Republicans and endorsed GOP nominee Charles Evans Hughes for President. Wilson defeated Hughes in one of the narrowest races in history, a 3,773 vote margin in California giving the President that state's pivotal electoral votes. The GOP also came within a hair's breadth of retaking the House in 1916. With war weariness setting in, the Republicans would seize control of both houses in 1918.

Despite abandoning temporarily his presidential ambitions, Roosevelt, with Massachusetts Senator Henry Cabot Lodge, continued to criticize Wilson sharply. Lodge and Roosevelt represented the internationalist wing of the GOP, whose strength was among the traditional elites and businessmen of the Eastern seaboard states. Early in the war, Roosevelt became one of the leading spokesmen for the so-called "preparedness" campaign, calling for a larger army and universal military training. More attuned than most U.S. politicians to the European balance of power, Roosevelt and Lodge argued that the United States had both a moral and a material interest in an Allied victory. After the sinking of the *Lusitania* on May 7, 1915, Lodge, Roosevelt, and former Secretary of War

Elihu Root took the lead in criticizing what they saw as Wilson's failure to defend U.S. rights as a neutral power. Seeking to mobilize a crusading U.S. idealism, Roosevelt and Lodge appealed to principles of honor, duty, and sacrifice in urging preparedness that, given the popularity of Wilson's determination to stay out of the war, they often couched in calls for a firm policy toward unrest in Mexico. They supported Wilson's decision to go to war in 1917 but feared lest the President make a compromise peace that did not destroy German militarism. When Wilson presented his Fourteen Points and plans for creating a postwar League of Nations, Roosevelt and Lodge denounced the President's abandonment of U.S. sovereignty. Although neither Lodge nor Roosevelt rejected the idea of a League in its entirety, they preferred an extension of the wartime alliance of democratic states to Wilson's universal League.

The Lodge/Roosevelt camp did not speak for the entire Republican Party, however. Several senators and congressmen, mostly from the rural West, opposed U.S. intervention and internationalism generally (though others, including former President William Howard Taft, supported a moderate form of internationalism). The Republican isolationists, whose most visible spokesmen were Senators William E. Borah of Idaho and Robert M. La Follette of Wisconsin, were usually drawn from the Progressive camp that had either defected to Roosevelt in 1912 or supported the GOP Progressive movement known as the Insurgency. Progressivism and pacifism were often linked. La Follette denounced the war for increasing the suffering of the poor while securing "privilege profits" for wealthy industrialists. The isolationists often objected to their own party's support for preparedness measures; their opposition forced Lodge to drop references to universal military service from the GOP's 1916 election platform. After the United States entered the war in April 1917, the isolationists faced charges of pro-German sympathies (La Follette had to defend his loyalty before a Senate investigation). Borah in particular led the "irreconcilable" opposition that ultimately scuttled the Treaty of Versailles, arguing that the League would entangle the United States in European politics and make future wars more likely.

Republicans and the War

Once the United States entered the war, Congressional Republicans criticized Wilson's handling of mobilization and made several attempts to wrest control over the economy from him. They also criticized Wilson for mishandling the large appropriations he demanded from Congress to prosecute the war, attempting unsuccessfully to establish a Committee on the Conduct of the War to combat waste and fraud, which they alleged to be widespread, especially in the Newton Baker's War Department. The struggles over the economy reflected sharp philosophical differences between Wilson and the GOP and highlighted the sectional divide between the major parties. Wilson wanted to pay for war expenses out of current revenues by raising taxes on income and profits. Although supported by GOP progressives like Borah, increased taxation was anathema to the Eastern Republicans. Conservatives like House Minority Leader James R. Mann of Illinois objected to the increased burdens on businessmen and favored issuing bonds and raising the tariff to pay for the expenses of preparedness and war. Republicans also objected to Wilson's attempts at regulating prices to combat shortages and profiteering. Congressional Republicans pointed out that, while wheat was subjected to price controls, cotton (produced in the heavily Democratic South) was not. This perceived pro-Southern bias was a boon to Republicans in the 1918 elections, in which they captured both houses of Congress from the Democrats.

Jeffrey Mankoff

See also: Elections of 1916 (WWI); Elections of 1920 (WWI); Progressivism (WWI); Biographies: Hughes, Charles (WWI); Lodge, Henry Cabot (WWI); Roosevelt, Theodore (WWI); Documents: Republican Party Platform, 1916

REFERENCES

Burgchardt, Carl R. *Robert M. LaFollette, Sr.: The Voice of Conscience.* Westport, CT: Greenwood Press, 1992.

Burton, David H. *Taft, Wilson, and World Order.* Madison, NJ: Fairleigh-Dickinson University Press, 2003.

Livermore, Seward W. *Politics Is Adjourned: Woodrow Wilson and the War Congress, 1916–1918.* Middletown, CT: Wesleyan University Press, 1966.

Margulies, Herbert F. *James R. Mann and the House Republicans in the Wilson Era.* Westport, CT: Greenwood Press, 1996.

Mayer, George H. *The Republican Party, 1854–1966.* New York: Oxford University Press, 1964.

Moos, Malcolm. *The Republicans: A History of Their Party.* New York: Random House, 1956.

Widenor, William C. *Henry Cabot Lodge and the Search for an American Foreign Policy.* Berkeley: California University Press, 1980.

Revivalism

For most Protestants in the United States, a "revival" signifies a widespread increase in spiritual devotion to God. Revivals are specifically considered a Protestant phenomenon because they are supported on the premise that Christians have been insufficiently devoted in the past and need to change their behavior in order to receive favor from God. The best-known revivals in U.S. history, the First and Second Great Awakenings, drew thousands to public church meetings and led to the growth of the Baptist and Methodist denominations, as well as many smaller religious groups. These revivals inspired American ministers to develop two theories about revivalism. Charles Finney argued that clergymen could start and orchestrate successful revivals with proper planning, and he published manuals for this purpose. On the other hand, American ministers like Jonathan Edwards argued that revivals would only happen through the intervention of God, which would be revealed in Christians' prayer, life, and actions. The question of whether or not World War I inspired religious revivals in the United States depends upon which interpretation one accepts.

Obstacles to Revivalism

Several characteristics of U.S. Christianity made it difficult for Protestant clergymen to manufacture a revival during World War I. First, the norms for church worship had changed since the eighteenth and nineteenth centuries. Mainline denominations, particularly in the North, eschewed the emotional, physically expressive worship prominent during the Great Awakening for more orderly signs of devotion. Rather than inspiring congregants to shout, faint, or rush to confess their sins at the altar, twentieth-century ministers more often asked laymen to silently indicate their change of heart on a "pledge card." By 1914, uncontrolled emotion had given way to

solemn conversion as a sign of revival, and the number of conversions did not increase dramatically enough to indicate that a U.S. revival was happening. Instead, U.S. Protestantism seemed to be in decline by the 1920s. Clergy judged the religious state of the nation by the soldiers' spirituality, but this perspective produced disappointing results. Though many soldiers freely admitted belief in God during battles and after being wounded, some clergy doubted whether such stress-induced confessions could be accepted as sincere Christian conversions. Also, newspapers published statements from soldiers who argued against the idea that Christianity was spreading in the trenches because chaplains had not done enough to spread the Gospel to soldiers. These arguments contradicted the widespread belief that the war would automatically increase faith among soldiers and around the world.

Many of the hopes for U.S. revivalism during World War I depended upon the spirituality of soldiers. Well-known clergymen, including the traveling evangelist Billy Sunday, discussed the war as if it was a crusade or holy war, comparing the German troops with the forces of hell. In this sense, U.S. soldiers were fulfilling their duty to God and the nation by fighting, which is why ministers often eulogized soldiers in terms of their "great sacrifice" or their "Christian duty." Chaplains in the field observed that soldiers seemed more interested in spiritual matters when confronted with death, and ministers hoped that other Americans would find a similar source of comfort when friends and family members died in the military. Because the wartime revival depended upon patriotism and national unity, its proponents rarely used specific terms to describe the type of spiritual devotion they hoped to inspire. The goal of the World War I revival seemed to be an ecumenical God who hated the Kaiser and would use U.S. soldiers to bring the nation's best interests to fruition.

The American Catholic Church stood out by endorsing a more specific vision of revivalism. Unlike most Protestant denominations, the Catholic Church did not participate in ecumenical organizations like the Federal Council of Churches or characterize the war as simply a reason for increased spirituality. Instead, Catholic leaders argued that World War I presented a key opportunity for U.S. Catholics to unify beyond the divisions of individual parishes. In particular, Cardinal James Gibbons used wartime patriotic rhetoric to craft a new American Catholic identity. Before 1908, the Vatican had only recognized Catholic presence in the United States as a foreign mission; likewise, U.S. Protestants often criticized Catholics as a religious minority under a style of monarchical leadership contrary to American ideals. However, the number of Catholics grew dramatically by the twentieth century, and World War I presented one of the first steps in an Americanization process that Gibbons had advocated since the 1890s. Father John Burke followed his lead; he argued that the Catholic faith constituted the only spiritual foundation that could enable someone to appreciate American values and become a true patriot. The confluence of American and Catholic identity seemed unrealistic considering that first- and second-generation European immigrants represented the majority of the U.S. Church in the early 1900s, and their parishes usually served as havens of foreign culture and language. Nevertheless, Catholics from many nations could agree to support the United States during the war, which made it easier to coordinate national service programs that contributed to Church-wide unity. Because of organizations like the National Catholic War Council, the phrase "American Catholic" became more meaningful and more popular after World War I.

Pentecostal Movement

A third group of U.S. Christians believed that God had already initiated a twentieth-century revival that would only grow stronger because of the war. The Pentecostal movement thrived on the conviction that the early 1900s were special years designated by God for inspiring holiness among believers and preparing for the end of the world. Pentecostal faith centered on the belief that God gave Christian converts the ability to speak in "tongues," or unknown languages, as the original disciples did in the second chapter of Acts. The first recorded example of an American speaking in tongues occurred in 1901, and it was followed by a major revival that started on Azusa Street in Los Angeles, California, in 1906. This revival led to the birth of several Pentecostal denominations that continued to proclaim revival throughout the 1910s and 1920s.

The Pentecostals were similar to Baptists, particularly Southern Baptists, in their conviction that the Bible should be interpreted literally. This belief inspired them to accept premillenialism, arguing that the Christ would return to Earth only after many years of war and destruction. Since World War I was the first major conflict to start after the Pentecostal movement began, Pentecostal leaders reasoned that the war represented a sign of the end times. Like premillenialists in other Protestant denominations, they argued that the Kaiser embodied the anti-Christ and that the battles fulfilled events prophesied in the Book of Revelations. Their willingness to characterize U.S. enemies as evil matched the rhetoric of patriotic Christian ministers in other denominations, but the Pentecostals distinguished themselves by arguing that the revival had already begun. For them, the main reward of revival was the imminent return of Christ, which did not necessarily depend upon church growth or military victory. Pentecostal leaders shared other ministers' hope that the violence and fatality associated with war would compel soldiers and other Americans to convert to Christianity, but their literal perspective made them more likely to believe that justice would not be realized on earth until God made it happen. Liberal critics argued that this perspective would diminish Americans' support for the war because it implied that human efforts to fight evil were comparatively unimportant. A Pentecostal could believe that Christ would return whether or not the United States and its allies won the war, and His return constituted the ultimate victory. The revival included the small percentage of U.S. Christians who agreed with this view and joined a Pentecostal church.

These three examples display the major interpretations of revival prominent during World War I. Most U.S. Christians, especially Protestants, felt that a nationwide revival depended upon an increase in spiritual piety among soldiers that would eventually inspire more Americans to convert to Christianity and join churches. This view of revival embraced ecumenical worship, using the war to characterize God as a symbol of freedom and salvation that all Americans could support in unison. Leaders of the American Catholic Church used similar rhetoric to raise support for the war, but they showed more interest in national Catholic unity than in interfaith cooperation. Their revival included a goal of Americanization for the relatively young national Church; Catholic leaders presented the war as a cause that millions of Catholic immigrants could support on the basis of a common faith as well as a widespread sense of American patriotism. On the other hand, U.S. Pentecostals saw wartime revival as simply a continuation of Divine intervention that began in the early 1900s. Rather than interpreting revival as an increase in ecumenical spirituality, they saw it as a movement restricted to Pentecostal churches in preparation for the imminent return of Christ and the violence that would precede it. As the movement grew, Pentecostals' hopes for revival were fulfilled during the war years, as were those of Catholic leaders who saw the American Catholic Church unify as never before. However, most scholars agree that the increase in conversions that mainline Protestant ministers interpreted as a revival never materialized.

Kimberly Hill

See also: Religion (WWI); Biographies: Sunday, Billy (WWI)

REFERENCES

Abrams, Ray H. "Preachers Present Arms: A Study of the War-Time Attitudes and Activities of the Churches and the Clergy in the United States, 1914–1918." Ph.D. dissertation, University of Pennsylvania, 1933.

Blumhofer, Edith L., and Randall Balmer. *Modern Christian Revivals.* Urbana: University of Illinois Press, 1993.

Dolan, Jay P. *In Search of an American Catholicism: A History of Religion and Culture in Tension.* Oxford: Oxford University Press, 2002.

Schweitzer, Richard. *The Cross and the Trenches: Religious Faith and Doubt among British and American Great War Soldiers.* London: Praeger, 2003.

Piper, John F., Jr. *The American Church in World War I.* Athens: Ohio University Press, 1985.

S

Sabotage and Spies

On February 4, 1917, a headline in the *New York Times* claimed that ten thousand spies for the Central Powers were at work in the United States. Responding to such reports, Americans were on edge in the months before war was declared, suspecting that anyone with a map or camera was engaged in espionage. Even during the "neutral" years, citizens or aliens with obvious ties to Germany, such as German cultural groups and readers of German-language magazines and newspapers, were suspect. Because the young Bureau of Investigation (later the FBI) was not prepared for combating the relatively sophisticated German intelligence system, fifty thousand U.S. government employees were recruited to help uncover espionage.

German Embassy Spy Ring

Documents found after the war revealed that, indeed, in the years 1914 to 1917, a spy ring was run from Germany through the German Embassy in Washington, D.C. The German ambassador, Count Johann von Bernstorff, was the heart of the operation, although he continued to deny any involvement. Two other embassy officials also participated: Captain Franz von Papen, the military attaché who was also attached to the German legation in Mexico City, and Captain Karl Boy-Ed, the naval attaché. Boy-Ed, who had served on the staff of Admiral Alfred von Tirpitz in Germany, directed sabotage on ships carrying munitions and supplies and arranged for false passports for German nationals returning home, while von Papen oversaw industrial sabotage.

Handling the funding for their operations was Dr. Heinrich Albert, the commercial attaché and an official with the Hamburg-Amerika steamship line with an office in New York City. He also directed activities intending to tie up Allied munitions orders. Joining them was Paul Koenig, known as "Triple X," a former detective with Hamburg-Amerika who recruited spies among the English-hating Irish, German nationals, and marginally employed Americans.

Initially, spying was simply information-gathering, with observers noting the production capabilities of U.S. and Canadian firms and determining which supplies were being readied for shipment to Europe. Activities were concentrated on the U.S.-Canada border and in the industrial Northeast. By 1914, espionage agents were more sophisticated and noted details of shipments, complete with times and routes for use by U-boats.

Communication with Germany became difficult once war was declared in Europe. In 1911, the German company Telefunken Communications had installed a huge radio tower at Sayville Station on Long Island, New York. For several years, it sent messages to Germany regarding the routes of transport ships leaving New York Harbor. In September 1914, the U.S. Navy seized the tower and arrested the internationally known radio engineer Jonathan Zenneck, who was interned on Ellis Island for the duration. After the tower was made inaccessible, German ships detained along the East Coast rigged concealed antennae in funnels or elsewhere on board to pick up radio transmissions coming directly from Germany or by way of Mexico or Sweden. Receiving stations were also set up in private homes.

On January 26, 1915, German Under Secretary of State Arthur Zimmermann sent a cablegram to Bernstorff stating: "In the U.S. sabotage can be carried out in every kind of factory for supplying munitions of war." From then on, a campaign was underway to impede or destroy the production of war matériel.

Conspirators met in a brownstone at 123 W. 15th Street in Manhattan to exchange information. The building, rented to the German opera singer Martha Held, was mistaken for a brothel by neighbors because of the frequent comings and goings of men and women and because of the large amount of alcohol consumed. Officers from interned German ships were frequently entertained there. From the later testimony of Mena Edwards, an occasional model who attended soirees at the house, discussions about the specifics of sabotage were common.

"Cigar" bombs made on shipboard were frequently used for sabotage. These small lead pipes were divided by copper discs into two compartments. One held potassium chlorate, the other sulfuric acid. When the acid ate through the disc, the two ingredients combined producing an explosion. TNT was also readily available to conspirators. International bridges were an early proposed target, but only a few plans were carried out. Werner Horn was found guilty of blowing up the international bridge at Vanceboro, Maine. Plans were made to demolish the Welland Canal between Lake Ontario and Lake Erie, but the act was not carried out. On May 30, 1915, a barge loaded with gunpowder from the Hercules Powder Company was dynamited in Tacoma Harbor in Washington State. Among the damage done by saboteurs, the most spectacular explosions were at Black Tom Island (now Liberty Park) and Kingsland in New Jersey.

Two million pounds of munitions were stored on Black Tom Island in New York Harbor when it exploded shortly after 2 a.m. on July 30, 1916. The promontory was the most important point in North America for the transfer of ammunition to Allied ships and was crisscrossed with railroad tracks leading to warehouses and piers. Guards reported seeing two fires before the explosion, one on a barge loaded with TNT and one on a railway car. When the eighty-seven railroad cars filled with dynamite began exploding, clouds of smoke were seen for miles and tons of glass in buildings in Manhattan and New Jersey shattered. With shells screaming and flaming rockets whizzing through the sky, residents were certain an invasion was underway. The result of the explosion was $25 million in property damage, thirteen warehouses leveled, six piers demolished, and hundreds of railroad cars and barges destroyed.

At Kingsland (now Lyndhurst), New Jersey, a shell-assembly plant owned by the Canadian

Car and Foundry Company burned on January 11, 1917. Workers evacuated the plant in time to escape injury. An employee was suspected of starting the fire, which began in an assembling shed, but he disappeared before he could be charged.

War Declared

As soon as war was declared on April 6, 1917, all German officials fled to Mexico. State sponsored spying and sabotage effectively ended. From that point, most arrests of spies and saboteurs were of unemployed or marginally employed men found lurking around naval yards, power plants, or munitions factories, probably with the hope of selling their information to Germany. Once a Military Intelligence Service was established, sabotage and spying were further curtailed.

At least $150 million damage was done in the United States by sabotage agents during the prewar years, not including the loss in profits to munitions makers and shippers. The Espionage Act of 1917 had no impact on German spies, but a few saboteurs were prosecuted by plant owners through the Mixed Claims Commission after the war.

Betty Burnett

See also: Federal Bureau of Investigation (WWI); Espionage Act (WWI); Zimmermann Telegram (WWI)

REFERENCES

Landau, Henry. *The Enemy Within: The Inside Story of German Sabotage in America.* New York: G. P. Putnam's Sons, 1937.
von Bernstorff, Johann. *My Three Years in America.* New York: Charles Scribner's Sons, 1920.
Witcower, Jules. *Sabotage at Black Tom: Imperial Germany's Secret War in America 1914–1917.* Chapel Hill, NC: Algonquin Books, 1989.

Sacco and Vanzetti Case

Charged with robbery and murder of a paymaster and his guard at a shoe factory in Massachusetts, on April 15, 1920, Nicola Sacco and Bartolomeo Vanzetti, both Italian immigrants and self-proclaimed anarchists, were executed amidst a storm of controversy on August 23, 1927.

As part of the postwar Red Scare, the Justice Department initiated a nationwide campaign to suppress Italian anarchists. Efforts to round up a group of Boston anarchists intensified when police began looking for suspects in the robbery-murder at the Slater and Morrill Shoe Factory in nearby South Braintree. Although they were not suspects in the case, police arrested Sacco, a skilled shoe worker, and Vanzetti, a fish seller, on a streetcar. Vanzetti was tried and convicted of an earlier robbery in Bridgewater, Massachusetts, and both men were found guilty of first-degree murder in the South Braintree case. Six years of unsuccessful appeals for a new trial followed, during which time Sacco and Vanzetti became internationally famous as symbols of an antilabor conspiracy. In the United States, their case garnered the attention of organized labor, the ACLU, and a host of prominent artists and intellectuals, including Edna St. Vincent Millay, John Dos Passos, and Felix Frankfurter. Comparing the Sacco-Vanzetti case to that of Tom Mooney, a labor organizer languishing in a San Francisco jail on trumped-up murder charges, defenders insisted the two men were victims of a frame-up by an anti-Italian, antiradical Massachusetts establishment in collusion with federal authori-

Convicted of armed robbery and murder after World War I, the case of Italian immigrants and anarchists Bar-tolomeo Vanzetti and Nicola Sacco became a cause celebre of leftists and civil libertarians in the United States and around the world during the 1920s. (Library of Congress)

ties. Despite demonstrations of support in the United States and abroad and requests for intervention from the Supreme Court, the men were executed at just after midnight on August 23, 1927. Thousands of men and women poured into Boston for the funeral procession, and thousands demonstrated in New York when the men's ashes were brought there days later. To this day, the guilt or innocence of Sacco and Vanzetti has never been definitively determined, and the case remains one of the most controversial episodes in U.S. history.

Mary Anne Trasciatti

See also: Anarchists (WWI); Italian Americans (WWI); Red Scare (WWI)

REFERENCES

Avrich, Paul. *Sacco and Vanzetti: The Anarchist Background.* Princeton, NJ: Princeton University Press, 1991.

Sacco-Vanzetti: Developments and Reconsiderations—1979. Boston: Trustees of the Boston Public Library, 1982.

Salvation Army

The Salvation Army is an international charitable organization that gained popularity as a result of its missionary work among Allied troops in France during World War I. The organization originally began in London as the East End Christian Mission. Founded in 1865 by London Minister William Booth, the East End Mission offered assistance and spiritual guidance to the city's poor. Booth renamed the organization the Salvation Army in 1878 to reflect its commitment to God's work. Booth took the title of General, while other members of the organization were given military ranks in accordance with their duties.

By the turn of the century, the Salvation Army's membership had grown to include officers in thirty-six countries around the world. Membership was especially strong in the United States due to a number of the organization's social work programs. However, it was the organization's missionary work in World War I that made it a household name.

Lieutenant Colonel William S. Barker and several other missionaries left for the French front in 1917. Upon their arrival, the group was received by the American Ambassador to France and General John J. Pershing. Barker asked Pershing for permission to counsel troops stationed with the Army's First Division in France. Pershing agreed and preparations were made for the first twenty-two volunteers to begin work.

Barker and the other volunteers, most of whom were women, set up camp in August 1917. They built a series of temporary shelters called *hutments* alongside the First Division's campsite. The hutments, which were long crude sectional buildings, served as gathering places for both the volunteers and the troops. The buildings housed song services, musical shows, and bible classes, but the hutments were available for use by other denominations as well. Volunteers built over four hundred hutments during the course of their fifteen-month stay.

The organization and its volunteers wanted to ease some of the heartache brought about by war by bridging the gap between home and the battlefront. One of the ways they did this was by establishing a safe money transfer system that allowed troops to send money back to the United States. Troops usually had extra money while stationed overseas and were prone to gambling it away or spending it all on alcohol. Salvation Army volunteers encouraged soldiers to send their money home to their families instead of spending it on various vices.

Volunteers also provided troops with fresh baked goods to remind them of the comfort of

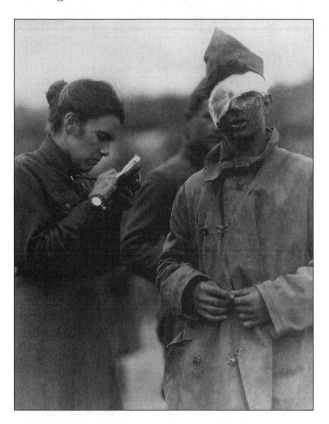

A Salvation Army worker writes a letter home for a wounded soldier in World War I. The organization was one of the main private providers of relief to U.S. soldiers fighting in Europe. (National Archives)

home. One baked good in particular was extremely popular among the soldiers. The doughnut became a symbol of the Salvation Army's dedication to improving the lives of troops stationed far away from home. The women volunteers, who were nicknamed *Sallies* by the troops, baked anywhere from 2,500 to 9,000 doughnuts a day. The program was so popular that it was resurrected during World War II and later turned into a national fundraiser. Doughnut Day was established in 1938 as a means of raising money for the Salvation Army's operating expenses and to honor the work of the men and women volunteers of World War I.

The Salvation Army had to finance the first phase of their missionary work with $125,000 borrowed from private lenders, but their efforts paid off. By the end of the war, the organization and its volunteers had raised $12.5 million in contributions. Volunteers continued to work with troops even after 1919. Sallies continued to make their rounds in army hospitals and to provide comfort for troops stationed in France, and the later occupied Germany.

During World War II, Salvation Army volunteers operated over three thousand service units for the U.S. Armed Forces, which eventually led to the formation of the United Service Organization (USO).

Catherine D. Griffis

See also: Religion (WWI); YMCA and YWCA (WWI)

REFERENCES

Bishop, Edward. *Blood and Fire: The Story of General William Booth and the Salvation Army*. London: Longmans, 1964.
Taiz, Lillian. *Hallelujah Lads and Lasses: Remaking the Salvation Army in America, 1880–1930*. Chapel Hill: University of North Carolina Press, 2001.
Winston, Diane. *Red-Hot and Righteous: The Urban Religion of the Salvation Army*. Cambridge: Harvard University Press, 2000.

Seattle General Strike

During World War I, Seattle shipyards achieved a miracle of production, turning out 26.5 percent of all ships constructed for the Emergency Fleet Corporation (EFC) to support the Allied war effort. During the war, Seattle's shipyards became completely unionized and represented by the American Federation of Labor. All disputes involving wages, hours, and working conditions were handled by the Shipbuilding Labor Adjustment Board, which included members from naval personnel and union officials, whose appeals to patriotism and steady wages kept the threat of strikes down.

After the signing of the Armistice in November 1918, shipyards began to lower wages. At the same time, government price controls were loosened and prices on products began to climb while wages continued to drop both in Seattle and around the nation. Unions that had gained power during the war lost ground as courts began upholding yellow-dog contracts, which forbid workers from joining unions.

Seattle in 1919 still retained the flavor of a western town complete with saloons, whorehouses, and mission churches. Its restless population included ship builders, dockworkers, lumberjacks, and sailors. The cut in wages hit Seattle hard, and union leaders struggled to maintain the gains they won during World War I. On January 21, 1919, 35,000 shipyard workers went on strike. A few days later, their employers left Seattle, signaling their intention not to negotiate and hopefully force, by hunger, the workers back to their jobs.

On January 23, the Seattle Central Labor Council adopted a resolution put forth by the

Metal Trades Council for a general strike in Seattle. Weeks of negotiations between Seattle unions passed. Hysteria built as newspapers warned of dire consequences if the unions went on strike: Homes would not have oil to heat them and meat, milk, and flour would vanish in two days. Both local and federal government officials refused to negotiate with the unions as rumors flew that the Bolsheviks, recently successful in seizing power in Russia, would use Seattle as a place to begin a revolution in the United States. Seattle's police chief deputized nearly three thousand sailors, soldiers, and ordinary citizens to meet the coming threat. On February 3, the official strike notice appeared in Seattle's daily newspaper and on February 6, a general strike in support of the shipyard strike began as members of 110 local unions participated in a massive walkout and the city ground to a halt. A General Strike Committee made sure that the city had light, heat, milk and mail deliveries, fire and police protection, and laundry services. The only vehicles moving along the streets were ambulances and hearses bearing signs that read "Exempted by the General Strike Committee." There was no revolution or violence in the streets.

Seattle newspapers and Mayor Ole Hanson claimed that the walkout was the beginning of a communist takeover of the United States. Hanson rode around town in a flag-draped car warning union leaders that he would use force to crush the strike. On the morning of February 7, Mayor Hanson led a regiment of soldiers from Fort Lewis into the city where they set up machine gun posts in the city's major intersections.

The head of the AFL, Samuel Gompers, came out against the strike and ordered its union members to quit supporting the shipyard workers. On February 9, workers began returning to their jobs. Police and vigilante squads began rounding up suspected radicals.

The Industrial Workers of the World hall and the Socialist Party headquarters were raided and several of their leaders arrested. A labor daily newspaper, the *Union Record,* was closed down and several of its staff arrested. On February 11, the Seattle General Strike ended. Shipyard workers went back to work but, as the EFC canceled existing orders, wages and employment in Seattle continued to fall.

The Seattle general strike set the pattern for dealing with strikes in the 1920s. Rather than focus on the real issues such as working conditions or wages, business leaders simply branded all strikes as radicalism and whipped up public anxiety about Bolsheviks and communism. The gains made by labor during the war were erased and labor spent most of the next two decades fighting for its survival.

Jason Dikes

See also: American Federation of Labor (WWI); Trade Unions (U.S., WWI); Biographies: Gompers, Samuel (WWI)

REFERENCES

Hawley, Ellis W. *The Great War and the Search for a Modern Order.* New York: St. Martin's, 1992.

Miller, Nathan. *New World Coming: The 1920s and the Making of Modern America.* New York: Scribner, 2003.

Perret, Geoffrey. *America in the Twenties, A History.* New York: Simon and Schuster, 1982.

Sedition Act

The Sedition Act was passed during World War I to punish people who made public comments deemed unpatriotic or supportive of the enemies of the United States. Signed into law on May 16, 1918, the Sedition Act was designed to close any loopholes that could be found in the Espionage Act, which was passed the previous year. The Sedition Act imposed a $10,000 fine and/or a prison term up to twenty years for anyone convicted of making or conveying "false reports or false statements with intent to interfere with the operation or success of the military or naval forces of the United States, or to promote the success of its enemies." The law also covered cases in which someone might ". . . incite insubordination, disloyalty, mutiny, or refusal of duty, in the military or naval forces of the United States, or shall willfully obstruct . . . the recruiting or enlistment service of the United States, or shall willfully utter, print, write, or publish any disloyal, profane, scurrilous, or abusive language about the government of the United States, or the Constitution of the United States, or the military or naval forces of the United States . . . or shall willfully display the flag of any foreign enemy, or shall willfully . . . urge, incite, or advocate any curtailment of production." The law was also designed to deal with those who did or said anything to obstruct the sale of Liberty Bonds. Despite its similarity to the Espionage Act, the Sedition Act's original roots lay in legislation passed in western states to muzzle labor radicals. But regardless of its origins, the law proved more sweeping in its intent to crush wartime dissent and criticism than anything previous. That fact was underscored when Congress, while debating the new law, voted against an amendment that would have stated that "nothing in this act shall be construed as limiting the liberty or impairing the right of any individual to publish or speak what is true, with good motives, and for justifiable ends." The law made it a crime to suggest higher taxes instead of bonds to pay for the war, or to urge that a referendum should have been held prior to declaring war. A film pro-

ducer even drew a ten-year prison sentence for making a movie on the American Revolution because it raised fears that it would stir sentiment against Britain. The inclusive nature of the act led some politicians to wonder just who the United States thought it was fighting. California Senator Hiram Johnson said: "It is war. But good God . . . when did it become war against the American people?"

Other leaders were not as concerned about the law's apparent assault on civil liberties. A New Mexico Congressman said: "I would have voted for it much more readily if it carried the death penalty."

The Sedition Act was used to convict more than one thousand people during the war years before it was repealed in 1921.

John Morello

See also: Alien Act (WWI); Espionage Act (WWI); Documents: Sedition Act, May 16, 1918

REFERENCES

Goldfield, David. *The American Journey: A History of the United States,* Vol. 2. Englewood Cliffs, NJ: Prentice-Hall, 1998.

Tindall, George Brown. *America: A Narrative History.* New York: W. W. Norton, 1988.

Sexuality (U.S.)

In the years prior to World War I, middle-class sexual values were beginning a transformation, creating tensions between the old Victorian values of the late nineteenth century and the newly rising modern values. Victorians had focused on sexual inhibition and self-control and the idea that the function of sex was procreation. Reformers and traditionalists, alarmed by the new values, had begun a social hygiene movement that aimed to stop the spread of venereal disease and prostitution. They objected to displays of female sexual desire outside of marriage and objected to the growing popularity of dance halls and movie theaters and fought for film production censorship and the prohibition of alcohol.

Meanwhile, medical and psychological professionals such as Sigmund Freud and Havelock Ellis began to emphasize sexual indulgence and open sexual expression. The emerging birth control movement, most widely associated with Margaret Sanger, played a key role in the emergence of new sexual attitudes and the move away from sex as merely procreation. It also helped women expand their roles beyond motherhood and opened the door for more female premarital sex. A small number of sexual radicals based in New York City's Greenwich Village sought to stretch the new sexual freedoms even farther, promoting free love and female sexual equality and speaking out against monogamy and the sanctity of marriage. Though small in numbers, many of these radicals were artists of various kinds whose ideas reached a wide audience.

World War I provided young men and women with new sexual opportunities and motives with which to explore the new sexual values. Sexual activity rose as people faced the social disruptions of mobilization and warfare with its accompanying fear of possible death. Enjoyment in the present day seemed more important than preparation for a distant future that may never come. Prostitutes saw an increase in business and marriage rates rose as many men married their sweethearts before leaving for duty. The war heightened some peoples' fears about a declining morality. Other concerns included the rising number of illegitimate "war babies," the cheating wives of ser-

vicemen, and "good time girls" with "khaki fever" who sought sexual relations with servicemen. There were also home front fears about enemy troops or spies. Propaganda and negative depictions of the enemy often contained sexual overtones and stories of the enemy's brutality and sexual depravity. Many of these fears had their foundations in the prewar era and proved to be exaggerated.

Women began working outside the home in record numbers as men left jobs for the military. Many women thus found increased freedom and independence. Some women became more knowledgeable about sexuality, but available information on birth control, sex, and bodily functions was still limited and many others remained sexually ignorant. Some feared that when women took advantage of the newfound freedom to dress in less restrictive clothing and to work outside the home, sexual experimentation would inevitably follow. Others feared that women would not want to return to the traditional role of mother and homemaker after the war. Even nursing concerned some, as it meant strong women caring for wounded and vulnerable men. At the same time, traditional gender roles remained strong as men were expected to courageously defend their country while women were expected to tend to the home.

The greatest sexual concerns within the military centered on venereal disease and prostitution. Widespread medical inspections and discipline among the large numbers of troops made it easier to openly talk about such previously guarded or taboo topics as venereal disease and sexuality. Most sexual activity among military forces took place behind the lines or on the home front. The military launched venereal disease campaigns in order to save manpower lost to the diseases. The military relied on posters, films, lectures, and prophylactic demonstrations to counter the spread of venereal disease and tried to offer healthy alternative activities to sex. In 1917, the newly created Committee on Training Camp Activities (CTCA) began to oversee draftee preparations for fighting and to prevent the moral dangers that could entrap young men. The group also pressured cities located near military bases to close their "red light" districts and sought to create five-mile "pure zones" around military camps.

After the war, gender imbalances caused by the number of war dead, family dislocations, and the mental and physical troubles of returning soldiers continued to affect sexuality. Many marriages hastily performed before servicemen left for duty and many marriages disrupted by returning servicemen's difficulties did not survive. Both government propaganda and popular culture emphasized motherhood and proper parenting techniques to counter these disruptions. More open discussions of sexual issues such as venereal disease and birth control continued. Many states enacted mandatory venereal disease reporting laws and began requiring blood tests before marriage. The U.S. Public Health Service now contained a Division of Venereal Disease. The war also popularized the use of condoms for the prevention of venereal disease. "Red light" prostitution districts containing brothels controlled by madams had almost disappeared by 1920, replaced by amateur streetwalkers and call girls controlled by male pimps.

The revision of sexual values, which had begun in the early 1900s, continued during the World War I period and reached its peak in the 1920s and 1930s. Changes included the positive view of sexual expression and female sexuality, more independence and sexual activity among the young, and sexual expression within commercialized leisure activities and popular culture. The idea of the companionate marriage based upon mutual sexual satisfaction became popular and widely accepted. Advice manuals instructed people on how to achieve sexual satisfaction through better techniques and many women began to enter marriage with more sexual knowledge and experience. Many people held the war responsible for hastening these changes in sexual morality.

David Treviño

See also: Anti-Prostitution Campaign (WWI); Women (U.S., WWI)

REFERENCES

D'Emilio, John, and Estelle B. Freedman. *Intimate Matters: A History of Sexuality in America.* New York: Harper and Row, 1988.

McLaren, Angus. *Twentieth Century Sexuality: A History.* Malden, MA: Blackwell, 1999.

Tannahill, Reay. *Sex in History.* Chelsea, MI: Scarborough House, 1992.

Shipping

During the first two years of World War I, the Wilson Administration struggled unsuccessfully to pass a bill through Congress that would give government the authority to own and operate a merchant fleet. Proponents of the legislation argued that a national merchant marine would augment the U.S. Navy and contribute to the nation's defense. But critics, which comprised the majority opinion, denounced the bill as socialistic and a threat to free enterprise. Opinion reversed, however, as German U-boats escalated attacks on U.S. merchantmen. In September 1916, Congress passed the Shipping Act, which gave government total control of the shipping industry and launched a massive shipbuilding program. As a result, the United

States emerged from the war as a maritime power, second only to England.

Prior to the outbreak of war in Europe in 1914, the Wilson Administration had identified the shortage of modern ocean-going flagships as the major obstacle to achieving the United States' international trade goals. The U.S. merchant marine comprised only 1,692 aging ships, most of which were employed in domestic coastwise trade or on routes connecting the mainland with outlying territories. As a result, more than 90 percent of the United States' international trade relied on foreign—mainly English—carriers. The start of the hostilities, which immediately diverted English and German merchant vessels away from regular trade routes and introduced raiding by German U-boats, crippled U.S. overseas commerce within three weeks. Goods piled up on docks because too few U.S. flagships were available to pick up the slack and because those vessels that could be obtained were kept moored for lack of war risk insurance.

The Wilson Administration responded to the emergency, which highlighted the deficiencies of a private and independent shipping industry, by proposing a bill that would establish a government-owned and -controlled merchant marine. Congress, rejecting such a drastic measure as premature, instead passed the Ship Registry Act on August 18, 1914. This legislation permitted foreign-built ships to register under the American flag, adding 148 vessels to the fleet by July 1, 1915. Simultaneously, Congress created the War Risk Insurance Bureau in the Treasury Department to protect shippers from losses due to mines, U-boat attacks, and the like.

While these preliminary actions put U.S. ships back on the seas, they did little to increase ship numbers. The small number of domestic shipyards plus high construction costs prevented private companies from meeting the growing demand for vessels. Naturally, shipping rates soared. As the war progressed, and German U-boats stepped up their raids, the ship shortage worsened. Finally, after the sinking of the *Lusitania* on May 7, 1915, killing 128 American passengers, as well as numerous U-boat attacks on U.S. merchantmen thereafter, Congress was persuaded to take further action. The Shipping Act, passed on September 7, 1916, provided for a Shipping Board, which, during the period of the war and five years afterward, had the authority to own, operate, and control every aspect of U.S. shipping.

The Shipping Board immediately requisitioned all seaworthy vessels plying domestic trade routes and transferred them to the Atlantic to carry war goods at assigned rates to the Allies. Simultaneously, it requisitioned all shipyards and ships under construction to serve government needs. On April 16, 1917, the Shipping Board created the Emergency Fleet Corporation to motivate private companies to expand existing shipyards and build new ones, and to contract with private companies the building of government shipyards and ships. By the end of the war, government subsidies and contracts had increased the number of shipyards in the United States from 61 to more than 200 and had delivered 592 merchant ships. These vessels were predominantly wooden-hulled, but a few had hulls that were composites (steel and wood) or concrete.

To man the new ships, the Emergency Fleet Corporation established a Recruiting and Training Service on June 1, 1917. Recruiting offices were opened in nearly seven thousand Liggett and Rexall drugstores in every one of the forty-eight states to sign up men between the ages of twenty-one and thirty. The Massachusetts Institute of Technology organized the first school to teach engineering and navigation courses to prospective officers. Later, more than forty-eight such schools sprouted up around the country.

Ships on both coasts were provided for seamen's training. On the Atlantic, the *Calvin Austin* and the *Governor Dingley*, antique coastwise passenger ships, were called into service. Each accommodated five to six hundred apprentice sailors. Later, other ships were added. The *Iris* was the first to do duty on the Pacific coast. Students trained at sea four to five days a week for a period of six weeks.

Madeleine Vessel

See also: Lusitania, Sinking of (WWI); Submarine Warfare (WWI)

REFERENCES

Branch, Alan E. *The Elements of Shipping.* London: Chapman and Hall, 1977.

Cafruny, Alan W. *Ruling the Waves: The Political Economy of International Shipping.* Berkeley: University of California Press, 1987.

Frankel, Ernst G. *Management and Operations of American Shipping.* Boston: Auburn House, 1982.

Jantscher, Gerald R. *Bread upon the Waters: Federal Aids to the Maritime Industries.* Washington, DC: The Brookings Institution, 1975.

Kennedy, David M. *Over Here: The First World War and American Society.* New York: Oxford University Press, 1980.

Kilgour, John G. *The U.S. Merchant Marine National Maritime Policy and Industrial Relations.* New York: Praeger, 1975.

Smith, J. Russell. *Influence of the Great War upon Shipping.* Preliminary Economic Studies of the War, no. 9, Carnegie Endowment for International Peace. New York: Oxford University Press, 1919.

Slackers

"Slackers" was a term of contempt used to identify those men who failed to register for military service during World War I. Stipulations of the May 18, 1917, Selective Service Act (and as amended) required men between the ages of twenty-one to thirty (later changed from ages eighteen to forty-five) to register for a new National Army draft on the first registration day, June 5, 1917. The government designated and publicized two other registration days: June 5, 1918, and September 12, 1918. By the end of the war, 24 million men had registered. The exact number of draft delinquents is unknown, but it is estimated that at least 10 percent of those eligible to register failed to sign up.

Concerned about the number of nonregistrants, the Justice Department and police coordinated nationwide punitive "slacker" raids to hunt down and arrest suspected draft dodgers. The majority of arrests occurred within ethnic, non-English-speaking immigrant communities within large cities and in itinerant labor camps and isolated rural areas. As the war persisted, U.S. officials realized they needed more men to serve. For three days prior to the September 12, 1918, registration day, the government used armed members of the military and citizen associates of the quasi-federal American Protective League to help search New York City for "slackers." By indiscriminately and illegally pursuing, questioning, and arresting thousands, authorities deprived innocent citizens of their civil liberties. The raids generated controversy, but not enough to stop them.

The press, novelists, and filmmakers drew attention to the problem of "slackers." In 1917 and 1918, films such as *The Slacker's Heart, Mrs. Slacker,* and two versions of *The Slacker* captured the public's imagination. One version of *The Slacker,* in which a man tries to resist service but proves to be a hero, was produced by the Peter P. Jones Photoplay Company, and is one of the earliest all-black features made by an African American production company.

Diane M. T. North

See also: American Protective League (WWI); Conscription (U.S., WWI); Vigilantism (WWI)

REFERENCES

Chambers, John Whiteclay. *To Raise an Army: The Draft Comes to Modern America.* New York: Free Press, 1987.

Harrison, Patricia K., ed. *The American Film Institute Catalog of Motion Pictures Produced in the United States,* Vol. F 1: *Feature Films 1911–1920.* Berkeley: University of California Press, 1988.

U.S. War Department. Final Report of the Provost Marshal General to the Secretary of War on the Operations of the Selective Service System to July 15, 1919. Washington, DC: 1920.

Socialist Party

The Socialist Party of America was the focus of a great deal of government scrutiny and censorship under the administration of President Woodrow Wilson due to its Marxist philosophy of society and pacifistic stance regarding World War I. The party took the unpopular view of opposing U.S. involvement in what the Socialists saw as a war for power between the capitalist ruling classes of Europe. The party was tolerated until the United States joined the fighting and the government cracked down on its members by invoking the Espionage Act, leading to the arrest of many leaders and the suppression of its newspapers and literature. These actions by the Federal government during the war as well as the postwar Red Scare severely weakened and eventually divided the Socialist Party.

The Socialist Party was formed in 1901 as an amalgamation of several leftist political groups. The party gained popularity among western farmers, factory workers, and northeastern intellectuals. By 1912, the Socialists claimed over 100,000 members and finished a respectable fourth in the presidential election, garnering nearly 900,000 votes. The party had made great strides in its first decade, but the advent of World War I would greatly challenge its ability to remain a viable political force.

The Socialists, like most Americans, were shocked by the onset of war in August 1914. The party issued a statement against the war soon after it began, referring to it as a battle of the ruling classes that the working classes would have to fight. To their dismay, their Socialist European counterparts overwhelmingly fell in line behind their respective governments and fully favored the war.

In 1916, the Socialists did poorly in the presidential elections, in part due to popular leader Eugene Debs's decision to stay out of the race. He was replaced on the ballot by the much less dynamic Allan Benson. Benson's star rose in the party when he proposed that the United States should not involve itself in the war unless it were attacked directly or the people voted for war through a national referendum. Benson, however, was a relative unknown outside the party and received about 35 percent fewer votes than Debs had in 1912.

Soon after Woodrow Wilson was reelected, it became obvious to the Socialists that he was leading the country to war. Debs rejected Wilson's "preparedness" as a scheme to turn the United States into a capitalist military despotism. In March 1917, the Socialist Party planned to meet in St. Louis to discuss what their reaction should be if the United States did actually go to war. The meeting took place shortly after the United States had joined the Allies. There they resolved to publicly oppose the war, the draft, war bonds, and any taxes specifically levied to aid the war effort. The Socialists also resolved to fight any restrictions the government should place on personal freedom.

Many prominent Socialists, such as Upton Sinclair, Charles Edward Russell, William English Walling, and even Allan Benson, left the party in disagreement with the majority opinion and decided to back the war effort. The national press picked up on this fact and reported the premature demise of the party as a whole. But in reality, the party was still strong, with over 90 percent of its members voting in agreement with the St. Louis Proclamation. However, the federal government soon began to take steps to ensure the ruin of the Socialist Party.

The tool used most effectively against the Socialists was the Espionage Act, which became law in June 1917. The act gave the government sweeping powers over free speech, including making public remarks against the war a criminal act and granting the Postmaster General the right to ban from the mails any publications thought to be un-American. Government agents began making regular appearances at Socialist Party meetings, trying to determine whether or not speeches given by members violated the law. Many borderline cases of alleged sedition by party leaders and sympathizers were prosecuted, including cases against Kate O'Hare, Morris Hillquit, Victor Berger, and Eugene Debs himself.

What affected the party more in the long term was the restriction of its mailing privileges. Postmaster General Albert Burleson was zealous in his duty to keep seditious materials out of the mail. He barred over a dozen socialist newspapers during the war and seized countless pamphlets and other publications. This restricted the recruiting power of the Socialists severely, especially in rural and western areas.

The Socialist Party's influence in the west was also adversely affected by an uprising by farmers in Oklahoma known as the Green Corn Rebellion. The ill-fated adventure was undertaken by a group of sharecroppers who felt betrayed by the Wilson Administration. Wilson, they believed, was ignoring their poverty and was now threatening to draft them into military service. The farmers planned to march to Washington, seize the government, and stop the war. Within a few days, all the rebels were arrested. The farmers were only loosely socialistic and the party had discouraged any violence by its members. Nevertheless, the Socialist Party of Oklahoma dissolved itself rather than have its members associated with the rebellion and negatively affect the ongoing trial of Victor Berger in Chicago.

The dissolution of the once-powerful Oklahoma party apparatus coupled with press and mailing restrictions and growing mob violence against party members led to a major shift in Socialist Party membership. The party of western farmers and sharecroppers became a party restricted to the East and Midwest.

The Red Scare that evolved immediately following World War I further hindered the Socialist Party's ability to function. Organizations such as the American Legion joined in the suppression of the party by disrupting meetings and renting out halls where meetings were to be held. Congress took overt action against the Socialists by refusing to seat Victor Berger, who had been elected by the citizens of Milwaukee, Wisconsin. Soon after these events, the Socialist Party spilt, with its more radical members leaving to help form the Communist Party USA.

Darron R. Darby

See also: Elections of 1916 (WWI); Pacifists (WWI); Red Scare (WWI); Biographies: Debs, Eugene V. (WWI); Berger, Victor (WWI)

REFERENCES

Critchlow, Donald T., ed. *Socialism in the Heartland: The Midwestern Experience, 1900–1925.* Notre Dame, IN: University of Notre Dame Press, 1986.

Miller, Sally M. *Victor Berger and the Promise of Constructive Socialism, 1910–1920.* Westport, CT: Greenwood Press, 1973.

Salvatore, Nick. *Eugene V. Debs: Citizen and Socialist.* Urbana: University of Illinois Press, 1982.

Shannon, David A. *The Socialist Party of America: A History.* New York: Macmillan, 1955.

Tussey, Jean Y., ed. *Eugene V. Debs Speaks.* New York: Pathfinder, 1970.

Weinstien, James. *The Decline of Socialism in America: 1912–1925.* New York: Monthly Review Press, 1967.

Songs (U.S.)

U.S. songwriters responded to the concerns of a nation at war by composing songs appealing to every conceivable feeling: nostalgia, reflection, fear, belligerence, sentimentalism, and humor. Ordinary Americans consumed more music than ever before; songwriters and publishers used the war to promote their industry as vital to asserting a collective national identity; and the U.S. government's Committee for Public Information distributed songbooks, encouraging national unity through singing. Throughout World War I, songwriters and publishers addressed the needs and concerns of Americans by changing their themes to accommodate shifting national sentiment.

Tin Pan Alley

Most of the songs produced during the war were written by songwriters working in New York's Tin Pan Alley, a section of 28th Street that housed hundreds of song publishers. The sound of composers pounding out tunes on cheap pianos filled the streets, a cacophony that reminded some listeners of banging tin—hence the name Tin Pan Alley. Though there were many publishers, the greatest bulk of songs were published by the six largest companies. These publishers had the most resources dedicated to advertising, promotion, and hiring the best songwriters.

The majority of popular songs were sold as sheet music, though records and rolls for player pianos were beginning to hedge into the market. Publishers marketed songs through "pluggers" hired to sing new songs at public venues such as moviehouses and department stores. Songs were also marketed through advertisements in popular magazines, many of which promoted songs as valuable to the war effort. The Aeolian Company, manufacturers of the Pianola player piano, and Columbia Grafonola marketed their products in patriotic, war-rallying campaigns. None were so vigorous as Leo Feist, whose advertisements boldly declared: "Music will help win the war!" In addition to producing sheet music and piano rolls, Feist also sold popular songbooks of war-related songs, including *Songs the Soldiers and Sailors Sing, Liberty Songs,* and *Songs of Cheer.* Songbooks were also produced as government propaganda through George Creel's Committee for Public Information.

Songs produced before the United States entered the war usually promoted neutrality or pacifism. "I Didn't Raise My Boy to Be a Soldier: A Mother's Plea for Peace" reflected this latter position. Other early songs adopted a more belligerent stance, including "Don't Bite the Hand That's Feeding You," a Feist song that anticipated the war and issued a sharp warning directed at immigrants, reminding them that their true alliance was to the United States. The diverse reactions to the specter of war were muted once combat began and songwriters unequivocally rallied behind the U.S. war effort.

The new confidence in U.S. troops overseas was captured in popular songs. Pride in the military was illustrated in "I'm Proud to Serve the Land that Gave Me Birth;" yearning for home was expressed in "Then I'll Come Back to You;" fear for the safety of troops motivated "Somewhere in France Is Daddy;" and the loneliness of lovers separated by an ocean was a central theme in "He's Had No Lovin' for a Long Long Time." Each of these songs responded to the concerns of those on the home front, offering a common vision of collective identity, shared fears, and united pride.

Nativism

Many songs of this time, such as "You Can Tell That He's an American," conveyed deeply held nativist sentiments, presenting the ideal American as one who was born in the United States. These songs encouraged anti-immigrant feelings and either ignored or caricatured the important contributions of ethnic Americans to the war effort. This tendency was reflected in songs poking fun at Italians ("Macaroni Joe"), as well as Irish in the immensely popular "Where Do We Go from Here?," but was challenged in songs like "It's Not Your Nationality (It's Simply You)." Songs like this latter one were rare after war was declared.

Though fears about unassimilated Americans on the home front were common in the songs of World War I, panic about the adulter-

ating influence of foreign cultures on soldiers overseas was also frequent. "How 'Ya Gonna Keep 'Em on the Farm (After They've Seen Paree?)" addressed these concerns by asking how U.S. farms could possibly match the decadence of Paris. The 1918 song "You'll Find Old Dixieland in France" responded to this fear by asserting the dominant influence of American culture on foreign lands. As was not uncommon, African American culture was made to stand in for the totality of American cultural expression, even though African American men were still not even allowed to fight alongside white troops in the war and Jim Crow remained an active deterrent to African American enfranchisement in the South.

The problems affecting African Americans on the home front were the subject of several songs, including "When the Good Lord Makes a Record of a Hero's Deed, He Draws No Color Line." This song, and others like it, envisioned the war as a site of racial reconciliation. Still, songwriters were generally insistent in their reliance upon gross stereotypes of African Americans, undercutting the reformist potential of such inclusive sentiments.

The most popular songs during World War I were far more innocuous than this. Leo Feist paid $25,000 for the rights to George M. Cohan's "Over There," which sold three million copies in sheet music and record sales, and Richard Whiting and Ray Eggan sold 3.5 million copies of sheet music for their "Till We Meet Again." These songs elicited the patriotic fervor and exuberant spirit of those on the home front, channeling their energy into songs that would become popular standards long after the war had been won.

The armistice brought an abrupt end to songs addressing wartime concerns. Though some songs of the era became standards and others were reintroduced with the beginning of World War II, most were quietly filed away and forgotten. The growing popularity of records, radio, and rock-and-roll, coupled with the decline of piano sales, spelled the end of Tin Pan Alley by the 1950s. Though most publishers survived through World War II, nothing could match the strength of popular songs and a singing nation during World War I.

Aaron Lecklider

See also: Cabarets (WWI); Jazz (WWI); Music (U.S., WWI); Propaganda (U.S., WWI); Biographies: Berlin, Irving (WWI); Cohan, George M. (WWI)

REFERENCES

Books

Ewen, David. *All the Years of American Popular Music.* Englewood Cliffs, NJ: Prentice-Hall, 1977.

Furia, Philip. *The Poets of Tin Pan Alley: A History of America's Great Lyricists.* New York: Oxford University Press, 1992.

Hamm, Charles. *Yesterdays: Popular Song in America.* New York: W. W. Norton, 1979.

Sanjek, Russell. *American Popular Music and Its Business: The First Four Hundred Years,* Vol. 3: *From 1900 to 1984.* New York: Oxford University Press, 1988.

Tawa, Nicholas. *The Way to Tin Pan Alley: American Popular Song, 1866–1910.* New York: Schirmer, 1990.

Songs

Bratton, John W. "Then I'll Come Back to You." New York: M. Witmark & Sons, 1917.

Bryan, Alfred, and Al Piantadosi. "I Didn't Raise My Boy to Be a Soldier." New York: Leo Feist, 1915.

Clarke, Grant, and George W. Meyer. "You'll Find Old Dixieland in France." New York: Leo Feist, 1918.

Cohan, George M. "Over There." New York: William Jerome, 1917.

Davis, Cliff, and Sam Brobst. "I'm Proud to Serve The Land That Gave Me Birth." Pittsburgh, PA: Liberty Music Co., 1918.

Donohue, James, Al Dubin, George Lyons, and Bob Yosco. "Macaroni Joe." New York: M. Witmark & Sons, 1917.

Egan, Raymond B., and Richard Whiting. "Till We Meet Again." Detroit, MI: Jerome H. Remick, 1918.

Great, Howard. "Somewhere in France Is Daddy." New York: Howard & LaVar Music Co., 1917.

Hoier, Thomas, and Jimmie Morgan. "Don't Bite the Hand That's Feeding You." New York: Leo Feist, 1915.

Johnson, Howard, and Joseph McCarthy. "It's Not Your Nationality (It's Simply You)." New York: Leo Feist, 1916.

Johnson, Howard, and Percy Wenrich. "Where Do We Go from Here?" New York: Leo Feist, 1917.

Johnson, Howard, and Percy Wenrich. "You Can Tell That He's an American." New York: Leo Feist, 1918.

Lewis, Sam M., Joe Young, and Walter Donaldson. "How 'Ya Gonna Keep 'Em Down on the Farm (After They've Seen Paree?)" New York: Waterson, Berlin & Snyder, 1919.

Tracey, William, and Maceo Pinckard. "He's Had No Lovin' for a Long, Long Time." New York: Broadway Music Corporation, 1919.

Trainor, Val, and Harry De Costa. "When the Good Lord Makes a Record of a Hero's Deed, He Draws No Color Line." New York: M. Witmark & Sons, 1918.

Stanford-Binet Test

The Stanford-Binet Test was an intelligence test administered by the Psychological Services branch of the military to nearly two million U.S. Army recruits from 1917 to 1919. Robert Yerkes (1876–1956), Lewis Terman (1877–1956), and Henry H. Goddard (1866–1957) designed the test consisting of Army Alpha for literate recruits and Army Beta for illiterate recruits. Results were ranked by examinees into superior, average, or inferior grades, which were then used to determine the placement of recruits either into officer training school or other units of the Army.

The Stanford-Binet test was adapted from the test created by French psychologist Alfred Binet who, at the behest of the French government, created a test to detect mental deficiency in children. U.S. psychologists interested in mental measurement adapted the test for a variety of uses, including Henry H. Goddard at the Vineland New Jersey, Training School for Feeble Minded Boys and Girls, and Robert Yerkes at the Boston Psychopathic Hospital. However, it was Stanford psychologist Lewis Terman who created the standard revision of the Binet test, known today as the Stanford-Binet. Terman's instrument added new dimensions to the test, including a measurement between the mental age of the subject, as measured by the test, and their chronological age in order to create an intelligence quotient, or I.Q. It was this version that laid the foundations for mental testing during World War I.

Robert Yerkes, the president of the American Psychological Association (APA) in 1917, offered to assist the War Department by devising a mental test for all new recruits to allow the military to either reject or place recruits based upon their mental ability. Under pressure from the APA and the National Research Council, chaired by George Ellery Hale, the army accepted the offer. In the spring of 1917, a committee consisting of Goddard, Terman, and Yerkes formed and developed a version of the test to be administered to a large number of subjects simultaneously. The Psychological Services branch of the U.S. army dispatched psychologists to all training camps.

Although the army terminated the examinations in 1919, psychologists emerged from the war with an enhanced status in the public mind, and mental testing, specifically the Stanford-Binet and the concept of the I.Q., entered the public lexicon. Psychologists trained during the war advocated the use of widespread mental testing, which then became a firmly established practice in public education throughout most of the twentieth century.

Timothy W. Kneeland

See also: Conscription (U.S., WWI)

REFERENCES

Cravens, Hamilton. *The Triumph of Evolution: The Hereditary Environment Controversy, 1900–1940.* Baltimore, MD, and London: Johns Hopkins University Press, 1988.

Kennedy, David. *Over Here: The First World War and American Society.* New York: Oxford University Press, 1980.

Kevles, Daniel. *In the Name of Eugenics: Genetics and the Use of Human Heredity.* Cambridge: Harvard University Press, 1995.

Steel Industry

By the beginning of World War I, the steel industry in the United States was in a state of high development. The ability to manufacture steel in great quantities had spurred the rise of the United States to a position of leadership in steel making throughout the world.

The manufacture of armored plates for ships began in the United States in the early 1880s when Congress authorized the construction of a number of steel ships. In the decades prior to World War I, an alliance had developed between the steel industry and the Navy. The Navy created a demand for technological developments in armament metals whether in armor plating or for milling guns.

By 1900, Andrew Carnegie had organized the Carnegie Company into an enormous operation integrated from iron mine to finished steel product. The whole process was thoroughly integrated and managed to the point that Carnegie had captured over 65 percent of the steel industry. However, well before 1914, Carnegie sold out to a steel trust that formed the United States Steel Corporation.

Prior to the entry of the United States into World War I, the steel industry was supplying great quantities of steel to the Allied powers at going prices. However, with the entry of the United States into the war, calls came from several quarters to fix steel prices in order to prevent price gouging by the steel industry.

In the spring of 1917, the Wilson Administration sought price reductions on government purchases of steel products. By the summer, steel prices had skyrocketed. On September 24, 1917, a price-fixing agreement was reached between the steel industry and the government. The agreement was the latest in a struggle over pricing policy.

Elbert H. Gary, chairman of the United States Steel Corporation and the president of the American Iron and Steel Institute, had been approached on March 30, 1917, by Bernard Baruch in an appeal for voluntary price reductions. Baruch was a member of the Advisory Commission of the Council of National Defense, which was in charge of raw materials and metals. Gary refused Baruch's request. From the point of view of the steel industry, the government was just one customer among many.

The steel industry was opposed to setting prices because of the uncertainty caused by the mobilization effort. Emergency agencies were proliferating in great numbers with competing authorities and demands. There was not yet a single source of authority for policy directions. Agreement on prices seemed premature and risky.

The Secretary of the Navy, Josephus Daniels, wanted to move toward nationalization of the industry; an idea that Wilson also bandied about briefly. Other radical ideas for regulating or fixing steel prices were also proposed. The success of ideas of this type would have probably been a disaster due to the lack of government expertise in running the industry.

As emotions increased, suspicions flourished on both sides. The steel companies balked at several government proposals because these would have negative consequences for the postwar market. A Federal Trade Commission report delivered to President Wilson showed that steel's profits were high. However, analysis showed that this was in part due to demand as well as the fact that about 20 percent of the steel being produced came from high-cost mills.

Eventually, calmer advice came in the form of the independently wealthy, "dollar-a-year" businessmen, who had entered the government war service. Experienced in business and its practices, they were able to remove the issue from public politics with its charges of immorality and the wanting of patriotism to a condition of business negotiations.

The War Industries Board (WIB) was formed in July 1917. Robert S. Brookings was made chairman of the Price Fixing Committee. He was a member of the National Civic Federation and in ideological agreement with Judge Elbert Gary. The eventual effect was that the WIB became a forum for business discussions about prices. In the end, prices were set where supplies were made abundant and the war effort was promoted in a cooperative capitalist-government agreement.

Andrew J. Waskey

See also: Mobilization (U.S., WWI); Shipping (WWI)

REFERENCES

Cooling, Benjamin Franklin. *Gray Steel and Blue Water Navy: The Formative Years of America's Military-Industrial Complex 1881–1917.* Hamden, CT: Archon, 1979.

Cuff, Robert D., and Melvin I. Urofsky. "The Steel Industry and Price-Fixing during World War I." *Business History Review* 44, no. 2 (Autumn 1970): 291–305.

Misa, Thomas J. *A Nation of Steel: The Making of Modern America 1865–1925.* Baltimore, MD: Johns Hopkins University Press, 1995.

Strikes, Labor

The United States saw a significant increase in strike activity during and immediately after World War I. The strike waves were related to the impact of war mobilization, which rapidly created dislocations in production, labor shortages, increases in the cost of living, and changes in the demographics of immigration as well as a general decline of immigration. During World War I, the labor market of the United States underwent a series of significant changes, especially in the expansion of federal involvement in economic production, labor industry relations, and surveillance and repression of strikes and related "subversive" labor organizing. World War I came immediately after a very violent period of confrontations between industry, allied private militia, and vigilante organizations on the one side and labor on the other. At the conclusion of World War I, the more radical components of the American labor movement, especially the Industrial Workers of the World (IWW) and associated labor organizations, were caught up in a "Red Scare," which was triggered by a combination of strikes and other forms of direct action. A wave of repression significantly disrupted the IWW and laid the foundations for the American Federation of Labor's dominance of labor organization and much diminished strike activity in the early 1920s.

General Patterns of Economic Stressors and Labor Strikes

Between the beginning of World War I in 1914 and the peak of U.S. military mobilization, the U.S. Army expanded dramatically. As an example of the rapidity of this expansion, and the not surprising stressors that this placed on labor markets and wages, between March 1917 and November 1918, the U.S. Army expanded from 189,674 to 3,554,000 soldiers, nearly a 2,000 percent increase. This drain of experienced workers, nearly 6 percent of the workforce, from economic production into war fighting triggered a labor market shortage that amplified the power of industrial and agricultural workers and heightened the impact of strikes. The cost of living also escalated significantly during the war, nearly doubling between August 1915 and the end of 1919. Federal intervention into labor markets also politicized the relationship between government, industry, and labor, and contributed to the impact of strikes that occurred throughout the war, notwithstanding the creation of a series of federal labor boards that were designed to both enforce prohibitions against strikes and also prevent strikes by mediating between labor organizations and industry.

Despite the efforts of the federal labor boards and the AFL's no-strike pledge, there was significant strike activity throughout the time period from 1914 to 1919. The Bureau of Labor Standards did not publish strike figures for the period 1905 to 1914, so comparisons to the period immediately before the war are not

Table 1: Strikes and Lockouts in World War I Era

Year	Number of Strikes	Lockouts	Total	Number of Employees Involved		
				Strikes	Lockouts	Total
1914	979	101	1,080	**	**	**
1915	1,246	159	1,405	468,983	35,292	504,275
1916	3,687	108	3,786	1,546,428	53,182	1,599,610
1917	4,233	126	4,359	1,193,867	19,133	1,213,000
1918	3,181	104	3,285	1,192,418	43,041	1,235,459
1919	3,253	121	3,374	3,950,411	162,069	4,112,507

**Figures not available for 1914.

Source: Bing, Alexander M. *War-Time Strikes and Their Adjustment.* New York: Arno and the *New York Times,* 1971 (reprint from 1921): 293.

possible. Additionally, the Labor Department's Bureau of Statistics changed how they compiled statistics on strikes and, therefore, comparisons between 1914 and 1919 data and previously collected data from 1881 to 1905 is problematic. Despite these caveats, the presence of significant strike activity is evident from the data related to strike activity, which is reflected in Table 1.

While the table demonstrates annual trends, there are some important monthly totals that stand out. The largest number of strikes and lockouts taking place in one month was during May 1916, with a total of 617 strikes (the May strike figures for other years were 1917, 1918, and 1919 were 463, 391, and 413, respectively). The total number of strikes is a bit misleading in terms of measuring the intensity of strike activity because, while 1917 had the largest number of strikes, the year with the largest number of employees involved was 1919. Strike activity did not diminish as the United States formally entered the war in 1917. Indeed, one author observed that the opening months of the war signaled a "Second Great Upheaval" of American labor, characterized by "unprecedented labor turmoil," according to historian Joseph McCartin. During the first full month of the war,

there were 438 strikes, and the first six months of the war saw the loss of 6,285,519 workdays in almost 3,000 strikes. This strike activity took place despite the invocation of patriotic duty to maintain war production on the part of political and industrial leaders and the pledge by the AFL to oppose strikes.

Strikes and Major Labor Organizations

The two most significant labor organizations during World War I were the American Federation of Labor and the International Workers of the World. These two organizations had been in conflict since the foundation of the IWW in 1903, with the AFL having a craft union organizational model and taking a more moderate course, and the IWW, which also organized the unskilled, African Americans, as well as women, taking a much more militant approach to labor organizing, strikes, and other forms of direct action, up to and including sabotage and other forms of violence against business and government forces. The AFL was involved in cooperating with the Wilson Administration in constraining strikes during the period before the U.S. entry into the war in exchange for the Wilson Administration's recognition of the right of labor to organize in the hopes of creating an alliance between government, industry, and labor that would produce a form of "industrial democracy." The Wilson Administration, which had endorsed the recommendations of the U.S. Commission on Industrial Relations and the Committee on Industrial Relations, drew upon the AFL for critical support in the 1916 presidential election. The IWW refused to oppose strikes and received much of the blame for strikes that were called by unions in industrial sectors that were critical to the war effort.

Federal Intervention in the Surveillance, Regulation, and Repression of Strikes

War mobilization involved the federal state in regulating the labor markets and strike activity in a number of different ways. As previously mentioned, the federal state created a number of labor boards and commissions that were designed to prevent or regulate conflict, including strikes, such as the Emergency Construction Wage Commission, Shipbuilding Labor Adjustment Board, National War Labor Board, and War Labor Policies Board. In addition to the regulation of labor markets, the Bureau of Investigation, U.S. Army Military Intelligence, state and local police, National Guard, and private security forces engaged in massive surveillance and disruption efforts aimed at suppressing and ending strikes. Some of the more dramatic instances of repression included the arrests and detention in makeshift prison camps of strikers in mining and lumber production areas in the American West. Repression of radical labor organizations, especially the IWW and allied unions, became truly massive during the "Red Scare" of 1919 and 1920 after World War I, but was directly related to the wave of strikes and labor militancy that occurred during the war and then spiked in 1919 after the removal of price controls.

Christian W. Erickson

See also: American Federation of Labor (WWI); Industrial Workers of the World (WWI); Seattle General Strike (WWI); Trade Unions (U.S., WWI); Biographies: Gompers, Samuel (WWI); Heywood, William "Big Bill" (WWI)

REFERENCES

Abrahamson, James L. *The American Home Front: Revolutionary War, Civil War, World War I, World War II.* Washington, DC: National Defense University Press, 1983.

Bing, Alexander M. *War-Time Strikes and Their Adjustment.* New York: Arno and the *New York Times,* 1971 (reprint from 1921).

Brecher, Jeremy. *Strike!* Boston: South End Press, 1997.

Edwards, P. K. "Strikes and Politics in the United States, 1900–1919." In *Strikes, Wars and Revolutions in and International Perspective: Strike Waves in the Late Nineteenth and Early Twentieth Century,* ed. Leopold Haimson and Charles Tilly. Cambridge: Cambridge University Press, 1989.

Eisner, Marc Allen. *From Warfare State to Welfare State: World War I, Compensatory State Building, and the Limits of Modern Order.* University Park: Pennsylvania University Press, 2000.

Haimson, Leopold, and Charles Tilly, eds. *Strikes, Wars and Revolutions in an International Perspective: Strike Waves in the Late Nineteenth and Early Twentieth Century.* Cambridge: Cambridge University Press, 1989.

Kornweibel, Theodore, Jr. *"Investigate Everything": Federal Efforts to Compel Black Loyalty during World War I.* Bloomington: Indiana University Press, 2002.

McCartin, Joseph A. *Labor's Great War: The Struggle for Industrial Democracy and the Origins of Modern American Labor Relations, 1912–1921.* Chapel Hill: University of North Carolina Press, 1997.

Preston, William. *Aliens and Dissenters: Federal Suppression of Radicals, 1903–1933*. 2d ed. Chicago: University of Illinois Press, 1994.

Rockoff, Hugh. "Until It's Over, Over There: The U.S. Economy in World War I." NBER Working Paper 10580. Cambridge, MA: National Bureau of Economic Research, 2004.

Theoharis, Athan G. *The FBI & American Democracy: A Brief Critical History*. Lawrence: University Press of Kansas, 2004.

Submarine Warfare

During World War I, Germany used the relatively unprecedented strategy of submarine warfare, which entailed attacks on surface ships by packs of *unterseeboots* (literally "under-sea boats," or "U-boats") to isolate and blockade Great Britain and the Allies. While German U-boats were enormously successful at sinking Allied shipping (over ten million tons in four years) and at inspiring terror in Allied countries, the strategy ultimately backfired when the United States entered the war against Germany in large part because of domestic anger over lost American lives and property.

In the period before the war, both Germany and Great Britain, like the United States, fashioned their naval strategies along the lines proposed by American Admiral Alfred Thayer Mahan, whose 1890 book, *The Influence of Sea Power Upon History*, had made him an internationally recognized expert on naval warfare. Mahan argued that great nations were nations that controlled the sea lines of communication—in other words, nations that had strong domestic economies, maintained significant merchant fleets, and possessed powerful navies that could attack enemy fleets, seize enemy merchant ships, and blockade enemy coasts. Mahan's theories, and especially his championing of the battleship as the most important weapon of naval warfare, helped instigate a naval race between Great Britain and Germany that in turn helped lead to World War I.

Blockade against Germany

While Germany had built a powerful surface fleet, Great Britain still had the most powerful navy in the world, and used that navy in 1914 to establish a naval blockade of Germany. Under this blockade, the British refused to allow war materials of any kind (including weapons, ammunition, heavy machinery, and even food) to get to Germany. Germany regarded this blockade as an illegal attempt to starve the German people into submission and responded by announcing its own blockade of Great Britain. Because Germany's surface fleet was outclassed by the British surface fleet, German strategists announced that they were going to enforce the blockade of England with submarines. In February 1915, Kaiser Wilhelm II of Germany announced that German U-boats would attack, without warning, *any* Allied ships, including warships, merchant vessels, and ships filled with refugees, around the British Isles. While the clearly understood rules of warfare from the period required that warring powers were to allow passengers and crews to abandon non-warships before sinking them, under this policy of unrestricted submarine warfare, U-boat commanders gave no warning, and thus condemned thousands to death by drowning.

The U-boats proved relatively effective, sinking almost 750,000 tons of British shipping in the first six months of 1915, but the Germans remained concerned about the effect that the U-boat campaign was having in the United States, where President Woodrow Wilson was urging Americans to be "neutral in thought and deed." By their very nature, U-boats broke what Americans saw as the rules of warfare. More importantly, German U-boat commanders had orders to attack any British ships and any ships carrying war materials to England. As many Americans were trading with England and France (between 1914 and 1916, that trade had increased from $824 million to $3.2 billion), and as many others were traveling aboard British ships, Germany's policy of unrestricted submarine warfare meant that it was nearly certain that American lives were going to be lost and American interests damaged.

An initial turning point in submarine warfare came late in 1915 after a number of U-boat attacks on Allied passenger ships had outraged the international community. The most shocking was the May 7, 1915, sinking of the *Lusitania*, a British passenger vessel. While the *Lusitania* was actually carrying munitions, and while Germany had actually placed an advertisement in the *New York Times* warning travelers to avoid the liner, Americans were horrified by the attack and by the deaths of 1,198 passengers, including 128 Americans, and by the depictions of the attack that they saw in many popular movies and cartoons. In response to international condemnation of the U-boat campaign, in September 1915, the Kaiser called off unrestricted submarine warfare.

Within a few months of this decision, however, Germany began to despair of winning the war unless they could effectively blockade the Allied powers and end the conflict, which was bleeding Germany dry. By March 1916, German naval authorities had ordered U-boat commanders to attack without warning all ships except for passenger vessels. The German strategy was one of attrition: German U-boats tried to sink Allied vessels faster than the tonnage could be made up with new construction.

United States Entry in War

After the United States entered the war in April 1917, and the Germans no longer had any incentive to limit their use of unrestricted submarine warfare, German U-boats became increasingly brazen and successful, sinking 181 ships in January, 259 in February, and 325 in March. The high point of the German submarine campaign came in April 1917, when U-boats sank 430 Allied vessels, totaling over 852,000 tons of shipping and representing one in every four of the merchant ships that had sailed from British ports. Before resuming unrestricted submarine warfare, Germany had predicted success if it could destroy 600,000 tons of Allied shipping per month; by April 1917, the German U-boat campaign was clearly having a decisive impact on the war.

April 1917 indeed proved to be the apex of German submarine warfare. In response to the threat posed by U-boats, the Allies had been developing and implementing the use of new technologies and strategies, including the convoy system and hydrophones. At the same time, the enormously productive U.S. shipyards were quickly replacing the lost Allied shipping and were providing many new destroyers to protect convoys and hunt down U-boats. Together, these new strategies and technologies, along with the increased Allied shipbuilding, shifted the equation of attrition, with Allied losses to submarines falling and U-boat losses to Allied warships steadily increasing.

Ultimately, even the power of the U-boats could not save Germany from defeat in World War I. Submarine warfare became an increasingly important naval strategy in the aftermath of the war, especially after the Washington Naval Conference in the 1920s restricted the total surface warship tonnage that nations were allowed to maintain. During World War II, Germany once again deployed U-boats to threaten Allied shipping (just as other countries, including the United States and the Soviet Union, deployed their own submarines against their enemies) and, once again, Allied and neutral observers reacted with anger and horror to the civilian casualties that resulted from what many saw as an especially cruel form of warfare.

Samuel Brenner

See also: Shipping (WWI); *Lusitania,* Sinking of (WWI)

REFERENCES

Alden, Carroll S. "American Submarine Operations in the War." *U.S. Naval Institute Proceedings* 46 (June 1920): 811–850, 1013–1048.

Ballard, Dr. Robert, and Spencer Dunmore. *Exploring the Lusitania.* London: Weidenfeld and Nicolson, 1995.

Blair, Clay. *Silent Victory: The U.S. Submarine War against Japan.* Annapolis, MD: Naval Institute Press, 2001.

Clark, William Bell. *When the U-Boats Came to America.* Boston: Little, Brown, 1929.

Gannon, Michael. *Black May: The Epic Story of the Allies' Defeat of the German U-Boats in May 1943.* New York: HarperCollins, 1998.

Grant, Robert M. *U-Boats Destroyed: The Effect of Anti-Submarine Warfare, 1914–1918.* London: Putnam, 1964.

Grove, Eric J. *The Defeat of the Enemy Attack on Shipping, 1939–1945,* Vol. 137. Navy Records Society, Burlington, VT: Ashgate, 1997.

Supreme Court

Throughout the years of U.S. involvement in World War I, the United States Supreme Court was headed by Chief Justice Edward Douglas White, a former Confederate soldier during the Civil War who had served on the Louisiana Supreme Court and in the U.S. Senate. He was appointed to the Court in 1894 by President William Howard Taft. President Grover Cleveland selected White to serve as the ninth Chief Justice of the Court in 1910, where he served until 1921. Only one other Southerner served on the Court, James Clark McReynolds, a former law professor at Vanderbilt University in Nashville, Tennessee, and was appointed by President Wilson in 1914. White and McReynolds, along with Willis Van Devanter, a former chief justice of the Wyoming Supreme Court appointed by President Taft in 1911, comprised the Court's conservative core.

Ideology of the Justices

The liberals, or progressives, on the Court were Louis Dembitz Brandeis and Oliver Wendell Holmes. Although both justices had been relatively mainstream previous to and during the war, wartime legislation that led to assaults on civil liberties under the guise of "emergency war powers" pushed both justices well to the left. Justice Brandeis, educated at Harvard Law School, had dedicated himself to social causes and to the Zionist movement during his tenure as a Boston lawyer. His efforts made him an enemy of the industrial giants of the day. President Wilson, a progressive himself, appointed Brandeis to the Court in 1916 over the vociferous protests of business interests and anti-Semites as well.

Holmes, son of the writer Oliver Wendell Holmes, was also educated at Harvard and, after a short tenure as professor of law at Harvard, was appointed to the Massachusetts supreme judicial court. After 20 years on the Massachusetts court, Holmes was appointed to the Supreme Court by President Theodore Roosevelt in 1902.

William Rufus Day, Joseph McKenna, Mahlon Pitney, and John Hessin Clarke rounded out the Court. Clarke was appointed to the Court by President Wilson in 1916 to fill the seat vacated by Charles Evans Hughes, a Republican progressive who resigned to run for president in the 1916 election. None of the four distinguished themselves as being particularly insightful jurists, although Pitney did write one opinion considered at the time to be quite progressive. That opinion, in *New York Central Railroad Co. v. White*, upheld a workman's compensation law in New York.

The nature of the work of the Supreme Court renders it a body that considers major issues of the day well after the fact. This was no less true of contentious issues that arose out of the national response to World War I. Before the war, the Court mainly looked to the past for guidance. Lacking what they perceived as valid precedent in U.S. law, both state and federal judges relied to a great extent upon eighteenth-century English common law as set out in *Blackstone's Commentaries*. War issues, especially First Amendment challenges over the rights of free speech and free expression, forced the Court to change its perspective and look instead to what part the Court would play in the future of a postwar America.

The Progressive Movement that preceded the war had instigated demands for change. Labor unions were strengthening and becoming more violent. Politicians were being exposed for their unscrupulous allegiance to big business to the detriment of the working public. In addition, war was imminent, and a huge body of citizens objected to U.S. involvement and especially to the draft. In response, Congress passed stricter laws invoking the police power of the state in hopes of suppressing conflict and quieting the storm brewing across the country. The judicial system upheld the laws and maintained the status quo until two

Supreme Court justices, Brandeis and Holmes, broke ranks with the mainstream Court and joined with the postwar civil libertarians. Brandeis and Holmes are not so much famous for their judicial opinions, although they wrote many, but instead are noteworthy for their eloquent dissents.

The issues before the Court during the war years principally involved federal police power and whether Congress's general delegated powers could be used more broadly to fulfill the progressive agenda. For example, the Court affirmed prohibition statues in 1917, upholding the Webb-Kenyon Act that allowed federal commerce power to assist states in enforcing prohibition statutes. Additionally, in 1918, the controversial Selective Service Act of 1917 was also upheld. That decision sustained the power of Congress to declare war and raise armies to support it, finding that compulsory service is fully legal and within the scope of federal power during war.

Wartime Legislation and Measures

The results of wartime legislation, meanwhile, did not reach the Court until well after the war ended. Once it did, the Court confirmed the legality of most wartime measures, producing a growing concern that the Court had allowed Congress to overstep its bounds in restricting the personal and civil liberties of U.S. citizens. Many progressives hoped that both the Espionage Act and the Sedition Act, passed in reaction to the war, would be struck down when they reached the Court. In *Schenck v. United States*, the first of six important cases challenging the constitutionality of these Acts to finally reach the Court in 1919, Schenck had been convicted of printing and distributing flyers denouncing the Conscription Act and protesting the draft. The Court unanimously affirmed his conviction. In another case, *Debs v. United States,* the Court unanimously upheld the conviction of Eugene Debs, who was found guilty of speaking out against the war, but the decisions led Justices Holmes and Brandeis to ponder the ramifications of the Court's actions in light of First Amendment free speech protections. In the fourth of the six cases, *Abrams v. United States,* in which Abrams was convicted of printing and distributing leaflets protesting U.S. intervention in the Russian Civil War, the Court upheld the conviction 7-2; both Holmes and Brandeis dissented, citing essentially the sanctity of free speech in the U.S. system of government. Indeed, the Acts were never struck down, but in every case thereafter involving these Acts, Holmes and Brandeis dissented or concurred apart from the rest of the Court. Although their concerns were not immediately shared by the other justices, their defense of free speech set the stage for future deliberations and helped prepare the Court for the next wave of social activism brought about by World War II and Franklin Roosevelt's New Deal.

Donna M. Abruzzese

See also: Espionage Act (WWI); Sedition Act (WWI); Biographies: Debs, Eugene V. (WWI); Holmes, Oliver Wendell (WWI); Hughes, Charles Evans (WWI); Documents: *Schenk v. U.S.,* 1919

REFERENCES

Harrell, Mary Ann. "A Heritage of Law." *Equal Justice under the Law.* Supreme Court Historical Society, 1965: 64–77.

Lewis, Anthony. "Civil Liberties in a Time of Terror." *Wisconsin Law Review.* 2003 Wis.L.Rev. 257, Westlaw.

Murphy, Paul. *The Constitution in Crisis Times 1918–1969.* New York: Harper & Row, 1972.

Steamer, Robert J. *The Supreme Court in Crisis: A History of Conflict.* Amherst: University of Massachusetts Press, 1971.

T

Taxation

The United States enacted a series of tax laws during the crisis of World War I that had a profound impact on the subsequent development of U.S. public finance. Beginning with the Revenue Act of 1916, which dramatically increased income tax rates and imposed a novel war profits tax on certain businesses, the World War I Revenue Acts redirected U.S. fiscal policy toward a new historical path—one that broke from an earlier reliance on tariffs and indirect consumption taxes and toward a new era marked by the direct and progressive taxation of individual and business income. More specifically, the 1916 Act initiated this radical shift in tax policy by raising the top personal income tax rate from 6 percent to 15 percent while maintaining high exemption levels of $3,000 for individuals and $4,000 for married couples. The law also doubled the corporate income tax rate to 2 percent, established a graduated federal estate tax, and imposed a 12.5 percent war profits tax on munitions makers. Thus, from the start, the United States appeared to be ushering in a "soak-the-rich" form of tax policy in order to finance the war.

War Financing: Taxes and Debt

In fact, by the time the United States officially entered World War I in the spring of 1917, President Woodrow Wilson and his administration were firmly committed to financing the war mobilization effort with an equal combination of taxes and debt. Treasury Secretary William G. McAdoo insisted that the financial sacrifice and fiscal burden of the war be borne substantially by the present generation of Americans, particularly the wealthy. Although the federal income tax had only recently become a permanent part of U.S. law—with the ratification of the Sixteenth Amendment in 1913 and the enactment of a modest income tax in that same year—a powerful coalition of Democratic and Progressive Republican lawmakers, led by Claude Kitchin (Democrat, North Carolina) and Robert La Follette (Republican, Wisconsin), were eager to exercise this nascent taxing power.

Yet, as the conflict in Europe continued, Wilson and McAdoo were forced to resort to more borrowing and less taxation than they initially anticipated. The 1917 Revenue Act certainly followed the premise of a steeply progressive tax structure, increasing marginal rates to over 60 percent for top bracket taxpayers, lowering exemption levels for personal filers, and enacting a controversial excess profits tax on businesses. But, as war expenditures continued to mount, the Treasury Department also began using bonds—patriotically dubbed "Liberty Loans"—to finance government expenditures. By the start of 1918, the Treasury Department had executed two very successful Liberty Loan campaigns, raising a total of approximately $4.6 billion from the two oversubscribed issuances. Over time, the reliance on debt financing coupled with easy monetary policy would provide for the bulk of wartime government revenues and, in the process, fuel skyrocketing inflation.

Tax rates during the war reached their peak with the 1918 Revenue Act, which was officially enacted in 1919. While the personal exemption levels remained the same as the previous year—$1,000 for individuals and $2,000 for families—the top marginal rate reached the wartime maximum of 77 percent. This law also added to the plethora of excise taxes on luxury goods and ordinary objects that had become commonplace during the war, such as taxes on beverages, telephone and telegraph messages, sporting goods, and numerous other sundry items.

Among the radical changes wrought by the wartime revenue laws, perhaps the most controversial were the new profits taxes on U.S. businesses. The 1916 law levied a flat 12.5 percent tax on the profits of all armament producers. Yet this measure seemed insufficient in light of the United States' official entry into the war. Thus, the 1917 Act dramatically raised the stakes; it enacted an excess profits tax that applied to profits "over a reasonable return on invested capital," and affected all businesses, not just those in the munitions industry. The "reasonable rate of return" was established as 8 percent, and all profits above that level were taxed at graduated rates ranging from 8 percent to a maximum of 60 percent on corporate profits that were in excess of 32 percent of invested capital.

The profits taxes were created to compel those businesses disproportionately profiteering from the war to pay their fair share of the burden of war financing. In this regard, they were quite successful, despite complaints from business leaders. Of the over $4 billion raised through internal revenue in 1918, close to 60 percent came from the war and excess profits levies. Given such success, some populist lawmakers contemplated making the excess profits tax a permanent part of U.S. tax law, as a way not only to raise revenue but to also curb the excesses of monopoly capitalism.

Wartime Taxes Repealed

Although many aspects of wartime tax policy, most notably the excess profits tax, were repealed in 1921 once the heavy national debt burden of the war was reduced, the administrative success of the wartime revenue laws had a lasting impact on the bureaucracy of U.S. public finance. The Revenue Acts passed during the war raised nearly $14 billion of revenue, but, more importantly, they set into motion the need for an enormous infusion of administrative resources within the Treasury Department. Managing a process as complex as financing a war—and a tax system that included such difficult to decipher provisions as the excess profits levy—required an immense infusion of resources into the administrative capacity of the emerging fiscal polity. The administrative apparatus installed at the national level to ensure the proper execution of the wartime system of taxation thus became a critical institutional component in the direct taxation of personal and corporate income.

Indeed, to levy the excess profits tax and to organize the other aspects of wartime fiscal policy, the Treasury Department itself underwent a major reorganization with the creation of several new Assistant Secretary positions and the significant expansion of rank-and-file personnel. The Bureau of Internal Revenue—a subdivision of the Treasury Department and the forerunner of the Internal Revenue Service—witnessed a nearly fourfold increase in personnel between 1913 and 1919, going from roughly four thousand employees to nearly sixteen thousand.

From a comparative perspective, the United States relied more on taxation to fund the war than any of the other nations engaged in the conflict. At the height of its participation, the United States was able to adhere to Wilson's decision to rely on taxation for 50 percent of the costs. But by the end of the war, as debt financing became more prominent, only about 35 percent of the total costs of the war were financed through taxes. Still, this was much more than other belligerent nations. By contrast, Britain financed approximately 30 percent of its war costs through taxation, and Germany, confident of victory, financed nearly all of its war expenditures with borrowing, save less than 2 percent that was raised through taxation.

Despite the shift in U.S. fiscal policy that was occasioned by the uncertainty of wartime expenditures, the tax laws enacted during World War I radically altered the incidence of taxation and hence the ultimate sources of government revenue. Before the war, nearly 75 percent of federal revenues came from indirect taxes related to the tariff and excise taxes on alcohol and tobacco. After the war, direct taxes on incomes, profits, and estates dominated federal revenues. In fact, by the end of hostilities, wealthy individuals and companies profiting from war conditions comprised the principal

sources of most federal tax revenue. With the top marginal rates for individuals reaching 77 percent, in 1918, the richest 1 percent of U.S. families accounted for approximately 80 percent of total federal personal income tax revenues. Similarly, the profits taxes on U.S. businesses accounted for about two-thirds of all federal tax revenues during World War I. Though income and profits tax revenue plateaued during the 1920s, as the revival of international trade reinvigorated the tariff and postwar political retrenchment reduced the impact of progressive taxes, the robust wartime tax regime signaled the beginning of the United States' commitment to the direct and progressive taxation of personal and business income.

Ajay Mehrotra

See also: Economic Policy (WWI); War Bonds (WWI)

REFERENCES

Brownlee, W. Elliot. "Economists and the Formation of the Modern Tax System in the U.S.: The World War I Crisis" in *The State and Economic Knowledge: The American and British Experiences,* eds. Mary O. Furner and Barry Supple, 401–435. New York: Cambridge University Press, 1990.

Gilbert, Charles. *American Financing of World War I.* Westport, CT: Greenwood, 1970.

Kennedy, David M. *Over Here: The First World War and American Society.* New York: Oxford University Press, 1980.

Technology

When the United States entered World War I in the spring of 1917, its technological advances had been limited at the military level by both civilian and military leaders. The former worried about added costs, while the latter resisted technical innovations. However, industry's rapid development in the nineteenth century combined with new governmental involvement allowed for some swift adjustments to military conditions, though the output remained limited. Thus, it is at the governmental level and those of specific industries that the impact of World War I on technology and applied science are most noticeable.

U.S. industry was well advanced by the time World War I broke out, and some companies made effective use of Taylorism (scientific management) and Fordism (chain assembly). However, this did not translate into uniformly standard technology in a country unaccustomed to governmental intervention.

The U.S. government noticed such shortcomings quickly, and had to move to take over several key technology areas on the home front. The railroad was taken over on January 1, 1918, thus allowing for the clearing of bottlenecks and forcing the resolution of various conflicts between private companies that had blocked the channeling of supplies. By March 1918, the War Industries Board, led by Wall Street financier Bernard Baruch, was in place. Its effectiveness, though limited, contributed to standardization of items produced with modern technology, from steel to baby carriages. It took several months to reach that stage, during which some industrial circles, such as the automobile industry, successfully opposed all efforts to curtail civilian automobile production until the spring of 1918. By then, the Ford Motor company relented under threat of having its coal and transport railroad car supplies cut.

Several government-sponsored organizations appeared in Washington, D.C. and continued to thrive after the war was over. The National Advisory Committee for Aeronautics (NACA), for example, was created in 1915 as part of that year's naval appropriations bill.

Established scientists were also pressed into service. Thomas Edison, upon recommendation of Navy secretary Josephus Daniels, chaired the Naval Consulting Board, an advisory committee created with the intention to help the Navy in technical matters. The principle of its function seemed simple enough: Inventors would send their proposals to the Board, which would in turn evaluate their value and screen out those deemed to be a waste. Eleven professional societies were asked to each recommend two members for the Board, but physicists were not included (they were deemed "nonpractical"), and neither was the National Academy of Science (see below). The group was not very successful: Of some 110,000 invention proposals sent, only 100 or so were deemed worthy of support by reviewers. This limited success reflected the fact that invention had entered an age of specialization that required more than genius, endeavor, or a tool shed. Knowledge of science and its applications was essential, though many failed to grasp this.

This lack of recognition also applied to scientists themselves. One of the high-level members of the National Academy of Science, astronomer George Ellery Hale, upset at not being included in Edison's board, went on to recommend the establishment of the National Research Council (NRC) to the government. Among other things, the NRC focused on devising a submarine-listening device (unrestricted German submarine warfare against Atlantic shipping had resumed in 1917). This research unit, though unsuccessful, was eventually deemed a scientific research arm of the U.S. government. Finally, select engineers and industrialists were invited to join the National Defense Advisory Commission (NDAC). The results of these multiple organizations were mixed. On the one hand, scientists and engineers made substantial contributions in highly advanced research areas like aviation and radio communication. However, effective application of such knowledge did not come until the 1920s.

At the level of private industry, several surges in applied science and technology are noticeable. Demand for war matériel predated the U.S. entry into the war, and the lack of access to European companies meant both challenge and opportunity for many firms. For example, chemical industries in the United States, accustomed to licensing brands from Germany and Switzerland, began developing their own lines of products.

E. I. Dupont de Nemours built new facilities to produce smokeless powder and explosives for the allies. The size of the wartime facilities prompted managers to plan for further expansion of their nitrocellulose technology, which included paint, varnishes, artificial leather, and fiber. Other companies followed similar paths by using their previous link to European companies as a learning base in order to develop new technologies and products.

In other realms, however, technological progress that had been swift at the turn of the century had slowed considerably. Despite being the first nation to successfully fly, by 1914, the United States ranked behind France, Great Britain, and Germany in many areas of technology. The latter had bested the United States in submarine design, while the British were pioneering naval gunfire control devices. Up to the war's end, U.S. troops would train and depend for the most part on foreign technology.

This is not to say that indigenous technology on the U.S. home front was nonexistent. On the contrary, it thrived, but was subject to the peculiarities of slow governmental involvement, economic and political imperatives, and the shortness of the war effort for the United States. However, the creation of various governmental offices for research as well as the War Industries Board established important foundations for the later successful development of U.S. technology in the interwar years and in World War II.

Guillaume de Syon

See also: Shipping (WWI); War Industries Board (WWI)

REFERENCES

Hughes, Thomas P. *American Genesis: A Century of Invention and Technological Enthusiasm.* New York: Viking, 1989.

Kevles, Daniel J. *The Physicists: The History of a Scientific Community in Modern America.* New York: Vintage, 1979.

McNeill, William H. *The Pursuit of Power: Technology, Armed Force, and Society since A.D. 1000.* Chicago: University of Chicago Press, 1982.

Roland, Alex. *Model Research: The National Advisory Committee for Aeronautics 1915–1958.* Washington, DC: NASA, 1985.

Theater

World War I came at a time of great change in U.S. theater. Vaudeville and variety were evolving into musical theater or devolving into burlesque; melodrama was giving way to more serious psychological drama; and a vigorous move toward community theater offered an alternative to the commercial and cultural power of Broadway.

The prewar building boom had resulted in dozens of elegant new theaters on Broadway, solidifying its prominence and ending the era of large touring companies whose employees earned a living on the road. In the 1917–1918 season, 156 productions ranging from serious drama to farcical revues opened, and the following year saw 149 new shows—few of them toured.

Americans away from New York were not willing to give up theatergoing. Local "little" theaters sprouted throughout the country, revitalizing the arts in small towns and large cities alike. These noncommercial ventures became centers for dramatic experimentation, rather than rehashes of Broadway hits. The staging called for simple sets and small arenas, allowing for intimacy between actors and audience. In 1911, there were three Little Theaters in the United States; by 1917, there were 250.

George Creel wanted his U.S. Committee on Public Information to exploit these resources for the war effort and recruited thousands of "four minute men" to speak in theaters throughout the country before performances in order to whip up enthusiasm for enlisting in the army and volunteering for the many homefront activities. He also encouraged the mounting of patriotic pageants across the nation with the goal of selling Liberty Bonds. Among those resisting Creel's urgings were the Lafayette Players in Harlem and the Provincetown Players in Greenwich Village.

Many theatrical offerings arose naturally from war concerns. *Friendly Enemies* explored the tensions and loyalties of German Americans. *Where Poppies Bloom, Under Orders, The Better 'Ole,* and *Arms and the Girl* were imports that exposed Americans to European reactions to the war. *Doing Our Bit, Over the Top* (introducing Fred and Adele Astaire), and *Out There* with Laurette Taylor were popular homegrown productions. The Ziegfeld Follies, in addition to offering patriotic songs and red-white-and-blue dance numbers, presented breathtaking tableaux, with beauties wrapped in French, British, and U.S. flags. The Follies refused to hire German-born actors for the duration of the war and fired any comedian who made a joke of the government or the military.

Productions staged by servicemen were enthusiastic and energetic, although short-lived. *Biff! Bang!* was a revue presented by a naval training camp, and *Yip-Yip-Yapahunk* came from the "boys of Camp Upton," which included Irving Berlin, whose "Oh, How I Hate to Get Up in the Morning!" became a solid hit.

Tin Pan Alley turned out scores of antiwar songs ("I Didn't Raise My Boy to Be a Soldier") until war was declared. Afterward, composers wrote patriotic marching songs as fast as they could put pen to paper. George M. Cohan responded to the declaration of war with a simple song that he brought to popular entertainer Nora Bayes, then appearing in her own revue. Her rendition of "Over There" brought the cheering audience to its feet.

Other milestones of the war years were: *Why Marry?*, a sophisticated look at marriage and the "new woman," won the first Pulitzer Prize for drama in 1917; *Maytime*, the Sigmund Romberg musical, turned Peggy Wood into a star. Helen Hayes made her acting debut as an ingénue in James Barrie's *Dear Brutus*. Al Jolson starred in *Sinbad*, singing "Sewanee" and "Mammy" in blackface. *Lightnin'* with Frank Bacon became one of the longest running plays in U.S. history. George Gershwin got his first Broadway job as a pianist in *Miss 1917*, which had music by Victor Herbert and Jerome Kern, and the Barrymores retained their position as America's "royal family."

Actors, actresses, and other theater people took the initiative in raising money for both humanitarian causes and war bonds, beginning with a mammoth Belgium Relief Benefit shortly after German forces invaded that country. For the event, dozens of top actors recreated their favorite roles and Irving Berlin's new composition "I Hear the Voice of Belgium" was sung. Julia Marlowe (reciting "In Flanders Field") and E. H. Sothern toured the United States to raise funds for the British Red Cross in the years before the United States was a combatant.

Once war was declared, performers organized a seventeen-city tour for the Red Cross, headlined by De Wolf Hopper and James Hackett. Laurette Taylor's benefit performances alone earned nearly $700,000 for the organization. Entertainers felt a special obligation to keep morale up in both the United States and Europe. Sothern, Cohan, and theater owner Winthrop Ames established the Over There League, which sent entertainment overseas under the auspices of the YMCA. Elsie Janis, the "Sweetheart of Broadway," put on her signature velvet tam-o'-shanter and performed for the troops just miles from the front. Others entertained at the dozens of military encampments scattered throughout the United States.

As manufacturing directed its efforts toward war, shortages became apparent. To conserve coal, marquees dimmed and some theaters went unheated on designated days. Inflation led to higher ticket prices. Congress imposed a war tax that added another 10 percent and tickets reached $3. Theatergoers rebelled at the cost, and some productions closed for want of an audience. At war's end, the flu epidemic also kept audiences sparse.

Despite the number of hastily crafted war plays, it wasn't until 1924 that the first significant one appeared, the Maxwell Anderson-Laurence Stalling comedy-drama *What Price Glory?*

Betty Burnett

See also: Committee on Public Education (WWI); Propaganda (U.S., WWI); Biographies: Barrymore, John (WWI); Cohan, George M. (WWI); Tucker, Sophie (WWI); Ziegfeld, Florenz (WWI)

REFERENCES

Brown, Gene. *Show Time: A Chronology of Broadway and the Theatre from Its Beginnings to the Present.* New York: Macmillan, 1997.

Churchill, Allen. "Over There!" in *The Great White Way.* Edited by Allen Churchill. New York: Dutton, 1962.

Hughes, Glenn A. *A History of the American Theater, 1700–1950.* New York: Samuel French, 1951.

Mackay, Constance D'arcy. *The Little Theater in the United States.* New York: Henry Holt, 1917.

Mantle, Burns, and Garrison P. Sherwood. *The Best Plays of 1909–1919.* New York: Dodd, Mead, 1943.

McArthur, Benjamin. *Actors and American Culture, 1880–1920.* Philadephia, PA: Temple University Press, 1984.

Trade

An important turning point in U.S. trade policy came after the election of 1912 when Woodrow Wilson, a former Princeton University professor of history and government and governor of New Jersey, triumphed over a divided Republican Party as his party gained control of the presidency and both houses of Congress for the first time since 1892. The Democrats moved quickly to reduce protective rates. The Underwood-Simmons Act of 1913 sharply lowered U.S. tariffs from an average of 19.3 percent on dutiable and free imports under the Payne-Aldrich Tariff of 1895 to 9.1 percent in 1916. Unfortunately, the Democrats ignored the opportunity to bargain down foreign trade barriers and, eager to redeem domestic campaign pledges to cut duties and aid consumers, they unilaterally lowered the U.S. tariff.

In the year before the outbreak of World War I, the share of world exports among the four major powers was:

France	7.97%
Germany	13.81%
Great Britain	14.69%
United States	13.95%

The outbreak of war in 1914 completely disrupted the existing network of trade and commercial treaties. When World War I began, there was little idea what impact the war would have on the economy and on public policy, but the war brought the federal government into the economy in ways that had been unimaginable in previous years. Congress passed the Lever Act (1917) and the Overman Act (1918), giving President Wilson absolute authority over farm production, commodity prices, and the uses and prices of industrial raw materials. When the United States finally entered the war—a war that had created unprecedented economic opportunities for U.S. businessmen, including the selling of goods to Germany or to Austria-Hungary—Congress passed the Trading With the Enemy Act (October 16, 1917), which prohibited all commercial activities with enemy nations and gave the president emergency powers, when necessary, to embargo exports and imports. To enforce this legislation, Wilson established the War Trade Board (October 12, 1917) while the Office of Alien Property Custodian was charged with the responsibility of supervising enemy assets that were seized in the United States. The law is still in effect today, with occasional amendments.

The war in Europe interrupted ocean shipping and provided a new form of temporary protection to U.S. industries during wartime, but as the conflict came to an end, the U.S. business community began to worry about cheap foreign competition, particularly from the German chemicals industry, and about how to negotiate access to closed European markets for U.S. exporters. The Wilson administration, preoccupied with its League of Nations and plans for global free trade, hoped to promote market access and reduce foreign trade barriers to U.S. exports that would continue the traditional Democratic remedy of a revenue tariff while endorsing the use of a nonpartisan tariff commission to suggest tariff revisions.

President Wilson

President Wilson did much to encourage the United States' changing role in the world economy. He believed that free trade promoted both universal prosperity and universal peace and democracy; international commerce led to a strong domestic economy; exports were essential for continued U.S. economic growth; restrictions on trade, such as tariffs and trade agreements, hindered efficiency and denied the natural cycle of the international economy; goodwill flowed along with goods; and commercial contacts were effective guarantors of peaceful relations among states.

As wartime government spending increased, the country's domestic economy benefited greatly. The War Industries Board, established in July 1917, endeavored to tap the nation's industrial resources while also protecting its basic economic infrastructure as a demand for supplies, weaponry, food, and other materials resulted in increased productivity among manufacturers and farmers. It was a boom time not only for large corporations, who increased their profit margins, but also for farmers, who saw a rise in agricultural prices, for blue-collar workers, whose wages increased, and for businesses, who expanded their global markets by exporting goods to European ally countries. However, other nations suffered more losses than gains during the course of the war.

After the defeat of the Central Powers (Austria-Hungary, Germany, and Italy) and the signing of an Armistice in 1918, the Triple Entente (France, Great Britain, and Russia) and its allies pressed for reparations from Germany, the nation held most responsible for the war. The Treaty of Versailles, signed on June 28, 1919, placed the bulk of financial responsibility on Germany and a Reparations Commission was established to determine the amount that the defeated nation would pay in damages to property and civilians. When the U.S. Senate refused to ratify the 1919 treaty, the United States forfeited its place on the commission, which decided in June 1920 that Germany would pay upward of three billion gold marks a year for thirty-five years.

Aftermath

World War I was enormously profitable to the United States; the U.S. economy boomed between 1914 and 1918 as it was protected from the physical ravages of the war by the Atlantic Ocean. It became the largest in the world in terms of gross national product (GNP) and the financial center of the world shifted from London to New York. Still, U.S. business worried about cheap foreign competition, particularly from the German chemicals industry, and about how to negotiate access to closed European markets for U.S. exporters. The Wilson administration, almost solely concerned about plans for global free trade and a League of Nations, hoped that international economic government would promote market access and reduce foreign trade barriers to U.S. exports.

U.S. participation in World War I resulted in, among other things, an increase in international trade that continued to raise profits for various industries, an economic boost that ushered in the prosperous 1920s. The war almost instantly reversed the credit standing of the United States. The nation, by the war's end, held billions of dollars in European debt obligations and was the globe's greatest creditor as well as its greatest economic power. By forcing the Europeans to accept goods instead of loans, the Wilson administration guaranteed that the country would be banker, arsenal, and breadbasket to the Allies. World War I set the foundation for the prosperity of the 1920s that eventually, as many economists argue, fostered the background for the Great Depression (1929–1939).

Martin J. Manning

See also: Business (U.S., WWI); Shipping (WWI); Submarine Warfare (WWI); War Industries Board (WWI)

REFERENCES

Beaver, Daniel R. *Newton D. Baker and the American War Effort, 1917–1919.* Lincoln: University of Nebraska, 1966.

Carson, Thomas, ed. Gale *Encyclopedia of U.S. Economic History.* Detroit, MI: Gale Group, 1999.

Curzon, Gerard. *Multilateral Commercial Diplomacy.* New York and Washington: Frederick A. Praeger, 1965.

Lovett, William A., Alfred E. Eckes, and Richard L. Brinkman. *U.S. Trade Policy: History, Theory, and the WTO.* Armonk, NY, and London: M. E. Sharpe, 1999.

Rosenberg, Emily S. *Financial Missionaries to the World: The Politics and Culture of Dollar Diplomacy, 1900–1930.* Cambridge: Harvard University Press, 1999.

U.S. Department of State. *Papers Relating to the Foreign Relations of the United States: 1917, Supplement 2: The World War, part 2.* Washington, DC: Government Printing Office, 1932. (This devotes an entire issue to the trade issues of World War I.)

U.S. Tariff Commission. *The Tariff and Its History.* Washington, DC: The Commission, 1934.

Trade Unions (UK)

British craft- and industrial-based trade unions entered World War I after a decade of struggle for better wages, traditional workplace rules, and union recognition. Despite this, the patriotism that swept through the general public in August 1914 found trade unionists willing converts, and soon its leadership swore off industrial militancy for the war's duration. As hopes for a short conflict waned, the realities of total war forced the government to reorganize the industrial home front. In this task, tripartite consultation between employers, the government, and unions was vital, and the government's intervention helped unions earn greater legitimacy and increased bargaining power. However, total war also increased the cost of living and forced many unions to accept concessions, particularly on the use of nonunion labor. Some union members fiercely resisted these efforts, leading to an increase in strike activity as the war continued. By war's end, trade union membership and legitimacy had increased considerably, but so to did militancy, as tripartite cooperation ultimately proved temporary.

Support for the War

Despite efforts by antiwar and pacifist elements in the union movement agitating against the war, the movement's initial responses were supportive. First, it voluntarily sought to curb industrial militancy during the war, with the Labour Party, the Trades Union Congress (TUC), and the General Federation of Trade Unions (GFTU) calling for the abandonment of all strikes and lockouts and the amicable settlement of industrial disputes. Second, it joined with representatives of the socialist and cooperative movements to establish the War Emergency Workers' National Committee (WEWNC), a body for advocating economic and social policies to protect worker living standards. These actions signaled the movement's willingness to cooperate during the national emergency.

However, the war had severely disrupted the British economy, and many trade unionists found themselves dealing with a rising cost of living and employer attempts to impose dilution of the worker power. These problems soon put to the test the leadership's capacity to control its own members, with mixed results. Dilution in particular was a contentious issue for many, because it meant the use of nonunion, semiskilled, and female labor in traditional skilled union jobs. Employers pushed for this because of the need to increase war production, and enlistment had resulted in a depletion of skilled workers in the munitions industries. Unions resisted this, often by taking unofficial strike actions, such as the strike around Glasgow in early February 1915 that brought out ten thousand engineering workers.

The Asquith Government's free market attitudes toward economic maintenance and war provisions proved inadequate in the face of total war. Following a shell scandal in 1915 over shortages on the Western Front and failed attempts to obtain union support for dilution in exchange for limits on munitions profits, David Lloyd George, as the new minister of munitions, pushed through Parliament in mid-1915 the Munitions of War Act. The Act declared strikes and lockouts illegal, required the relaxation of restrictive work practices, limited the free movement of labor through the Leaving Certificate, and created penalties for noncompliance. The Leaving Certificate, a document employees had to receive from their employer before changing jobs, was designed to stop other employers from raiding employees in the labor-short business climate of World War I. To balance this, it also required mandatory arbitration of disputes handled by a new Committee on Production, thereby encouraging cooperation. Unions grudgingly accepted this, though in engineering areas like Glasgow and Sheffield resistance, organized by militant shop stewards, was dogged, forcing the government to back down and make adjustments to female pay rates and the leaving certificates. After that, dilution proceeded rapidly, although the introduction of conscription in 1916 caused further tensions, as the spread of female labor to non-munitions industries like textiles, printing, and transport met some resistance.

As the war continued, strike activity remained at remarkably low levels, reflecting both the success of the government's industrial relations strategies and union restraint. In 1915–1916, there were 1,204 strikes, less than half the number for 1913 alone. Despite the problems with dilution, most strikes were unsanctioned, concerned pay and working conditions, and reflected growing perceptions among workers that the burdens of war were not being shared equally. Syndicalist sentiments arguing for greater worker control of industry had a limited impact on strike activity. However, in 1917–1918, with war weariness setting in, the Russian Revolution's example, and discontent over high prices, strike actions increased, reaching nearly 1,900 strikes.

Fostering Industrial Peace

Despite these struggles, attempts were made to develop policies to foster lasting industrial peace. In 1916, the government appointed a special commission charged with submitting proposals for improved industrial relations. Called the Whitley Committee after its chairman J. H. Whitley, its membership contained employer association and union representatives, government officials, and academics. Its report rejected the notion of expanding government control and instead proposed a voluntary system of joint consultation at the national and district levels and work committees at the factory level. These councils were designed to serve as bodies to adjudicate industrial disputes and manage collective bargaining. They also served as notice that the government had accepted, if not embraced, unionism and collective bargaining as fundamental processes in industrial relations. The big unions in coal, engineering, shipbuilding, and iron and steel ignored the Whitley recommendations, as they favored more radical solutions. However, unions in newer and less organized industries, such as vehicle assembly, chemicals, the civil service, and pottery, seized the chance Whitley gave them to achieve recognition and collective bargaining rights. By 1918, twenty-six Joint Industrial Councils were in existence with another fourteen planned.

The war years also witnessed increased union growth, a trend that continued until 1920. New sectors achieved union recognition while older unions made moves toward consolidation and amalgamation. Union membership jumped from over 4 million in 1914 to 6.5 million in 1918, reaching a density of nearly 36 percent. This included over one million female trade unionists representing 17 percent of all organized workers, an increase of 160 percent over 1914. Transport and general labor unions accounted for much of this increased female membership, as well as the clothing, printing, and clerical sectors, but larger unions, such as the Amalgamated Engineering Union (AEU), still resisted female members.

Andrew D. Devenney

See also: Conscription (UK, WWI); Economy (UK, WWI); Labour Party (UK, WWI); Liberal Party (UK, WWI); Mobilization (UK, WWI); Biographies: Asquith, Herbert Henry (WWI); Lloyd George, David (WWI)

REFERENCES

Boston, Sarah. *Women Workers and the Trade Union Movement.* London: Denis-Poynter, 1980.

Campbell, Alan, Nina Fishman, and David Howell, eds. *Miners, Unions and Politics 1910–47.* Aldershot, UK: Scolar Press, 1996.

Clegg, Hugh A. *A History of British Trade Unions Since 1889, Volume II, 1911–1933.* Oxford: Clarendon Press, 1985.

Fraser, W. Hamish. *A History of British Trade Unionism, 1700–1998.* London: Macmillan, 1999.

Kirby, Maurice W. "Industry, Agriculture and Trade Unions." In *The First World War in British History,* ed. Stephen Constantine, Maurice W. Kirby, and Mary B. Rose, 51–80. London: Edward Arnold, 1995.

Laybourn, Keith. *A History of British Trade Unionism, c. 1770–1990.* Phoenix Mill, UK: Alan Sutton, 1992.

McIvor, Arthur J. *Organised Capital: Employers' Associations and Industrial Relations in Northern England, 1880–1939.* Cambridge: Cambridge University Press, 1996.

Middlemas, Keith. *Politics in Industrial Society: The Experience of the British System since 1911.* London: Andre Deutsch, 1979.

Price, Richard. *Labour in British Society: An Interpretative History.* London: Croom Helm, 1986.

Robb, George. *British Culture and the First World War.* Basingstoke: Palgrave, 2002.

Thorpe, Andrew. *The Longman Companion to Britain in the Era of the Two World Wars, 1914–45.* London: Longman, 1994.

Wrigley, Chris. "The First World War and State Intervention in Industrial Relations." In *A History of British Industrial Relations 1914–1939,* ed. Chris Wrigley, 23–70. Aldershot, UK: Gregg Revivals, 1987.

Trade Unions (U.S.)

Trade unions and the United States worked together during World War I in an effort to prevent work stoppages. The federal government believed that the outbreak of worker strikes would ultimately hinder the nation's ability to produce military supplies during the war.

Prior to the outbreak of World War I, the American Federation of Labor (AFL) was comprised of skilled workers. Samuel Gompers, who served as the president of the AFL, regarded World War I as an event that would serve the interests of labor organizations and guarantee union recognition. To accomplish these gains, Gompers realized that he needed to strengthen the organization by extending membership to immigrants and employees in the mass production industries. By 1916, the AFL reported a membership of more than two million people. Following the U.S. intervention into the war, Gompers asserted that members of the labor organization would not engage in strikes to force the federal government to recognize the union. Upon learning of Gompers's statement, members of the AFL criticized the union leader for his statement because they believed that the war would worsen working conditions and extend working hours within the various industries. Nevertheless, Gompers's pledge resulted in improved relations between unions and the federal government during the war.

During the early 1910s, the Industrial Workers of the World (IWW, or Wobblies), encouraged workers to seize control of the nation's factories and called for the establishment of a workers' republic. Additionally, members of the IWW argued against the U.S. intervention into the war. For instance, Wobblies asserted that the conflict in Europe would only serve the interests of merchants and bankers. By 1916, the IWW drew support from miners, lumberjacks, and farmers throughout the nation. As the United States mobilized its industries, the Wobblies encouraged workers to wage strikes in order to force employers to address the workers' grievances. Thus, the federal government viewed the Wobblies as a threat toward industrial mobilization. Nevertheless, since the majority of workers in the United States opposed the labor organization's radical ideology, members of the IWW represented only a minority within the various trade unions.

Following the U.S. entry into World War I, business managers refused to recognize the demands of union leaders. Factory owners also fired labor activists and hired private agents to destroy the trade unions. Workers responded to these measures by engaging in strikes, sabotage, and attacking replacement workers. For instance, nearly three thousand strikes occurred on an annual basis between 1914 and 1920.

President Woodrow Wilson regarded these labor problems as a serious issue as the nation prepared for war. Consequently, the president implemented various measures designed to incorporate workers into the war effort and subvert any groups or organizations that opposed the war. For instance, Congress enacted various laws designed to protect unions, provide representation for workers dealing with managers, limit child labor, and reduce working hours for women. The federal government also exempted trade unions from the antitrust stipulations within the Clayton Anti-Trust Act. Additionally, Wilson offered Samuel Gompers a position within the National Council of Defense (CND), and also Wilson became the first president to address a labor convention. Although some worker strikes still occurred during World War I, the president's actions caused some union leaders to support the Wilson Administration throughout the war.

In September 1917, Felix Frankfurter, who served as head of the President's Mediation Commission, asserted that federal officials should not favor a policy of union recognition but rather they should encourage shop committees or work councils. Frankfurter justified his actions by noting that the government would ultimately hinder the war effort if it supported unionism. He maintained that workers could utilize shop committees or work councils to discuss issues relating to wages and working conditions with their employers. Upon learning of Frankfurter's proposal, the majority of the labor leaders approved the idea of shop committees and work councils. Nevertheless, members of the IWW opposed Frankfurter's recommendation because they believed that these measures would not serve the workers' interests. Gompers and other AFL members countered the IWW's response to the government's policy by asserting that shop committees and work councils would empower union leaders and increase membership within the various labor organizations. While the outbreak of World War I did not cause the federal government to recognize trade unions, the labor policy that the Wilson Administration adopted during the war improved relations between workers and employers.

In 1918, the United States witnessed an increase in worker strikes as a result of rising prices and wartime employment. After consulting with Secretary of Labor William B. Wilson and AFL leaders, President Wilson decided to create a federal agency designed to mediate disputes between workers and employers. On April 8, 1918, the president issued an executive order that established the National War Labor Board (NWLB). By the summer of 1918, workers utilized the NWLB to seek higher wages, improve working conditions, and assure worker representation within the various industries. The NWLB secured some of the workers' demands, but the conclusion of the war caused employers to ignore the federal agency's recommendations.

World War I represented limited benefits for trade unions. While the war caused workers to receive higher wages, labor leaders failed to obtain their main goal of gaining union recognition. The aftermath of World War I resulted in even fewer gains for trade unions because as the Red Scare gained momentum in the United States, the U.S. public increasingly came to oppose organized labor.

Kevin M. Brady

See also: American Federation of Labor (WWI); Industrial Workers of the World (WWI); Red Scare (WWI); Strikes, Labor (WWI); War Labor Board (WWI); Biographies: Gompers, Samuel (WWI); Heywood, William "Big Bill" (WWI)

REFERENCES

Conner, Valerie Jean. *The National War Labor Board: Stability, Social Justice, and the Voluntary State in World War I.* Chapel Hill: University of North Carolina Press, 1983.

Kennedy, David M. *Over Here: The First World War and American Society.* New York: Oxford University Press, 1980.

Koistinen, Paul A. C. *Mobilizing for Modern War: The Political Economy of American Warefare, 1865–1919.* Lawrence: University Press of Kansas, 1997.

Larson, Simeon. *Labor and Foreign Policy: Gompers, the AFL, and the First World War, 1914–1918.* Rutherford, NJ: Fairleigh Dickinson University Press, 1975.

McCartin, Joseph A. *Labor's Great War: The Struggle for Industrial Democracy and the Origins of Modern American Labor Relations, 1912–1921.* Chapel Hill: University of North Carolina Press, 1997.

V

Vigilantism

Vigilantism includes actions indicative of self-interested citizens who either individually or collectively take the law into their own hands to suppress dissent, gain political power, maintain social order, or punish others. The presence of legal authority does not dissuade vigilantes. During World War I, vigilantes often acted with the approval and cooperation of the state. This collusion contributed to the erosion of personal liberty that defined the wartime legacy.

As the nation mobilized for war, vigilantism took several forms. First, a national network of volunteer informants paralleled the rise of a government-sponsored domestic security system, resulting in attacks upon civil liberties and civil rights. Congress passed laws and the president issued executive orders to identify alien enemies and ferret out spies, traitors, saboteurs, draft dodgers, and those suspected of disloyalty, including the press as well as pacifists, socialists, communists, and members of the Industrial Workers of the World (IWW). The government also sought to identify and reprimand citizens caught hoarding food, fuel, and other rationed items. Because the Justice Department permitted members of the private American Protective League (APL) to work alongside its field investigators, almost every agency of the federal government relied upon the APL for information.

Although each branch of the military conducted its own investigations, the Military Intelligence Division (MID) of the War Department initiated a nationwide domestic surveillance operation and also created a volunteer spy corps. Fear and intimidation in the name of patriotism was widespread. Federally mandated State Councils of Defense instituted loyalty committees. The Minnesota legislature established a Commission of Public Safety that relentlessly attacked the militant farmer's organization and the Nonpartisan League, and also condoned the persecution of the state's sizable German American population. Other mid-Western states such as Iowa and North Dakota also vilified their German American communities. New York, Pittsburgh, Chicago, and Los Angeles used volunteers to help round up and detain thousands of innocent men presumed to be "slackers," or those who neglected to register for the draft. There were instances around the country where mobs captured, tortured, and killed suspected German sympathizers.

Other patriotic organizations like the Minute Men, which operated in the Pacific Northwest, or the Nathan Hale Volunteers, which had a national following, cooperated with business leaders to maintain order. Corporate executives also took the law into their own hands by hiring Pinkerton detectives to serve as strikebreakers or to spy on employees in mines, factories, oil fields, lumber and steel mills, shipyards, and farms. Worried that the IWW would influence migrant workers, the head of the California Commission of Immigration and Housing personally paid a spy to infiltrate labor camps. Antilabor violence that resulted from a workers' strike in the Bisbee, Arizona, copper mines in 1917 led to the mass detention and deportation of over 1,200 men, women, and children who were hoarded onto trains and taken to the desert town of Hermanas, New Mexico. Over two thousand deputized citizens and private detectives participated in the round up. Backed by industry and the states, the federal government carried out a series of raids, arresting, prosecuting, and unjustly jailing IWW leaders and numerous members who posed no real threat to the country. At the conclusion of the war, Washington officials launched the "Red Scare," which was aimed at silencing critics of the government and at arresting, detaining, or deporting dissidents.

Although Washington's propaganda touted the significance of fighting a war to maintain democratic ideals, African Americans, including African American soldiers, continued to be mistreated throughout the country. The National Association for the Advancement of Colored People (NAACP) petitioned the government for help, but President Woodrow Wilson did little to stop the violence against African Americans. Angry citizens shot, burned, and lynched African Americans, including African American veterans. Forty-eight persons were lynched in 1917, Sixty-three in 1918, and seventy-eight in 1919. Even the government treated its African American soldiers with extreme harshness. In 1917, African American soldiers stationed near Houston, Texas, got into trouble with the local police and white citizens. The military's punishment of eighty-eight soldiers ended with nineteen men being hanged. During and immediately after the war, race riots or mob violence against African Americans broke out in South Carolina, Texas, Tennessee, Alabama, Nebraska, Washington, D.C., Missouri, Arkansas, Oklahoma, and Illinois. The 1919 Chicago race riot, which left 537 wounded and 38 dead, pitted blacks against whites at a time when both vied for limited economic and social opportunities in the postwar downturn. The 1920s saw the rise of the Ku Klux Klan, which further threatened the lives and property of African Americans.

Diane M. T. North

See also: American Protective League (WWI); German Americans (WWI); Race Riots (WWI)

REFERENCES

Christian, Garna. *Black Soldiers in Jim Crow Texas, 1899–1917.* College Station: Texas A&M University Press, 1995.

Dubofsky, Melvin. *We Shall Be All: A History of the Industrial Workers of the World.* New York: Quadrangle/The New York Times Book Co., 1969.

North, Diane M. T. "Civil Liberties and the Law: California during the First World War." In *Law, Society, and the State: Essays in Modern Legal History,* ed. by Louis A. Knafla and Susan W. S. Binnie, 243–262. Toronto: University of Toronto Press, 1995.

Tuttle, William M., Jr., ed. *Race Riot: Chicago in the Red Summer of 1919.* New York: Atheneum, 1977.

W

War Bonds

The tremendous expense of the United States' participation in World War I was supported in part by the public sale of war bonds. The U.S. Treasury supported the production and sale of the bonds, which ultimately raised $21.5 billion for the war effort. In addition to their financial impact, the war bonds were envisioned as a tool that would positively affect public morale. In particular, Treasury Secretary William G. McAdoo argued that the bond program could primarily function as a tool for shaping public support for the war. By saturating the home front with bond publicity, he argued, the war bond program could raise money for the military while simultaneously raising public support for the war. In retrospect, however, the program's various problems—including low sales among average citizens and a coercive atmosphere that led to widespread abuse—tarnished its legacy.

After the United States declared war in 1917, the Treasury proposed its Liberty Bond program to raise money for the conflict. In previous wars, the Treasury had generally used heavy war taxes or attempted to sell bonds to wealthy investors. The new approach, in contrast, would attempt to spread the war debt among many members of the public. Additionally, rather than emphasizing the potential (and often risky) financial benefits of purchasing bonds, McAdoo insisted that the new bond program should focus on patriotic themes in its advertising and other forms of publicity. In this way, he reasoned, the public's bond purchases would not only help the war economy, but also reflect increased morale on the home front.

McAdoo's patriotic approach to war bond sales borrowed heavily from a military philosophy. Calling his program the Treasury's "financial front," he insisted that home front Americans would come to exhibit "the same qualities of discipline, self-sacrifice, and devotion that characterized those who served in the trenches." The Treasury's war bond program, he felt, would use its patriotic appeals to militarize the public. As he later argued, "any great war must necessarily be a popular movement. It is a kind of crusade . . . [that] sweeps along on a powerful stream of romanticism."

To support this patriotic and militarized approach, McAdoo's Treasury ultimately engineered four Liberty Loan drives during the war. These drives were intense periods of nationwide sales pressure, with a strong emphasis on themes of liberty and freedom. For instance, the First Liberty Loan in May and June

1917 presented the ever-present poster of a humanized Liberty pleading for average citizens to save her by purchasing war bonds. This first drive raised $1.9 billion for the war effort, while the Fourth Liberty Loan raised $6.9 billion in October 1918. A postwar Victory Loan completed the Treasury's World War I bond operations by raising an additional $4.5 billion in April 1919.

The relatively new art of propaganda had a strong influence on the Treasury's efforts in these bond drives. The Treasury's planners forged several connections with the government's official propaganda agency, George Creel's Committee on Public Information (CPI). Liberty Bonds were a favorite topic, for instance, of CPI's "four-minute men," a program in which government-trained speakers blanketed the country with programmed material. Moreover, most of the war bond program's marketing material—including posters, newspaper advertisements, billboards, and so on—was designed by CPI's propagandists.

In spite of its carefully planned propaganda, though, the Treasury's appeals often failed to motivate the public. The average American was unfamiliar with public bond offerings, and for this reason many rejected the government's propaganda. In fact, most of the campaign's sales resulted from investments by large financial interests that sought a good investment, not a patriotic gesture. Although McAdoo claimed that the Treasury's successful sales record reflected high public morale, the truth was that his program fostered inflationary pressure on the economy because the public's money remained in circulation, driving up the prices of scarce consumer goods. Even worse, the negotiable nature of the war bonds caused many private citizens to lose their investment when the postwar economy sagged.

But perhaps the least attractive aspect of the Treasury's Liberty Loan program was its tacit encouragement of coercive pressure to increase sales. People who were unwilling to purchase bonds were popularly known as "slackers." Occasionally, such individuals found their homes had been painted yellow, or that their cars had been stolen and sold for a large bond purchase. Even those unable to afford bonds—including recent immigrants and school children—were shamed or bullied into stealing or borrowing money to avoid being called a "slacker."

The final product of McAdoo's war bond program was thus an unexpectedly low number of sales to the common investor, a number that was probably inflated by coercive sales tactics. Although his patriotic approach would be influential for the war bond program adopted in World War II, the tarnished legacy of the Liberty Loan operation served as a cautionary note to both the public and the government in the later war.

James J. Kimble

See also: Advertising (WWI); Committee on Public Information (WWI); Propaganda (U.S., WWI); Taxation (WWI); Biographies: McAdoo, William (WWI)

REFERENCES

Gilbert, Charles. *American Financing of World War I.* Westport, CT: Greenwood Press, 1970.

McAdoo, William G. *Crowded Years.* Boston: Houghton Mifflin, 1931.

Mock, James R., and Cedric Larson. *Words that Won the War: The Story of the Committee on Public Information, 1917–1919.* Princeton, NJ: Princeton University Press, 1939.

St. Clair, Labert. *The Story of the Liberty Loans: Being a Record of the Volunteer Liberty Loan Army, Its Personnel, Mobilization and Methods, How America at Home Backed Her Armies and Allies in the World*

War. Washington, DC: James William Bryan Press, 1919.

War Industries Board (WIB)

World War I brought an enormous growth in the size and influence of the national government in the United States as it did elsewhere. The mobilization of the nation's economic and industrial resources required an increase in centralized control. The War Industries Board (WIB) was established on July 28, 1917, as the central federal agency and became the most important war agency in the United States. It was responsible for coordinating the United States' industrial mobilization, fixing prices, allocating raw materials, and determining production levels during the war. Such was the eventual power of the WIB that some commentators viewed it as a form of "war socialism." However, the Board developed only slowly and relied upon the participation and largely voluntary cooperation of businessmen. In large measure, the Board witnessed the integration of business and government interests. Certainly, it marked a major increase in the regulatory authority of the federal government and, although abolished at the war's end, the WIB set an important precedent for future action.

The WIB had its origins in the Munitions Standards Board, later the General Munitions Board, created by the Council of National Defense in March 1917. When the earlier bodies proved unwieldy, the War Industries Board was established by presidential authority to "act as a clearing house for the war industry needs of the Government" and "the most effective ways of meeting them." It was to encourage production and to determine priorities between different government agencies. The Board consisted of a chairman, representatives of the army and navy, and three members, each responsible for raw materials, finished products, and priorities respectively. The WIB was intended as a coordinating body. Initially it had no price-fixing powers and significant authority still remained within military bureaus. This division of authority hampered the WIB's operation and, consequently, the first two chairmen, Cleveland manufacturer Frank Scott and Daniel Willard of the Baltimore and Ohio Railroad, resigned in frustration.

Problems with coal production and rail transportation in the harsh winter of 1917–1918 threatened to bring the United States' wartime industrial mobilization to a halt. As a result, in March 1918, the WIB's powers were further increased. Bernard Baruch, a successful Wall Street banker and head of the Drexel Institute, was appointed chairman. The Board's new powers included creating new production facilities or converting existing ones, conserving resources, determining priorities of production, making purchases for the allies, and advising government purchasing agents on prices. The new Board established a number of divisions responsible for different aspects of war production and, to that end, utilized the enormous number of committees established by the Council of National Defense staffed primarily with "dollar-a-year men" from business who could afford to work for a nominal salary.

Between April 6, 1917, and June 1, 1919, the WIB handled 300,000 contracts worth an estimated $14.5 billion. While agreement on most of these was reached by a process of negotiation, the WIB did have enforcement powers it could use if necessary. Baruch wrote afterward of the huge savings in steel resulting from the alteration in the design of bicycles and the removal of stays from women's corsets. Automobile tire sizes, plow designs, and typewriter spools were also standardized. When Henry

Ford refused to limit private automobile production and Elbert Gary of U.S. Steel refused to accept the steel price set by the government, Baruch forced them to back down when he threatened to order the military to take over their production.

Most of the WIB's controls came to an end shortly after the Armistice on November 11, 1918, and the Board was officially abolished in January 1919. A number of its officials later found work in New Deal agencies during the 1930s, and the WIB provided a model for the National Recovery Administration created in 1933 to revive the flagging economy.

Neil Alan Wynn

See also: Business (U.S., WWI); Council of National Defense (WWI); Food Administration (WWI); Fuel Administration (WWI); Mobilization (U.S.); Biographies: Baruch, Bernard (WWI)

REFERENCES

Baruch, Bernard M. *American Industry in the War: A Report of the War Industries Board, March 1921.* New York: Prentice Hall, 1941.

———. *Baruch: The Public Years.* New York: Holt, Rinehart and Winston, 1960.

Clarkson, Grosvenor B. *Industrial America in the World War: The Strategy behind the Lines.* Boston: Houghton Mifflin, 1923.

Crowell, Benedict, and Robert F. Wilson. *How America Went to War.* 6 vols. New Haven, CT: Yale University Press, 1921.

Cuff, Robert D. *The War Industries Board: Business-Government Relations During World War I.* Baltimore, MD: Johns Hopkins University Press, 1973.

Eisner, Marc Allen. *From Warfare State to Welfare State: World War I, Compensatory State Building, and the Limits of the Modern Order.* University Park: Pennsylvania State University Press, 2000.

Kennedy, David M. *Over Here: The First World War and American Society.* New York: Oxford University Press, 1980.

Schwarz, Jordan A. *The Speculator: Bernard M. Baruch in Washington, 1917–1965.* Chapel Hill: The University of North Carolina Press, 1981.

Wynn, Neil A. *From Progressivism to Prosperity: World War I and American Society.* New York and London: Holmes and Meier, 1986.

War Labor Board (WLB)

The need to maximize production in order to feed and supply an army, as well as support the Allies, required the mobilization of all the resources of the United States, human as well as industrial. The war brought full employment and labor shortages, enabling workers to improve wages and trade unions in order to exercise greater influence. However, despite the American Federation of Labor's (AFL) no-strike pledge and the involvement of labor leader Samuel Gompers in the war administration, there was an outbreak of industrial unrest in 1917 that threatened the war effort. Key industries such as copper mining and lumber production were particularly badly affected. These strikes often led to vigilante action, such as the deportation of 1,186 strikers from Bisbee, Arizona, in July 1917. Such acts of repression seriously challenged the Wilson administration's claims to be fighting a "war for democracy." As a result, a Mediation Commission was established in September 1917 to investigate and settle disputes and bring about better labor-management relations. As well as settling some disputes, the Commission recommended the creation of a unified labor administration. After further consideration by a War Labor Conference Board, President Wilson established a National War Labor Board (WLB) by executive order on April 9, 1918, to mediate in labor-management disputes in defense industries and lessen the potential disruption of the war effort by strikes.

The WLB was chaired jointly by former President William Howard Taft and Frank P. Walsh, the chairman of the prewar Commission on Industrial Relations. The other members were five labor representatives (Frank J. Hayes, William L. Hutcheson, Thomas A. Rickert, Thomas J. Savage, and Victor Olander), and five business representatives (Loyall A. Osborne, William H. VanDervoort, Leonor F. Loree, B. L. Worden, and C. Edwin Michael). An economist and statistician, W. Jett Lauck, was appointed secretary.

The WLB established certain basic principles for its operation. In return for a suspension of strikes and lockouts for the duration of the war, the Board recognized the workers' right to free collective bargaining and union membership, accepted the principle of the eight-hour day and of equal pay for women for equal work. It also adopted the principle of a basic minimum wage depending upon local conditions as a basis for pay settlements. In total, the WLB adjudicated in 1,245 cases, involving 670,000 workers in over 1,000 establishments. In some instances, the Board actually awarded more than striking workers were asking for in order to bring them up to the established minimum of 40 cents an hour. The Board's decisions also helped further the spread of the eight-hour day, and it was believed that more than 250,000 additional union members joined as a result of the WLB's decisions, although in some instances it had to accept the creation of company unions.

Although in keeping with other war agencies, the Board relied upon voluntary cooperation; in three instances, it used or threatened the use of force to impose its decisions: It took over the running of Western Union and the Smith and Wesson Company in April and September 1918 respectively, and when strikers at the Remington Arms Plant in Bridgeport, Connecticut, refused to accept wage increases negotiated by the Board, they were warned that exemptions from the draft could be rescinded. The WLB continued to function until June 1919, but by then the divisions between employers and the union representatives rendered it increasingly ineffective. Nonetheless, the WLB had given organized labor unprecedented equal representation with business in establishing a federal labor policy. Significantly, Walsh described the WLB as "a new deal for American labor," and it brought enormous recognition for trade unions and, like the War Industries Board, set important precedents for policies in the 1930s.

Neil Alan Wynn

See also: American Federation of Labor (WWI); Trade Unions (U.S., WWI); War Industries Board (WWI); Biographies: Gompers, Samuel (WWI)

REFERENCES

Bing, Alexander M. *War-Time Strikes and Their Adjustment.* New York: E. P. Dutton, 1921.

Breen, William J. *Labor Market Politics and the Great War: The Department of Labor, the States, and the First U.S. Employment Service, 1907–1933.* Kent, OH: Kent State University Press, 1997.

Chambers, Frank P. *The War behind the War, 1914–1918: History of the Political and Civilian Fronts.* New York: Harcourt, Brace, 1939.

Conner, Valerie Jean. *The National War Labor Board: Stability, Social Justice, and the Voluntary State in World War I.* Chapel Hill: University of North Carolina Press, 1983.

Dubofsky, Melvyn, *Industrialism and the American Worker 1865–1920.* Arlington Heights, IL: Harlan Davidson, 1985.

Kennedy, David M. *Over Here: The First World War and American Society.* New York: Oxford University Press, 1980.

Koisten, Paul A. C. *Mobilizing for Modern War: The Political Economy of American Warfare, 1865–1919.* Lawrence: University Press of Kansas, 1997.

Watkins, Gordon S. *Labor Problems and Labor Administration in the United States during the World War: Part II: The Development of War Labor Administration,* Vol. VIII, No. 4, University of Illinois Studies in the Social Sciences. Urbana: University of Illinois, Sept. 1919.

Women (Canada)

Canadian women proudly contributed to the war effort in Canada during World War I. When the men left for war, women filled many job positions that were left vacant by the departing soldiers. But they also maintained more traditional roles, such as nursing. Women became involved in business, industry, and agriculture. Over thirty thousand Canadian women worked in factories making guns, bullets, bomb uniforms, ships, tanks, and planes. They were also employed as welders, machinists, fitters, riveters, and other jobs that were originally considered men's work. The women who could not work for some reason or another contributed in other capacities, such as knitting heavy scarves and socks that were sent to the soldiers overseas. They kept the Canadian economy strong throughout the war and did a superb job of proving that they could handle so much more than running a home and raising a family.

Posters throughout Canada encouraged women to give their husbands and sons permission to join the Canadian Armed Forces. Some women walked the streets encouraging able-bodied men to enlist. Still, there were many women who refused to give their husbands permission to enlist. Thousands more spent their time raising money for the war. Many Canadian women tried to do more but were discouraged by their social status and by rules created by the Canadian government. For instance, women in Toronto tried to form the "Women's Home Guard" (a group of women to be trained as soldiers to protect Canada's home front and free up men in the official "Home Guard" for overseas duty) but it failed because of strong opposition within Canada. Canadian women did form the "Suffragists' War Auxiliary," designed to provide women to do the jobs of men in order to free men up for overseas duty.

From the nineteenth century onward, female employment beyond the domestic sphere had been growing in Canada. Women had become involved in school teaching, medical care, store and office work, and in clothing plants and garment workshops, thanks to the sewing machine. But the impact of war magnified the role of Canadian women both in the economy and society. In addition to breaking down old prejudices and misconceptions about women in business and industry, working women proved that they were as proficient and reliable as men, and consequently gained a sizeable place in society as solid wage earners.

Many Canadian women volunteers were active at the battlefront as nurses or organizing hospitals at home. About 2,500 women went overseas as nurses to casualty-clearing stations near the front lines in France and Belgium. These women joined the Canadian Army Medical Corps Force. Forty-six women died during the war from diseases and air raids that struck the field hospitals. They also served at base hospitals and staff offices in Britain. Volunteers also set up nursing homes and canteens. They organized charitable organizations and sent food and supplies to the soldiers overseas. Over one thousand women were employed by the Canadian Royal Air Force, performing a variety of tasks like truck driving, mechanical work, and ambulance driving.

After the war, women were discouraged from continuing to work in business and industry. There was no longer a shortage of labor. In fact, some posters in Ontario acknowledged that the large number of men unemployed put the economy in a serious and dire situation. These numbers increased daily as more and more men came home after the conflict. Posters directed at both female employees and their employers encouraged women to go back to the domestic sphere to take care of hearth and family.

In the 1890s, there had been movements in Canada to grant women the right to vote. These movements were met with a great deal of male hostility, and male politicians refused to take women seriously, claiming that women would vote the same as their husbands. World War I, however, changed these perceptions. The war had given women great economic and political clout. In 1916, Manitoba's provinces granted women the right to vote in provincial elections. British Columbia and Ontario followed suit in 1917. The Maritimes did so a little later, but Quebec did not grant women the right to vote until 1940. On the federal level, a 1917 act gave the Dominion vote to women who were in military service or were relatives of servicemen. In 1918, all female citizens aged twenty-one and over received vote equality with men, a monumental event for Canadian women. This, coupled with working women, was the significant impact of World War I on Canadian society.

David Treviño

See also: Mobilization (Canada, WWI); Biographies: McClung, Nellie (WWI)

REFERENCES

Bourne, John. *Who's Who in World War One.* London: Routledge, 2001.

Clint, M. B. *Our Bit: Memories of War Service by a Canadian Nursing Sister.* Montreal: Barwick, 1934.

Gilbert, Martin. *The First World War: A Complete History.* New York: Henry Holt, 1994.

Kealey, Linda. "Women and Labour during World War I: Women Workers and the Minimum Wage in Manitoba," in *First Days, Fighting Days: Women in Manitoba History,* ed. Mary Kinnear, 76–99. Regina: Canadian Plains Research Center, University of Regina, 1987.

Nicholson, G. W. L. *Canada's Nursing Sisters.* Toronto: S. Stevens, Hakkert, 1975.

Phillips, Paul, and Erin Phillips. *Women and Work: Inequality in the Canadian Labour Market.* Toronto: James Lorimer, 1983.

Ramkhalawansingh, Ceta. "Women during the Great War," in *Women at Work: Ontario, 1850–1930,* ed. Janice Acton, et al, 261–307. Toronto: Canadian Women's Educational Press, 1974.

Wilson-Simmie, Katherine M. *Lights Out: A Canadian Nursing Sister's Tale.* Belleville, Ontario: Mika, 1981.

Women (UK)

At the outbreak of World War I, the British establishment saw no place for women in Britain's war effort. A woman's place was clearly in the home. However, as the advances in technology placed an ever increasing demand on the limits of British manpower, entrenched ideologies changed and a role was found for those women determined to establish their place within society. They toiled in factories, served in the uniformed services, and volunteered for any duty that would in some way help the nation. Thus, they were able to identify, in some way at least, with their men folk fighting the war at the front.

Workplace

The popular perception is that women did not work before the war. However, while the scope for female employment did widen due to the necessities of the war effort, it would be wrong to assume that women had not contributed to the economy of prewar Britain. In July 1914, the female workforce stood at just under five million, only increasing by 25 percent during the war to 6.2 million in 1918. The greatest changes came about in the type of work undertaken by women. The highest sector of prewar female employment was in domestic service, which fell by 400,000 during the war, while the outbreak of war created high unemployment among female-dominated industries like the textiles and garment trades. These industries were affected by the loss of raw materials and the European marketplace for the finished products. Over 40 percent of working women were unemployed by September 1914. The hardship was so great that charities were formed to find employment for those made redundant by the war. However, those undertaking work created by such charities as Queen Mary's Work for Women Fund were deliberately paid lower than average wages to ensure that only those in dire need would be attracted to the charities. Other groups, such as the National Guild of Housecraft, were created to teach those unemployed members of the so-called luxury trades—musicians, artists, and actresses—how to be good housewives and prepare for the return of the men from the front. Those workforces that experienced a significant growth in female employment included commerce, finance, and banking, which grew by 429,000 women and became synonymous with postwar low-status female employment. During the war, almost 700,000 women worked in transport, farming, and industry, while some one million were employed in white-collar or service industries.

Those women entering employment during the war, at least industrial employment, were for the most part married women who, having left employment when they were married, returned when their husbands entered the army or when they were widowed or had to support crippled husbands demobilized from the army without support. For some, it was a means to identify with the war and the suffering of their men folk. While for thousands of families the gender of the breadwinner changed and women returned to the employment market. For the middle classes, the opportunity to work was a new phenomenon but only in as much as they undertook paid employment. They tended to center on the professional and caring professions, with less than 10 percent of industrial munitions workers coming from the upper and middle classes, and those who did were predominantly in supervisory positions.

The stumbling block to female employment in industry was the concept of dilution, which meant that a job previously undertaken by a man was reorganized so that the relatively low-skilled component tasks could be undertaken by unskilled workers. Trade union reluctance was eventually overcome, but it was not until 1915 that new avenues and new, previously male-dominated, occupations opened for women. Women were now employed as tram drivers, dairy workers, clerks, ticket-collectors, shell-makers, motor-van drivers, van guards, and railway-carriage cleaners.

Military Service

Once it became apparent that the war was not a short-term conflict, attention turned to means of utilizing women in the various branches of the military. Established in 1916, the Women's Royal Naval Service (WRENS) was the first of its kind to recruit women for military service. Its members took over the role of cooks, electricians, code experts, and wireless telegraphists. By the end of the war, some 5,000 ratings and 450 officers had joined the unit. The success of the WRENS led to the creation of female branches of the other armed services later in the war. Established in January 1917, the Women's Auxiliary Army Corps (WAACS) allowed women to take over a number of roles in the British Army such as drivers, clerks, cooks, and telephonists. Women would also be used on the Lines of Communication and at General Headquarters on tasks that did not require heavy labor. Between January 1917 and the end of the war, over 57,000 women had served in the WAAC, enlisting for a year or the duration, with some 10,000 serving in France and Flanders. Later still, in March 1918 when the Royal Flying Corps and the Royal Naval Air Service merged to form the Royal Air Force, the Women's Royal Air Force (WRAF) was brought into being, with its members fulfilling the same role as that of the WAACS.

Under the umbrella of the Board of Agriculture and Fisheries, the Women's Land Army was formed in January 1917 in an attempt to regulate the agricultural workforce. However, the work was dangerous and dirty, with poor accommodation, long hours, and low pay. In 1918, only sixteen thousand members assisted with the harvest and those women who joined were never fully accepted into the agricultural community, while the adoption of male dress by the members, not only for work but also in their leisure hours, outraged conservative sections of British rural society.

The Women's Police Service (WPS) was a voluntary organization that came into being to oversee and protect the morals of those women who were experiencing their newfound freedom for the first time. It was thought that the newfound wealth of those in employment would lead inevitably to a decline in the nation's morality. The women police patrolled cinemas, camps, ports, and parks—indeed any area where soldiers might gather and so corrupt the morals of young women. The main aim was to prevent a rise in prostitution and, to this end, the WPS printed posters and pamphlets warning young women of the dangers of working on the street.

Other women's organizations included the Territorial Force Nursing Service, an auxiliary nursing service created as a backup for the army's regular nursing service, and the Women's Forage Corps, which assisted in providing forage for the huge number of horses and mules used in the British Army. The Women's Forestry Corps had the task of maintaining the supply of wood for use as a construction material in the theaters of war, as lining for the trenches, and for the production of paper.

Medicine

Many women turned to nursing as a means of contributing to the war effort, but the work was considered suitable only for middle- and upper-class girls. By July 1917, some 45,000 young ladies had turned to nursing. The First Aid Nursing Yeomanry (FANY) was established in 1907. During World War I, as well as driving ambulances and running field hospitals, it operated troop canteens and soup kitchens. However, the majority of the work undertaken by FANY was in Britain. In August 1918, there were only some 120 members of the organization actually in France.

Voluntary Aid Detachments (VADs) were formed in August 1909, and consisted of nurses who would provide medical assistance in time of war. By the outbreak of war in 1914, the organization had an establishment of over 2,500 Voluntary Aid Detachments in Britain with a strength of 47,000 members. Initially, the War Office was reluctant to use VADs at the front but, by 1915, realized their usefulness and allowed foreign service for female volunteers over the age of twenty-three and with more than three months of experience. These volunteers served on the Western Front, Gallipoli, and Mesopotamia. During the period of the war, some 38,000 women worked as ambulance drivers and assistant nurses and served in VAD hospitals abroad and in most major British towns. Both the FANY and the VADs recruited from the upper and middle classes, since caring was assumed to be a gentile occupation. Furthermore, as a byproduct of the medical needs of the British Army, the demand for male doctors for military duty created a vacuum that allowed those women with the necessary qualifications to establish themselves as doctors, allowing their gender to become firmly established in the medical profession.

The Women's Hospital Corps was formed as early as September 1914 by Dr. Flora Murray and Dr. Louisa Garrett Anderson, who, having been rejected by the British authorities, proceeded to establish military hospitals for the French at Wimereux and Paris. It was only later when needs overtook the objections of the British that they were able to establish a hospital in London that was fully staffed by women.

Dr. Elsie Inglis

Dr. Elsie Inglis was a Scottish Doctor, born in India in 1864 and educated in Edinburgh at the Edinburgh School of Medicine for Women. Having already established her own medical college, Inglis approached the War office in

February 1915 with a proposal to form a women's ambulance detachment, but this offer was turned down. However, never one to admit defeat, she took her offer directly to the French government, which quickly accepted. She proceeded to France and quickly established a Scottish Women's Hospital at the Abbaye de Royaumont Hospital by December 1914, a mere five months after the outbreak of war. A second hospital was later established in 1917 at Cotterets in France. She also established Scottish Women's Hospitals in the Balkans (Serbia, Romania, Corsica, Russia, and Malta) and, by 1918, she had established fourteen such hospitals that worked closely with all of the Allied armies except the British. Inglis herself served in Serbia, which included a period of captivity, as well as Russia before falling ill and returning to England, where she passed away on November 26, 1917, the day after her arrival in Newcastle.

Edith Cavell

British nurse Edith Cavell was executed on October 12, 1915, by German firing squad for her part in assisting captured Allied soldiers escape from German hands. Born in Norfolk, England, on December 4, 1865, Cavell trained as a nurse at the London Hospital and subsequently, in 1907, became the matron of the Berkendael Medical Institute in Brussels, Belgium. In the autumn of 1914, an "underground" escape line was organized from Belgium into neutral Holland, and Cavell began to assist stranded Allied soldiers evade capture. Over two hundred men escaped in this fashion before the organization was betrayed. Arrested on August 5, 1915, she was detained in solitary confinement for nine weeks. At her trial, Cavell admitted her involvement and, along with a Belgian accomplice, Philippe Baucq, was sentenced to death by firing squad. The case found widespread press coverage and Cavell became a worldwide heroine and martyr, unifying condemnation of German behavior in Belgium, uniting neutral opinion against Germany, and stimulating military recruitment in Britain for several weeks after her death.

Derek Rutherford Young

See also: Mobilization (UK, WWI)

REFERENCES

Beckett, Ian. *The Great War 1914–1918.* Harlow: Pearson Education, 2001.

Bond, Brian. *War and Society in Europe 1870–1970.* Stroud: Sutton, 1998.

DeGroot, Gerard. *Blighty: British Society in the Era of the Great War.* London: Longman, 1996.

Marwick, Arthur. *The Deluge: British Society and the First World War.* London: Macmillan, 1991.

Strachan, Hew. *The First World War; Volume 1: To Arms.* Oxford: Oxford University Press, 2001.

Women (U.S.)

World War I accelerated social change in the United States on many levels, affecting most profoundly women between the ages of eighteen and forty. During the war, service to one's country took precedence over service to family and, for a select group of women, this was a door to wider opportunity.

Women's Committee of the Council of National Defense

By 1917, the suffrage, labor, and temperance movements had already organized great numbers of women into clubs, associations, and unions. The government was quick to use women's traditional strengths—housewifery, nurturance, and the ability to maintain social control—on the home front by tapping into those organizations immediately after war was declared. The Women's Committee of the Council of National Defense (WCCND) was appointed on April 21, 1917. Its mandate was to advise and support existing programs, not to create new ones.

Journalist Ida Tarbell, a member of the Council, wrote: "Quietly, almost unconsciously, there is going on in this country, an extraordinary gathering of its women power." And Carrie Chapman Catt spoke of how easy it was "to unite all these organizations in this tremendous machinery, which has been perfected and adjusted with amazing efficiency."

Suffrage leader Dr. Anna Howard Shaw was appointed chairman of the WCCND. Some of the organizations united under the Council's banner were the General Federation of Women's Clubs, the National League for Women's Service, National Association for Woman Suffrage, National Council of Women, Daughters of the American Revolution, Colonial Dames, and garment workers unions. The aim of the Council was to coordinate the activities and resources of women for war work. Its major chores were conserving food, attending to child welfare, mitigating the problems of working women, monitoring the social life of soldiers, and raising money for the war effort through the Liberty Loan program.

A goal of the Council was to register every woman in the United States fit for war work. Unlike registration for the military, this was a voluntary program dependent upon the wave of patriotism that ignited the nation. Although it had the potential for mobilizing energy, skills, and experience, women's recruitment was only partially successful. Bureaucratic confusion stalled the program in many areas, and the government's efforts were criticized for being patronizing and the concept dictatorial. Shaw complained that government officials "think that women, like little children, ought to obey without the whys or wherefores of anything."

Despite the problems with the structure of the Council (Shaw considered resigning several times), its work was prodigious and far-reaching. The campaign for the elimination of waste in food management was the epitome of frugal housewifery. Enough bread was saved each day to feed a million people. Some $350 million worth of produce was raised in backyard gardens, 460 million quarts of fruits and vegeta-

American women, like these workers on the Great Northern Railway in Montana, replaced male workers who were drafted or enlisted to fight in World War I. (National Archives)

bles were preserved, and recipes for "wheatless, meatless" meals were circulated. Women's groups knit $36 million worth of gloves, scarves, caps, socks, and other necessities for soldiers. They also rolled hundreds of thousands of bandages and dressings.

The Women's Council spearheaded a campaign to implement the Child Labor Law, which went into effect on September 1, 1917. State chairs were requested to send out investigators to locate children under fourteen who were not in school. As children's advocate Julia Lathrop wrote: "The least a democratic nation can do, which sends men into war, is to give a solemn assurance that their families will be cared for."

As part of their motherly role, women were assigned the task of making life comfortable for young soldiers in the hastily thrown together camps. They sponsored various kinds of healthy recreation and chaperoned their activities. Alice Dunbar-Nelson wrote that it was the duty of women to overcome the "lure of the khaki" by carefully watching over young girls in the area. Women's groups also provided home-like furnishings for camp common rooms, as well as games, books, pianos, Victrolas, and endless refreshments. Librarians with the American Library Association, women's associations at local churches, the YWCA, Red Cross, and WCTU were especially active in camp work.

Each state was organized into its own WC-CND committee and from there into county, city, and town groups. These groups were allowed creative latitude, the freedom to develop their own agenda, and methods for achieving it. In Southern states, the United Daughters of the Confederacy established day care facilities for factory-working mothers; women in Chicago created a "flag hospital" to clean and mend American flags; and a "Better Babies"

The struggle for women's right to vote did not stop for World War I, as this 1917 picket line in front of the White House makes clear. (Library of Congress)

campaign in Idaho urged mothers to take their infants and toddlers to doctors for checkups.

An important part of WCCND work was the education of adult, white immigrant women. Patriotic women's organizations saw their mission as Americanizing the foreign-born. Their members volunteered to see that at least one immigrant became a citizen and to teach English to at least one foreign-born woman. Women in Midwestern states, especially Minnesota, Nebraska, Illinois, and Michigan, excelled at this task. Pacifist and suffrage leader Carrie Chapman Catt saw the educational mission in a broader context, feeling it was a necessity "if future generations were to be protected from the menace of an unscrupulous militarism."

The Liberty Loan campaign was established to raise funds for the government's war chest. The women's effort was led by Eleanor Wilson McAdoo, Woodrow Wilson's daughter and wife of future Treasure Secretary William G. McAdoo. More than one million women sub-

scribed to the loan campaign, convinced that it was a good investment with its 3.5 percent interest. Although women were exhorted to give, no matter how low their income—African American women working in a tobacco factory in Norfolk, Virginia, raised $91,000—in most communities, women were not allowed to handle the money collected.

Some two million women were already in the workforce when war was declared. At least one million more entered or reentered the work force in 1917 as salaried employees. Immigration was halted in 1914, drying up that seemingly endless labor pool, and "Women Wanted!" ads appeared for manufacturing firms even before war was declared. As men left for military service, women became more visible in the professions, especially in the sciences as physicists, chemists, engineers, and medical doctors, as well as office managers. Lesser educated women sought out skilled work. The number of women store clerks increased by more than 300 percent, while those in domestic service decreased by about 250 percent. The number of women employed in industry and offices also grew by about 300 percent.

African American Women

African American women were urged to "come out of the kitchen, Mary" and were taught motor mechanics in Missouri and Florida. Others took over "men's" work in cotton fields and on tobacco farms. White women throughout the breadbasket found themselves as farm and ranch managers. Eastern European women in the Northeast were hired as streetcar conductors and railroad workers. The Remington Arms plant in Bridgeport, Connecticut, took on five thousand women; the Curtiss aircraft factory employed four hundred.

Women workers were paid less than men workers, and African American women less than white women, but nonetheless, both groups received more money than they had ever earned. Women elevator operators or trolley conductors might receive $18.50 per week, while machine shop operators could expect $35 per week. Dormitories for women were set up at some munitions factories, and Briggs & Stratton in Milwaukee designed their new factory with women workers in mind.

The Department of Labor hastily created a new agency, Women in Industry Service (WIS), to oversee the conditions of working women. Accepting the ideas from trade unionists, WIS called for an eight-hour day instead of the standard ten hours, with rest breaks and access to clean restrooms. (After the war, WIS became the Women's Bureau, a permanent part of the bureau.) Flexing their muscle, some women's leaders, such as Carrie Chapman Catt, called for equal pay for equal work.

Some 16,500 women were employed by the AEF overseas as members of the army or as civilian employees in 1917–1918, while 12,000 joined the Navy as Yeomenettes and the Marine Corps. Most were used as office workers in both the United States and abroad. Most notable were the "Hello Girls," scores of telephone operators who emerged in this period. Other women found employment with the armed forces as domestics and nurses in National Guard camps.

As women were perceived as coworkers in the war effort, the momentum for woman suffrage took a surge forward. Nine states granted suffrage to women during the war, and demonstrations for a constitutional amendment on the issue continued in force.

The changes in lifestyles were most marked in young women who embraced the period's symbols of freedom—smoking, bobbed hair, shorter skirts, looser waistlines, and fewer "foundation garments" or corsets. These daring innovators would become "the modern women" of the 1920s, seeking fulfillment through independence. Margaret Sanger opened her first birth control clinic in 1916, offering education and contraceptives to women suffering under the burden of many and frequent pregnancies.

Alice Dunbar-Nelson summed up the American woman's experience during World War I: She "shut her eyes to past wrongs and present discomforts and future uncertainties, stood large-hearted, strong-handed, clear-minded, splendidly capable, and did not her bit, but her best . . ."

Betty Burnett

See also: Anti-Prostitution Campaign (WWI); Daughters of the American Revolution (WWI); Fashion (WWI); National Consumer's League (WWI); Sexuality (WWI); Women's International League for Peace and Freedom (WWI); YMCA and YWCA (WWI); Documents: Women's Suffrage Speech to Congress, 1917

REFERENCES

Blatch, Harriot Stanton. *Mobilizing Women-Power.* New York: The Women's Press, 1918.

Clarke, Ida C. *American Women and the World War.* Boston: D. Appleton, 1918.

Dunbar-Nelson, Alice. "Negro Women in War Work" in *Scott's Official History of the America Negro in the World War,* ed. Emmett J. Scott. New York: Arno Press and the *New York Times,* 1969.

Fraser, Helen. *Women and War Work.* New York: G. Arnold Shaw, 1918.

Gavin, Lettie. *American Women in World War I: They Also Served.* Niwot: University Press of Colorado, 1997.

Greenwald, Maurine Weiner. *Women, War, and Work The Impact of World War I on Women Workers in the United States.* Westport, CT: Greenwood Press, 1980.

Steinson, Barbara J. *American Women's Activism in World War I.* New York and London: Garland, 1982.

Zeiger, Susan. *In Uncle Sam's Service: Women Workers with the American Expeditionary Forces.* Ithaca, NY: Cornell University Press, 1999.

Zeiger, Susan. "She Didn't Raise Her Boy to Be a Slacker: Motherhood, Conscription, and the Culture of the First World War." *Feminist Studies* 11, no. 1 (Spring 1996).

Women's International League for Peace and Freedom

The Woman's International League for Peace and Freedom, or WILPF, began as the Woman's Peace Party, founded by a convention lead by Jane Addams in January 1915. Established in the sprit of Progressive reform that characterized early twentieth-century U.S. society and politics, the Woman's Peace Party advocated a variety of policies including disarmament, women's suffrage, increased cooperation among the nations of the world, and the cessation of war. The decision to form a gender-exclusive peace organization was reached by Jane Addams and her supporters because they were tired of occupying secondary roles in existing male-dominated pacifist organizations, and because popular philosophy of the period held that women were more pacific than men.

Within its first year, forty thousand people joined the Woman's Peace Party, but membership numbers fell in the environment of patriotism and war enthusiasm that surrounded the U.S. entry into World War I in April 1917. Prior to U.S. entry into the war, leaders of the Woman's Peace Party traveled around Europe attempting to form a conference of neutral nations who would persuade the belligerent powers to accept a cease-fire agreement and begin peace negotiations. While many of the leaders of neutral nations seemed receptive to the idea, the effort ultimately failed. Jane Addams and other leaders of women's peace organizations were, however, able to form the International Committee of Women for Permanent Peace, an international peace organization based in The Hague, in the spring of 1915.

U.S. participation in the war in Europe badly damaged popular support for the young Woman's Peace Party. People despaired of the movement because it had failed to influence Woodrow Wilson's decision to go to war, and because once war had been declared, antiwar organizations were believed by the majority of Americans to be unpatriotic. Nevertheless, the Woman's Peace Party and the International Committee of Women for Permanent Peace worked to position themselves in place to influence the peace negotiations at the end of the war. The members of the women's peace movement were encouraged by Wilson's announcement in January 1918 that he would advocate a lenient peace and the creation of an international League of Nations once the war ended.

The peace treaty that eventually resulted from the negotiations at Versailles disappointed both the members of the International Committee of Women for Permanent Peace and Wilson. The principle of leniency toward the defeated Germans was abandoned, and the League of Nations did not promise to become the benevolent international peace organization that its strongest advocates had hoped. In response to this disappointment, the leaders of the International Committee of Women for Permanent Peace decided to continue their work by converting into a new organization, the Women's International League for Peace and Freedom in 1919. In the United States, the Woman's Peace Party became the U.S. section of the new organization.

After a struggle among the leaders and members over the precise ideals and purpose of the league, the WILPF emerged as a moderate women's peace organization in the wake of Versailles. Its members decided to promote peace by advocating disarmament and opposing forms of universal military training and overseas economic imperialism. In the period between the world wars, the WILPF gained members and greater recognition in the United States, despite attempts to brand the women's peace movement as unpatriotic during the Red Scare. Its members supported disarmament initiatives such as the Washington Naval Treaty and the Kellogg-Briand Pact, although they viewed both realistically as imperfect peace measures, designed as stepping-stones on a path to genuine international peace. Prior to the outbreak of World War II, the members of the WILPF promoted initiatives to produce cooperation between the United States and other nations in order to provide relief for European Jews.

Incorrectly labeled isolationist, the WILPF was one of the most ardent organizations favoring international cooperation for permanent peace during the interwar period. WILPF members remained vocal opponents of militarism and war, and the only two American women to be awarded the Nobel Peace Prize to date, Addams and Emily Greene Balch, served as leaders of the league during this period. The women's peace movement survived World War I and, after some changes in its organization and its principles, the WILPF became one of the most prominent peace organizations in the United States by World War II.

Thomas I. Faith

See also: Pacifists (WWI); Women (U.S., WWI); Biographies: Addams, Jane (WWI); Catt, Carrie Chapman (WWI)

REFERENCES

Alonso, Harriet Hyman. *Peace as a Woman's Issue: A History of the U.S. Movement for World Peace and Women's Rights.* Syracuse, NY: Syracuse University Press, 1993.

Foster, Carrie A. *The Women and the Warriors: The U.S. Section of the Women's International League for Peace and Freedom, 1915–1946.* Syracuse, NY: Syracuse University Press, 1995.

Foster, Catherine. *Woman for All Seasons: The Story of the Woman's International League for Peace and Freedom.* Athens and London: University of Georgia Press, 1989.

Y

YMCA and YWCA

When the United States entered World War I, the U.S. branch of the Young Men's Christian Association was over sixty years old. This organization and its counterpart, the Young Women's Christian Association, had grown dramatically and developed large goals for U.S. cities. The war presented opportunities to enact those goals among military personnel and the increasing numbers of young urbanites. Industrialization increased from 1917 to 1918, bringing more workers to U.S. cities and placing pressure on YMCA and YWCA branches to serve them.

The YMCA and YWCA grew from prayer groups in England that catered to young adults who had moved from rural areas to the cities. In the midst of the Industrial Revolution, middle-class Christians worried that financial concerns and urban entertainment would corrupt moral youth. Because American Protestants harbored similar fears, they supported local YMCA organizations as a form of ecumenical Christian outreach. Originally, YMCA chapters hosted weekly gatherings of men and encouraged them to convert to Christianity; the YWCA had a similar agenda for women, with the added intention of sheltering them from sex-

ual promiscuity. These goals matched the rhetoric of the foreign missionary and social gospel movements from the 1880s into the early 1900s. They expressed the conviction that Protestant values guaranteed physical and spiritual success and should be shared by all people.

The YMCA and YWCA seemed like most other social reform efforts until both organizations expanded their goals to embrace secular interests after the U.S. Civil War. More U.S. businessmen provided financial support to YMCA chapters because the organization's target population represented potential workers for urban corporations. With these funds, many YMCA chapters established their own buildings and replaced volunteers with professional staff. They also established gymnasiums, cafeterias, and dormitories to compete with the sordid entertainment and subpar accommodations usually offered at nightclubs and hotels. These new amenities set the model for the type of YMCA that became common during and after World War I; the organization was perceived less as a Christian institution than as a set of "manhood factories" teaching Protestant, capitalist ethics to the next generation of U.S. workers. Many local chapters specifically catered to railroad workers, using games like billiards to catch their interest. After the wartime rations on building

YMCA facilities, like this one in London, provided much needed recreational opportunities for off-duty Allied servicemen during World War I. (Hulton-Deutsch Collection/Corbis)

materials ended, the YMCA National Board standardized all U.S. YMCA facilities, ensuring that every local chapter would focus on physical health, employment, and morality.

The YWCA did not organize its National Board until 1906, but its chapters expressed similar concerns. By 1917, YWCA leaders advocated for safe work environments and adequate wages to protect females' moral integrity. Most YWCA members worked in factories or service positions, earning so much less than male counterparts that their wages could barely cover rent. The organization leaders argued that such women were more likely to turn to prostitution, thereby degrading the morals of urban males. The organization appointed labor leaders as national staff, inspected and improved working conditions in large factories, and officially supported unionism and labor reform in 1920. The YWCA established dormitories and advocated workers' rights on the common Victorian assumption that this protection enabled single members to marry well and thereafter quit the job market.

After 1910, the YWCA started providing similar accommodations for foreign immigrants but, unlike most U.S. reform programs, the YWCA did not force its members to conform to U.S. culture. Instead, local branches celebrated immigrants' ethnicity and eased their cultural adjustment. The YWCA also sponsored segregated chapters for African Americans, which were especially active during World War I. The organization first gained national prominence because the federal government gave the YWCA and the YMCA responsibility for organizing recreational activities for troops. The African American YWCA responded by establishing "Hostess Houses" to provide refuge and support in military camps within the United States and abroad. This program helped YWCA membership increase substantially, local chapters gain influence, and African American leaders gain national staff positions. After the war, black YWCA chapters served as forums promoting better race relations.

The YMCA and YWCA blended Christianity with secular urban culture in unprecedented ways, which inadvertently created spaces for homosexual activity. The gender-segregated dormitories had provided opportunities for sexual encounters since the late 1800s. This activity increased during both world wars, as many soldiers and defense workers moved to cities and joined local chapters. Most military YMCA patrons stayed for short periods, and YMCA officials were more likely to either ignore their homosexual behavior or never notice it. The

YMCA did not officially condone homosexuality, but its role as a major source of urban recreation and housing ensured that it continued to play a role in gay culture until the 1960s.

Kimberly Hill

See also: Religion (WWI); Salvation Army (WWI); Sexuality (U.S., WWI)

REFERENCES

Ahlstrom, Sydney L. *A Religious History of the American People.* New Haven, CT: Yale University Press, 1972.

Mjagkij, Nina, and Margaret Spratt. *Men and Women Adrift: The YMCA and the YWCA in the City.* New York: New York University Press, 1997.

Z

Zimmermann Telegram

The Zimmermann Telegram was a telegram sent in January 1917 by German Foreign Minister Arthur Zimmermann to German Minister to Mexico Heinrich von Eckardt ordering the ambassador to offer Mexico the states of Texas, New Mexico, and Arizona in exchange for Mexico's assistance in any war between Germany and the United States. The telegram was intercepted by British intelligence, and when it was produced by Britain several weeks later at a crucial moment in international affairs, it provoked an anti-German furor in the United States. This anti-German feeling, combined with U.S. anger over Germany's resuming unrestricted submarine warfare, helped bring the United States into World War I on the side of the Allies. According to David Kahn, author of *The Codebreakers,* "No other single cryptanalysis has had such enormous consequences."

By the time Zimmermann sent the telegram in January 1917, tensions were already escalating between Germany and the United States. Up until this point in World War I, the United States under President Woodrow Wilson had struggled to remain out of what it saw as a European conflict. "We must remain neutral in thought and deed," Wilson had declared, and

Americans took this charge so seriously that, when they were shown newsreels of how the war was progressing, audiences in movie theaters were encouraged not to cheer, lest their noise be taken as partisanship.

The most significant issue between the United States and Germany was the question of Germany's submarine warfare. To enforce a blockade of England, German submarines (*unterseeboots,* or "U-boats") were waging "unrestricted" submarine warfare, and so were inevitably destroying U.S. property and killing Americans. While after 1916, Germany agreed to restrict its U-boat attacks, by early 1917, German strategists had concluded that they could not win the war unless they resumed unrestricted submarine warfare.

Believing that the U-boat controversy would propel Germany and the United States into war, Zimmermann decided to try to enlist Mexico in the coming fight. Announcing that Germany intended to resume unrestricted submarine warfare in February, Zimmermann explained in his January 19 message that, while he wanted the United States to remain neutral, he was proposing an alliance with Mexico in case of war. Germany would provide Mexico with funds, Zimmermann continued, and together they could invite Japan into an alliance.

Mexico ultimately decided that it would not be able to pacify the Anglo population in Texas, New Mexico, and Arizona, and so officially declined Zimmermann's proposal on April 14, by which time Germany and the United States were already at war.

The Zimmermann Telegram might not have come to light had British Naval Intelligence not been eavesdropping on the U.S. diplomatic communications. At the time Zimmermann dispatched his message, Woodrow Wilson was trying to arrange peace talks between the belligerent European nations. As part of these talks, Wilson had given Germany access to the U.S. diplomatic telegraph cable. Aware that the United States as a matter of principle refused to read other countries' diplomatic correspondence or to break codes, Zimmermann actually used the United States' own telegraph to send the encrypted telegram to the German ambassador in the United States with orders that the message be forwarded to Mexico. British Naval Intelligence was tapping the U.S. cable, and so was in a position to intercept the telegram and break the code.

The British were faced with a serious dilemma: While they wanted to use the telegram to convince the United States to enter the war on the Allied side, they knew that if they made the telegram public they would reveal that they had broken the latest German codes and that they were illegally spying on the United States. The British decided to try to intercept the message again, this time after it was sent on to Mexico. A British agent ultimately found a copy of the telegram (which had been re-encrypted with an outdated code) in a public telegraph office. Not only did this mean that the British did not have to reveal that they were reading U.S. diplomatic correspondence, but also that they could keep secret the fact that they had broken the latest German codes. The British

delivered the telegram to the U.S. ambassador on February 23, who on February 25 passed it on to Wilson. Shortly afterward, the text of the telegram was on the front page of every newspaper in the United States.

When Americans read about the telegram they were already irritated with Mexico because of the cross-border raids conducted by Mexican bandit Pancho Villa, and were increasingly concerned with Germany's resumption of unrestricted submarine warfare. Nonetheless, many Americans seized upon German, Mexican, and Japanese accusations that the document was fake, and concluded that the telegram was a fraud designed by the British to bring the United States into war. Remarkably, this conclusion was refuted by Arthur Zimmermann himself, who in speeches on March 3 and March 29 admitted that he had sent the telegram, that he continued to hope that the United States would remain neutral in the conflict, and that the joint German-Mexican plan would be implemented only if the United States went to war with Germany.

Anti-German sentiment in the United States increased quickly and dramatically after Zimmermann confirmed that the telegram was real and, late in March, Wilson asked Congress to arm U.S. ships so that they could fight off German U-boat attacks. On April 2, 1917, Wilson asked Congress to declare war on Germany, exclaiming: "We must make the world safe for democracy!" Congress complied on April 6, 1917.

Samuel Brenner

See also: Lusitania, Sinking of (WWI); Sabotage and Spies (WWI); Submarine Warfare (WWI); Biographies: Villa, Pancho (WWI)

REFERENCES

Bridges, Lamar W. "Zimmermann Telegram: Reaction of Southern, Southwestern Newspapers," *Journalism Quarterly* 46, no.1 (1969): 81–86.

Friedman, William F. *The Zimmermann Telegram of January 16, 1917, and Its Cryptographic Background.* Laguna Hills, CA: Aegean Park Press, 1976.

Kahn, David. *The Codebreakers: The Comprehensive History of Secret Communication from Ancient Times to the Internet,* rev. ed. New York: Scribner, 1996.

Kahn, David. "Edward Bell and His Zimmermann Telegram Memoranda." *Intelligence and National Security* 14, no. 3 (1999): 143–159.

Spencer, Samuel R. *Decision for War, 1917; The Laconia Sinking and the Zimmermann Telegram as Key Factors in the Public Reaction Against Germany.* Rindge, NH: R. R. Smith, 1953.

Tuchman, Barbara W. *The Zimmermann Telegram.* New York: Macmillan, 1966.